Lonely Planet Publications
Melbourne | Oakland | London

Andrew Bender &
Wendy Yanagihara

Tokyo

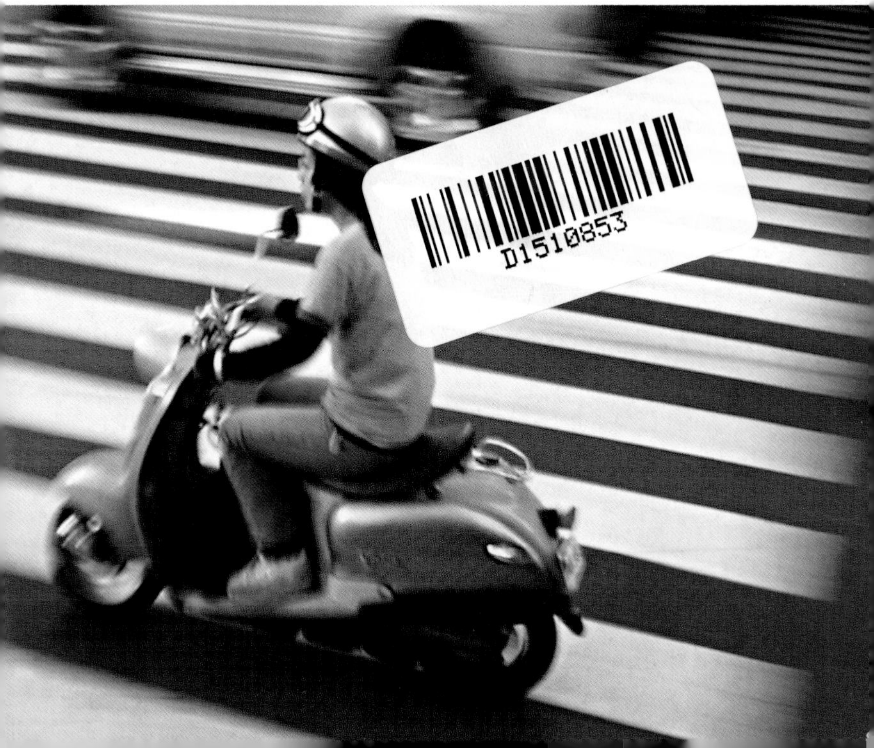

The Top Five

1 Sumida-gawa Cruise
Imagine old Edo as you journey through modern Tokyo (p87)

2 Omote-sandō
See unique boutiques with haute couture and riotous teen togs (p98)

3 Sensō-ji
Visit the city's spiritual anchor (p85)

4 Roppongi Hills
Eat, drink, play, get lost and enjoy amazing views in this architectural playground (p93)

5 Tsukiji Central Fish Market
Note, a fish is just a fish, but a million fish are a must-see (p75)

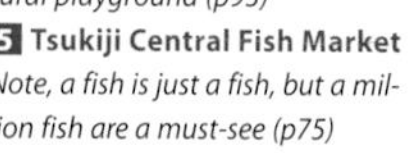

Published by Lonely Planet Publications Pty Ltd
ABN 36 005 607 983

Australia Head Office, Locked Bag 1, Footscray, Victoria 3011, ☎ 03 8379 8000, fax 03 8379 8111, talk2us@lonelyplanet.com.au

USA 150 Linden St, Oakland, CA 94607, ☎ 510 893 8555, toll free 800 275 8555, fax 510 893 8572, info@lonelyplanet.com

UK 72–82 Rosebery Ave, Clerkenwell, London, EC1R 4RW, ☎ 020 7841 9000, fax 020 7841 9001, go@lonelyplanet.co.uk

Printed by SNP Security Printing Pte Ltd, Singapore

Contents

The Authors

Andrew Bender

France was closed, so after college Andy moved to Tokyo instead. It ended up being a life-changing sojourn, as visits to Japan so often are. Yet another Lonely Planet author with an MBA, he worked with Japanese companies in the finance, film and animation industries in both Tokyo and Los Angeles, before doing what every MBA secretly dreams of: travelling the world and writing about it. His writing has since appeared in dozens of publications including *Forbes, Travel + Leisure* and the *Los Angeles Times*. Dividing his time between Los Angeles and New York, Andy keeps up his business chops with cross-cultural consulting and strategising about ways to spoil his nieces and nephews. Find out more at www.andrewbender.com.

For this book, Andy was the coordinating author. He wrote the Introducing Tokyo, City Life, Arts & Architecture, History and Sights chapters.

Wendy Yanagihara

Wendy first toured Tokyo perched on her mother's hip at age two. Between and beyond childhood summers spent in Japan, she has roamed around Mexico, Central America, Europe, Southeast Asia and New Zealand. She spent stints as a psychology and art student, bread peddler, espresso puller, jewellery pusher, graphic designer, and more recently as Lonely Planet author for titles including *Japan* and *Best of Tokyo*. When not on the road or tapping at the laptop, Wendy paints, tangos and prowls around the San Francisco Bay Area.

For this edition Wendy wrote the Walking Tours, Eating, Drinking, Entertainment, Shopping, Sleeping, Excursions and Directory chapters.

CONTRIBUTING AUTHOR

PHILIP BROPHY

Philip Brophy (www.philipbrophy.com) wrote the boxed text Manga & Anime (p29). Philip is a film director, composer and writer. One of his specialities is Japanese pop culture. His most recent book is *100 Anime* for the British Film Institute.

PHOTOGRAPHER

Greg Elms

Lured by magazine images of exotic locales, Greg has always dreamed of becoming a travel photographer. He has photographed numerous award-winning books, and was commissioned to photograph the World Food Guides to Mexico, India, Turkey, France and China. He has worked from Melbourne for 12 years, for a variety of magazines, ad agencies, designers and, of course, book publishers such as Lonely Planet.

This *Tokyo* guide was Greg's seventh Lonely Planet commission.

ANDY'S TOP TOKYO DAY

This day begins, like every good day, with food: a visit to the Tsukiji Central Fish Market (p75) and its Outer Market (p76) for a browse, maybe a quick visit to the shrine, and sushi, breakfast of champions. A quick hop on the subway takes us to Roppongi (p92), and the latest and greatest at the Mori Art Museum (p92). A quick circumnavigation of the Tokyo City View observatory helps us decide where to head next. 'Ryōgoku', we think, where if there's a sumō tournament (p106) on we'll try for the cheap seats as the big guys battle it out. Or else an excursion to the Kabuki-za (p66) is always an adventure. Nightfall demands a stop in Shibuya (p96), when its neon never seems brighter, before adjourning to dinner at a high-rise restaurant in Shinjuku (p138), with the city spread out and glistening before us like a rainbow-coloured electronic carpet.

Introducing Tokyo

A bowl of whisked green tea in the teahouse of Hama Rikyū Onshi-teien is about as Japanese as it gets. The garden was once a pleasure dome for the shōgun, but now you too can pause and savour the moment, as ducks glide by in the pond at your feet and precision-plucked pines pose like puffed clouds.

But cross the narrow wooden bridge over the pond and look backward: framing the teahouse, the pond and the pines are the skyscrapers of Shiodome, gleaming glass and granite and all built since the turn of the millennium. If that's not an only-in-Tokyo moment, then nothing is.

But that's just one of hundreds – indeed thousands – of inimitable moments in the Japanese capital. You might find *your* moment crammed on the morning train, cheek-to-jowl among millions of commuters. Or maybe it will be finding fish fin-to-fin in the cavernous Tsukiji Central Fish Market, before arriving on your plate as sashimi that evening, arranged atop rough-hewn ceramic and garnished with a young chrysanthemum.

Perhaps it will be in catching a cluster of school kids in sailor suits and matching yellow backpacks, or the impeccably dressed ladies strolling Ginza or Aoyama, or the not-to-be-forgotten costumes of the kabuki stage, or the ignore-me-if-you-can get-ups of the cos-play kids by Harajuku Station. You might indeed lose yourself in Hokusai's great wave or the neon forests of Shinjuku or Shibuya, beneath the sweep of a torii (gate) or in a high-rise panorama with Mt Fuji beckoning from the west.

It might simply be in the taxi door that magically opens and closes for you. You can, if you choose, be alone in any crowd, but if you do happen to drop your wallet, three strangers will reach down to return it to you.

Other cities may be more historic, they may indeed be more beautiful or more laid-back, but few are more ambitious or have weathered disasters – both natural and manmade – with such grit, style and grace. In barely 140 years, Tokyo has transformed itself from a provincial town in a nation that knew nothing of the

LOWDOWN

Time zone Japan Standard Time (GMT plus nine hours)

Population 12 million (greater metro area 33.4 million)

Commuters who pass through Shinjuku Station daily approximately two million

Market capitalisation of Tokyo Stock Exchange ¥541,670,370,000,000

Time in business of some Tsukiji Market vendors 20 generations

Subway ticket from ¥160

Three-star room ¥20,000

Cup of coffee ¥400

outside world, surviving social upheaval, earthquake, war, boom and recession to come out on top. And we dare you to find another city anywhere in the world to match Tokyo's sheer, crackling energy.

Today's Tokyo is as Ultraman as it is Hello Kitty, as worldly as it is homebound, as demure as it is unremitting. It's a place where you may find a rustic Shintō shrine in the busiest of business districts, where a shop selling the latest in computers might calculate your bill using an abacus, where people cherish their personal space yet may insist on walking you to your destination if you are lost.

Tokyo may be one of the world's most high-powered cities, noted as a capital of politics, finance, fashion and design, yet in this city even the humblest of tasks carries great nobility. Watch as a gardener sweeps with a broom made of tiny switches so as not to displace a single piece of gravel, as the mistress of a tiny coffee shop prepares that perfect cup with all her concentration, or as a shopkeeper wraps even the simplest of gifts so elegantly that the recipient will surely know it came from the heart of the giver.

Finding *your* Tokyo moment requires only one thing – observation; and that is one of the pleasures of this city. Yet, like the nation it leads, Tokyo requires decades of experience to truly understand it.

And that is also one of its pleasures.

ESSENTIAL TOKYO

- Asakusa (p83)
- Shibuya (p96)
- Roppongi Hills (p93)
- Sumida-gawa Cruise (p87)
- Tsukiji Central Fish Market (p75)

City Life

City Life

TOKYO TODAY

As one look at the train map will tell you, Tokyo is a vast, knotted web. It's remarkable, really, that a city of 12 million people (expand that to 33.4 million if you include the greater metropolitan area) can function at all, let alone with the efficiency for which Tokyo is so famous.

Tokyo works because, perhaps more than any other big city in the world, its residents work together – even if they don't recognise it. Step onto one of those trains, and you may well find that it's completely silent; talking would disrupt the ride for others. An 'office lady' exiting an elevator might press the 'door close' button as she leaves, so as to lessen the inconvenience to the other riders. Even the brashest of punks may offer a '*sumimasen*' (excuse me) and a smile if they've inadvertently bumped into someone.

Of course Tokyo's social order has begun to change, largely due to the recession of the 1990s and the first half of this decade. It took its toll in terms of unemployment (now at around 4.5% from a postwar historic high of 5%) and birth rates; Tokyo now reproduces at less than one child per couple.

Thankfully, many Tokyoites used that period to rebuild, both architecturally and in many cases personally. Entrepreneurship is up, from the boardroom to buskers, and the last two decades have seen the construction of some of the city's grandest structures: new art venues, hotels, restaurants and entertainment options.

More than anything else, this rebuilding is proving, once again, that this oft-devastated city usually survives, and often triumphs.

CITY CALENDAR

Tokyo's hectic schedule is a mix of *matsuri* (festivals), trade shows covering everything from motorcycles to design, and flower viewings. Depending on the season, you may be able to check in on all three at once. For a list of Japan's national holidays see p242.

TOP FIVE QUIRKY EVENTS

- Hari-kuyō (February; opposite) Mourn the passage of broken pins and needles by pushing them into blocks of tender tofu.
- Setsubun (February; opposite) Out, out with the Devil at this bean-throwing event.
- Design Festa (May & November; p10 & p12) International artists and designers gather twice-yearly to show their wares.
- Samba Carnival (August; p11) The fierce competition is almost as obvious as the dancers are naked. Ancient Asakusa gets an eyeful.
- Takigi Noh (July & August; p11) Perhaps less quirky and more hypnotic, these evening stagings of medieval *nō* dramas happen outdoors by firelight at parks, shrines and temples around the city.

JANUARY & FEBRUARY

SHŌGATSU (NEW YEAR'S HOLIDAY)

1 to 3 January

Sensō-ji (p85) & Meiji-jingū (p98)

While Tokyo comes to a virtual halt on the first few days of the year (also referred to as O-Shōgatsu, 'Honourable New Year'), the city's large Shintō shrines and Buddhist temples swell with visitors; Sensō-ji and Meiji-jingū are good places to start. Although both places are crowded (Meiji-jingū gets millions of visitors), it can be a particular thrill to be part of the crowds of people from all walks of life, many dressed in fine kimono and purchasing seasonal trinkets. You may also want to stop in at **Yasukuni-jinja** (p89), where the shrine's dramatic *nō* dance of the year is performed in honour of the shrine's god. On 2 January the emperor and imperial family make a brief appearance in one of the Imperial Palace's inner courtyards; it's one of the very rare occasions when visitors are allowed a glimpse into imperial life behind bulletproof glass.

A masked participant celebrating Seijin-no-hi (below)

SEIJIN-NO-HI (COMING-OF-AGE DAY) — 15 January

Meiji-jingū (p98)

Arrows fly during traditional archery displays in the celebration of the world of the grown-up.

AKŌ GISHI-SAI — Late January

Sengaku-ji (p110)

The tale of the 47 *Rōnin,* loyal retainers who avenged the death of their former master and then committed ritual suicide, still resonates with many in Tokyo. Crowds turn out for two days of Buddhist rites and bouts of less ceremonial partying.

SETSUBUN — 3 or 4 February

Sensō-ji (p85) & Zōjō-ji (p94)

Setsubun marks the first day of spring in the traditional calendar, a shift once believed to bode evil and bring disaster. To ward off the oncoming evil, temples erupt into metaphysical food fights as rowdy suppliants throw tiny sacks of roasted beans and shout, *'Oni wa soto! Fuku wa uchi!'* ('Devil out! Fortune in!').

HARI-KUYŌ — Early February

Sensō-ji (p85)

Mourn the passing of broken pins and needles at Sensō-ji temple in Asakusa, where women bury their beloved sartorial pals in cubes of tofu or in radishes.

MARCH & APRIL

HINA MATSURI (GIRLS' DAY) — 3 March

Sumida River (Map pp296-7)

Homes and public spaces are decorated with squat dolls in the traditional dress of the *hina* (princess). Around this time, dolls made by children are set adrift on the Sumida River (Sumida-gawa), from Sumida-kōen near Azuma-bashi. There's also a boy version held in May (see Otoko No Hi; p10).

UME HANAMI — Early March

Mt Takao

Before the riot of cherry blossoms comes to town, the plum trees do their own number. Mt Takao, in far western Tokyo, fairly explodes with them.

HIWATARI MATSURI — Mid-March

Mt Takao

Mountain monks lead this festival, in which they walk over hot coals. If you're feeling invincible, or drunk, you're also welcome to try.

ST PATRICK'S DAY PARADE — Mid-March

www.inj.or.jp/stpatrick_e.html; Omote-sandō (p284)

This parade may not be exactly on 17 March, but the crowds line the Omote-sandō route rain or shine for the wearin' and sometimes the drinkin' of the green. It's usually led by local Irish dignitaries and well attended by Tokyo's sizable, cohesive Irish community.

HANAMI (CHERRY-BLOSSOM VIEWING) — Late March to April

Late March through April sees the much-anticipated and glorious reign of the cherry blossom. See p12 for details on the best spots for these blossom-viewing parties.

TOKYO INTERNATIONAL ANIME FAIR — Late March or early April

www.taf.metro.tokyo.jp/en; Tokyo Big Sight (Map p289)

Tokyo's *anime* scene is the real deal, and this trade fair brings in everyone from the 12-year-old *anime*-tor next door to big-screen voice actors and some 170 exhibitors. Sorry, cos-play (see p14) is not permitted inside.

MATSURI

Tokyo's civic calendar is marked by an abundance of *matsuri* (festivals). *Matsuri* originated in farming communities as expressions of Shintō, according to the seasonal planting and harvesting of rice. Spring festivals were held to supplicate the local gods and to secure a plentiful harvest. Autumn festivals were held in thanks and celebration of a rich harvest. Summer and winter *matsuri* were less common, although summer festivals were sometimes held to ward off the natural disasters that could ravage a crop before harvest. Summer *matsuri* became more common with the rise of large urban settlements like Edo, where they were held in the hope of circumventing pestilence and plague.

One element common to many *matsuri* is a boisterous crowd of men clad in *happi* (half-length coats) and *fundoshi* (loincloths) and not much else, puffing and heaving beneath the weight of a *mikoshi* (portable shrine) before swilling large amounts of sake along with the rest of the crowd. Tokyo's rowdiest and best *matsuri* are Sanja (below), Sannō-sai (below) and Kanda (below).

HANA MATSURI — First week in April

Sensō-ji (p85) & Zōjō-ji (p94)

Happy birthday Buddha celebrations happen across Japan. Look for the parade of children in Asakusa, pulling a white papier-mâché elephant.

TOKYO MOTORCYCLE SHOW — Early April

Tokyo Big Sight (Map p289)

The biggest motorcycle show in Japan has been letting the good times roll since the 1970s.

MAY & JUNE

OTOKO NO HI (BOYS' DAY) — 5 May

This is the male counterpart to Hina Matsuri (see p9). Homes where boys live fly *koinobori*, banners or windsocks in the shape of a carp, a symbol of strength, never-ending struggle and other masculine virtues.

KANDA MATSURI — Mid-May

www.kandamyoujin.or.jp; Kanda Myōjin (p77)

One of the city's three big *matsuri*. Like other major *matsuri*, this one has music and dancing and a good dose of sake. The highlight is the parade of *mikoshi* (portable shrines).

SANJA MATSURI — Mid-May

☎ 3844-1575; Asakusa-jinja (p84)

This three-day festival attracts around 1.5 million spectators. The highlight is watching half-naked men (and women, although not half-naked) carry more than a hundred *mikoshi* around the shrine and neighbouring Sensō-ji. The crowd sheds its reserve and things get rowdy, just in time for you to do the same.

DESIGN FESTA — Mid- to late May

www.designfesta.com; Tokyo Big Sight (Map p289)

This two-day arts and design fair brings in 6000 exhibitors (professionals and nonpros) and some 51,000 visitors, making it the biggest art event in Asia. Also held in mid-November (see p12).

IRIS VIEWING — Early to mid-June

Mizumoto-kōen (3-2 Mizumoto-kōen, Katsushika-ku) & Horikiri Iris Garden (2-19-1 Horikiri, Katsushika-ku)

These parks on the eastern side of town show off more than 100 iris species. Saturdays and Sundays bring drum performances and larger crowds; weekdays are better for a quiet walk. The park is best reached by taking the Keisei Line to Kanamachi Station.

SANNŌ-SAI — Mid-June

Hie-jinja (p90)

Edokko (natives of Tokyo) turn out for this *matsuri* with music and dancing and the usual frenetic procession of *mikoshi*, at the former protector shrine for Edo Castle.

JULY & AUGUST

INTERNATIONAL GAY AND LESBIAN FILM FESTIVAL — Mid-July

www.tokyo-lgff.org/2006/index.html; various venues

An outgrowth of the Gay Art Project, in 2007 IGLFF will be in its 17th season. Features come from around the world, although some programmes focus on Japanese queer cinema. Many films shown are in English.

SUMIDA RIVER HANABI — Last Saturday in July

Sumida River (Map pp296-7)

Summertime in Japan is synonymous with exhibitions of fireworks *(hanabi)*, which happen throughout the country. The ones on the Sumida River are among the most spectacular. Although you may have seen fireworks displays elsewhere, they probably haven't prepared you for the grandness of this one, which goes on, marvellously, for hours.

TAKIGI NOH
July or August

Meiji-jingū (p98), Kichijoji Gesoji (Map pp278-9) & Shinjuku (p100)

As the weather cools, shrines, temples and parks stage outdoor nō dramas backlit by bonfires. Meiji-jingū, Kichijoji Gesoji and Shinjuku offer evening performances within the city limits.

O-BON
Mid-August

Yasukuni-jinja (p89)

For several days, Japanese city dwellers return to their ancestral provinces to gather with family and visit the graves of ancestors, marking the time when Buddhist teaching says the dead revisit the earth. *Bon-odori* (folk dances) by people in *yukata* (light cotton kimono) are held throughout Japan, but the one at Yasukuni-jinja is famous, illuminated by *bonbori* (paper lanterns).

KŌENJI AWA ODORI
Late August

Kōenji Station (Map pp278-9)

More than 10,000 participants do the Fool's Dance along a 2km stretch. If you're there, you're welcome to break into your own rendition.

SAMBA CARNIVAL
Last Saturday in August

Asakusa (p83)

Put on by Nikkei Brazilians and those who love them (and who doesn't?), roughly 3500 dancers move their fleshy way down Kaminarimon-dōri past a half-million spectators. The dancing is top-notch and the judged competition fierce, drawing dancers all the way from Rio.

SEPTEMBER & OCTOBER

TOKYO GAME SHOW
Mid-September

www.tgs.cesa.or.jp; Makuhari Messe

Get your geek on when the Computer Entertainment Suppliers Association stages this massive expo at a convention centre on the way to Narita Airport (Makuhari Messe is about 29 minutes east of Tokyo, via the JR Keiyō Line from Tokyo Station to Kaihin Makuhari Station). The holding of the event in 2006 marks its 16th year. Expect over 130 exhibitors and 175,000 visitors over three days.

NINGYŌ-KUYŌ
Late September

Kiyōmizu Kannon-dō (p81)

Childless couples pray for children by offering dolls to Kannon (Buddhist goddess of mercy). More interesting for spectators is the ceremonial burning by priests of all the dolls held in the temple precinct from the previous year.

TOKYO INTERNATIONAL FILM FESTIVAL
Late October

www.tiff-jp.net

Bigger doesn't necessarily mean better when it comes to film festivals. TIFF is the biggest in Asia, but it maintains its integrity by keeping a feature-length film competition at its core. Special attention is paid to films from Asia, although there are always selections in English.

EDO TENKA MATSURI
Late October

Marunouchi (Map pp294-5)

This festival began in 2003 to commemorate the 400th anniversary of Edo and is held every two years (next is 2007). You'll find exhibits and demonstrations of traditional Edo crafts, as well as a parade of *mikoshi*.

TOKYO METROPOLITAN CHRYSANTHEMUM FESTIVAL
Late October to mid-November

Hibiya-kōen (p65)

Chrysanthemums are the flower of the season (as well as of the imperial family), and here you'll see some 2600 of them at once. The festival has been going on since 1914. You can also catch dazzling chrysanthemum displays at Shintō shrines, including Meiji-jingū (p98) and Yasukuni-jinja (p89), 10am to 6pm daily.

NOVEMBER & DECEMBER

TOKYO JIDAI MATSURI (FESTIVAL OF THE AGES)
3 November

Asakusa (p83)

On National Culture Day locals dressed in splendid costumes representing figures from Japanese history parade around the Sensō-ji temple precincts. This festival takes

TOKYO IN BLOOM

Owing to the seasonal nature of Japanese culture, monitoring the progress of spring blossoms and autumn foliage is an obsession up and down the archipelago – the national news carries maps of their progress. Even though Tokyo is famously hemmed in by concrete, blossom-viewing and leaf-peeping are a big deal.

Hanami

Cherry blossoms seem to burst out overnight sometime between the end of March and the beginning of April, representing the climax of spring. *Hanami* (cherry-blossom viewing) parties begin with the earliest buds and endure to the last clinging blossoms. Both daytime parties and moonlit soirees are standard, as crowds flood the parks with beer and good humour.

- Hama Rikyū Onshi-teien (p75) There are about a hundred cherry trees here, including a few wild varieties. An admission fee keeps the crowds at bay and the rest of the garden is pleasant as well.
- Zōjō-ji (p94) About a hundred trees are found here at Shiba-kōen, with the temple for a backdrop.
- Shinjuku-gyōen (p102) A prime cherry-blossom attraction, this garden has several varieties of cherry trees, including *yaezakura* (double-blossoming cherries).
- Ueno-kōen (p81) Ground zero for the *hanami* explosion. Enthusiasts vie for the best angle on Ueno's 1000 flowering trees.
- Yasukuni-jinja (p89) There are more than a thousand cherry trees in the grounds of the shrine; check out the cherry trees lining the nearby Imperial Palace moat as well.
- Yoyogi-kōen (p100) There is plenty of space here to admire the park's 500 or so cherry trees.

Kōyō

During the autumn foliage season *(kōyō)*, which runs from about mid-October to early November, Tokyo's trees virtually explode in colour. Look especially for the maple, which goes through a minor spectrum of yellows and oranges before climaxing in a fiery red. Some of the best spots include the following.

- Kitanomaru-kōen (p63) Just north of the Imperial Palace, a great place for an autumn stroll or picnic.
- Koishikawa Kōrakuen (p88) A lovely pond and surrounding gardens make it perhaps Tokyo's best foliage spot.
- Shinjuku-gyōen (p102) This sprawling garden's many leaf-peeping locales include the Western-style garden.
- Ueno-kōen (p81) As popular for autumn foliage as for cherry blossoms.
- Yasukuni-jinja (p89) Note especially the tree-lined walkway.
- Yoyogi-kōen (p100) Sprawling park with ginkgo, zelvoka and cherry trees.

after a much bigger (and older) one in Kyoto, held a couple of weeks earlier.

TOKYO DESIGNERS' WEEK Early November

www.tdwa.com

Video, furniture and fashion are a few of the genres represented at venues around the city, mostly in arts enclaves such as Aoyama, Harajuku and Roppongi. Parties happen in the evenings.

SHICHI-GO-SAN (SEVEN-FIVE-THREE FESTIVAL) Early to mid-November

Meiji-jingū (p98), Yasukuni-jinja (p89) & Hie-jinja (p90)

This incredibly sweet festival celebrates children of these tender ages, who were once thought to be in danger of imminent misfortune. Parents dress girls aged seven and three and boys aged five in wee kimono and head to Shintō shrines and Buddhist temples throughout town, grandparents often in tow. It's a prime photo opportunity.

KŌYŌ (AUTUMN FOLIAGE SEASON)

The city's trees undergo magnificent seasonal transformations during *kōyō*. For listings of optimum foliage-viewing pleasure, see above.

DESIGN FESTA Mid-November

Tokyo Big Sight (Map p289); www.designfesta.com

An enormous art and design festival held twice-yearly. See also p10.

INTERNATIONAL ROBOT EXHIBITION Late November to early December

In 2005 nearly 100,000 people joined the Japan Robotics Association and friends to take in the latest (in the Robo-One Grand Prix) and the classics (a robo-dino). Held biennially (next is in 2007).

CULTURE

It's not practical to try to ascribe a uniform culture to a metro area of 33-plus million people. That said, we can offer a few observations to give you some insight into daily interactions and life in Tokyo.

Over the years, we've boiled it down to one truism about Tokyo: 'things are what they are, except when they aren't'. Pedestrian traffic generally travels on the left (following vehicular traffic)...unless it's on the right. The same *obaasan* (grandma) who spikes you with her razor-sharp elbows trying to get a seat on the subway might serve tea that evening with the grace of a geisha. Office workers may be buttoned down during the daytime, but when you put a few drinks in them anything goes. But the difference from other societies is that even this divergence has its rules.

IDENTITY

Tokyo's civic identity has been formed and reformed by fluctuating cycles of disaster, exodus, growth and change; and the social system has created buffer zones and boundaries to help deal with such things.

For most of the time since WWII, stability came through work. Lifetime employment was the rule, and a single breadwinner (the husband in virtually every case) was enough for one household, while the wife tended to young Kenji and Miyuki and managed the family finances. Divorce was extremely low by standards of industrialised countries (around 10%). Even if the lifestyle wasn't extravagant, families were comfortable enough, and few of the neighbours had significantly more than anyone else (roughly 90% of Japanese consider themselves middle class).

Since the bubble burst in the early 1990s, family structures have changed. Lifetime employment or social security are no longer givens, nor is a tax structure that helps young people afford their own apartments. Yet some ideas seem to endure as part of the social fabric.

Thinking Socially

Much has been made for an awfully long time about the affinity Japanese people have with groups, yet it remains largely true. Japanese friendships often last for a lifetime, and it's not unusual for high-school chums, members of a club or colleagues in an 'entering class' of a company to keep tabs on each other well after any day-to-day association is over, into middle age or even old age.

MASAKO, THE RELUCTANT PRINCESS

Crown Princess Masako's biography may be one of the most perplexing in recent memory. Born in 1963, Owada Masako was the daughter of a diplomat, raised in cosmopolitan locales around the world (she speaks several languages) and educated at Harvard and Oxford. In 1993 she passed the notoriously difficult Japanese Foreign Ministry exam and was on her way to following in her father's footsteps, despite the fact that Japan's Crown Prince, Naruhito, had twice asked her to marry him.

The third time was the charm, though, as she accepted Naruhito's offer of marriage after he reputedly promised to protect her from the legendary rigidity of the Imperial Household Agency, which oversees imperial life.

It was a promise he would ultimately find difficult to fulfil. Prior to their highly publicised marriage in 1993, Masako seemed poised to become a sort of Japanese Princess Diana, an attractive, well-spoken royal envoy, but it soon became clear that her primary role was to produce an heir. Fertility eluded the couple, until at long last Masako gave birth in 2001, to Princess Aiko. However, a law dating from more than a century ago means that Aiko cannot become heir to the throne (see the boxed text, p55). Meanwhile, pressure continues on Masako to produce a male heir, even as she enters her mid-forties.

No doubt this, among other strains, contributed to Masako developing a 'nervous disorder', treated with counselling, therapy and medication. Prince Naruhito, for his part, has broken with imperial practice and valiantly spoken up on behalf of his wife. As we went to press, Masako has finally begun to emerge from isolation within the palace. Only time will tell whether the imperial family will be able to make some changes to its stiff structure.

URBAN ANTHROPOLOGY

Tokyoites may seem monolithic at first glance, but look closely and you'll notice great variation. Here are some types you may encounter.

Bosozoku These 'speed tribes' are motorcycle gangs who dye their hair and wear bright, flashy clothes. Typically, they'll spend a night loudly revving their motorcycle engines and speeding off tailed by the police, who never catch them. Like *chimpira,* some of the wilder *bosozoku* go on to become *yakuza.*

Chimpira This is often a *yankii* who has taken rebellion a step further and hopes to attract the attention of *yakuza* and be asked to join the gang as a junior *yakuza.*

Freeters A legacy of the recession, people in their 20s with little ambition. Equivalent to drifters in other societies, they typically work in places like convenience stores (the name comes from 'freelance') and make just enough money to get by.

Cos-play Typically high-school girls who dress up to attract attention (the name comes from *cos*tume *play*). The get-up as we went to press was sort of 'Gothic Lolita', frilly dresses and Little Bo Peep bonnets offset by gothic make-up. Prime spotting is on the bridge by Harajuku Station on weekend afternoons. Manga characters are also favoured in certain circles.

Obatarian This word combines the Japanese word *obasan* (aunt or older woman) and the English suffix '-genarian', as in someone who has reached a certain age, with all its negative stereotypes. *Obatarian* are known for shouldering their way onto trains and buses, terrorising shop assistants and generally getting their way. The male equivalent, *ojitarian* (from *ojisan* – uncle or older man), are generally uncommunicative and sour, wear unfashionable clothes and pick their teeth in public.

Office Ladies Also known as OLs, these women may be secretaries, but may equally be women who do the same work as their male bosses for significantly lower pay. OLs usually travel in small groups wearing matching uniforms of skirts, white blouses and vests. Other places to find them are in Italian cafés and on overseas trips (the latter without the uniforms).

Ojōsan Literally 'young woman', usually refers to a college student or graduate, who is middle class and headed for marriage to a young salaryman. An *ojōsan*'s dress is conservative, with the exception of the occasional miniskirt.

Otaku People (usually male and younger, though not exclusively either) who are unusually obsessed with electronics, manga, *anime*, a certain musical style etc. They're like 'nerds' but even more so.

Parasite singles These are single women who continue to live with their parents well into their 20s and 30s, hence the name 'parasite'. They are part of what is known in Japan as the *mukekkon sedai* (nonmarriage generation).

Salarymen These are just what you'd expect: businessmen, identifiable by their dark suits with the company logo pinned into the lapel. Often found in matching groups.

Yakuza These are the real thing: Japanese mafia. They used to stand out, with tight 'punch-perms' and loud suits, but modern *yakuza* are hardly noticeable, except perhaps for their swagger and black Mercedes with tinted windows.

Yan-mama This word is formed from the English word 'young' or the Japanese *yankii* and *mama* (mother). A *yan-mama* is a woman who has had children at a very early age (usually as a high-school student) and continues to dress in miniskirts and platform shoes, to the great horror of conservative weekly magazines in Japan.

Yankii (yahn-kee) A member of this tribe of low-grade punks prefers brown or blond hair, sports flashy clothes and has a mobile phone permanently glued to one ear. Male *yankii* often work in the construction industry, where their penchant for loud clothes is expressed in the brightly coloured *nikka-bokka* (from the English word 'knickerbockers') pants that they wear.

If you're let into a friendship or a group of friends, it's expected that you will always – *always* – consider the members of your circle in your words and deeds. This means watching what you say, taking care to avoid conflict, taking gifts to someone's home if you've been invited or if you haven't seen them for a long time, and apologising profusely when there's a problem, even if it may not be your fault. All of this reverses if you're out drinking or, more specifically, are drunk, when people often feel free to say whatever they want without fear that it will be brought up later.

Yet while it's true that relationships, families and networks remain extremely important, the idea that individual members of a social set *think* identically is absurd.

Inside & Out

Part of thinking about someone else's feelings can mean keeping yours to yourself. Thus *honne* (personal views) are often kept private and are sometimes never expressed. *Tatemae* (the safer views demanded by one's position within a group, a company or a family) are expressed often and sometimes act as a social lubricant to help things run smoothly. Trying to squeeze personal views out of a Japanese friend may be as uncomfortable for them as silence might be for you. There are myriad exceptions to this practice, particularly among young Japanese, who seem to feel more comfortable telling you what's on their minds; usually this begins with an expression such as *hitotsu itte ii?* ('may I say one thing?').

See Space & Silence (below) for practical uses of inside and out.

Space & Silence

Part of giving someone space, which you'll notice there isn't much of in Tokyo, means allowing downtime for someone to think and say what they find most appropriate. Hold on to your stopwatch – this stretch of quiet sometimes lasts as long as 30 seconds. Of course, the exceptions are numerous. Intimate friends may have an exchange that flies as fast as a table tennis ball, and older women often will tell you, point blank, what they think as they're thinking it. The drunk rule also applies here: when the sake's flowing, so are the thoughts.

Seasonality

Japanese culture is deeply keyed into the seasons, even in the big city. You won't have to look far to notice seasonal reminders: seasonal dishes at meals (both the food and the dishes they're served on), the changing of the plastic greenery over Asakusa's Nakamise-dōri (p179), ikebana (flower arrangements) in hotel lobbies and office buildings, plum blossoms in late winter, cherry blossom–viewing parties in spring, the switch to chilled *mugi-cha* (barley tea) in summer, the return of *oden* (fish-cake stew) to convenience stores each autumn, and the display of *mikan* (mandarin oranges) and *mochi* (cakes of pounded glutinous rice) before New Year's. Seasonality can also have its drawbacks, as in when a hotel won't turn on its air conditioning on an otherwise hot day because it's out of season.

BEING POLITE

In Tokyo, there are scores of unwritten rules visitors can't be expected to know, but here are a few simple practices to adopt and gaffes to avoid. See also p34 for eating etiquette.

- Shoes – Take them off whenever you enter a home, public bath and many temples, shrines and restaurants. Shoes without laces come in handy. Even if you are given slippers to wear, never step on tatami (tightly woven floor matting) in anything heavier than your socks. Public facilities often have racks or lockers for your shoes.
- Umbrellas – Umbrellas are for outdoors and should not be carried indoors when wet – use the umbrella stand by the entrance, or many businesses keep a supply of plastic sheaths by the entrance for you to insert your umbrella in before carrying it inside.
- Punctuality – Being on time in Tokyo means arriving a few minutes early, so that your meeting or event can start at the designated hour. This is particularly important in the business world.
- Mobile (cell) phones – Don't use them to speak while on trains, although many Japanese happily sit quietly on the train and text message friends, family and colleagues. Turn phones off completely near priority seating for the elderly and pregnant women.
- Noses – Blow them on the sly. Blowing your nose in public is considered disgusting. Carry tissues, as pocket handkerchiefs are not used for nose-blowing but instead for drying hands after using public rest rooms (many public rest rooms don't have towels or hand dryers).
- Gifts – Whenever you've accepted an invitation to someone's home, a gift is in order. Same goes if you're about to see someone you haven't seen for ages, or for neighbours in your new apartment building (for whom dish towels are a gesture of good will). Nearly as important as the gift itself is its presentation: attractively wrapped and offered with both hands and a slight bow. Also see the boxed text, p178, for more information on the custom of gift-giving.

LIFESTYLE

If you were to look into a typical Tokyo home, in a 2LDK apartment (two bedrooms with a living, dining and kitchen area) in a neighbourhood like Otsuka near Ikebukuro, you might find morning beginning at 6am. Mother prepares breakfast (traditionally rice, miso soup, some grilled fish and tea, but now more likely toast and coffee) for father before he takes off on his 12-minute walk to the train station in order to be at work by 8.30am.

Father may be a salaryman, a white-collar office employee who works for a large company five days a week and looks forward to retiring in 10 years so that he can finally focus on his watercolours. His wife may be college-educated but is from a generation of women who didn't see careers as an option. She probably takes classes during the day – perhaps at an English conversation school or a yoga studio – and spends a lot of time with her daughter, who is part of that generation of Japanese kids, the first really, to grow up as only children (Tokyo's birth rate is below 1%, even lower than in the rest of Japan).

Rounding out the household is their daughter, in her late 20s and, like the majority of women her age in the city, lives with her parents. This is nothing unusual or new; young Tokyoites (for practical and social reasons) have for generations lived with their parents until marriage, often helping with the care of a grandparent. But there's a key difference with this young woman who, college-educated like her mother, has a good job and a decent salary that could enable her to live on her own. The Japanese press has dubbed her, and others like her, a 'parasite single', even though she might pay her parents rent. Her mother probably does her laundry for her, and it's likely that she spends most of her disposable income on Prada shoes and European vacations, which she sometimes takes with her mother.

RELIGION

Ask Japanese friends about their religion, and they're likely to tell you that they are born Shintō, marry Christian and die Buddhist. The two big traditions here are Shintō (approximately 1400 Shintō shrines in Tokyo) and Buddhism (approximately 1850 Buddhist temples in Tokyo). Yet many Japanese find puzzling the notion that one should have to subscribe to only one religion. Rather, Japanese tend to observe life rites of different religions at the appropriate times.

Shintō, Japan's native religion, goes back to prehistory and holds that objects in nature contain a *kami* (god), many of which harbour special powers; sometimes a great person can become a *kami* as well. Shintō is also about purity, so people tend to visit Shintō shrines to commemorate new beginnings: parents bring babies to the shrine to be blessed and return for the Shichi-go-san festival (p12), and traditional weddings – the start of a new life – are held at Shintō shrines. If you have a new car, you might bring it to the shrine for a blessing. For more information on shrines and temples, see p86.

The central act of Buddhism, which arrived from India via China and Korea, is to achieve enlightenment, in order to escape the cycle of reincarnation and move on to Nirvana. Even if different Buddhist sects have different interpretations of the path to enlightenment – chanting, silent meditation, good works etc – Buddhism in Japan ultimately concerns itself with the afterlife. Buddhist altars are common in Japanese homes and businesses – their owners make regular offerings to their ancestors. Most Japanese funerals are held at Buddhist temples, as are festivals such as Setsubun (p9) and O-bon (p11). For more information on Buddhism in Japan, see p212.

The percentage of practising Christians in Japan is less than 1%, yet people who would otherwise never set foot in a church might marry in a Christian ceremony. The white wedding-dress aesthetic has trumped the solemnity of the traditional Shintō ceremony; Christian ceremonies also tend to accommodate much larger crowds than Shintō ceremonies, which are traditionally for family only. Christmas is also a big deal in Tokyo, although it tends to focus on Santa Claus and not Jesus Christ.

FASHION & DESIGN

Visitors to Tokyo are often in awe of this city's incredible sense of style. From the chaotic get-ups worn by Harajuku girls (and boys) to the sleek black shoes that click along the avenues in Ebisu, people here think carefully about design, trends and beauty.

Ever since the Edo period, this city has been Japan's most fashion-forward. Edokko (children of Edo) found a way to make chic the drab kimono imposed by the Tokugawa shōgunate, with handsomely crafted pouches closed with sculptural clasps called *netsuke*.

In the last couple of decades, Tokyo's fashion scene has been loosely organised around the work of Issey Miyake (p185), Yohji Yamamoto (p186) and, more recently, Rei Kawakubo of Commes des Garçons (p115), who show worldwide in addition to maintaining their presence in Tokyo.

Young designers have initiated an anti-fashion movement, designing clothes meant to be worn with comfort inside and outside of the house. Bathing Ape (aka BAPE) is the label *du jour*. Even casual wear may not be inexpensive compared to your home; Tokyo's parasite singles have money. Districts to see the newest and most fashionable are Omote-sandō and Aoyama, Daikanyama and Shimo-kitazawa; see p184 for more details.

Design in Tokyo is everywhere, from the marvellous Tōkyū Hands (p184), which carries wonderfully crafted furniture in addition to anything else you might want to put together an incredible apartment, to exquisite design stores in Roppongi and the Omote-sandō area. Electronics junkies already know about Akihabara and its plasma television screens, mobile-phone accessories and robot stores (see p77). Tokyo also hosts Asia's largest design show (Design Festa; p10 and p12) and an enormous robot exhibition (p12).

THE DECORATED SKIN

Japanese *irezumi* (tattooing) is widely considered the best of its kind. Usually completed in blue and red natural dyes, the tattoos often cover the whole body, with intricate designs featuring auspicious animals, flowers, Buddhist deities or folktale characters. In feudal times, the authorities tattooed criminals, thus stigmatising them as 'branded'. In due course, those who had been tattooed exhibited a defiant pride in these markings that set them apart from the rest of society. As a sop to foreign sensibilities, tattooing was banned during the Meiji era, but was promptly reinstated after the Prince of Wales (later to become King George V) took a liking to the art and had a dragon tattooed on his arm in 1881. Today the *yakuza* (Japanese mafia) are the only ones to stand out with magnificent *irezumi*, although to have a chance to see their exquisite body art you may have to visit *sentō* (public baths) regularly.

SPORT

Tokyo may be constantly on the go, but you'll see crowds often by the hundreds slow and then stop beneath one of the city's giant TV screens when an important moment in a sporting match is being broadcast. This pause testifies to the city's enthusiasm for its revered sports triumvirate: sumō, baseball and soccer (football).

The object of sumō is deceptively simple: knock the other guy off his feet or out of the ring. This 2000-year-old sport, derived from Shintō ritual, attracts huge crowds at the Kokugikan stadium (p106) in Tokyo's Ryōgoku district and on TV. Sumō *bashō* (tournaments) take place six times a year in Japan, three of which are in Tokyo (in January, May and September). Most popular are matches where one of the combatants is a *yokozuna*, a grand champion. At the moment, sumō's hottest ticket is Asashoryu, a Mongolian-born master who, as we went to press, had an unprecedented seven consecutive tournament championships and broke previous records with 84 wins out of 90 bouts in 2005.

Baseball *(yakyū)* was introduced to Japan in 1873 and became a fixture in 1934 when the *Yomiuri Shimbun* newspaper started its own team to capitalise on the fervour of a visit by US legends Babe Ruth and Lou Gehrig. That fervour continues through to the 21st century: the Japanese national team won the inaugural World Baseball Classic in March 2006. Today, Tokyo has two teams, the Yomiuri Giants and the Yakult Swallows (teams continue to be named largely for their corporate sponsors, rather than for their home cities). Japanese baseball rules allow a limited number of foreign players on each team. More to the point, some of the most talented Japanese players have been recruited to play in the Big Leagues in the USA – think Ichirō Suzuki, Hideki 'Godzilla' Matsui and Tadahito Iguchi; if a Japanese player is playing in the USA, the game is usually broadcast live in Japan (regardless of the hour). See the Baseball Hall of Fame & Museum (p88) for more information, and check out p173 for where to watch a game.

Fans at a Yomiuri Giants baseball game (see p17), Tokyo Dome

While soccer does not have baseball's storied history, it has gripped Japan like nothing else, especially in the last decade. Tokyo has two top-notch J-League (Japan League) teams, FC Tokyo and the Tokyo Verdies, that play from March to October. In 2002, when Japan and South Korea co-hosted the World Cup, two of the venues were just outside Tokyo, in Saitama and Yokohama. Like baseball leagues, soccer teams have recently seen an influx of international players and coaches and an export of Japanese talent to teams abroad.

MEDIA

Tokyo is Japan's media capital. TV *(terebi)* networks based here include NHK (the national broadcaster), Fuji Television, Nippon Television, TBS and TV Asahi; their headquarters are destinations for Japanese visitors. Breakfast broadcasts vary from sober reporting of world news to chipper chatter about the latest pop-star gossip. Daytime TV focuses on cooking and chat shows for housewives, with late-afternoon *anime* (p29) for kids. Info-tainment, variety and quiz shows are popular night-time fare.

Programming from overseas is typically dubbed, but many Japanese TVs have a 'bilingual' button for watching shows in their original language.

Major newspapers *(shimbun)* include the grey-lady *Asahi Shimbun*, the financial daily *Nihon Keizai Shimbun* (aka *Nikkei*) and the more populist *Mainichi Shimbun*, *Sankei Shimbun* and *Yomiuri Shimbun*. Sports newspapers are targeted at male readers (often with racy photos to match), and the *shūkanshi* (weekly magazines) compete intensely for the most sensational stories – you'll see them advertised on trains citywide. See p245 for English-language publications.

ECONOMY & COSTS

Although it looked as if Japan was going to take over the world economically through the 1980s, by the 1990s Japan's economy was in a certifiable recession and remained so until recently. Unemployment hovered around 5% (high by national standards), homelessness rose (visible in major encampments in districts like Ueno and Shinjuku), corporations approached bankruptcy and bank loans turned into bad debts. The result: deflation, increased public debt and growing concern over how to support a greying populace (Japan has one of the world's oldest populations, with life expectancies over 77 for men and 85 for women). However, 2005 marked the beginning of a turnaround, which appears, finally, to have traction; land values in the city rose for the first time since 1991.

Some smart Tokyoites used the bubble to regenerate. People under 40 began to reject the stability of lifetime employment in favour of more compelling, often more flexible, independent jobs. The emblem of this movement was Horie Takafumi, who in 1995 dropped out of Tokyo

University (Japan's most prestigious) at the age of 23 to found a consulting company which eventually morphed into Livedoor, one of Japan's leading Internet services and DVD-rental empires. Horie's showy personal trappings – fast cars, T-shirts instead of suits, brash corporate takeover bids and being a general media hound – infuriated the old-line corporate world. They also landed him in a book-cooking scandal which was headline news for months as we went to press.

Tokyo, once known as an impossibly expensive city, has become a lot more affordable in the last 10 years (or, at least, prices have frozen, giving the rest of the world a chance to catch up). As a rule, anything that requires a lot of space costs a lot (eg bowling alleys, cinemas, domestic produce). Most museums and cinemas don't generally offer discounts to adults, but concessions are usually available to students and the youngest children can often enter free. Senior discounts are sometimes available too.

HOW MUCH?

Cinema ticket ¥1800

Newspaper (in English) ¥150

One apple ¥100

2km taxi ride ¥660

Nappies (diapers; 32) ¥1300

Chewing gum ¥110

Pack of cigarettes ¥280

'Morning set' breakfast at a coffee shop ¥ 450 to ¥ 600

Beer at a bar ¥700

Beer from a vending machine ¥300

GOVERNMENT & POLITICS

Tokyo is the capital of Japan as well as the seat of national politics and, accordingly, is at the eye of the nation's parliamentary storm. The governing body, known as the Diet, is divided into two houses: the lower, House of Representatives, and the upper, House of Councillors. The party that controls the majority of seats in the Diet is the ruling party and has the right to appoint the prime minister – usually the party's president. The prime minister then appoints his cabinet, which is usually constituted entirely of Diet members. In theory, the Diet is a multiparty governing body; in practice, it is controlled by the conservative Liberal Democratic Party (LDP), which since its formation in 1955 has held sway with the exception of a few years in the mid-90s. See p91 for information about tours of the National Diet.

Although Diet members are elected by popular vote, real power is held by the bureaucracies of the ministries' powerful political cliques descended from generations of the nation's elite and Japan's dominant *keiretsu* (business cartels; see below). In addition, Tokyoites have long complained that the allocation of Diet seats gives the countryside much more power (and appropriations) per capita than the big cities. These factors, plus the recent recession and the charisma of the current, wild-maned Prime Minister Koizumi Junichirō have led the Japanese to begin to demand greater transparency.

WHAT'S IN A KEIRETSU

Businesspeople from abroad who come to work in Tokyo are often mystified by the structure of companies and interpersonal relationships. Business, they quickly learn, is never just business, but depends on a complex set of social relationships and corporate bonds that can never be accessed in a few meetings but must be built over years.

At the centre of this system, and of the economy, are *keiretsu,* alliances of businesses based on cross-shareholding (aka business cartels). This configuration, with a bank at its core, links a number of companies together. Each *keiretsu,* however, has only one enterprise in each industry, preventing competition within the group.

Although for years foreign companies, especially those from the USA, whinged about the exclusivity and seeming impracticality of the *keiretsu's* tight-knit alliance, they have recently begun to adopt the model themselves. As for Japanese views on the same, *keiretsu* are often viewed as safety zones for lifetime employment, with employees being shifted horizontally from one enterprise to another as components of the group become less fiscally viable. It remains to be seen whether such loyalty will stand as the prospect of lifetime employment continues to evaporate and ageing baby boomers find themselves – sometimes literally – out in the cold.

ENVIRONMENT

Perhaps the most remarkable thing about Tokyo is that the environment supports it at all. Comprehensive pollution laws (introduced in 1967), one of the best public-transit systems in the world and an ongoing commitment to recycling programmes continue to make it one of Asia's most environmentally viable supercities.

Adding to the liveability of the city are the numerous parks (there are thousands from pocket parks to riverside promenades and sprawling affairs dating back to samurai times) that dot the landscape. These are frequented year-round as Tokyo's mild climate makes them accessible and the marked changes in seasons make them appealing.

THE LAND

Tokyo lies at the southern end of the Kantō Plain, the largest stretch of lowland in Japan, and is surrounded by nearby prefectures of Kanagawa, Yamanashi, Saitama and Chiba, and Tokyo Bay, which opens into the Pacific Ocean. The city is famously earthquake prone, in part because it lies at the junction of the Eurasian, Pacific and Philippine tectonic plates. To compound the problem, much of the city and many crowded residential areas are built on loosely consolidated landfill, which could theoretically mix with underground water during a big trembler, causing portions of the city to collapse. To learn about earthquake safety, see the Ikebukuro Bōsai-kan (p103).

THE BIG ONE

On 17 January 1995, the city of Kōbe (about 600km from Tokyo) was devastated by an earthquake measuring 7.2 on the Richter scale, and it left Tokyoites wondering 'what about us?'

Although imperceptible earthquakes happen nearly every day in Japan, the last one to give Tokyo a major shakedown was the 1923 Great Kantō Earthquake (p53). Thankfully, Tokyo is not the city it was in 1923. Its architects have been leaders in designing buildings to withstand earthquakes; some skyscrapers are on rollers or casters, others are reinforced at intervals etc. Yet the prospect of another major quake remains a grim one, and the devastation in Kōbe served as a reminder that that no amount of earthquake preparation is too much.

GREEN TOKYO

Tokyo has an excellent recycling system duly enforced by garbage collection services. In apartments, homes and businesses, all garbage must be separated into burnable, nonburnable and recyclable bags. Garbage that is not appropriately bundled is simply not picked up.

Foreign visitors are often surprised at the lack of garbage bins in public places. Eating while walking in Japan is almost never done, except at fairs or the occasional ice-cream cone. Otherwise, the rule is to hold on to your rubbish (trash) until you get home. Under duress, train stations and convenience stores usually have bins, typically separated into those for paper (sometimes newspapers and magazines), cans, bottles, and other rubbish, with handy pictures.

URBAN PLANNING & DEVELOPMENT

Tokyo probably has looser building restrictions than many giant cities, yet its growth has been carefully planned since the Meiji era. Most recently, the Metropolitan Government Bureau of City Planning has recognised that the declining birth rate means that more space will open up. It has also turned away from the anticontrol policies that drove a frenzied building boom in the late '80s and early '90s and has set out to encourage the renovation of decrepit office buildings. Other improvements on the horizon include additional train services, to decrease congestion enough that commuters will have room to read a newspaper.

On a greener note, laws passed in 2002 require all new and reconstructed buildings to include a roof garden. The measures were adopted to combat Tokyo's infernal summer heat – temperatures have risen 3°C in the last hundred years – and also to beautify its concrete expanse. Noncompliant property owners are subject to hefty fines.

Arts & Architecture

Arts & Architecture

TRADITIONAL ARTS

From Old Edo to Ultra Tokyo, Edokko have always lived for art, even if it isn't where you'd expect to see it. There's fine art from ancient Japanese traditions, of course, such as *ukiyo-e* wood-block printing and ikebana flower arranging, but it can also take the form of something as simple as the adorable, expressive graphics in advertisements or the way a department store clerk wraps a package.

If it's Art with a capital A you're after, Tokyo is experiencing a renaissance. You'll find it in the large museums, in matchbox-sized galleries, decorating the streets, at train stations and convention halls, in hulking stages and tiny underground theatres in quiet neighbourhoods, and, incredibly, a lot of it is really good.

ARTS & CRAFTS

Painting

From AD 794 to 1600, Japanese painting borrowed from Chinese and Western techniques and media, ultimately transforming these towards its own aesthetic end. By the beginning of the Edo (the pre–Meiji Restoration name for Tokyo, 1600–1867) period, which was marked by a wide range of painting styles attracting enthusiastic patronage, Japanese art had come completely into its own. The Kanō school, initiated more than a century before the beginning of the Edo period, continued to be in demand for its depiction of subjects connected with Confucianism, mythical Chinese creatures or scenes from nature. The Tosa school, which followed the *yamato-e* style of painting (often used on scrolls during the Heian period, 794–1185), received commissions from nobility eager for scenes from ancient classics of Japanese literature.

Finally, the Rimpa school (from 1600) absorbed the earlier styles of painting and progressed beyond conventions to produce a strikingly decorative and delicately shaded form of painting. The works produced by a trio of outstanding artists from this school – Tawaraya Sōtatsu, Hon'ami Kōetsu and Ogata Kōrin – rank among the finest of this period.

Ukiyo-e

Far from the Chinese-inspired landscapes and religious-themed paintings, *ukiyo-e* (literally 'pictures of the floating world'; wood-block prints) were for the common people, used in advertising or much in the way posters are used today. The subjects of these wood-block prints were images of everyday life, characters in kabuki (p24) plays and scenes from the 'floating world', a term derived from a Buddhist metaphor for life's fleeting joys.

Edo's particular floating world revolved around pleasure districts such as the Yoshiwara (see also p51). In this topsy-turvy kingdom, an inversion of the usual social hierarchies imposed by the Tokugawa shōgunate, money meant more than rank, actors and artists were the arbiters of style, and prostitutes elevated their art to such a level that their accomplishments matched those of the women of noble families.

The vivid colours, novel composition and flowing lines of *ukiyo-e* caused great excitement when they finally arrived in the West; the French came to dub it 'Japonisme'. *Ukiyo-e* was a key influence on impressionists and post-impressionists (eg Toulouse-Lautrec, Manet and Degas). Yet among the Japanese, the prints were hardly given more than passing consideration – millions were produced annually in Edo, often thrown away or used as wrapping paper for pottery. For many years, the Japanese continued to be perplexed by the keen interest foreigners took in this art form.

The compact but exceptional Ukiyo-e Ota Memorial Art Museum (p99) has rotating exhibitions, while the Edo-Tokyo Museum (p105) has a section describing *ukiyo-e* and how they were made.

Mingei

The *mingei* movement had its heyday in the early and mid-20th century, but its impact on the Japanese aesthetic has been profound. *Mingei* is often translated as 'folk crafts', though that rather misses the point. Central to the *mingei* philosophy is *yo no bi* (beauty through use), where everyday objects should bring pleasure through their aesthetics, touch and ease of use. *Mingei* movement leaders included potters Hamada Shoji (1894–1978) and Kawai Kanjirō (1890–1966), the eccentric genius potter and painter Munakata Shikō (1903–75), Serizawa Keisuke (1895–1984) for his amazing textiles and the British-born potter Bernard Leach (1887–1979).

To see some *mingei* works, visit the Crafts Gallery (p64) of Kokuritsu Kindai Bijutsukan (National Museum of Modern Art), or the Nihon Mingeikan (p109).

TOP FIVE TRADITIONAL ART VENUES

- Bijutsukan Kōgeikan (Crafts Gallery; p64) of Kokuritsu Kindai Bijutsukan (National Museum of Modern Art)
- Musée Tomo (p93)
- Nihon Mingeikan (p109)
- Tokyo Kokuritsu Hakubutsukan (Tokyo National Museum; p80)
- Ukiyo-e Ota Memorial Art Museum (p99)

Ikebana

Key differences between ikebana (flower arranging) and western forms of flower arranging are the illusion of space, the interplay between the flowers and the vessels or baskets used to display them, and the sense of balance created when a flower is placed just so. The popularity of ikebana is evident in the eye-pleasing creations in the city's shop windows and the *tokonoma* (sacred alcoves) of its private residences.

See p238 for information about ikebana classes.

Ceramics

Japan has one of the world's great ceramic traditions, from early Jōmon earthenware to the humble aesthetic of the tea ceremony and brightly coloured vessels sold overseas for big prices. Tokyo is not a significant centre for ceramic making, but has extensive descriptions about ceramic styles and their appreciation.

Various museums around town host ceramics exhibitions – Tokyo Kokuritsu Hakubutsukan (Tokyo National Museum; p80) and Hatakeyama Collection (p109) are particularly good examples. Department-store art galleries are also good places to catch a show. The remarkable online gallery www.e-yakimono.net has all the information you need about ceramic styles and appreciation.

Tea Ceremony

First things first: the tea ceremony is not about drinking tea (well, only a little). As much a philosophy as an art, *sadō,* or the 'way of tea', combines a host of related arts and crafts: ceramics, kimono, calligraphy, ikebana, food, traditional architecture and garden design.

The art of the tea ceremony

Originally the pastime of samurai and Zen priests, *sadō* placed great emphasis on the aesthetic qualities of simplicity and naturalness, which together with humility create a spirit called *wabi-sabi.* Tea-master Sen no Rikyū codified the practice in the Momoyama period. Today a proper tea ceremony takes place in a tea room of 4.5 tatami mats. Seasonal ikebana and scroll paintings, the selection of ceramics and utensils used in the preparation and serving of the tea, the sweets accompanying the tea, and the design of the adjoining garden should all unite to create an 'only-in-this-moment' experience.

TRADITIONAL CRAFTS

In lacquerware (*shikki* or *nurimono*), multiple layers of lacquer are painstakingly applied to a wood surface, left to dry, and polished to a luxurious shine. A decorative technique called *maki-e* involves the sprinkling of silver or gold powder onto liquid lacquer to form a picture. After the lacquer dries, another coat seals the picture.

Bamboo crafts (*take-seihin* or *take-kōgei*) are another specialty. Bamboo baskets, remarkable for their complexity and delicacy, are popular for use in ikebana. Bamboo is also commonly used in tea-ceremony ladles and whisks.

Folding fans *(sensu)* are still a practical and fashionable way of dealing with Tokyo's sweltering summers. Some shops in town also specialise in the large, elaborate types used in *nō* drama and classical dance.

Handmade paper *(washi)* was introduced from China in the 5th century. The arrival of Western paper in the 1870s caused the craft to plummet, but *washi* has enjoyed a revival with some amazing new techniques that, for example, highlight the wood pulp.

There are many opportunities to see these works in Tokyo's museums, galleries, department stores and shops.

Opportunities to participate in a full-on tea ceremony are exceedingly rare anywhere in Japan; if you are invited, *accept* (but not so eagerly as to show immodesty). Otherwise, many places around town offer the same sort of whisked green tea *(matcha)* with a sweet in far less formal settings. The teahouse at Hama Rikyū Onshi-teien (p75) is particularly lovely, in the centre of a pond, or inquire at shrines, temples and smaller museums.

PERFORMING ARTS

See p145 for publications and websites where you can find listings of what's on.

Nō

Nō originated from the combination of indigenous Shintō-related dance and mime traditions, and dance forms that originated elsewhere in Asia, and it really came to the fore in Kyoto between 1350 and 1450. Rather than a drama in the usual sense, a *nō* play seeks to express a poetic moment by symbolic and almost abstract means: glorious movements, grand and exaggerated costumes and hairstyles, sonorous chorus and music, and subtle expression. Actors frequently wear masks while they perform before a spare, unchanging set, which features a painting of a large pine tree.

Most *nō* plays centre around two principal characters: the *shite,* who is sometimes a living person but more often a demon or a ghost whose soul cannot rest; and the *waki,* who leads the main character towards the play's climactic moment. The elegant language used is that of the court of the 14th century.

Some visitors find *nō* rapturous and captivating; others (including many Japanese) find its subtlety all too subtle. If you are going to take in a *nō* performance, familiarise yourself with the story and characters beforehand. If all else fails, the intermissions of *nō* performances are punctuated by *kyōgen,* short, lively comic farces.

For performance information, see p145.

Kabuki

If *nō* has a history of catering to the elites, with themes of the afterlife and classical Japanese legend, kabuki originated as art for the common people, with dialogue, lively music, breathtaking costumes, an absence of masks, casts of dozens and stagecraft that was – and remains – unique in the world.

Although kabuki is most closely associated with Edo, it began in Kyoto around 1600 when a charismatic shrine priestess called Okuni and her troupe started entertaining crowds with a new type of dance people dubbed 'kabuki', a slang expression that meant 'cool' or 'in vogue'.

Okuni's dancers were not above prostituting their talents, and when fights for the ladies' affections became a bit too frequent, order-obsessed Tokugawa officials declared the entertainment a threat to public morality. Women's kabuki was banned, and troupes of adolescent men took over the female roles, a development that only fed the flames of samurai ardour. Finally, in 1653, the authorities mandated that only adult men with shorn forelocks could perform kabuki, which gave rise to one of kabuki's most fascinating and artistic elements, the *onnagata* (an actor who specialises in portraying women).

Over several centuries, kabuki has developed a repertoire of popular themes, such as famous historical accounts and stories of love-suicide, while also borrowing copiously from *nō* (opposite), *kyōgen* (short comic farces) and bunraku (below). Many kabuki plays border on melodrama, while others vary from stories of bravery to elaborate dance pieces.

Unlike Western theatre, kabuki is actor-centred. Kabuki actors are born to the art form – the leading families of modern kabuki go back many generations – and training begins in childhood; the Japanese audience takes great interest in watching how different generations of one family perform the same part. Actors today enjoy great social prestige, and their activities on and off the stage attract as much interest as those of film and TV stars.

Ingenious features of kabuki include the revolving stage (a kabuki invention), the *hanamichi* (a raised walkway connecting the stage to the back of the theatre, which is used for dramatic entrances and exits), *koken* (on-stage assistants) and *hiki-nuki* (on-stage costume changes).

Another unique aspect of kabuki is the *kakegoe*, enthusiastic fans who shout out the name of the *yago* (home studio; below) of their favourite actors at pivotal moments such as well-known lines of dialogue or poses called *mie*. Actors note they miss this reinforcement when performing overseas (but don't try it yourself!). See Kabuki-za (p66 and p145) for more details.

Bunraku

Japan's traditional puppet theatre developed at the same time as kabuki, when the *shamisen* (a three-stringed lute), imported from Okinawa, was combined with traditional puppetry techniques and *joruri* (narrative chanting). Bunraku, as it came to be known in the 19th century, addresses many of the same themes as kabuki, and in fact many of the most famous plays in the kabuki repertoire were originally written for the puppet theatre. Bunraku involves large puppets – nearly two-thirds life size – manipulated by up to three black-robed puppeteers. The puppeteers do not speak; a seated narrator tells the story and provides the voices of the characters, expressing their feelings with smiles, weeping and starts of surprise and fear. Although bunraku is most closely associated with Ōsaka, the best place to see it in Tokyo is the New National Theatre (Shin Kokuritsu Gekijō; p147).

Rakugo

A traditional Japanese style of comic monologue, *rakugo* (literally, 'dropped word') dates back to the Edo period (1600–1867). The performer, usually in kimono, sits on a square cushion on a stage. Props are limited to a fan and hand towel. The monologue begins with a *makura* (prologue), which is followed by the story itself and, finally, the *ochi* (punch line, or 'drop', which is another pronunciation of the Chinese character for *raku* in *rakugo*). Many of the monologues in the traditional *rakugo* repertoire date back to the Edo and Meiji periods, and while well known, reflect a social milieu unknown to modern listeners. Accordingly, many practitioners today also write new monologues addressing issues relevant to contemporary life.

WAX ON, WAX OFF

As anyone who's seen *The Karate Kid* can tell you, learning in Japan traditionally takes place through apprenticeship at the feet of one's elders and betters. In the world of kabuki (stylised Japanese theatre; opposite), for example, sons often follow their fathers into the *yago* (studio) to train in order to perpetuate the father's name on stage. Thus, the generations of certain families (eg Bando and Ichikawa) run into the double digits. Traditional painters and musicians are often associated with a 'school', which may refer both to where they trained and the style of art they create.

The early years of training tend to be arduous and seemingly unrelated to anything artistic: cleaning the studio, assisting with costumes, carrying instruments. But through this process, a young artist gets to know his or her craft inside out, and by the time he (or more recently, she) is finally ready to take the mantle, preparation is complete. A similar system applies in fields from sumō to cuisine to the corporate world – one has to earn one's dues before receiving a promotion.

Given the quickened pace of life in postwar Japan, Western-style art schools have long since come into their own. Still, in the traditional arts, apprenticeship remains the tried-and-true way to earn respect.

CONTEMPORARY ARTS

VISUAL ARTS

Tokyo has one of the world's most vibrant contemporary art scenes and dozens of galleries throughout the city at which to view it.

The opening of the Mori Art Museum in 2003 was something of a watershed for the contemporary arts. More than a dozen excellent art galleries are consolidated in buildings such as Complex in Roppongi (p92) and near the eastern bank of the Sumida River (p104). It's fair to say that the city's contemporary aesthetic heartbeat has never been heard more clearly.

Artists to look for include Miyajima Tatsuo, whose sculptures and installation pieces often incorporate numeric LCD displays; Sugimoto Hiroshi, famous for his time-transcending photos (eg exposing the film to a movie screen while the entire movie runs); and Nara Yoshitomo and Murakami Takashi, both heavily influenced by manga (Japanese comics, p29). The signature style of Kusama Yayoi is motifs of dots and nets, which make their way onto hanging art, sculptures and even clothing. Ishiuchi Miyako appeared in the Japan pavilion at the 2005 Venice Biennale, with her collection *Mother,* exploring artefacts of her own mother's turbulent life in penetrating photographs.

MUSIC

Tokyo has a huge, shape-shifting music scene supported by a local market of audiophiles willing to try almost anything. International artists make a point of swinging through on global tours, and the local scene surfaces every night in one of the city's thousands of 'live houses'.

Western classical music (p163) is performed by several outstanding local orchestras, such as the NHK Symphony Orchestra and the Tokyo Philharmonic Orchestra, and by visiting ensembles. Opera (p163) too has come to stay. Notable companies include the Fujiwara Opera, which specialises in French and Italian operas, and the Nikkai opera, which mounts performances of Mozart and Wagner.

The jazz scene is enormous (see p165), as are the followings for rock, house, electronica and Latin jazz.

Mainstream music is dominated by the commercial J-Pop. Some of the biggest acts are young *aidoru* (idol) singers who owe their popularity to cute looks and a flood of media appearances. The all-girl group Morning Musume has been the standard in recent years, keeping things fresh by regularly 'graduating' some of its dozen-or-so members and holding auditions for new ones. The boy-band equivalent is SMAP, which has prospered since 1991 with about half as many members. Other current top J-Pop artists include singer-songwriter Utada Hikaru, the Korean-born Boa, Hamasaki Ayumi and long-time favourite Southern All Stars. Japanese bands also follow Western music trends like hip-hop and rap.

Tokyo is famous for its cutting-edge club music scene. DJs here are as numerous as they come, but some of the biggest names are DJ Cornelius, Ken Ishii and DJ Kentaro.

Enka is a musical style popular among older generations but its nostalgic charm occasionally attracts younger audiences too. Its lyrics and emotions emphasise themes of longing and tears, and musically it's usually languidly paced and in a musical scale that borrows from traditional Japanese music.

Tokyo is also one of the only cities in Asia where you may have the luxury of seeing up-and-coming performers playing in intimate venues. See p163 for more on these styles.

And no discussion of the Tokyo music scene can be complete without a mention of karaoke. Karaoke started in Japan in 1971 and remains wildly popular, as a walk down just about any alley at night will evidence. Go with a group, and you'll almost certainly be expected to perform; most karaoke bars and 'karaoke boxes' (private rooms with karaoke equipment) have at least a few English songs.

TOP FIVE CONTEMPORARY ART VENUES

- Complex (p92)
- Kokuritsu Kindai Bijutsukan (National Museum of Modern Art; p63)
- Mori Art Museum (p92)
- Museum of Contemporary Art, Tokyo (p107)
- Tokyo Opera City (p101)

THEATRE & DANCE

Commercial Theatre

Theatre performer in traditional dress

Commercial theatre in Tokyo encompasses classical and contemporary dramas and musicals, both home-grown and imported, staged by large entertainment companies and starring well-known actors, singers and other celebrities. If you're struck by a sudden hankering for a Royal Shakespeare Company production of *Romeo and Juliet,* or a Japanese-language performance of the *Phantom of the Opera* you might just be in luck.

Popular but quirky, the all-female Takarazuka troupe offers a musical experience unlike any other. Founded in 1913, partially as an inversion of the all-male kabuki theatre and partially as a form of entertainment for a growing male middle-class with money to burn, Takarazuka combines traditional Japanese elements with Western musical styles. Interestingly, in light of its history, its most devoted admirers are young women who swoon with romantic abandon over the troupe's beautiful drag kings. Takarazuka adopted its present revue format in the late 1920s, and except for the WWII years – during which the troupe proved an ideal propaganda tool – has continued to perform musicals and revues set in exotic locations.

Underground Theatre

Theatre the world over spent the 1960s redefining itself, and it was no different in Tokyo. The *shōgekijō* (little theatre) movement, also called *angura* (underground), has given Japan many of its leading playwrights, directors and actors. Like their counterparts in the West, these productions took place in any space available – in small theatres, tents, basements, open spaces and on street corners.

Today's *shōgekijō* take on realistic themes, such as modern Japanese history, war and environmental degradation. Socially and politically critical dramas (such as those by Kaneshita Tatsuo and Sakate Yōji), psychological dramas (eg by Iwamatsu Ryō, Suzue Toshirō and Hirata Oriza) and satirical portrayals of modern society (eg by Nagai Ai and Makino Nozomi) have come to the fore and even attracted attention overseas.

Venues include the Suzunari Theatre outside of the city centre in Shimokitazawa, and Die Pratze. And there always seems to be at least one troupe performing English-language theatre. See p146 for listings.

Butō

In many ways, *butō* is Japan's most exciting dance form. It is also the newest, dating only from 1959, when Tatsumi Hijikata (1928–86) gave the first *butō* performance. *Butō* was born out of a rejection of the excessive formalisation that characterises traditional forms of Japanese dance and of an intention to return to the ancient roots of the Japanese soul.

Butō performances are best likened to performance art rather than traditional dance. During a performance, one or more dancers use their naked or semi-naked bodies to express the most elemental and intense human emotions. Nothing is forbidden in *butō,* and performances often deal with taboo topics such as sexuality and death. For this reason, critics often describe *butō* as scandalous, and *butō* dancers delight in pushing the boundaries of what can be considered tasteful in artistic performance.

CINEMA

Japan has a vibrant, proud, critically acclaimed cinematic tradition. Renewed international attention since the mid-1990s has reinforced interest in domestic films, which account for an estimated 40% of box-office receipts – nearly double the level of most European countries. This includes not only artistically important works, but also films in the science-fiction, horror and 'monster-stomps-Tokyo' genres for which Japan is also known.

The golden age of Japanese cinema began with Kurosawa Akira's *Rashōmon,* winner of the Golden Lion at the 1951 Venice International Film Festival and an Oscar for best foreign film. The increasing realism and high artistic standards of the period are evident in such milestone films as *Tōkyō Monogatari* (Tokyo Story; 1953), by the legendary Ōzu Yasujirō; Mizoguchi Kenji's classics *Ugetsu Monogatari* (Tales of Ugetsu; 1953) and *Saikaku Ichidai Onna* (The Life of Oharu; 1952); and Kurosawa's 1954 masterpiece *Shichinin no Samurai* (The Seven Samurai); the latter was remade as the classic Western *The Magnificent Seven.*

The 1960s gave the world such landmarks as Ichikawa Kon's *Chushingura* (47 Samurai, 1962, based on the Akō incident; see p110) and Kurosawa's *Yōjimbo* (1961).

Up against TV and, later, video, cinema attendance in Japan declined through the 1980s, yet Japanese filmmakers continued to set standards: Kurosawa garnered acclaim worldwide for *Kagemusha* (The Shadow Warrior; 1980), which shared the Palme d'Or at Cannes, and *Ran* (1985). Imamura Shōhei's heartrending *Narayama Bushiko* (The Ballad of Narayama) won the Grand Prix at Cannes in 1983. Itami Jūzō became perhaps the most widely known Japanese director outside Japan after Kurosawa with such biting satires as *Osōshiki* (The Funeral; 1985), *Tampopo* (1986) and *Marusa no Onna* (A Taxing Woman; 1988). Ōshima Nagisa scored critical success with *Senjo no Merry Christmas* (Merry Christmas Mr Lawrence) in 1983.

In the 1990s, Japanese directors received top honours at two of the world's most prestigious film festivals: *Unagi* (Eel), Imamura Shōhei's black-humoured look at human nature's dark side won the Palme d'Or in Cannes – making him the only Japanese director to win this award twice; and 'Beat' Takeshi Kitano took the Golden Lion in Venice for *Hana-bi,* a tale of life and death, and the violence and honour that links them. The undisputed king of current Japanese cinema, 'Beat' Takeshi is a true renaissance man of the media; he stars in and directs his films, and is an author, poet and frequent TV personality.

These days, a new generation of directors is emerging; it includes Koreeda Hirokazu, with *Dare mo Shiranai* (Nobody Knows; 2004), winner of the Best Actor prize at the Cannes Film Festival for its young star Yagira Yūya, and Kurosawa Kiyoshi, with *Cure.*

Naturally, of course, the world's blockbusters also play here in Tokyo. See p147 for cinemas.

TOKYO ON FILM

- *Tokyo Story* (*Tokyo Monogatari;* 1953) Ōzu Yasujirō's story of an older couple who come to Tokyo to visit their children only to find themselves treated with disrespect and indifference.
- *Godzilla* (*Gojira;* 1954) It's become almost a cliché, but watch it again and you'll find a powerful metaphor in this city that spent the first half of the 20th century being beaten down and getting right back up again.
- *The Bad Sleep Well* (*Warui Yatsu Hodo Yoku Nemuru;* 1960) Kurosawa Akira's first film after breaking from Toho studios centres on a protagonist who marries the boss' daughter as part of an intricate plan to avenge his father's death.
- *Tokyo Pop* (1988) Fran Rubel Kuzui's breezy comedy about a lonely American songstress who finds redemption, fame and love in the here-today-gone-tomorrow world of J-pop.
- *Shall We Dance ?* (1997) A bored salaryman risks it all to learn the low-brow art of ballroom dancing. Footage includes some wistful shots of Tokyo at night.
- *Distance* (2001) A subtle meditation on togetherness and loneliness, Koreeda Hirokazu's follow-up to *After Life* follows four people into the woods as they seek the truth about lovers and friends who belonged to a murderous cult. Though clearly an examination of the phenomena of Aum Shinrikyō (see p56) and the subway sarin attacks, this film is blissfully free of dogma.
- *Lost in Translation* (2003) Tokyo takes on a muted gleam in Sofia Coppola's Oscar-winner about two guests at the Park Hyatt, sharing a moment away from loveless marriages. Bill Murray is in finest deadpan form, and the movie made Scarlett Johansson a star.
- *Tokyo Godfathers* (2003) Kon Satoshi's animated film uses a group of homeless men to explore the city's post-bubble underside. They come across a baby and don't quite know what's hit them.
- *Nobody Knows* (*Dare mo Shiranai;* 2004) Koreeda Hirokazu's slow and depressing but somehow life-affirming tale of four children forced to fend for themselves after their heinous mother abandons them. Based on true events.
- *Kamikaze Girls* (*Shimotsuma Monogatari;* 2004) One of the daffiest buddy movies ever made, and the only one we know that pairs a country girl obsessed with Lolita outfits from Tokyo boutiques with a biker chick who spits to punctuate her sentences. Written and directed by Tetsuya Nakashima.

MANGA & ANIME *Philip Brophy*

Despite a half-century of denial by Japanese cultural officialdom, manga (comics) and *anime* (animation) are among the most recognised signs of Japan to the West. Twenty years ago, many would offer bonsai, kimonos and tea ceremonies as emblems of Japan. Now it's garage kits (homemade model kits), character costumes and fan conventions.

Symbolised by the *otaku* social phenomenon (a reviled yet resounding 'fan/nerd' subculture), manga and *anime* are prime entertainment industries and major cultural forces. Japanese pop culture is possibly the most potent globally due to its saturation, range and extremities. Of course Japan is a lot more than manga and *anime*. But the manga and *anime* that proliferates is of a monumental scale.

Manga in 2004 accounted for 37% of all publications sold. *Shonen Jump* – the most popular of the giant weekly compendiums of manga – notches a circulation of three million copies. Weekly. Back in 1995 it did six million weekly. The overall downturn is largely attributed to the spread of secondhand manga stores, libraries and cafés – which means that the popularity of the medium is undiluted.

Gradually the West is realising that manga/*anime* is of a more complex nature than that established by Western superhero comics and series. Japan's most revered animator Hayao Miyazaki enjoyed international respect by winning the 2003 Oscar for Best Animated Feature for *Spirited Away* – the most successful Japanese movie of all time in Japan. Like all Miyazaki's films, it's noticeably devoid of the paternal patronising which characterises Western children's fare. By extension, the culture of manga/*anime* in Japan can decimate your assumptions about something as 'crass' as cartoony images.

Encountering this culture in Japan is not only easy – it's inescapable. Cute cartoon characters are everywhere and in the most unlikely places. Many Japanese treat this iconography as indifferently as we might treat the ubiquitous Helvetica lettering on freeway signs.

To gauge the economic might of manga/*anime*, you could attend the Tokyo International Animation Fair (March at Tokyo Big Sight; p120). It's a one-stop hit for proving exactly how big *anime* is in Japan. Some estimates have it that nearly 5000 titles of *anime* are currently produced annually (covering features, TV episodes and Original Video Animation (OVAs; animation released directly to retail sale on DVD). The number of booths, companies and buyers at Tokyo International Animation Fair supports these estimates.

Less corporate in its orientation is Comiket (short for 'Comic Market') held twice yearly in Tokyo (August and December, also at Tokyo Big Sight). This is the massive gathering of fan-produced amateur manga known as *doujinshi*. To the untrained eye, *doujinshi* looks like 'official' manga, but most are parodies of famous manga characters. Complete subgenres exist here, from gag-strips to sexual re-imaginings of popular titles. Unlike the copyright-neurotic West, the Japanese manga/*anime* industries support the *doujinshi* networks. The last decade witnessed many a famous manga artist emerge from this sprawling subculture. Also at Comiket one can experience the *kosu-purē* phenomenon: 'costume play' where fans dress up in their favourite character's attire. It's a bit nerdy, but the Japanese kids take it to another level. Your scepticism may melt into admiration. Branching out from these events into the everyday, there are hundreds of *anime*/manga stores throughout Tokyo. Current districts to explore include Kōenji and Nakano where many secondhand collectors' stores have sprouted. A major chain is Mandarake with a superstore in Nakano that will require many hours of your time. It houses thousands of rare and affordable merchandise of every kind. Don't be dismissive of what appears like a teenage overload; the age demographic of those who shop here will surprise you. And they're not just men.

But if you want to dive in and truly get lost, head to Akihabara. Many guides still tag Akihabara's 'Electric Town' as the electronics district. True, that sector survives there, but a closer look reveals a massive increase in manga/*anime* stores lining the strip. Notably, the upper floors of these stores withhold the more perverse *(hentai)* end of the spectrum with PC games, magazines *and* DVDs. The stores are incredibly crowded and narrow, plus any one store will simultaneously be playing 10 CDs and 10 DVDs. If you think you know noise, you don't. Free admission and an exhausting ride.

A final admonition. Forget the old binaries of new-versus-old, natural-versus-artificial, past-versus-future. In Tokyo they circulate freely like carp in an ornamental pond. The thrill in experiencing manga/*anime* culture lies in its demolition of high-versus-low paradigms familiar to us in the West. The images of *anime*/manga will retain their effect when you return home. After Tokyo, your own city can appear like a strangely artificial theme park. A great place to live.

LITERATURE

Fiction

Most of Japan's national literature since the Edo period has been penned by authors who have written about or spent most of their lives in Tokyo. From Natsume Soseki to Mishima Yukio to Murakami Haruki, the literature written in and about the metropolis has served as the playground of the national imagination. Not surprisingly, both of Japan's Nobel Laureates, Kawabata Yasunari and Ōe Kenzaburo spent the bulk of their writing lives in Tokyo (Ōe eventually left to escape the Japanese press).

And the trend continues as a new generation of Tokyo writers takes the stage. In April 2004, the Akutagawa Prize – one of the nation's most prestigious – was awarded to the two youngest Japanese writers to have ever received it, both of them women: Kanehara Hitomi (19) and Wataya Risa (20). The previous youngest winners included Ōe Kenzaburo and current Tokyo governor Ishihara Shintarō, who were both 23 at the time.

Poetry

While Japanese traditional poetry, such as the 17-syllable haiku or the 31-syllable *waka,* is most closely associated with the ancient capital of Kyōto, it has a history in Tokyo as well. Japan's most famous poet of all time, Matsuo Bashō, led a literary society here and began his journey to write his renowned work *Oku no Hoso-michi* on the banks of the Sumida River.

TOKYO FICTION

- *I Am a Cat,* Natsume Soseki – Soseki's best known for *Kokoro,* but this merciless turn-of-the-century narrative, told from the point of view of a cat, is way more fun.
- *Now Country,* Kawabata Yasunari – Written in the years just before WWII, this novel by one of Japan's two Nobel Laureates tells the tale of a Tokyo dilettante's cruel, tragic affair with a mountain geisha.
- *Monkey Brain Sushi: New Tastes in Japanese Fiction,* eds Birnbaum & Luke – The stories in this collection are a mind scramble. The best offering is Murakami Haruki's 'TV People'. Other stories titillate and satirise, and often attempt to shock.
- *Best Japanese Science Fiction,* eds Apostolou & Greenberg – Interestingly free of gadgets and gimmicks, this decently written collection (which includes work by Abe Kobo) of psychologically driven narratives asks questions about conformity and politics, and the cultural implications of keeping silent.
- *The Sailor Who Fell from Grace* and *After the Banquet,* Mishima Yukio – If you're looking for unsettling beauty, reach for the former. History buffs will want the latter tome, which was at the centre of a court case that became Japan's first privacy lawsuit.
- *Coin Locker Babies,* Murakami Ryu – A coming-of-age tale centred on the lives of Kiku and Hashi, two boys left to die in coin lockers by their mothers. Both survive. The latter part of the book follows Hashi through Toxictown, a futuristic danger zone. This is Murakami at his most poetic.
- *The Waiting Years,* Enchi Fumiko – Winner of the Noma Prize, Japan's highest literary award, *The Waiting Years* tells the story of Tomo, a woman who humiliatingly sets out to find a mistress for her husband, and Suga, the girl who is taken into the household thinking she is to become a maid.
- *The Cape and Other Stories from the Japanese Ghetto,* Nakagami Kenji – Often compared to William Faulkner, Tokyo author Nakagami provides rare insight into the world of the *burakumin,* often described as Japan's untouchable caste. The stories are set in the slums and alleyways of Kishu province.
- *Norwegian Wood,* Murakami Haruki – Set in the late '60s against the backdrop of student protests, Norwegian Wood is both the portrait of a young artist (as recounted by a reminiscent narrator) and an ode to first loves. Murakami is perhaps Japan's most celebrated novelist, and this is his most celebrated work.
- *A Wild Sheep Chase,* Murakami Haruki – A mutant sheep with a star on its back generates a search that takes a 20-something ad man to the mountainous north. The hero eventually confronts the mythical beast while wrestling with his own shadows.
- *A Personal Matter,* Kenzaburo Ōe – A 27-year-old school teacher's child is born brain-damaged. His life claustrophobic, his marriage failing, he dreams of escaping to Africa while planning the murder of his son.
- *Kangaroo Notebook,* Abe Kobo – The last novel Abe wrote before his death charts the route of an everyman who has begun to grow radish sprouts on his shins. He visits the hospital, only to find himself propelled towards a hallucinatory hell.
- *Kitchen,* Yoshimoto Banana – Yoshimoto gets a bad rap as a smooth operator of surfaces. It's true, *Kitchen* relentlessly chronicles Tokyo's fast-food menus and '80's pop culture, though underlying the superficial digressions are hints at a darker and deeper world of death, loss and loneliness.
- *Idoru,* William Gibson – This novel paints Tokyo's dark future, after the earthquake, after the grim reconstruction made possible by ominous nanotechnology. Shinjuku looms large, as does megawatt Akihabara.
- *Audrey Hepburn's Neck,* Alan Brown – Life in Tokyo in the 1990s, a story of life and love, city and country, straight and gay, Japanese and foreign.
- *On Parole,* Yoshimura Akira – After serving a prison term for murdering his wife, Shiro Kikutani learns to navigate daily life on the outside in a city that overwhelms and contains him. An accurate portrayal of claustrophobia and confusion in the megalopolis.
- *Out,* Kirino Natsuo – A gritty thriller about downtrodden female employees of a *bentō* (boxed-lunch) factory who become a band of murderesses. Winner of Japan's grand prize for crime fiction.

Contemporary poetry in Tokyo is alive and well…and read mostly by the dedicated. One exception to this trend is Tanikawa Shuntaro *(Map of Days, Naked)*, whose inspired verse has earned him not only a loyal following, but interviews in fashion and pop culture magazines. Also of note is Shiraishi Kazuko *(Let Those Who Appear)*, whose rowdy, lyrical poetry has earned her comparisons to American Beat poet, Allen Ginsberg.

ARCHITECTURE

Due to 20th-century disasters – and the fact that Tokyo is barely 400 years old to begin with – few ancient buildings remain here compared to other Japanese cities. But contemporary Tokyo architecture is among the world's most exciting and influential. The traditional Japanese preference for simple, natural and harmonious spaces is much in evidence in the work of modern architects – think post-and-beam construction and strong geometry – but this is now combined with high-tech materials and building techniques that originated elsewhere.

Japan first opened its doors to Western architecture with the Meiji Restoration. Japanese architects immediately responded to these new influences, but some 20 years later, a nationalistic push against the influence of the West saw a resurgence in the popularity of traditional Japanese building styles.

This ambivalence towards Western architecture continued until after WWI, when foreign architects, such as Frank Lloyd Wright came to build the Imperial Hotel in Tokyo (since demolished for safety reasons, although the façade can be seen at Meiji Mura, a culture/history park near Nagoya, two hours from Tokyo on the bullet train). Wright introduced the International Style, characterised by sleek lines, cubic forms and materials such as glass, steel and brick. Other prewar monoliths still stand in Marunouchi and Yūrakuchō opposite the east side of Hibiya Park; American bombers spared them and they were used for postwar command facilities.

After WWII, the aggressively sculptural stone and concrete work of French architect Le Corbusier exerted strong influence on Japanese architects, and by the mid-1960s Japanese architects were beginning to attract attention on the world stage for their unique style.

The best known was Tange Kenzō (1913–2005). The mixing of Le Corbusier and traditional Japanese forms can be seen in Tange's buildings, including the National Gymnasium (1964; p100) in Yoyogi-kōen, Hanae Mori Building (p115) and Sōgetsu Kaikan (1977; p91). His skyscraping Tokyo Metropolitan Government Offices (1991; p101) was modelled after the great European cathedrals – look up from the plaza below and see if it doesn't remind you of Notre Dame in Paris. Also look out for the Fuji TV Headquarters (1996, p107)

TOP 10 CONTEMPORARY BUILDINGS

- National Gymnasium (1964; p100) Avant-garde before this city knew the meaning of the words.
- Spiral Building (1985; p99) Clean lines and a user-friendly interior have made this design by Maki Fumihiko one of Aoyama's best-loved buildings.
- Asahi Flame (1989; Map pp296–7) Famously capped by a representation of a golden flame come to be known as the 'golden turd', Philippe Starck's late Bubble-era design is one of Tokyo's most recognisable modern structures.
- Tokyo Metropolitan Government Offices (1991; p101) Tange Kenzo's new city hall has both heft and airiness; great, free observatories mean it's popular too.
- Edo-Tokyo Museum (1992; p105) Architect Kikutane seems to have thumbed his nose at time in designing a history museum that so clearly represents a vision of the future. Wonderful *Star Wars* feel.
- Fuji TV Headquarters (1994; p107) The signature building of Odaiba, and well worthy of the title.
- Museum of Contemporary Art, Tokyo (1995; p107) Yanagisawa Takahiko's wild design feels like an experiment in outrageous geometry. Steel and concrete blend harmoniously into the surrounding urban park.
- Tokyo International Forum (1996; p64) This wonder of glass verticality stands tall in Ginza.
- Prada Aoyama (2003; p115) Pritzker winners Jacques Herzog and Pierre de Meuron's creation is a marvel of white-on-white, encased in a crystalline honeycomb.
- Roppongi Hills (2003; p93) Jon Jerde created a phenomenon of East-meets-West, ancient-meets-the-future and stark beauty-meets-crass-commercialism.

TEMPLE OR SHRINE?

The quickest way to distinguish a Buddhist temple from a Shintō shrine is to examine the entrance. The main entrance of a shrine is customarily a torii (Shintō shrine gate), usually composed of two upright pillars, joined at the top by two horizontal cross-bars, the upper of which is normally slightly curved. Torii are often painted a bright vermilion, though some are left as bare wood. In contrast, the *mon* (main entrance gate) of a temple is often a much more substantial affair, constructed of several pillars or casements, joined at the top by a multitiered roof. Temple gates often contain guardian figures, usually *Niō* (deva kings). Keep in mind, though, that shrines and temples sometimes share the same precincts, and it is not always easy to tell where one begins and the other ends.

in Odaiba; its latticelike frame suspends a giant orb that looms like the Death Star over Tokyo Bay.

In the 1960s, architects such as Shinohara Kazuo, Kurokawa Kisho, Maki Fumihiko and Kikutake Kiyonori began a movement known as Metabolism, which promoted flexible spaces and functions at the expense of fixed forms in building. Kurokawa's **Nakagin Capsule Tower** (Map pp290–1; 8-16-10 Ginza, Chūō-ku; Ⓢ Ōedo line to Tsukijishijō) is a seminal work, designed as pods which could be removed whole from a central core and replaced elsewhere. Shinohara finally came to design in a style he called Modern Next, incorporating both modern and postmodern design ideas combined with Japanese influences. This style can be seen in his Centennial Hall (1987) at Tokyo Institute of Technology, an elegant and uplifting synthesis of clashing forms in a shiny metal cladding. Maki, the master of minimalism, pursued design in a modernist style while still emphasising elements of nature – such as the roof of his Tokyo Metropolitan Gymnasium (1990; p172), which takes on the form of a sleek metal insect. Another Maki design, the Spiral Building (1985; p99) is a favourite with Tokyo residents for its user-friendly design, gallery space, café and shops.

Isozaki Arata, who originally worked under Tange, also promoted the Metabolist style before becoming interested in geometry and postmodernism. His work includes the Cultural Centre (1990) in Mito, about an hour from Tokyo, which contains a striking geometric, snake-like tower clad in different metals, and the Museum of Contemporary Art in Los Angeles.

Kikutake, meanwhile, went on to design the Edo-Tokyo Museum (1992; p105). This enormous structure, encompassing almost 50,000 sq metres of built space and reaching 62.2m (the height of Edo-jō) at its peak.

For more information on the city's architecture, visit www.tokyoarchitecture.info.

Another Tokyo architect to break onto the international scene in recent years is Taniguchi Yoshio. He had some important commissions in Japan – including the Gallery of Hōryū-ji Treasures, p81, at Tokyo Kokuritsu Hakubutsukan (Tokyo National Museum) – but his first overseas project was as big as they get: the 2004 renovation and expansion of the Museum of Modern Art in New York.

In the 1980s, a second generation of Japanese architects began to gain recognition within the international architecture scene, including Ito Toyo, Hasegawa Itsuko and Andō Tadao. This younger group has continued to explore both modernism and postmodernism, while incorporating the renewed interest in Japan's architectural heritage. Ito's most recent design is Tod's **Omote-sandō building** (2004; Map p284; 5-1-15 Jingūmae, Shibuya-ku), which looks as if it was wrapped in surgical tape. Andō's architecture utilises materials such as concrete to create strong geometric patterns that have so regularly appeared in Japan's traditional architecture. Two of his landmarks are around Omote-sandō: **Collezione** (6-1-3 Minami-Aoyama, Minato-ku) and **Omote-sandō Hills** (Map p284; 4-12 Jingūmae, Shibuya-ku; also see p114).

Across the street from Omote-sandō Hills is the new **Christian Dior store** (5-9-11 Jingūmae, Shibuya-ku) by a young protégée of Ito's, Sejima Kazuyo, together with her partner Nishizawa Ryūe in the firm Sanaa. They and others like them are quietly becoming the next generation of great Japanese architects; projects include museums in Spain, in New York and Toledo, Ohio, USA.

PRITZKER PRIZE–WINNING TOKYO ARCHITECTS

- Tange Kenzō (1987)
- Maki Fumihiko (1993)
- Andō Tadao (1995)

Food & Drink

Food & Drink

If you're reading this in your hotel room in Tokyo, go turn on the TV. We bet you won't have to scroll far through the channels to find some show involving food: a chef cooking, a host sampling the wares at a restaurant, an introduction to the latest and greatest speciality shop. With all the time and energy Tokyoites devote to food, it's a wonder they're so thin.

Even if you're already a fan of *Nihon ryōri* (Japanese cuisine), you're likely to be surprised by how delicious the original is when served on its home turf. Adventurous eaters will be delighted to find brave new worlds beyond sushi, tempura and sukiyaki.

No city in Japan can match Tokyo for the sheer variety and quality of its restaurants. This chapter concentrates on Japanese cuisine, but Tokyo is filled with many great international options. Really serious gourmands can visit the excellent Tokyo food pages at www.bento.com.

Many restaurants, especially high-end eateries, have some kind of English menu, though this is never guaranteed. Others, especially *izakaya* (pub chains) and other daily spots, have picture menus; most staff will understand 'picture menu'. Otherwise, many restaurants have plastic models in the window, making it easy to point and eat.

If you're looking for a place to grab a bite, you'll find plenty to choose from in Eating (p122) or consider a convenience store (see Beam Me to the Konbini, p41). In each of our restaurant listings throughout this book we denote a price guide; for more information and an explanation of the general costs of meals see p122).

CULTURE

ETIQUETTE

If you're worried about putting your foot in it, relax – the Japanese don't expect you to know everything and are unlikely to be offended as long as you follow the standards of politeness of your own country. Just follow the locals for things like lifting soup bowls and slurping noodles.

Among the more important rules are those regarding chopsticks. Don't stick them upright in your rice – that's how rice is offered to the dead! Passing food from your chopsticks to someone else's is a similar no-no. When taking food from shared plates, avoid using the end of the chopsticks that's already been in your mouth – invert your chopsticks before reaching for that tasty morsel. When there are shared dishes, you will usually be given a small plate *(torizara)* to use as your own.

Before digging in, it's polite to say *itadakimas[u]* (literally 'I will receive'). At the end of the meal you should say *gochisō-sama deshita* (literally 'it was a feast') a respectful way of saying that the meal was good. Even if you're just enjoying a cup of coffee or sampling some snacks at a shop, it's polite to use these expressions.

If you're out drinking, remember that you're expected to keep the drinks of your companions topped up – beer bottles in Japan are typically large (at least 500mL) and the glasses small. Hold your glass with both hands while it's being filled, and don't fill your own glass; wait for someone to do this for you, and if you're done just leave your glass full. The Japanese equivalent of 'cheers' is *kampai!* Don't use the Mediterranean toast *cin cin* unless you want to induce peals of laughter (it translates to what little boys have and little girls don't).

The word for 'delicious' is *oishii.* If there's something you don't like, just leave it on your plate or in your bowl and don't make a big deal of it. If you're at a group dinner and have eaten enough, and the server brings more food, it's best just to accept it and leave it, rather than send it back.

If someone invites you to eat or drink with them, they will be paying. In any case, it's unusual for bills to be split. Generally at the end of the meal, something of a struggle ensues to see who gets the privilege of paying. If this happens, it is polite to at least make an effort to pay the bill – it is extremely unlikely that your hosts will acquiesce. Exceptions are likely among younger people or co-workers, for example, out for lunch together.

If you're arriving at someone's home, it is polite to bring a gift. See p178 for suggestions. And if you have been someone's guest, be sure to thank them upon leaving. Following up with a thank you note is an excellent touch.

HOW LOCALS EAT

Unless it's at a noodle shop or the equivalent, it's rare to see someone eating out alone in Tokyo. Generally, meal times are social affairs where families or colleagues get together, sometimes around a *kotatsu* (a heated table with a quilted cover that reaches to the floor), although this has given way to Western-style seating in many private homes. At night, many restaurants host large groups enjoying many dishes meant to be sampled by everyone at the table. These social gatherings almost always include liquor, meaning that the volume can rise to decibel levels not heard in the rest of daily life. If you find yourself alone at an *izakaya*-type restaurant (see p38 for details), you can pretty well expect that someone will strike up a conversation, especially if he (usually) has been drinking.

EATING IN A JAPANESE RESTAURANT

When you enter a restaurant, often the entire staff will shout a hearty *irasshaimase!* (welcome!). In all but the most casual places the waiter or waitress will next ask you, *nan-mei sama?* (how many people?). Indicate the answer with your fingers, which is what the Japanese do, or respond with the number (eg *san-nin* for 'three people'). You may also be asked if you would like to sit at a low table on the tatami *(zashiki)* or at a table *(tēburu)* or counter *(kauntā)*. More and more restaurants these days offer the fun compromise of *hori-kotatsu* seating: you sit on the tatami, but there's a well beneath the table for you to place your legs.

Once seated you will be given an *o-shibori* (hot towel), a cup of tea or water and a menu. The *o-shibori* is for wiping your hands and face. When you're finished with it, just roll it up and leave it next to your place. Now comes the hard part: ordering. If you don't read Japanese, you can use the Romanised translations in this chapter to help you, or direct the waiter's attention to the Japanese script. If this doesn't work, there are two phrases which may help: *o-susame wa nan desuka?* (what would you recommend?) and *o-makase shimasu* (I leave it to you). If you're still having problems, you can try pointing at other diners' food or dragging the server outside to point at the plastic food displays in the window if the restaurant has them.

When you've finished eating, you can signal for the bill by crossing one index finger over the other to form an X. This is the standard sign for 'cheque please'. You can also say *o-kanjō o kudasai*. Remember, there is no tipping in Japan and tea and tap water are free of charge. Usually you will be given a bill to take to the cashier at the front of the restaurant. At more upmarket places, the host of the party will discreetly ask to be excused and pay before the group leaves. Only the bigger and more international places take credit cards.

When leaving, it is polite to say to the restaurant staff *gochisō-sama deshita* ('it was a real feast').

'CAN YOU EAT NATTŌ?'

Some Japanese seem to take perverse pleasure in challenging foreign visitors to try uniquely Japanese foods. Here's a rogue's gallery you may encounter:

- *nattō* (納豆) Fermented soybeans that are firm in the centre and malodorous outside. When you pick one soybean up with your chopsticks, it usually leaves gooey strings behind it.
- *shiokara* (塩辛) Squid intestines that are pickled until they're pink. Verrry salty. Served as a side dish.
- *basashi* (馬刺し) Raw horsemeat.
- *fugu* (ふぐ) Globefish, aka puffer fish or blowfish. Also see p41.
- *kujira* (鯨) Whale meat. Need we say more?

If there are foods you can't eat for health, religious or personal reasons, it's OK to refuse (politely). Preferably, inform your hosts before you decide on a restaurant, as once you get there it may be difficult to find something suitable.

STAPLES

RICE

Rice is more than just food in Japan; it's an essential component of Japanese culture. Over millennia, communities sprang up over rice farming. It is so central to the Japanese idea of eating that the word for rice, *gohan* (ご飯), is also the word for a meal, for example (*asagohan*, 'morning rice', is one way to say 'breakfast'). Despite the influx of foreign cuisines, rice remains the centrepiece of a Japanese meal, and everything else is *okazu* (side dishes).

Rice may appear at any Japanese-style meal of the day, but don't be surprised if it does not appear until the end, especially at more formal dinners. A current popular trend is *takikomigohan*, rice mixed with other ingredients, typically bits of stewed vegetable, fish or chicken. Plain rice is also about the only food in Japan for which a refill *(okawari)* is typically free.

FISH & SEAFOOD

The tonnes of fish that pass through the fish market in Tsukiji are the telltale signs of what locals are eating, and the variety of fish and seafood available in Tokyo can be overwhelming. Almost every Japanese meal you eat will probably include something fishy, whether or not you recognise it. For example, the first ingredient in many Japanese dishes is *dashi* (fish stock), made from shavings of dried bonito (a tuna-like fish).

Typical serving styles include sushi (すし or 寿司) and sashimi (opposite) or *yakizakana* (grilled fish; 焼き魚). Rrestaurants serving one style probably won't carry the other (pubs are the exception).

SOY

Like rice and fish, the humble soybean has a revered place in the Japanese food pantheon, simple, versatile and monstrously good for you. You probably are familiar with soy sauce (*shōyu*, しょうゆ) but may not know that miso (味噌, fermented soybean paste) also comes from the soybean. Miso comes in several varieties and is found most often in soup, made from *dashi* and typically includes cubes of tofu, strips of *wakame* seaweed and some chopped *negi* (green onion). Miso can also be a flavouring for other dishes. When sweetened and served atop something grilled, it's called *dengaku*.

Tofu (豆腐), soybean curd, is another soy staple, and many visitors to Japan are surprised at how much better it tastes when it is made fresh daily. Tofu appears in dozens of dishes, or for an unadulterated flavour try *hiya-yakko* (冷奴) at a pub, which is a small block of fresh tofu topped with grated ginger, which you drizzle with soy sauce. Another popular pub dish is *edamame* (枝豆), which is whole soybean pods that have been quickly boiled; pop the soybean from the shell into your mouth.

PICKLES

For centuries, *tsukemono* (漬物) were essential to the diet of Japanese who had no way of procuring fresh vegetables much of the year. Pickles are made from *daikon* (大根, a large, long white radish), eggplant, cucumber, various greens and more.

NOODLES

It's hard to imagine how the city could function without noodles. Shops range from ultra-refined to simple stand-and-eat (*tachikui*, 立ち食い) stands. Also see Soba & Udon (p38) and Rāmen (p38) for more information.

JAPANESE BREAKFAST

A traditional Japanese breakfast consists of rice, miso soup and pickles, some kind of cooked egg, a piece of grilled fish, and a cup of green tea. Tokyoites are also known to be fond of *nattō* (p35) for breakfast, mixed into the rice with a dab of hot mustard.

That said, the breakfast of choice for more and more Japanese these days is a cup of coffee, a thick slab of white toast, an egg and a small green salad. You can enjoy this as a *mōningu setto* (morning set) at small coffee houses for between ¥450 and ¥600. Many hotels serve both Western- and Japanese-style breakfasts.

STANDARDS

SUSHI & SASHIMI

Sashimi (刺身) is slices of raw fish served with soy sauce for dipping, while sushi is raw fish served with sweetened, vinegared rice.

There are two main types of sushi: *nigiri-zushi* (a small slice of fish served on a small pillow of rice) and *maki-zushi* (served in a seaweed roll). Lesser-known varieties include *chirashi-zushi* (a layer of rice covered in strips of fish, julienned egg, and vegetables), *oshi-zushi* (fish pressed in a mould over rice) and *inari-zushi* (rice in a pocket of sweet, fried tofu). *Nigiri-zushi* and *maki-zushi* usually contain a bit of *wasabi* (hot green horseradish).

If you're seated at the sushi counter, you can simply point at what you want; most of the selections are visible in a refrigerated glass case between you and the *itamae* (sushi chef). One portion *(ichi-nin mae)* usually means two pieces of sushi. If ordering à la carte feels like a chore, you can order a *mori-awase* (assortment, generally six or seven pieces); prices vary according to the type of fish used.

Sushi dish

Unless the sushi is already dressed with a sauce, you'll probably want to dip it in *shōyu* before popping it into your mouth. Pour just a little soy sauce at a time from the bottle on the counter into the small saucer provided (don't fill the saucer), and if there is a side of wasabi, add a little at a time – it can be very hot! Remember, the soy sauce is used to flavour the fish and not the rice, so don't dip your sushi rice-side down (plus, the rice tends to fall apart in the soy sauce). If you're not good at using chopsticks, don't worry, sushi is one of the few foods in Japan that it is perfectly acceptable to eat with your hands. Slices of *gari* (pickled ginger) are served to help refresh the palate. The beverage of choice with sushi is beer or sake, with a cup of cloudy green tea at the end of the meal.

ama-ebi	甘海老	sweet shrimp
awabi	あわび	abalone
ebi	海老/エビ	prawn or shrimp
hamachi	はまち	yellowtail
ika	いか	squid
ikura	イクラ	salmon roe
kani	かに	crab
katsuo	かつお	bonito
maguro	まぐろ	tuna
tai	鯛	sea bream
tamago	たまご	sweetened egg
toro	とろ	the choicest cut of fatty tuna belly
unagi	うなぎ	eel with a sweet sauce
uni	うに	sea urchin roe

SOBA & UDON

Soba are thin, brownish buckwheat-based noodles and udon are thick, white wheat noodles. *Soba* is more closely associated with the Kantō region, which includes Tokyo, while udon are more reminiscent of Kansai (around Ōsaka); however many restaurants throughout the country serve both. When hot, both varieties are served in a large bowl of light, bonito-flavoured broth; you can also order them served cold and piled on a bamboo mat, very refreshing in warm weather. It is customary to slurp your noodles, both to cool them (when hot) and to enhance the flavour.

The most popular type of cold noodles is *zaru soba,* topped with slivers of dried *nori* (seaweed). They come with a cup of cool broth and small plate of wasabi and sliced spring onions – stir these into the cup of broth and eat the noodles by dipping them in this mixture. Do not pour the broth over the noodles – it creates a huge mess! At the end of your meal, the server may give you some of the hot water used for boiling the noodles to mix with the leftover broth, which you drink like tea.

kake	かけ	*soba*/udon in broth
kitsune	きつね	*soba*/udon with fried tofu
soba	そば	buckwheat-based noodles
tempura	天ぷら	*soba*/udon with tempura shrimp
tsukimi	月見	*soba*/udon with egg on top
udon	うどん	thick, white wheat noodles
zaru	ざる	cold *soba*/udon served on a bamboo mat, topped with *nori*

RĀMEN

Rāmen originated in China, but its popularity in Japan is epic. Your basic *rāmen* is a big bowl of noodles in broth, served with toppings such as sliced pork, bean sprouts and leeks. Some *rāmen* restaurants also serve fried rice (*chāhan* or *yaki-meshi*), and *gyōza* (pork potsticker dumplings).

Rāmen restaurants are easily identified by the red *noren* (cloth awning) out front. As with *soba* and udon, slurping is *de rigueur*.

chānpon-men	ちゃんぽんメン	Nagasaki-style *rāmen* (noodles in meat broth with toppings)
chāshū-men	チャーシューメン	*rāmen* topped with slices of roast pork
miso-rāmen	味噌ラーメン	*rāmen* with miso-flavoured broth
rāmen	ラーメン	noodles in soup, topped with meat and vegetables
shio-rāmen	塩ラーメン	*rāmen* with salt-flavoured broth
shōyu-rāmen	醤油ラーメン	*rāmen* with soy sauce-flavoured broth
wantan-men	ワンタンメン	*rāmen* with meat dumplings

IZAKAYA

Izakaya translates as 'drinking house', the Japanese equivalent of a pub. They're great places for a casual meal, with a wide selection of food, hearty atmosphere and, of course, plenty of beer and sake. *Izakaya* can be identified by their rustic façades and the red lanterns outside their doors.

Patrons typically order a few dishes at a time, from a selection of Japanese foods such as *yakitori* (skewers of grilled chicken), *kushiyaki* (other grilled skewers, often vegetables), sashimi and grilled fish, as well as Japanese interpretations of Western foods like French fries and beef stew. Say *toriaezu* ('that's all for now') when finished ordering each set of dishes.

Izakaya food is usually fairly inexpensive. Depending on how much you drink, you can expect to get away for ¥2500 to ¥5000 per person.

Special types of *izakaya* include *robata-yaki* (a long counter with a busy grill behind it) and *yakitori-ya* (which specialises in *yakitori*). At either, you sit around a counter with the other patrons and watch the chef grill your selections over charcoal.

agedashi-dōfu	揚げだし豆腐	deep-fried tofu in a fish-stock soup
aspara-batā	アスパラバター	buttered asparagus
chiizu-age	チーズ揚げ	deep-fried cheese
ebi	エビ	shrimp
ginnan	ぎんなん	ginkgo nuts
gyū-niku	牛肉	pieces of beef
hasami/negima	はさみ/ねぎま	pieces of white meat alternating with leek
hiya-yakko	冷奴	a cold block of tofu with soy sauce and scallions
ika	いか	squid
jaga-batā	ジャガバター	baked potatoes with butter
kata yaki-soba	固焼きそば	hard fried noodles with meat and vegetables
kawa	かわ	chicken skin
niku-jaga	肉じゃが	beef and potato stew
piiman	ピーマン	small green peppers
poteto furai	ポテトフライ	French fries
rebā	レバ	chicken livers
renkon	れんこん	lotus root
sasami	ささみ	skinless chicken-breast pieces
sashimi mori-awase	刺身盛り合わせ	a selection of sliced sashimi
shiitake	しいたけ	Japanese mushrooms
shio-yaki-zakana	塩焼魚	a whole fish grilled with salt
shishamo	ししゃも	pregnant smelts, grilled and eaten whole
tama-negi	たまねぎ	round, white onions
tebasaki	手羽先	chicken wings
tsukune	つくね	chicken meat balls
tsuna sarada	ツナサラダ	tuna salad over cabbage
yaki-onigiri	焼きおにぎり	triangle of grilled rice
yaki-soba	焼きそば	fried noodles with meat and vegetables
yakitori	焼き鳥	skewers of grilled chicken
yasai sarada	野菜サラダ	mixed vegetable salad

TEMPURA

Tempura is portions of fish, prawns and vegetables cooked in fluffy, nongreasy batter. There are speciality tempura restaurants, but tempura is common elsewhere as well, such as at *izakaya*. Tempura is served with a small bowl of *ten-tsuyu* (a light brown sauce) and a plate of grated *daikon* to mix into the sauce ahead of time. Dip each piece of tempura into this sauce before eating it. Tempura is best when it's hot, so don't wait too long – use the sauce to cool each piece, and dig in.

kakiage	掻き揚げ	tempura cake of shredded vegetables
kakiage-don	掻き揚げ丼	*kakiage* served over a large bowl of rice
shōjin age	精進揚げ	vegetarian tempura
tempura moriawase	天ぷら盛り合わせ	a selection of tempura
ten-don	天丼	tempura shrimp and vegetables over a large bowl of rice

SUKIYAKI & SHABU-SHABU

Sukiyaki and *shabu-shabu* are favourites of most foreign visitors to Japan, perhaps because you get to cook them yourself at the table. Sukiyaki consists of thin slices of beef cooked in a broth of soy sauce, sugar and sake together with a variety of vegetables and tofu. After cooking, dip the ingredients one by one in raw egg before eating. When made with high-quality beef, such as that from Kōbe, it is a sublime experience.

Shabu-shabu consists of thin slices of beef and vegetables cooked by swirling the ingredients in a light broth light broth (*'shabu-shabu'* is an onomatopoeia for the 'swish-swish' sound the beef makes in the pot), then dipping them in special sesame seed and/or citrus-based sauce.

Both of these dishes are prepared in a pot over a fire at your table; your server will usually help you get started and keep a close watch. Take your time, add the ingredients little by little and savour the flavours as you go.

TONKATSU

Tonkatsu is a deep-fried, crumbed pork cutlet served with a savoury sauce. It is found both at speciality restaurants and elsewhere.

hire katsu	ヒレカツ	*tonkatsu* (crumbed pork) fillet
katsu-don	カツ丼	*tonkatsu* and egg on rice
kushi katsu	串カツ	deep-fried pork and vegetables on skewers
minchi katsu	ミンチカツ	minced pork cutlet
rōsu katsu	ロースカツ	fattier cut of pork, which some consider more flavourful
tonkatsu teishoku	トンカツ定食	a set meal of *tonkatsu*, rice, *miso shiru* and shredded cabbage

OKONOMIYAKI

The name means 'cook what you like', and *okonomiyaki* is an inexpensive opportunity to do just that. Sometimes described as Japanese pizza or pancake, the resemblance is in form only. At an *okonomiyaki* restaurant you sit around a *teppan* (iron hotplate), armed with a spatula and chopsticks to cook your choice of meat, seafood and vegetables in a cabbage and vegetable batter.

Some restaurants will do most of the cooking and bring the nearly finished product to your hotplate for you to season with *katsuo bushi* (bonito flakes), soy sauce, *ao-nori* (a sea green similar to parsley), Japanese Worcestershire-style sauce and mayonnaise. Cheaper places, however, will simply hand you a bowl filled with the ingredients and expect you to cook it for yourself. If this happens, don't panic. First, mix the batter and filling thoroughly, then place it on the hot grill, flattening it into a thick pancake. After five minutes or so, use the spatulas to flip it and cook for another five minutes. Then season and dig in. Most *okonomiyaki* places also serve *yaki-soba* (fried noodles) and *yasai-itame* (stir-fried vegetables). All of this is washed down with mugs of draught beer. Also look for *okonomiyaki* at festivals and street fairs.

gyū okonomiyaki	牛お好み焼き	beef *okonomiyaki*
ika okonomiyaki	イカお好み焼き	squid *okonomiyaki*
mikkusu	ミックス焼き	mixed fillings of seafood, meat and vegetables
modan-yaki	モダン焼き	*okonomiyaki* with *yaki soba* and a fried egg
negi okonomiyaki	ネギお好み焼き	thin *okonomiyaki* with scallions

SHOKUDŌ

A *shokudō* is the most common type of restaurant in Japan, and is found near train stations, tourist spots and just about any other place where people congregate. Easily distinguished by the presence of plastic food displays in the window, these inexpensive places usually serve a variety of *washoku* (Japanese) and *yōshoku* (Western) dishes.

BEAM ME TO THE KONBINI

Convenience stores *(konbini)* are a way of life for many Tokyoites, and even if you had never set foot in one at home you may find yourself visiting them daily here; there seems to be a Sunkus, AM-PM, Lawson, 7-Eleven or Family Mart on just about every corner. Here's the difference: Japanese convenience-store food tends to be both fresh and of decent quality, and whether you're going home after a late night or heading out on a hike, it's hard to do better. Some of our favourite *konbini* foods:

- *onigiri* – King of them all. A triangle of rice with a dollop of some treasure inside (salmon, tuna salad, marinated kelp etc), wrapped in a plastic sheath together with a sheet of *nori* (seaweed).
- *inari sushi* – Sushi rice in a tofu pouch. If you find it a little sweet, cut it with soy sauce.
- *goma-ae* – Vegetables (typically spinach) mixed with sesame sauce.
- *oden* – Fish cakes, hard-boiled egg, vegetables and more, stewing in a *dashi* (fish-stock) broth. Enjoy with hot mustard. It's not winter without it.
- *niku-man* and friends – Steamed buns filled with pork, pizza flavourings, curry sauce and more. If you've had dim sum, you'll get the picture.

At lunch, and sometimes at dinner, the easiest meal to order at a *shokudō* is a *teishoku* (set-course meal), which is sometimes also called *ranchi setto* (lunch set), or *kōsu* (set meal). This usually includes a main dish of meat or fish, a bowl of rice, miso soup, a small salad and some *tsukemono*. In addition, most *shokudō* serve a fairly standard selection of *donburi-mono* (a large bowl of rice topped with egg or meat) and *menrui* (usually *soba* or udon; see p38 for more details), which can also be served pan-fried instead of in soup. Another speciality is *karē-raisu* (curry rice), a bowl filled with hot rice on one side and beef, chicken or other meats and/or vegetables in a thick curry sauce on the other of the bowl.

karē-raisu	カレーライス	rice topped with ingredients in curry sauce
niku-don	肉丼	rice topped with thin slices of cooked beef
omu-raisu	オムライス	rice flavoured with ketchup, served inside a thin omelet
oyako-don	親子丼	rice topped with egg and chicken

SPECIALITIES

UNAGI

Even if you can't stand the creature, you owe it to yourself to try *unagi* (eel) at least once while in Tokyo. It's cooked over hot coals and brushed with a rich sauce composed of *shōyu* and sake. Often you can sprinkle it with powdered *sanshō*, a pungent herb that has numbing properties in the mouth. Some *unagi* restaurants keep barrels of live eels to entice passers-by.

kabayaki	蒲焼	skewers of grilled eel without rice
unadon	うな丼	grilled eel over a bowl of rice
unagi teishoku	うなぎ定食	full-set *unagi* meal with rice, grilled eel, eel-liver soup and pickles
unajū	うな重	grilled eel over a flat tray of rice

FUGU

The deadly *fugu* (globefish, aka puffer fish or blowfish) is eaten more for the thrill than the taste. The liver of this fish is highly poisonous, and chefs who serve it are required to have a licence and extensive training. *Fugu* is best eaten in winter. *Fugu* is usually served only in *fugu* speciality restaurants, so it's highly unlikely that you'll be served it unknowingly.

The actual meat is rather bland but acclaimed for its fine texture. Nonetheless, if you have the money to lay out for a *fugu* dinner (around ¥10,000), it makes a good 'been there, done that' story.

Although the danger of *fugu* poisoning is negligible, some Japanese joke that you should always let your dining companion try the first piece of *fugu* – if they are still talking after five minutes, you can consider the dish safe. For some liquid courage, try a glass of *hirezake* (toasted *fugu* fin in hot sake), the traditional accompaniment to a *fugu* dinner.

If you're eating *fugu* because you've been challenged by a Japanese friend, and you want to repay them with a cruel joke, hold your hand still and let your chopsticks drop onto the table (in case of poisoning, the extremities go first). On second thought, don't do this, as it will probably alarm everyone else in the restaurant.

EKIBEN – LUNCH IN LOCOMOTION

A contraction of the words *eki* (train station) and *bentō* (boxed lunch or dinner), every big train station has an *ekiben* stand, and some of them are quite famous.

Legend has it that the first *ekiben* were served in 1885 at Utsunomiya Station, not far from Tokyo. Back in the day, pickles and rice balls were standard fare. Now there are close to 3000 varieties of *ekiben*, and stations contend to produce ever more exotic morsels – a station might feature mushroom, marinated boar or trout *ekiben*. Because meals here are always taken to go, prices are pretty reasonable.

fugu chiri	ふぐちり	a stew made from *fugu* and vegetables
fugu sashimi	ふぐ刺身	thinly sliced raw *fugu*
fugu teishoku	ふぐ定食	a set course of *fugu* served several ways, plus rice and soup
yaki fugu	焼きふぐ	*fugu* grilled on a *hibachi* (a small earthenware grill) at your table

KAISEKI

Kaiseki (elegant ceremonial-type Japanese food) is the pinnacle of Japanese cuisine, where ingredients, preparation, setting and presentation come together to create a dining experience quite unlike any other. Born as an adjunct to the tea ceremony, *kaiseki* is a largely vegetarian affair (though fish is often served, meat never appears on the *kaiseki* menu). One usually eats *kaiseki* in the private room of a *ryōtei* (an especially elegant style of traditional restaurant), often overlooking a tranquil garden. The meal is served in several small courses, giving the diner an opportunity to admire the plates and bowls, which are carefully chosen to complement the food and season. Rice is eaten last (usually with an assortment of pickles) and the drink of choice is sake or beer.

VEGETARIAN OPTIONS

Until recently the only option for vegetarians was *kaiseki* (an exquisite culinary artform, see above) or *shojin ryōri* (special dishes in the Buddhist tradition). Today, however, most of the more cosmopolitan neighbourhoods like Harajuku boast several vegetarian eateries, many of them serving vegan meals and exclusively organic produce (see Top Five Spots for Vegetarians, p137).

OTHER CUISINES

Being the cosmopolitan city that it is, Tokyo has long had cuisines from around the world; many Japanese chefs pride themselves on having trained in high-powered cooking schools overseas. French and Italian have long figured prominently, and Indian, Thai and, of course, Chinese are all easy to find. The current rage is Korean, with an exploding number of *yakiniku* (Korean barbecue) places and *kimchi* (Korean pickled cabbage) finding its way into all kinds of menus.

SWEETS

Although most Japanese-style restaurants don't serve dessert (plates of sliced fruit are sometimes served at the end of a meal), there is no lack of sweets in Japan. Traditional Japanese sweets (known generically as *wagashi*) are sold in speciality stores for you to eat at home. Many of the more delicate-looking ones are made to balance the strong, bitter taste of the special *matcha* (whisked green tea) served during the tea ceremony.

Even if you have the sweetest tooth in the world and have sampled every type of sweet that's come your way, you may find yourself surprised by Japanese confectionery. Many sweets contain the red adzuki-bean paste called *anko*. This earthy, rich filling turns up in a variety of pastries, including those you pick up at the corner bakery shop. Legions of foreign visitors have been surprised – not altogether unpleasantly – expecting chocolate and finding *anko* instead.

With such a wide variety of sweets, it's impossible to list all the names. However, you'll probably find many variations on the *anko* with *mochi* (glutinous rice) theme. Sweet shops are easy to spot; they usually have open fronts with their wares laid out in wooden trays to entice passers-by.

For Western-style sweets, try cafés, coffee shops and pastry shops for a variety of cakes, muffins and the like; these are also abundant in Tokyo. If all else fails, duck into a convenience store for *aisukurīmu* (ice cream) or *chokorēto* (chocolate).

anko	あんこ	sweet paste or jam made from red adzuki beans
mochi	餅	cakes of pounded glutinous rice
wagashi	和菓子	Japanese-style sweets
yōkan	羊羹	sweet red-bean jelly

DRINKS

Drinking plays a big role in Japanese society, and there are few social occasions where beer or sake is not served. Alcohol (in this case sake) also plays a ceremonial role in various Shintō festivals and rites, including the marriage ceremony. As a visitor to Tokyo, you'll probably find yourself in situations where you are invited to drink, and tipping back a few beers or glasses of sake is a great way to get to know the locals. However, if you don't drink alcohol, it's no big deal to order *oolong cha* (oolong tea) or a soft drink in place of beer or sake.

ALCOHOLIC DRINKS

Beer

Introduced in the late 19th century, *biiru* (beer) is now the favourite tipple of the Japanese. The quality is generally excellent and the most popular type is light lager, although recently some breweries have been experimenting with darker brews. The major breweries are Kirin, Asahi, Sapporo and Suntory. Sapporo also produces the currently popular Yebisu brand. Beer is dispensed everywhere, from vending machines to beer halls, and even in some temple lodgings. A standard can of beer from a vending machine is about ¥250, although some of the gigantic cans cost over ¥1000. At bars and restaurants, a beer starts at ¥500 and the price climbs upwards, depending on the establishment. *Nama biiru* (draught beer) is widely available, as are imported beers.

Sake

Sake (rice wine) has been brewed for centuries in Japan. Once restricted to imperial brewers, it was later produced at temples and shrines across the country. In recent years, consumption of beer and *shōchū* (p44) has overtaken that of sake, but it's still a standard item in homes, restaurants and drinking places. Large casks of sake are often seen stacked up as offerings outside temples and shrines, and the drink plays an important part in most celebrations and festivals.

Casks of sake (p43)

There are several types of sake, of which clear sake is by far the most common. Premium clear sake are classified into grades according to how much of the rice kernel is milled away before brewing begins; in descending order of refinement (and usually price) they are *daiginjō* (50% or less of the kernel remaining), *ginjō* (60%) and *honjōzōshu* (70%). Any of these can also be *junmaishu*, made only from rice, *kōji* (a brewing micro-organism) and water. Other clear sakes are called *futsūshu* (ordinary sake); these tend to be the least expensive and most hangover-inducing. Sake can be further divided into *karakuchi* (dry) and *amakuchi* (sweet). Rarer varieties of sake include *nigori* (cloudy) and *nama* (unrefined).

As well as the national brewing giants, there are thousands of provincial brewers producing local brews called *jizake*. Tokyo is not well known as a sake-producing region, but you can look for the locally brewed brands Sawanoi, Tama Jiman and Ginsetsu.

Sake is served *atsukan* (warm) and *reishu* (cold). Warm sake tends to be more popular in winter, but purists will tell you that a fine sake should always be served chilled.

Sake is usually served in a small flask called *tokkuri*, in two sizes, *ichi-gō* (small) or *nigō* (large). From these flasks you pour the sake into small ceramic cups called *o-choko* or *sakazuki*. Another way to sample sake is to drink it from a small wooden box called *masu*, sometimes served with a bit of salt on the rim.

With a 15% to 17% alcohol content, sake, particularly the warm stuff, is likely to go to your head quickly, and you'll soon understand why it's drunk from such small cups!

Final note: the correct pronunciation is *'sakay'* (rhymes with 'hey') and not *'saki'* (rhymes with 'he').

Shōchū

This distilled spirit with an alcohol content of about 30% also used to be the province of those looking for a quick and cheap escape from the sorrows of the world (it was used as a disinfectant in the Edo period). Yet *shōchū* has been resurrected from its previous lowly status to become a trendy drink. You can drink it *oyu-wari* (with hot water) or *chūhai* (with soda and lemon or other flavours).

Wine & Spirits

Most visitors to Japan are disappointed by the wine selection outside of tippy-top restaurants (where you'll pay handsomely for it). Japan does produce wine, in the mountainous regions of Honshū and Hokkaidō, often blended with imports from South America or Eastern Europe. Note that Japanese restaurants tend to serve both red and white wines chilled.

Whisky is also available at most drinking establishments and is usually drunk *mizuwari* (with water and ice) or *onzarokku* (on the rocks). Local brands, such as Suntory and Nikka, are sensibly priced, and most measure up to foreign standards. Expensive foreign labels are popular as gifts.

Most other imported spirits are available at drinking establishments in Japan. Bars with a large foreign clientele, including hotel bars, can usually mix any type of drink you request.

aka wain	赤ワイン	red wine
amakuchi	甘口	sweet (sake)
atsukan	熱燗	warm sake
biiru	ビール	beer
chūhai	チューハイ	*shōchū* with soda and lemon
ikkyūshu	一級酒	first-grade sake
jizake	地酒	locally brewed sake
karakuchi	辛口	dry (sake)
mizu-wari	水割り	whiskey, ice and water
nama	生	regular clear sake
nama biiru	生ビール	draught beer
nigori	にごり	cloudy sake
nikkyūshu	二級酒	second-grade sake
o-choko	お猪口	ceramic sake cup
onzarokku	オンザロック	whiskey with ice
oyu-wari	お湯割り	*shōchū* with hot water
reishu	冷酒	cold sake
sakazuki	杯	ceramic sake cup
sake	酒	Japanese rice wine
shiro wain	白ワイン	white wine
shōchū	焼酎	distilled grain liquor
tokkyūshu	特級酒	premium-grade sake
whiskey	ウイスキー	whiskey

NONALCOHOLIC DRINKS

Most soft drinks you may be be used to at home will be available in Japan, with a few colourfully named additions like Pocari Sweat (a sports drink) and Calpis Water (a yogurt-based drink). With six million vending machines across the city, refreshment is rarely more than a few steps away. Fun fact: vending machines throughout Japan dispense both hot and cold drinks. A blue bar near the can or bottle indicates that it's cold, and red means hot (including canned coffees and soups). Tokyo tap water is safe to drink, or if you prefer, bottled water is available from vending machines and convenience stores.

Juice drinkers, take note: what's called 'juice' *(jūsu)* in Japan might be closer to commercially available fruit punch in your home country, with just a splash of fruit juice. If you're looking for the real thing, look for '100%' on the label.

Japanese Tea

Green tea contains loads of vitamin C and a good dose of caffeine. The powdered form used in the tea ceremony is called *matcha* and is drunk after being whipped into a frothy consistency. The more common form, a leafy green tea, is simply called *o-cha,* and is drunk after being steeped in a pot. In addition to green tea, you'll probably drink a lot of roasted tea called *hōjicha,* which restaurants serve for free. In summer, cold *mugicha* (roasted barley tea) is served in restaurants and private homes.

Coffee & Tea

When ordering *kōhii* (coffee) at a coffee shop in Japan, you'll be asked whether you like it *hotto* (hot) or *aisu* (cold). Black tea also comes hot or cold, with *miruku* (milk) or *remon* (lemon).

American kōhii	アメリカンコーヒー	weak coffee
bancha	番茶	ordinary-grade green tea, has a brownish colour
burendo kōhii	ブレンドコーヒー	blended coffee, fairly strong
kafe ore	カフェオレ	*café au lait*, hot or cold
kōcha	紅茶	black, British-style tea
kōhii	コーヒー	regular coffee
matcha	抹茶	powdered or whisked green tea used in the tea ceremony
mizu	水	water (cold)
mugicha	麦茶	roasted barley tea
o-cha	お茶	leafy green tea
orenji jūsu	オレンジジュース	orange juice
sencha	煎茶	medium-grade green tea
yu	湯	water (hot)

USEFUL WORDS & PHRASES

Note that the letters enclosed in square brackets are not pronounced.

A table for two/five people, please.	(二人/五人)お願いします。	*(futari/go-nin) onegai shimas[u].*
Do you have an English menu?	英語のメニューがありますか。	*eigo no menyū ga arimas[u] ka?*
Can you recommend any dishes?	おすすめの料理がありますか。	*osusume no ryōri ga arimas[u] ka?*
Is this self-service?	ここはセルフサービスですか。	*koko wa serufu sābis[u] des[u] ka?*
Is service included in the bill?	サービス料は込みですか。	*sābis[u] ryō wa komi des[u] ka?*
Cheers!	乾杯！	*kampai!*
[before eating]	いただきます！	*itadakimasu!*
Delicious!	おいしい！	*oishii!*
Thank you. (after a meal)	ごちそうさまでした。	*gochisō sama deshita.*
assortment of foods	盛り合わせ	*moriawase*
set menu (with rice and soup)	定食	*teishoku*
restaurant	レストラン	*resutoran*
Please bring...	をお願いします。	*...o onegai shimas[u]*
the bill	お勘定	*o-kanjō*
chopsticks	はし	*hashi*
a fork	フォーク	*fōku*
a glass (of water)	コップ(一杯の水)	*koppu (ippai no mizu)*
a knife	ナイフ	*naifu*
a spoon	スプーン	*supūn*
I can't eat…	が食べられません。	*…ga taberaremasen.*
I can't eat meat.	肉は食べられません。	*niku wa taberaremasen.*
I can't eat chicken.	鶏肉は食べられません。	*toriniku wa taberaremasen.*
I can't eat pork.	豚肉は食べられません。	*butaniku wa taberaremasen.*
I can't eat seafood.	シーフードは食べられません。	*shīfūdo wa taberaremasen.*
I'm a vegetarian.	私はベジタリアンです。	*watashi wa bejitarian des[u].*
I'm allergic to (peanuts).	私は(ピーナッツ)アレルギーです。	*watashi wa (pīnattsu) arerugī des[u].*

History

History

THE RECENT PAST

The last 25 years – indeed the entire postwar period – have been a roller coaster for Tokyo. If Japan seemed to be on a course for world domination in the 1980s, the 1990s and first half of this decade saw what some would call a long-overdue comeuppance: shrinking economy, rising unemployment, declining birth rate, deflation and political stagnation.

Yet as we went to press, Tokyo was finally shaking its post-millennial blues to become perhaps the city it was always meant to be: a vigorous economic and cultural powerhouse minus the late-20th-century hubris. Share prices, construction and new businesses were all on the rise, unemployment was falling from its historic 5% highs, and the overall mood was more palpably upbeat.

Certainly concerns remain: the birth rate in Tokyo is below 1% per year (even lower than the Japanese average of 1.24%), while Japan's elderly continue to make up an ever-larger share of the population. No one really knows how the system will manage to support the 30% of the population that is projected to be over the age of 65 in the next 25 years.

Japan is also struggling with its international role, particularly the leeway allowed by its 'Peace Constitution'; in 2003 some 50,000 demonstrators protested the decision of the cabinet of Prime Minister Koizumi Junichirō to send the National Self-Defence Force members to the War in Iraq. Meanwhile, relations with many of Japan's Asian neighbours are less than cordial, ostensibly over Japan's lack of reckoning with its conduct in WWII, and also, some analysts say, because growing economic might, notably in China and South Korea, means greater world political clout.

But for the first time in a decade and a half, both visitors and locals have the sense that things are about to get better rather than worse, and that's cause for – cautious – satisfaction.

FROM THE BEGINNING

It's believed that Tokyo's first permanent inhabitants were a pottery-producing culture whose main concern was fertility. They inhabited the area during the late Neolithic Jōmon period (Jōmon means 'rope marks' for the design on pottery fragments discovered from this time) around 10,000 BC. People at that time lived as fishers, hunters and food-gatherers, and may have benefited from the fauna-rich, marshy area that was left behind after what is now Tokyo Bay rose to cover most of the valley where Tokyo now sits.

Some 4000 years later, during the Yayoi period, wet-rice farming techniques were introduced from Korea, and Shintō – Japan's native religion – began to develop. Shintō is similar to animism, with many gods who inhabited animals and objects in nature. By AD 300, Japan was already, more or less, a unified nation, with its cultural base in the Kansai area (around the present day cities of Nara, Kyoto and Osaka), while the Kantō area (present-day Tokyo and its surrounds) was something of a distant backwater.

The nation came under the control of the Yamato clan (forerunners of the current imperial family), who claimed a handy direct descent from the sun goddess Amaterasu and introduced the title of *tennō* (emperor) around the 5th century. This was called the Kofun period, named for the earthen mounds in which the nobility were interred.

But the most important event in Japan's early history was the arrival of Buddhism in the 6th century, from India via China and Korea. Buddhism introduced a highly evolved system of metaphysics, codes of law and the Chinese writing system, a conduit for the principles of Confucian statecraft.

TIMELINE

4000 BC
Tokyo Bay floods, sparing the high areas located within the area of the present-day Yamanote Line

552
Buddhism arrives via China and Korea

THE RISE OF THE SAMURAI

From the earliest days of the Yamato court, it was the custom to relocate the capital following the death of an emperor (presumably to free the capital from the taint of death). However, this custom was altered in 710 with the establishment of a Japan's first permanent capital at Nara.

By the end of the 8th century, the Buddhist clerical bureaucracy had become vast, threatening the authority of the imperial administration. The emperor responded by relocating the capital once again and establishing a new seat of imperial power at Heian (modern-day Kyoto). From that point on, Kyoto by and large served as the capital until the Meiji Restoration (1868; see p52 for more information) and the establishment of Tokyo as Japan's capital.

From Kyoto's early days, a *samurai* (warrior; see also p50) class in the employ of *daimyō* (feudal lords) emerged. Much of Japan's subsequent history chronicled struggles for power among the *daimyō* while the emperor mostly watched impotently from the haven of Kyoto's Imperial Palace.

The one interruption came when the warlord Minamoto Yoritomo defeated the ruling Taira clan and established the first shōgunate in Kamakura (about 50km southwest of Tokyo) in 1185. Although the emperor remained the nominal ruler in Kyoto, the Minamoto clan ruled a *bakufu* (military government) from Kamakura until 1333, when it was toppled by a rebellion and official power reverted to Kyoto.

Near the mid-15th century, a *waka* (31-syllable poem) poet named Ōta Dōkan constructed the first castle at Edo (the pre-Meiji Restoration name for Tokyo) on the site of an old fortress above Hibiya Cove. By 1467, when the disastrous Ōnin civil war was devastating the capital in Kyoto, many aristocrats and monks had fled the capital to become supplicants in Dōkan's secure eastern hold. This might have been the beginning of explosive growth for Edo (that was to come soon enough), but Dōkan's overlord ordered Dōkan's assassination.

HISTORICAL PERIODS

For the last two millennia, the eras of Japanese history were named mostly for the location of the capital. From 1868 on, eras have been named for the Japanese emperor reigning at the time. For example, the current era is Heisei, after the official name of the current emperor, Akihito. Many Japanese calendars reckon 2006 as year 18 of the Heisei era; the Western calendar is also used.

Period	Date
Jōmon	10,000-300 BC
Yayoi	300 BC-AD 300
Kofun	300-710
Nara	710-94
Heian	794-1185
Kamakura	1185-1333
Muromachi	1333-1576
Momoyama	1576-1600
Edo	1600-1868
Meiji	1868-1912
Taishō	1912-26
Shōwa	1926-89
Heisei	1989-present

THE PORTUGUESE ARRIVE

By the time Portuguese traders and missionaries arrived in 1543, Japan was a divided realm of feudal fiefs. One of the most powerful *daimyō*, Oda Nobunaga of the Chūbu region, near present-day Nagoya, was quick to see how the Portuguese could support his own ambitious plans. He viewed Christianity as a potential weapon against the power of the Buddhist clergy and made ample use of the firearms brought by the God-fearing Portuguese. By the time he was assassinated in 1581, Oda had united much of central Japan. He was succeeded by Toyotomi Hideyoshi, who continued unification but looked less favourably on the growing Christian movement, subjecting it to systematic persecution.

Toyotomi's power was briefly contested by Tokugawa Ieyasu, son of a minor lord who had been allied to Oda. After a brief struggle for power, Tokugawa agreed to a truce with

ca. 1450
Construction of first Edo Castle

1853
'Black Ships' of the US navy arrive

Toyotomi; in return, Toyotomi granted him eight provinces in eastern Japan, including all of the Kantō region (Edo and its surrounding provinces). While Toyotomi intended this to weaken Tokugawa by separating him from his ancestral homeland Chūbu, the young Tokugawa looked upon the gift of land as an opportunity to strengthen his power. He set about turning Edo into a real city.

When Toyotomi Hideyoshi died in 1598, power passed to his son, Toyotomi Hideyori. However, Tokugawa Ieyasu had been busily scheming to secure the shōgunate for himself and soon went to war against those loyal to Hideyori. Tokugawa's forces finally defeated Hideyori and his supporters at the Battle of Sekigahara in 1600, moving him into a position of supreme power. He chose Edo as his permanent base and thus began two-and-a-half centuries of Tokugawa rule.

TOKUGAWA EDO

In 1603, the emperor appointed Tokugawa Ieyasu as shōgun (military administrator), and the Tokugawa family ruled from Edo Castle, on the grounds of the current Imperial Palace. One of the most important acts of the Tokugawa regime in its quest to achieve total control of the country was to implement the *sankin kōtai* system. This demanded that all *daimyō* in Japan spend at least one year out of two in Edo. Their wives and children were to remain in Edo while the *daimyō* returned to their home provinces. This dislocating ransom policy made it difficult for ambitious *daimyō* to usurp the Tokugawas.

SAMURAI

The prime duty of a samurai, a member of the warrior class, was to give faithful service to his feudal lord or *daimyō*. In fact, the origin of the term 'samurai' is closely linked to a word meaning 'to serve'. Over the centuries, the samurai established a code of conduct that came to be known as *bushidō* (the way of the warrior), drawn from Confucianism, Shintō and Buddhism.

Confucianism required a samurai to show absolute loyalty to his lord. Toward the oppressed, a samurai was expected to show benevolence and exercise justice. Subterfuge was to be despised, as were all commercial and financial transactions. A real samurai had endless endurance and total self-control, spoke only the truth and displayed no emotion. Since his honour was his life, disgrace and shame were to be avoided above all else, and all insults were to be avenged.

From Buddhism, the samurai learnt the lesson that life is impermanent – a handy reason to face death with serenity. Shintō provided the samurai with patriotic beliefs in the divine status both of the emperor and of Japan – the abode of the gods.

Seppuku (ritual suicide), also known as *hara-kiri*, was a practice to which Japanese Buddhism conveniently turned a blind eye and was an accepted means of avoiding dishonour. *Seppuku* required the samurai to ritually disembowel himself, watched by an aide, who then drew his own sword and lopped off the samurai's head. One reason for this ritual was the requirement that a samurai should never surrender but always go down fighting. Since surrender was considered a disgrace, prisoners received scant mercy. During WWII this attitude was reflected in the Japanese treatment of prisoners of war – still a source of bitter memories.

In quiet moments, a samurai dressed simply but was easily recognisable by his triangular *eboshi*, a hat made from rigid black cloth.

The samurai's standard battle dress or armour (*yoroi* in Japanese, usually made of leather or maybe lacquered steel) consisted of a breastplate, a similar covering for his back, a steel helmet with a visor, and more body armour for his shoulders and lower body. Samurai weaponry – his pride and joy – included a bow and arrows (in a quiver), swords and a dagger; and he wasn't complete without his trusty steed.

Before entering the fray, a samurai was expected to be freshly washed and groomed. The classic samurai battle took the form of duelling between individuals rather than the clashing of massed armies.

Not all samurai were capable of adhering to their code of conduct – samurai indulging in double-crossing or subterfuge, or displaying outright cowardice, were popular themes in Japanese theatre.

1868

Meiji Restoration; Imperial residence moves to Edo, which is renamed Tokyo

1872

Japan's first train line connects Tokyo with Yokohama

Society was made rigidly hierarchical, comprising (in descending order of importance) the nobility, who had nominal power; the *daimyō* and their samurai; the farmers; and finally the artisans and merchants. Class dress, living quarters and even manner of speech were all strictly codified, and interclass movement was prohibited.

When Ieyasu died in 1616, his ashes were briefly laid to rest in Chūbu before being moved to Nikkō (p221). Generations of Tokugawas made improvements to the vast Tōshō-gu Shrine dedicated to his memory there, transforming it into one of the grandest in all Japan. A smaller version stands in the large park Ueno-kōen (p81) in Tokyo.

In 1638, concerned that missionaries were gaining too much power, Ieyasu's grandson, Tokugawa Iemitsu, massacred a number of Kyūshū Christians and closed the country to almost all foreign trade; only a limited number of Dutch and Chinese traders were permitted access to Japan, and even then only from the island of Dejima, off Nagasaki (about as far as one could go from Edo). This radical isolation policy, known as *sakoku,* was to remove Japan from the world stage for nearly 250 years.

Page from Edo period samurai clothing catalogue, Tokyo Kokuritsu Hakubutsukan (Tokyo National Museum; p80)

These sudden changes led to the rapid growth of the previously small town of Edo. By the early 1700s the population had grown to more than one million, making it the largest city in the world. Meanwhile, the caste-like society imposed by Tokugawa rule divided Edo into a high city (Yamanote) and a low city (Shitamachi). The higher Yamanote (literally 'hand of the mountains') was home to *daimyō* and their samurai, while the lower orders of Edo society were forced into the low-lying Shitamachi (literally 'downtown').

One distinguishing feature of those days was the pleasure quarters, where samurai would come to indulge in activities forbidden in the Yamanote: wine, women and song and not necessarily in that order. The most legendary of these districts was the Yoshiwara, to the northeast of present-day Asakusa.

Otherwise the typical residential neighbourhood of the Shitamachi featured squalid conditions, usually flimsy wooden structures with earthen floors. These shantytowns were often swept by great conflagrations, which locals referred to as *Edo-no-hana,* or flowers of Edo (see p52). The cocky bravura of the expression sums up the spirit of the Shitamachi. Under great privation and in accordance with a social order set by the Tokugawa regime, the Shitamachi produced a flourishing culture that thumbed its nose at social hardships and the strictures of the shōgunate. Today, the best glimpses we have into that time come from *ukiyo-e* (wood-block prints; see p22).

Another feature of Edo that has left its mark on today's Tokyo was the division of the city into *machi* (towns) according to profession. Even today it is possible to stumble across small enclaves that specialise in particular wares. Most famous are Jimbōchō, the bookshop area; Kappabashi, with its plastic food and kitchen supplies; and Akihabara, which now specialises in electronics and manga (comic books), but in the past has been a bicycle retailing area, an area specialising in domestic household goods and a freight yard.

1923

Great Kantō Earthquake kills more than 140,000 and razes over half the city's wooden structures

1926

Hirohito ascends to become the Shōwa emperor

TOKYO RISING

The turning point for the city of Edo, indeed for all of Japan, was the arrival of US Navy Commodore Matthew Perry's squadron of 'black ships' at Edo-wan (now known as Tokyo Bay) in 1853. Perry's expedition demanded, in the name of US President Millard Fillmore, that Japan open itself to foreign trade. Other Western powers were quick to follow in demanding the Japanese open treaty ports and end the policy of isolation. The coming of Westerners heralded a far-reaching social revolution against which the antiquated Tokugawa regime was powerless. In 1867–68, faced with widespread antigovernment feeling and accusations that the regime had failed to prepare Japan for the threat of the West, the last Tokugawa shōgun resigned and power reverted to Emperor Meiji. In 1868 Meiji moved the seat of imperial power from Kyoto to Edo Castle, renaming the city Tokyo ('eastern capital'). This was known as the Meiji Restoration; in other words, power was restored to the emperor, and the imperial and political capitals were once again unified.

The Meiji Restoration was not an entirely peaceful handover of power. In Edo some 2000 Tokugawa loyalists put up a futile last-ditch resistance to the imperial forces in the brief Battle of Ueno. The struggle took place around the beautiful temple, Kanei-ji (p82), which, along with Zōjō-ji (p94), was one of Edo's two mortuary temples for the Tokugawa shōgunate.

In some ways it was less a restoration than a revolution, as the Japanese underwent a crash course in industrialisation and militarisation. In 1872, the nation's first railroad opened, connecting Tokyo with the new port of Yokohama, south along Tokyo Bay, and by 1889 the country had instituted a Western-style constitution. In a remarkably – some would say disturbingly – short time, Japan achieved military victories over China (1894–95) and Russia (1904–05) and embarked on modern, Western-style empire-building, with the annexation of Taiwan (1895), then Korea (1910) and Micronesia (1914).

Nationalists were also transforming Shintō into a jingoistic state religion. Seen as a corrupting foreign influence, Buddhism suffered badly – many valuable artefacts and temples were destroyed, and the common people were urged to place their faith in the pure religion of 'State Shintō'.

During the Meiji period, and the following Taishō period, changes that were taking place all over Japan could be seen most prominently in the country's new capital city. Tokyo's rapid industrialisation, uniting around the nascent *zaibatsu* (huge industrial and trading combines), drew jobseekers from around Japan, causing the population to grow rapidly.

FLOWERS OF EDO

Fire, earthquake and war have meant that there is little left today of the Shitamachi ('downtown' districts) of old Edo, although some parts of town – notably Asakusa, Nippori and Fukagawa – still retain some of that character and feel. About the best way to get an idea of the look of these lower-class neighbourhoods is to stroll through Nippori (p118) or visit museums like the Shitamachi Museum (p80) in Ueno or the Fukagawa Edo Museum (p105).

Edo was a city built of wood, and its natural stained frontages and dark-tiled roofs gave the city an alluring attractiveness. Yet this same construction also left Edo subject to huge fires, periodically purging the congested city. In a perverse attempt to make the best of misfortune, Edo-dwellers seemed almost to take pride in these fires, calling them *Edo-no-hana* (literally 'flowers of Edo').

The flowers of Edo bloomed with such frequency that it has been estimated that a Shitamachi structure could reckon on a life span of around 20 years, often less, before being destroyed by fire. Preventive measures included building houses that could be completely sealed at the approach of a fire and keeping belongings in baskets for easy removal when fires came; candles would be left burning inside, starving the houses' interior of oxygen. Private fire brigades operated with standard-bearers who would stake out their territory close to a burning building and exact payment if they managed to save it.

1927

Opening of Japan's first subway in Tokyo

1944–45

US firebombs Tokyo and drops two atomic bombs on Hiroshima and Nagasaki; US occupation begins

ALL ABOARD!

Just as arteries and veins pump blood through the body, Tokyo's trains are the circulatory system of this city. Japan's first train line was built in 1872, connecting Tokyo with Yokohama; visitors can still see the original station and locomotive near present-day Shimbashi Station. But even the most enthusiastic trainspotter of those days could not have imagined today's *rāmen* bowl of a train map, a tangle of lines now operated by the JR (Japan Rail) and 13 subway lines operated by not one but two municipal systems.

Tokyo's transit system also stands out for its network of privately operated commuter train lines, ferrying suburbanites into hubs along the JR Yamanote Line, which loops around the city centre. The Tōbu Line was the first in 1899, followed by the Musashino (now Seibu), Keio, Odawara Kyūkō (now Odakyū) and Meguro-Kamata (now Tōkyū) Lines just for starters. Some of these early trains were streetcars connecting neighbourhoods of this fast-growing city, others shuttled holidaymakers as far as Nikkō (p221) and Hakone (p216), some 100km away.

If the names of these private lines remind you of Tokyo department stores, you're very perceptive. In 1929, Ōsaka-based Hankyū Railway became the pioneer in the train-line-as-real-estate-mogul concept, developing residential suburbs along its rail routes and connecting them to large retail complexes at its hubs. Tokyo rail operators followed suit, particularly after WWII; major hubs now include Shinjuku, Shibuya and Ikebukuro. Up to that point, department stores catered to well-heeled consumers in chi-chi neighbourhoods like Ginza and Nihombashi, but the train-affiliated stores were more democratic. That pattern continues today.

To find out more, see Train (p231), visit the Transportation Museum (p78) or the department stores or just take a ride and see what new horizon you encounter.

In the 1880s electric lighting was introduced. Western-style buildings began to spring up in fashionable areas such as Ginza. In 1904, Mitsukoshi became Japan's first Western-style department store, and its annexe in Nihombashi (1914) was called the grandest building east of the Suez Canal. However, if the Meiji Restoration sounded the death knell for old Edo, there were two more events that were to erase most traces of the old city.

THE GREAT KANTŌ EARTHQUAKE

The Great Kantō Earthquake struck at noon on 1 September 1923. More than the earthquake itself, it was the subsequent fires, lasting some 40 hours, that laid waste to the city, including some 300,000 houses. A quarter of the quake's 142,000 fatalities occurred in one savage firestorm in a clothing depot. (There are some sombre reminders of the earthquake exhibited at the Kantō Earthquake Memorial Museum; see p106.)

1947	1952
New Constitution adopted, including Article 9 'peace clause'	US occupation ends

TOP FIVE BOOKS

- *Edo, the City that Became Tokyo* (2003), Naito Akira – This beautifully illustrated history begins with primeval Edo, continues on to evil Edo, and concludes with the surrender of Edo Castle to the emperor. There are wonderful maps throughout.
- *Low City, High City* (1983), Edward Seidensticker – Chronicles the decline of Edo between the time of the Meiji Restoration and the Great Kantō Earthquake. A follow-up to this book, *Tokyo Rising*, charts the capital's postwar growing pains.
- *Shocking Crimes of Post-War Japan* (1996), Mark Schreiber – Worth the read because of the first chapter, which investigates the ins and outs and cultural implications of the sarin attack on the Tokyo subways in 1995. Also a good reminder of the fact that Japanese cops are tough cookies.
- *Tokyo: City of Stories* (1991), Paul Waley – Tales of Tokyo's neighbourhoods and how they developed as part of the greater megalopolis.
- *Underground* (2001), Murakami Haruki – One of Japan's most celebrated authors interviews dozens of Tokyoites impacted by the 1995 sarin gas attack on the Tokyo subway. A fascinating look into the mindset of ordinary people.

In true Edo style, reconstruction began almost immediately. The spirit of this rebuilding is perhaps best summed up by author Edward Seidensticker (see *Low City, High City*; above): popular wisdom had it that any business which did not resume trading within three days of being burnt out did not have a future. Opportunities were lost in reconstructing the city – streets might have been widened and the capital transformed into something more of a showcase. Yet with the slate wiped clean, Tokyoites were given a second opportunity.

THE BEGINNING OF SHŌWA & WWII

From the accession of Emperor Hirohito (Showa to the Japanese) and the initiation of the Shōwa period in 1926, Japanese society was marked by a quickening tide of nationalist fervour. In 1931 the Japanese invaded Manchuria, and in 1937 embarked on full-scale hostilities with China. By 1940 a tripartite pact with Germany and Italy had been signed and a new order for all of Asia formulated: the 'Greater Asia Co-Prosperity Sphere'. On 7 December 1941 the Japanese attacked Pearl Harbor, bringing the USA, Japan's principal rival in the Asia-Pacific region, into the war.

Despite initial successes, the war was disastrous for Japan. On 18 April 1942, B-25 bombers carried out the first bombing and strafing raid on Tokyo, with 364 casualties. Much worse was to come. Incendiary bombing commenced in March 1944, notably on the nights of the 9th and 10th, when some two-fifths of the city, mainly in the Shitamachi area, went up in smoke and 70,000 to 80,000 lives were lost. The same raids destroyed Asakusa's Sensō-ji (p85), and later raids destroyed Meiji-jingū (p98). By the time Emperor Hirohito made his famous address to the Japanese people on 15 August 1945, much of Tokyo had been decimated and sections of it almost completely depopulated as surely as if it had shared the same fate (atomic-bomb explosions) as Hiroshima and Nagasaki.

POSTWAR YEARS

Tokyo's phoenix-like rise from the ashes of WWII and its emergence as a major global city is something of a miracle. Once again, Tokyoites did not take the devastation as an opportunity to redesign their city (as did Nagoya, for example), but rebuilt where the old had once stood.

1964	1966
Tokyo Olympic Games	The Beatles play the Budōkan

During the US occupation in the early postwar years, Tokyo was something of a honky-tonk town. Now-respectable areas such as Yūrakuchō were the haunt of the so-called *pan-pan* girls (prostitutes), and areas such as Ikebukuro and Ueno had thriving black-market zones. The remains of Ueno's black market can be seen in the Ameyoko Arcade (p79), which is still a lively market, though there is no longer anything very black about it.

In 1947 Japan adopted its postwar constitution, with the now-famous Article 9, which bars the use of military force in settling international disputes and maintaining a military for warfare (although the nation does maintain a self-defence force).

By 1951, with a boom in Japanese profits arising from the Korean War, Tokyo rebuilt rapidly, especially the central business district, and the subway began to take on its present form. The city has never looked back.

During the 1960s and '70s, Tokyo re-emerged as one of the centres of growing Asian nationalism (the first phase was in the 1910s and '20s). Increasing numbers of Asian students came to Tokyo, taking home with them new ideas about Asia's role in the postwar world.

One of Tokyo's proudest moments came when it hosted the 1964 summer Olympics. In preparation the city embarked on a frenzy of construction unequalled in its history. Many Japanese see this time as a turning point in the nation's history, the moment when Japan finally recovered from the devastation of WWII to emerge as a full fledged member of the modern world economy.

THE UYOKU

Since the end of WWII, right-wing and nationalist sentiments have generally taken a back seat to moderate political views or outright apathy. However, there remain pockets of right-wing sentiment. These are most visible to the visitor in the form of sinister black buses and vans, which ply the streets of big cities blaring patriotic Japanese songs (that unfortunately always sound like the TV theme songs for kids' manga cartoons) at ear-splitting volume. These vehicles represent the propaganda arm of the *uyoku* – far-right political parties and organisations.

When not playing music, speakers deliver lengthy diatribes against Japanese politicians or a litany of nationalist sentiments. Japanese pedestrians studiously ignore black buses blaring 100 decibels of noise. When regular citizens pay them any notice at all, it's usually to dismiss them as cranks. There is, however, a dark side to the *uyoku:* it acts as a volunteer police force for right and right-leaning politicians, effectively prohibiting criticism of the emperor. This is done by intimidating would-be critics with threats of violence, which are occasionally carried out.

AN EMPRESS AT LAST?

On 1 December 2001, Crown Princess Masako gave birth to a baby girl, whom she and Crown Prince Naruhito named Aiko. Princess Aiko's birth was a huge relief to the nation, since the royal couple had previously been childless, but it also rekindled a debate as to whether a female has the right to ascend to Japan's throne.

It seems safe to say that women's equality has not been high on the 'to-do' list of the Imperial Household Agency, which controls all things royal in Japan. For example, as we went to press, imperial daughters were required to relinquish their royal status upon marriage. Thus when Princess Aiko's aunt, the former Princess Nori, married an employee of the Tokyo Metropolitan Government in 2005, she changed her name to the distinctly nonroyal Kuroda Sayako and moved with her husband into an ordinary 1LDK condominium (one bedroom with living room and dining room/kitchen).

There have been empresses in Japan's distant past, but the succession laws were modified in the 19th century such that only men could be emperor. The rub, though: the imperial family has been without a male child since the mid-1960s. As we went to press, the Diet (parliament) had been considering a proposal allowing the first child of either gender to become emperor, but it was put on hold with news that the wife of the Crown Prince's brother had become pregnant - with presumably the chance of a baby boy.

1968–69

Tokyo University students take over administrative buildings to protest the Vietnam War

1989

Death of Emperor Hirohito; Heisei era begins; stock market decline begins

Construction and modernisation continued at a breakneck pace through the '70s, with the interruption of two Middle East oil crises, to reach a peak in the late '80s, when wildly inflated real-estate prices and stock speculation fuelled what is now known as the Bubble Economy. Based on the price paid for the most expensive real estate at the time, the land value of Tokyo exceeded that of the entire United States, and Japanese companies went on a purchasing spree of international icons including Pebble Beach Golf Course, Rockefeller Center and Columbia Pictures movie studio. When the bubble began to burst in 1989 with the crash of the stock market, the economy went into a protracted slump that was to last over 15 years.

In March 1995, members of the Aum Shinrikyō cult released sarin nerve gas on a crowded Tokyo commuter train, killing 12 and injuring more than 5000. This, together with the Kōbe earthquake of the same year, signalled the end of Japan's feeling of omnipotence, born of the unlimited successes of the '80s.

1995	2005
Sarin attacks on Tokyo subway kill 12 and injure over 5000	Protest against the changing the 'Peace Constitution' draws more than 10,000 demonstrators

Sights

Sights

Like Edo before it, Tokyo has long thought of itself in terms of high city and low city. The high city (or Yamanote), home of the shōgun and the nobles and samurai who served him, and later the emperor, was a rarefied place, while the low city (Shitamachi) was for the commoners.

If you look at a transit map today, you'll notice a green ring around the centre. This is the JR Yamanote Line, which loops around the heart of the city, connecting east and west, old and new. Transit, among other things, has eliminated the distinctions between high city and low city, but the visitor can still enjoy the heritage and idiosyncrasies of the city's neighbourhoods.

We begin at the centre of it all, the Imperial Palace and neighbouring Marunouchi, from where we progress east towards Ginza and the Sumida River (Sumida-gawa). Then it's north, through Akihabara and Kanda en route to the venerable cultural centres of Ueno and Asakusa.

West of the Imperial Palace are pleasure gardens ancient and modern, the government district of Akasaka, and the party town-turned-design centre of Roppongi. In Ebisu, in the city's southwest corner, we pick up the JR Yamanote Line again, on its way north through the teen fashion hub of Shibuya and the high-rise-meets-low-rise cacophony of Shinjuku and Ikebukuro, detouring at Harajuku Station for a walk down the grand boulevard Omote-sandō.

Finally, we'll cross the river to Ryōgoku, seat of sumō culture, and continue through historic Kiyosumi and Fukagawa until we end at Odaiba, a manmade island with no intention whatsoever of taking you back to Old Edo.

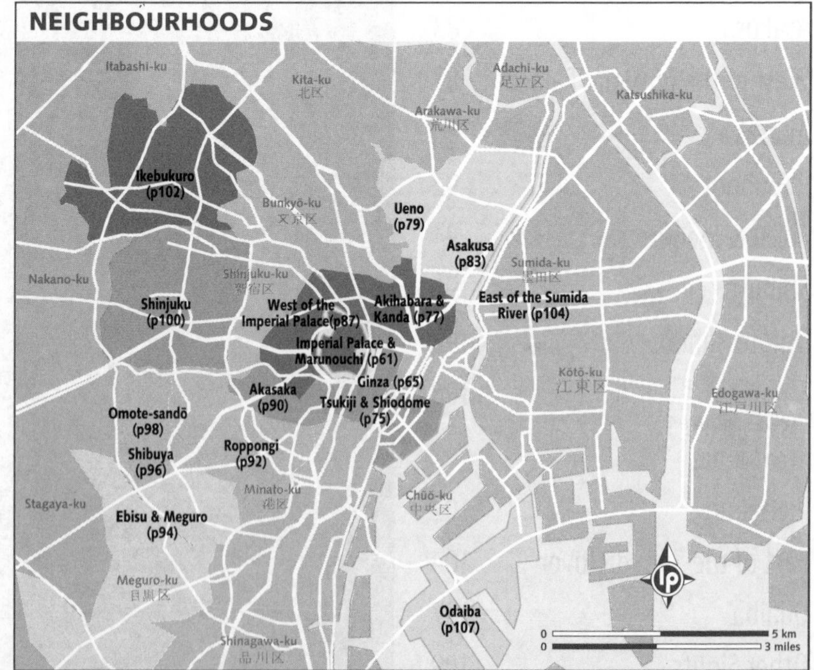

CHŌME THE WAY TO GO HOME...

In Tokyo, finding a place from its address can be difficult, even for locals. The problem is twofold: first, addresses are given within a district rather than along a street (only major streets have names or numbers); and second, building numbers are not necessarily consecutive, as prior to the mid-1950s numbers were assigned by date of construction. During the US occupation after WWII, an attempt was made to impose some 'logic' upon the system and main streets were assigned names, but the city reverted to its own system after the Americans left.

Tokyo, like most Japanese cities, is divided first into *ku* (wards – Tokyo has 23 of them), which in turn are divided into *chō* or *machi* (towns) and then into numbered *chōme* (*cho*-may), areas of just a few blocks. Subsequent numbers in an address refer to blocks within the *chōme* and buildings within each block. In English, addresses are most often written, for example, '3-5-1 Marunouchi, Chiyoda-ku, Tokyo': the '3' refers to the *chōme;* the '5' narrows down the field to a single block within the *chōme;* and the '1' indicates a specific building, all within the Marunouchi district of Chiyoda ward (head here to visit the Tokyo International Forum; p64). A number followed by an F in an address indicates the floor within the building. Note that when written in Japanese the order is reversed ('Tokyo, Chiyoda-ku, Marunouchi 3-5-1'). Of course!

Generally you have to ask directions. Numerous *kōban* (local police boxes) are there largely for this purpose. Businesses often include a small map on their advertisements or business cards, or most are happy to fax you a map. It was not too long ago that you needed this map to show to a taxi driver, but nowadays if you have the address they can generally get you there by means of a navigation system. If you're arriving by train or subway, be sure to also get the closest exit number from the station. We've provided transit information throughout this guidebook, including exit numbers where useful.

Otherwise, you can pick up a bilingual road atlas (Kodansha publishes the excellent *Tokyo City Atlas*) or buy a map that shows every building in every *chōme*. More and more there are also directional signs in English to important locations.

ITINERARIES

One Day

Jet lag will probably provide the wake-up call you need to get up and moving towards **Tsukiji Central Fish Market** (p75) before the sun rises. As dawn breaks, you'll see rubber-booted stall owners and an army of hydraulic lifts doing their daily work of selling a fish every four seconds. The sushi breakfasts here are great – the freshest available probably anywhere in the world. As the market gets ready to close, walk up wide Harumi-dōri to **Kabuki-za** (p66), where you can pop in for one or more acts of white-faced drama. That afternoon, hop on the subway to **Asakusa** (p83), once the bustling centre of the old city and still the spiritual heart of Tokyo, where **Sensō-ji** (p85) is Tokyo's grandest and most-frequented Buddhist temple. At night, head to the lights of **Shinjuku** (p100) and dine above the riveting views at the **New York Grill** (p139).

Three Days

In addition to the one-day itinerary, head to the **Imperial Palace** (p63), giving yourself time to wander the broad lawns of **Higashi-gyōen** (p62), the only royal garden open to the public. That afternoon it's off to Harajuku, the fashion and design centre of Tokyo. The forested Shintō shrine **Meiji-jingū** (p98) is majestic and peaceful. Walk down Omote-sandō, taking time to duck off into its side streets with their funky shops, the **Ukiyo-e Ota Memorial Art Museum** (p99) and wonderful small galleries and boutiques. That evening, poke around Shibuya, visiting the **Hachikō the Dog statue** (p97) and heading up Dōgenzaka into the excellent rock, rap and blues clubs. Another day gives you time to walk through **Ueno-kōen** (p81), with its myriad museums.

One Week

If you're craving some open air after the three-day itinerary, follow the Tokyoites onto the train to charming **Kamakura** (p210) and a glimpse into other eras and enormous Buddhas. Back in the city, head to Roppongi, where the **Mori Art Museum** (p92) offers marvellous panoramic views and compelling contemporary art exhibits. For a totally different view, trek to **Shizen Kyōiku-en** (p95), a forest in the middle of Meguro. Afterwards, stop by the controlled chaos of **Tonki** (p134) for a bite, and then head up to Ebisu, past **Yebisu Garden Place** (p183), with its excellent art-house cinema and photographic museum, and through the harebrained buildings and funky shops that open up onto Daikanyama.

A MEDLEY OF MUSEUMS

There are some 240 museums in Tokyo, ranging from the grand and world-scale to quirky one-room affairs of mind-boggling specificity. If you're planning on visiting any of them, here are some tips to keep in mind.

- Museum hours are generally 10am to 5pm and nearly all museums are closed Mondays. Hours in this book refer to closing times, not to last-admission times.
- Student discounts are common by school type (university, high school etc), and for the youngest visitors admission is usually free. Seniors discounts are less frequent. You may be required to show ID for any discount.
- The GRUTT Pass allows free or discounted admission to some 45 attractions around town within two months, and it can be an excellent value. It costs ¥2000 and can be purchased at tourist offices, Lawson convenience stores, some hotels and the venues themselves. Inquire at tourist information offices.
- The *Handy Guide* and *Handy Map* published by the Tokyo Metropolitan Government come with tear-off coupons for discounted admission.

ORGANISED TOURS

Though exploring Tokyo on your own offers distinct pleasures, it can be daunting at first. Listed are several touring companies that can help introduce you to the metropolis by land, sea, air or even on foot. Most have websites and English-speaking staff on hand.

Boat

KOMATSUYA

☎ 3851-2780; www.komatuya.net in Japanese; tours per person ¥10,000-20,000

If you've come with a gang and want a very Japanese experience, Komatsuya arranges for groups of 15 and up to cruise the city's waterways while enjoying Japanese cuisine in a tatami-room setting on a Japanese-style boat. Even the website is in Japanese.

SUMIDA-GAWA WATERBUSES

☎ 3841-9178; www.suijobus.co.jp/english/; tours ¥200-800; Ⓜ Ginza Line to Asakusa (exit 5), or Toei Asakusa Line to Asakusa (exit A5) for Azuma-bashi Pier

Offers extremely reasonable ferry rides under the 12 bridges up and down the Sumida River. Destinations include Tokyo Big Sight (p120) in Odaiba, Asakusa (p83) and the lovely Hama Rikyū Onshi-teien (Detached Palace Garden; p75). A special new boat, *Himiko,* was designed especially for Suijō Bus by the cartoonist Matsumoto Reiji and looks like a bug from the future.

SYMPHONY

☎ 3798-8101; www.symphony-cruise.co.jp; tours adult ¥1500-3800, child ¥750-1900; JR Yamanote Line to JR Hamamatsu-cho (south exit) for Hinode Pier

Symphony offers two-hour day and evening cruises around the bay, which depart from Hinode Pier. If you lunch or dine on board, you'll pay ¥5000 to ¥21,000 (including passage) depending on the type of meal you choose (options include French and Italian).

VINGT-ET-UN

☎ 3436-2121; cruises from ¥2040, dinner cruises from ¥7000; Ⓜ Yurikamome Line to Takshiba for Takeshiba Pier

This restaurant boat offers evening dinner excursions as well as afternoon cruises on weekends. The evening dinner cruises usually include excellent French meals. Reservations are essential. Passengers may be able to board without purchasing a meal, but there are no special seats and, no, you can't bring your own food.

Bus

These well-established, commercial tour operators all have an extensive line-up of tours, including many in English. While buses are their stock-in-trade, they also offer boat and walking tours.

GRAY LINE

☎ 3595-5948; www.jgl.co.jp/inbound/index.htm; tours ¥4000-9600

Without getting fancy, Gray Line buses chug along to places like the Imperial Palace, Asakusa, Sensō-ji and the National Diet. Tours run for either a half- or full day and sometimes include meals, usually at traditional Japanese restaurants. Pick-up and drop-off is available at dozens of hotels.

HATO BUS TOURS

☎ 3435-6081; www.hatobus.com; tours ¥3500-12,000

One of the longest-standing tour operators, Hato Bus offers half- and full-day tours around the city. It hits big spots like Sensō-ji and Tsukiji Central Fish Market, or offers tourists the chance to head out on the bay. If you're feeling daunted by the subway, check out the subway tour that alights at sites that recount the importance and beauty of the Edo era. Some tours include meals.

If your time is limited, Hato also operates tours aboard the Hello Kitty Bus (adult/child ¥1300/760, one hour) departing from Tokyo Station (check for departure times). One route covers basics like Nihombashi, Akihabara and Asakusa, and the other goes west of the Imperial Palace. Unlike other tours, you stay on the bus the whole time and guides narrate in Japanese only; English narration is available via headphones. Apart from that it's a pretty typical tour bus, although it is decorated with the cat with no mouth.

SUNRISE TOURS

☎ 5796-5454; www.jtbgmt.com/sunrisetour/ex/; tours ¥3500-9800

Within the city, Sunrise's offerings are not much different from those of other companies, but as a subsidiary of Japan Travel Bureau (JTB), Japan's largest travel company, it boasts an extensive roster of day trips and tours in other parts of Japan. Some are round trips from Tokyo, while others originate in other big Japanese cities. If you've got time to kill at the airport, it even has a worthwhile tour of Narita city.

Helicopter

EXCEL AIR

☎ 047-380-5555; www.excel-air.com; Urayasu Heliport; flights adult/child from ¥8000/4000; 🕑 2pm-dusk; Ⓡ JR Keiyo Line to Urayasu then 15 minutes by taxi

These five- to 20-minute flights are a dramatic way to take in the skyline of Ginza, the Imperial Palace or Akihabara during the day, at sunset or after dark. Helicopters fly up to eight people. Saturday and Sunday flights cost about 25% more. Flights depart from Urayasu city, east of Tokyo in Chiba Prefecture. Reserve in advance.

Walking

VOLUNTEER GUIDE TOURS

www.tourism.metro.tokyo.jp; free-¥2860 for the first person, may be less for additional people

Operated by the Tokyo Metropolitan Government, these guide services allow you face-to-face contact with real Tokyoites. Some volunteers speak better English than others, but you can't beat the price. Since the guides work on a volunteer basis, visitors pay only admission and transport fees for themselves and the two guides. Itineraries that involve no transport or admissions cost nothing. The 10 routes include the well-touristed (eg Asakusa) and the under-touristed (department-store food floor). Tour sizes are limited to a handful of people per tour; apply at least a few days in advance.

IMPERIAL PALACE & MARUNOUCHI

Eating p124, Shopping p177, Sleeping p194

Around 1600 the district that now makes up the imperial grounds suddenly became the centre of national affairs in Japan. Under the watch of shōgun Tokugawa Ieyasu and his descendants, the outpost of Edo expanded at a breakneck pace, on its way to becoming a military stronghold and one of the world's largest cities. Edo Castle (Edo-jō) grew to include high, thick, stone walls and a great keep. The new fortification would remain the locus of the shōgun's power for more than two centuries.

Although only a few vestiges of the castle remain, its imposing grounds still house the Imperial Palace. Yet in truth most of the area's power brokering takes place a short walk away at the city's centre of capital, Marunouchi. Together, Marunouchi and the Imperial Palace recall times when this small tract of land was the command post for a nation. The monolithic ministry and insurance industry buildings fronting the palace were among the few places in Tokyo to be spared bombing in WWII; American forces later used them to set up postwar command.

TRANSPORT

Train The JR Yamanote Line stops at brick-fronted Tokyo Station and is the best, most convenient way to reach the area. Yūrakuchō Station, one stop south, may be more convenient to some destinations.

Metro The Marunouchi Line runs along the east side of the Imperial Palace and connects with Tokyo Station. The Toei Mita, Chiyoda and Hanzōmon Lines also have stops near Tokyo Station and around the Imperial Palace.

Orientation

Northeast of here lie remnants of Edo's rough-and-tumble low city. To the south is glitzy Ginza and the fish market at Tsukiji.

Once you've arrived at Tokyo Station, the western exit will take you out towards the Imperial Palace. It is an easy, accessible five-minute walk through Marunouchi's rows of banks and blue suits and onward to one of the most open spaces in the city, within which live perhaps the most cloistered family in Japan. The eastern exit takes you to Yaesu and more of the financial district.

BRIDGESTONE MUSEUM OF ART

Map pp294-5

☎ 3563-0241;www.bridgestone-museum.gr.jp/en/; adult/senior/student/under 15 ¥800/600/500/free; 10am-8pm Tue-Sat, 10am-6pm Sun; Ginza or Tozai Line to Nihombashi (Takashimaya exit), Ginza Line to Kyōbashi (Meidi-ya exit) or JR Yamanote or Marunouchi Line to Tokyo (Yaesu Central exit)

Tokyo embraces all things French and so French impressionist art looms large in the civic imagination. The Bridgestone Tyre Company's collection, once kept privately by Bridgestone founder Ishibashi Shojiro, rates highly. Though French painting is the star (think Renoir, Ingres, Corot, Matisse et al), the museum also exhibits sculpture and some works by Japanese impressionists as well as European pieces that employ abstract or neoclassical aesthetics.

HIGASHI-GYŌEN Map pp294-5

Imperial Palace East Garden; ☎ 3213-2050; admission free; 9am-4.30pm Tue-Thu, Sat & Sun Mar-Oct, closed for imperial functions & from 4pm Nov-Feb; Marunouchi, Tozai, Chiyoda or Hanzōmon Line to Ōtemachi (exits c13b or c8b)

Higashi-gyōen is the only corner of the Imperial Palace (opposite) proper that is regularly open to the public, and it makes for a pleasant retreat. You can get up-close-and-personal views of the massive stones used to build the castle walls and climb the ruins of one of the keeps, off the upper lawn. Although entry is free, the number of visitors at any one time is limited, so it never feels crowded.

Entry is through one of three gates, **Ōte-mon** on the east, or via **Hirakawa-mon** or **Kita-hanebashi-mon** on the north, but most people enter through Ōte-mon, which is closest to Tokyo Station. This was the principal entrance to Edo Castle for more than 200 years. Here you may want to make a stop at the **Museum of Imperial Collections**, which mounts small exhibits of the 5000-plus artworks held within the palace.

It is worth buying a map too. Check out the list of prohibited behaviour on the back, including the stricture against making 'hideous noises'.

CASTLES

Japan's first castles were simple mountain forts that relied more on natural terrain than structural innovations for defence, making them as inaccessible to their defenders as to invading armies. The central feature was the *donjon* (keep), surrounded by several smaller towers. The buildings, which sat atop stone ramparts, were mostly built of wood covered with plaster to protect against fire.

The 210,000 sq metres of Edo Castle (Edo-jō) were composed of the Honmaru (inner citadel), second and third citadels (called Ninomaru and Sannomaru, respectively) as well as a western citadel, Nishinomaru. The grounds of the Honmaru are now part of the Higashi-gyōen, where you can see the ruins of the main *donjon*. The citadels and gardens were ringed by a series of moats (*hori* or *-bori* in Japanese). Many of these moats are still visible, sometimes under expressways in central Tokyo.

Many historic castles were destroyed by the Edo government; under the *sankin kōtai* system (p50), *daimyō* (feudal lords) were permitted only one castle each in their home territories, so any left over after conquering territory, for example, had to be dismantled. The Meiji government, for its part, demolished still more castles to de-emphasise the feudal connotation and increase loyalty to the emperor. Still more were flattened in WWII.

The 1950s and '60s saw a boom in castle reconstructions, most built of concrete and steel and like Hollywood movie sets – authentic-looking when viewed from a distance but modern inside.

Although Edo Castle (Edo-jō) is long since gone, its grounds and some peripheral buildings give you some idea of the mass of the place. Four castles remain in their original condition and are national treasures. Of these, the closest is in Matsumoto, about 2½ hours by train from Shinjuku Station.

IDEMITSU MUSEUM OF ARTS Map pp290-1

☎ 3213-9402; www.idemitsu.co.jp/museum in Japanese; 9th fl, 3-1-1 Marunouchi, Chiyoda-ku; adult/student ¥800/500; 🕒 10am-5pm Tue-Thu, Sat & Sun, 10am-7pm Fri; JR Yamanote Line to Yūrakuchō, or subway Chiyoda or Toei Mita Line to Hibiya (exit A1 or B3)

This excellent collection of Japanese art, sprinkled liberally with Chinese and Korean pottery and a few stray Western pieces, is the result of the lifetime passion of petroleum magnate Idemitsu Sazo. Exhibits change every few months; there is no permanent display. The museum provides broad views across the grounds of the Imperial Palace and is next door to the characterful Teikoku Gekijō Theatre (Imperial Theatre), which shows high-stepping foreign musicals.

IMPERIAL PALACE Map pp294-5

Called the *kōkyo* in Japanese, this is the home of Japan's emperor and imperial family. Completed in 1968, the palace itself is a contemporary reconstruction of the Meiji Imperial Palace, destroyed during devastating aerial bombing in WWII. On these grounds once stood Edo Castle, in its time the largest castle in the world. The first Edo Castle was home to a feudal lord who was assassinated in 1486. The castle then fell into disuse until 1590, when Tokugawa Ieyasu chose it as the site for an unassailable castle from which the shōgun was to rule all Japan until the Meiji Restoration.

Edo Castle was fortified by a complex system of moats, and the grounds included numerous watch towers and armouries. By the time the Emperor Meiji moved to Edo in 1868, after the arrival of Commodore Perry and the black ships brought about the end of shōgunal rule, large sections of the old castle had been destroyed in the upheavals leading to the transfer of power. Much that remained was torn down to make way for the new Imperial Palace.

The palace itself is closed to the public for all but two days a year, 2 January (New Year's holiday) and 23 December (the emperor's birthday). But it is possible to wander around its outskirts and to visit the gardens, from where you can catch the double-barrelled bridge (and the palace's most famous landmark), **Nijū-bashi**, in the foreground.

Irises in bloom, Higashi-gyōen (opposite)

KITANOMARU-KŌEN Map pp294-5

Ⓜ Hanzōmon Line or Shinjuku or Tōzai Line to Kudanshita (exit 2), or Tōzai Line to Takebashi (exit 1a)

This large park north of the Imperial Palace grounds is home to a few noteworthy museums and **Nihon Budōkan** (☎ 3216-5123; 2-3 Kitanomaru-kōen). Westerners know the 14,000-plus-seat Budōkan as Tokyo's legendary concert hall for big acts from the Beatles to Beck, but it was built as the site of martial arts (judō, karate, kendō, aikidō) championships for the 1964 Olympics (*budō* means 'martial arts'). These arts are still practised and exhibited here today; see p169 and p238.

Southeast of the Budōkan is **Kagaku Gijitsukan** (Science Museum; ☎ 3212-2440; www.jsf.or.jp; 2-1 Kitanomaru-kōen, Chiyoda-ku; adult/child ¥600/250, student ¥400-600; 🕒 9am-4.50pm), which has good exhibits aimed primarily at children and teens. There's little in the way of English explanations, but there's an excellent bilingual guidebook (¥200); even without, you can stand inside a soap bubble or visit the 'methane boy' (he emits what you think he emits).

In the south of the park, facing the Imperial Palace East Garden, is the contemporary art museum **Kokuritsu Kindai Bijutsukan** (National Museum of Modern Art, MOMAT; ☎ 5777-8600; www.momat.go.jp/english; 3-2 Kitanomaru-kōen, Chiyoda-ku; adult/senior & child ¥420/free, student ¥130-420; 🕒 10am-5pm Tue-Thu, Sat & Sun,

SEE ALSO

Mitsukoshi (p177) Japan's first department store. Whatever you think of the shopping, the art galleries attract world-class exhibits.

10am-8pm Fri). All pieces date from the Meiji period onwards and impart a sense of a more modern Japan through portraits, photography and grim wartime landscapes. Its collection of over 9000 works is arguably the best in the country.

Nearby, MOMAT also operates the **Bijutsukan Kōgeikan** (Crafts Gallery; 1 Kitanomaru-kōen, Chiyoda-ku; adult/senior & under 15 ¥200, student ¥40-70; 10am-5pm Tue-Sun), an excellent museum staging changing exhibitions of *mingei* crafts (see p23): ceramics, lacquerware, bamboo, textiles, dolls and more. Artists range from living national treasures to contemporary artisans. Its red-brick building is an important cultural property in its own right; it dates from 1910, when it was the headquarters of the imperial guards, and was rebuilt after destruction in WWII.

The gate at the northern end, **Tayasu-mon**, dates from 1636, making it the oldest remaining gate in the park.

NIHOMBASHI Map pp294-5

Ginza Line to Mistukoshimae (exits b5 or b6) or Nihombashi (exits b11 or b12)

Even with the bronze lions guarding it, you could be forgiven for walking right past this granite bridge under an expressway, where Chūō-dōri meets Nihombashi-gawa. Still, it bears mention for its historic significance. Nihombashi ('Japan bridge') was the point from which all distances were measured during the Edo period, the beginning of the great trunk roads (the Tōkaidō, the Nikkō Kaidō etc) that took *daimyō* between Edo and their home provinces. To see a replica of the original wooden bridge, visit the Edo-Tokyo Museum (p105).

TOKYO INTERNATIONAL FORUM Map pp290-1

5221-9000; 3-5-1 Marunouchi, Chiyoda-ku; admission free; JR Yamanote Line to Yūrakuchō, or Yūrakuchō Line to Yūrakuchō (exit a4b)

The Forum is truly one of Tokyo's architectural marvels. Between Tokyo and Yūrakuchō Stations, it's used principally for its meeting halls and convention venues, but for the casual visitor there are restaurants, cafés and shops throughout. Architect Rafael Viñoly won Japan's first international architecture competition with his design that matches a building with this sort-of-trapezoidal lot, hemmed in by train tracks on the east side (the land had been the site of the Tokyo Metropolitan Government Offices before they were moved to their present location (see p101). It was completed in 1996. The glass eastern wing looks like a fantastic ship plying the urban waters, while the west wing is a phantasma of cantilevered spaces and cavernous atria. At night, the glass hall takes on the appearance of a space colony.

TOKYO STOCK EXCHANGE Map pp294-5

3665-1881; www.tse.or.jp; 2-1 Nihombashi Kabutocho, Chūō-ku; admission free; 9am-4pm on trading days; Tōzai Line to Kayabacho (exit 11) or Toei Asakusa Line to Nihombashi (exit D2)

Though the Tokyo Stock Exchange no longer echoes with the flurry of unbridled activity (the trading floor closed in the spring of 1999, and now all trading is by computer), it's worth a visit to contemplate the sheer amount of capital that passes through here daily (the market value of domestic stocks alone was nearly ¥541,670,370,000,000 in 2005). You may do your own walk-through the visitors galleries, or inquire about the 40-minute guided English-language tour (with video presentation). Also see the boxed text, below.

KNOW YOUR NIKKEI

The Tokyo Stock Exchange (TSE; above) has been operating since 1878, and today it is the world's second-largest capital market after the New York Stock Exchange. The two main indices of the TSE are the benchmark Nikkei (an index of 225 companies selected by the *Nihon Keizai Shimbun*, Japan's leading economic daily) and the broader TOPIX index, which covers all 1600 companies on the TSE's prestigious 1st Section. The Nikkei average hit its all time high of 38,915 points in 1989, just before the massive crash that lasted some 16 years before finally showing signs of recovery in 2005; it bottomed out around 7600 in 2003, at the beginning of the Iraq War. As we went to press, it was climbing back up through 16,700.

GINZA

Eating p124, Shopping p177, Sleeping p192

In the 1870s, Ginza was one of the first areas to modernise and featured novel (for Japan) brick buildings, department stores, pavements, gas lamps and other Western emblems of modernity.

Though some might say it has lost a bit of its edge and glamour as other districts such as Aoyama, Ebisu and Daikanyama have taken off, Ginza, or 'silver mint', is still where Tokyoites determined to shop often begin their mission. The crowds, mostly women, head for top-notch department stores like Wakō, Mitsukoshi and Matsuya. If you're not inclined to follow them, make a day of visiting the excellent small galleries, museums or showrooms in the neighbourhood. Also here is Japan's finest kabuki theatre, Kabuki-za.

On Sundays, many Ginza streets close to motor vehicles to allow the lively alleyways and lanes to come alive with foot traffic.

Orientation

Ginza is bounded to the north by the Imperial Palace and commercial Marunouchi. To the east and south are Tsukiji, with its fish and grocery markets, and the brand new skyscrapers of Shiodome.

Ginza itself, almost completely encircled by the Shuto Expressway, is about as grid-like as Tokyo gets. Within these confines, the neat rows of squares make for easy navigation through the boutiques, galleries and cafés.

GALLERY KOYANAGI Map pp290-1

☎ 3561-1896; www.gallerykoyanagi.com; 8th fl, 1-7-5 Ginza; admission free; 🕒 11am-7pm Tue-Sat; Ⓜ Ginza, Hibiya or Marunouchi Line to Ginza (exit A9), or Yūrakuchō Line to Ginza-itchōme (exit 7)

This gallery exhibits photography and prints in a space conspicuously set off by blinding white light. The staff speaks fluent English and is willing to talk about the work on the walls, which includes some of the leading artists of Japan and abroad, like Sugimoto Hiroshi (p26) and Marlene Dumas. Enter around the rear of the building housing the White Bell jewellery shop on Chūō-dōri.

TRANSPORT

Train The JR Yamanote Line stops at Shimbashi Station, which borders Ginza to the west. It's a five- to 10-minute walk to reach central Ginza.

Metro The Ginza and Marunouchi Lines are the best way to get to Ginza.

TOP FIVE – GINZA & TSUKIJI

- Department stores of Ginza (p66) Browse, people-watch and snack, view in-store art galleries or – just maybe – buy something.
- Hama Rikyū Onshi-teien (p75) At some point you'll want a break from the madness. These manicured gardens, whose grounds once belonged to the shōgun, provide the appropriate respite.
- Kabuki-za (p66) Japan's most revered kabuki theatre lies midway between Ginza and Tsukiji Central Fish Market, and makes for an excellent afternoon stopover.
- Tokyo Gallery (p66) Well-connected to the avant-garde art scene in Beijing, Tokyo Gallery is an excellent place to take in what's going on with Asian art.
- Tsukiji Central Fish Market (p75) This market is set to pick up stakes and move. Catch it while it occupies its current riverside home.

HACHIMAN-JINJA Map pp290-1

7-4 Ginza; admission free; Ⓜ JR Yamanote Line to Shimbashi (Ginza exit) or Toei Asakusa Line to Shimbashi (exits 1 & 3)

It's so small that you might stroll past and not notice it – which is exactly what makes Hachiman-jinja worth pausing for. Real-estate values in Ginza have generally forced places of worship elsewhere (or relocated them to the rooftops of Ginza's temples of commerce). Near Shimbashi Station, this is one shrine that remains at street level, a feat that was achieved by building over the top of it.

HIBIYA-KŌEN Map pp290-1

admission free; Ⓜ Chiyoda, Hibiya or Toei Mita Line to Hibiya (exits A5 & A13)

The park just west of Ginza was Tokyo's first Western-style park (built at the turn of the 20th century); you'll instantly notice similarities to public spaces in London, Paris and New York. If you're in need of a break on a quiet afternoon, find your way to one of the two ponds for a cup of tea at a pavilion.

DEPARTMENT STORES OF GINZA

There are clusters of department stores throughout Tokyo, but Ginza's have long been the leaders. The department stores here are shopping extravaganzas, to be sure, but they're so much more: highlights include traditional Japanese products and kimono displayed as if in art galleries, in-store art galleries that actually are art galleries of current up-and-coming artists, and wildly bustling food floors called *depachika* (p124). Check out Matsuya (p177), Mitsukoshi (a branch of the landmark Nihombashi store; p177) and Wakō (p178).

KABUKI-ZA Map pp290-1

☎ 3541-3131; www.shochiku.co.jp/play/kabukiza/theater/index.html; 4-12-5 Ginza, Chūō-ku; Ⓢ Hibiya or Toei Asakusa Line to Higashi-Ginza (exit 3)

To the east, along Harumi-dōri, is this famed kabuki theatre. Even if you don't plan to attend a performance, take a look at the building, a 1950s replica of a 1920s fusion of Western and Japanese architecture. If you do plan on sitting in on a few acts, keep in mind that it's OK to bring your lunch and something to sip on. See p145 for information on attending shows or p24 for more background on this fabulous art.

SHISEIDO ART HOUSE Map pp290-1

☎ 3571-0401; www.shiseido.co.jp/house-of-shiseido; 7-5-5 Ginza, Chūō-ku; admission free; ⏲ 11am-7pm Tue-Sun; Ⓢ JR Yamanote Line to Shimbashi (Ginza exit) or Toei Asakusa Line to Shimbashi (exits 1 & 3)

Underwritten by the cosmetics giant Shiseido, this new space is also a classic Ginza concoction: soft-sell corporate promo. Most will be drawn by the alluring, wonderfully displayed themed exhibitions (past ones have included speciality handbags and cosmetics for men), and along the way you might find yourself distracted by icons of the history of Shiseido (advertising etc).

SHISEIDO GALLERY Map pp290-1

☎ 3572-3901; www.shiseido.co.jp/e/gallery/html; 8-8-3 Ginza, Chūō-ku; admission free; ⏲ 11am-7pm Tue-Sat, 11am-6pm Sun; Ⓢ JR Yamanote Line to Shimbashi (Ginza exit) or Toei Asakusa Line to Shimbashi (exits 1 & 3)

This gallery in the basement of Shiseido's Ginza boutique is more experimental than the house thereof. The result is an ever-changing selection, particularly of installation pieces, which lend themselves well to the tall-ceilinged space. It's also one of the oldest galleries in the area (since 1919).

SONY BUILDING Map pp290-1

☎ 3573-2371; Sukiyabashi Crossing; admission free; ⏲ 11am-7pm; Ⓢ Marunouchi, Ginza or Hibiya Line to Ginza (Exit B9)

Right on Sukiyabashi Crossing is the Sony building, which attracts gadget hounds in search of gizmos that have yet to be released. Although there's often a wait, kids love the free video and virtual reality games on the 6th floor. If nothing else, you can put your feet up and relax for a while in one of the building's two Hi-Vision theatres.

TOKYO GALLERY Map pp290-1

☎ 3571-1808; 8-6-18 Ginza; admission free; Ⓢ Ginza Line to Shimbashi (exit 1)

One of our favourites, Tokyo Gallery collaborates with a large studio in Beijing and shows challenging, often politically pointed works by Japanese and Chinese artists. The staff speak English and are wonderfully friendly.

SHOWROOMS & CORPORATE GALLERIES

Ever since Tokyo was Edo, the city's residents have been attracted to the newest, coolest and most cutting-edge. So perhaps it's no surprise that soft-sell showrooms are attractions in their own right. We've listed some of the biggest in the neighbourhood sections, but here are some others worth a visit if you're nearby.

Pen Station (Map pp290–1; ☎ 3538-3840; www.pilot.co.jp; 2-6-21 Kyōbashi, Chūō-ku; ⏲ 9.30am-5pm Mon-Fri, 11am-5pm Sat; Ⓢ Ginza Line to Kyōbashi, exit 6) Museum and café owned by Pilot Pen company, with writing implements from antiques to the latest.

Toto Super Space (Map p282; ☎ 3345-1010; 26th & 27th fl, Shinjuku L Tower, 1-6-1 Nishi-Shinjuku; ⏲ 10am-6pm, closed 1st and 3rd Mon of the month; Ⓢ JR Yamanote Line to Shinjuku, west exit) This shrine to Japan's leading toilet maker gives entirely new meaning to 'praying to the porcelain god'.

Toyota Amlux (Map p280; ☎ 5391-5900; www.amlux.jp/english/floor/l_f.shtml; admission free; ⏲ 11am-9pm Tue-Sun; Ⓢ Marunouchi Line to Ikebukuro, east exit) Yes, Amlux is trying to sell you a car, but the ambient sound effects, movie theatre in an orb and virtual test drives make it almost painless. See also Toyota Mega Web (p109).

(Continued on page 75)

ongi Hills (p93),
gi **2** *Sky Bar Polestar*
Shinjuku **3** *Tokyo Big*
120), Odaiba

1 *Shinjuku (p100)* **2** *Sens (p85), Asakusa* **3** *Fortun paper tying, Sensō-ji (p8 Asakusa*

1 *Sumō wrestlers, Ryōgoku Kokugikan (p106), Sumida-ku* **2** *Geisha* **3** *Gallery of Hōryū-ji Treasures (p81), Tokyo Kokuritsu Hakubutsukan (Tokyo National Museum), Ueno* **4** *Shinjuku Station*

1 *Nakamise-dōri (p179), Asakusa* **2** *Shibuya (p96)* **3** *Ginza (p65)*

1 *Shinjuku (p100)* **2** Pachinko *(vertical pinball-game)*
3 *Shopping, Shibuya (p183)*
4 *Harajuku (p98), Omote-sandō*

1 *Japanese breakfast (p36)*
2 *Sake (p43)* **3** *Chef serving* oden *(fish-cake stew)* **4** *Red lantern*

1 *Produce at Tsukiji Outer Market (p76), Tsukiji* **2** *Noren (split doorway curtains)* **3** *Plastic food displays (p35)* **4** *Tuna for sale, Tsukiji Central Fish Market (p75), Tsukiji*

1 *Street art, Jingūmae*
2 *Traditional theatre perf ance (p24)* **3** *Design Festc (p10)*

(Continued from page 66)

TSUKIJI & SHIODOME

Eating p126, Shopping p177

Before 1923, the city's fish market was ensconced in Nihombashi as it had been throughout the Edo era. Of course the whole place smelled, well, fishy, and the market's well-off neighbours had grown weary of looking at its ugly façade. They got a reprieve when the deadly Great Kantō Earthquake flattened it. Though some of the more stubborn stall keepers insisted on returning to the old location, the market was officially moved to the old naval lands at Tsukiji, where it is now the world's largest fish market.

But not for much longer; the market is scheduled to move east to the Toyosu neighbourhood, east of the Sumida River, in 2012. For a good bet to see what the neighbourhood will look like once the move is complete, look just a little south, past the glorious garden, Hama Rikyū Onshi-teien (Detached Palace Garden). Here you'll find the skyscrapers of Shiodome; pretty much all the construction you see here has been done in the new millennium.

TRANSPORT

Metro For Tsukiji, the Hibiya Line stops at Tsukiji Station, while the Toei Ōedo Line stops at nearby Tsukijishijō. Shimbashi Station (JR and subway lines) is the transit hub for Shiodome. Shimbashi is also the terminus for the Yurikamome Line for Odaiba.

Waterbus Sumida River (Sumida-gawa) water taxis stop at the pier on the east end of Hama Rikyū Onshi-teien (Detached Palace Garden; Map pp290–1). Destinations include Asakusa and Odaiba.

Orientation

The fish market and outer market rest on the banks of the Sumida River on what were once old naval lands. Heading away from Tsukiji to the northwest on foot via Hanatsubaki-dōri will land you on the west end of Ginza, while walking just a few minutes to the southwest will bring you to the gates of Hama Rikyū Onshi-teien, one of Tokyo's most expansive gardens. Shiodome is the cluster of tall buildings on the other side of the Shuto Expressway.

ADVERTISING MUSEUM TOKYO

Map pp290-1

☎ 6218-2500; www.admt.jp; B1 fl, 1-8-2 Higashi Shimbashi, Minato-ku; admission free; 🕑 11am-6.30pm Tue-Fri, 11am-4.30pm Sat & public holidays; Ⓜ Ginza, Toei Asakusa or JR Yamanote Line to Shimbashi (Shiodome Shio-site exit or exit A3)

Dentsu, Japan's largest advertising agency, operates this rather extensive museum of Japanese advertising in the basement of the Caretta building. The collection covers wood-block printed handbills from the Edo period, through sumptuous Art Nouveau and Art Deco Meiji and Taisho era works, to the best of today. Although there's not a lot of English signage, the strong graphics of many of the ads stand in good stead, and there's a video room where you can watch award-winning TV commercials from around the world.

HAMA RIKYŪ ONSHI-TEIEN Map pp290-1

Detached Palace Garden; ☎ 3541-0200; adult/senior ¥300/150; 🕑 9am-5pm; Ⓜ Toei Ōedo Line to Shiodome (A2 or A3 exit) or Tsukijishijō (exit A2)

Once a shōgunal palace extending into the area now occupied by the fish market, this garden is one of Tokyo's finest. It features a large duck pond with an island that's home to a charming tea pavilion, and wonderful manicured trees (black pine, Japanese apricot, hydrangeas, camellias etc), some of them hundreds of years old. Besides visiting the park as a side trip from Ginza or Tsukiji, consider arriving by boat from Asakusa via the Sumida-gawa cruise aboard the Suijō Bus (p87).

TSUKIJI CENTRAL FISH MARKET

Map pp290-1

www.tsukiji-market.or.jp; admission free; 🕑 closed 2nd & 4th Wed of most months, Sun & public holidays; Ⓜ Toei Ōedo Line to Tsukijishijō (exit A1) or Hibiya Line to Tsukiji (exit 1 or 2)

If it lives in the sea, it's probably for sale here, where acres and acres of fish and fish products pass hands in a lively, almost chaotic atmosphere. Everything is allotted its own area, and a quick scan of the loading docks will reveal mountains of octopus, rows of giant tuna, endless varieties of shellfish and tanks of live unnameable fish.

About 2246 tonnes of fish, worth over 1.8 billion yen (US$15.5 million), are sold here daily; that's 615,409 tonnes of fish

Fish for sale, Tsukiji Central Fish Market (p75)

worth some US$4.25 billion a year. It's not unheard of for a single tuna to fetch an incredible ¥20 million.

The auctions are not officially open to the general public, but if you are of a mind to go you have to be there well before 5am to see the action. You are free to visit the wholesalers' market, though, and wander around the stalls set up to sell directly to restaurants, retail stores and such; some of the hundreds of merchants have been here for 20 generations. The hustle and bustle can be intoxicating, and as long as you're there before 8am, some kind of push and pull will doubtless be going on. The market shuts completely by 1pm for cleaning. Although the market is not as odoriferous as you might think, you still don't want to wear your nicest clothing (and especially not your best shoes).

Tradition has it that you should finish your visit here with a sushi breakfast. Daiwa Sushi (p126) is within the market itself and gathers long, long lines. For other choices, check out Edogin (p126) and Takeno (p126).

Between Tsukiji Central Fish Market and the Tsukiji Outer Market (below) is **Namiyoke-jinja**, the Shintō shrine where wholesalers and middlemen come to pray before work. Highlights are the giant gold parade masks used for the lion dance and the dragon-shaped taps over the purification basins.

TSUKIJI OUTER MARKET Map pp290-1

admission free; ⏲ closed 2nd & 4th Wed of most months, Sun & public holidays; Ⓜ Toei Ōedo Line to Tsukijishijō (exit 1) or Hibiya Line to Tsukiji (exit 1 or 2)

So you've arrived too late to see the fish auctions, or maybe you just can't stand the thought of sea creatures. Even you will probably find something in Tsukiji's Outer Market.

The Outer Market is neither as famous nor as breathtakingly busy as its inner counterpart, but that is usually a blessing. It gives you the time you need to browse all kinds of seafood (naturally) and produce, noodle shops, tiny cafés and cooking-supply shops, in addition to boots, baubles, baskets, plates, picks (of the tooth variety) and pottery, all at reasonable prices. It can be quite an education to see how those foods you've always loved are actually made or to wonder what those tiny bowls are used for. There are loads of tasting opportunities as well. In short, it's one-stop shopping for anything you need to prepare and serve that next great Japanese meal, though check your country's import restrictions if you plan to take any food products out of the country.

If you hate food in general, we can't help you.

GINZA, TSUKIJI & SHIODOME FOR FREE

- Advertising Museum Tokyo (p75) Japan's dominant ad firm, Dentsū, operates this gallery of advertisements historic and modern.
- Gallery Koyanagi (p65), Tokyo Gallery (p66) and the art galleries of the cosmetics giant Shiseido (p66) You never know what surprises you might find.
- Hachiman-jinja (p65) This tiny shrine has managed to hold its own as land prices soar and Ginza destroys and reconstructs itself around it.
- Hibiya-kōen (p65) Literally a breath of fresh air in the middle of the city.
- Tsukiji Central Fish Market (p75) and Tsukiji Outer Market (left) A fish is sold every four seconds, though it won't cost you a dime to watch.

AKIHABARA & KANDA

Eating p127, Sleeping p194

Akihabara's Electric Town (Denki Gai) is Tokyo's – and indeed Japan's – centre for electronics. Its street touts and electronic bells still ring with inimitable sound and fury, and the scene is a whirl of lights, beeps and foot traffic.

Nearby, Kanda was a bustling commercial and residential district during the Edo period. The vibrant green banks of the Kanda-gawa (Kanda River) and clear blue waters were famously depicted in woodblock prints. Streets in the neighbourhood were lined with artisans' shops and a residential district served as a rowdy, overcrowded home to workers and craftsmen. A quick look around will tell you that Kanda has seen happier days; the big attraction remains the lovely, atmospheric restaurants that have been around since the Edo period.

Yet Kanda's vital spirit has been channelled by the thousands of students who inhabit Ochanomizu, the area that lies north of Kanda proper. Nihon University and Meiji University, two of Japan's most prestigious private universities, are located nearby, and a couple of enclaves cater to them with clusters of shops as in days of old. A musical-instrument district sells mostly guitars and drums along Meidai-dōri, while Jimbōchō (along Yasukuni-dōri) houses a wonderful warren of antiquarian bookstores, shelves overseen by bookish staff who can help you locate even the most obscure texts. For purveyors of books in English, see p182.

TRANSPORT

Train The JR Yamanote and Keihin-Tōhoku Lines both stop at Akihabara and Kanda. Akihabara is also served by the JR Sōbu Line.

Metro Although the Hibiya Line stops east of the main electronics neighbourhood, the JR is more convenient. For Kanda, the Marunouchi Line stops at Awajichō, close to the traditional restaurant neighbourhood. To get to Jimbōchō, take either the Toei Shinjuku or the Hanzōmon Lines to Jimbōchō Station.

Orientation

Akihabara and Kanda lie firmly within the bounds of the old city, between the Tokyo Station and Ueno areas. Electric Town is west of Akihabara Station. West of Kanda are the Kiyōmizu Moat and the grounds of the Imperial Palace.

AKIHABARA ELECTRIC TOWN Map pp294-5

Denki-gai; west of JR Akihabara; Ⓜ JR Yamanote or JR Sōbu Line to Akihabara (Denki-gai exit)

What the Tsukiji Central Fish Market is to the food trade, Akihabara is to Japan's legendary electronics industry: bustling, busy and fun to watch. Bonus: you don't have to get up early in the morning to catch the action (afternoon is prime time). Big box retailers (Ishimaru Denki, Laox, Onoden, Satō Musen and Yamagiwa among them), wholesale shops and tiny stalls all compete to sell you everything from big appliances to microscopic components, robots, mouse pads and next year's computers, some at a steep discount from prices on the outside. Some items are intended for export (make sure the voltage and plugs match what you use at home), others are just coming on the market, so even if you have no intention of shopping now it's worth a peek to see what you may be buying two years hence.

Akihabara can no longer claim exclusive rights to the title of the city's electronic centre (thanks to increased competition from denser hubs like Shinjuku and Ikebukuro), yet it is still quite a scene. As the electronics business has moved elsewhere (and competition has come in from – gasp! – Korea, China and Taiwan), Akihabara has turned to the boom market in cartoon manga (comics; p29), often of the pornographic variety, to round out its fiscal activity.

KANDA MYŌJIN Map pp294-5

☎ 3254-0753; www.kandamyoujin.or.jp; 2-16-2 Sotokanda, Chiyoda-ku; admission free; Ⓜ Marunouchi Line to Ochanomizu (exit 2)

Hidden behind the main streets, this large, quietly splendid Shintō shrine boasts vermillion-coloured halls surrounding a stately courtyard. It traces its history back to AD 730 and moved here in 1616. The *kami* (gods) enshrined here are said to bring luck in business and finding a spouse. It is the home shrine of the Kanda Matsuri (Kanda Festival; p10) in mid-May, one of the largest festivals in Tokyo.

BULLETS & HORSES

Tokyo Station dates from 1914 after a design inspired by Amsterdam's Centraal Station; you can see the resemblance on Tokyo Station's red-brick Marunouchi side. Today, Tokyo Station is the hub of *shinkansen* (bullet train) traffic from around the nation.

There's one door train travellers never use, however. The elegant Marunouchi main entrance is reserved for state guests and the imperial family. About 60 times a year, new ambassadors ride from here to the Imperial Palace by horse-drawn carriage to present their credentials to the emperor.

NICHOLAI CATHEDRAL Map pp294-5

☎ 3295-6879; hrc@gol.com; 4-1 Surugadai, Kanda, Chiyoda-ku; donation ¥300; 1-4pm Tue-Fri Apr-Sep, 1-3.30pm Tue-Fri Oct-Mar; Chiyoda Line to Shin-Ochanomizu (exit C12)

This Russian Orthodox cathedral is named for St Nicholai of Japan (1836–1912), who first arrived as chaplain of the Russian consulate in the port city of Hakodate (Hokkaidō), and through missionary work soon amassed about 30,000 faithful. The Tokyo building, complete with a distinctive onion dome, was first constructed in 1891. The original copper dome was, like parts of so many grand buildings, damaged in the 1923 earthquake, forcing the church to downsize to the (still enormous) dome that's now in place. If you're interested in attending worship services, inquire for times.

TOKYO ANIME CENTER Map pp294-5

☎ 5298-1188; www.animecenter.jp; 4th fl, Akihabara UDX Bldg, 4-14-1 Soto-Kanda, Chiyoda-ku; admission free; 11am-7pm; JR Yamanote or JR Sōbu Line to Akihabara (Electric Town or Denki-gai exit)

Due to open as we were going to press, the Anime Center is less a museum than a place for promoting the latest and greatest in the world of *anime* (animation) and its merchandising. Facilities include exhibit halls, a shop and a theatre for cinematic screenings of *anime* as well as appearances by voice actors and *anime* creators (some 200 events annually). Displays are planned to be in four languages, including English.

TOKYO WONDER SITE Map pp294-5

☎ 5689-5531; www.tokyo-ws.org in Japanese; 2-4-16 Hongo, Bunkyō-ku; admission free; 11am-7pm Tue-Sun; JR Sōbu Line to Ochanomizu or Suidōbashi

Operated by the Tokyo Metropolitan Government, Tokyo Wonder Site comprises three floors of galleries with the aim of promoting new and emerging artists. There is a regularly changing programme of exhibitions, competitions and lectures in media ranging from painting to video art.

TRANSPORTATION MUSEUM Map pp294-5

☎ 3251-8481; www.kouhaku.or.jp; 1-25 Kanda Sudachō, Chiyoda-ku; adult/child ¥310/150; 9.30am-5pm Tue-Sun; Marunouchi Line to Awajichō (exits A3 & A5)

Try not to be deterred by this museum's unimpressive shell; inside it is a hoot for kids and any inner children you may have along. The museum covers all manner of transport, but – since this is Japan afterall – the emphasis is on trains. You can drive simulators of favourite routes (for example the JR Yamanote train around Tokyo or a *shinkansen* bullet train), marvel at the hulking engines and cars or gasp for at least a half-hour at the giant model-train set. The gift shop sells all manner of train-themed souvenirs that won't break the bank (at least not by Tokyo standards); we admit we've had hours of fun playing with the coloured pencils painted with train patterns.

YUSHIMA SEIDŌ Map pp294-5

☎ 3251-4606; 1-4-25 Yushima, Bunkyō-ku; admission free; 9.30am-5pm Apr-Sep, 9.30am-5pm Oct-Mar; Marunouchi Line to Ochanomizu (exit 2)

Established in 1632 and later used as a school for the sons of the powerful during the Tokugawa regime, Yushima Seidō is one of Tokyo's few Confucian shrines. There is a Ming dynasty bronze statue of Confucius in its black-lacquered main hall, which was rebuilt in 1935. The sculpture is visible only from 1 to 4 January and the fourth Sunday in April, but you can turn up at weekends and holidays for a chance to see the building's interior.

UENO

Eating p128, Sleeping p195

Geographically, Ueno Hill is one of the five rises that originally demarcated the edge of the Kantō Plain as it met Edo Harbour, now known as Tokyo Bay.

Historically, the hill, northeast of Edo Castle, is most famous as the site of a last-ditch defence of the Tokugawa shōgunate by roughly 2000 loyalists in 1868. Devoted to preventing the restoration of the emperor (though the shōgun himself had already willingly abdicated power), these adherents stationed themselves at Kanei-ji, a grand temple compound on the hill. They were duly dispatched by the imperial army, and the new Meiji government decreed that Ueno Hill would become one of Tokyo's first parks.

Today, that park, Ueno-kōen, is Ueno's foremost attraction, with a wealth of museums and a zoo that is small but fun, especially for kids. Expect lots of company during cherry-blossom season (p12), as well as the occasional homeless encampment.

Opposite Ueno Station is Ameyoko Arcade, which was once the site of one of the city's two largest postwar black markets (the other was in Ikebukuro), and today, more or loss legit, it still teems with atmosphere. West of the park are the hallowed precincts of Tokyo University, Japan's most prestigious institution of higher learning.

Orientation

The large Ueno Station is the hub of the area, with the greater Asakusa area to the east, Nippori to the north and Kanda and Akihabara to the south. In Ueno itself, all things lead to the park with its myriad art museums; take the Ueno-kōen (Ueno Park) exit from Ueno Station.

TRANSPORT

Train The JR Yamanote Line stops at Ueno Station and is the best transport option. The private Keisei Line also terminates here, with cheap connections to Narita airport.

Metro The Hibiya and Ginza Lines connect with Ueno Station and let you off near the park. If you're heading to Tokyo University or Yushima Tenjin, take the Chiyoda Line to Yushima.

TOP FIVE – UENO & ASAKUSA

- Ameyoko Arcade (below) Don't come here seeking glamour. But this one-time black-market district does its best to sell you cut-rate goods.
- Kappabashi-dōri (p87) The place to pick up those over-easy plastic eggs you've seen in so many noodle-shop windows.
- Kokuritsu Kagaku Hakubutsukan (p80) This newly renovated science museum is well worth a stop for its amazing displays.
- Sensō-ji (p85) Tokyo's only agreed-upon tourist attraction and a spiritual centre. Locals visit too.
- Tokyo Kokuritsu Hakubutsukan (p80) The Tokyo National Museum holds the largest collection of Japanese art on the planet.

AMEYOKO ARCADE Map pp296-7

10am-8pm; Yamanote Line to Okachimachi (north exit) or Ueno (south exit), or Ginza Line to Ueno Hirokōji or Hibiya Line to Naka-Okachimachi (both exit A5)

Ameya Yokochō (its full name) is one of the few areas in which some of the rough readiness of old Shitamachi lingers. Step into this alley paralleling the JR Yamanote Line tracks south of JR Ueno Station, and ritzy, glitzy Tokyo may seem like a distant memory.

Ameyoko was famous as a black-market district in the years following WWII, and it's still a lively bargain-shopping area. Simple shops spill out into the alleys, selling block after block of cheap clothing (for Japan, anyway), produce, dried fruit, dried *nori* (seaweed), dried mushrooms and dried squid and outdoor goods (also dried, we hope), plus DVDs that didn't look authentic to us, but what do we know? Some of the same tourist items on sale in Ginza sell here at more reasonable rates. Shopkeepers also stand on less ceremony than those in other shopping areas in Tokyo, brazenly hawking their goods with guttural cries to the passing crowds. In the **Ameyoko Center building**, Chinese, Korean and Southeast Asian merchants have set up their own shopping arcade where you'll find exotic cooking spices, fresh seafood, durian fruit and other unusual imported items.

Ameyoko is also one of the few places in this city where it pays to watch your purse. Probably nothing will happen, but better to be safe than sorry.

Frankenstein and other figures, Ameyoko Arcade (p79)

KOKURITSU KAGAKU HAKUBUTSUKAN (NATIONAL SCIENCE MUSEUM) Map pp296-7

☎ 3822-0111 Mon-Fri, 3822-0114 Sat, Sun & holidays; www.kahaku.go.jp; 7-20 Ueno Kōen, Taitō-ku; adult/child ¥500/free; 9am-5pm Tue-Sun; JR Yamanote Line or Tokyo Metro Ginza or Hibiya Line to Ueno (Ueno Kōen exit)

Broadly speaking, there are two components to this large, sprawling, multistorey museum. The older part was closed for a massive overhaul as we went to press and should have reopened by the time you read this, but the 'new annexe' (opened November 2004) is packed with delights. Displays (eg of the forest or animals of the savannah) are imaginatively presented, some allowing kids to climb up, down, around and even within. Other displays explain concepts of physics and mechanics by showing just how mystical things like magnets do what they do. And of course, dinosaurs, dinosaurs, dinosaurs.

There is English signage throughout, though it's not nearly as extensive as the Japanese signage; however, an English-language audio guide is available (¥300). Note the different contact number for weekends and holidays.

KOKURITSU SEIYŌ BIJUTSUKAN (NATIONAL MUSEUM OF WESTERN ART) Map pp296-7

☎ 3828-5131; www.nmwa.go.jp; 7-7 Ueno Kōen, Taitō-ku; adult/child ¥420/free, student ¥70-130; 9.30am-5pm Tue-Sun, 9.30am-8pm Fri; JR Yamanote Line or Tokyo Metro Ginza or Hibiya Line to Ueno (Ueno Kōen exit)

Designed by Le Corbusier in the late '50s, this museum has its roots in French impressionism but runs the gamut from medieval Madonna & Child images to 20th-century splatter painting. All the big names are here, particularly Manet, Rodin, Miró and the Dutch Masters. It also hosts wildly popular temporary exhibits on loan from such stalwarts as the Prado Museum in Madrid.

Much of the original collection was amassed by Matsukata Kōjiro (1865–1950), president of a shipbuilding company and later a politician. He would travel frequently to Europe on business and bring back treasures to inspire young, up-and-coming Japanese painters. Some 400 of his works were impounded in France during WWII, and it was only after Matsukata's death that they were allowed to be shipped to Japan.

SHITAMACHI MUSEUM Map pp296-7

☎ 3823-7451; 2-1 Ueno Kōen, Taitō-ku; adult/child/student ¥300/free/100; 9.30am-4.30pm; JR Yamanote Line or Tokyo Metro Ginza or Hibiya Line to Ueno (Ueno Kōen exit)

Take off your shoes and look inside an old tenement house or around an old sweet shop. This museum re-creates life in the plebeian quarters of Tokyo during the Meiji and Taishō periods through an exhibition of typical Shitamachi buildings. Pick up the English-language leaflets describing the various buildings in detail. On weekends the museum stages *kamishibai*: narratives told by performers using lovely painted cards.

TOKYO KOKURITSU HAKUBUTSUKAN (TOKYO NATIONAL MUSEUM) Map pp296-7

☎ 3822-1111; www.tnm.jp; 13-9 Ueno Kōen, Taitō-ku; adult/child ¥420/free, student free-¥130, additional charges for special exhibitions; 9.30am-5pm Tue-Sun; JR Yamanote Line or Tokyo Metro Ginza or Hibiya Line to Ueno (Ueno Kōen exit)

If you visit only one museum in Tokyo, make it this one. Its grand, recently renovated buildings hold the world's largest collection of Japanese art and you could easily spend a day here.

The museum has four galleries, the most important of which is the **Honkan** (Main Gallery). For an introduction to Japanese art history from Jōmon to Edo in one fell swoop, head to the 2nd floor. Other galleries include ancient pottery, religious sculpture, arms and armour, exquisite lacquerware and calligraphy. The building dates from 1939 and is in the imperial style, fusing Western and Japanese architectural motifs. The **Tōyōkan** (Gallery of Eastern Antiquities) boasts a collection of art and archaeological finds from all over Asia, with an emphasis on Chinese arts and archaeology. **Heiseikan** (Heisei Hall) is the newest, open in 1999 to commemorate the marriage of Crown Prince Naruhito, and it is used for exhibitions of Japanese archaeology. Finally, there is the **Gallery of Hōryū-ji Treasures**, which displays masks, scrolls and gilt Buddhas from Hōryū-ji, the first Buddhist temple in Japan. This wing may be shut when it's raining or humid, in order to protect artefacts that are more than 1000 years old.

A fifth building, Hyōkeikan was built in 1909, with Western-style architecture that might remind you of museums in Paris; it is used for special exhibitions.

One caveat: during blockbuster exhibitions like the 2005 showing of the woodblock prints of Hokusai, crowd control can be a problem with visitors three or more deep.

TOKYO METROPOLITAN MUSEUM OF ART Map pp296-7

☎ 3823-6921; www.tobikan.jp; 8-36 Ueno Kōen, Taitō-ku; admission free, charges for special exhibits vary; 9am-5pm Tue-Sun; JR Yamanote Line or Tokyo Metro Ginza or Hibiya Line to Ueno (Ueno Kōen exit)

Established in 1926, this museum hosts special exhibitions of everything from traditional Japanese arts, such as ink brush and ikebana (flower arranging), to avant-garde shows paid for by groups of artists who collaborate to rent gallery space. One annual event (most of November) that consistently draws hundreds of thousands is the exhibit of the Nitten, considered the leading association of Japanese artists, in Japanese- and Western-style painting, calligraphy, sculpture and craft as art. The museum has an excellent, free art library.

TOKYO UNIVERSITY Map pp296-7

Chiyoda Line to Nezu (exit 2) or Yushima (exit 1)

Most kids in Japan dream of gaining admission to Tōdai, as Japan's most prestigious institution of higher learning is known; admission here practically ensures later admission to the halls of power in both business and government. With that in mind, high-school students spend years studying at home and in cram schools for Tōdai's admission exam.

The campus is not beautiful, but does hold historical interest. In 1968 and 1969 Tōdai became the centre of a national crisis when students thrice took over the main administrative building, Yasuda Hall, ousting the school's president and other administrators before finally being ousted themselves. In order to make an example of the students, police used tear gas and blasted the students' stronghold with fire hoses on national TV in what came to be called the battle of Yasuda castle.

UENO-KŌEN Map pp296-7

☎ 3828-5644; admission free; 5am-11pm; JR Yamanote Line or Tokyo Metro Ginza or Hibiya Line to Ueno (Ueno Kōen exit)

This park has several names: its Sunday name, which no-one ever uses, is Ueno Onshi Kōen; some locals dub it Ueno no Oyama (Ueno Mountain); and English speakers call it Ueno Park. Whichever you prefer, there are two entrances. The main one takes you straight into the museum and art-gallery area, a course that might leave you worn out before you get to Ueno's temples. It's better to start at the southern entrance between Ueno JR Station and Keisei Ueno Station, and do a little temple viewing en route to the museums. From the JR Station, take the Ikenohata exit and turn right. Just around the corner is a flight of stairs leading up into the park.

Slightly to your right at the top of the stairs is the mother of all meeting places, a **statue of Saigō Takamori** (p82) walking his dog.

Bear to the far left and follow a wide tree-lined path until you reach **Kiyōmizu Kannon-dō**, modelled after the landmark Kiyōmizu-dera in Kyoto. During Ningyō-kuyō (p11) those wishing to conceive a child leave a doll here for the Senjū Kannon (the 1000-armed Buddhist goddess of mercy), and the accumulated dolls are burnt ceremoniously each 25 September.

From the temple, continue down to the narrow road that follows the pond, Shinobazu-ike. Through a red torii (gate), on an island in the pond, is **Benten-dō**, a memorial to Benten, a patron goddess of the arts. Behind the temple you can hire a **small boat** (☎ 3828-9502; row boats per hr ¥600, paddle boats per 30min ¥600; 🕑 9am-5pm Mar-Nov) to take out on the water, weather permitting.

Make your way back to the road that follows Shinobazu-ike and turn left. Where the road begins to curve and leaves Shinobazu-ike behind, there is a stair pathway to the right. Follow this path and take the second turn to the left. This will take you into the grounds of **Tōshō-gū** (☎ 3822-3455), which was established in 1627 (the present building dates from 1651). This is a shrine which, like its counterpart in Nikkō, was founded in memory of Tokugawa Ieyasu (p224). Inside, beyond the subdued worship hall, Ieyasu's shrine is all black lacquerwork and gold leaf. Miraculously, the entire structure has survived all of Tokyo's many disasters, making it one of the few early Edo structures still extant. There's a good view of the 17th-century, five-storey pagoda **Kanei-ji**, now stranded inside Ueno Zoo, to your right as you take the pathway into the shrine. The pathway itself is fronted by a stone torii and lined with 200 stone lanterns rendered as gifts by *daimyō* in the Edo period.

UENO ZOO Map pp296-7

Ueno Dōbutsu-en; ☎ 3828-5171; www.tokyo-zoo.net/english/index.html; 9-38 Ueno Kōen, Taitō-ku; adult/child/senior ¥600/200/300; 🕑 9.30am-5pm Tue-Sun; Ⓜ JR Yamanote Line or Tokyo Metro Ginza or Hibiya Line to Ueno (Ueno Kōen exit)

Japan's oldest zoo (1882) includes all the lions, tigers and bears that zoos normally have, although the sweet and sleepy pandas are by far the most popular. You can also check out the Bengal tigers, snow leopards and lowland gorillas, all of whom live in somewhat natural habitats.

If you're visiting the zoo with the kids, you can take a ride on the monorail to the petting zoo, where your precious wee ones can gently run their small, sticky hands over ducks, horses and goats.

YUSHIMA TENJIN Map pp296-7

Yushima Tenmangū; ☎ 3836-0753; 3-30-1 Yushima, Bunkyō-ku; admission free; 🕑 8am-5pm; Ⓜ Chiyoda Line to Yushima (exit 1)

Across the way from Tokyo University, this particularly attractive Shintō shrine traces its lineage back to the 5th century. In the

THE 'REAL' LAST SAMURAI

Saigō Takamori (1827–1877) looms large in Ueno-kōen, and that is fitting. He was a giant of a man for his day, at about 180cm (6ft) tall, with a big build and large eyes, and he became a giant of Japanese history.

Originally from Satsuma province on the southern island of Kyūshū, Saigō was an ardent supporter of the emperor Meiji, and in 1868 he led the defence against the rebellion of Tokugawa loyalists here on Ueno Hill, thus cementing the Meiji Restoration.

But things did not turn out as he had hoped. Not long after the Meiji Restoration, the samurai system was abolished and by 1872 the military system of professional warriors gave way to a Western model of conscription. By 1874, small samurai-led riots had broken out around the country, put down by the new army. Meanwhile, Saigō's own advice to the Meiji government (including an invasion of Korea) was rejected. A dispirited Saigō resigned his government post and returned to Satsuma.

Other former samurai rallied around Saigō and urged him to lead a rebellion against the imperial forces. The subsequent siege of Kumamoto Castle lasted for 54 days, with a reported 40,000 men, including both samurai and armed peasants, arrayed against the imperial army. Other skirmishes followed, and the rebellion gradually dwindled. Finally, in September 1877, a small remaining cadre of rebel samurai faced the imperial army at an outpost on the most distant corner of Kyūshū. Vastly outnumbered and outgunned, they committed *seppuku* (ritual suicide by self-disembowelment) rather than face the humiliation of defeat.

The Satsuma Rebellion soon gained the status of legend among the common Japanese. The Meiji government, capitalising on this fame, posthumously pardoned Saigō and granted him full honours, and today he remains an exemplar of the samurai spirit.

Fans of the movie *The Last Samurai* may recognise elements of this story in Katsumoto, the character played by Watanabe Ken. However, there is no evidence that any Western soldier, such as the one played by Tom Cruise, had any role in these events.

DETOUR

Asakura Chōso Museum (Map pp296-7; ☎ 3821-4549; 7-18-10 Yanaka, Taitō-ku; adult/student ¥400/150; 9.30am-4.30pm Tue-Thu, Sat & Sun; JR Yamanote Line to Nippori, north exit) The primary work of sculptor Asakura Fumio (1883–1964) consisted of realistic sculptures of people and cats, but the real attractions are the Japanese house, studio and garden, designed by the artist himself. Upstairs in the Morning Sun Room and the Poised Mind Room are some excellent ink scrolls and beautiful old *tansu* (wooden chests). See also the Nippori to Nishi-Nippori walking tour, p118.

14th century the spirit of a renowned scholar was also enshrined here, which leads to Yushima Tenjin's current popularity: it receives countless pilgrims in search of academic success. Amid the buildings with their painted accents and gold trim (the latest reconstruction was in 1995), students hang messages written on wooden tablets called *ema*, left in hope that lofty exam scores will gain hopeful high-school students admission to the power generator across the street or universities nationwide.

ASAKUSA

Eating p129, Shopping p178, Sleeping p197

Asakusa (say a-*sock*-sa) is where the spirit of Old Edo proudly lives. Asakusa's grandest sight is the temple Sensō-ji, also known as Asakusa Kannon-dō. It was founded in the 7th century, not only before Tokyo was Edo, but before Edo was a glimmer of an idea. As Edo rose, Asakusa emerged as a bustling commercial centre and bawdy entertainment area, becoming the sturdy beat of Shitamachi's rowdy heart.

Like Ueno, Asakusa recommends itself to the directionless stroll – up one alley you'll find a charming ryokan (traditional inn) or a fastidious *sembei* (rice cracker) maker, while down the next lane will be a marvellous public bath frequented by the *yakuza* (Japanese mafia).

In early Edo times, Asakusa was a halfway stop between the Yamanote and the pleasure quarters of the Yoshiwara, but in time the area emerged as a pleasure quarter in its own right, eventually becoming the hub of that most beloved of Edo entertainments, kabuki theatre (p24). In the very shadow of Sensō-ji, a fairground atmosphere harboured a wealth of decidedly secular entertainment – from kabuki to brothels.

When Japan ended its isolation with the Meiji Restoration, it was in Asakusa that the first cinemas, music halls and Western operas appeared. It was also in Asakusa that another Western export – the striptease – first found a Japanese audience. It almost failed to catch on, such was the popularity of a rival form of risqué entertainment – female sword fighting. The inspired introduction of a bubble-bath show saved the day; you can still see girlie-show venues at the fringes of central Asakusa. Famed movie-maker and comedian Kitano Takeshi (Beat Takeshi) got his start in showbiz here, doing comic riffs between acts. (For more information on film in Tokyo see p27.)

Asakusa had never fully recovered from the great earthquake of 1923, before it was flattened once again by aerial bombing in the closing months of WWII. Sensō-ji was rebuilt and the area remains undeniably bustling and fun. Even if the brightest lights have shifted elsewhere, that works to Asakusa's advantage: it retains a close-to-the-ground feeling of the common people not readily visible in other parts of town; just visit the smoke-filled floors of WINS Asakusa, the off-track betting hall operated by the Japan [horse-] Racing Association.

Orientation

Asakusa is bounded on the east by the Sumida River, with its small barges and waterbuses; to the west by Ueno.

All of the destinations in this section are easiest reached via Asakusa Station on the Ginza Line. There is also an Asakusa Station on the Toei Asakusa Line, a slightly longer walk.

TRANSPORT

Train The Tōbu Nikko Line terminates at Asakusa Station, offering the most convenient connections to Nikko (p221).

Metro The Ginza Line stops at Asakusa, just in front of Azuma-bashi. The Toei Asakusa Line also stops at a separate Asakusa Station nearby.

Waterbuses Water taxis arrive and depart regularly from beneath Azuma-bashi.

From either subway station, head away from the river along Kaminarimon-dōri; the Kaminarimon Gate marks the entrance to Sensō-ji. Through the gate, the lively Nakamise-dōri shopping arcade leads straight to the temple.

ASAKUSA-JINJA Map pp296-7

Asakusa Kannon-dō; 2-3-1 Asakusa, Taitō-ku; Ⓢ Ginza Line to Asakusa (exit 1) or Toei Asakusa Line to Asakusa (exit A5)

The proximity of this Shintō shrine, behind Sensō-ji and to the right, testifies to the comfortable co-existence of Japan's two major religions. Asakusa-jinja was built in honour of the brothers who discovered the Kannon statue and is renowned as a fine example of an architectural style called *gongen-zukuri*. It's also the site of one of Tokyo's most important festivals, the Sanja Matsuri (p10), a three-day extravaganza of costumed parades, about 100 lurching *mikoshi* (portable shrines) and stripped-to-the-waist *yakuza* sporting remarkable tattoos.

The gate **Niten-mon** marks one of the entryways to Asakusa-jinja. It was erected in 1618 as a private entrance to the temple for the Tokugawa shōgun, and it is the only structure in the temple precincts to have survived Asakusa's various disasters. It was built here at the same time as Tōshō-gū (p82), which burned at this location and was moved to Ueno for fire prevention. The gate's weathered wooden pillars, plastered with votive papers left by Shintō pilgrims, and its enormous red paper lantern merit a stop on your way out of the compound.

Tanuki *(racoon dog statues), Chingodō-ji (above)*

CHINGODŌ-JI Map pp296-7

admission free; Ⓢ Ginza Line to Asakusa (exit 1) or Toei Asakusa Line to Asakusa (exit A5)

This odd, peaceful little shrine on the banks of Dembō-in (below), pays tribute to *tanuki* (raccoon dogs who figure in Japanese myth as mystical shape-shifters and merry pranksters). *Tanuki* are normally depicted with enormous testicles on which they can fly and have been known to pop up in Japanese wood-cuts like Utagawa Kuniyoshi's *The Seven Wonders of the Clowning Raccoon*, in which the *tanuki* is shown cheerily dancing his way round a geisha house.

DEMBŌ-IN Map pp296-7

☎ 3842-0181; admission free; Ⓢ Ginza Line to Asakusa (exit 1) or Toei Asakusa Line to Asakusa (exit A5)

To the left of the temple precinct lies Dembō-in, a garden that adjoins the residence of the chief priest of Sensō-ji. The grounds are thought to have been designed sometime in the late 18th century to resemble those of Katsura-rikyu, the sprawling imperial villa in Kyoto. Dembō-in is not usually open to the public, but if you'd like to take a peek at the 12,000-sq-metre area, whose pond is reputedly shaped like the Chinese character for 'heart', call ahead to the main office, which is to the left of the five-storey pagoda.

EDO SHITAMACHI DENTŌ KŌGEIKAN

Map pp296-7

Traditional Crafts Museum; ☎ 3842-1990; 2-22-13 Asakusa, Taitō-ku; admission free; 🕑 10am-8pm; Ⓢ Ginza Line to Asakusa (exit 1) or Toei Asakusa Line to Asakusa (exit A5)

Gallery Takumi, as this hall is also known, is a great place to view dozens of handmade crafts that still flourish in the heart of Shitamachi. The gallery on the 2nd floor is crammed with a rotating selection of works by neighbourhood artists: fans, lanterns, knives, brushes, gold leaf, precision woodworking and glass just for starters. Craft demonstrations take place most Saturdays and Sundays around noon.

If anything you see strikes your interest, staff can direct you to artisans or shops selling their work.

JAPANESE GODS & MYTHICAL CREATURES

You can see representations of a myriad of folk gods in temples, shrines and artwork. Common deities and supernatural creatures include the following.

Benzaiten The goddess of art is skilled in eloquence, music, literature and wisdom. She holds a *biwa* (lute) and is often escorted by a sea snake.

Bishamon The god of war wears a helmet and a suit of armour, and brandishes a spear. As a protector of Buddhism, he can be seen carrying a pagoda.

Daikoku The god of wealth has a bag full of treasures slung over his left shoulder and a lucky mallet in his right hand.

Ebisu The patron of seafarers and a symbol for prosperity in business, Ebisu carries a fishing rod with a large, red sea bream dangling on the line and can be recognised by his beaming, bearded face.

Fukurokuju This god looks after wealth and longevity. He has a bald, dome-shaped head, a dumpy body and wears long, flowing robes.

Jurojin This god also covers longevity. He sports a distinguished white beard and holds a cane to which is attached a scroll listing the life-spans of all living beings.

Hotei The god of happiness is instantly recognisable (in Japan and elsewhere in Asia) by his large paunch and Cheshire-cat grin. Originally a Chinese beggar-priest, he is the only god in this group whose antecedents can be traced to a human being. His bulging bag provides for the needy and is never empty.

Jizō Bodhisattva and protector of children, the infirm, the aged and travellers. Often seen by the side of the road, and wearing a red bib and sometimes a cap, and often in clusters where tragedies have taken place.

Kappa These are amphibious creatures about the size of a 12- or 13-year-old child. They have webbed hands and feet and a reputation for mischief, such as dragging horses into rivers or stealing cucumbers. The source of their power is a depression on top of their heads that must always contain water. A crafty method to outwit a *kappa* is to bow to it. When the *kappa* bows back, it empties the water from its head and loses its power. The alternatives are not pleasant: *kappa* are said to enjoy ripping out their victim's liver through the anus!

Kitsune This creature is a fox that has strong connections with the supernatural and is worshipped at over 30,000 Inari shrines as the messenger of the harvest god. Fushimi Inari Taisha, a shrine near Kyoto, is the largest of its kind and is crammed with fox statues.

Maneki-neko The Beckoning Cat is a very common sight outside shops or restaurants. The raised left paw attracts customers – and their money.

Shichifuku-jin The seven gods of luck are a happy band of well-wishers plucked from Indian, Chinese and Japanese sources. Their images are popular at New Year, when they are, more often than not, depicted as a group on a *takarabune* (treasure ship).

Tanuki This creature is often translated as 'badger', but bears a closer resemblance to a North American raccoon. Like the *kitsune,* the *tanuki* is thought of as a mischievous creature and is credited with supernatural powers, but it is more a figure of fun than the fox. Statues usually depict the *tanuki* in an upright position with straw headgear, clasping a bottle of sake.

Tengu The mountain goblin has a capricious nature – sometimes abducting children, sometimes returning those who were missing. Its unmistakable feature is a long nose, like that of a proboscis monkey.

SENSŌ-JI Map pp296-7

☎ 3842-0181; 2-3-1 Asakusa, Taitō-ku; admission free; 🕑 24hr; Ⓢ Ginza Line to Asakusa (exit 1) or Toei Asakusa Line to Asakusa (exit A5)

Asakusa's *raison d'-être,* Sensō-ji enshrines a golden statue of Kannon, the Goddess of Mercy, which was miraculously fished out of the nearby Sumida River by two fishermen in AD 628. In time, a structure was built to house the image, which has remained on the spot through successive rebuildings of the temple, including a complete postwar reconstruction following the aerial bombings at the end of WWII.

The temple precincts begin at the majestic **Kaminarimon** (Thunder Gate), which houses a pair of ferocious protective deities: Fūjin, the god of wind, on the right; and Raijin, the god of thunder, on the left.

Straight on through the gate is the lively shopping street **Nakamise-dōri**. Everything is sold here from tourist trinkets like purses made from obi (kimono sash) fabric to Edo-style crafts and wigs to be worn with a kimono. Along this route are also stands that specialise in salty, crunchy *sembei*, and *ningyō-yaki* (snacks in the shape of pagodas, fish and more), made of pancake batter with a dollop of *anko* (bean paste) baked inside.

Nakamise-dōri leads north to another gate, **Hōzōmon**, whose fierce guardians you must pass to reach the main temple compound. To your left stands a 53m-high **five-storey pagoda**, a 1973 reconstruction of a pagoda built by Tokugawa Iemitsu. The current structure is the second-highest pagoda in Japan.

The temple grounds buzz and click with cameras and voices with accents from across the country and around the world. The Kannon image (a tiny 6cm) is cloistered within, but despite its seclusion, a steady stream of worshippers makes its way up

TEMPLE & SHRINE ETIQUETTE

Visitors to Tokyo are often nervous about committing some dreadful faux pas at a temple or shrine. Relax – as with most other aspects of their lives, the Japanese are not particularly rigid in these matters and certainly wouldn't judge a foreign visitor for not adhering to ritual.

If photography is forbidden at a shrine, it will be posted as such; otherwise, it is permitted and you should simply use your discretion when taking pictures so as not to interfere with other visitors.

At both shrines and temples, you can buy amulets called *omamori*, for traffic safety, academic success, good health, safe pregnancy and more, usually for ¥300 to ¥500. *Omamori* run the gamut from minimalist paper or wooden charms to small but elaborate brocade bags embroidered with the name of the shrine or temple and your wish. Another popular memento is *shūin-chō* (pilgrimage books; around ¥1000), which are blank fanfold books; purchase one at the first shrine or temple you visit, and then have it inscribed at each subsequent shrine or temple (around ¥300), usually with lovely calligraphy.

Shintō Shrines

Just past the torii (gate) at most larger Shintō shrines is a *chōzuya* (trough of water) with long-handled ladles perched on a *hishaku* (rack) above. This water can be used to purify yourself before entering the sacred precincts. Some Japanese forego this ritual and head directly for the main hall. The traditional way to purify oneself is to take a ladle, fill it with fresh water from the tap, pour some over one hand, transfer the ladle and pour water over the other hand, then pour a little water into a cupped hand, rinse your mouth and spit the water out. Make sure that any water you have used for washing or rinsing goes on to the ground beside the trough (not into the trough, which would make it impure).

Once you have purified yourself, head to the *haiden* (hall of worship), which sits in front of the *honden* (main hall) enshrining the *kami* (god or gods) of the shrine. Here you'll often find a thick rope hanging from a gong, in front of which is an offerings box. Toss in a coin, ring the gong by pulling on the rope (to summon the deity), bow twice, place your hands in the prayer position to pray silently, clap twice, bow once more and then back away. Some Japanese believe that a ¥5 coin is the luckiest offering at a temple or shrine (the word for ¥5, *go-en*, is a homonym for fate), and that the blessing engendered by the offering of a ¥10 coin will come in the future (since 10 can be pronounced 'tō' in Japanese, which also means 'far').

Many shrines sell *ema* (wooden votive plaques), on which you can write a wish before hanging it on a rack for the purpose. Your wish does not have to be in Japanese.

Buddhist Temples

Unless the temple contains a shrine, you will not have to purify yourself before entry. The place of worship in a temple is in the *hondō* (main hall), which usually contains a Buddhist altar and one or more Buddha images. The standard practice is to toss some change into the offering box, which sits in front of the altar, step back, place your hands together, pray and then bow to the altar before backing away.

Most temples sell *omikuji* (fortunes written on little slips of paper). These usually cost ¥100. Either pay an attendant or place the money in an honour-system box. Fortunes are dispensed randomly from a special box containing sticks with different numbers written on their ends. Shake the box until one stick pops out of a hole in the box's top. Show this to the attendant and you will be given a fortune matching the number on the stick (remember to return the stick to the box!). This will be written in Japanese under one of four general headings: *dai-kichi* (big luck), *kichi* (luck), *sho-kichi* (small luck) and *kyō* (bad luck). *Kichi* is considered best – your luck is good, but getting better – whereas *dai-kichi* implies that it's great now but otherwise all downhill. *Sho-kichi* is moderately grim and *kyō* is the worst. Some fortunes are translated into English, or you can ask someone on the temple grounds to read your fortune for you. Once you've read it, fold the fortune and tie it to a nearby tree branch so that the wind can disperse the bad luck; there's always a tree nearby festooned with the white fortunes, or sometimes there's a clothesline-type contraption for the same purpose.

the stairs to the temple, where they cast coins, pray and bow in a gesture of respect. In front of the temple smoke winds its way up from a huge incense cauldron around which supplicants stand wafting the smoke and its scent to their bodies and over their heads to ensure good health.

SUMIDA-GAWA CRUISE Map pp296-7

Suijō Bus; ☎ 0120-977-311; www.suijobus.co.jp; Ⓢ Ginza Line to Asakusa (exit 5), Toei Asakusa Line to Asakusa (exit A5) for Azuma-bashi Pier

Though the Sumida River is no longer a quaint river, it is still famous for its 12 bridges, and a trip by waterbus is an excellent way to survey Tokyo's old corners and new quarters. The Suijō Bus departs from a pier by Asakusa's Azuma-bashi for the stately garden Hama Rikyū Onshi-teien (p75; ¥620, 35 minutes) and Hinode Pier (¥660, five minutes further). From Hinode Pier you can continue on to Odaiba Marine Park (¥400, 20 minutes) or the Museum of Maritime Science (p108; ¥520, 25 minutes). Boats leave once or twice per hour between 9.45am and 6.30pm (until 7.10pm on Saturday and Sunday), and English leaflets describe the dozen-or-so bridges you'll pass under en route.

TAIKO-KAN Map pp296-7

Drum Museum; ☎ 3842-5622; 2-1-1 Nishi Asakusa, Taitō-ku; adult/child ¥300/150; ⏲ 10am-5pm Wed-Sun; Ⓢ Ginza Line to Tawaramachi (exit 3)

More than 600 drums make up this collection from around the world, though only about 200 are available at any one time in the splendidly interactive drum exhibit. You have free rein to touch or play any instrument with no mark; those with a blue dot should be handled carefully, while a red dot means 'off limits'. If you're inspired, you can buy a Japanese-style drum and lots of other festival products at Miyamoto Unosuke Shoten (p179).

WHERE A RUBBER CHICKEN IS NO YOLK

A 10-minute walk west of Sensō-ji, **Kappabashi-dōri** (Map pp296–7; Ⓢ Ginza Line to Tawaramachi, exit 3) is the country's largest wholesale kitchenware and restaurant-supply district. Gourmet accessories include colourful, patterned *noren* (split doorway curtains), pots and pans, restaurant signage, tableware, and kitchen gadgets to make you go '*hmmm?*'

But the key drawcard for overseas visitors is the plastic models of food, such as you see in restaurant windows throughout Tokyo. Whether you want steak and chips, a lurid pizza, a bowl of *rāmen* (see p38) or a plate of spaghetti bolognaise complete with an upright fork, you'll find it. Good bets are the model shops **Maiduru** (Map pp296–7; ☎ 3483-1686; 1-5-17 Nishi-Asakusa, Taitō-ku; Ⓢ Ginza Line to Tawaramachi, exit 3) and **Satō Sample** (Map pp296–7; ☎ 3844-1650; 3-7-4 Nishi Asakusa, Taitō-ku; Ⓢ Ginza Line to Tawaramachi, exit 3).

Kappabashi-dōri is several compact blocks between Asakusa-dōri on the south and Kototoi-dōri on the north. If you're not walking from Sensō-ji, the closest subway stop is Tawaramachi. Also see p178.

WEST OF THE IMPERIAL PALACE

Eating p130, Sleeping p194

More a collection of contiguous neighbourhoods than one unified district, this area spans the spectrum from historic gardens and samurai quarters to baseball, amusement parks and war memorials.

Closest to the palace is Yasukuni-jinja, controversial shrine to Japan's war dead. Kōrakuen, north and west of the palace, was originally the pleasure garden of the nobility, and it continues to be a place of amusement. Here, Tokyo Dome stadium is the home of the Yomiuri Giants, Japan's most storied baseball team, and there's an adjacent amusement park. Also in the shadow of the dome is Koishikawa Kōrakuen, one of the city's loveliest gardens.

Heading west is Kagurazaka, with quaint old-Edo streetscapes and hide-and-seek alleys, the better for a tryst or a backroom deal. Other sights include some interesting speciality museums of cameras and Meiji period art.

Orientation

This district, bordered roughly by the Imperial Palace grounds on the east, the government district to the south and greater Shinjuku to the west, starts with Yasukuni-jinja (basically north of the palace grounds) and curves around past the Tokyo Dome and Koishikawa areas through the area immediately west of the palace. Sotobori-dōri pretty well bisects the district.

TRANSPORT

Train The JR Chūō and JR Sōbu Lines stop at Iidabashi and Suidōbashi, at the centre of this area.

Metro Useful stations include Iidabashi (Toei Ōedo Line), Kōrakuen (Marunouchi Line), Kagurazaka (Tōzai Line) and Hanzōmon (Hanzōmon Line).

BASEBALL HALL OF FAME & MUSEUM Map pp278-9

☎ 3811-3600; 1-3-61 Kōraku, Bunkyō-ku; adult/child ¥400/200; ⏲ 10am-6pm Tue-Sun Mar-Sep, 10am-5pm Tue-Sun Oct-Feb; Ⓜ Marunouchi Line to Kōrakuen, or JR Chūō or JR Sōbu Line to Suidōbashi (west exit)

Baseball arrived in Japan in 1872, courtesy of an American teacher at the school that eventually became Tokyo University, and it has been an obsession among Japanese ever since. From college baseball leagues to the professional leagues in 1922, to Oh Sadaharu becoming the world's home-run king and the Japanese team winning the bronze medal at the 2004 Olympics, this museum at the Tokyo Dome walks you through it all. Be sure to pick up the comprehensive English-language pamphlet.

Enter next to Gate 21 of the Tokyo Dome (right).

JCII CAMERA MUSEUM Map pp294-5

☎ 3263-7100; www.jcii-cameramuseum.jp; 25 Ichiban-cho, Chiyoda-ku; adult/child/student ¥300/free/100; ⏲ 10am-5pm Tue-Sun; Ⓜ Hanzōmon Line to Hanzōmon (exit 4)

What? You didn't know that Japan is obsessed with photography? This museum, established in 1989 by the Japan Camera Industry Institute, takes it a step further, for those for whom equipment is the thing. Holdings consist of over 10,000 cameras, of which as many as 600 may be on show at any one time. Highlights of the collection include the world's first camera, the 1839 Giroux daguerreotype (one of an estimated seven worldwide) and the prototype for the original digital camera, the Sony Mavica, from which images had to be downloaded to a floppy disk.

Behind the museum is the JCII **photo salon** (☎ 3261-0300; admission free; ⏲ 10am-5pm Tue-Sun) with a changing roster of photography exhibits.

Exiting Hanzōmon Station, walk around the Diamond Hotel. The photo salon is in this alley, while the museum entrance is through to the next street.

KAGURAZAKA Map pp294-5

Tōzai Line or Yūrakuchō Line to Iidabashi (exit B3)

Kagurazaka is worth a visit more for an atmospheric stroll than for any particular sights. Its intimate *kakurenbo yokochō* (hide-and-seek alleys) recall bygone days of Edo, or a city like Kyoto which wears its history on its sleeve. But this is Tokyo, which means that the denizens of the nearby government and business districts come to broker their power, and deals are being made behind the wooden façades and sliding gates of the expensive restaurants and nightspots.

From Sotobori-dōri, head up Kagurazaka Hill and turn right at Royal Host restaurant. The back alleys will be on your left in a few blocks.

KOISHIKAWA KŌRAKUEN Map pp294-5

☎ 3811-3015; 1-6-6 Kōraku, Bunkyō-ku; adult/senior & child ¥300/free; ⏲ 9am-5pm; Ⓜ Toei Ōedo Line to Iidabashi (exit C3)

This 70,000-sq-metre formal garden is one of Tokyo's most beautiful and least visited (by foreigners at least). Any visitor with even the slightest interest in gardens should make a bee line. Established in the mid-17th century as the property of the Tokugawa clan, it incorporates elements of Chinese and Japanese landscaping, although nowadays the *shakkei* (borrowed scenery) also includes the otherworldly cool of the Tokyo Dome. The garden is particularly well known for plum trees in February, irises in June and autumn colours, and the Engetsu-kyō (full moon bridge) dates from the early Edo period.

Kōrakuen means 'the garden of later enjoyment'; it comes from a Chinese proverb about maintaining power first and enjoying it later. We assume this sounds better in Chinese.

TOKYO DOME CITY Map pp278-9

☎ 5800-9999; www.tokyo-dome.co.jp/e; 1-3-61 Kōraku, Bunkyō-ku; all-day pass adult/child ¥4000/3000, night ticket (after 5pm) ¥3000/2800; ⏲ 10am-10pm; Ⓜ Marunouchi Line to Kōrakuen, or JR Chūō or JR Sōbu Line to Suidōbashi (west exit)

Kōraku-en stadium dates back to 1937, and in 1988 it reopened as the Tokyo Dome (aka 'Big Egg') and has never looked back. The dome's Teflon roof is supported by nothing but air (the pressure is 0.3% higher indoors than out – what will they think of next?). You can take a **stadium tour** (☎ 3817-6086; adult/child from ¥1000/600) on the rare occasions when no events are on (telephone the stadium for tour hours).

The dome is surrounded by an amusement park with the usual assortment of coasters and spinners, as well as shops. If you don't want to invest in an all-day pass offering access to all rides (see information at the beginning of this listing), tickets are available for individual rides (¥400 to ¥1000).

Also see the Baseball Hall of Fame & Museum (opposite).

YAMATANE BIJUTSUKAN (YAMATANE MUSEUM OF ART) Map pp294-5

☎ 3239-5911; 2 Sanbanchō, Chiyoda-ku; adult/student ¥600/500, special exhibitions extra; 10am-5pm Tue-Sun; Hanzōmon Line to Hanzōmon (exit 5)

This exceptional collection includes some 1800 Japanese paintings dating from the Meiji Restoration and onward, of which around 50 are on display at any one time; exhibits change approximately every two months. Some names to look for: Hayami Gyoshū (1894–1935), whose *Dancing Flames* is an important cultural property; and Okumura Togyū (1889–1990), whose *Cherry Blossoms at Daigoji Temple* is a masterpiece in pastel colours. It's on the ground floor of the KS Building.

YASUKUNI-JINJA Map pp294-5

☎ 3261-8326, Yūshūkan ☎ 3261-0998; www.yasukuni.or.jp; 3-1-1 Kudankita, Chiyoda-ku; shrine admission free, Yūshūkan admission adult ¥800, student ¥300-500; 9am-5.30pm Mar-Oct, 9am-5pm Nov-Feb; Tōzai, Hanzōmon or Toei Shinjuku Line to Kudanshita (exit 1)

You know that shrine that causes such controversy every year when the Prime Minister visits? This is it. Literally 'For the Peace of the Country Shrine', Yasukuni is the memorial shrine to Japan's war dead, some 2.5 million souls who died in combat.

The shrine dates back to 1869, and in the years leading up to and during WWII it became Tokyo's chief shrine of State Shintō (p52). Despite a postwar constitutional commitment to the separation of religion and politics, and a renunciation of militarism, in 1979 a group of class-A war criminals (as determined by postwar American occupying forces) was enshrined here. The current controversy comes from the visits by leading Liberal Democratic Party (LDP) politicians on the anniversary of Japan's defeat in WWII (15 August), including prime ministers.

Yasukuni-jinja's enormous torii at the entrance are, unusually, made of steel; and the second set is made of bronze. The beautiful inner shrine is laid out in the style of Japan's most important Shintō edifice, Ise Shrine (100km southeast of Kyoto), and there are often seasonal displays of ikebana (p23) in the inner courtyard. The grounds are charmingly home to a flock of doves.

Tokyo Dome City (opposite)

Visitors are likely to come away with mixed feelings about the shrine's museum, the **Yūshūkan**, Japan's oldest museum (1882), which was renovated in 2002. It starts fittingly enough for a war memorial, with stately cases depicting Japan's military heritage and traditions, punctuated with displays of swords and samurai armour, and art and poetry extolling the Yamato spirit. Gradually you progress through Japan's 19th- and early-20th-century military conflicts: the Meiji Restoration, Satsuma Rebellion, tussles in Russia, occupation in Korea, and elsewhere.

But the source of the most controversy is the section of the museum covering the 'Greater East Asian War', which you probably know as WWII. While there is undoubtedly value in offering the Japanese perspective, one can also understand the anger of Japan's neighbours at the apparent watering down of the hardships they endured at Japan's hands. Consider this gem about the Rape of Nanjing (here called the 'Nanking Incident') of December 1937: 'The Chinese were soundly defeated, suffering heavy casualties. Inside the city, residents were once again able to live their lives in peace.' Or you might learn that Japan was forced into attacking Pearl Harbor due to American and British foreign policy of the time, or that 'The US had no interest in bringing the war to an early end.' If this strikes you as revisionism, many of Japan's neighbours feel the same.

That said, many of the exhibits are fascinating and harrowing. Note the *kaiten* (human torpedo), essentially a submarine version of the kamikaze aeroplane. You can listen to the final message of a *kaiten* pilot to his family – it's in Japanese but it's easy to remark how young he sounds. There's also the 'miracle coconut' inscribed and set afloat by a Japanese soldier in the Philippines shortly before his death in 1944. The coconut floated in the Pacific for 31 years before washing up very near his widow's hometown. You can still make out the Japanese characters. The walls of the last few galleries of the Yūshūkan are covered with seemingly endless photos of the dead, enough to leave a lump in many throats and make one wonder about the value of any war.

Finally, it appears unseemly to us to have to pay to visit a memorial, and it's at best of questionable taste to have a gift shop selling gaily decorated biscuits, chocolates and curry in a place of such solemnity.

AKASAKA

Eating p131, Sleeping p198

During the Meiji era, Akasaka was the district of Tokyo most densely populated by geisha. These trained female companions (though mistakenly called prostitutes, history has shown them to be highly trained artists and masters of conversation) continued to occupy the area during both world wars. Following the occupation, the area's geisha houses served as the settings for notorious backroom deals that influenced the economy and sealed political alliances.

Today, Akasaka is still one of Tokyo's centres of both explicit and exclusive power. With the National Diet just a few minutes' walk away in the Nagatachō area, Akasaka fills with bureaucrats and politicians at the end of the day. Also here is Hie-jinja, which comes alive in the spring when the cherry blossoms complement its row of rust-red torii, and in autumn when children arrive for Shichi-go-san (p12), dressed in traditional costume. One of Tokyo's most exuberant *matsuri* takes place here, offering an excellent chance to see one of the rowdy, colourful processions of *mikoshi*.

Orientation

Akasaka lies southwest of the Imperial Palace and due north of the better part of Roppongi. To the west it melts into Aoyama and Shibuya.

Once in the area, you'll find that Hie-jinja seems to be literally at the centre of things, though the pull of the National Diet buildings to the shrine's east is strong. Nearby is a cadre of luxury hotels, most notably the Hotel New Ōtani, which is known for its splendid garden and intimate art gallery.

HIE-JINJA Map pp290-1

☎ 3581-2471; www.hiejinja.net/eindex.htm; 2-10-5 Nagatachō, Chiyoda-ku; admission free; Ⓜ Ginza or Namboku Line to Tameike-Sannō (exit 5 or 7)

This Shintō shrine traces its roots to the sacred Mt Hiei, northeast of Kyoto, and it

TRANSPORT

Metro The Yūrakuchō, Hanzōmon, Namboku, Chiyoda, Marunouchi and Ginza Lines all converge in the Akasaka area, including Nagatachō, Akasaka, Akasaka-Mitsuke and Tameike-Sannō Stations.

TOP FIVE – WEST OF IMPERIAL PALACE, AKASAKA & ROPPONGI

- Koishikawa Kōrakuen (p88) Sprawling and lovely strolling garden in the shadow of the Tokyo Dome.
- Mori Art Museum (p92) Tokyo's highest museum, with changing contemporary exhibits that are a cut above.
- Musée Tomo (p93) For some of the finest in Japanese ceramics.
- National Diet Building (right) You're here in the capital already; see where national politics are made.
- Yasukuni-jinja (p89) Stately, controversial and very handsome Shintō shrine.

has been the protector shrine of Edo Castle since it was first built in 1478; it was moved to its present site in 1659. The shrine was destroyed in the 1945 bombings and the current buildings date from 1967. These days it is chiefly known as host to one of Tokyo's three liveliest *matsuri,* Sannō-sai (p10, 15 June); given the shrine's protector status, the festival was regularly attended by the shōgun, and even now the route of the festival's *mikoshi* terminates at the Imperial Palace. When the festival's not on, the shrine makes for a colourful yet quiet break. A highlight is the walk up through a 'tunnel' of orange torii, especially dramatic on a sunny day; the shrine is also pretty when the cherry blossoms are out. If you're wondering about the carved monkey clutching one of her young, she is emblematic of the shrine's ability to offer protection against the threat of a miscarriage.

HOTEL NEW ŌTANI Map p286

☎ 3265-1111; www1.newotani.co.jp/en/tokyo/index.html; 4-1 Kioi-chō, Chiyoda-ku; Ⓜ Ginza or Marunouchi Line to Akasaka-mitsuke (Belle Vie exit)
The New Ōtani was a showplace when it opened in 1964 to coincide with the Tokyo Olympics, and even if the mantle of tippy-top hotel has since gone elsewhere it remains worth visiting: chiefly for its 400-year-old strolling **garden** (admission free; 🕑 6am-10pm) that once belonged to a Tokugawa regent, and for the **New Ōtani Art Museum** (☎ 3221-4111; hotel guests free, nonguests from ¥500; 🕑 10am-6pm Tue-Sun), which displays a decent collection of modern Japanese and French paintings as well as wood-block prints. Otherwise, visitors may be blown away by the hotel's sheer mass: two towers, 1533 guest rooms, nearly three dozen banquet rooms and 37 (!) restaurants and bars. Be sure to pick up a map. Also see p199.

NATIONAL DIET BUILDING Map pp290-1

☎ 3581-3111; www.sangiin.go.jp; 1-7-1 Nagatachō, Chiyoda-ku; 🕑 8am-5pm Mon-Fri, closed national holidays; Ⓜ Yūrakuchō, Hanzōmon or Namboku Line to Nagatachō (exit 1), or Marunouchi or Chiyoda Line to Kokkai-gijidōmae (exit 1)
Built on a site once inhabited by feudal lords, the current building was completed in 1936 with its landmark pyramid-shaped dome. The chambers – the Shūgi-in or House of Representatives (sometimes called the Upper House) and the Sangi-in or House of Councillors or Lower House – have been the scene of fist fights and wrestling matches over the occasional hot-button issue. Recently things have been a bit more tame, though you can still take in the occasional hot-tempered plenary session.

Free 60-minute **tours** (☎ 5521-7445) of the Sangi-in are available when the Diet is not in session, taking in the public gallery, the emperor's room (from where he addresses the Diet at the start of each session) and central hall (featuring a floor mosaic of one million pieces of marble and murals depicting the four seasons). For the tours, it is best not to arrive before 9am to avoid the largest tour groups. And unless you're here for a protest, leave your red headbands in your suitcase (though they are de rigueur among demonstrators).

SŌGETSU KAIKAN Map p286

☎ 3408-1126; www.sogetsu.or.jp/english/index.html; Sōgetsu Kaikan Bldg, 7-2-21 Akasaka, Minato-ku; 🕑 10am-5pm Mon-Thu & Sat, 10am-8pm Fri; Ⓜ Ginza, Hanzōmon or Toei Ōedo Line to Aoyama-itchōme (exit 4)
Sōgetsu is one of Japan's leading schools of avant-garde ikebana (p23) offering classes in English (p238). Even if you have no interest in flower arranging, it's worth a peek in for the building (1977) designed by Tange Kenzō (p31) and the giant, climbable piece of installation art that occupies the lobby, by the revered Japanese-American sculptor Isamu Noguchi.

> **DETOUR**
>
> **Akasaka Detached Palace** (Map p286) This edifice, officially known as Geihinkan, was built in 1909, with an eye to Versailles and the Louvre, to be used as the residence of the crown prince (later Emperor Hirohito). Today it serves as a guesthouse for visiting dignitaries. Although closed to the public, Geihinkan can be viewed from the outside at its west entry gate, about 15 minutes' walk west of central Akasaka.

ROPPONGI

Eating p131, Shopping p180, Sleeping p200

Ten or 20 or 50 years ago any Tokyo local could tell you exactly what you could do during the day in Roppongi: nothing. Night-time was another story, however. Since the end of WWII, Roppongi has been a seedy, somewhat changeable area, the site of murders, home of Occupation forces' barracks, turf of gangs of dancing kids, and haunt of hordes of partying expats and soldiers on leave.

Yet in 2003, the opening of Roppongi Hills (a shopping/dining/arts/office/hotel/etc complex) created a centre for this diffuse culturescape. The apex is the Mori Art Museum, the world's highest exhibition space (it's situated 52 floors up). Nearby are a number of interesting galleries of both the practical and fine arts.

And of course the reasons you have always wanted to come here still exist. At night, the bars still fill with an international crowd that sticks around until the small hours of the morning, when the trains finally resume service.

Orientation

Roppongi lies between Aoyama and Harajuku to the west and greater Ginza/Shiodome to the east, while to the north it eventually turns into stately Akasaka.

The centre here is Roppongi Crossing *(Roppongi kōsaten)*, where Roppongi-dōri meets Gaien-highashi-dōri in the shadow of the expressway. The legendary meeting place here is in front of Almond *(āmondo)* coffee shop. Roppongi Hills lies west along Roppongi-dōri (if you're facing Almond, head right). Within Roppongi Hills, the most obvious place to meet is by *Maman*, the giant sculpture of a spider in the main plaza.

From the crossing, heading down the hill towards Azabu-jūban Station, you'll pass most of the expat nightspots and a number of really good restaurants.

AXIS Map pp290-1

☎ 3587-2781; 5-17-1 Roppongi, Minato-ku; admission free; 🕑 11am-7pm Mon-Sat; Ⓜ Hibiya or Toei Ōedo Line to Roppongi (exit 3)

One of the most respected design showcases in Tokyo, as well as the publisher of a well-regarded design magazine, Axis is a multistorey, multigenre gallery and retail building. There's always something new and daring in its art galleries, and the shops, chosen with care, include home design at **Living Motif** (☎ 3587-2784, 1st & 2nd fl), fabulously innovative textiles at **Nuno** (☎ 3582-7997; www.nuno.com; B1 fl) and flashy duds and accessories for your inner auto mechanic at **Le Garage** (☎ 3587-2785; 1st fl). Also see p180.

COMPLEX Map p286

☎ 5411-7510; admission free; Ⓜ Hibiya or Toei Ōedo Line to Roppongi (exit 3)

If you're only here for a few days and are seeking a peek into the Tokyo art scene, stop here. Several of the best commercial galleries in town inhabit the five-storey, aptly named Complex. Spaces are a mix of styles and intentions, a conflation of more established exhibitors such as Ota Fine Arts, known for showing big names like Kusama Yayoi (p26), as well as newer galleries.

MORI ART MUSEUM Map p286

☎ 5777-8600; www.mori.art.museum; Mori Tower, Roppongi 6-chōme; admission varies; 🕑 10am-10pm Wed-Mon, 10am-5pm Tue; Ⓜ Hibiya or Toei Ōedo Line to Roppongi (exit 1c)

Perched on the 52nd and 53rd floors of Mori Tower in the Roppongi Hills complex, the high ceilings, broad views and thematic

> **TRANSPORT**
>
> **Metro** The Hibiya and Toei Ōedo Lines both run through Roppongi. The Hibiya Line drops you closer to Roppongi Crossing, Roppongi's main intersection.

programmes of this new museum have somehow managed to live up to all the hype. Exhibits are consistently beautifully presented and run the gamut from Bill Viola and Sugimoto Hiroshi to the Da Vinci Codex and the silver of Georg Jensen.

Admission to the museum also includes **Tokyo City View** (☎ 6406-6652; www.tokyocityview.com; adult/child/student ¥1500/500/1000 if purchased separately; 9am-1am), on the 52nd floor. (The observatory is open longer than the museum. If you're visiting the museum, you also get admission to the observatory, otherwise you have to purchase a separate admission.) There are observatories atop other tall buildings in town, but none can match Roppongi Hills for its central location.

The museum is subject to closure between exhibitions, but Tokyo City View is open daily.

MUSÉE TOMO Map pp290-1

☎ 5733-5311; 4-1-35 Toranomon, Minato-ku; adult ¥1300, student ¥500-800; 11am-6pm Tue-Sun; Hibiya Line to Kamiyachō (exit 4b)

This marvellous museum that opened in 2003 may be one of Tokyo's most elegant and tasteful. It is named for Kikuchi Tomo, whose collection of contemporary Japanese ceramics wowed them in Washington and London before finally being exhibited in Tokyo. Exhibitions change every few months and might include highlights of the Kikuchi collection or a special study of *raku* pottery; you can bet that the displays will be atmospheric and beautiful. The museum is behind the Hotel Ōkura.

ROPPONGI HILLS Map p286

☎ 6406-6000; Roppongi 6-chōme; admission free; Hibiya or Toei Ōedo Line to Roppongi (exit 1c)

Opened in 2003, Roppongi Hills was the dream of real-estate developer Mori Minoru, and the rest of us are very fortunate that it's become a reality. The centrepiece of the complex is the 54-storey Mori Tower, home to some of the world's leading companies, the Mori Art Museum (opposite) and Tokyo City View (above). At the base of the tower are the marvellous Grand Hyatt Tokyo (p200) and some 200 shopping, drinking and dining establishments to the west and east (both geographically and culturally), including internationally known brands and chefs (eg Joël Robuchon). On the plaza below, the TV Asashi network headquarters adjoins an ancient samurai garden and the Roppongi Hills Arena, where you can often catch outdoor performances. Just beyond, the shops ascending the street Keyakizaka are marvels of design.

Spider sculpture called Maman, *Roppongi Hills (left)*

Roppongi Hills' architecture is a feast for the eyes, enhanced by public art such as Louise Bourgeois's giant, spiny alfresco spider called *Maman*, and the benches-cum-sculptures on Keyakizaka. You'll probably get lost, but Roppongi Hills guide maps are available.

TOKYO TOWER Map pp290-1

☎ 3433-5111; www.tokyotower.co.jp; 4-2-8 Shiba-kōen, Minato-ku; adult/child ¥820/460; observation platforms 9am-10pm; Toei Ōedo Line to Akabanebashi (Akabanebashi exit)

When it was built as a broadcast tower in 1958, this 333m-high orange and white Eiffel Tower wannabe was the tallest structure in the city (it's actually 13m taller than the one in Paris). Today its observatory is more relic than cause for amazement, and places elsewhere offer views at least as good.

All of which kind of makes it a tourist trap, complete with **aquarium** (adult/child ¥1000/500) and **wax museum** (¥870/460), yet it retains a retro-popularity; bus tours visit by the bundle.

DETOUR

Zōjō-ji (Map pp290-1; ☎ 3432-1431; Shiba-kōen; admission free; ⏰ dawn-dusk; Ⓜ Toei Ōedo Line to Akabanebashi, Akabanebashi exit) Behind Tokyo Tower is this former funerary temple of the Tokugawa regime, one of the most important temples of the Jōdō (Pure Land) sect of Buddhism. It dates from 1393, yet like many sights in Tokyo, its original structures have been relocated and subject to war, fire and other natural disasters. It has been rebuilt several times in recent history, the last time in 1974.

Nevertheless, Zōjō-ji remains one of the most monumental temples in town. The main gate, Sanmon, was constructed in 1605, and its three sections were designed to symbolise the three stages one must pass through to achieve nirvana. The giant bell (1673; 15 tonnes) is considered one of the Great Three Bells of the Edo period. On the temple grounds there is a large collection of statues of the Bodhisattva *jizō,* said to be a guide during the transmigration of the soul (see p85 for more details).

EBISU & MEGURO

Eating p133, Shopping p181, Sleeping p200

Ebisu is one of Tokyo's best-kept secrets, home to a smart, stylish set. To the west and up the hill towards Daikanyama lies a matrix of funky shops run by eccentric proprietors, crazy buildings designed by local visionaries, and unique restaurants. Also here are the Beer Museum Yebisu (with bargain tasting room!) and the Tokyo Metropolitan Museum of Photography, a point of pilgrimage for devout shutterbugs.

One stop south on the JR Yamanote Line is Meguro, with the intimate and haunting Daien-ji temple, the intimate and artful Meguro Museum of Art and the intimate and, frankly, icky Meguro Parasitological Museum. Also nearby are the forests of the Shizen-Kyōiku-en, a nature preserve right in the middle of the big city.

Orientation

Ritzy Ebisu lies south of Shibuya, and to its south is more working-class Meguro. From JR Ebisu Station, the east exit opens onto the Yebisu Sky Walk, a series of conveyor belts that will eventually deposit you in the courtyard of Yebisu Garden Place. This is the side of Ebisu designed for visitors, tourists and hardcore shoppers. If you want to see where locals live and play, head for the west exit and up the hill towards glitzy Daikanyama.

From Meguro Station, Daien-ji, Meguro Gajoen and the Meguro Museum of Art are west of the station, while the Teien Art Museum and National Park for Nature Study are east along Meguro-dōri.

BEER MUSEUM YEBISU Map p288

☎ 5423-7255; www.sapporobeer.jp/english/when/museum/museum.html; 4-20-1 Ebisu, Shibuya-ky; admission free; ⏰ 10am-6pm Tue-Sun, last entry 5pm; Ⓜ Hibiya or JR Yamanote Line to Ebisu (main exit)

Let's cut to the chase. Yes, this is the site of the original Yebisu brewery (1889; now owned by the giant brewer Sapporo). And yes, inside are giant pot-bellied beer vats, antique signage, cute beer ads and a suitably cheesy Magic Vision Theatre. But really you've come for the Tasting Room, where you can try cheap draughts of Weizen or Ale (such as a four-glass tasting set for ¥400). We give a big thumbs-up to the beer *natto* (fermented soybeans) snacks.

DAIEN-JI Map p288

☎ 3491-2793; 1-8-5 Shimo-Meguro, Meguro-ku; admission free; ⏰ 9am-5pm; Ⓜ JR Yamanote Line or subway Namboku or Mita Line to Meguro (west exit)

Established sometime around 1615, this small, photogenic temple hemmed in by trees commemorates stillborn and miscarried children and aborted foetuses. In the rear of the temple precinct is a separate tribute to the 14,700 people who died in the fire of 1772, which in addition to flattening most of the wooden houses in surrounding Meguro, burned the original temple structure to the ground. As you enter, you'll see red-bonneted *jizō* figures (small stone statues of the Buddhist

TRANSPORT

Train The JR Yamanote Line stops at Ebisu and Meguro Stations.

Metro The Hibiya Line runs through Ebisu and connects with the main JR station. Meguro is served by the Namboku and Toei Mita Lines. Some locations east of Meguro are closest to Shirokanedai Station on the Namboku Line.

protector of travellers and children; for more details see p85). Further into the temple precinct and completely lining one of its walls are Arhat (atonement) statues of the Gohyakurakan (the 500 followers of Buddha). Each of these exquisite stone markers, made to appease the souls that departed in the great fire, has its own design and facial expression. Water is often placed in front of the statues to ease the degree of the victims' suffering.

MEGURO GAJOEN Map p288

☎ 3491-4111; 1-8-1 Shimo-Meguro, Meguro-ku; admission free; Ⓜ JR Yamanote Line or subway Namboku or Mita Line to Meguro (west exit)

One look at the ads on virtually any subway car will tell you that wedding halls are big business in Tokyo. For better or for worse, Gajoen is one of the biggest, and as a study in anthropology you can hardly beat it. 'Wedding hall' doesn't do justice to its many storeys of chapels, banquet halls, expensive restaurants and hotel rooms. The impossibly long corridor connecting them is lined with friezes of geisha and samurai and often festooned with flowers, while floor-to-ceiling windows look out on a drop-dead hillside garden. OK, we'll get married here too.

MEGURO MUSEUM OF ART, TOKYO Map p288

☎ 3714-1201; www.mmat.jp mostly in Japanese; 2-4-36 Meguro, Meguro-ku; adult/concession ¥1000/700; 🕑 10am-6pm Tue-Sun; Ⓜ JR Yamanote Line or subway Namboku or Mita Line to Meguro (west exit)

Half local, half global, one part of this museum exhibits the work of Meguro artists, while the other is dedicated to fine art and craft exhibits from around the world (think the work of Charles and Ray Eames). The building is a delight – it's airy, spacious and well-lit compared with many other Tokyo art museums, which can want for space – and there is a coffee shop on the 1st floor with pleasant views of the grounds.

Take the west exit of Meguro Station, walk straight ahead down Meguro-dōri and turn right just after crossing Meguro River (Meguro-gawa). Walk along the river and the museum is on your left, past the tennis court and swimming pool.

MEGURO PARASITOLOGICAL MUSEUM Map p288

☎ 3716-1264; 4-1-1 Shimo-Meguro, Meguro-ku; admission free; 🕑 10am-5pm Tue-Sun; Ⓜ JR Yamanote Line or subway Namboku or Mita Line to Meguro (west exit)

Yeah, ew. Probably the grossest museum in Japan, this spot was established in 1953 by Satoru Kamegai, a local doctor concerned by the increasing number of parasites he was encountering in his practice due to unsanitary postwar conditions. The grisly centrepiece is an 8.8m-long tapeworm found ensconced in the body of a 40-year-old Yokohama man. Although there's not a lot of English signage, you can easily see how some of these nasties might set up house inside you. Those into bugs will love it.

SHIZEN KYŌIKU-EN Map p288

Institute for Nature Study; ☎ 3441-7176; www.kahaku.go.jp/english/visitor_info/shizenen/index.html; 5-21-5 Shirokanedai, Minato-ku; adult/child to 18 & seniors ¥300/free; 🕑 9am-4.30pm Tue-Sun Sep-Apr, 9am-5pm Tue-Sun May-Aug, last admission 4pm year-round; Ⓜ Namboku Line to Shirokanedai (exit 1)

Although the 200,000 sq metres of this land was the estate of a *daimyō* some six centuries ago and was the site of gunpowder warehouses in the early Meiji period, you'd scarcely know it now. Since 1949, this garden has been part of the Kokuritsu Kagaku Hakubutsukan (p80) and preserves the local flora in undisciplined profusion. There are some wonderful walks through its forests, marshes and ponds, making this one of Tokyo's least known and most appealing getaways. Bonus: admission is limited to 300 people at a time.

TOKYO METROPOLITAN MUSEUM OF PHOTOGRAPHY Map p288

☎ 3280-0099; www.syabi.com; 1-13-3 Mita, Meguro-ku; admission ¥500-1500; 🕑 10am-6pm Tue-Sun; Ⓜ Hibiya or JR Yamanote Line to Ebisu (main exit)

In a corner of Yebisu Garden Place, this five-storey museum chronicles the history and contemporary use of still and moving images. it holds 23,000 works, roughly 70% of them Japanese. Displays are often comprised of exceptional work by photographers from both Japan and abroad, and there's an extensive library of photographic literature from throughout the world.

TOKYO FOR CHILDREN

Tokyo deliberately cultivates spaces for children. Parks, museums and other venues are designed with wee ones in mind and, even on a limited budget, you'll find things here reasonably accessible. The following should get you started.

Ikebukuro Bōsai-kan (p103) Younger children may be rattled, literally, by the simulations of earthquakes and fires, but it's important preparation for older kids.

Meguro Parasitological Museum (p95) This museum is ideal for kids who like big worms and other scary bugs.

Miraikan (National Museum of Emerging Science & Innovation; p108) Offers interactive exhibits where kids can manipulate robots and micromachines, and explore the principles of superconductivity.

Mori Art Museum (p92) This is a dramatic place to introduce kids to contemporary art. If they weary of the exhibits, excellent views await on the 52nd-floor observation decks and food kiosks serve kid-appropriate snacks.

Museum of Maritime Science (p108) Filled with detailed model ships, hands-on displays and a cool pool for piloting remote-control submarines.

National Children's Castle (Kodomo-no-Shiro; Map p284; www.kodomono-shiro.jp/english/index.html; adult/child over 3 ¥500/400; JR Yamanote Line to Shibuya, east exit, or Ginza Line to Omote-sandō, B2 exit) Has playrooms, puppet theatres, a swimming pool and a music lobby where kids can make noise until the rafters shake. The Children's Castle Hotel (p201) next door was built especially for those with young children and can be a convenient refuge for travelling families. It's located off Aoyama-dōri.

Tokyo Metropolitan Children's Hall (Tokyo-to Jido Kaikan; Map p284; ☎ 3409-6361; www.fukushihoken.metro.tokyo.jp/jidou/English/index.html; 1-18-24 Shibuya, Shibuya-ku; admission free; JR Yamanote Line to Shibuya, east exit [Miyamasuzaka]) Has six kid-friendly storeys and a number of ingenious play areas. Check out the human body maze or get messy in the hands-on art studio, where children can make pottery and origami. It's 300m north-east of Shibuya Station, next to Mitake-kōen.

Transportation Museum (p78) Has trains and steam engines for climbing and riding. Simulators allow kids to play conductor.

Ueno Zoo (p82) Has the usual monkeys and tigers and bears. The petting zoo, with its goats and ducks, is the real attraction if you've come with little ones.

There are a number of amusement parks, including the humble **Hanayashiki Amusement Park** (☎ 3482-8780; www.hanayashiki.net in Japanese; 2-28-1 Asakusa, Taitō-ku; 10am-6pm; adult/child under 5/5-12 years ¥900/400/free) in Asakusa (rides cost extra) and the more razzle-dazzle-y **Tokyo Dome City** (p88) or the indoor amusements and food theme-parks of **Namco Namjatown** (p103), and the world's tallest **Ferris wheel** (p109) in Odaiba.

TOKYO METROPOLITAN TEIEN ART MUSEUM Map p288

☎ 3443-0201; www.teien-art-museum.ne.jp; 5-21-9 Shirokanedai, Minato-ku; admission around ¥1000; 10am-6pm, closed 2nd & 4th Wed of the month; Namboku Line to Shirokanedai (exit 1)

Although this museum hosts art exhibitions (eg Meissen porcelain or pottery by important Japanese artists), its appeal lies principally in the building itself: it's an Art Deco structure built in 1933, designed by French architect Henri Rapin. The interior details remain alluring, including etched tile trim, light fixtures sculpted to look like peaches and pumpkins, and the 'perfume fountain', sort of an early day aromatherapy device. The house was originally home to Prince Asaka-no-miya (1887–1981), Emperor Hirohito's uncle, who was pardoned for his part in the 'Rape of Nanjing'. It became a museum in 1983. The museum sits in the southwest corner of the Shizen Kyōiku-en (separate entrance and admission).

SHIBUYA

Eating p134, Shopping p183, Sleeping p201

Step out of Shibuya Station onto Hachikō Plaza, just after dark, and you're in the Tokyo of your dreams. The grand square is a spectacle in neon, streets radiate out like a starburst, and the crowd is a mix of diligently acquired elegance and adolescent exuberance. Shibuya is not rich in historical sights, but it is perhaps the best place to take the pulse of the city by browsing, shopping, dining and watching the outrageous get-ups that have most recently come off the runways at Tokyo's fashion shows.

The area is studded with department stores that vie for the patronage of cash-loaded young Japanese. The offshoots of the Tōkyū and Seibu department stores tend to be funkier than in other parts of the city; Tōkyū Hands (p184) is perhaps the gem among them.

Orientation

Shibuya, the neighbourhood, is at the centre of Shibuya ward, with nearly a million people within its bounds. Harajuku and Shinjuku border it to the north, while Aoyama and Roppongi lie to the east. To the south is sophisticated Ebisu. The only real meeting place by Shibuya Station is the Hachikō the Dog statue. He even has his own exit from the station named after him, which is the exit you should use for all of the sights in the section.

BUNKAMURA Map p284

☎ 3477-9111; www.bunkamura.co.jp; 2-24-1 Dōgenzaka, Shibuya-ku; admission varies by event; ⏲ vary by event; Ⓜ JR Yamanote Line or subway Ginza Line to Shibuya (Hachikō exit)

'Bunkamura' means 'culture village' and it was Japan's first crosscultural centre. Spin-the-globe exhibits feature the work of artists from Grandma Moses to Monet to Munakata Shikō (1903–75; also see p23), as well as photographic displays by the likes of Man Ray. It's also a busy theatre, art house cinema and concert hall. It's about seven minutes' walk from Shibuya Station (turn right at the Shibuya 109 building).

HACHIKŌ THE DOG STATUE Map p284

Ⓜ JR Yamanote Line or subway Ginza Line to Shibuya (Hachikō exit)

In the 1920s, a professor who lived near Shibuya Station kept Hachikō, a small Akita dog, who came to the station every day to await his master's return. The master died while at work in 1925, but the dog continued to show up and wait at the station until his own death 10 years later. Hachikō's faithfulness was not lost on the Japanese, who built a statue to honour his memory. The story is more interesting than the statue itself, but Hachikō is usually surrounded by young Tokyo cool dudes and dudettes.

TRANSPORT

Train The JR Yamanote Line stops at Shibuya Station. You can also connect here to suburban private trains operated by the Tokyu and Keio Lines (eg to Shimokitazawa and Komaba-Todaimae).

Metro The Hanzōmon and Ginza Lines stop at Shibuya.

LOVE HOTEL HILL Map p284

Ⓜ JR Yamanote Line or subway Ginza Line to Shibuya (Hachikō exit)

Take the road up Dōgenzaka to the left of the Shibuya 109 building. At the top of the hill, on the side streets that run off the main road, is a concentration of love hotels (see p235 for more details) catering to all tastes. The buildings alone are interesting and represent a range of architectural pastiche, from miniature Gothic castles to kitsch Arabian Nights. Nearby are shops selling amenities you might want to use in a love hotel.

TEPCO ELECTRIC ENERGY MUSEUM Map p284

☎ 3477-1191; 1-12-10 Jinnan, Shibuya-ku; admission free; ⏲ 10am-6pm Thu-Tue; Ⓜ JR Yamanote Line or subway Ginza Line to Shibuya (Hachikō exit)

Called Denryokukan, the Tepco Electric Energy Museum is the building on Jingū-dōri with the R2D2-shaped silver dome; it's visible from the Hachikō statue. Operated by the Tokyo Electric Power Company, it offers seven floors of knowledge about electricity production and consumption; if you're not fortunate enough to be invited to a Japanese home, the 4th-floor collection will give you a good idea of the state of the art. There are lots of hands-on exhibits, normally a hit with kids. Signage is almost entirely in Japanese, but there's an excellent English handout on each floor.

TOBACCO & SALT MUSEUM Map p284

☎ 3476-2041; www.jti.co.jp/Culture/museum/Welcome.html; 1-16-8 Jinnan, Shibuya-ku; admission ¥100; ⏲ 10am-6pm Tue-Sun; Ⓜ JR Yamanote Line or subway Ginza Line to Shibuya (Hachikō exit)

For years, smokers have found solace in Tokyo's cafés and bars, and for much of that time the government was in the business of supplying them through a tobacco monopoly. That company has since been privatised to Japan Tobacco Inc, which is the owner of this museum, a shrine to the bitter leaf, complete with pipes, paraphernalia and wood-block prints.

Downstairs is a homage to Japanese modes of salt production, which until recently was conducted by cumbersome harvests from a reluctant sea. Among the exhibits is a grey, crystalline salt cylinder whose circumference could match that of a small whale. English signage is limited.

TOGURI MUSEUM OF ART Map p284

☎ 3465-0070; www.toguri-museum.or.jp; 1-11-3 Shōto, Shibuya-ku; adult ¥1030, student ¥420-730; 9.30am-5.30pm Tue-Sun; JR Yamanote Line or subway Ginza Line to Shibuya (Hachikō exit)

A few minutes' walk from Bunkamura, the Toguri displays about 100 pieces at a time from its 7000-piece collection of fine Japanese, Korean and Chinese porcelain. The galleries are reasonably sized, there's a pretty garden, and the residential neighbourhood is so quiet that you'd never guess you're just steps away from Shibuya's bustle.

OMOTE-SANDŌ

Eating p135, Shopping p184

The grand, calming, tree-lined precincts of the Meiji-jingū are an anchor to the west end of this district, but step just outside this shrine and all serenity is forgotten. On the bridge over the tracks of Harajuku Station, the girls of whom Gwen Stefani sings hang out and pose in cos-play (p14) outfits.

Head east, and the study in contrasts continues. Omote-sandō is home to the *haut*-est of *haute couture*, yet its side streets – notably the cacophonous Takeshita-dōri – teem with teenagers on the hunt for the next big thing. Yet another block away, the shrine Tōgō-jinja hosts regular flea markets for folk seeking the next old thing.

At the boulevard's other end is Aoyama, domain of chic boutiques and ersatz Parisian cafés. Here too are fine museums, galleries and design stores, most notably Watari-Um (Watari Museum of Contemporary Art) and the Nezu Institute of Fine Arts, with its collection of traditional painting and calligraphic works on paper.

Beyond Omote-sandō the street, Gaien-nishi-dōri is better known as Killer-dōri, for its very fashionable (ie 'killer') boutiques. Kottō-dōri, which runs southeast off Aoyama-dōri, very close to the Spiral building, has a number of fine, high-end antique stores.

Orientation

Omote-sandō links Harajuku with Aoyama, which lie at the centre of the greater Shibuya ward. To the west is busy Shibuya and the expanse of Yoyogi-kōen, while to the east is Aoyama Rei-en (Aoyama Cemetery) and, beyond that, Roppongi.

MEIJI-JINGŪ Map p284

Meiji Shrine; ☎ 3379-5511; www.meijijingu.or.jp; Kamizono-chō, Yoyogi, Shibuya-ku; admission free; dawn-dusk; JR Yamanote Line to Harajuku (Omote-sandō exit) or Chiyoda Line to Meiji-Jingūmae (exit 3)

Tokyo's grandest Shintō shrine, this 1920 edifice enshrines the Emperor Meiji and Empress Shōken, under whose rule Japan ended its isolation from the outside world. Destroyed in WWII bombings and reconstructed in 1958, the shrine buildings occupy just a corner of the precinct's 70 forested hectares (175 acres); its 100,000 trees are said to have been donated by 100,000 visitors from all over Japan.

Meiji-jingū might be a reconstruction of the original but, unlike so many of Japan's postwar reconstructions, it is altogether authentic. The main structure was built with prized *hinoki* cypress from the Kiso region of Nagano-ken (Nagano prefecture), while the cypress for the huge torii was imported from Alishan in Taiwan. If you're there when a wedding is in progress, the procession is pure photographic gold.

The grounds are home to the **Meiji-jingū Gyōen** (admission ¥500; 9am-4.30pm), a lovely strolling garden. Once the property of two *daimyō* families, after it came under imperial control, Meiji himself designed the garden as a gift to the Empress Shōken. There are peaceful walks to the pond and teahouse and a good dose of privacy on weekdays, and spectacular irises and *satsuki* azaleas in season.

TRANSPORT

Train The JR Yamanote Line stops at Harajuku Station.

Metro The Chiyoda Line runs beneath Omote-sandō, stopping at Omote-sandō Station and Meiji-jingūmae Station. The Ginza and Hanzōmon Lines also both stop at Omote-sandō Station.

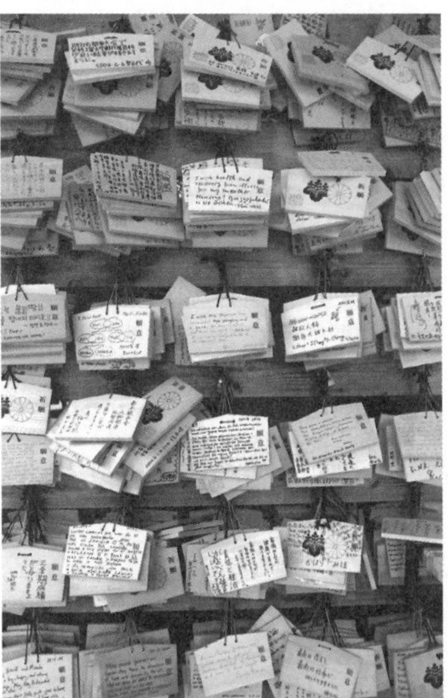

Ema *(wooden votive plaques), Meiji-jingū (opposite)*

NEZU INSTITUTE OF FINE ARTS Map p286

☎ 3400-2536; www.nezu-muse.or.jp; 6-5-1, Minami-Aoyama, Minato-ku; admission ¥1000; 9.30am-4.30pm Tue-Sun; Chiyoda, Ginza or Hanzōmon Line to Omote-sandō (exit A5)

This striking museum houses a well-known collection of Japanese art, including paintings, calligraphy and sculpture all displayed on a rotating basis. Seven of these works are National Treasures and 84 are Important Cultural Properties. Also on display is Chinese and Korean art, and teahouses where tea ceremonies are performed. The exhibits are well displayed and nestled within a wonderful, slightly wild, ornamental garden.

SPIRAL BUILDING Map p284

☎ 3498-1171; www.spiral.co.jp; 5-6-23 Minami-Aoyama, Minato-ku; hours vary; Chiyoda, Ginza or Hanzōmon Line to Omote-sandō (exit B1)

Maki Fumihiko's 1985 building is always a hit with architecture fans, and fun and busy for the general public too. Its very subtle spiral is laden with boutiques (see Spiral Records; p186), the lively café is great for a rest, and its gallery features ever-changing modern art exhibitions.

TAKESHITA-DŌRI Map p284

JR Yamanote Line to Harajuku (Takeshita-dōri exit)

This teeming alley (say ta-*kesh*-ta-dōri) represents Tokyo's propensity for both teenage kitsch and subcultural fetish. Boom boxes blare at full volume while young, angst-decorated adolescents browse through racks of cheap versions of the day's latest trend. This is the place to look for outrageously gaudy jewellery, punk accessories, trendy hair boutiques, fast-food joints and cuddly toys. Also see p186.

UKIYO-E OTA MEMORIAL ART MUSEUM Map p284

☎ 3403-0880; www.ukiyoe-ota-muse.jp/english.html; 1-10-10 Jingūmae, Shibuya-ku; adult ¥700, student ¥200-500 Tue-Sun, student free-¥250 Sat & Sun; 10.30am-5.30pm Tue-Sun, closed 27th-end of the month; JR Yamanote Line to Harajuku (Omote-sandō exit), or Chiyoda Line to Meiji-jingūmae (exit 5)

This cosy museum, which asks that you trade your shoes for a pair of slippers at the door, has an excellent collection of *ukiyo-e* (wood-block prints; see p22). The original collector, Ota Seizo, former head of the Toho Life Insurance Company, began to buy *ukiyo-e* when he realised that many important examples of Japanese wood-block prints belonged to foreign museums, making it impossible for Japanese to view many of the genre's masterworks. The museum usually displays no more than a few dozen works at a time from its collection of over 10,000 prints, including those by masters of the art such as Hokusai and Hiroshige.

TOP FIVE – OMOTE-SANDŌ

- Meiji-jingū (opposite) Tokyo's stateliest Shintō shrine, so forested that you'd scarcely believe you're still in the world's largest metropolis.
- Nezu Institute of Fine Arts (left) Stellar collection of Asian arts in a luxe setting.
- Spiral Building (left) Architectural landmark which always houses something cool and design-y.
- Takeshita-dōri (above) Head here to see the world's most fashion-forward teens in their element.
- Ukiyo-e Ota Memorial Art Museum (above) The panoply of wood-block print art, presented in digestible bits.

WATARI-UM (WATARI MUSEUM OF CONTEMPORARY ART) Map p284

☎ 3402-3001; www.watarium.co.jp; 3-7-6 Jingūmae, Shibuya-ku; adult/student ¥1000/800; 11am-7pm Tue & Thu-Sun, 11am-9pm Wed; Gaienmae (exit 3)

This progressive and often provocative museum was built in 1990 to a design by Swiss architect Mario Botta. Exhibits are always cutting-edge and sometimes arty-farty – think push-the-envelope photos by Larry Clark, or vacuum-cleaner ballets choreographed by visiting Scandinavians. There's an excellent art bookshop called **On Sundays** (☎ 3470-1424; hours vary) where you can browse through its enormous collection of obscure postcards.

YOYOGI-KŌEN Map p284

admission free; dawn-dusk; JR Yamanote Line to Harajuku (Omote-sandō exit)

Sunday in Yoyogi-kōen used to be one of Tokyo's prime attractions, when local bands gathered to give free concerts on the park's pathways and kids in wild hairdos and 1950s get-ups gathered to gyrate to recorded rock and roll. Sadly, the police have put a stop to this and now Yoyogi-kōen is just another park. That said, with lots of wide open spaces and some flowering trees, it's not a bad place for a picnic or playing some sport on the grass. It's also worth a stop to view an early piece by Tange Kenzō, the National Gymnasium, built for the 1964 Olympics; you can view it from the footbridge by Harajuku Station.

SHINJUKU

Eating p138, Shopping p187, Sleeping p202

We weren't at all surprised that Sofia Coppola used Shinjuku to give Bill Murray his first, jet-lagged glimpses of Tokyo in *Lost in Translation*. More than anyplace else, Shinjuku represents Tokyo's sensory overload and breakneck pace. Its neon canyons crackle with an energy from somewhere in the future, and its laissez-faire attitude draws 20- and 30-something party people to tiny nightspots stacked storeys high.

Shinjuku is effectively divided into two sides by the massive JR station that delivers millions of commuters to and from work each day. The west side, Nishi-Shinjuku, was once the site of a sizable reservoir and now dominated by skyscraping office towers, luxury hotels and the imposing Tokyo Metropolitan Government Offices, all connected by wide avenues that are definitely not of old Edo. Compelling museums have brought contemporary art to the area.

Shinjuku's east side is spontaneous chaos, an area to wander with your neck craning up and around. Chief attractions here include the shrine Hanazono-jinja, site of a great Sunday morning flea market, some block-long department stores and the colourful, if sleazy, Kabukichō and Golden Gai areas. Tokyo's gay district, Shinjuku-nichōme, is also here, one of the liveliest queer neighbourhoods in Asia. Just beyond, the park Shinjuku-gyōen remains one of Tokyo's favourite spots for cherry-blossom viewing in the spring, and a calming respite at other times.

Orientation

Shinjuku is bordered by Harajuku to the south, greater Akasaka and the outskirts of the Imperial Palace to the east, and the Takadanobaba district (home of Waseda University) to the north.

Shinjuku Station is the city's biggest transit hub and the one everyone's warned you about: take the wrong exit and you may find yourself a half-hour away from your destination. Yes it is daunting, but here are some general guidelines.

The classic rendezvous point opposite the station's east exit, across Shinjuku-dōri, is in front of the Studio Alta building with its huge video screen. Continuing through the side streets away from the station, you'll reach Yasukuni-dōri with its neon buildings, and beyond that the bawdy district of Kabukichō. Isetan and Mitsukoshi department stores and Shinjuku-nichōme are to the east via Shinjuku-dōri or Yasukuni-dōri (Shinjuku-sanchōme Station is the closest station for these locations).

The west side of the station takes you by Keio and Odakyū department stores. If you're heading for the skyscrapers, there is a pedestrian tunnel towards Tochōmae Station on the Toei Ōedo Line, which may be the easier stop depending on your destination. There's also a south exit, which is the closest access to Shinjuku-gyōen and the Takashimaya Times Square shopping complex.

TRANSPORT

Train The JR Yamanote Line, JR Chūō Line and several other commuter lines stop at Shinjuku Station. Travellers may find that the private Keio and Odakyū Lines come in handy for destinations west of the Yamanote Line.

Metro The Marunouchi, Toei Shinjuku and Toei Ōedo Lines run through Shinjuku.

WEST SIDE

JAPANESE SWORD MUSEUM Map p282

☎ 3379-1386; 4-25-10 Yoyogi, Shibuya-ku; adult/student ¥525/315; 9am-4.30pm Tue-Sun; Keio New Line to Hatsudai (east exit)

In 1948, after American forces returned the swords *(katana)* they'd confiscated during the postwar occupation, the Ministry of Education established a society to preserve the feudal art of Japanese sword-making. There are about 120 swords with their fittings in the collection, of which about one-third are on view at any one time. The museum also showcases crafts of tempering and polishing steel. Its location, in a residential neighbourhood, is not obvious, but if you ask for the *Token Hakubutsukan,* someone should be able to help you.

SOMPO JAPAN MUSEUM OF ART Map p282

☎ 5777-8600; www.sompo-japan.co.jp/museum/english/index.html; 42nd fl, 1-26-1 Nishi-Shinjuku, Shinjuku-ku; adult/student ¥500/300; 10am-6pm Tue-Sun; JR Shinjuku (west exit)

The private museum of the Sompo Japan insurance company concentrates most heavily on the lithography, sculpture and painting of Tōgō Seiji (1897–1980), whose subjects, most often women, resemble luminescent *anime* figures set off against backdrops that hover between cubist and Art Deco. Tōgō was closely associated with the Sompo Japan's forerunner, Yasuda Fire & Marine Insurance Company, and donated many of his works for the museum. The museum also caused a stir back in the 1980s bubble, when it famously purchased van Gogh's *Sunflowers* for a cool ¥5 billion; there are also a limited number of works by Gauguin, Cézanne and Van Gogh. The museum's 42nd floor location also affords excellent views.

TOKYO METROPOLITAN GOVERNMENT OFFICES Map p282

☎ 5321-1111; 2-8-1 Nishi-Shinjuku, Shinjuku-ku; admission free; observatories 9.30am-11pm, north observatory closed 2nd & 4th Mon of the month, south observatory closed 1st & 3rd Tue of the month; Toei Ōedo Line to Tochōmae, (exit A3)

Known as Tokyo Tochō, this grey granite complex designed by Tange Kenzō has stunning, distinctive architecture and great views from the **observatories** (☎ 5320-7890) on the 45th floor of the twin towers of building 1. On a clear day, look west for a glimpse of Mt Fuji. Back on the ground, stand in the Citizens Plaza and look up at Building 1 and see if it does not remind you of a computer-chip version of the great cathedrals of Europe. There's even a 'rose window', only this being Tokyo the rose is replaced by a gingko leaf, in honour of the city's official tree. With several modern sculptures scattered about, this is a good spot for a picnic lunch.

There's also a **tourist information centre** (☎ 5321-3077; 9.30am-6.30pm) on the lobby floor. It's a great place to stock up on info and is also the meeting place for the volunteer guide–led tours.

TOKYO OPERA CITY Map pp278-9

☎ 5353-0770; www.operacity.jp; 3-20-2 Nishi-Shinjuku, Shinjuku-ku; Keio New Line to Hatsudai (north exit)

Since opening in 1997, Tokyo Opera City has been recognised as one of the world's most acoustically perfect **concert halls**, and this in a city that embraces classical music with fervour. It's also one of the most architecturally daring, like a giant indoor A-frame.

Even if you can't make a concert, Opera City is home to two of Tokyo's best art spaces. The two storeys of the **Tokyo Opera City Art Gallery** (☎ 5353-0756; www.operacity.jp/ag; 3rd fl; admission varies by exhibition; 11am-7pm Tue-Thu & Sun, 11am-8pm Fri & Sat) showcase new and established Japanese artists. Meanwhile the **NTT Intercommunication Centre** (ICC; ☎ 0120-144-199; www.ntticc.or.jp; 4th fl; adult ¥800, student ¥600-400; 10am-6pm Tue-Sun) has an excellent collection of cutting-edge works and installations that address the myriad intersections of art and technology. Its superlative video library includes works by Idemitsu Mako, Bill Viola and Nam June Paik, while installations include dreamy pieces such as works by Laurie Anderson, or Mikami Seiko's *World, Membrane and the Dismembered Body*, designed for the museum's eerie, echo-free chamber.

EAST SIDE

GOLDEN GAI Map p282

Marunouchi Line to Shinjuku-sanchōme (exit B3)
This ramshackle block of tiny *boîtes* became golden just in time for the '64 Olympics. By day, there's not much going on here except for dozens of stray cats. But by night, the closet-sized bars, some accessed by stairways steep enough to bruise your shins as you ascend, light and fill up, mostly with off-duty office workers. There's been much speculation about the demise of Golden Gai's rickety structures and narrow alleyways, but for the moment it seems a new generation is buying in and quietly setting up shop.

HANAZONO-JINJA Map p282

3200-3093; 5-17 Shinjuku, Shinjuku-ku; 24hr; Marunouchi or Shinjuku Line to Shinjuku-sanchōme (exit B3 or B5)
During the day merchants from nearby Kabukichō come to this Shintō shrine to pray for the solvency of their business ventures, but at night the spotlights come on, gangs of high school kids and salarymen show up, and action spills over from nearby Golden Gai and from further-away Yasukuni-dōri. On Sunday the grounds become a **marketplace** (8am-4pm), where you'll find bargains on knick-knacks and, possibly, some antiques. For more information on other markets around town, see p176.

KABUKICHŌ Map p282

JR Yamanote Line to Shinjuku (east exit)
Tokyo's notorious red-light district lies east of Shinjuku Station and north of Yasukuni-dōri. It's made up of soaplands (massage parlours), love hotels, peep shows, pink cabarets, porn booths, prostitutes and strip shows, all well attended by drunken salarymen out for a night on the make. Female voices wail out invitations, while Japanese (and, increasingly, foreign) punks eke out a living passing out ads for karaoke boxes and peep shows. Remarkably, the area is generally safe (and much more interesting) to walk through at night, though it's wise to go with a friend or more or you may find yourself the object of unwanted, and irritating, attention (both for males and females).

SEE ALSO

Omoide-yokochō (Piss Alley; p139) As aromatic as its name sounds, a by-the-tracks throwback that's been serving down 'n' dirty *yakitori* (meat or vegetable on skewers) for generations. It's due to be razed for new development in 2008, so get in while you can.

SHINJUKU-GYŌEN Map p282

3350-0151; www.shinjukugyoen.go.jp; 11 Naito-chō, Shinjuku-ku; adult/child under 6/6-15 yrs ¥200/free/50; 9am-4.30pm Tue-Sun; Marunouchi Line to Shinjuku-gyōenmae (exit 1)
Though Shinjuku-gyōen was designed as an imperial retreat (completed 1906), it's now definitively a park for everyone. The wide lawns and diverse design (the garden applies French, English and Japanese horticultural principles) make it a favourite of urbanites in need of a quick escape. To make an afternoon of it, head for the east side where the glassed-in **greenhouse** displays subtropical waterlilies the size of party platters. Alternatively, park yourself in the southern part of the park in the **traditional teahouse.** Expect lots of company during cherry-blossom season.

IKEBUKURO

Eating p140, Shopping p187, Sleeping p205

Never quite part of Shitamachi and in the postwar years the site of an enormous, gang-controlled black market, Ikebukuro seemed destined to be the sleaziest of the three main Yamanote hubs. Yet it's evolved into a well-grounded, working-class neighbourhood that feels wonderfully lived in. Perhaps because the rents have stayed relatively stable, young families, students and senior citizens have been able to set up shop here without going broke.

Two of the world's biggest department stores, Tōbu and Seibu, are here, as are an entire complex built around one of the tallest buildings in Asia, Sunshine City, and the second-busiest station in Tokyo.

Orientation

Takadanobaba, the eccentric student district, is south of Ikebukuro, as are the lights of Shinjuku. To the east lie quiet lowland residential districts, while the west stretches into some of Tokyo's more remote wards.

The JR Yamanote Line runs smack through the middle, dividing Ikebukuro into east and west. Like Shinjuku, Ikebukuro's east and west sides have different identities. The west end has the lion's share of bars and good restaurants, while the east is home to the towering Sunshine City complex.

IKEBUKURO BŌSAI-KAN Map p280

☎ 3590-6565; 2-37-8 Nishi-Ikebukuro, Tōshima-ku; admission free; 9am-5pm Wed-Mon, closed 3rd Wed of the month; JR Yamanote Line or Marunouchi Line to Ikebukuro (Metropolitan exit)

Quick: what should you do in case of an earthquake? What if your house is on fire? This facility operated by the Tokyo Fire Department prepares you for these and other disasters by means of videos (available in English) and incredibly realistic simulations; it's hard not to be rattled once the room starts a-shaking. A visit here is important preparation if you're planning on living in Japan, and even if you're not it's an important insight into a possibility that's never far from the mind of any Japanese.

JAPAN TRADITIONAL CRAFT CENTER Map p280

☎ 5954-6066; www.kougei.or.jp/english/center.html; 1st fl, Metropolitan Plaza Bldg, 1-11-1 Nishi Ikebukuro, Toshima-ku; admission free; 11am-7pm; JR Yamanote Line or Marunouchi Line to Ikebukuro (Metropolitan exit)

Operated by the Ministry of Economy, Trade and Industry, this showroom is less a museum than a resource for working artisans and crafts collectors. You'll find on display some 130 different types of crafts, from lacquerwork boxes to paper, textiles to earthy pottery. You can also buy much the same from the discriminating collection. If you've recently broken your favourite ceramic cup or damaged your kimono, the centre also conducts repair clinics (which are inside the massive Metropolitan Plaza building). Also see p188.

TRANSPORT

Train The JR Yamanote Line conveniently runs through Ikebukuro, terminus of the Tōbu and Seibu commuter lines.

Metro The Marunouchi Line terminates at Ikebukuro, while the Yūrakuchō Line also runs through it.

SUNSHINE CITY Map p280

☎ 3989-3331; JR Yamanote Line to Ikebukuro (east exit)

A complex of four buildings, Sunshine City stands on the former site of Sugamo Prison where General Tojo, and others deemed Class A war criminals by occupying forces, were executed. All echoes of that past are gone now, though, and this 'city within a building' – the buildings are connected by interior walkways – is now focused on that quintessential Japanese pastime: shopping.

If retail therapy isn't your thing, the complex includes **Sunshine 60**, an office tower and one of the tallest buildings in Japan (the 60 refers to the number of floors). What's billed as the world's second-fastest lift whisks you to the top-floor **observatory and sky deck** (adult/child ¥620/310; 10am-9.30pm) where you can gaze out at the Lego blocks below or perhaps Tokyo's horizon beyond.

On the top floor of the World Import Mart building is the **Sunshine International Aquarium** (☎ 3989-3466; adult/child ¥1800/900; 10am-6pm), home to more than 20,000 fish, while on the same floor the planetarium at the **Sunshine Starlight Dome** (☎ 3989-3475; adult/child ¥800/500; noon-5.30pm Mon-Fri, 11am-6.30pm Sat & Sun) is a nice diversion for space heads (shows in Japanese only). If you plan to visit more than one of these three venues, discounted combination tickets are available.

Families with kids may want to visit **Namco Namjatown** (☎ 5950-0765; 2nd fl, World Import Mart bldg; adult/child ¥300/200; 10am-10pm). Namjatown is owned by the arcade-game company Namco, which should tell you all you need to know about one half of the activities here (it can be pretty cacophonous!). The other half consists of three food theme parks (see p141 for more information). In the **Ikebukuro Gyoza Stadium**, 23 vendors from all over Japan compete for your business with their version of pan-fried dumplings. Denizens of the **Tokyo Chou Crème Hatake** peddle dozens of varieties of cream puffs, while **Ice Cream City** showcases innovative takes on the world's favourite dessert – check out the **Cup Ice Museum**, displaying packaged ice cream in flavours from vanilla and chocolate to octopus and grilled eggplant.

Finally, on the 7th floor of the Bunka Kaikan Centre you'll find the quiet **Ancient Orient Museum** (☎ 3989-3491; admission ¥500; 10am-5pm). It displays art and antiquities, sculpture and fragments,

DETOUR

Gokoku-ji (Map pp278–9; ☎ 3941-0764; admission free; 🕑 dawn-dusk; Ⓜ Yūrakuchō Line to Gokokuji, exit 1) Though this temple has been declared an Important Cultural Property, it gets surprisingly few visitors. One of the few surviving Edo temples, it dates from 1680 and was built by the fifth Tokugawa shōgun for his mother. Exiting the temple grounds and turning to the left, you'll soon reach Toshimagaoka Goryo, an imperial mausoleum that is closed to the public.

Rikugi-en (Map pp278-9; ☎ 3941-2222; 6-16-3 Hon-Komagome; admission ¥300; 🕑 9am-5pm; Ⓜ JR Yamanote Line to Komagome, south exit) This fine garden has landscaped views unfolding at every turn of the pathways that crisscross the grounds. The garden is rich in literary associations: its name is taken from the six principles of *waka* poetry (31-syllable poems), and the landscaping invokes famous scenes from Chinese and Japanese literature.

amulets and idols from Iran, Iraq, Uzbekistan and especially Syria. Exhibits change every six months; there are about 600 pieces on display at any one time.

EAST OF THE SUMIDA RIVER

The area east of the Sumida was – and remains – little visited by sightseers, but some new sights worth seeing have sprung up in the last few years, and now visitors are discovering the old sights too.

We've lumped together three districts in this section. Ryōgoku is the centre of sumō culture, with sumō *heya* (stables) in the neighbourhood. The nearby Edo-Tokyo Museum gives a marvellous presentation of city history. To the south, the neighbourhoods of Kiyosumi and Fukagawa retain a Shitamachi feel not gussied up for tourists, with some wonderful old gardens and temples. Stroll Eitai-dōri east of Monzen-nakachō Station on the 1st, 15th and 28th of each month for a street market with lots of local colour. Kiyosumi is also where you'll find the Museum of Contemporary Art, a quietly remarkable building with consistently smart exhibitions. Perhaps because of this museum, or because rents remain relatively low, private galleries from other parts of Tokyo have begun to move here. Finally, Fukagawa is also known for its association with Japan's most noted poet, Matsuo Bashō.

Orientation

This area is more a collection of distinct districts than one single unit. Ryōgoku (north side) is a quick train ride from Akihabara or a quick taxi ride from the Asakusa area. Kiyosumi and Fukagawa are neighbours on the south side in Kōtō-ku, just across the river from the greater Ginza area.

ART GALLERIES Map pp278-9

1-3-2 Kiyosumi, Kōtō-ku; Ⓜ Hanzōmon or Toei Ōedo Line to Kiyosumi Shirakawa (exit A3)

As we were going to press, a number of important galleries in town were moving out of central Tokyo to an edgy space such as you might expect in New York or Los Angeles. The building faces the Sumida River on one side and a cement plant on the other, and downstairs are loading docks for a department store. But no matter: the gallery owners present some of the city's most cutting-edge work. Galleries are on the 5th through 7th floors. **Taka Ishii Gallery** (☎ 5646-6050; www.takaishiigallery.com), **Shugoarts** (☎ 5621-6434; www.shugoarts.com) and **Tomio Koyama Gallery** (☎ 3462-4090; www.tomiokoyamagallery.com) should give you a good start. Check for exhibitions and opening hours before setting out.

BASHŌ KINENKAN Map pp278-9

Bashō Museum; ☎ 3631-1448; 1-6-3 Tokiwa, Kōtō-ku; admission ¥100; 🕑 9.30am-5pm Tue-Sun; Ⓜ Toei Ōedo Line to Morishita (exit A1)

Although it now takes just a matter of minutes from the central Nihombashi district, Fukagawa was considered a very remote area of Edo in 1680, when the revered poet Matsuo Bashō (see the boxed text, opposite) arrived here. At this compact museum, you can see some scrolls of poetry written by Bashō and those inspired by him, as well

TRANSPORT

Train The JR Sōbu Line is a main approach to Ryōgoku. It is the most convenient access to the sumō district and slightly less convenient to the Edo-Tokyo Museum.

Metro The Toei Ōedo Line connects the Ryōgoku, Kiyosumi and Fukagawa districts via Ryōgoku, Kiyosumi-Shirakawa and Monzen-Nakachō Stations. The Hanzōmon and Tōzai Lines also serve the last two stations, respectively.

as souvenirs of his journeys. There's no English signage, but it's a unique opportunity nonetheless to enter his world. There's a small garden out back, or walk out to the Sumida River and take a left for a lookout where you can view the skyscrapers while contemplating Bashō's Edo.

EDO-TOKYO MUSEUM Map pp278-9

☎ 3626-9974; www.edo-tokyo-museum.or.jp/english/; 1-4-1 Yokoami, Sumida-ku; adult/child ¥600/free, student ¥300-450; 9.30am-5.30pm Tue, Wed, Sat & Sun, 9.30am-8pm Thu & Fri; Toei Ōedo or JR Sōbu Line to Ryōgoku (main exit)

This massive, futuristic building is by far the best city-history museum we've ever encountered. At 62.2m tall, it is the height of Edo Castle and its structure, perched above an outdoor plaza, recalls an old granary. Once inside, the permanent collection on the upper floors starts with a reconstruction of one-half of the bridge at Nihombashi (p64), on either side of which are thorough histories of Edo and Tokyo respectively, mostly with excellent English signage. Highlights are too numerous to mention, but we like the sections on the lodgings of the *daimyō*, wood-block printing, the evolution of kabuki and Tokyo's headlong rush to Westernise. There are often special exhibits, but the permanent collection is usually plenty for most visitors.

FUKAGAWA EDO MUSEUM Map pp278-9

☎ 3630-8625; 1-3-28 Shirakawa, Kōtō-ku; adult ¥300, student ¥50-300; 9.30am-5pm, closed 2nd & 4th Mon of the month; Toei Ōedo or Hanzōmon Line to Kiyosumi-shirakawa (exit A3)

This museum is small but fine. In a multistorey room, it re-creates a 17th-century Edo neighbourhood with fire lookout tower, life-sized façades and buildings you can enter. Explore the shops like the greengrocer's and rice shop, or slip off your shoes to enter the tenement homes and handle the daily utensils and children's toys. Be sure to note the Inari shrine and the *kura* (storehouse) where belongings were kept for protection from fire and, just as big a danger, Edo's legendary humidity.

FUKAGAWA FUDŌ-DŌ Map pp278-9

Fukagawa Fudō Hall; ☎ 3461-8288; 1-17-13 Tomioka, Kōtō-ku; admission free; Tōzai or Toei Ōedo Line to Monzen-nakachō (exit 1)

The history of this giant temple dates from 1703 (with reconstructions), as a subtemple of Shinshō-ji in the city of Narita, one of the head temples of Shingon Buddhism. The main image, in a recently constructed inner hall is Fudōmyō, a venerable Buddha depicted in murals by Nakajima Chinami (2004);

MATSUO BASHŌ

Matsuo Bashō (1644–1694) was born in what is now Mie prefecture in western Japan and by the age of 10 he began to compose haiku, the seasonal-themed Japanese poetry of 5 syllables in the first line, 7 in the second and 5 in the third. In 1671 he published his first set of poems. By 1680 he became the leader of a literary circle in Edo. In 1681 one of his disciples planted a banana tree *(bashō)* by Matsuo's cottage here in Fukagawa; the cottage came to be known as Bashō-an (banana house) and from that Matsuo took his pen name.

Bashō soon embarked on an additional career, travel writer. He wandered the length of his homeland, documenting what he saw, Edo's own Mark Twain, Bill Bryson or Pico Iyer. Here is one of his most famous verses, from 1686:

Furu-ike ya
Kawazu tobikomu
Mizu no oto.

The ancient pond
a frog leaps in.
The sound of the water.

In 1689, he departed Fukagawa to research what would become one of his most famous works, *Oku no Hosomichi no Tabi* (the Narrow Road to the Deep North), then later to the Kyoto area where he wrote *Saga Nikki* (Saga Diary). Upon returning home to Fukagawa, he wrote the verse:

Moon viewing at my hut.
Let me hang on the pillar
like a banana leaf

In 1694, he took one last journey, to the great city of Ōsaka, where he fell ill. His last poem before dying that October:

On a journey, ailing
My dreams roam about
Over a withered moor.

The above haiku are translated from Japanese and don't conform exactly to the 5-7-5 rule, but one of haiku's great legacies is its easy adaptability to other languages. To try one in English, use the 5-7-5 syllabication, include a reference to the season, and throw in a twist, so that by the end of the haiku, readers are transported somewhere they couldn't anticipate.

take the elevator to the 4th floor. On the 2nd floor is a gallery depicting all 88 temples of the 1400km pilgrimage route on the island of Shikoku; it is said that offering a prayer at each alcove has the same effect as visiting each temple.

One of the best times to visit is around 3pm, when priests read sutras in a thunder of *taiko* drums and fire.

KANTŌ EARTHQUAKE MEMORIAL MUSEUM Map pp278-9

☎ 3622-1208; Yokoami-kōen, Sumida-ku; admission free; 🕑 9am-5pm Tue-Sun; Ⓜ Toei Ōedo Line to Ryōgoku (exit A1)

This museum presents sombre exhibits about the 1923 earthquake that destroyed more than 70% of the city and killed more than 50,000 people. Maps chart the course of the devastating fires while cases display glassware, eyeglasses, binoculars, tools and other objects convoluted by heat. There is also a harrowing collection of photographs and paintings of the aftermath. The museum has generalised to cover other disasters to strike Tokyo prefecture, including WWII air raids and the volcanic eruption on one of the prefecture's southern islands. The museum sits in **Yokoami-kōen** (Yokoami Park), with other memorial buildings and a garden dedicated to quake victims.

A pleasant walk connects the park and the Ryōgoku Kokugikan (right) through the **former Yasuda garden** (admission free; 🕑 9am-4pm), once the site of the Edo home of a *daimyō*.

KIYOSUMI TEIEN Map pp278-9

Kiyosumi Gardens; ☎ 3641-5892; 3-3-9 Kiyosumi, Kōtō-ku; adult/child/senior ¥150/free/70; 🕑 9am-5pm; Ⓜ Toei Ōedo or Hanzōmon Line to Kiyosumi-shirakawa (exit A3)

This marvellous garden was the first location to be designated a site of scenic beauty by the Tokyo Metropolitan Government, and it's easy to see why. It dates back to 1721 as a villa for a *daimyō*. The villa itself was destroyed in the 1923 earthquake, and thereafter the property was purchased by Iwasaki Yatarō, founder of the Mitsubishi Corporation. He was able to use company ships to transport prize stones to here from all over Japan – count all 50 (they're numbered). They're set around a pond ringed with Japanese black pine, hydrangeas, Taiwan cherries and other plants designed to bloom at different times of the year.

RYŌGOKU KOKUGIKAN Map pp278-9

www.sumo.or.jp/eng/index.html; 1-3-28 Yokoami, Sumida-ku; admission free; 🕑 10am-4.30pm Mon-Fri; Ⓜ JR Sōbu or Toei Ōedo Line to Ryōgoku (main exit)

Just north of Ryōgoku Station is this **sumō stadium** with its adjoining **Sumō Museum** (☎ 3622-0366). Fifteen-day tournaments *(basho)* take place here three times a year (January, May and September); three other tournaments are held in other cities in March, July and November. It is these *basho* that decide the *yokozuna* (grand champion). The museum is quite small but displays a rotating selection of interesting artefacts of sumō history and art (mostly wood-block prints). When sumō tournaments are on at the stadium, only those holding tickets to the matches can enter the museum.

See p17 for an introduction to sumō and p172 for details on watching tournaments. See also Tomioka Hachimangū (opposite) and Tomoegata (p142).

VISITING A SUMŌ STABLE

Sumō stables, called *heya* or *beya* in Japanese, are where the *sumōtori* (wrestlers) live and train. There are over 50 *heya* in Ryōgoku, along with shops catering to their clothing needs as well as restaurants. *Heya* are not normally in the business of hosting guests, but a few of them occasionally open to allow visitors to observe training sessions. Some things to know:

- Times of visits are limited. Stables close during tournaments and for one to three weeks immediately before or after.
- Training usually begins around 6am and finishes by 10am, with the lower-rank wrestlers training earliest. The best time to see the wrestlers is usually around 8.30am. For most visitors, a half-hour visit is sufficient.
- Most *heya* prefer visits arranged in advance. Ask at tourist information offices or check out www.sumo.or.jp for information on which stables are open and how to arrange a visit, and do not be a no-show or cancel at the last minute.
- Discipline is a key element of sumō training, and you should also exercise discipline as a visitor. Sit quietly outside the *dohyō* (ring) and do not make noise or take photographs without permission.

Iron railing sculpture of sumō wrestlers, Sumida River (p104)

MUSEUM OF CONTEMPORARY ART, TOKYO Map pp278-9

☎ 5245-4111; www.mot-art-museum.jp; 4-1-1 Miyoshi, Kōtō-ku; adult/child ¥500/free, student ¥250-400; 10am-6pm Tue-Sun; Hanzōmon or Toei Ōedo Line to Kiyosumi-shirakawa (exit B2)

Dedicated to showcasing postwar artists and designers from Japan and abroad, MOT also holds some 3800 pieces exhibited in rotation in its permanent collection gallery, by the likes of David Hockney, Sam Francis and Andy Warhol, as well as Japanese artists such as Yokō Tadanori. Special exhibits, meanwhile, are significant and exhausting. The building's stone, steel and wood architecture by Yanagisawa Takahiko is a work of art in its own right; highlights include a sunken garden, V-shaped structural supports, and a water and stone promenade.

The museum is located in Metropolitan Kiba Park. It takes about 10 well-signposted minutes on foot from the subway station.

TOMIOKA HACHIMANGŪ Map pp278-9

Tomioka Hachiman Shrine; ☎ 3462-1315; 1-20-3 Tomioka, Kōtō-ku; admission free; Tōzai or Toei Ōedo Line to Monzen-nakachō (exit 1)

Next door to Fukagawa Fudō-dō, this large shrine dates from 1627 and is closely associated with the world of sumō. Around the back of the main building is the *yokozuna* stone, carved with the names of each of these champion wrestlers. Also of note are two treasured *mikoshi*, used in the Fukagawa Hachiman festival in mid-August. The current *mikoshi* date from 1991 and are encrusted with diamonds and rubies – look in the eyes of the phoenix and other birds on top.

A flea market takes place here on the 15th and 28th of most months, from around 8am to sunset.

ODAIBA

Eating p142, Shopping p188

Odaiba is a manmade island, cobbled together from the heady dreams of the Bubble Era. Reaching Odaiba is a journey, not so much in length but in attitude. You board a train with no conductor somewhere around Shimbashi, and as it takes you across the width of Tokyo Bay, Odaiba's futuristic buildings beckon while the skyline you just left continues to tempt.

The architectural centrepiece of the island is the Fuji TV Headquarters (see p31 for other examples of contemporary architecture), whose 25th-floor observation deck opens onto views of the city and on rare

TRANSPORT

Train Odaiba is on the Yurikamome Line from Shimbashi, which crosses the majestic, 918m-long Rainbow Bridge. An ¥800 day pass makes sense unless you plan to make a simple round trip. The Rinkai Line also approaches from the south and east.

Waterbus The Suijo Bus stops at Odaiba Marine Park and Palette Town. Catch the waterbus (see Sumida-gawa River Cruise, p87) from Hinode Pier (Map pp278–9).

clear days provides a glimpse of majestic Mt Fuji in the distance. Mega malls like Aqua City Odaiba, Decks Tokyo Beach (p188) and Venus Fort (p188) dominate the rest of the landscape, with heaps of shopping, theme dining and game arcades.

Across the flats, the science museum Miraikan, the Museum of Maritime Science and Ō-edo Onsen Monogatari are all excellent alternatives.

Orientation

Most of Odaiba is navigable by foot, though jumping on and off the Yurikamome Line train can be wonderfully convenient. The western part of the island, fronted by Odaiba Marine Park, is home to luxury hotels, shopping and arcades and a great number of eateries. The museums and other attractions generally lie to the east.

MUSEUM OF MARITIME SCIENCE
Map p289

Fune no Kagaku-kan; ☎ 5500-1111; www.funenokagakukan.or.jp/english/index.html; 3-1 Higashi Yashio, Shinagawa-ku; adult/child ¥700/400; Ⓡ Yurikamome Line to Fune-no-kagakukan

This museum is ship-shape, literally. From the outside it looms like an ocean liner by the water's edge, and inside are four floors of excellent displays related to every aspect of ships; don't miss the stunningly crafted replicas of Japanese ships, or try the navigation simulator. Outside, the 83.7m icebreaker Sōya is preserved. The museum is full of activities for kids, including a pool next door used for swimming and demonstrations and instruction of small craft. There's limited English signage but an English audio guide is available (¥500).

MIRAIKAN Map p289

National Museum of Emerging Science & Innovation; ☎ 3570-9151; www.miraikan.jst.go.jp; 2-41 Aomi, Kōtō-ku; adult/child ¥500/200; ⏲ 10am-5.30pm Wed-Sun; Ⓡ Yurikamome Line to Fune-no-kagakukan or Telecom Center

In the 20th century, '2001' had overtones of the future. 'Miraikan' means 'hall of the future', so it's somehow fitting that that's the year this futuristic building opened. It's been a favourite for travellers with kids ever since. Robotics (check out Asimo), home and automotive technology figure prominently, as do the newest in space and the life sciences. The Gaia planetarium, in its own orb, almost always books out – get a reservation ticket when you arrive. The building itself is as futuristic as its exhibits; glass of different degrees of clarity has been used for different parts of the exterior shell, to allow for capture of natural light, and 'through holes' and 'wind gardens' provide ventilation.

Ō-EDO ONSEN MONOGATARI Map p289

☎ 5500-1126; 2-57 Aomi, Kōtō-ku; adult ¥1575-2827, child ¥840-1575; ⏲ 11am-9am; Ⓡ Yurikamome Line to Telecom Center, or Rinkai Line to Tokyo Teleport (free shuttle bus)

Public bathing in *onsen* (hot springs) is a Japanese obsession (see p170), and believe it or not they've managed to find an actual hot spring 1400m below this giant complex. Bathing opportunities (most separated by gender) include indoor and outdoor pools, a foot bath, a bed of hot stones, and the opportunity to be buried in hot sand. Massage services are available, as are relaxation spaces in case all that pampering makes you sleepy. Bathing products and rental of towels and *yukata* (light cotton kimono) are included.

It's more than just hot springs, though. Like the food theme parks around town Onsen Monogatari has re-created an old Japanese downtown indoors, selling old-timey foods, toys and souvenirs. Wander around in your colourful *yukata* and you'll fit right in. Sure it's kitschy, but what the hey…

Note: Discounts are available if you arrive late at night or early in the morning; admission prices are highest between 11am and 6pm, and lowest between 5am and 8am. Visitors with tattoos will be denied admission.

TOYOTA MEGA WEB Map p289

☎ 3599-0808; www.megaweb.gr.jp; 1 Aomi, Kōtō-ku; admission free, virtual test drives ¥600; 11am-9pm; Yurikamome Line to Aomi (main exit), or Rinkai Line to Tokyo Teleport (main exit)

In the Palette Town development, Mega Web was designed to display the wares of the Toyota corporation. Yes, it's a showroom, but against all odds it's actually also fun. Test drive vehicles (advance reservation required), try the Mega Theater motion simulator or poke around in the History Garage with cars from the Golden Age. Some facilities close earlier; call ahead to confirm. Next door, don't miss the world's tallest **Ferris wheel** (Dai-kanransha), as high as the second viewing platform of the Eiffel Tower (Paris).

OTHER SIGHTS

GHIBLI MUSEUM Map pp278-9

general information ☎ 0570-055777, tickets ☎ 0570-000777; www.ghibli-museum.jp/ticket_info.html; 1-1-83 Shimorenjaku, Mitaka-shi; adult ¥1000, child ¥100-700; 10am-6pm Wed-Mon; Tōzai or JR Chūō Line to Mitaka (south exit)

When you saw *Spirited Away* by Miyazaki Hayao (or *Princess Mononoke, Howl's Moving Castle, My Neighbour Totoro* and so on) you probably fell in love with its mythical themes, fanciful characters and outrageous landscapes. So did every kid in Japan, which means you need to arrange tickets long before you arrive at this museum of the work of Ghibli, Miyazaki's animation studio.

Galleries walk you through the process of animation from concept to screen (English-speaking docents are usually on hand). Other highlights include a zoetrope presentation of a half-dozen Ghibli characters in motion, a minitheatre presenting short films (in Japanese but usually easy enough to follow), 5m worth of robot from the *Castle in the Sky* in a garden on the roof, and a gift shop with exclusive themed merchandise (though much of it at exclusive prices). Special exhibits change annually. To top off the visit, every visitor is given an original frame from one of Miyazaki's films.

From Mitaka Station, follow the sign-posted walk along the Tamagawa Waterworks for 15 minutes to Inokashira Park, and turn right. Alternatively, a community bus (one way/return ¥200/300, approximately every 10 minutes) goes directly to the museum from the Mitaka Station.

HARA MUSEUM OF CONTEMPORARY ART Map pp278-9

☎ 3445-0651; www.haramuseum.or.jp; 4-7-25 Kita-Shinagawa, Shinagawa-ku; adult ¥1000, student ¥500-700; 11am-5pm Tue & Thu-Sun, 11am-8pm Wed; JR Yamanote Line to Shinagawa (Takanawa exit)

South of the city in Shinagawa, this museum is one of Tokyo's more adventurous art spaces. Given that exhibitions change often, it is a good idea to check what's on before making your way out here. The Bauhaus design and the café, which overflows into a delightful garden, are attractions in themselves.

HATAKEYAMA COLLECTION Map pp278-9

☎ 3447-5787; www.ebara.co.jp/socialactivity/hatakeyama/english/; 2-20-12 Shirokanedai, Minato-ku; adult/student ¥500/300; 10am-5pm Tue-Sun Apr-Sep, 10am-4.30pm Tue-Sun Oct-Mar; Asakusa Line to Takanawadai (exit A2)

This undervisited museum should be high on the list for anyone with an interest in Japanese ceramics and the tea ceremony. It was the private collection of Hatakeyama Issei, an industrialist who dedicated himself to the way of tea and also designed the museum. You'll find seasonal displays of priceless works of tea ware from the Muromachi, Momoyama and Edo periods, some of them important cultural properties. The muted lighting in the exhibit hall seems inspired by the mock-up of a teahouse in the corner (you can have tea hall for an additional ¥400). It's all reached via a lovely garden.

NIHON MINGEIKAN Map pp278-9

Japan Folk Crafts Museum; ☎ 3467-4527; www.mingeikan.or.jp/english/; 4-3-33 Komaba, Meguro-ku; adult ¥1000, student ¥200-500; 10am-5pm Tue-Sun; Keio Inokashira Line to Komaba-tōdaimae

The collection of this lovely museum numbers some 17,000 pieces of *mingei* (called folk crafts but really a philosophy, p23). Most of the work is from Japan, but there are also pieces from Europe, Africa and other Asian countries. No surprise that the museum's pioneers were Yanagi Sōetsu, Hamada Shōji and Kawai Kanjiro, three of the leaders of the *mingei* movement itself; the impressive building (1936) was Yanagi's house. In addition to changing exhibits of *mingei*, the museum also sponsors an annual competition of new works.

TOKYO CEMETERIES

Strolling through a cemetery may seem like a grim pastime, but in Tokyo the grave markers can be quite elegant, making the experience both historical and pleasant. As all good things must come to an end, thus we finish this chapter.

Aoyama Rei-en (Map p286; Aoyama Cemetery; 24hr; Chiyoda Line to Nogizaka (main exit)) John Manjiro, the famously shipwrecked young fisherman who became the first Japanese to go to America, is buried here, as is professor Ueno, the master of Hachikō the Dog (p97). It's a good alternative to the crowds at Ueno or Yoyogi-kōen during *hanami* (cherry-blossom viewing) season. You can stroll from either Roppongi or Aoyama.

Yanaka Cemetery (Map pp296-7; dawn-dusk; JR Yamanote Line to Nippori (south exit))One of Tokyo's oldest cemeteries, it's worth strolling the narrow lanes and continuing to Ueno on foot. Beyond the cemetery, the quiet Yanaka area has many old Buddhist temples and speciality shops. For a walking tour of the area, see Nippori to Nishi-Nippori (p118).

Zōshigaya Cemetery (Map p280; dawn-dusk; Yūrakuchō Line to Higashi-ikebukuro (exit 5)) Not far south of Ikebukuro's commercial hub is the old residential district of Zōshigaya. This cemetery, a collection of weathered headstones surrounded by small paths and greenery, is the final resting place of authors Lafcadio Hearn, Nagai Kafu and Soseki Natsume.

SENGAKU-JI Map pp278-9

☎ 3441-5560; 2-11-1 Takanawa, Minato-ku; admission free; 7am-6pm Apr-Sep, 7am-5pm Oct-Mar; Toei Asakusa Line to Sengakuji (exit A2)

This temple of the Soto Zen sect is included in Tokyo's sights primarily for the dramatic story that surrounds it, that of the 47 *rōnin* (masterless samurai), also called the Akō Incident. This story, with its theme of paying the supreme sacrifice in the name of loyalty, has captured the Japanese imagination like no other, and has been adapted into countless films and plays (usually by the name *Chushingura*).

These *rōnin* plotted for two years (1701–03) to have vengeance on the man who caused what they believed to be the unjust and humiliating death of their master, Lord Asano of Akō province. They sought revenge even knowing that they too would have to forfeit their lives. After having brought the head of his enemy to their master's grave, 46 of the *rōnin* were condemned to commit *seppuku* (ritual suicide by self-disembowelment) in the samurai fashion – the 47th apparently escaped this communal fate on a technicality.

The cemetery here is quite dramatic as there always seems to be incense burning; you can buy your own to add for ¥100. There is also a new **museum** (adult/child/student ¥500/250/400; 9am-4pm daily) on the premises; there's not much English explanation, but a video presentation in English is available.

Walking Tours

Walking Tours

'Nobody walks in LA', the song goes, but *everybody* walks in Tokyo. It's the best way to get to know the idiosyncratic districts of the city, where even along the widest boulevards, the tiniest of cobbled alleys veer off into intriguing niches and neighbourhoods. From the street, you'll notice the otherwise undetectable waft of incense, the narrow shop window displaying a sprout of bonsai, or the temple gateway guarded by stone fox gods, carefully preserved between the modern concrete buildings alongside.

SHITAMACHI

If you squint a little, the Shitamachi (low city) you'll see before you still looks something like the settings depicted in the woodblock prints famously produced here in Edo times. Luckily, the area retains much of its traditional working-class feel – sort of a rough, gruff, friendly spirit distinctly different from other zones of reinvention-addicted Tokyo.

To start your walk, exit Sensō-ji the way you'd normally enter it – through Hōzōmon at the temple end of Nakamise-dōri. Turn right here and follow the road around the perimeter of the temple grounds. When you've walked along the walled area for

WALK FACTS

Start Asakusa subway station (exit 6)

End Tawaramachi subway station

Distance 2km

Duration Two hours

Fuel Stop Asakusa Imahan (p129)

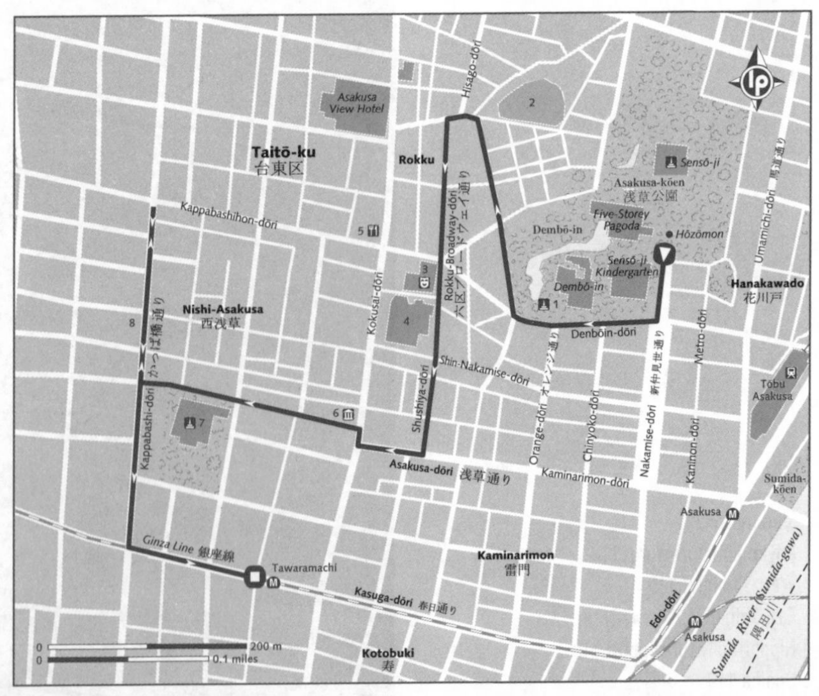

a minute or so, look for **Chingodō-ji** 1 (鎮護寺; p84) on your right, next door to the back entrance of Dembō-in. This temple is an interesting oddity: founded in 1883, it was constructed for the *tanuki* (raccoon dogs) living in the Sensō-ji precincts. These beasts, which local lore has as relentless shape shifters and hedonists, are sculpturally depicted with enormous testicles. As you enter, also notice the *jizō* statues, protectors to travellers and children. There are often stalls set up along the stretch of road outside of the temple precincts. Along with workaday clothing and shoes, you can find interesting festival accessories here.

If you follow the road round to the right, you will enter an area dense with shops, and finally pass an arcade selling traditional items like *yukata* (belted cotton robes) and kimono at reasonable prices. Further along is the **Hanayashiki Amusement Park** (2; ☎ 3842-8780; 2-28-1 Asakusa; adult/child ¥900/400; ⏰ 10.30am-6pm Wed-Mon), dating back to 1853 – listen for delighted shrieking, and the rollercoaster creaking and whooshing along its wooden tracks.

Entrance to Hanayashiki Amusement Park (left)

From Hanayashiki take a left and then another and you will enter what is left of Rokku (Block 6), Asakusa's old cinema district. It is all a little down-at-heel nowadays, and the few remaining cinemas don't screen much besides Japanese pornography. As you wander through, consider that this was once the most lively of Tokyo's entertainment districts, home to prostitutes and gangsters, and the haunt of novelists and artisans. A feature of the area today is **Asakusa Engei Hall** 3 (p148) where *rakugo* (performances of stand-up comedy or long tales) are held. Dominating the skyline is the **Rox building** 4, a shopping centre notable only for its immaculate **sentō** (public bath; p169) on the 7th floor, Matsuri-Yu (☎ 3836-7878; 1-25-15 Asakusa; ⏰ 10.30am-9am Mon-Sat, 10.30am-11pm Sun).

Ahead is another arcade, this one filled with Japanese restaurants specialising in tempura and other Japanese treats. Look for the traditional *sembei*-making shops here, some of which are open-fronted and allow you to watch these popular, crunchy, savoury rice crackers being made.

The arcade takes you back onto Kaminarimon-dōri, which is lined with Japanese restaurants perfect for a lunch break. Or take a detour along Kappabashihon-dōri for red meat at **Asakusa Imahan** 5. Turn right here and cross over Kokusai-dōri. On your right, just as you cross the street, is the **Taiko-kan** 6 (Drum Museum; p87) where you can sample the sounds and tones of drums from distant shores. Following the small road that runs to Kappabashi-dōri, to your left is a block dotted with temples, most of them quite small. The largest is **Tokyo Hongan-ji** 7 (東京本願寺), which is on your left just before you get to Kappabashi-dōri.

Kappabashi-dōri is Tokyo's wholesale restaurant supplies area. It's shop upon shop selling plastic food models, bamboo cooking utensils, batik cushions and even the *aka-chōchin* (red lanterns) that light the back alleys of Tokyo by night. Turn right into **Kappabashi-dōri** 8 and you can explore for several blocks before crossing the road and heading back south towards Asakusa-dōri.

You'll know you've reached the end of your Shitamachi tour when you come upon the Niimi building, crowned with an enormous chef's head – you can't miss it. It's on the corner of Asakusa-dōri, and a few minutes down the road to your left is Tawaramachi subway station on the Ginza Line, which can shuttle you into central Tokyo and beyond.

AOYAMA ARCHITECTURE

From cos-play kids (p14) to Commes des Garçons, Omote-sandō stretches out in a veritable catwalk of fashion and architecture.

At Harajuku Station, take the Omote-sandō exit and begin your stroll down Omote-sandō. At the large intersection of Meiji-dōri, turn left and look for the rounded exterior of the **Laforet building 1** (p185). Ascend the circular interior as if in a shopping-focused video game, and you'll soon discover the uniquely confusing half-floors of this building.

WALK FACTS

Start Harajuku JR Station (Omote-sandō exit)
End Omote-sandō subway station
Distance 2.5km
Duration One to two hours with stops
Fuel Stop Home (p136), Hiroba (p136)

Continue down Meiji-dōri and cross the street at Harajuku-dōri, where secondhand and local designers' shops are crammed upstairs and down. Meander down Harajuku-dōri, and just before you encounter a fairly large intersection, you'll see a building with huge windows and a dark-grey granite façade. Turn left here and continue walking until the street looks as if it's about to veer left. On your right, you should see a building that looks like an industrial, spiderwebbed diorama. Behold **Design Festa** (**2**; ☎ 3479-1433; 3-20-18 Jingūmae; 🕑 11am-8pm), a warren of rental galleries. Design Festa is responsible for an enormous art and design festival (p10) that takes place biannually at Tokyo Big Sight.

Coming back out to Harajuku-dōri, turn left and continue a short distance to a large four-way intersection, where you'll turn right. On this street you'll pass skateboard shops and a series of outrageous, experimental storefronts, many of them belonging to cutting-edge fashion boutiques. Eventually this street will intersect with Omote-sandō. Turn left onto Omote-sandō and on your left, you'll pass the latest, ungreatest Mori development that is **Omote-sandō Hills 3**. Slated to house upscale boutiques and apartments, its long glass façade replaced the crumbling but charming apartment buildings originally built for public housing after the Great Kantō Earthquake (p53).

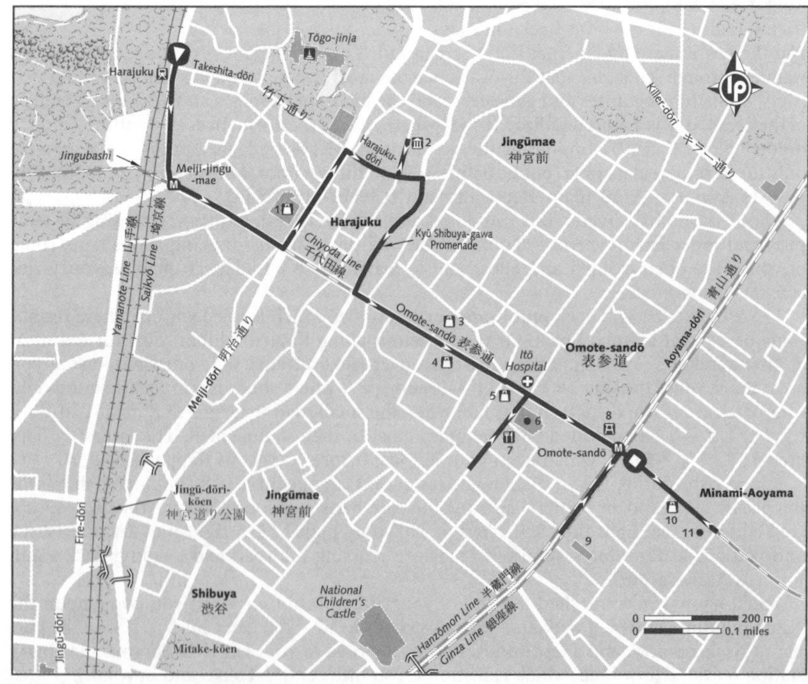

Across from Omote-sandō Hills, scan across the street for the blocky **Louis Vuitton building** (4; ☎ 3478-2100; 5-7-5 Jingūmae; ⏰ 11am-8pm). Meant to evoke a stack of clothes trunks, Jun Aoki's design features offset panels of tinted glass behind sheets of metal mesh of varying patterns, creating a fabric-like effect. When you encounter the pedestrian bridge in front of Itō Hospital, cross to the other side and you'll be heading straight for the Tokyo home of Italian footwear designer **Tod's** (5; ☎ 6419-2055; 5-1-15 Jingūmae). Wrapped in glass and supporting beams whose shapes reflect the winter-bared branches of the Zelkova trees along Omote-sandō, architect Toyo Ito's structure makes a statement while echoing the elements of its environment.

Moving further down the block, look for the exquisitely mirrored surface of the **Hanae Mori building** 6 (p185) on your right – designed by Tange Kenzō, one of Japan's most influential architects. If you're ready for a bite to eat, duck down the alley to the right of the Hanae Mori building and take lunch in either Home or Hiroba in the **Crayon House building** 7.

After lunch, retrace your steps to Omote-sandō and then turn right towards Aoyama-dōri. Just before the intersection, consider a quick detour across Omote-sandō to the quaint neighbourhood shrine, **Akiba-jinja** 8. Cross Aoyama-dōri, turn right, and in a few short blocks the **Spiral building** 9 (p99) will appear on your left. Designed by Tokyo architectural luminary Fumihiko Maki, its interior, 1st-floor gallery is dramatically crowned by a semicylinder. Just inside the door is a listening station featuring Japanese and world music. Exhibitions in the main hall range from fashion to sculpture to photography, and you can ascend the spiral ramp to a museum-style gift shop on the 2nd floor.

Retrace your steps along Aoyama-dōri and turn right at the Omote-sandō intersection. Just after the first block, peer into the sloped windows of Future Systems' **Commes des Garçons building** 10 (p184). Inside, Kawakubo Rei's wares occupy minimalist, curvaceous display spaces arranged in a mildly disorienting maze of tilted walls. Continue on to the end of the block for your final, dazzling destination: the **Prada Aoyama building** (11; ☎ 6418-0400; 5-2-6 Minami-Aoyama). Swiss architects Jacques Herzog and Pierre de Meuron created a weirdly organic, bubble-surfaced crystal of a venue in which the goods almost play a secondary role. The exterior itself is stunning, with its panels of convex glass, but the design of the interior's six floors almost deceives the senses into seeing the space as a seamless whole.

Once you've had your fill of architecture, turn back towards the Omote-sandō intersection; it's just a few minutes' walk to the Omote-sandō subway station.

WEST SHINJUKU

Looking up as you walk the streets of west Shinjuku (Nishi-Shinjuku) may put a kink in your neck, while peering down from those skyscrapers will make your jaw drop (smog willing). Within these towering structures lie delights as unexpected as a toilet gallery, the world's largest pendulum clock and Matisse originals.

The west exit of Shinjuku Station leads into an underground mall lined with shops and restaurants. Follow the mall to the Shinjuku post office exit and take the stairs to the right. One block ahead and to your right is the **Shinjuku L Tower**, which houses the high-tech bathroom showroom **Toto Super Space** (1; ☎ 3345-1010; 1-6-1 Nishi-Shinjuku; ⏰ 10am-6pm, closed 1st & 3rd Mon) on its 26th and 27th floors. Test-drive the latest in bidet technology in the facility's facilities. Opposite is the Sompo Japan Headquarters building, with the **Sompo Japan Museum of Art** 2 (p101) on the 42nd floor. The museum is known mainly for its purchase of Van Gogh's *Sunflowers* for a whopping ¥5 billion. The work it showcases, however, is the largely figurative work of Japanese artist Tōgō Seiji.

Even nonphotography buffs will appreciate the photography exhibits at the **Pentax Forum** (3; ☎ 3348-2941; 2-1-1 Nishi-Shinjuku; ⏰ 10.30am-6.30pm), on the 1st floor of the Shinjuku Mitsui building. For gearheads, however, the best part is the vast

WALK FACTS

Start Shinjuku Station (west exit)

End Tochō-mae subway station

Distance 3km

Duration Two hours

Fuel Stop Park Hyatt Delicatessen

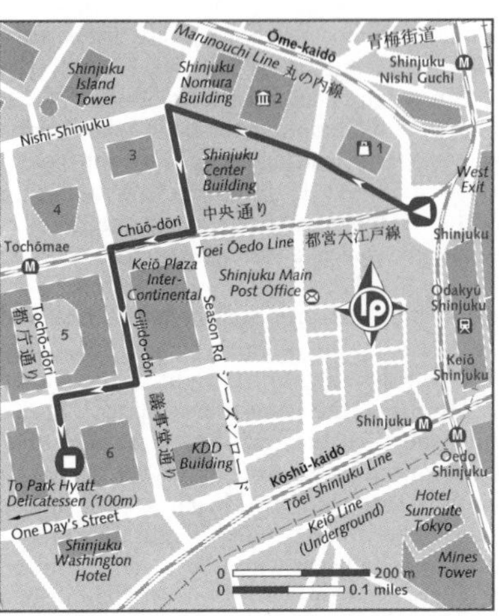

array of Pentax cameras, lenses and other optical equipment on display. It's completely hands-on – you can snap away with the cameras and spy into neighbouring buildings through the huge 1000mm lenses.

On the opposite corner of the intersection is the **Shinjuku Sumitomo building** 4, which has a hollow core. The ground floor and basement feature a jewellery shopping mall and a general shopping centre, but the attraction here is the free observation platform on the 51st floor.

By now you've noticed the towering **Tokyo Metropolitan Government Offices** 5 (p101), whose 45th-floor views (from building No 1) are the real reason you came. Some 13,000 government workers sweat over the administrative paperwork of running Tokyo in these buildings. The Citizen's Plaza features shops, restaurants, a passport section and, curiously, a blood donation room.

If you are in the mood for a bit of eccentric high tech, the interior of the **Shinjuku NS building** 6, just down the road, is hollow, like the Sumitomo building, featuring a 1600 sq metre area from which you can gaze upward at the transparent roof. Overhead, at 110m, is a sky bridge. The square itself features a 29m pendulum clock, listed by the *Guinness Book of Records* as the largest in the world. From here, head west about 200m down One Day's Street for a rewarding nosh at the **Park Hyatt Delicatessen** (☎ 5323-3635; 3-7-15 Nishi-Shinjuku; 🕑 8am-8pm Mon-Fri, 11am-8pm Sat & Sun).

EAST SHINJUKU

This walking tour is best begun about an hour before dusk falls, when you'll observe the perceptible change of east Shinjuku's day life turn over to night. The neon burns brighter against the darkening sky, and the seamier side of Kabukichō likewise comes into sharper contrast.

From inside Shinjuku Station, follow the east exit or Kabukichō exit signs. Once you've passed through the ticket gates, take the 'My City' exit. As you surface, directly ahead of you is the **Studio Alta building** 1 and its enormous video screen.

Continue walking east down Shinjuku-dōri past the bargain men's clothing and shoe stores. A little further on is **Kinokuniya bookshop** (2; ☎ 3354-0131; 3-17-7 Shinjuku; 🕑 10am-8pm), where you can pop in to browse its superb collection of foreign-language books on the 7th floor. Keep walking and you pass **Mitsukoshi department store** 3 (p177) on the right; on the left is the Art Deco **Isetan building** 4 (p187), packed with fashionable boutiques and the **Isetan Art Gallery** (admission free; 🕑 hours vary) on the 5th floor. The gallery hosts print, ceramic, and fine art exhibits by Japanese artists.

Turn left at Isetan and walk down to Yasukuni-dōri. A lane on the opposite side of the road leads to **Hanazono-jinja** 5 (p102), which nestles so close to Tokyo's most infamous red-light district that its clientele can make for some interesting people-watching. The shrine has a reputation for bringing success to business ventures – both legit and not-so.

Exit the shaded grounds of Hanazono-jinja onto **Golden Gai** 6 (p102), a tiny warren of alleyways devoted entirely to small, stand-up watering holes. Traditionally the haunt of bohemian Tokyoites, it's a safe

WALK FACTS

Start Shinjuku Station (east exit)

End Shinjuku Station

Distance 2km

Duration Two hours

area to walk around at night (by day it's deserted). If you decide to stop for a drink, keep in mind that some bars serve regulars only. It's said that the block is gradually being bought up by Seibu department store, but for now Golden Gai hangs tight.

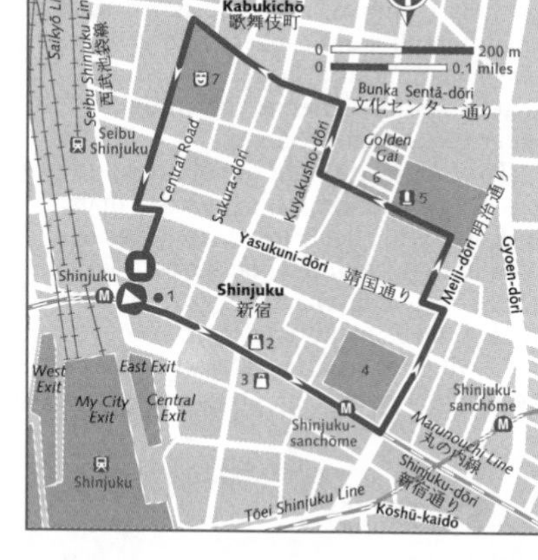

Continue in the same direction along the alleyways running parallel to Yasukuni-dōri and you reach **Kabukichō** (p102), Tokyo's notorious red-light district. Despite its reputation among locals, it's a relatively safe area to stroll around. Most of what goes on in these environs is pretty much off-limits to foreigners, though single men are likely to be approached by touts offering to take them to one of the 'pink cabarets'.

Kabukichō has a distinctly Japanese red-light district, with 'soaplands' (massage parlours), love hotels, peep shows, porno-video booths and strip shows that involve audience participation. As you walk through streets lined with neon signs and crowded with drunken salarymen, high-pitched female voices wail invitations to their establishments through distorting sound systems, and black-suited, spiky-pompadoured punks earn extra yen passing out advertisements for telephone clubs.

Continue along the perimeter of Kabukichō and look for the enormous **Koma Theatre** 7, which started off as a cinema, but quickly switched to stage shows. It still hosts performances of a more mainstream variety than those elsewhere in Kabukichō. The square facing the Koma is ringed by cinemas and is also a popular busking spot at night, though *yakuza* (mafia) are usually quick about moving anyone too popular along. Take any of the lanes radiating off the square to see Kabukichō at its best.

From this point wander back through to Yasukuni-dōri and take one of the lanes that connect it with Shinjuku-dōri.

Kabukichō district (above) at dusk

NIPPORI TO NISHI-NIPPORI

Spared from aerial bombing during WWII, the area around Nippori and Nishi-Nippori stations is imbued with the slowness of a former age. This nook of Tokyo is filled with small temples, atmospheric old cemeteries and little shops. Take the following route between stations as a suggested outline, from which you should deviate at your whim. Note that admission is free to the grounds of the temples listed here, though some fees apply to enter their inner precincts.

To start, take a right out of the south exit from Nippori Station. Walk across the railway tracks to a stairway leading up to Yanaka Cemetery (Yanaka Reien). You can orient yourself here using the large area-map at the base of the stairs. At the top of the stairs, walk about 60m until on your left you see **Tenno-ji 1** (天王寺), which belongs to the Tendai Buddhist sect. In the main courtyard there's a large Buddha image cast in 1690, reminiscent of the Great Buddha in Kamakura (p213).

Leaving Tenno-ji, enter **Yanaka Cemetery 2** (p110) proper. Roam around the cemetery a bit, and keep an eye out for the shy, stump-tailed cats in residence. Continue straight down the main road, which leads past a police box. Make your way to the public toilet about 100m past the police box and turn right (west) through the graves towards a residential area. After a quick dogleg, this will bring you out in front of a quaint shop selling Buddhist religious goods. Turn right here.

WALK FACTS

Start Nippori Station (south exit)

End Nishi-Nippori Station

Distance 2km

Duration Three hours with stops

Fuel Stop Chalet Swiss Mini (p128)

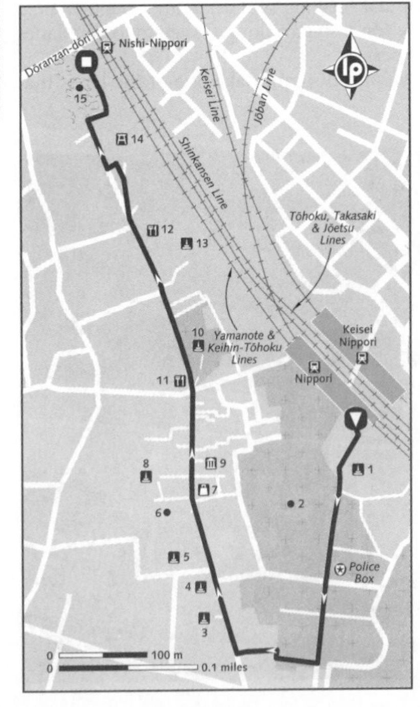

After the shop, you'll pass **Jōzai-ji 3** (常在寺), a temple that's worth a quick look. The next temple on the left is **Chōan-ji 4**, a Rinzai sect temple that was established in 1669.

Next, about 30m further on the left is **Kannon-ji 5** (観音寺), a Shingon sect temple consecrated to Kannon (Buddhist goddess of mercy). The temple grounds contain another small cemetery, pleasant for stealing views of the modern city beyond. Continuing on, you'll pass **Kaizō-in 6** (海蔵院), an administrative centre that can be safely missed.

Diagonally across from Kaizō-in, the **Sandara Kōgei 7** (さんだら工芸屋) basket store displays a rustic collection of Japanese crafts. Past this on the left, you'll see **Ryūsen-ji 8** (龍泉寺), another small Nichiren temple with a cemetery on its grounds.

Soon after Ryūsen-ji, on the right, you'll see **Asakura Chōso Museum 9** (p83), a charming collection of Asakura's quirky sculptures (many of them cats) with a marvellous Japanese garden behind the main building. After leaving the museum continue on for another 100m or so to the next main intersection. Here, in front of you on the right is the entrance to **Keiō-ji 10** (経王寺), a pleasant Nichiren temple with an old wooden *honden* (main hall).

After leaving Keiō-ji, you can walk to nearby **Darjeeling 11** for a curry lunch; or if you've a yen for pastry or fondue, head in the opposite direction up narrow Suwadai-dōri to the charming **Chalet Swiss Mini 12** (p128).

As you continue north, you'll pass several small temples. The most notable of these is **Yōfuku-ji 13** (養福寺), the gate of which houses two fierce-looking *niō* (temple guardian) figures. Not far beyond this the road leads you straight into **Suwa-jinja 14** (諏訪神社), a shrine, established in 1205, with good views from the grounds.

After the shrine, the road leads straight on to **Nishi-Nippori-kōen 15**, home to a dozen well-fed wild cats. Turn right and then left and you'll find yourself at Nishi-Nippori Station, where you can catch the JR Yamanote Line.

ODAIBA

Pick and choose your stops on this walk. The entertainments of Odaiba are so humungous and sprawling that browsing one mall and one museum could take an entire day.

To start, take the Yurikamome Line from Shimbashi Station to Daiba Station. The ride itself affords excellent views of the bay area as it crosses Rainbow Bridge. Upon arrival at Daiba, don't miss Tokyo's very own **Statue of Liberty 1**, studiously turning its back to the Rainbow Bridge.

Decks Tokyo Beach 2 (p188), **Mediage 3** and **Aqua City 4** house dozens of trendy restaurants, including **Tsukiji Tama Sushi 5** (p142), and shops and the chichi Sony Style showroom. You could easily while away an entire rainy day in here.

The **Fuji Television Japan Broadcast Center observatory 6** is on the upper floors of the ball-shaped structure. On clear days, you'll get great views of the bay and Rainbow Bridge. A ticket to the observatory (adult/child ¥500/300) also gets you into the Fuji Studio Tour (conducted in Japanese).

WALK FACTS

Start Daiba Station (main exit)

End Kokusai-Tenjijō Seimon Station

Distance 2.5km

Duration Three to four hours with stops

Fuel Stop Tsukiji Tama Sushi (p142)

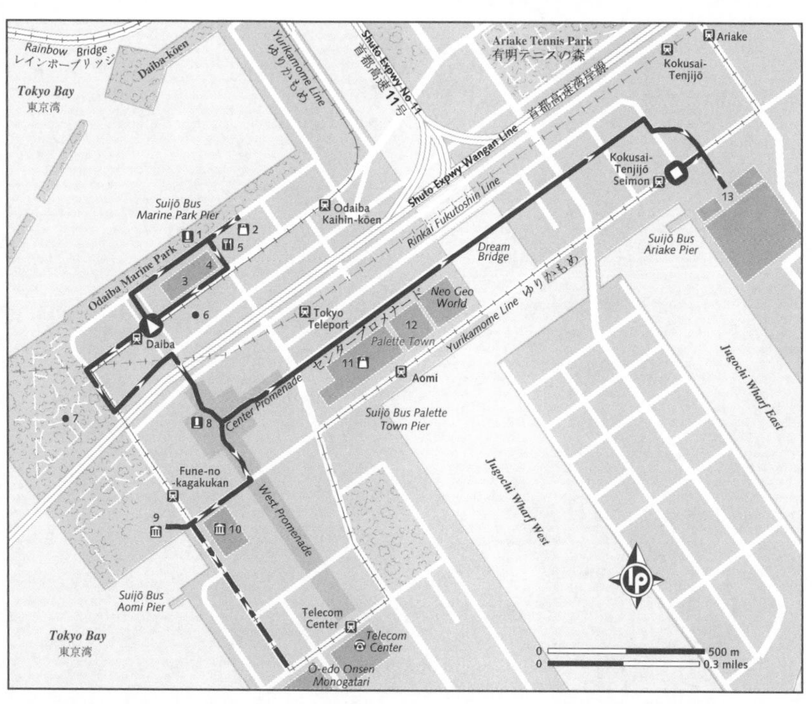

Shiokaze-kōen 7 is a good park for a waterside picnic on warmer days. From here, head for the giant gold needle that is the **Flame of Freedom** 8 statue.

The next stop is either the ship-shaped **Museum of Maritime Science** 9 (p108), or the marvellous, hands-on **Miraikan** 10 (National Museum of Emerging Science & Innovation; p108). If you visit the latter, add at least an hour or two to your itinerary.

From here, you can continue walking south to end your day with a bath, massage and dinner at **Ō-edo Onsen Monogatari** (p171). If you're not ready to jump in the bath just yet, take the train or walk to Palette Town, complete with humungous Ferris wheel, Italian Renaissance–themed shopping mall **Venus Fort** 11 (p188) and state-of-the-art **Toyota Mega Web** 12 (p109) showroom.

Once more you can walk or take the train to the next stop: **Tokyo Big Sight** 13, also known as the Tokyo International Exhibition Centre. The walk along the 'Center Promenade' leads across the flat middle of the island and takes about 20 minutes. After crossing Dream Bridge, Tokyo Big Sight comes into view.

The Big Sight's main hall looks like an Egyptian pyramid that fell to earth upside-down – certainly one of Tokyo's architectural wonders. For a good view of the bay, you can take the lifts or escalators to the roof of the hall, which is open to visitors any time a conference is not in session.

From Tokyo Big Sight walk straight ahead and then left to find yourself at Kokusai-Tenjijō Seimon Station.

Eating

Eating

From the simple knowledge that Japan's most refined cuisine – *kaiseki ryōri* (p42) – traces its roots to the tea ceremony, one can surmise that Japanese food has always been about more than basic sustenance. A stroll through any *depachika* (p124) will reveal rows of neatly boxed *bentō* (boxed lunches) featuring a natural balance of colours, subtle tastes and textures within. Even in prosaic convenience store cases, humble rice balls are pleasingly triangular in shape and surprisingly wholesome.

So it would follow that the aesthetics and feel of a dining room are often as important as the food itself, as you might observe even in a simple, busy train station *rāmen* (p38) counter. And like their Japanese counterparts, which are often exquisitely designed in wood, bamboo and tatami, nearly every French bistro and good tandoori kitchen has invested almost as much time in the interior design as that of the menu. This is not to suggest that quality ever takes a back seat to appearances; on the contrary, the breadth and calibre of Tokyo's international cuisine scene, which rivals that of Paris and New York, often surpasses both.

Opening Hours

Restaurants in hubs like Shinjuku, Ikebukuro or Shibuya are usually open seven days a week from 11am or noon until 9pm or 10pm, with many offering set specials during lunch hours. In smaller eateries in less central areas like Ebisu or Asakusa, hours often run shorter, and it's not unusual to find some places shuttered on Sunday, Monday or Tuesday. Generally, the lunch hour goes from 11am or noon to 2pm or 3pm, while dinner is served from 5pm or 6pm to 9pm or 10pm. Last orders are usually taken an hour or half-hour before the kitchen closes.

How Much?

Haute cuisine fetches high prices here, as anywhere else in the world. An upscale sushi dinner can easily run to ¥20,000. But despite what you've heard about Tokyo's exorbitant prices, it's possible to eat very well on a midrange or even modest budget without needing to raid the shelves of the convenience stores or to eat curried rice twice a day. Good *tonkatsu* (deep-fried crumbed pork cutlet) can be had for around ¥3000, and a

JAPANESE CUISINE TYPES

Sorting through the different types of Japanese cuisine can be confusing and daunting at first. To help you along, we've categorised specialist Japanese eateries along the following lines. For more information, see p34.

izakaya – Japanese version of a pub

kaiseki – beautifully presented Japanese banquet cuisine in which every small detail of the repast is carefully controlled

rāmen – noodles served in meat broth with a variety of toppings

shabu-shabu & sukiyaki – these two dishes are cooked at your table and consist of sautéed meat and vegetables

soba & udon – buckwheat and wheat noodles served in a light broth

sushi & sashimi – raw fish and rice dishes

tempura – food fried in a fluffy, nongreasy batter

tonkatsu – deep-fried crumbed pork cutlet

traditional – this includes *kushiage* (skewered meat and vegetables), *kaiseki* (a traditional multicourse meal) and other specialities like tofu and river fish

yakitori – skewers of grilled chicken

tremendous bowl of noodle soup might set you back around ¥850. You should know, too, that Tokyo's little-kept secret, the bargain lunch set, can sometimes put your foot in the door at places that might otherwise be beyond your budget.

Cheap Eats listings will cost around ¥1000 or less for lunch, or ¥2000 or less for dinner. Remember that tipping is not customary, and if you try it, you may get chased down the street by staff wanting to reunite you with your change.

PRICE GUIDE

¥¥¥	over ¥4000 a meal
¥¥	¥2000-4000 a meal
¥	¥2000 a meal or less

Booking Tables

Reservations are essential at many top-end spots. Some of the finer Japanese restaurants will be able to reserve a table for you over the phone, though in some cases it helps if you can speak some Japanese. If you don't, your hotel can usually make the booking for you. As for midrange and budget spots, reservations are unnecessary except in the case of larger groups.

Self-Catering

Even if you're here with money to burn, a visit to an everyday market or to the food halls in the more elegant department store basements (p124) is well worth the time. Traditional family-owned shops are dotted around the city; most sell seasonal produce (like summer melons, autumn persimmons and winter strawberries) and daily basics like fish, seaweed and rice. International supermarkets like those listed cater to Western palates and charge import prices; any would be great one-stop shops to pick up victuals for picnics in the park.

KINOKUNIYA INTERNATIONAL SUPERMARKET Map p284 Supermarket

☎ 3409-1236; 3-11-7 Kita-Aoyama, Minato-ku; 9.30am-8pm; Chiyoda, Ginza or Hanzōmon Line to Omote-sandō (exit B2)

Kinokuniya carries expat lifesavers like marmite and peanut butter, Belgian chocolate and herbal tea. Foreign imports like cheese, salami and Finnish bread generally fetch high prices, much like the flawless fruit in the produce section. If this branch is still under renovation when you visit, head to its interim store (Map p284; ☎ 3409-1231; 3-11-13 Minami-Aoyama), further south along Aoyama-dōri.

MEIDI-YA Map p286 Supermarket

☎ 3401-8511; 7-15-14 Roppongi, Minato-ku; 10am-9pm; Hibiya Line to Roppongi (exit 2)

Established in the 19th century, not too long after strangers in black ships started arriving on Japan's shores, Meidi-ya specialises in higher-end groceries for foreign predilections. It's a midsized store with a corresponding selection of goods, so you should find ample fixings for a picnic. Other locations throughout the city include a branch in Ginza (Map pp290–1).

NATIONAL AZABU Map pp278-9 Supermarket

☎ 3442-3181; 4-5-2 Minami-Azabu, Minato-ku; 9.30am-7pm; Hibiya Line to Hiro-o (exit 2)

Based in Azabu, where a high concentration of expats also happen to base themselves, National Azabu carries an impressive array of expat staples like imported cheeses, wines, Vegemite and natural foods as well as hard-to-find produce. Also notable is the pharmacy with English-speaking staff (p245) and the small bookshop upstairs.

NATURAL HOUSE Map p284 Natural Grocery

☎ 3498-2277; 3-6-18 Kita-Aoyama, Minato-ku; 10am-10pm; Chiyoda, Ginza or Hanzōmon Line to Omote-sandō (exit B4)

Natural House serves the eco-conscious trendsters around Aoyama, meeting a growing demand for whole foods and organic produce. Along with bricks of rye loaves and pricey but nutritious *bentō*, Natural House also peddles natural beauty products and health supplements.

YAMAYA Map pp290-1 Supermarket

☎ 3583-5657; 2-14-33 Akasaka, Minato-ku; 10am-9pm; Chiyoda Line to Akasaka (exit 2)

Yamaya's shelves are stuffed primarily with European wines, though there's also a

DEPACHIKA

Hungry for the next culinary novelty, OLs (office ladies) and *obaasan* (grandmotherly types) alike prowl the mazes of *depachika,* the cavernous food halls in department store basements. *Depachika* often take up several floors, housing a staggering array of foodstuffs of the highest order, freshly prepared and often gorgeously packaged for presentation as gifts. Depending on the most *au courant* food trends, you could find black truffle oil or dessert vinegar just round the corner from the more traditional 573 grades of the season's green tea and *wagashi* (delicate candies). Though samples are harder to come by these days, the sharp-eyed will find nibbles of sublime chocolate, sesame-seed *sembei* (crunchy rice crackers) and dried squid.

Large department stores are often attached to major train stations – *über*-convenient for picking up museum-quality *bentō* for dinner, picnic items for a sunny afternoon or a fancy gift of flower-shaped *okashi* (sweets).

If you can read Japanese, do as obsessive OLs do and monitor the day's specials on www.depachika.com. If not, descend into one of the following basements, among Tokyo's best *depachika*.

Isetan (Map p282; ☎ 3352-1111; 3-14-1 Shinjuku, Shinjuku-ku; 🕑 10am-8pm; Ⓜ Marunouchi Line to Shinjuku-sanchōme, exits B2, B3, B4 & B5) The grandmother of them all.

Matsuya (Map pp290–1; ☎ 3567-1211; 3-6-1 Ginza, Chūō-ku; 🕑 10.30am-7.30pm; Ⓜ Ginza, Hibiya or Marunouchi Line to Ginza, exits A12 & A13) An upscale Ginza stalwart.

Mitsukoshi (Map pp290–1; ☎ 3241-3311; 4-6-16 Ginza, Chūō-ku; 🕑 10am-7.30pm Mon-Sat, 10am-7pm Sun; Ⓜ Ginza, Hibiya or Marunouchi Line to Ginza, exit A7) Classic style and status at this Ginza institution.

Seibu (Map p280; ☎ 3981-0111; 1-28-1 Minami-Ikebukuro, Toshima-ku; 🕑 10am-9pm, closed some Tue; Ⓜ JR Yamanote Line to Ikebukuro, east exit) Spanning several city blocks, with a particularly comprehensive spice market.

Takashimaya Times Square (Map p282; ☎ 5361-1111; 5-24-2 Sendagaya, Shibuya-ku; 🕑 10am-8pm, closed some Wed; Ⓜ JR Yamanote Line to Shinjuku, south exit) Like the 15-storey department store above it, this *depachika* is enormous.

representative selection of American and Australian grape as well. Most branches are discount retailers and offer some imported packaged foods in addition to wines and liquors.

IMPERIAL PALACE & MARUNOUCHI

Despite the number of luxury hotels in the proximity of Tokyo Station and the Imperial Palace, good restaurants can be hard to find around Marunouchi. But between the shopping centres within the large Marunouchi Buildings and the avenues lined with luxury retailers, a few decent restaurants serve this business and commercial district.

KUA 'AINA Map pp294-5 Café ¥

☎ 5220-2440; 5th fl, Marunouchi Bldg, 2-4-1 Marunouchi, Chiyoda-ku; mains from ¥600; 🕑 11am-11pm Mon-Sat, 11am-10pm Sun; Ⓜ JR Yamanote or Marunouchi Line to Tokyo (Marunouchi exits)

From the Haleiwa shore comes this Hawaiian burger chain, serving up mahi-mahi and microbrew. Lovers of avocado, fabulous chips and massive, juicy burgers would be wise to pop by for lunch if a boat-sized bowl of *rāmen* (noodles in broth) sounds too skimpy.

MIKUNI'S CAFÉ MARUNOUCHI

Map pp294-5 Continental Café ¥¥

☎ 5220-3921; 2-6-1 Marunouchi, Chiyoda-ku; meals from ¥1260; Ⓜ JR Yamanote or Yūrakuchō Line to Yūrakuchō (exit A4b)

Civilised multicourse Italian lunch sets fortify the diner for gallery-hopping and window-shopping. The circular pastry counter beckons the sweet-tooth – and the tiny, floury scones verge on perfection.

GINZA

Ginza has always been a stronghold of the city's finest restaurants, with excellent sushi, marvellous French *haute cuisine* and ethereal surroundings. It can be challenging to find in Ginza a modestly priced meal in the evenings, but poking around the restaurant towns of department stores can turn up good lunch deals.

KYŪBEI Map pp290-1 Sushi & Sashimi ¥¥¥

☎ 3571-6523; 8-7-6 Ginza, Chūō-ku; lunch from ¥4000, dinner from ¥10,000; 🕑 11.30am-2pm & 5-10pm Mon-Sat; Ⓜ Ginza Line to Shimbashi (exit 1)

Established in 1936, Kyūbei's raw fish is still revered in restaurant-rich Ginza. If you request it beforehand – and reservations are recommended – the owner will arrange for your meal to be served on fine pottery thrown by Rosanjin Kitaoji (p126). In a city reluctant to apply sushi superlatives, this spot is truly considered one of the best.

L'OSIER Map pp290-1 French ¥¥¥

☎ 3571-6050; 7-5-5 Ginza, Chūō-ku; dishes ¥6000-10,000; 🕑 noon-2pm & 6-9.30pm; Ⓜ Ginza, Hibiya or Marunouchi Line to Ginza (exit B6)

Many local gourmets consider L'Osier to be the best French restaurant in Tokyo; and if bookings signify popularity, you might agree based on this evidence alone. But if you wish to analyse the foie gras yourself, you'll need to book as far in advance as possible. This is tremendously rich *haute cuisine* in Deco-inspired surroundings.

NAIR'S Map pp290-1 Indian ¥¥

☎ 3541-8246; 4-10-7 Ginza, Chūō-ku; dishes ¥1500-2500; 🕑 11am-8.30pm; Ⓜ Hibiya or Toei Asakusa Line to Higashi-Ginza (exit A2)

Like Japan's foremost living novelist, Murakami Haruki, Nair's was born in 1949, signalling a shift in tone in postwar Tokyo. Though curry restaurants are now a dime a dozen, this was one of the first to introduce cardamom and spice to Tokyo. Since good, midrange fare is a rare find in Ginza, lunch here tends to be extremely busy.

TOP FIVE PLACES TO GO FOR BROKE

- Inakaya (p132) Very fancy grilling, and maximum fun with a merry group.
- Kyūbei (above) Stupendous and seriously costly sushi.
- L'Osier (above) Reserve ahead (by weeks or months), and the payoff is what many call Tokyo's best French cuisine.
- New York Grill (p139) An impressive venue for special occasion dinners or decadent Sunday brunches.
- Rakutei (p131) A much-celebrated establishment for its incredibly light, heavenly tempura.

Tempura dish

NATARAJ Map pp290-1 Indian Vegetarian ¥¥

☎ 5537-1515; 7th-9th fls, 6-9-4 Ginza, Chūō-ku; set meals from ¥2800; 🕑 11.30-11pm; Ⓜ Ginza, Hibiya or Marunouchi Line to Ginza (exit A2)

Herbivores have reason to rejoice. Nataraj brings its warm colours, low-key elegance and Indian vegetarian cuisine to its three-storey branch here. Sizable set meals include appealing choices such as pumpkin curry and chickpea pakora. The English menu also lists beer and wine.

ROBATA Map pp290-1 Traditional ¥¥

☎ 3591-1905; 1-3-8 Yūrakuchō, Chiyoda-ku; dishes ¥2000-4000; 🕑 5-10.30pm Mon-Sat; Ⓜ Chiyoda or Hibiya Line to Hibiya (exit A4)

From the rustic, weathered exterior to the ceramic bowls along the counter inside, Robata's looks are well-matched to the Japanese country-style food served here. Though the chef doesn't speak English, requesting *omakase* (chef's suggestion) will put your course choices in his capable hands; less hearty appetites should opt for the point-and-eat method.

TEN-ICHI Map pp290-1 Tempura ¥¥¥

☎ 3571-1949; 6-6-5 Ginza, Chūō-ku; lunch ¥5000, dinner from ¥8500; 🕑 11.30am-9.30pm; Ⓜ Ginza, Hibiya or Marunouchi Line to Ginza (exits A1, B3 & B6)

Tempura at the esteemed Ten-Ichi has rightfully earned its reputation as supernaturally light and nongreasy, and since 1930 it has enjoyed steady fame as some of the best in Tokyo. The dignified dining area at the flagship Ginza shop is a pleasure – and one for which you'll spend significant coin. It has an English menu; reservations recommended.

THE WORK OF ROSANJIN KITAOJI

Rosanjin Kitaoji (1883–1959), who was born in a small town just north of Kyoto, won notoriety as the winner of a national calligraphy competition and then spent the better part of his life shuttling between his shop in Tokyo and his intimate pottery studio in Kamakura. He despised ugly things and the people that created and condoned them, and quite rancorously attacked any form of sloppiness or mediocrity that dared call itself art.

Not surprisingly, Rosanjin was also a gourmand who was drawn to food in all its forms. As with everything else, in food he sought the ideal, the beautiful, the perfect. This greatly influenced his pottery, which often seems to be a kind of meditation on the perfect container for the perfect dish. And so a square plate with a silver overglaze serves as the backdrop for the shimmery scales of a small pile of fresh fish, or a shoe-shaped bowl acts as a tureen. If you're interested in experiencing Rosanjin's pottery at first hand, you can do so by calling ahead to Kyūbei (p125) whose attention to detail and beautiful arrangement pay fitting tribute to works whose form so closely follows beauty.

CHEAP EATS

SAKATA Map pp290-1 Soba & Udon ¥

坂田; ☎ 3563-7400; 2nd fl, 1-5-13 Ginza, Chūō-ku; dishes from ¥850; 11.30am-2pm & 5.30-10pm Mon-Fri, 11.30am-2pm Sat; Yūrakuchō Line to Ginza-itchōme

If you eat only one meal out, you'd do well to eat it here. Sakata is widely recognised as the city's best noodle spot, and the *sanuki udon* (a thick, silky noodle of exceptional firmness) is divine. Gracious Sakata-san doesn't speak English but will go out of his way to feed you. Look for the 2nd-floor sign reading *ishokuya* (menu).

YŪRAKUCHŌ YAKITORI ALLEY

Map pp290-1 Yakitori ¥

dishes from ¥1000; Chiyoda or Hibiya Line to Hibiya (exit 1)

Follow the smoke and steam that's looping its way up from under the railway tracks to this warren of rickety outdoor *yakitori* stands. Each open-air corner is tended by its own chef who knows everything you'd ever need to about grilling chicken. These stands offer little shelter from the elements, so dress accordingly.

TSUKIJI & SHIODOME

Right on the waterfront of Tokyo Bay, the Tsukiji neighbourhood encircles the busiest fish market on earth. It is here, any hard-working, tough-talking fisherman will tell you, that you'll find the best sushi breakfast in Japan and the freshest sashimi in the world. Enjoy it now while you can, as the ageing market will uproot for bigger digs across Tokyo Bay by 2015.

DAIWA SUSHI Map pp290-1 Sushi & Sashimi ¥¥

大和寿司; ☎ 3547-6807; Bldg 6, 5-2-1 Tsukiji, Chūō-ku; set meals from ¥2100; 5am-1.30pm Mon-Sat, closed 2nd Wed of the month; Toei Ōedo Line to Tsukijishijō (exit A2)

Lines are pretty much unavoidable at Tsukiji's best and most famous sushi bar, but once you're past the *noren* (curtains) and your first piece of sushi hits the counter, gratification is inevitable. Unless you're comfortable ordering in Japanese, the chef's sushi sets are a good bet. Though it may be too polite to say so, you're expected to eat and run.

EDOGIN Map pp290-1 Sushi & Sashimi ¥¥

☎ 3543-4401; 4-5-1 Tsukiji, Chūō-ku; dishes ¥1000-3000; 11am-9.30pm Mon-Sat; Toei Ōedo Line to Tsukijishijō (exit A2)

Fat pieces of superfresh sashimi and sushi draw the crowds at this little spot just up the way from Tsukiji Central Fish Market. The *teishoku* (lunchtime set) is a steal at ¥1000. Though there's nothing in the way of atmosphere, the locals who come here to eat provide all the colour you need.

CHEAP EATS

TAKENO Map pp290-1 Sashimi & Tempura ¥

☎ 3541-8698; 6-21-2 Tsukiji, Chūō-ku; dishes ¥1000-1200; Mon-Sat; Hibiya Line to Tsukiji (exit 1)

Catering mostly to the fishermen who flow in after the market has closed, Takeno serves only sashimi and tempura. If your Japanese is limited, consider ordering the *moriawase* (assortment) of either of the house specialities. Prices vary depending on the day's market activity next door. There's no English sign here, but the address is posted above the doorway.

AKIHABARA, KANDA & AROUND

The neighbourhood Kanda has perhaps the city's largest concentration of long-standing, excellent traditional eateries, some specialising in dishes as simple as *soba*, others serving prewar favourites on traditional tatami. In manic Akihabara, in contrast, cheap eateries abound though only a few stand out.

BOTAN Map pp294-5 Traditional ¥¥¥

☎ 3251-0577; 1-15 Kanda-Sudachō, Chiyoda-ku; mains ¥7000; 🕒 11.30am-8.30pm Mon-Sat; Ⓜ Marunouchi Line to Awajichō (exits A3 & A5) or Toei Shinjuku Line to Ogawamachi (exits A3 & A5)

Botan has been making a single, perfect dish in the same button-maker's house since before the turn of the last century. Sit cross-legged on bamboo mats as chicken *nabe* (meat cooked in broth in an iron pan with vegetables) simmers over a charcoal brazier, allowing you to take in the scent of prewar Tokyo.

ISEGEN Map pp294-5 Traditional ¥¥¥

☎ 3251-1229; 1-11-1 Kanda-Sudachō, Chiyoda-ku; mains from ¥4000; 🕒 11.30am-2pm & 4-9pm Mon-Sat, closed Sat Jun-Aug; Ⓜ Marunouchi Line to Awajichō (exits A3 & A5) or Toei Shinjuku Line to Ogawamachi (exits A3 & A5)

From early autumn to mid-spring, this restaurant reminiscent of the Edo era dishes up monkfish stew in a splendid communal tatami room. The rest of the year, when monkfish is out of season, expect the same traditional surroundings and a menu offering fresh river fish.

MARUGO TONKATSU

Map pp294-5 Tonkatsu ¥¥

☎ 3255-6595; 1-8-14 Soto-Kanda, Chiyoda-ku; mains ¥2000; 🕒 11.30am-3pm & 5-9pm Fri-Wed, closed every 3rd Wed; Ⓜ JR Yamanote or JR Sōbu Line to Akihabara (Denki-gai exit)

In Akihabara's megawatt circus, Marugo sits serenely unplugged. Set in one of the few prewar houses remaining in the area, this spot serves good *tonkatsu* atop piles of fresh shredded cabbage. English menus are available – ask when you enter.

MUANG THAI NABE

Map pp294-5 Asian Fusion ¥

☎ 3239-6939; 2-1 Jimbōchō, Chiyoda-ku; lunch from ¥1200, dinner from ¥3000; 🕒 11.30am-3pm & 5.30-10pm Mon-Sat; Ⓜ Toei Mita or Toei Shinjuku Line to Jimbōchō (exits A6 & A7)

Jimbōchō's office workers come out of the woodwork at lunchtime for Thai-spiced sukiyaki. Its location makes it the perfect midday stop for poring over your used copy of *Akira* with a dish of coconut-milk-based curry at your elbow.

MUITO BOM Map pp294-5 Café ¥

☎ 3238-7946; 2nd fl, 2-1 Jimbocho, Chiyoda-ku; mains from ¥1200; 🕒 11.30am-3pm & 5.30-10pm Mon-Sat; Ⓜ Toei Mita or Toei Shinjuku Lines to Jimbōchō (exits A6 & A7)

From the same restaurateurs who bring you Muang Thai Nabe, this warmly-lit Brazilian café just upstairs brings you a local rendition of Brazilian barbecue. Though tailored to Tokyo palates, it's a departure from the usual if you're not in the mood for noodles.

CHEAP EATS

JANGARA RĀMEN Map pp294-5 Rāmen ¥

☎ 3251-4059; 3-11-6 Soto-Kanda, Chiyoda-ku; mains ¥800; 🕒 10.30am-11pm; Ⓜ JR Yamanote Line to Akihabara (Denki-gai exit)

While not exactly a refuge, as this branch of Jangara Rāmen might well be the most cramped, the big bowls of Kyūshū-style *rāmen* is good reason to take a breather. Try the *tonkotsu* (pork bone), *rāmen* while rubbing elbows with the *otaku* (computer geeks) at the counter.

TOP FIVE CENTRAL TOKYO CLASSICS

- Botan (left) Traditional chicken sukiyaki served in an old button-maker's house.
- Daiwa Sushi (opposite) Tsukiji Central Fish Market's best sushi breakfast.
- Isegen (left) The monkfish stew here tastes the better for being served in an open, airy tatami room.
- Kanda Yabu Soba (p128) The mother of all Yabu Sobas and a delish dish of noodles.
- Sakata (opposite) Tokyo has gone udon crazy in the last few years; this is the nexus of so much of the madness.

KANDA YABU SOBA
Map pp294-5 Soba & Udon ¥
☎ 3251-0287; 2-10 Kanda-Awajichō, Chiyoda-ku; mains from ¥630; 11.30am-8pm; Marunouchi Line to Awajichō (exits A3 & A5) or Toei Shinjuku Line to Ogawamachi (exits A3 & A5)
A wooden wall and a small garden enclose this venerable buckwheat noodle shop. When you walk in, the staff singing out the orders will be one of the first signs that you've arrived in a singular, ageless place. Raised tatami platforms and a darkly-wooded dining room set the stage for show-stopping *soba*. Has an English menu.

MATSUYA Map pp294-5 Traditional ¥
☎ 3251-1556; 1-13 Kanda-Sudacho, Chiyoda-ku; mains from ¥900; 11.30am-8pm Mon-Sat; Marunouchi Line to Awajichō (exits A3 & A5) or Toei Shinjuku Line to Ogawamachi (exits A3 & A5)
Behind the traditional façade, you'll enter a room full of crammed tables and a glassed-in kitchen, where you can watch noodles emerge from a floury mass of dough under the *soba*-maker's hands. Slightly less formal than Kanda Yabu Soba but just as serious about *soba,* it's a good lunch stop for celebrating midday with a beer.

UENO

Beyond the park, Ueno's a fairly mundane part of town, and it probably doesn't warrant a trip on the train just for dinner. But after a long day of meandering the halls of Ueno-kōen's many museums, you may want to stick around for dinner. While the local restaurants aren't doing anything cutting-edge, they are satisfyingly down-to-earth and modestly priced.

FUTABA Map pp296-7 Traditional ¥¥
☎ 3835-2672; 2-8-11 Ueno, Taitō-ku; dishes ¥1500-3000; JR Yamanote Line to Ueno (Hirokō-ji exit)
Like so many home-style eateries, this place doesn't look like much, in its nondescript corner building, but who needs charm when you make the best *tonkatsu* on the block? It's a bit like a diner with matter-of-fact service, but it knows its stuff and needs no gimmicks beyond the edges of the plate.

HANTEI Map pp296-7 Traditional ¥¥¥
☎ 3828-1440; 2-12-15 Nezu, Bunkyō-ku; dishes ¥2700; noon-2.30 & 5-10pm Tue-Sun; Chiyoda Line to Sendagi (south exit)
Skewers of *kushiage* (fried meat, fish and vegetables) arrive at your table six at a time, counterbalanced with small, refreshing side dishes. Though courses are predetermined, and well worth the wait, you'll have to decide when you've had enough (or they'll keep coming) and whether to drink sake or beer. The backdrop is a lovely wood-and-bamboo Meiji-era house.

IZU-EI Map pp296-7 Traditional ¥¥
☎ 3831-0954; 2-12-22 Ueno, Taitō-ku; meals from ¥2500; JR Yamanote Line to Ueno (Hirokō-ji exit)
Try to get seated near an upstairs window for the best views of the large lilypads of Shinobazu-ike. Izu-ei specialises in *unagi* (eel), which you can take in two ways: in a *bentō* that includes tempura and pickled vegetables, or charcoal-grilled, sauced and laid on a bed of steamed rice, as *unagi* purists might insist. Order from a limited picture menu.

SASA-NO-YUKI Map pp296-7 Traditional ¥¥
☎ 3873-1145; 2-15-10 Negishi, Taitō-ku; dishes ¥1500-4200; 11am-9pm Tue-Sun; JR Yamanote Line to Uguisudani (north exit)
Sasa-no-Yuki opened its doors in thriving Edo and continues to present tofu in elegant arrangements and surprising variety, served in traditional surroundings. The house recommends *kuya tōfu* (tofu steamed with egg custard), but set meals allow you a broader sampling. Strict vegetarians should note that many dishes include chicken and fish stock, if not the meat itself.

CHEAP EATS

CHALET SWISS MINI Map pp296-7 Swiss ¥
☎ 3822-6034; 3-3-12 Nishi-Nippori, Arakawa-ku; dishes ¥200-1500; 10am-6.30pm Tue & Wed, 10am-9pm Thu-Sat, 10am-6pm Sun
Somehow this odd little school and café works. Nestled among the temples and shrines on a hill Shitamachi, which was spared of the bombing during the war, it looks just like a Swiss chalet on a Hollywood movie set. It serves, not surprisingly, very good fondue, pastries and sandwiches, often to children who are just being let out of class

upstairs. If you opt to do the Nishi-Nippori walk (p118), this could be a charming rest stop or a place to pick up a flaky pastry on your way down to the train station.

IKENOHATA YABU SOBA

Map pp296-7 Soba & Udon ¥

☎ 3831-8977; 3-44-7 Yushima, Taitō-ku; dishes ¥1000-2000; Ⓜ Chiyoda Line to Yushima (exit 1)

Soba, even if eaten solo, feels like a communal dining experience with its soundtrack of a roomful of customers solemnly slurping. Nothing beats a lunch of cold *soba* with *tsuyu* (dipping sauce) on a humid summer afternoon, while *soba* in hot broth warms you from the inside in winter. Luckily, branches of Yabu Soba extend all over Tokyo.

ASAKUSA

Despite the fact that Sensō-ji (Asakusa Kannon-dō) is Tokyo's most-frequented tourist attraction, the neighbourhood itself retains its own working-class, laugh-out-loud character. Delightfully, almost none of the restaurants cater to tourists, and so, here you are, just another person in the neighbourhood to be fed and then sent gently on your way. As a note of warning, most Asakusa shops shut down around 8pm.

ASAKUSA IMAHAN

Map pp296-7 Shabu-shabu & Sukiyaki ¥¥¥

☎ 3841-1114; 3-1-12 Nishi-Asakusa, Taitō-ku; dishes ¥3000-8500; ⏲ 11.30am-9.30pm; Ⓜ Ginza Line to Tawaramachi (exit 3)

Here in Shitamachi, this original branch of Imahan feels appropriately dignified for cooking your *shabu-shabu* and seasonal vegetables at low tables on tatami. Yet it's not so staid that you can't get happy on sake while you let your dinner simmer. There's an English menu here.

ASAKUSA MANOS Map pp296-7 Russian ¥¥

☎ 3843-8286; 2-7-14 Kaminarimon, Taitō-ku; dishes ¥1500-4000; ⏲ 11.30am-2pm & 4.30-10.30pm; Ⓜ Ginza or Toei Asakusa Line to Asakusa (exits A4 & 2)

Asakusa Manos is an incongruous spot in Asakusa, with its red tablecloths and borscht. Dine as the locals do on stuffed cabbage rolls and pirozhki; very good food served in a kitschy, somewhat incongruously un-Japanese atmosphere.

DAIKOKUYA Map pp296-7 Tempura ¥¥

☎ 3844-1111; 1-38-10 Asakusa, Taitō-ku; dishes ¥1500-3000; ⏲ 11.30am-8.30pm Mon-Fri, 11.30am-9pm Sat; Ⓜ Ginza or Toei Asakusa Line to Asakusa (exit 6)

The long line snaking around the building should tell you something about this much-loved tempura place before you even catch the unmistakable fragrance of it. Sneak off to the other branch around the corner if the line seems to put too much distance between you and your *ebi tendon* (shrimp tempura over rice). It has an English menu.

ICHIMON Map pp296-7 Izakaya ¥¥

☎ 3875-6800; 3-12-6 Asakusa, Taitō-ku; dishes ¥1500-3000; ⏲ 6-11pm Mon-Fri, noon-2pm & 5-10pm Sat & Sun; Ⓜ Ginza Line to Tawaramachi (exit 3)

Though primarily an *izakaya*, as the sake barrel over the door might suggest, the proprietress back in the kitchen whips up some of the best *oden* (stewed meat, vegetables and tofu) in town. There's an English menu and an unusual payment

Diners at an izakaya in Asakusa

system here – before sitting down, patrons buy wooden chips, which they spend as the night goes on.

KOMAGATA DOJŌ Map pp296-7 Traditional ¥¥
☎ 3842-4001; 1-7-12 Komagata, Taitō-ku; dishes ¥1500-3000; 11am-9pm; Ginza or Toei Asakusa Line to Asakusa (exits A2 & 4)
The sixth-generation chef running this marvellous restaurant will continue the tradition of transforming the humble river fish called the *dojō* (something like an eel) into various incarnations: grilled to miso-simmered to stewed. The open seating around wide, wooden planks heightens the traditional flavour.

OMIYA Map pp296-7 French ¥¥
☎ 3844-0038; 2-1-3 Asakusa, Taitō-ku; dishes from ¥2000; 11.30am-2pm & 5-9pm Tue-Sun; Ginza or Toei Asakusa Line to Asakusa (exit 6)
Even Asakusa, Tokyo's most traditional district, has its little neighbourhood French joint. Omiya serves a lovely set meal, backing it up with à la carte beef and fish if the day's selection doesn't move you. The wine list, however, is startlingly long and will turn on oenophiles who stray into this charming spot.

CHEAP EATS

NAMIKI YABU SOBA
Map pp296-7 Soba & Udon ¥
☎ 3841-1340; 2-11-9 Kaminarimon, Taitō-ku; dishes ¥1000-2000; Fri-Wed; Ginza or Toei Asakusa Line to Asakusa (exit A4)
Another member of the Yabu Soba family that has withstood the encroachment of high-rises, this little brown house continues to thrive as it has for almost 100 years. It specialises in tempura *soba,* still served at communal tables.

SOMETARO
Map pp296-7 Traditional ¥
☎ 3844-9502; 2-2-2 Nishi-Asakusa, Taitō-ku; meals ¥1000; noon-10pm; Ginza Line to Tawaramachi (exit 3)
Sometaro is a fun, funky place to try *okonomiyaki* – cabbage-batter pancakes filled with meat, seafood and vegetables that you cook yourself. It's a friendly spot, where the English menu even includes a how-to guide. Look for the rustic, overgrown façade.

WEST OF THE IMPERIAL PALACE

On the JR Sōbu Line and easily accessed via several subway lines, Iidabashi Station lies alongside a canal that once formed a part of the outer moat of the Imperial Palace grounds. Uphill and west of the canal lies the former geisha quarter of Kagurazaka, whose narrow alleys are home to small temples and hundreds of tiny restaurants; larger, more accessible ones, like those following, do business along the main avenue.

CANAL CAFÉ Map pp294-5 Italian ¥¥
☎ 3260-8068; 1-9 Kagurazaka, Shinjuku-ku; dishes around ¥1800; Tue-Sun; Namboku, Tōzai, Yūrakuchō or Toei Ōedo Line to Iidabashi (exit B3)
When summer evenings hang heavy with humidity, you may long for a leisurely cocktail on some riverside. Though Tokyo has a regrettable dearth of alfresco restaurants with breathing room, rare canal-side spots like this one do exist. Decent pizzas and Italian dishes seem a smidge overpriced, but the tangible sense of relaxation is worth the surcharge.

HANA NOREN Map pp294-5 Izakaya ¥¥
☎ 5261-4881; 2nd fl, 2-10 Kagurazaka; Shinjuku-ku; 5-11.30pm Mon-Sat, 4-10pm Sun; Namboku, Tōzai, Yūrakuchō or Toei Ōedo Line to Iidabashi (exit B3)
Located up the Kagurazaka slope above the Wendy's restaurant, this great *izakaya* occupies an atmospheric corner of Tokyo. The beers are cold, and the pub grub – such as the grilled fish and *yakisoba* (fried noodles) – are well-executed and reasonably priced. There's a picture menu but none in English.

LE BRETAGNE Map pp294-5 French ¥¥
☎ 3235-3001; 1st fl, 4-2 Kagurazaka, Shinjuku-ku; dishes ¥1800; Tue-Sun; Namboku, Tōzai, Yūrakuchō or Toei Ōedo Line to Iidabashi (exit B3)
Up Kagurazaka slope, you'll find this outpost of Le Bretagne (p137) tucked in the alley opposite the temple gate of Zenkoku-ji. Oddly, the cobbled alley is reminiscent of both old Edo and the French countryside.

AKASAKA

This is where both fiscal and governmental business gets done. Good portions of it empty at night as limousines take officials and luminaries elsewhere for secret suppers behind thick doors. But since low-key, non-power lunches need to happen and movers and shakers often work late, Akasaka has a few real finds in comfortable quarters.

ASTERIX Map p286 French ¥¥

☎ 5561-0980; B1 fl, 6-3-16 Akasaka, Minato-ku; lunch/dinner from ¥1500/2500; Mon-Sat; Chiyoda Line to Akasaka (exit 7)

Lunch at Asterix is a smashing deal, but dinner has its own merits – not as rushed, so you can linger over your wine while you mull the meal that is pleasantly dulling your senses just so. Portions here are large, but the dining room is petite, so reservations are advised. The menu is in French but not English.

RAKUTEI Map pp290-1 Tempura ¥¥¥

☎ 3585-3743; 6-8-1 Akasaka, Minato-ku; dinner from ¥10,000; 6-10pm; Chiyoda Line to Akasaka (exit 5)

If the Japanese have elevated the deep-fried to an art form, then the chefs at Rakutei create masterpieces nightly. The freshest seafood and the lightest tempura batter are prepared to order, resulting in tender prawn and sweet potato that actually does melt in your mouth.

SUSHI-SEI Map pp290-1 Sushi & Sashimi ¥¥

☎ 3582-9503; 3-11-14 Akasaka, Minato-ku; lunch/dinner ¥1500/4000; 11.30am-2pm & 5-10.30pm; Ginza or Marunouchi Line to Akasaka-mitsuke (Belle Vie exit)

Tracing its bloodline back to Tsukiji, Sushi-Sei has exactly the kind of ancestry every little sushi bar wishes it could have. The atmosphere here, created by escapees from Akasaka's nearby commercial and governmental office blocks, sometimes borders on sombre.

TŌFU-YA Map pp290-1 Traditional ¥¥

豆腐家; ☎ 3582-1028; 3-5-2 Akasaka, Minato-ku; lunch ¥1000, dinner ¥4000; 11.30am-1.30pm & 5-10.30pm Mon-Fri; Chiyoda Line to Akasaka (exit 2)

Don't be put off by the name if you don't happen to be a vegetarian. There's grilled fish and sashimi on the menu. But if you're sceptical about how versatile tofu could possibly be, the *bentō* here are a terrific introduction, packed with lotus root, pickled vegetables and morsels like *gammo-doki* (fried tofu-and-veggie cakes).

CHEAP EATS

DELHI Map pp290-1 Indian ¥

☎ 3560-5188; 2-14-34 Akasaka, Minato-ku; mains from ¥800; 11.30am-9.30pm; Chiyoda Line to Akasaka (exit 2)

Tropical cultures tout the numerous benefits of eating spicy foods; among them, the flushing of toxins when one begins perspiring with the endorphin rush (or pain, as the case may be). For those who like it hot, Delhi serves a fiery Kashmir curry. Patrons with milder tastes will find equally delicious options on the menu.

ROPPONGI

At any given hour, the population of Roppongi probably maintains the highest saturation of ethnic diversity (and perhaps also the highest saturation, drink-wise) in Tokyo. Long the district favoured by randy foreigners on R&R and Tokyo party people, it's also adjacent to nearby embassies and upscale hotels. So while some Roppongi restaurants serve indifferent sustenance to those merely fuelling up for a long night, some of Tokyo's more refined culinary experiences exist amid the madness.

FUKUZUSHI Map p286 Sushi & Sashimi ¥¥¥

☎ 3402-4116; 5-7-8 Roppongi, Minato-ku; meals ¥10,000; Mon-Sat; Hibiya or Toei Ōedo Line to Roppongi (exit 3)

Arguably some of Tokyo's best sushi is served at Fukuzushi's lovely wooden counter, where the chefs can satisfy your palate with conventional favourites but could just as easily piece together something more innovative, if you wish. Reservations aren't taken at this popular spot, so plan a few minutes' wait.

GINO'S Map p286 Italian ¥¥¥

☎ 3402-2227; 3-10-9 Roppongi, Minato-ku; dishes ¥5000; Mon-Sat; Hibiya or Toei Ōedo Line to Roppongi (exit 5)

Rumour has it that former American first couple Jimmy and Roslyn Carter shucked their sticky Secret Service bodyguards not once, but twice, to dine quietly in Gino's close quarters (their picture still hangs on the wall). The menu is a short but confident list of Italian comfort foods, such as brisket and pasta, never containing more than several items nightly.

INAKAYA Map p286 Traditional & Robatayaki ¥¥¥

☎ 3408-5040; 5-3-4 Roppongi, Minato-ku; meals from ¥10,000; 5pm-5am; Hibiya or Toei Ōedo Lines to Roppongi (exit 3)

Once you're bombarded with greetings at the door, the action doesn't stop at this old-guard *robatayaki* (a place that grills food that goes beautifully with booze). It's a party, it's joyous, it's boisterous – and that goes for the profusion of toothsome dishes as well as the attitude one must have when the bill arrives. Live large!

KISSO Map pp290-1 Kaiseki ¥¥¥

☎ 3582-4191; B1 fl, 5-17-1 Roppongi, Minato-ku; lunch/dinner ¥1200/8000; 11.30am-2pm & 5.30-9pm Mon-Sat; Hibiya or Toei Ōedo Line to Roppongi (exit 3)

Wonderfully accessible without compromising on aesthetics, Kisso is the perfect venue for sampling *kaiseki ryōri* (beautifully presented multicourse meals). The dining experience doesn't disappoint, served on beautiful ceramics and lacquerware in artistically arranged surroundings. Order a set meal and allow the chef free rein for the most transcendent culinary experience.

LILLA DALARNA Map p286 Swedish ¥¥

☎ 3478-4690; 5-9-19 Roppongi, Minato-ku; lunch ¥1000, mains from ¥2000; Mon-Sat; Hibiya or Toei Ōedo Line to Roppongi (exit 3)

Yes, this snug Swedish kitchen has very good meatballs…as well as tart lingonberry jam for the homemade rye rolls. But perhaps the best thing about this place is its tiny interior, littered with Scandinavian knick-knacks, lending the feeling that upon leaving, you might find yourself lost in the middle of a Swedish forest.

MOTI Map p286 Indian ¥

☎ 3479-1939; 6-2-3 Roppongi, Minato-ku; lunch ¥1000, mains ¥1100-3000; Hibiya or Toei Ōedo Line to Roppongi (exits 1c & 3)

Loved by local expats, Moti maintains a loyal base of foodies who come for the set lunches and well-seasoned curries. Settle into one of the comfortable booths and watch as first one embassy staffer and then another comes and goes. Moti can fill to the rafters around noon, as do its other branches in Akasaka (Map pp290–1).

CHEAP EATS

BIKKURI SUSHI Map p286 Sushi & Sashimi ¥

☎ 3403-1489; 3-14-9 Roppongi, Minato-ku; dishes ¥1000-2000; 11am-5am; Hibiya or Toei Ōedo Line to Roppongi (exit 3)

If you haven't yet had the pleasure of picking your sushi from a slow-moving conveyor belt as a fast-handed chef manages to fill any cavity left by your choices, here's your chance. Sushi starts at ¥130 per piece of tuna, salmon or shrimp, though you may want to dig deeper to go for more interesting choices like *aji* (horse mackerel).

SICILIA Map p286 Italian ¥

☎ 3405-4653; B1 fl, 6-1-26 Roppongi, Minato-ku; dishes ¥1200; 11.30am-2am Mon-Sat, 11am-1am Sun; Hibiya or Toei Ōedo Line to Roppongi (exit 3)

Lines up the stairs and out the door on any given Friday or Saturday testify to the delicacy of the pizza crust at this basement Italian joint. The garden salads are unexpectedly beautiful (cucumbers as sculpture) and refreshing after a day of riding trains and climbing stairs, but you'll need to carb-load with pizza before that long night out dancing.

NISHI-AZABU

BINDI Map p286 Indian/Pakistani ¥¥

☎ 3409-7114; B1 fl, 7-10-10 Minami-Aoyama, Minato-ku; dishes ¥2000; noon-2pm & 6-9pm; Hibiya Line to Hiro-o (exit 3) or Roppongi (exits 1b & 2)

Wonderful Bindi lies almost in the shadow of the freeway, which does nothing to deter the aspiring painters, writers and poets who gather here for their lunch. The Mehtas, who own the place, serve up the best curry and the liveliest conversation in town, and that humble plastic squeeze bottle contains the tangiest, most delectable mango chutney this side of London.

BISTROT DE LA CITÉ Map p286 French ¥¥¥
☎ 3406-5475; 4-2-10 Nishi-Azabu, Minato-ku; lunch/dinner ¥2500/7500; ⌚ noon-2pm & 6-10pm Tue-Sun; Ⓜ Hibiya Line to Hiro-o (exit 3) or Roppongi (exits 1b & 2)
Established in 1973, Bistrot de la Cité was one of the first of a new wave of French bistros to sweep the city. Its quaint glass front, steep stairwell and warm, well-lit interior are reminiscent of small cafés off alleyways on the Left Bank. The menu, of course, consists of French favourites whipped up with beef, fish and duck.

EBISU & AROUND

Ebisu, though not on most short-term visitors' radar, is home to a grown-up creative community of 30- and 40-something designers, artists and architects. As such, the area – particularly around Daikanyama – is usually full of independent boutiques and European-style cafés, the area's sophisticated aesthetics and flavours reflecting a hip and worldly population. Dining areas tend to be small here, so reservations are a good idea unless you're headed for a café or one of the famous *rāmen* shops.

KATSUYOSHI Map p288 Tonkatsu ¥
☎ 5421-0355; B2 fl, Yebisu Garden Place Tower; lunch ¥1500, mains from ¥2500; Ⓜ JR Yamanote Line to Ebisu (east exit to Skywalk)
Here, everyone sits at huge, communal oak tables with little dishes of radish to their right. Staff deliver a patch of spicy mustard just before setting down the *tonkatsu*, which seems like it has never known oil. Go to the basement's 2nd floor (underneath the 1st basement floor), and look for the Kurumaya sign; Katsuyoshi is next door.

KM FILS Map p288 French ¥¥
☎ 5457-1435; 1-30-14 Ebisu, Shibuya-ku; lunch/dinner from ¥1000/3700; ⌚ noon-3pm & 6-11pm Mon & Wed-Fri, 11.30am-2pm & 6-9pm Sat & Sun; Ⓜ Hibiya or JR Yamanote Line to Ebisu, exit 4 & west exit)
The initials KM behind this sophisticated, Mediterranean-leaning menu at this chic French bistro is respected chef Kiyoshi Miyashiro. Complementing the gorgeous Gallic cuisine is the jazz in the background and the knowledge that you're enjoying a sweet deal – all of which more than compensates for sometimes stilted service.

MONSOON Map p288 Asian Fusion ¥¥
☎ 5789-3811; www.global-dining.com; 4-4-6 Ebisu, Shibuya-ku; dishes ¥2000-3000; ⌚ 11.30am-3.30am Mon-Sat; Ⓜ JR Yamanote Line to Ebisu (east exit)
Like its lower-key branch in Aoyama (Map p286), this Monsoon serves pan-Asian cuisine in a tropics-evocative café setting. Alfresco seating and fruity cocktails help stave off the oppression of Tokyo's notoriously muggy summers. Small plates such as satay and steamed shrimp dumplings hit the spot whatever the season.

MUSHROOM Map p288 French ¥¥¥
☎ 5489-1346; 2nd fl, 1-16-3 Ebisu-Nishi, Shibuya-ku; dishes ¥5000-7000; Ⓜ JR Yamanote Line to Ebisu (west exit)
Chef Yamaoka's obsession with the taming of the 'shroom has sprouted this very cosy little French bistro – whose décor is dominated by a mushroom motif, of course. Three-course set lunches (¥2500 to ¥3500) are amazing value and will transport you elsewhere – without the mind-altering side effects. Japanese or French skills will help in making a reservation or interpreting the menu.

NANAKI SOBA Map p288 Soba & Udon ¥
☎ 3496-2878; 1-13-2 Ebisu-Nishi, Shibuya-ku; dishes ¥1000-3000
One of the best little *soba* shops in the area, this wooden house is hidden in an alleyway leading around Ebisu-jinja. It may not look like much, but these buckwheat noodles are

The venerable soba *dish*

just the right tenderness, and if you're not in a noodle mood, you can order *izakaya*-style dishes to go with your beer.

CHEAP EATS

BIKKURI SUSHI Map p288 Sushi & Sashimi ¥

☎ 5795-2333; 1-12-1 Ebisu, Shibuya-ku; dishes ¥1000-2000; 11am-4am; JR Yamanote Line to Ebisu (east exit)

This branch of Bikkuri is a bit more private and less gritty than its Roppongi relation (p132). Same idea: inexpensive sushi, festive atmosphere and an English menu detailing sushi pieces that start at ¥200.

GOOD HONEST GRUB Map p288 Café ¥

☎ 3710-0400; 1-11-11 Ebisu-Minami, Shibuya-ku; meals ¥1500; 9am-4.30pm Sat, Sun & holidays; JR Yamanote Line to Ebisu (west exit)

If it's one of those weekend mornings when you require hydraulics to haul yourself into an upright position, and upon gaining full consciousness you begin jonesing for strong coffee and bacon, then brush your tongue and aim yourself at Ebisu. Good Honest Grub will make you human again with comforting brunch classics, loads of vegetarian-friendly options and vitamin-rich smoothies.

IPPŪDŌ Map p288 Rāmen ¥

☎ 5420-2225; 1-3-13 Hiro-o, Shibuya-ku; dishes ¥800; 11am-4pm; JR Yamanote Line to Ebisu (west exit)

So, there are two great *rāmen* shops within a short stroll of the west exit of Ebisu Station. Kazuki Rāmen (below) is to the west, Ippudō to the east. Ippudō specialises in rich pork broth, so this is the direction to head if you prefer a meatier taste. Grate some fresh garlic and toss some beansprouts into the broth, and savour.

KAZUKI RĀMEN Map p288 Rāmen ¥

☎ 3496-6885; 1-10-8 Ebisu-Nishi, Shibuya-ku; dishes ¥800; 11am-6pm Mon-Sat, 11am-5pm Sun; JR Yamanote Line to Ebisu (west exit)

Steam rises above chrome as you sit on your stool at the counter and watch the calm *rāmen* cooks methodically moving that line of customers along the wall and back out the door, as they'll do all night. When your massive, well-balanced bowl arrives, be stingy with extra condiments. Propriety demands you take no more than 20 minutes to eat.

DAIKANYAMA

CAFFÉ MICHELANGELO Map p288 Café ¥

☎ 3770-9517; 29-3 Sarugakuchō, Shibuya-ku; dishes ¥1500; JR Yamanote Line to Ebisu (west exit)

Stylish Daikanyama is exactly the locale this Parisian-style café is meant to occupy. The smart set comes here to be seen, but you could just as easily blend into the background. Sidewalk seating makes it a fine summertime lunch stop, with lovely reasonably-priced lunch sets to enjoy with wine.

Cheap Eats

CAFÉ ARTIFAGOSE Map p288 Café ¥

☎ 5489-1133; 20-23 Daikanyama, Shibuya-ku; dishes ¥900; JR Yamanote Line to Ebisu (west exit)

The alfresco café seating in Daikanyama is one of the appealing features of this neighbourhood. Follow your nose toward the yeasty scent of baking bread, and you'll wind up at Café Artifagose where strong coffee and fine cheese and bread are your reward. If the neighbourhood shops tempt you more than a leisurely lunch does, pick up a pastry for later.

MEGURO

TONKI Map p288 Tonkatsu ¥

☎ 3491-9928; 1-1-2 Shimo-Meguro, Meguro-ku; dishes ¥1500; 4-11pm Wed-Mon; JR Yamanote Line to Meguro (west exit)

Tonki's chaotic kitchen turns out *tonkatsu* that's worth the wait, as the line out the door will attest. The brisk staff will take your order when you arrive – perhaps the *hirekatsu* (leaner pork) this evening? – and then let you relax with a beer until they call you to the squeaky clean counter when your dish has been plated.

SHIBUYA

Along with the teenagers cruising Shibuya crossing and clusters of young fashionistas awaiting their cohorts at Hachikō Plaza, your attention span might only allow you a quick bite at a greasy spoon near the station before darting back into the melee. But for those nights when you need a bigger gastronomic thrill, stray outward onto the streets spoking away from Shibuya Station and discover the neighbourhood's more sophisticated delights.

EL CASTELLANO Map p284 Spanish ¥¥

☎ 3407-7197; 2nd fl, 2-9-12 Shibuya, Shibuya-ku; dishes ¥2000-4000; 6-11pm Mon-Sat; JR Yamanote Line to Shibuya (east exit)

El Castellano's success could be attributed to the warmth of its owner, who casts a friendly eye over the evening's progress and affectionately greets his regulars with sunny Spanish hospitality. But that would discount the definite draw of his homestyle cooking, including a mean paella and the sangria that goes so well with it. Call ahead for reservations.

KANTIPUR Map p284 Nepalese ¥

☎ 3770-5358; B1 fl, 16-6 Sakuragaokachō, Shibuya-ku; mains around ¥850; 11.30am-3pm & 5-11pm Mon-Fri, 11.30am-11pm Sat; JR Yamanote Line to Shibuya (south exit)

After you've spotted its colourful sandwich boards on the street, make your way down the narrow stairway into the warmly lit dining room. Kantipur offers generous portions and a bountiful selection of vegetarian choices. Much of the cuisine is of the familiar Indian bent, like good tandoori chicken and fish tikka, with uncommon snacks balancing out the mix.

SAKANA-TEI Map p284 Izakaya ¥¥

☎ 3780-1313; 4th fl, 2-23-15 Dōgenzaka, Shibuya-ku; dishes ¥1000-3000; 5.30-11.30pm Mon-Sat; JR Yamanote Line to Shibuya (Hachikō exit)

Though it will serve beer, this casual *izakaya* is sought out by connoisseurs of high-quality sake, of which many varieties flow freely every night. Salty, savoury pub snacks boast flavours undiminished by forbidden cigarette smoke. Despite the rough-edged, home-style décor, this place expects you to mind your manners and keep your mobile phone turned off. Reservations recommended.

SONOMA Map p284 Californian ¥¥

☎ 3462-7766; 2-25-17 Dōgenzaka, Shibuya-ku; mains ¥1000-1500; 6-11.30pm Sun-Thu, 6pm-4am Fri & Sat; JR Yamanote Line to Shibuya (Hachikō exit)

Favourites like polenta fries and pork chops with sage, brown sugar and apples form the mainstay of this unpretentiously inspired and priced Californian fusion menu. The interior resembles a Sonoma wine country restaurant and the menu is complemented with a strong selection of California wines. Swing by on weekends, when Sonoma patrons gain free entry into the Ruby Room (p149).

CHEAP EATS

MYŌKŌ Map p284 Traditional ¥

☎ 3499-3450; 1-17-2 Shibuya, Shibuya-ku; dishes from ¥800; 11am-10pm; JR Yamanote Line to Shibuya (east exit)

The wooden waterwheel outside is the sign you've arrived. Inside intimate rooms you'll be served hearty mountain stews made with seasonal vegetables and *kimchee* (pickled cabbage) and a helping of oysters, if you so choose. The coterie of *obaasan* (grandmotherly types) who run the place speak absolutely no English but will help you choose from a picture menu.

SHIZENKAN II Map p284 Vegetarian ¥

☎ 3486-0281; 3-9-2 Shibuya, Shibuya-ku; dishes ¥900-2000; 11am-8pm Mon-Sat; JR Yamanote Line to Shibuya (east exit)

Strict vegetarians looking to sample Japanese favourites may find it tough in Tokyo. Shizenkan II fills the gap with gluten cutlets and substantial lunch sets of prettily arranged piles of veggies. Though the food is flavourful and packs a nutritional wallop, Shizenkan's atmosphere is decidedly anaemic. You could instead pick up picnic components at the health food grocery in the front part of the restaurant.

OMOTE-SANDŌ

Like the boutiques and galleries that flank Omote-sandō and the winding lanes that diverge from it, the cafés and eateries in this area experiment relentlessly and insist on finding new directions. New takes on old standards – French may fuse with Japanese, organic vegetarian options might stand in for normally meaty favourites – dominate menus and chefs must become inventors to make a name. Surprisingly, all this innovation can be had without sacrificing comfort and beauty in the name of economy. Following are a good number of eateries that will satisfy a number of tastes while serving a variety of budgets.

CAM CHIEN GRIPPE Map p284 French ¥¥

☎ 3400-6885; 5-46-12 Jingūmae, Shibuya-ku; dishes ¥3500-5000; 11.30am-2pm & 6-9pm; Chiyoda, Ginza or Hanzōmon Line to Omote-sandō (exit B2)

Any Japanese chef worth their *shōyu* (soy sauce) will take themselves seriously enough to consistently make food pleasing to all the senses. But one who marries the formal aesthetics of Japanese *kaiseki* cuisine with French fare should also have sense enough to have fun with it. Chef Asano's Cam Chien Grippe (Dog with the Flu) proves itself to be just such a delightful animal.

FONDA DE LA MADRUGADA
Map p284 Mexican ¥¥¥

☎ 5410-6288; B2 fl, 2-33-12 Jingūmae, Shibuya-ku; dishes ¥6000; 5.30pm-2am Sun-Thu, 5.30pm-5am Fri & Sat; JR Yamanote Line to Harajuku (Takeshita exit)

Mariachis stroll through the enclosed courtyard – in a basement hacienda! – as you tuck into *chiles rellenos* (stuffed chillies) or appraise the *mole* (savoury, spicy chocolate sauce) drizzled over chicken or enchiladas. This is the only Mexican restaurant in Tokyo free of grim guacamole and unfortunate Californian-Mexican flourishes – and, we think, the best.

FUJIMAMAS Map p284 Asian Fusion ¥¥

☎ 5485-2283; www.fujimamas.com; 6-3-2 Jingūmae, Shibuya-ku; dishes around ¥1500; 11am-11pm; Chiyoda Line to Meiji-jingūmae (exit 4) or JR Yamanote Line to Harajuku (Omote-sandō exit)

Once a tatami-maker's workshop, both the airy upstairs dining room and the breezy, open ground-floor space now echo the freshness and vitality of Fujimamas' fusion food. Dishes come from multi-ethnic backgrounds, much like the people who come here to enjoy it, and portions are generous. Staff speak fluent English, and there's an English menu.

FU-MIN Map p284 Chinese ¥¥

☎ 3498-4466; 5-7-17 Minami-Aoyama, Minato-ku; dishes ¥1600-6000; Mon-Sat; Chiyoda, Ginza or Hanzōmon Line to Omote-sandō (exits B1 & B3)

Most who come are lured by tales of garlic, but stay for the *negi* (onion) wonton. The décor is understated, the service quick and the whole placed filled with the divine steam of deeply seasoned stir-fry. As good as it is, it's no secret – so you may have to wait.

HIROBA Map p284 Vegetarian ¥

☎ 3406-6409; B1 fl, 3-8-15 Kita-Aoyama, Minato-ku; lunch ¥1260; Chiyoda, Ginza or Hanzōmon Line to Omote-sandō (exits B2 & B4)

If you've come with kids this makes a great afternoon outing and lunch spot. Upstairs lives Crayon House (p182), with sweet children's books in several languages. In the basement, you can browse through the small grocery store or sit down for a quick lunch at Hiroba, which specialises in Japanese vegetarian cookery.

HOME Map p284 French ¥

☎ 3406-6409; B1 fl, 3-8-15 Kita-Aoyama, Minato-ku; dishes from ¥1200; Chiyoda, Ginza or Hanzōmon Line to Omote-sandō (exits B2 & B4)

Like its neighbour in the Crayon House building, Hiroba, Home has lots on hand for vegetarians…and it also has a decent wine list. The cuisine here leans towards a French flavour, and the atmosphere invites longer, leisurely lunches.

A pasta dish at Las Chicas (opposite), Jingūmae

LAS CHICAS Map p284 Continental Modern ¥¥

☎ 3407-6865; 5-47-6 Jingūmae, Shibuya-ku; dishes ¥1500; 🕑 11am-11pm Sun-Thu, 11am-11.30pm Fri & Sat; Ⓜ Chiyoda, Ginza or Hanzōmon Line to Omote-sandō (exit B2)

Urbane and relaxed, Las Chicas draws an international crowd with its artsy location, unfussy cuisine and friendly foreign staff. Its inviting terrace being a rarity in Tokyo, you might have to – sigh – settle for a place at the bar. An English menu details comfort foods with fun twists, like the Caligula, its version of the Caesar salad.

LE BRETAGNE Map p284 French ¥¥

☎ 3478-7855; 4-9-8 Jingūmae, Shibuya-ku; dishes ¥1800; 🕑 10am-11pm Mon-Sat, 10am-10pm Sun; Ⓜ Chiyoda, Ginza or Hanzōmon Line to Omote-sandō (exit A2)

The Brittany-born man behind Le Bretagne is so committed to producing authentic *galettes* (buckwheat crêpes) that, along with the *jambon* (ham), he's also imported his chefs from France. So turn your back to the window and pair a crispy-edged, tender-centred *galette* with a cup of cider, and imagine yourself in France. Afterwards, back in Harajuku, browse art books at NADiff (p182), next door.

MAISEN Map p284 Tonkatsu ¥

☎ 3470-0071; 4-8-5 Jingūmae, Shibuya-ku; dishes ¥1500-3000; 🕑 11am-10pm; Ⓜ Chiyoda, Ginza or Hanzōmon Line to Omote-sandō (exit A2)

Set in a converted public bathhouse, Maisen is rightfully famous for its *tonkatsu* – choose from shrimp, pork or premium *kurobuta* (black pig). Vegetarian offerings, though few, include new takes on old standards, like green tea *soba* with wild potatoes. There's also a takeaway window for picking up *bentō* of *tonkatsu* accompanied by packets of Maisen's savoury dipping sauce.

MOMINOKI HOUSE

Map p284 Japanese Health Food ¥¥

☎ 3405-9144; 2-18-5 Jingūmae, Shibuya-ku; lunch/dinner sets from ¥1050/2800; 🕑 11am-11pm; Ⓜ JR Yamanote Line to Harajuku (Takeshita exit)

Boho Tokyoites and personages such as Paul McCartney and Stevie Wonder have descended into Mominoki House's multi-level, rabbit warren of a dining room since 1976. Chef Yamada's menu consists mostly of Japanese whole foods, much of it vegetarian but also including organically-raised Australian perch and Hokkaidō venison. Food here is lovingly prepared – enriching to body and soul.

TOP FIVE SPOTS FOR VEGETARIANS

- Hiroba (opposite) Downstairs in the Crayon House Building, you'll find organic and veggie versions of Japanese and French standards.
- Mominoki House (left) More macrobiotic than vegetarian; still, most menu items are veg-friendly, and the English-speaking proprietor is more than happy to satisfy your preferences.
- Natural Harmony Angolo (below) Tokyo's best spot for health freaks and dyed-in-the-wool vegans. The occasional dish includes fish, but strict veggies can easily feast without worry.
- Nataraj (p125) Strictly vegetarian and positively delectable – vegans will have to watch out for paneer and other pitfalls.
- Shizenkan II (p135) This diner-ish spot in Shibuya dishes up veggie takes on Japanese favourites.

NATURAL HARMONY ANGOLO

Map p284 Vegetarian ¥¥

☎ 3405-8393; www.naturalharmony.co.jp in Japanese; 3-38-12 Jingūmae, Shibuya-ku; lunch/dinner from ¥1200/3000; 🕑 11.30am-2.30pm & 6-9pm Tue-Sun; Ⓜ Ginza Line to Gaienmae (exit 2)

Downshift to the pace of Natural Harmony, where the wholesome food is pure and so is the smoke-free air. The menu is largely vegetarian, augmented with some fish dishes; set meals featuring the delicately prepared vegetables *du jour* come with a choice of white or brown rice. Try some cold, cloudy sake with your meal and meditatively decompress.

NOBU Map p286 Modern Japanese ¥¥¥

☎ 5467 0022; 6-10-17 Minami-Aoyama, Minato-ku, Tokyo; lunch/dinner from ¥3000/10,000; 🕑 11.30am-3.30pm & 5.30-10pm Mon-Fri, 6-11.30pm Sat & Sun; Ⓜ Chiyoda, Ginza or Hanzōmon Line to Omote-sandō (exit B1)

Stemming from a childhood wish to become a sushi chef, Nobu Matsuhisa now has namesake restaurants in cities on four continents. His 1993 foray into the New York scene was financed by Robert De Niro, with subsequent Nobu restaurants established in Milan, Paris, London and Tokyo. His stunning, cutting-edge Japanese food doesn't come cheap – but it is phenomenal.

CHEAP EATS

JANGARA RĀMEN Map p284 Rāmen ¥

☎ 3404-5405; 1-13-21 Jingūmae, Shibuya-ku; dishes ¥800; 11am-2am Sun-Thu, 11am-3.30am Fri & Sat; Chiyoda Line to Meiji-jingūmae (exit 3)

Just a few dozen steps and a left turn away from the Harajuku JR station, the Omotesandō branch of Jangara Rāmen dishes up the same pungent, potent broth as its cousin in Akihabara (p127).

NEWS DELI Map p284 Delicatessen ¥

☎ 3407-1715; 3-6-26 Kita-Aoyama, Minato-ku; dishes ¥500-800; 9am-midnight Mon-Fri, 11am-4am Sat, 11am-11.30pm Sun; Chiyoda, Ginza or Hanzōmon Line to Omote-sandō (exit B4)

Sunk just below street level, this New York–style deli has the embrace of a comfy but stylish easy chair. There's an ever-changing selection of ethnically-diverse deli goodies to peruse, as well as cold drinks and a few sweet treats. Have a nosh, flip through Japanese- or English-language magazines and relax over coffee. It's open late and usually plays eclectic tunes.

PAMPKIN COOK KATSURA

Map p284 Vegetarian ¥

☎ 3403-7675; 4-28-28 Jingūmae, Shibuya-ku; lunch/dinner ¥850/1500; Wed-Mon; JR Yamanote Line to Harajuku (Takeshita exit) or Chiyoda Line to Meiji-jingūmae (exit 5)

You have to give it up for Tokyo chefs with one-track minds, cranking out imaginative variations on their favourite foods – from the delicious fungus at Mushroom (p133) to the eleventy-seven ways to cook a *kabocha* (Japanese pumpkin) here at the charmingly spelt Pampkin Cook. Set meals offer the best breadth of dishes. Look for the tiny shop-front down Takeshita-dōri (p181) adorned with…guess.

SPYRO'S Map p284 Greek ¥

☎ 5786-4446; www.spyros.jp; 3rd fl, 4-26-28 Jingūmae, Shibuya-ku; lunch sets from ¥650, dinner mains around ¥1250; noon-midnight Tue-Sun; Chiyoda Line to Meiji-jingūmae (exit 5)

Inside this glass-walled café, the scents of a Mediterranean climate are brought to you by a Japanese-Greek owner. If you hanker for a good *tzatziki* (yogurt and garlic dip) or succulent souvlaki, the authentic Greek flavours here will appease and please. A beautiful bar with real liquor is the decorative centrepiece and makes this a good dinner-and-drinks stop at night.

SHINJUKU

At the end of the work day, a few million sturdy pairs of shoes carry Shinjuku's workforce out of office doors towards the train stations. To avoid the worst of rush hour, most stop along the way for *yakitori* or *rāmen* or a more convivial sit-down affair with colleagues. Once inside most eateries on the east side of the station, the pace slows and the light-show outside disappears. On the west side, restaurants within the towers of the luxury hotels are designed for the view-hungry.

CHRISTON CAFÉ Map p282 Izakaya

☎ 5287-2426; 8th fl, 5-17-13 Shinjuku, Shinjuku-ku; dishes ¥2000; 5-11pm Mon, 5pm-5am Tue-Sat; Marunouchi Line to Shinjuku-sanchōme (exit B5)

Irreverent in the most orthodox sense of the word, this cathedral-like *izakaya* fetishises the Catholic aesthetic and turns this dining experience into something your inner goth will love. Reservations are definitely required to feast on small plates to share with your brethren under gigantic altars and doleful images of the pietà. There's a small cover charge (¥300).

IMAHAN Map p282 Shabu-shabu & Sukiyaki

☎ 5361-1871; 14th fl, 5-24-2 Sendagaya, Shibuya-ku; lunch/dinner from ¥1575/5565; 11am-11pm; JR Yamanote Line to Shinjuku (new south exit)

Upstairs from the huge Takashimaya Times Square branch of Tōkyū Hands department store, Imahan is all about beef. Apart from the house specialities of sukiyaki and *shabu-shabu*, Imahan serves such delicacies as *fugu* (blowfish), marbled beef sashimi and scaled-down but beefy *kaiseki* dinners. Come with comrades, as this cookery is meant to be shared for maximum merriment. There's an English menu.

NEW YORK GRILL

Map p282 Continental Modern ¥¥¥

☎ 5323-3458; 52nd fl, 3-7-1-2 Nishi-Shinjuku, Shinjuku-ku; Sun brunch ¥5800, dinner from ¥10,000; 11.30am-2.30pm & 5.30-10.30pm; Toei Ōedo Line to Tochōmae (exit A4)

You may not be staying here, but don't let that stop you from ascending to the 52nd floor to swoon over the stunning views of the city below. Splurge on a romantic, sumptuous supper backlit by sparkling night-time lights and live jazz. Reservations are advised, especially on weekends and for brunch.

RAJ MAHAL Map p282 Indian ¥¥

☎ 5379-2525; 5th fl, 3-34-11 Shinjuku, Shinjuku-ku; buffet lunch ¥1000, mains from ¥1800; 11.30am-9pm; JR Yamanote Line to Shinjuku (east exit)

The wonderful carved chairs and a continuous stream of Bollywood flicks set the scene for Raj's bottomless lunch buffet (11.30am to 3pm). It usually includes several vegetarian options and a pile of tandoori chicken; halal options are also available. If you're arriving with a group of more than five, you'll need to call ahead.

TSUNAHACHI Map p282 Tempura ¥¥

☎ 3352-1012; 3-31-8 Shinjuku, Shinjuku-ku; lunch sets from ¥1100; 11.30am-10pm; JR Yamanote Line to Shinjuku (east exit)

Tsunahachi operates several branches of its tempura restaurants in East Shinjuku, of which this is the flagship. Even the cheapest of lunch sets is an undertaking, with several healthy-sized, perfectly crispy tempura shrimp atop a bed of hot rice. If you're coming in a group, call ahead to reserve one of the tatami rooms. It has an English menu.

CHEAP EATS

CAPRICCIOSA Map p282 Italian ¥

☎ 3341-6066; B1 fl, 3-27-2 Shinjuku, Shinjuku-ku; dishes from ¥900; noon-10.30pm; JR Yamanote Line (east exit)

Ubiquitous Capricciosa is the standby for reliable, inexpensive pasta, which the waiters always follow up with a demitasse of strong coffee, gratis. The Shinjuku branch is buried (beneath the Zara store) in the basement of its building whose corrugated skeleton is left charmingly exposed overhead. Branches all over Tokyo have English menus.

COURT LODGE Map p282 Sri Lankan ¥

☎ 3378-1066; 2-10-9 Yoyogi, Shibuya-ku; lunch sets from ¥800; 11am-11pm; JR Yamanote Line to Shinjuku (south exit)

In this cramped, clean, cheerily busy restaurant, the superfriendly and efficient staff serve Sri Lankan specialities. It's possible that one could live on their *dotamba* (flatbread) alone. However, you're better off accompanying it with its yummy curries. While its lunch sets are an excellent deal, you can also pick up takeaway at its streetside counter.

OMOIDE-YOKOCHŌ Map p282 Yakitori ¥

Nishi-Shinjuku 1-chōme, Shinjuku-ku; dishes ¥1000-3000; JR Yamanote Line to Shinjuku (west exit)

Literally translated as 'Memory Lane' (and less politely known as 'Piss Alley') Omoide-yokochō will be but a memory when it's razed to make way for new development by late 2008. A remnant of postwar Tokyo, the alley is lined with wooden shacks selling *yakitori* and cold beers to longtime regulars – stop by around 7pm to indulge in noodles and pre-emptive nostalgia.

SHINJUKU NEGISHI Map p282 Traditional ¥

新宿根岸; ☎ 3232-8020; 2-45-2 Kabukichō, Shinjuku-ku; dishes from ¥1300; 11am-3pm & 5.30-10.30pm; JR Yamanote Line to Shinjuku (east exit)

Slow-boiled beef, carrot and onion stew is Negishi's main dish, though you might also want to try the signature beef tongue. The worn-wood place feels like a diner, not least because most things come with pickles on the side. This branch is well-frequented by neighbourhood denizens, giving you the chance to take in some local colour.

TAKADANOBABA

At the crossroads of several universities, Takadanobaba has its bookshops and dark basement bars, and cafés catering to students with big appetites and smaller budgets. Happily, along with the Starbucks and burger chains one might expect, these back streets thrive with inexpensive and cheery bistros of all backgrounds. Cosy establishments serve Turkish food or Thai, and social hour can stretch out till late at the local deli or dive bar. Wherever you decide to dine, you and the students at the next table will be getting more bang for your buck here in Baba.

LA DINETTE Map p280 French ¥

☎ 3200-6571; 2-6-10 Takadanobaba, Shinjuku-ku; lunch/dinner set ¥1000/2200; 11.30am-1.30pm & 6-9pm Mon-Sat; JR Yamanote Line to Takadanobaba (main exit)

Tucked down a small street in Waseda's cash-strapped student district, La Dinette serves French fare in a quaint café complete with chequer tablecloths. Reservations are required for dinner when the seven or eight tables are in high demand. For the incredibly cheap three-course lunch, walk on in.

MARMARA Map p280 Turkish ¥¥

☎ 3227-5940; 4-9-9 Takadanobaba, Shinjuku-ku; dishes ¥1000-2000; JR Yamanote Line to Takadanobaba (main exit)

The tiny wooden shack that marks the entrance and dispenses dirt-cheap take-away kebab is so small you might pass it by without remark. Once through the door, however, you'll see the stairs leading down to the spacious seating area where there's sometimes live music, but always solicitous staff and a dizzying choice of Turkish delights listed on an English menu.

TAVERNA Map p280 Italian ¥¥

☎ 3232-1997; 2-5-10 Takadanobaba, Shinjuku-ku; dishes ¥2000; 5-10.30pm Mon-Sat; JR Yamanote Line to Takadanobaba (main exit)

There are reasons why some people eat here every night, and why the sommelier, who started hanging around 23 years ago while still a student at Waseda, finally landed a job with owner Ide-san. Authenticity's part of it, but the charm of the owner probably clinches such unflagging loyalty. Easily the warmest cheap Italian joint in the city.

CHEAP EATS

BEN'S CAFE Map p280 Café ¥

☎ 3202-2445; 1-29-21 Takadanobaba, Shinjuku-ku; mains from ¥1000; 11.30am-11.30pm Sun-Thu, 11.30am-12.30am Fri & Sat; JR Yamanote Line to Takadanobaba (main exit)

Local students and expats come to Ben's to quell cravings for bagels or Belgian beer – or just to chill. The patio out front is a good place to sip on wine and watch life amble by on warm evenings. Ben's also hosts poetry readings and rotating art exhibitions by local artists, and it has wi-fi access.

KAO TAI Map p280 Thai ¥

☎ 3204-5806; 2-14-6 Takadanobaba, Shinjuku-ku; mains from ¥1000; 11.30am-2pm & 5-10pm; JR Yamanote Line to Takadanobaba (main exit)

From the bamboo-framed doorway leading downstairs to its snug dining room, Kao Tai feels like a warm slice of Southeast Asia. Most dishes are small-plate affairs, allowing you to sample and share while swigging a Singha. While not the most complicated Thai food around, the room's feel more than makes up for it. There's an English menu; best to book ahead.

IKEBUKURO

After an afternoon spent wandering around Ikebukuro, you'll have noticed that many of the area's cheaper eateries are jammed with young salarymen with a bit of time on their hands. Accordingly, many places are very cheap and rather uninspired. But there's no reason to suffer. Along with fabulous *yakitori* and Vietnamese food, you'll find a couple of restaurant 'theme parks' (opposite) in the neighbourhood, specialising in *rāmen* and *gyōza* (pork dumplings). As in most hubs in Tokyo, the trick to finding good food here is to distance yourself from the train tracks.

AKIYOSHI Map p280 Yakitori ¥¥

☎ 3982-0601; 3-30-4 Nishi-Ikebukuro, Toshima-ku; dishes ¥3000; 5-11pm; JR Yamanote Line to Ikebukuro (west exit)

If in the mood for *yakitori*, Akiyoshi is an approachable, ebullient place to partake. The open grill at centre stage ignites a festive, sociable space. The chefs work quickly to help move traffic along, but that doesn't mean you can't sit comfortably through several small courses and at least one conversation. Ordering is simple with the picture menu.

MALAYCHAN Map p280 Malaysian ¥¥

☎ 5391-7638; 3-22-6 Nishi-Ikebukuro, Toshima-ku; dishes ¥2000; 11am-2.30pm & 5-11pm Mon-Sat, 11am-11pm Sun; JR Yamanote Line to Ikebukuro (west or south exits)

With a sweet location next to a small park, Malaychan welcomes a steady stream of clientele who come back again and again for lunchtime doses of nasi goreng and roast duck. The menu covers an impressive breadth of culinary styles that comprise Malaysian cookery, from its Indonesian roots to its Chinese, additionally distinguishing itself by featuring certified halal food.

SAIGON Map p280 Vietnamese ¥

☎ 3989-0255; 3rd fl, 1-7-10 Higashi-Ikebukuro, Toshima-ku; mains from ¥750; 🕑 11.30am-2.30pm & 5-10.30pm Mon-Fri, 11.30am-10.30pm Sat & Sun; Ⓜ JR Yamanote Line to Ikebukuro (east exit)

Though not quite as far away as its namesake, Saigon isn't really on the way to anything unless you're shopping at Bic Camera (p187). If you're on this side of town, though, it's a lovely spot you'll want to look for above the sleazy peepshows and convenience stores. Viet-pop ballads set the mood for a peaceful lunch with iced artichoke tea.

SASASHŪ Map p280 Izakaya ¥¥¥

笹周; ☎ 3971-9363; 2-2-6 Ikebukuro, Toshima-ku; meals from ¥6000; 🕑 5-10pm Mon-Sat; Ⓜ Marunouchi Line to Ikebukuro (exit C5)

Sasashū's Japanese-style façade is easy to pick out between the modern concrete strip joints nearby. This relaxed *izakaya* is known for its highbrow sake selection (see p154) and its traditional hearth. Typical offerings on the menu are *kamonabe* (duck stew) and smoked salmon; Japanese skills are helpful here, but you can also point at what others are enjoying to order for yourself.

SUSHI KAZU Map p280 Sushi & Sashimi ¥¥

☎ 3590-4884; 2-10-8 Ikebukuro, Toshima-ku; dishes ¥3500; Ⓜ Marunouchi Line to Ikebukuro (exit C6) or JR Yamanote Line to Ikebukuro (west exit)

Off the main boulevards of west Ikebukuro, Sushi Kazu is a welcome, low-key place to take refuge from the neighbourhood hawkers, *pachinko* (vertical pinball-game) parlours and seedy bars. The sushi is served at the counter, where you can watch the chef as he slices, presses and arranges, or at one of the low tables that rest on tatami.

CHEAP EATS

MYUN Map p280 Vietnamese ¥

My Dung; ☎ 3985-8967; 2nd fl, 5-1-6 Nishi-Ikebukuro, Toshima-ku; lunch ¥500, mains from ¥1200; 🕑 11am-2pm & 5-11pm; Ⓜ Marunouchi Line to Ikebukuro (exit C2) or JR Yamanote Line to Ikebukuro (west exit)

It may not look like much either from the outside or in, but the proof is in the corn

RESTAURANT TOWNS & THEME PARKS

On the upper floors of most big department stores and on the basement floors of some large office buildings, you'll find what the Japanese call *resutoran-gai* (restaurant towns). Within the space of a few hundred metres, these places contain almost every major type of Japanese restaurant, plus a variety of Western favourites like Italian, French and the inevitable fast-food joints. Despite the sometimes featureless surroundings, the food quality at these spots is high, making them a better bet than many of the anonymous streetside *rāmen* (noodles in broth) or *kaiten-zushi* (conveyor-belt sushi restaurant) shops when you find yourself in unfamiliar neighbourhoods.

At lunch and dinner most eateries in *resutoran-gai* display their specials (or plastic food models) outside their entrances. Either way, they make ordering a snap.

Campier than restaurant towns are restaurant 'theme parks' which usually specialise in one kind of food, perfect for those moments when your cravings are particularly decisive. Try these foodie-themed destinations:

Daiba Little Hong Kong (Map p289; ☎ 3599-6500; 6th & 7th fl, Decks Tokyo Beach, Odaiba, Minato-ku; 🕑 11am-9pm; Ⓜ Yurikamome Line to Odaiba Kaihin-kōen, main exit) If the restaurant towns aren't kitschy enough for you, try this made-in-Japan plastic toy of Hong Kong.

Hikarichō Rāmen Meisakuza (Map p280; 1-14 Higashi-Ikebukuro, Toshima-ku; 🕑 11am-4am; Ⓜ JR Yamanote Line to Ikebukuro, east exit) Sample the diversity of *rāmen* in the regional specialities from Kyūshū to Hokkaidō, all on one block.

Ikebukuro Gyōza Stadium (Map p280; ☎ 5950-0765; 2nd fl, World Import Mart Bldg, 3-1-2 Higashi-Ikebukuro, Toshima-ku; admission ¥300; 🕑 10am-10pm; Ⓜ JR Yamanote Line to Ikebukuro, east exit) Here you'll find this gluttonous paradise of *gyōza* (pork dumplings) done 1001 ways, from regions all over China and Japan. Also see Sunshine City (p103).

tapioca pudding…and the Vietnamese curry, and the *bun* (rice noodles). Order from the picture menu, pour yourself some iced jasmine tea from the plastic jugs on the utilitarian tables and await a respectably good taste of Vietnam.

OOTOYA Map p280 Japanese ¥

☎ 3989-1555; 2nd fl, 1-17-6 Nishi-Ikebukuro, Toshima-ku; lunch sets from ¥570; 🕑 11am-11pm; Ⓜ JR Yamanote Line to Ikebukuro (west exit)

A notch above most budget chain restaurants, Ootoya specialises in *teishoku* (Japanese lunch sets) for cheap. Offering selections from grilled fish to *tonkatsu* to fried chicken, each set comes with rice, vegetables (like lotus root and pickled eggplant) and miso soup. This chain originated in Ikebukuro and remains great value. Check out the picture menu to order.

TONCHIN Map p280 Rāmen ¥

☎ 3987-8556; 2-6-2 Minami-Ikebukuro, Toshima-ku; dishes from ¥850; 🕑 11am-4am; Ⓜ JR Yamanote Line to Ikebukuro (east exit)

While hundreds of *rāmen* shops populate Ikebukuro, some are necessarily much better than others – not only for the complex, deep flavours of their broth or the tender chewiness of their noodles, but also for the warm and efficient feel of their shops that speaks quietly of their confidence and expertise. Try Tonchin to taste what this means.

EAST OF THE SUMIDA RIVER

There are lots of little neighbourhood spots in these eastern district, but the draw is to eat as the sumō wrestlers do, in Ryōgoku.

TOMOEGATA Map pp278-9 Nabe ¥¥

☎ 3632-5600; www.tomoegata.com in Japanese; 2-17-6 Ryōgoku, Sumida-ku; lunch ¥840-2100; Ⓜ JR Sōbu Line to Ryogoku (west exit)

Given the preponderance of sumō stables in Ryōgoku, it's only natural that you'd find restaurants serving the sumō wrestler's staple: *chanko nabe*. Recipes vary for this hearty stew, but count on beef, chicken, pork, fish and/or seasonal vegetables. Tomoegata has been serving it for generations. Go with a group, or eat it all by yourself if you want to become big like a wrestler.

ODAIBA

Eating in Odaiba should mean food with a view, so we've listed places with big windows overlooking the bay. If you're willing to empty your wallet, hit the top-end hotels for grand panoramas and high-style dinners. Those on more modest budgets can instead make an expedition to Odaiba for lunch or coffee at one of the perfectly fine spots at Decks Tokyo Beach (p188).

KHAZANA Map p289 Indian ¥¥

☎ 3599-6551; 5th fl, Decks Tokyo Beach, 1-6-1 Daiba, Minato-ku; lunch ¥800, mains from ¥1200; Ⓜ Yurikamome Line to Odaiba Kaihin-kōen (main exit)

From your seat in the warm, wood-floored dining room, ponder birds in flight over the bay through windows edged with arches. The curry is good and spicy – nice on one of Odaiba's many cool, windy days.

ŌSHIMA ENDOMAE-DOKORO
Map p289 Sushi & Sashimi ¥¥¥

☎ 5556-4808; 30th fl, Hotel Grand Pacific Le Meridien, 2-6-1 Daiba, Minato-ku; lunch/dinner ¥2500/10,000; Ⓜ Yurikamome Line to Daiba (south exit)

The 30th floor of the Meridien affords broad views of the cranes, lifts and skyscrapers on the opposite shore. How charming then at such a soaring height that this little spot, with its tiny counter and virtuosic sushi chefs, makes you feel like a bird in a very warm nest.

TSUKIJI TAMA SUSHI
Map p289 Sushi & Sashimi

☎ 3599-6556; 5th fl, Decks Tokyo Beach, 1-6-1 Daiba, Minato-ku; dishes ¥2000-4000; Ⓜ Yurikamome Line to Odaiba Kaihin-kōen (main exit)

Settle yourself near the windows and sip from a huge, earthy cup of green tea while you wait for your sushi, which will come immaculately presented and perfectly fresh. The menu also includes set meals and udon, if you prefer; either way, this is a pleasant corner from which to take in good Japanese food and bay views.

Entertainment

Entertainment

Tokyo is the entertainment capital of Japan, with events running the gamut from arthouse cinema to sumō. Not surprisingly, there are wonderful venues across the city that cater to very specific tastes, so whether you're in search of an ear-splitting live house or a side-splitting comedy club, you should find yourself in luck.

The one challenge you'll obviously come across is the language barrier. If your Japanese is rudimentary or nonexistent, some of the contemporary theatre and traditional storytelling forms might not feel terribly compelling. We've tried to be mindful of this and to point you to things that are local but accessible. One last word here – because of fierce competition, venues close and open at lightning speed in Tokyo. Unless you've seen a very current listing in one of the English dailies or weeklies, you should at the very least call to make sure the venue is still there and still open.

TOKYO FOR FREE

If you've been here for a few days, you've probably learned that yen spend quickly in the metropolis. To balance out your budget, which will be taxed by simple things such as cinema tickets, consider the many things to do that are completely free. These suggestions will cost no more than the train ticket to get to them.

For an idea of current goings-on, including some freebies, check the website of **Japan National Tourist Organization** (JNTO; www.jnto.go.jp).

Parks

Unlike Tokyo's gardens, most of Tokyo's parks are free (Shinjuku-gyōen is the big exception to this rule), and provide a welcome escape from the omnipresent concrete and urban sprawl. Just grab a *bentō* (boxed lunch) and/or some baked bread and you've got yourself a picnic. Good spots are **Kitanomaru-kōen** (p63), **Yoyogi-kōen** (p100) near Harajuku, **Ueno-kōen** (p81) in Ueno and **Hibiya-kōen** (p65) near Ginza.

Galleries

Most private galleries don't charge admission. Indeed, these galleries are often rented by individual artists who are delighted to help cultivate interest in their work. Ginza and Harajuku are the best places to hunt for them. Department store galleries (on upper floors) are another good bet; if these are not free, admission is often cheaper than a museum entry fee.

Temples & Shrines

Shrines are almost always free in Tokyo and most temples only charge to enter their *honden* (main hall). **Sensō-ji** (p85) in Asakusa and **Meiji-jingū** (p98) in Harajuku are two good places to start.

Company Showrooms

So they're really just another form of advertising, but some showrooms in Tokyo are like small museums and most have hands-on displays and test-drives – all are free. Auto enthusiasts will love **Toyota Mega Web** (p109) in Odaiba, and just about everyone will find something intriguing at the **Sony building** (p66) in Ginza. One floor is devoted to free video games. Other showrooms can be found in Ginza, Shinjuku and Harajuku/Aoyama.

Tsukiji Central Fish Market

Wander the world's biggest fish market (p75) and its great Tsukiji Outer Market (p76) for hours at no cost.

Skyscrapers

Several skyscrapers have free observation floors, eg **Tokyo Metropolitan Government Offices** (Tokyo Tochō; p101), **Shinjuku Sumitomo building** (p116) and **Tokyo Big Sight** (Tokyo International Exhibition Centre; p120).

Bookshops

Unlike some other countries, in Japan no one will object to your spending hours reading books and magazines on display in bookshops. There's even a word for the practice: *yomitachi* (a standing read). See Tokyo's Bookshops (p182) for listings.

WHERE TO FIND WHAT'S ON

Because of Tokyo's sizable expat community, there is loads of English-language information available about what's going on in town. Below are several options, many of which you can pick up around town in hard copy, usually at music stores or in international supermarkets.

Japan Times (www.japantimes.co.jp/entertainment.html) Comprehensive movie listings service, also available in the hard-copy newspaper.

Metropolis (http://metropolis.japantoday.com/default.asp) An excellent free resource that lists and reviews events, including contemporary film. Available in record stores and expat-frequented cafés and restaurants.

Tokyo Journal (www.tokyo.to) Has some useful listings in the Cityscope section that detail goings-on in Tokyo.

Tokyo Q (www.tokyoq.com) Run by long-time expats who adore Tokyo, *Tokyo Q* is an excellent place to catch glimpses of the city from the inside. Reviews and listings cover clubs and bars – colourful, thoughtfully crafted and discriminating. Many listings include fairly detailed maps.

Tokyo Weekender (www.weekender.co.jp) This is another expat publication with its fingers firmly on the city's pulse. It's available in hard copy at some hotels, international supermarkets and music stores around Tokyo.

TRADITIONAL THEATRE

Tokyo has one of the best, if not *the* best, traditional theatre scene in Japan. The Kabuki-za is splendid, as is the Kokuritsu Nō-gakudō (National Nō Theatre). You've probably already been warned, but keep in mind that *nō* (stylised Japanese dance-drama) performances in particular can feel like they're crawling at a snail's pace (see p24 for more information). You can generally get more from the experience if you do as the locals do and pack a lunch or snack. Believe it or not, it's even considered acceptable to doze (though not so to snore).

CERULEAN TOWER NŌ THEATRE Map p284

☎ 3476-3000; B2 fl, 26-1 Sakuragaokachō, Shibuya-ku; admission varies; Ⓡ JR Yamanote Line to Shibuya (south exit)

Performances in Japanese are held here in Tokyo's newest traditional theatre, situated discreetly in one of its most stunning hotels. Fairly intimate quarters make for close-ups of improvisational *nō* dances, while walls made of Japanese cypress contribute to the excellent acoustics. Purchase tickets at the **Cerulean Tower Tōkyū Hotel** (p201).

KABUKI-ZA Map pp290-1

☎ 5565-6000; Ginza; www.shochiku.co.jp/play/kabukiza/theater/index.html; 4-12-5 Ginza, Chūō-ku; tickets ¥2520-16,800; Ⓡ Hibiya or Toei Asakusa Line to Higashi-Ginza (exit 3)

Performances and times vary from month to month at Kabuki-za (p66), so check with the TIC (Tourist Information Center; p248) or the theatre for programme information. Be sure to rent a headset for blow-by-blow explanations in English, and pick up a *bentō* downstairs. A full kabuki performance (see p24) comprises three or four acts (usually from different plays) over an afternoon or an evening (typically 11.00am to 3.30pm or 4.30pm to 9pm), with long intervals between the acts. If four-plus hours sounds too long, you can purchase last-minute tickets for a single act, although seats are only on the highest balcony. Since some acts tend to be more popular than others, inquire ahead as to which to catch and arrive well in advance.

KANZE NŌ-GAKUDŌ Map p284

Kanze Nō Theatre; ☎ 3469-6241; 1-16-4 Shōtō, Shibuya-ku; tickets from ¥3000; Ⓡ JR Yamanote Line to Shibuya (Hachikō exit)

Kanze Nō-gakudō is one of Tokyo's most highly regarded *nō* troupes. By far the most exciting are the occasional outdoor night performances of Takigi Nō, where the masked actors are illuminated by huge burning torches. It's a transporting experience (and only a 15-minute walk from Shibuya Station).

KOKURITSU NŌ-GAKUDŌ Map p282

National Nō Theatre; ☎ 3423-1331; 4-18-1 Sendagaya, Shibuya-ku; tickets ¥2800-5600; Ⓡ JR Chūō Line to Sendagaya (west exit)

Built in the early 1980s as a public performance space, this theatre stages the traditional chants and dances *nō* is famous for,

TOP FIVE PERFORMANCE VENUES

- Aoyama Enkei Gekijō (right) A lovely round theatre nestled in the National Children's Castle.
- Bunkamura Theatre Cocoon (right) Hosts many experimental modern dance troupes of international renown.
- Kabuki-za (p145) This lovely building, whose façade is reminiscent of Edo Castle, is simply the best kabuki venue in the world.
- Kanze Nō-gakudō (p145) Kabuki, taken in while taking the fresh air in the torchlit night, is something else altogether.
- Session House (opposite) This small theatre hosts traditional, folk and modern dance. Check the notice board to find out what else is on in town.

as well as the *kyōgen* (short, lively comic farces) interludes that serve as cathartic comic relief. The stark legends and historical dramas unfold on an elegant cypress stage. Performances are held on weekends only.

TAKARAZUKA GEKIJŌ Map pp290-1

☎ 5251-2001; http://kageki.hankyu.co.jp/english/index.html; 1-1-3 Yūrakuchō, Chiyoda-ku; tickets from ¥3500; Ⓢ Chiyoda, Hibiya or Toei Mita Line to Hibiya (exits A5 & A13)

An all-female revue with a bloodline running back to 1914, Takarazuka Gekijō is one of those things that exposes Tokyo's knack for complexity. Though the performances of these musicals are in Japanese, English synopses are available. These days, performances are taken in by a mostly female audience that swoons over actresses dressed in drag.

CONTEMPORARY THEATRE

Tokyo has a lively contemporary theatre scene tucked away and often off the beaten track. Language can be a barrier, as most of the productions taking place in these alternative performance venues are in Japanese.

DIE PRATZE Map pp278-9

☎ 3235-7990; 2-12 Nishi-Gokenchō, Shinjuku-ku; Ⓢ Tōzai Line to Kagurazaka (exit 1)

Home to experimental theatre group OM-2, this small space features a variety of genres, from ballet to *butō* (contemporary dance style; p27) to experimental performance pieces. Die Pratze is northwest of the Imperial Palace, near Kagurazaka Station.

SUZUNARI THEATRE

☎ 3469-0511; admission varies; 1-45-15 Kitazawa, Setagaya-ku; Ⓢ Odakyū or Keiō Inokashira Line to Shimokitazawa (main exit)

A good bit of Japanese would be helpful in getting the gist of these underground theatre pieces. Like most avant-garde theatre, plays here tend towards experimental explorations of contemporary issues.

TOKYO INTERNATIONAL PLAYERS

☎ 090-6009-4171; www.tokyoplayers.org; adult/student or child ¥4000/2500

Since 1896, this theatre troupe has been performing plays in English; in the last few years, productions have included Steve Martin's *Picasso at the Lapin Agile* to the Oscar Wilde classic *The Importance of Being Earnest*. Shows run at various venues around Tokyo; check the website for the current schedule and detailed directions.

DANCE

Tokyo's dance scene is a mix of international and indigenous styles. At venues around the city you'll find all the Western forms – ballet, modern, jazz and experimental – in abundance. You may also be able to see *butō* in its home environment, if your trip happens to coincide with a performance.

AOYAMA ENKEI GEKIJŌ Map p284

Aoyama Round Theatre; ☎ 3797-5678; 5-31-1 Jingūmae, Shibuya-ku; admission varies; Ⓢ Chiyoda, Ginza or Hanzōmon Line to Omote-sandō (exit B2)

Found within the **National Children's Castle** (p96), this midsized round theatre stages musicals, ballet and modern dance. Though the theatre is lovely, performances tend toward the conservative. Because of the venue's location, many programmes are ideal for kids.

BUNKAMURA THEATRE COCOON

Map p284

☎ 3477-9999; www.bunkamura.co.jp/english; 2-24-1 Dōgenzaka, Shibuya-ku; admission varies; Ⓢ JR Yamanote Line to Shibuya (Hachikō exit)

This dance space in one of Tokyo's liveliest arts complexes (p97) shows occasional experimental works by international dance troupes. It has also been known to stage musical dramas, though these take place less frequently than dance programmes.

NEW NATIONAL THEATRE Map pp278-9

Shin Kokuritsu Gekijō; ☎ 5351-3011; www.nntt.jac.go.jp/english/index.html; 1-1-1 Honmachi, Shibuya-ku; admission varies; Ⓢ Toei Shinjuku Line to Hatsudai (Theatre exit)

Part of the New National Theatre's arts complex, the Playhouse and the Pit are performance venues for modern dance, with the latter hosting just about every international dance luminary who passes through. The Opera House programmes also feature the occasional ballet.

SESSION HOUSE Map pp278-9

☎ 3266-0461; 158 Yaraichō, Shinjuku-ku; admission varies; Ⓢ Tōzai Line to Kagurazaka (exit 1)

Most dance aficionados consider Session House one of the best traditional, folk and modern dance spaces in the city. The small theatre seats only 100 people, which means that all performances have an intimate feel to them. For news about what's on in the rest of the city, check the crowded notice board in the lobby.

SETAGAYA PUBLIC THEATRE

☎ 5432-1526; www.setagaya-ac.or.jp/sept; 4-1-1 Taishidō, Setagaya-ku; Ⓢ Tōkyū Denentoshi Line to Sangenjaya (Sangenjaya exit)

Though dedicated performances of *butō* are rarer these days since the closure of founding theatre Asbestoskan, you can sometimes catch *butō* and other performances of dance and experimental theatre at Theatre Tram, a part of Setagaya Public Theatre.

SPACE ZERO Map p282

☎ 3375-8741; B1 fl, 2-12-10 Yoyogi, Shinjuku-ku; admission varies; Ⓢ Toei Ōedo or Shinjuku Line to Shinjuku (exit 6)

This is a 550-seat, fine-art performance venue that happens to be located centrally in Shinjuku. Space Zero is host to contemporary dance performances and experimental theatre productions. You'll find it in the basement of the Zenrōsai Kaikan building.

CINEMAS

Tokyo cinemas show blockbuster movies in small spaces, while charging you a cool ¥1800 (on average). Shibuya, Shinjuku and Ginza all have major movie-houses that list screenings in either hard copy or online at **Japan Times** (www.japantimes.co.jp/entertainment.html). While they're easy to find, you may find the English-language films have already played in and disappeared from your hometown. Quirkier arthouse cinemas are harder to track down, so we've listed several following. Most independent films in English are not dampened by dubbing and some of the more avant-garde theatres show films you might not see anywhere else.

At larger theatres, getting seated is a free-for-all once the doors open, so it's a good idea to show up an hour before the film to

Posters at Shinjuku Station

shove your way to a decent seat. If you're catching a mainstream flick, the most stress-free theatres are **Virgin Toho Cinemas Roppongi Hills** (below) and **Yebisu Garden Cinema** (right), which each have their own seating systems.

CINE AMUSE EAST/WEST Map p284

☎ 3496-2888; 4th fl, 2-23-12 Dōgenzaka, Shibuya-ku; JR Yamanote Line to Shibuya (Hachikō exit)

This well-known arthouse standby screens Japanese and foreign classics, as well as new independent releases. Coffee, beer and snacks are available at the small café in the lobby. This is a great place to take a break from Shibuya's hectic pace while taking in a matinée.

CINEMA RISE Map p284

☎ 3464-0051; 13-17 Udagawachō, Shibuya; JR Yamanote Line to Shibuya (Hachikō exit)

Located near the Parco conglomeration north of Shibuya Station, Cinema Rise screens independent international cinema, but very few indie Japanese films. Just around the corner is an even more avant-garde space called **Rise X** (☎ 3464-8555), a tiny offshoot of Cinema Rise that screens mostly Japanese digital films.

EUROSPACE Map p284

☎ 3461-0211; 1-5 Maruyamachō, Shibuya-ku; JR Yamanote Line to Shibuya (Hachikō exit)

In its new digs on the far side of Love Hotel Hill, the focus at this fine theatre remains unwaveringly on small European films not shown elsewhere in town. Eurospace also occasionally hosts documentary or feature-film festivals, which will be listed in the major English-language weeklies; and sometimes screens late shows.

VIRGIN TOHO CINEMAS ROPPONGI HILLS Map p286

☎ 5775-6090; www.tohotheater.jp/theater/roppongi/index.html; 6-10-2 Roppongi, Minato-ku; adult ¥1800-3000, child ¥1000, 1st day of month ¥1000, women on Wed ¥1000; 10am-midnight Sun-Wed, 10am-5am Thu-Sat; Hibiya or Toei Ōedo Line to Roppongi (Roppongi Hills exit)

Virgin's nine-screen multiplex has the biggest screen in Japan, as well as luxurious reclining seats and Internet booking up to two days in advance for reserved seats. This state-of-the-art theatre also holds all-night screenings on nights before holidays.

WASEDA SHOCHIKU Map p280

☎ 3200-8968; 1-5-16 Takadanobaba, Shinjuku-ku; tickets ¥1800; JR Yamanote Line to Takadanobaba (main exit)

Waseda Shochiku softens the blow by screening two films for the price you'd normally pay to see one. A favourite among students and cash-strapped expats, the bills normally feature second-run double features, some of an artsy bent.

YEBISU GARDEN CINEMA Map p288

☎ 5420-6161; Yebisu Garden Place, 4-20-2 Ebisu, Shibuya-ku; adult/child ¥1800/1000, 1st day of month ¥1000; 10am-11pm; JR Yamanote Line to Ebisu (east exit, then Skywalk)

This small, comfortable movie house is at the far end of Yebisu Garden Place and screens foreign independent films, many of them in English. Tickets are numbered as they are sold and theatre-goers are called to screenings as their numbers come up, preventing competition for seats.

COMEDY

Though expat stand-up comics do have their limitations in terms of content (that wacky culture shock), they can also provide insight into the quirks, kinks and frustrations of living in this incredibly complex place. In addition to the few English comedy troupes that make the rounds of town, Asakusa Engei Hall is one venue that puts on *rakugo* performances (Edo-era comic monologue with killer punch lines). Though these comic storytelling shows will invariably be in Japanese, the chance for you to see the costume design and the subtle use of simple props can themselves be rewarding.

ASAKUSA ENGEI HALL Map pp296-7

☎ 3841-6545; 1-43-12 Asakusa, Taitō-ku; adult/student/child ¥2500/2000/1100; Ginza Line to Tawaramachi (exit 3)

Asakusa Engei Hall hosts traditional *rakugo*, with all performances conducted in Japanese. The linguistic confusion is mitigated by lively facial expressions and traditional props (performers use only a hand towel and a folding fan), which help translate comic takes on universal human experiences.

TOKYO COMEDY STORE

www.tokyocomedy.com

You probably know the type – the class clown, the merry exhibitionist – who joins this kind of comedy troupe. Basically, this is a funny bunch of expatriated amateurs and professionals doing their shtick. Shows take place at various venues; check the website for current schedules.

TOKYO CYNICS

The idiosyncrasies of Tokyo's expat comics are sometimes funny and always free. The show goes on primarily at the **Fiddler** (p152) and **Footnik** (p153).

CLUBBING

The economy comes and goes, dips and dives, but the clubs groove on. You'll find lots of techno and disco and house in the city, with most of the music starting when doors open usually around 8pm – you won't really want to arrive until 10pm or so, when the volume increases and the floor fills. Many clubs claim they close at midnight (they're legally required to tell you so), but don't buy it. At most places, you can dance until dawn. Your biggest concern is when the trains stop and start running.

AGEHA

☎ 5534-1515; www.ageha.com; 2-2-10 Shin-Kiba, Kōtō-ku; 🕑 11pm-5am Thu-Sat; admission ¥4000; Ⓜ Yūrakuchō Line to Shin-Kiba (main exit)

This gigantic club on the waterside rivals any you'd find in LA or Ibiza. Mostly international DJs appear here, with Japanese DJs filling out the mix. Counterbalancing the thumping dance floors are lounge spaces and a little pool area. Free buses run to the club every half hour from the east side of Shibuya Station on Roppongi-dōri; bring photo ID.

CLUB 328 Map p286

☎ 3401-4968; B1 fl, 3-24-20 Nishi-Azabu, Minato-ku; admission ¥2000-2500; 🕑 8pm-5am; Ⓜ Hibiya or Toei Ōedo Line to Roppongi (exit 1)

DJs at San-ni-pa (aka San-ni-hachi) spin a quality mix, from funk to reggae to R&B. With its refreshing un-Roppongi feel and a cool crowd of Japanese and *gaijin* (foreigners), 328 is a fabulous place to boogie 'til the break of dawn. Two drinks are included in the cover charge.

CLUB ASIA Map p284

☎ 5458-1996; 1-8 Maruyamachō, Shibuya-ku; admission around ¥2500; 🕑 11pm-5am; Ⓜ JR Yamanote Line to Shibuya (Hachikō exit)

This massive club is worth a visit if you're on the younger end of twentysomething. Events here are usually jam-packed every night. Occasionally the club hosts some of Tokyo's bigger DJ events and hip-hop acts. There's also a good restaurant serving Southeast Asian food, if you need more fuel to burn on the dance floor.

LEXINGTON QUEEN Map p286

☎ 3401-1661; B1 fl, 3-13-14 Roppongi, Minato-ku; admission from ¥2000; 🕑 8pm-5am; Ⓜ Hibiya or Toei Ōedo Line to Roppongi (exit 3)

The Lex was one of Roppongi's first discos and is still the place where every visiting celebrity ends up. The cover here starts at around ¥2000 unless you've had your visage on the front of *Vogue* or *Rolling Stone*. But, even noncelebrities get a free drink with admission. Things only start heating up after midnight.

RUBY ROOM Map p284

☎ 3780-3022; www.moderndining.com/RubyRoom/index.shtml; 2nd fl, 2-25-17 Dōgenzaka, Shibuya-ku; admission ¥1500; 🕑 9pm-late; Ⓜ JR Yamanote Line to Shibuya (Hachikō exit)

This cool, sparkly gem of a cocktail lounge is on a hill behind the Shibuya 109 building. With both DJed and live music, the Ruby Room is an appealing spot for older kids hanging in Shibuya. The cover includes one drink, but if you dine downstairs at **Sonoma** (p135), admission is free.

TOP FIVE CLUBS

- Ageha (left) Glam, gigantic Ageha is worth the haul to Shin-Kiba for a big night of clubbing on the waterfront.
- Club 328 (left) In Nishi-Azabu, the best balance of *gaijin* (foreigners) and locals, and a good mix of beats.
- Lexington Queen (above) This queen's seen better days, but she's still got a reliable pulse in Roppongi.
- Ruby Room (above) Sophisticated in the most fun, relaxed way, this Shibuya spot mostly brings in international DJs.
- Space Lab Yellow (p150) Subterranean, cool, with several dance floors and stellar sound.

SALSA CARIBE Map p286

☎ 3746-0244; 2nd fl, 5-3-4 Roppongi, Minato-ku; admission Fri & Sat ¥1500; 7pm-5am Sun-Thu, 7pm-7am Fri & Sat; Hibiya or Toei Ōedo Line to Roppongi (exit 3)

The narrow bar Salsa Caribe has long been a gathering place for an internationally diverse crowd that usually arrives at midnight and leaves in the early hours of the morning – only after every man has danced with almost every woman in the room. On weekends, the room can feel like rush hour on the subway though probably more festive.

SALSA SUDADA Map p286

☎ 5474-8806; 3rd fl, 7-13-8 Roppongi, Minato-ku; admission Fri & Sat ¥1500; 6pm-6am; Hibiya or Toei Ōedo Line to Roppongi (exit 4)

Tokyo's sizable population of Peruvian and Colombian workers, many of whom grind away at factories in Kawasaki and Yokohama, come here to salsa and merengue, as do many salsa-mad locals. If you don't know how to dance, they'll teach you (lessons held nightly). On weekends, the room is a mad, joyful mass of hot, hip-shaking humanity.

SPACE LAB YELLOW Map p286

☎ 3479-0690; B1 & B2 fls, 1-10-11 Nishi-Azabu, Minato-ku; admission ¥2000-3500; 8.30pm-late; Hibiya & Toei Ōedo Line to Roppongi (exit 2)

Located by Nishi-Azabu crossing, Yellow spins everything from house to acid jazz, Brazilian samba to techno. Foreign DJs are sometimes spotlighted; regardless of who it is, the sound is always excellent. Look for the entrance to this inky basement space next to the coin parking lot.

VANILLA Map p286

☎ 3401-6200; www.clubvanilla.com; 7-14-30 Roppongi, Minato-ku; admission from ¥1500; 7pm-late; Hibiya or Toei Ōedo Line to Roppongi (exits 2 & 4)

Attracting a mostly Japanese clientele, Vanilla attracts fewer drunken *gaijin* kooks than nearby clubs. Three floors of dance space are filled with different beats and crowds of peeps. It's at the end of a small alley off of Roppongi-dōri, close to Roppongi crossing.

WOMB Map p284

☎ 5459-0039; www.womb.co.jp; 2-16 Maruyamachō, Shibuya-ku; admission ¥1500-4000; 8pm-late; JR Yamanote Line to Shibuya (Hachikō exit)

'Oomu' (as pronounced in Japanese) is all about house, techno and drum 'n' bass. All four floors get jammed on weekends. Bring a flyer and they'll knock ¥500 to ¥1000 off the cover – check around Shibuya music shops beforehand, or print one from Womb's website. Picture ID required at the door.

BARS

A lot of heavy drinking goes on in Tokyo, something you will realise very quickly if you happen to hop on any train after 10pm. And while it's true that you may need to look out for the occasional tippler who will pass out or throw up on the station platform, amazingly, any form of violence is quite rare.

Not surprisingly, all that drinking makes for a lot of bars. Roppongi, which has been the *gaijin* bar capital of Tokyo for years, probably has the lion's share per square metre, though Shinjuku could give it a run for its money. Quieter but excellent watering holes can be found in less-central neighbourhoods such as Harajuku, Aoyama, and Nishi-Azabu.

For practicality's sake, we've noted when cover charges are applicable, though even places that don't normally charge an entrance fee may do so when hosting a special event, like live music. Most bars in the city officially claim to be open from 5pm or 6pm until midnight, though many stay open until late becomes early again. Those we've listed stay open past the official witching hour.

ADVOCATES BAR Map p282

☎ 3358-8638; B1 fl, 2-18-1 Shinjuku, Shinjuku-ku; 8pm-4am; Marunouchi or Toei Shinjuku Line to Shinjuku-sanchōme (exits C7 & C8)

This bar is so small that as the crowd magically expands during the course of an evening, it becomes more like a block party and takes to the streets. Advocates welcomes people of all genders, identities and nationalities.

DRINKS WITH A VIEW

One of the best methods to decompress from pounding the pavement all day is to rise to a different atmosphere. Savour spectacular views while sipping a vodka martini at one of the following bars with views.

Aurora Lounge (Map p282; ☎ 3344-0111; 45th fl, 2-2-1 Nishi-Shinjuku, Shinjuku-ku; 🕑 11.30am-11.30pm; Ⓜ Toei Ōedo Line to Tochōmae, exit B1) In west Shinjuku, the stately Aurora Lounge, which is perched 150m up in the **Keiō Plaza Hotel** (p203), offers great views and drinks (from ¥1100). On the same floor, the crisp, elegant **Sky Bar Polestar** (Map p282; ☎ 3344-0111; 45th fl, 2-2-1 Nishi-Shinjuku, Shinjuku-ku; 🕑 5-11.30pm Mon-Sat, 4-11.30pm Sun & public holidays; Ⓜ Toei Ōedo Line to Tochōmae, exit B1) is built for gazing out over the city, with each seat facing the windows. Drinks start at ¥1500.

Bello Visto (Map p284; ☎ 3476-3000; 40th fl, 26-1 Sakuragaokachō, Shibuya-ku; 🕑 4pm-midnight Mon-Fri, 3pm-midnight Sat, Sun & public holidays; Ⓜ JR Yamanote Line to Shibuya, south exit) The Cerulean Tower's 40th floor eyrie keeps the interior lights dim so that you can see the lights on the far horizon. The 95-seat capacity ensures the atmosphere is always intimate. Cocktails and wine start at ¥1155.

New York Bar (Map p282; ☎ 5322-1234; 52nd fl, 3-7-1-2 Nishi-Shinjuku, Shinjuku-ku; 🕑 5pm-midnight Sun-Wed, 5pm-1am Thu-Sat; Ⓜ Toei Ōedo Line to Tochōmae, exit A4) You may not be lodging at the Park Hyatt, but that doesn't mean you can't ascend to the 52nd floor to swoon over stunning views of Mt Fuji and the city below. There's a cover charge of ¥2000 after 8pm.

Top of Akasaka (Map pp294–5; ☎ 3234-1111; 40th fl, 1-2 Kioi-chō, Chiyoda-ku; 🕑 5pm-2am Mon-Fri, noon-2am Sat; Ⓜ Ginza & Marunouchi Lines to Akasaka-mitsuke, exit 7, or Hanzōmon, Namboku & Yūrakuchō Lines to Nagatachō, exits 5, 7 & 9) If you're planning an intergalactic rendezvous, this is the place. Like the rest of the **Akasaka Prince Hotel** (p198), the purple-and-pink 40th-floor cocktail lounge would fit seamlessly onto a *Star Trek* set. Drinks start at ¥1300.

AGAVE Map p286

☎ 3497-0229; B1 fl, 7-15-10 Roppongi, Minato-ku; 🕑 6.30pm-2am Mon-Fri, 6.30pm-4am Sat; Ⓜ Hibiya or Toei Ōedo Line to Roppongi (exit 2)

Rawhide chairs, *cruzas de rosas* (crosses decorated with roses) and tequila shots for the willing make Agave a good place for a long night in search of the sacred worm. Luckily, this amiable spot is more about savouring the subtleties of its 400-plus varieties of tequila rather than tossing back shots of Cuervo.

ARTY FARTY Map p282

☎ 5362-9720; www.arty-farty.net; 2nd fl, 2-11-7 Shinjuku, Shinjuku-ku; 🕑 5pm-5am Mon-Sat, 4pm-5am Sun; Ⓜ Marunouchi or Toei Shinjuku Line to Shinjuku-sanchōme (exits C7 & C8)

This bar for boys and the guys who love them has been the gateway to Tokyo's gay neighbourhood, Ni-chōme, for many a man and many a moon. Women are allowed only on Sundays and only with gay male friends; exceptions are rarely made.

AUX AMIS DES VINS Map pp290-1

☎ 3567-4120; 2-5-6 Ginza, Chūō-ku; 🕑 5.30pm-2am Mon-Fri, noon-midnight Sat; Ⓜ Yūrakuchō Line to Ginza-itchōme (exits 5 & 8)

Even when it snows, the plastic tarp comes down and good wine is drunk alleyside. The enclosed upstairs seating area is warm and informal, and you can order snacks to go with your wine, or full prix-fixe dinners. A solid selection of wine comes by the glass (¥800) or by the bottle.

BAR PLASTIC MODEL Map p282

☎ 5273-8441; 1-1-10 Kabukichō, Shinjuku-ku; 🕑 8pm-5am Mon-Sat, 6pm-midnight Sun; Ⓜ Marunouchi or Toei Shinjuku Line to Shinjuku-sanchōme (exit B5)

It's true that in the last few years construction has started around Golden Gai, but some of those hammers are wielded by a new generation of iconoclastic bar masters rather than, as previously feared, a major developer. Bar Plastic Model is one of the new joints, with an '80s soundtrack and decorated with *tchotchkes* (knick-knacks) c 1980.

BOBBY'S BAR Map p280

☎ 3980-8875; 3rd fl, 1-18-10 Ikebukuro, Toshima-ku; 🕑 from 6pm Mon-Thu, from 7pm Fri & Sat; Ⓜ JR Yamanote Line to Ikebukuro (west exit)

One of Tokyo's longest-standing and best-known *gaijin* bars, perfect for those in need of a warm barstool, a dartboard and reasonably priced drinks (from ¥500). The crowd here is always international – a good mix of long-time expats and travellers.

BON'S Map p282

☎ 3209-6334; 1-1-10 Kabukichō, Shinjuku-ku; admission ¥500; 🕑 7pm-5am; Ⓜ Marunouchi or Toei Shinjuku Line to Shinjuku-sanchōme (exit B5)

There's a sign reading 'American Bar' out front, but Bon's is about as American as *anko* (azuki bean paste). Look for this cosy dive on the Golden Gai's (p102) southeast corner, next to the police box. It's one of the few bars in the neighbourhood that will accommodate the odd nonregular patron.

BUL-LET'S Map p286

☎ 3401-4844; www.bul-lets.com; B1 fl, 1-7-11 Nishi-Azabu, Minato-ku; admission ¥2000; 🕑 from around 6pm; Ⓜ Hibiya or Toei Ōedo Line to Roppongi (exit 2)

This mellow basement space plays worldwide trance and ambient sounds for barefoot patrons. Mattresses in the middle of the floor provide refuge from the madding crowd, but don't get the wrong idea – it's not always tranquillity and deadbeats. You can also groove on to live-wire electronica and experimental rhythms.

CLUBHOUSE Map p282

☎ 3359-7785; www.clubhouse-tokyo.jp; 3rd fl, 3-7-3 Shinjuku, Shinjuku-ku; 🕑 from 5pm Mon-Fri, from 3pm Sat & Sun; Ⓜ Marunouchi or Toei Shinjuku Line to Shinjuku-sanchōme (exit C3)

This clubhouse looks like the kind of wood-trimmed beer bar you'd find at any ski lodge, and it's a magnet for Tokyo's diehard rugby fans. Its comfortable, rugged interior is a friendly place to settle in for one of the fine imported or domestic beers and whatever game's on the telly.

DEN AQUAROOM Map p284

☎ 5778-2090; B1 fl, 5-13-3 Minami-Aoyama, Minato-ku; admission ¥500-1000; 🕑 6pm-2am Mon-Thu, 6pm-4am Fri, 6-11pm; Ⓜ Chiyoda, Ginza or Hanzōmon Line to Omote-sandō (exit B1)

Darting fish within the walls of immaculate blue aquariums make a visual counterpoint to the bop of jazz basslines. But even prettier than the dark décor is the chic clientele hanging out here for the evening. Chill with a fruity cocktail in this velvety lounge and enjoy the view.

DUBLINERS Map p282

☎ 3352-6606; 2nd fl, Lion Beer Hall Bldg, 3-28-9 Shinjuku, Shinjuku-ku; 🕑 noon-1am Mon-Sat, noon-11pm Sun; Ⓜ JR Yamanote Line to Shinjuku (east exit)

The strains of an old Irish tune may meet you at the door. Live music, good beer and a warm break from Tokyo's smooth, cool rhythm have made this one of the city's most frequented international watering holes. Pub grub includes a few Irish standards in portions that are larger than normal for Tokyo. There's a second branch in **Ikebukuro** (Map p280).

FIDDLER Map p280

☎ 3204-2698; www.thefiddler.com; B1 fl, 2-1-2 Takadanobaba, Shinjuku-ku; 🕑 from 6pm; Ⓜ JR Yamanote Line to Takadanobaba (main exit)

As close to a real British pub as you'll get this side of London, this spot is completely relaxed. Mostly foreign bands play here some nights with no cover charge and comedy troupes lighten things up a bit every second Tuesday.

FOOTNIK Map p288

☎ **5795-0144; www.footnik.net; 1-11-2 Ebisu, Shibuya-ku; 11.30am-1am Mon-Fri, 3pm-1am Sat & Sun; JR Yamanote Line to Ebisu (east exit)**
Cold pints cost only ¥700, and the big-screen TVs broadcast – what else? – footy (er, soccer) for the footniks. Find this friendly pub downstairs from **Good Day Books** (p182), probably the best secondhand English-language bookshop in town.

GARAM Map p282

☎ **3205-8668; www17.big.or.jp/~kamal; 7th fl, 1-16-6 Kabukichō, Shinjuku-ku; admission from ¥1500; 8pm-5am; JR Yamanote Line to Shinjuku (east exit)**
Garam is a cool little reggae club with a friendly owner and no Rasta poseurs. The house DJ spins a mix of dub, hip-hop and roots reggae, but guest DJs also make appearances. The cover includes one drink.

GAS PANIC Map p286

☎ **3405-0633; www.gaspanic.co.jp; 2nd & 3rd fls, 3-15-24 Roppongi, Minato-ku; 6pm-5am; Hibiya or Toei Ōedo Line to Roppongi (exit 3)**
Gas Panic has been split into three *gaijin* bars, forming one of Roppongi's rowdier cul-de-sacs. They're cheap places to drink, but predictably, this tends to attract unpredictable yahoos. Its policy is that you can't stay unless you're holding a drink – and it means it. Look for the seizure-inducing neon.

HOBGOBLIN Map pp290-1

☎ **6229-2636; www.hobgoblin-tokyo.com; 1st fl, 2-13-19 Akasaka, Minato-ku; 11am-2pm & 5pm-1am Mon-Fri, 5pm-1am Sat; Chiyoda Line to Akasaka (exit 2), Ginza & Namboku Lines to Tameike-sannō (exit 9)**
Far better than your average Britpub replica, Akasaka's Hobgoblin is run by an Oxfordshire brewery. It serves good pub fare, like toad in the hole, with excellent microbrews. You'll find this Hobgoblin lurking in the basement of the building next to the clearly marked Marugen 23 building.

HUB PUB Map p284

☎ **3770-4524; 25-9 Udagawachō, Shibuya-ku; noon-midnight Sun-Thu, noon-2am Fri & Sat; JR Yamanote Line to Shibuya (Hachikō exit)**
A generally English ambience, pub food and a decent selection of beers attract a mixed crowd of 20-somethings, especially on weekends. The Hub has branches all over the city, though this is probably the most comfortable of the lot.

INSOMNIA 2 Map p284

☎ **3476-2735; B1 fl, 26-5 Udagawachō, Shibuya-ku; 6pm-5am; JR Yamanote Line to Shibuya (Hachikō exit)**
Insomnia 2 is that rare Shibuya find: a bar for grown-ups. Good food, low music and a cosy, mirrored red interior make it the kind of place to come when you're in the mood for conversation. The kitchen's open late, and the oddly eyeball-esque mirrored wall behind the bar will induce insomnia if you're not already feeling it.

KINSWOMYN Map p282

☎ **3354-8720; 3rd fl, 2-15-10 Shinjuku, Shinjuku-ku; 8pm-4am Wed-Mon; Marunouchi or Toei Shinjuku Line to Shinjuku-sanchōme (exit C8)**
Since women are excluded from many of the boy-bars in Ni-chōme, the sisters decided to do it for themselves. This girls-only spot is welcoming and comfortable, and is run by a lesbian activist. English is spoken here, making it a perfect stop for visitors.

LA JETÉE Map p282

☎ **3208-9645; 1-1-8 Kabukichō, Shinjuku-ku; 7pm-late Mon-Sat Marunouchi or Toei Shinjuku Line to Shinjuku-sanchōme (exit B5)**
Kawai-san, the proprietor of this Golden Gai bar, knows more about film (especially that of Chris Marker) than most of us ever will. No English is spoken here, though you're more than welcome to practise your rusty Français. Unlike many Golden Gai establishments, this one is amenable to foreign visitors.

LAS CHICAS Map p284

☎ **3407-6865; 5-47-6 Jingūmae, Shibuya-ku; 11am-11pm Sun-Thu, 11am-11.30pm Fri & Sat; Chiyoda, Ginza or Hanzōmon Line to Omote-sandō (exit B2)**
Yes, it's also a restaurant (p137) and one of Harajuku's core art spaces. But that doesn't

mean you can't come here just to hang out in the bar area, which is especially comfortable – the kind of place you want to sit and sip for hours. The crowd here is as eclectic as the mostly Australian staff is eccentric.

LION BEER HALL Map pp290-1

☎ 3571-2590; 7-9-20 Ginza, Chūō-ku; 11.30am-11pm; Ginza, Hibiya or Marunouchi Line to Ginza (exits A2 & A3)

What luck. An almost-Bavarian beer hall smack in the middle of the otherwise ritzy, retail-crazed Ginza. Good pub food and a lovely 1930s mural on the wall only add to the atmosphere on weekend nights, which have been known to erupt into song.

MOTOWN HOUSE 1 & 2 Map p286

☎ 5474-4605; www.motownhouse.com; 2nd fl, 3-11-5 Roppongi, Minato-ku; 6pm-5am Hibiya or Toei Ōedo Line to Roppongi (exit 3)

The crass may call it 'ho town', but on the pick-up front it's no worse (or better?) than its neighbours, and since it expanded to two venues, it can actually be quite relaxed. Drinks start at ¥800. Funk, soul, R&B and hip-hop dominate here, of course. Requests are gladly taken.

OH GOD Map p284

☎ 3406-3206; B1 fl, 6-7-18 Jingūmae, Shibuya-ku; 6pm-6am; Chiyoda to Meiji-jingūmae (exit 4)

It's been trucking for years and miraculously still is; nightly movie screenings and pool tables do the trick. Quite a way from the main streets, the bar can be difficult to find: from Meiji-jingūmae Station, head southeast down Omote-sandō and take the first lane on the right after Meiji-dōri. Oh God is in the building at the end of the lane.

PADDY FOLEY'S Map p286

☎ 3423-2250; www.paddyfoleystokyo.com; B1 fl, 5-5-1 Roppongi, Minato-ku; noon-2am; Hibiya or Toei Ōedo Line to Roppongi (exit 3)

Happy-hour pints of Guinness at ¥750 and the relatively early opening time make this awesome Irish pub a favourite stop for drinks after the weekday grind. It's a popular place with expats, and the friendly Japanese staff and good Irish beer packs the place to the rafters on weekends.

PINK COW Map p284

☎ 3406-5597; www.thepinkcow.com; B1 fl, 1-3-18 Shibuya, Shibuya-ku; 5pm-late, Tue-Sun; Chiyoda, Ginza or Hanzōmon Line to Omote-sandō (exit B2)

With its animal-print décor, rotating display of local artwork and terrific all-you-can-eat buffet (¥2625) every Friday and Saturday, the Pink Cow is a funky, friendly place to hang out. Also host to stitch-and-bitch evenings, writers' salons and indie film screenings, it's a good bet if you seek some artistic stimulation. Check the website for directions and events.

PROPAGANDA Map p286

☎ 3423-0988; 2nd fl, 3-14-9 Roppongi, Minato-ku; 6pm-dawn Mon-Sat; Hibiya or Toei Ōedo Line to Roppongi (exit 3)

A shot bar calling itself Propaganda couldn't possibly take itself too seriously, and it doesn't. Happy hour (6pm to 9pm) specials cost around ¥400, and it's sort of a pick-up scene if this is on your agenda. Look for the technicolour Rosie the Riveter on the sign upstairs.

SASASHŪ Map p280

笹周; ☎ 3971-9363; 2-2-6 Ikebukuro, Toshima-ku; meals from ¥6000; 5-10pm Mon-Sat; Marunouchi Line to Ikebukuro (exit C5)

The proprietor here is famous for having been a kamikaze pilot whose number was just about up when the war ended. To celebrate his good fortune in evading an irrevocable nose dive, he has dedicated himself to knowing all there is to know about sake, making Sasashū a favourite of curmudgeonly connoisseurs and those seeking a dignified *izakaya* (Japanese pub/eatery) experience (p141).

SPACE PUNCH Map p288

☎ 3496-2484; 8pm-3am; 1-13-5 Ebisu-nishi, Shibuya-ku; 8pm-3am Mon-Sat; JR Yamanote Line to Ebisu (west exit)

Orange, white and lit all over, this view to the future is located up the street from Ebisu-jinja, a weathered shrine that is a vision of Tokyo's sturdy past. Look out for the action figures in the blue-lit window of Sand the televisions beaming out across the hazy, mirrored surface of the bar.

(Continued on page 163)

1 *Commes des Garçons (p184), Omote-sandō* **2** *Plaza of Tokyo Metropolitan Government Offices (p101), Shinjuku* **3** *Japanese girls in cos-play (p14)*

1 *Digital screen, Shibuya (p96)* **2** *Tokyo Kokuritsu Hakubutsukan (Tokyo National Museum; p80) Ueno* **3** *Chopsticks for sale* **4** *Ginza Station*

-jingū (p98), Omote-
2 Games arcade
ō wrestlers (p172),
ku Kokugikan,
a-ku

1 *Manga (comic) on sub*
2 *Manga cartoon charac*
(p29) **3** *Roadside manga*

1 Gas Panic (p153), Roppongi
2 Absinthe and champagne
3 Karaoke venue, Kabukichō (p102), Shinjuku
4 Roppongi (p92)

1 *Chingodō-ji (p84), Asc*
2 *Fish in pond, Sensō-ji*
Asakusa **3** *Higashi-gyōe*
(Imperial Palace East Gc
p62), Imperial Palace **4**
kōen (p100), Omote-sar
5 *Class photo, Nijū-bash*
Imperial Palace

2
3

1 *Fans for sale* **2** *Buddh*
statue, Sensō-ji (p85), A
3 *Entrance to tradition*
restaurant, Asakusa (p1

(Continued from page 154)

TOKYO APARTMENT CAFÉ Map p284
☎ 3401-4101; 1-11-11 Jingūmae, Shibuya-ku; 11am-3am; Chiyoda Line to Meiji-jingūmae (exit 1)
This subterranean room with a view doubles as a cool daytime coffee house and eatery. At night, the atmosphere goes a shade hipper and cocktails are served until closing. This is a good place to hole up for the evening if you're out for the night on Omote-sandō, which otherwise shuts its doors pretty early.

TOKYO SPORTS CAFÉ Map p286
☎ 3404-3675; www.tokyo-sportscafe.com; 7-15-31 Roppongi, Minato-ku; 6pm-5am Mon-Sat; Hibiya or Toei Ōedo Line to Roppongi (exit 4)
With Kilkenny beer on tap, a pool table and a talking computerised alcohol tester, this friendly sports bar is the obvious choice for cheering on your favourite team. Sports-wise, it's more Rotherham United than Chicago Bulls, and many events here are broadcast live. By the early morning, just before train service kicks in, it can get quite rowdy.

WHAT THE DICKENS Map p288
☎ 3780-2099; 4th fl, 1-13-3 Ebisu-Nishi, Shibuya-ku; 5pm-1am Tue & Wed, 5pm-2am Thu-Sat, 3pm-midnight Sun; Hibiya Line to Ebisu (exit 2) or JR Yamanote Line to Ebisu (west exit)
What the Dickens occupies the 4th floor of the Roob building, whose outstanding façade looks as if it's finished with a layer of mud, and adorned with the mirrored replica of a hummingbird. The beer and pub grub are up to snuff, and good live music and the occasional poetry reading keep things rolling, if not necessarily rockin'.

BEER HALLS & BEER GARDENS

A way around seasonal humidity and summer temperatures in July/August is to head to one of Tokyo's many beer halls and beer gardens. Most offer some kind of outdoor seating and an array of salty, tasty beer food.

ANA Hotel Beer Garden (ANA Hotel Tokyo; Map pp290–1; ☎ 3505-1111; 1-12-33 Akasaka, Minato-ku; 6-9.30pm Jul-Sep; Ginza Line to Tameike-sannō,exit 13, or Namboku Line to Roppongi-itchōme, exit 3) During the dog days of summer, the ANA serves up cold beer and hot barbecue.

Lion Beer Hall (p154) An occasionally rowdy 1930s beer hall smack in the middle of Ginza's chichi shopping arcade. Unfortunately, there's no outdoor seating.

Shibuya Tōkyū Honten (Map p284; ☎ 3477-3111; 2-24-1 Dōgenzaka, Shibuya-ku; 5-9.30pm) *Yaki-niku* (Korean barbecue) and beer on the roof of the Tōkyū department store.

OPERA

In Tokyo, opera companies don't own the venues where they perform. Its three major companies, Fujiwara Opera, Nihon Opera Kyokai and Nikkai Opera perform around the city, most often at the **New National Theatre** (p147). Check for information at www.operajaponica.org/tokyocompanies.htm. Or check out the English listings services (p145) for performance times and venue locations.

CLASSICAL MUSIC

You probably have some idea that many of the world's top-flight classical musicians are currently trained in Japan and that much of the nation's talent makes its home in Tokyo. The city has more than one symphony orchestra, and a thumb through one of the English dailies or a quick navigation through their websites will give you some idea what's on in classical venues.

TOKYO SYMPHONY ORCHESTRA
www.tokyosymphony.com/e-tokyo
One of Tokyo's best, established in 1946, this orchestra premieres works by contemporary Japanese composers, such as Ikumu Dan and Yoshiro Irino. It also performs traditional works by Western masters, such as Berlioz, Mahler and Schoenberg. Check its website for performance times and venues.

LIVE MUSIC

Though the live-music scene keeps geriatric hours (shows often end around 9pm), rock, house, blues, jazz and electronica are thriving in Tokyo. Big international acts, particularly from the UK and US, often appear at one of the city's megastadiums such as the **National Stadium** (p174) in Yoyogi or **NHK Hall** (Map p284).

But you won't need to subject yourself to the giant venues if you're seeking aural satisfaction; instead, head for one of the city's

TOP FIVE LIVE-MUSIC VENUES

- Blue Note (opposite) Tokyo's finest jazz club attracts the cream of the blues and jazz world. Tickets here cost more than at most places, but then virtuosity shouldn't come cheap.
- Crocodile (right) Emerging bands play here on their way to something bigger.
- Hot House (p166) This jazz club is so tiny that only two dozen people fit inside. If you arrive late, wait to enter until the end of the song or face the consequences of tripping over the pianist on your way in.
- Liquid Room (right) One of the bigger live music venues in Tokyo, this is where to look for bigger international and Japanese acts.
- Milk (opposite) Milk has long been home to most of Tokyo's underground acts and the weirdos who love them.

many good live houses. Shibuya is particularly ripe with such spots, in fact, Shibuya has its own sound, dubbed 'Shibuya-kei' or 'Shibuya type'. Exceptional, idiosyncratic music venues are also scattered throughout the city. The choices are endless, so if you have no idea what you'd like to hear, check out the current listings either at *Tokyo Q* or *Metropolis* (see p145).

CAVERN CLUB Map p286

☎ 3405-5207; 5-3-2 Roppongi, Minato-ku; admission ¥1500; from 6pm; Hibiya or Toei Ōedo Line to Roppongi (exit 3)

The heartfelt, adeptly executed covers performed at Cavern Club continue to shine on after all these years. The name of the spot, as any good John, Paul, George or Ringo fan would know, is the same as that of the Liverpool club that first featured the fabulous four flopheads. Reserve a seat for your two sets of yeah, yeah, yeah.

CLUB QUATTRO Map p284

☎ 3477-8750; 32-13 Udagawachō, Shibuya-ku; admission ¥3000-4000; JR Yamanote Line to Shibuya (Hachikō exit)

This venue feels more like a concert hall, but it's actually more along the lines of a slick club. It books local and international bands of generally high quality. Though there's no explicit musical focus, emphasis is on rock and roll with leanings toward world music.

CROCODILE Map p284

☎ 3499-5205; B1 fl, 6-18-8 Jingūmae, Shibuya-ku; admission ¥2000-3000; 6pm-2am; Chiyoda Line to Meiji-jingūmae (exit 1)

In the basement of the New Sekiguchi building in Jingūmae, Crocodile has something happening almost every night. It could be jazz, it could be rock, it could even be country and western or Cuban. Get here early, as things are known to fill up fast, especially on Friday and Saturday nights.

EGGMAN Map p284

☎ 3496-1561; 1-6-8 Jinnan, Shibuya-ku; admission ¥1000-3000; JR Yamanote Line to Shibuya (Hachikō exit)

Follow the spiral staircase down to the basement to hear blues, rock or light jazz musicians get low down. Most acts are local, and of the lighter, sweeter variety. Show up to see if tickets aren't completely sold out on a given night, and take a quick listen at the door to sample before committing. Most shows start around 7pm.

LA.MAMA Map p284

☎ 3464-0801; B1 fl, 1-15-3 Dōgenzaka, Shibuya-ku; admission ¥2000; JR Yamanote Line to Shibuya (Hachikō exit)

Just about every Japanese band from Buck-Tick to Melt Banana has passed through here at some time. Who knows if the band you see here will be the next indie darling. The room is fairly spacious, but even when the place gets crowded you'll never be far from the stage. Shows usually begin around 7pm.

LIQUID ROOM Map p288

☎ 5464-0800; www.liquidroom.net; 3-16-6 Higashi, Shibuya-ku; admission varies; 7pm-late; JR Yamanote Line to Ebisu (east exit)

Some of the world's greatest performers have graced the stage of the Liquid Room, from The Flaming Lips to Linton Kwesi Johnson. This is an excellent place to see an old favourite or find a new one, but you'll have to buy tickets as soon as they go on sale.

LOFT Map p282

☎ 5272-0382; B2 fl, 1-12-9 Kabukichō, Shinjuku-ku; admission ¥1500-3000; 5pm-late; JR Yamanote Line to Shinjuku (east exit)

This well-respected, quarter-century-old Tokyo live house, whose chequerboard stage has hosted the feedback and reverb of many a Tokyo punk, is often grungy and smokey – with just the right level of sweaty intimacy. The music is always loud and usually good. The walls are so acoustically sound that quiet conversations can be held just outside the door.

MILK Map p288

☎ 5458-2826; B1 fl, 1-13-3 Ebisu-Nishi, Shibuya-ku; admission ¥1000-3000; 8pm-4am; Hibuya Line to Ebisu (exit 2) or JR Yamanote Line to Ebisu (west exit)

In Ebisu, this is one of Tokyo's best small live clubs, featuring international punk, hard rock and alternative, along with some Tokyo dub, hip-hop and electronica. This cool space comprises three underground levels housing a crowd of weirdos and punks. On the 4th floor of the building is **What the Dickens** (p163), a much more sedate British pub.

SHIBUYA O-EAST Map p284

☎ 5458-4681; 2-14-9 Dōgenzaka, Shibuya-ku; admission varies; JR Yamanote Line to Shibuya (Hachikō exit)

Shibuya O-East is the big mama of several related venues forming a compound of clubs up Love Hotel Hill. With its sheer size, this house draws bigger-name international and domestic acts. If tickets to a show are sold out, stop by an hour before showtime to see if you can't snag one of the last-minute tickets they sometimes release.

JAZZ

Tokyo has long loved jazz, and affections don't seem to be on the wane. Major international artists invariably stop in the city, often at the Blue Note, and Japan's emerging improvisers most often get their start here at one of the smaller clubs. This is generally a hip, well-informed scene where audiences come with the intention of focusing on the music (and they'll expect the same of fellow clubgoers).

B-FLAT Map pp290-1

☎ 5563-2563; B1 fl, 6-6-4 Akasaka, Minato-ku; admission from ¥2500; 6.30-11pm Mon-Sat; Chiyoda Line to Akasaka (exits 5A & 5B)

Located in a part of Akasaka that empties and grows quiet at night, this hip jazz club often features local and European talent, as well as healthy doses of Latin jazz. As the owner recently passed away, so too may the club – check locally when you're in town.

BLUE NOTE Map p286

☎ 5485-0088; 6-3-16 Minami-Aoyama, Minato-ku; admission ¥6000-15,000; 5.30pm-1.30am Mon-Sat; Chiyoda, Ginza or Hanzōmon Line to Omote-sandō (exit B3)

Serious cognoscenti roll up to Tokyo's prime jazz spot in Aoyama to take in the likes of Maceo Parker, Herbie Hancock and Doctor John. Like its sister acts in New York and Milan, the digs here are classily decorated with dark wood and deep velvet,

Live-music performance (p163)

THE MODERN FLOATING WORLD

During the late-Tokugawa period, a colourful world was born in which kabuki actors, prostitutes, poets and high-living merchants cavorted in pleasure quarters such as Tokyo's Yoshiwara district. This was the so-called 'floating world' *(ukiyo)*, an ephemeral world of night pleasures (called *mizu shōbai* or 'the water trade') centred on geisha houses, brothels and drinking establishments.

Although prostitution was made illegal during the Allied occupation of Japan following WWII, the water trade is alive and well in Japan. A new form of floating world exists, one in which gaily painted kimonos and decorative hair combs have been replaced by gaudy miniskirts and flashing neon lights, particularly in the modern red-light districts of Shinjuku's Kabukichō and the areas around Ikebukuro Station.

While it is easy to romanticise the exploits of those otherworldly figures who live on in *ukiyo-e* (wood-block prints), the modern floating world allows for little in the way of sentimentality – today it is primarily a sleazy underworld of illegal Southeast Asian sex workers and economically poor, young Japanese women controlled by thoroughly unromantic *yakuza* (Japanese mafia) bosses. Unfortunately, there are few legal protections for sex workers – and immigrant women in the sex trade are completely vulnerable to the whims of the law and the street.

making this a good spot for a slow night of cool sounds.

HOT HOUSE Map pp278-9

☎ 3367-1233; 3-23-5 Takadanobaba, Shinjuku-ku; admission varies; 8.30pm-2am; JR Yamanote Line to Takadanobaba (main exit)

This must be the smallest jazz dive in the world. Musicians play in twos and threes (there's no room for more). Audiences are usually a few dozen; get here early if you're set on sitting in for the evening.

JAZZ SPOT INTRO Map p280

☎ 3200-4396; B1 fl, 2-14-8 Takadanobaba, Shinjuku-ku; admission ¥1000; from noon; JR Yamanote Line to Takadanobaba (main exit)

It's a good sign when a little club allows a quarter of its floor space to be monopolised by a sexy grand piano. It also bodes well when the place is staffed by musicians who love to talk shop all night – which is how long the Saturday-night jam sessions can last. At Jazz Spot Intro, all the omens are favourable.

JZ BRAT Map p284

☎ 5728-0168; 2nd fl, 26-1 Sakuragaokachō, Shibuya-ku; admission varies; from 6pm Mon-Sat; JR Yamanote Line to Shibuya (south exit)

This lovely, airy venue in the Cerulean Tower Tōkyū Hotel books consistently solid acts from Tokyo and abroad. The space seats just over 100 audience members, who are always treated to an intimate ambience. Though there's no formal dress code, you'll feel better dressing up rather than down.

ROPPONGI PIT INN Map pp290-1

☎ 3585-1063; B1 fl, 3-17-7 Roppongi, Minato-ku; admission from ¥3000; 6.30-10pm; Hibiya or Toei Ōedo Line to Roppongi (exit 3)

This recently renovated, spacious spot books fusion and jazz-rock in addition to more traditional jazz forms. Because of its progressive programming, the Roppongi Pit Inn is a magnet for younger jazz fans who tend to be most interested in the riffs of the future.

SHINJUKU PIT INN Map p282

☎ 3354-2024; B1 fl, 2-12-4 Shinjuku, Shinjuku-ku; admission ¥3000-10,000; from 7.30pm Mon-Fri, from 2pm Sat & Sun; Marunouchi Line to Shinjuku-sanchōme (exit C5)

Shinjuku Pit Inn, which has been around for over 35 years, is not the kind of place you come to talk over the music. Aficionados come here to listen in silence to Japan's best jazz performers. Weekend matinées are half the price of evening performances.

SWEET BASIL 139 Map p286

STB 139; ☎ 5474-0139; http://stb139.co.jp; 6-7-11 Roppongi, Minato-ku; admission ¥3000-7000; 6-11pm Mon-Sat; Hibiya or Toei Ōedo Line to Roppongi (exit 3)

Sweet Basil has a large, lovely space that draws big-name domestic and international jazz acts. Performances range the gamut of the genre; check the calendar on the website for the current line-up. This classy joint is a good place to have an Italian dinner before a show; call for reservations between 11am and 8pm Monday to Saturday.

Activities

Activities

Everyone needs to let off some steam once in awhile, and though you may be working up a sweat navigating the streets, you may crave a more intense workout than subway station stairs can offer. Most Tokyoites join private gyms or clubs to participate in recreational sports, which is why most facilities in the city are closed to nonmembers. But if you're in need of a vigorous swim, or a series of transcendental asanas, all is not lost. You'll find that visitors do have access to some of the city's excellent, and heavily subsidised, public sports facilities. Also open to the public are Tokyo's many baths and hot springs, which are an excellent antidote to a hard workout at the gym or a long day of circuit-training on the streets and subways.

CYCLING

Tooling around Tokyo on a bike can turn you onto some wonderful alleys and back streets, but you'll have to sharpen your senses to avoid opening taxi doors and pedestrians suddenly veering into your path. The city is pretty flat, so most of the challenge will come from finding your way between points B and A. Some ryokan (traditional Japanese inns) rent or loan out bicycles to their guests, and there are a few mellow cycling courses in the city parks. Always lock up your bike, as theft does happen.

EIGHT RENT Map p284

☎ 3462-2382; 31-16 Sakuragaokachō, Shibuya-ku; rentals per day ¥1920; JR Yamanote Line to Shibuya (south exit)

Near the south exit of Shibuya Station, this place requires a passport to rent a bicycle; call ahead for an appointment. It's an OK deal if you're only renting for one day, but if you plan to get around on a bike for the duration of your stay, you might be better off purchasing a cheap bike from **Tōkyū Hands** (p184) and selling it when you leave. Call ahead for an appointment.

IMPERIAL PALACE CYCLING COURSE Map pp294-5

☎ 3211-5020; 10am-3pm Sun; Chiyoda Line to Nijūbashimae (exit 2)

Every Sunday, 500 free bicycles are lent out for use along the 3.3km Imperial Palace cycling course. Bikes are given on a first-come, first-served basis and can be picked up next to the Babasakimon police box just outside the station exit.

MEIJI-JINGŪ OUTER GARDENS Map p286

☎ 3405-8753; 9am-4pm Sun & holidays; Toei Ōedo Line to Kokuritsu-Kyōgijō (exit A2)

On Sundays and holidays, 400 bicycles are lent to ride the road that encircles Meiji-jingū's outer gardens. Pick up these free bikes outside the office near the National Stadium.

TAMA RIVER Map pp278-9

☎ 3731-9388; 9am-noon; Keihin-Kyūkō Line to Rokugō-dote

A limited number of bicycles are available for the 6.5km ride that runs along the river between Maruko-bashi and Daishi-bashi. Free bikes can be picked up outside the station. From the station exit, turn left and continue until you pass under another set of train tracks. Turn left again and find the office on your right.

GOLF

Many golfers who live in Tokyo claim it's cheaper to tee off in Hawaii because the trip costs less than booking a space at one of the 500 local courses. Tokyo does have 19 public golf courses, the most conveniently located of which is listed here.

TOKYO TOMIN GOLF COURSE Map pp278-9

☎ 3919-0111; 1-15-1 Shinden, Adachi-ku; admission from ¥5000; Namboku Line to Shimo

If you dream of sand traps and short puts, give this place a go. Some ability to speak Japanese will be useful when making a reservation, though most hotel staff can easily help you past this obstacle. Keep in mind that spring and autumn tend to be when the weather is fine and the courses are often full.

MARTIAL ARTS

Small *dōjō* (place of practice) of Japanese martial arts disciplines exist in neighbourhoods all over Tokyo, but most instruction and practice is conducted in Japanese. The following organisations can point you to *dōjō* where you may be able to take lessons or attend a training session; see p238 for more resources.

INTERNATIONAL AIKIDŌ FEDERATION Map pp278-9

☎ 3203-9236; www.aikido-international.org; Aikikai Foundation, 17-18 Wakamatsuchō, Shinjuku-ku; 6am-7.30pm Mon-Sat, 8.30-11.30am Sun; Toei Ōedo Line to Wakamatsu-Kawada (main exit)

Practicing at the Aikikai Foundation requires filling out an application form and paying a registration fee in addition to a monthly course fee. Shorter-term visitors should stop by during office hours to ask about *dōjō* where it's possible to drop in for training.

KŌDŌKAN JUDŌ INSTITUTE Map pp278-9

☎ 3818-4172; www.kodokan.org; 1-16-30 Kasuga, Bunkyō-ku; open practice 3.30-8pm Mon-Fri, 4-7.30pm Sat; Toei Mita or Toei Ōedo Line to Kasuga (exits A1 & A2)

Students of judō who wish to keep up their practice while in Tokyo are welcome to stop by Kōdōkan Judō Institute in the afternoons for open practice. Lessons are also available here on a long-term basis, and visitors are welcome to observe training during practice hours.

KYŪMEIKAN Map pp278-9

☎ 3930-4636; 2-1-7 Akatsuka-Shinmachi, Itabashi-ku; Yūrakuchō Line to Chikatetsu-Narimasu (main exit)

Kyūmeikan *dōjō* welcomes foreign observers as well as practitioners of *kendō* (meaning 'way of the sword'), a discipline of wooden sword fighting that evolved from actual sword techniques used by samurai in battle. There's a fee of around ¥5000 for a lesson lasting one hour or more; those seeking to practice here can usually reach an English speaker on the phone at the *dōjō*.

PUBLIC BATHS & HOT SPRINGS

It has been said that a few minutes in a public bath will teach you more about daily life in Tokyo than any book you could ever read. These incredible venues, which locals still seem to frequent though almost all apartments in Tokyo have their own shower and bath, continue to be some of the most inclusive, amazing social spaces in the city.

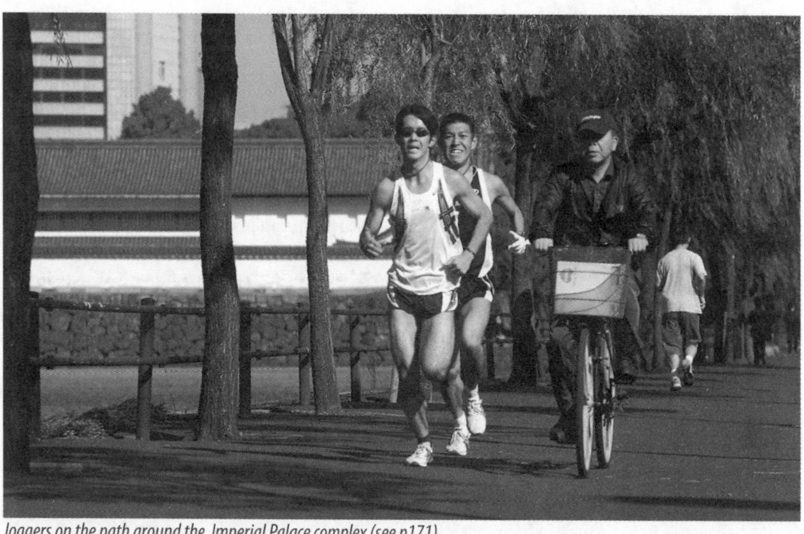

Joggers on the path around the Imperial Palace complex (see p171)

Luckily, the metropolitan government seems to recognise this and so every *sentō* (public bath) and *onsen* (hot spring) in the city is generously subsidised. This means you'll usually only be charged around ¥500 for the perfect soak – what a steal. It also means you'll encounter people from all walks and at all stages of life – mafia bosses bathe solemnly alongside splashing toddlers and nobody bats an eye. If you're craving a detour that will take you off the beaten tourist path, this is it.

Though typically associated with mountain resorts and small ryokan, several *onsen* are found in Tokyo. Most of these *onsen* draw their mineral water from deep underneath Tokyo Bay – by definition, what sets an *onsen* apart from a *sentō* is that *onsen* water must issue from a natural hot spring. *Sentō*, happily, can heat plain tap water to deliciously excruciating temperatures and bring baths to the city-dwelling masses.

ASAKUSA KANNON SENTŌ Map pp296-7

☎ 3844-4141; 2-7-26 Asakusa, Taitō-ku; admission ¥700; 🕑 6.30am-6pm Fri-Wed; Ⓜ Ginza, Hibiya or Toei Asakusa Line to Asakusa (exit 6)

Near Sensō-ji, the water at this traditional bathhouse is a steamy 40°C. Asakusa's historic ambience makes this a great place for a soul-soothing soak.

JAKOTSU-YU Map pp296-7

☎ 3841-8645; 1-11-11 Asakusa, Taitō-ku; admission ¥400; 1pm-midnight Wed-Mon; Ⓜ Ginza Line to Tawaramachi (exit 3)

This Edo-era bath is our favourite in Tokyo (and the preferred place of repose for neighbourhood *yakuza,* Japanese mafia, as well). First, be warned: the bathers here adore this place and initially will watch you carefully to make sure no dirty or soapy bodies make their way into the sacred tub. Once you've convinced them you're up to scrubbing every inch (yes, that means *every* inch), head into the incredibly hot indoor soaking area where you'll be massaged by tea-coloured water that is propelled by vigorous jets. Once you're cooked, you're ready for the real treat: the lovely, lantern-lit, rock-framed *rotemburo* (outdoor bath) that's just outside. The water in this little pool is much more temperate and now that your muscles have been turned to loose string by the heat, you could sit here for hours, perhaps wandering occasionally to the cold bath a few steps away, just to keep yourself awake. Keep in mind that the sauna is off limits unless you pay an additional fee.

SENTŌ PRIMER

Until quite recently, most private homes in Japan did not have baths, so every evening people gathered their toiletries into a bowl and headed off to the local neighbourhood *sentō* (public bath). More than just a place to wash oneself, the *sentō* served as a kind of community meeting hall, where news and gossip were traded and social ties strengthened.

Unfortunately, the number of *sentō* in Japan is rapidly declining, but there are still enough left in Tokyo and Yokohama for you to sample this most traditional aspect of Japanese life. More than just a cultural experience, however, a soak in a *sentō* is the ideal way to cure the sore muscles born of a day of sightseeing.

Sentō can be identified by their distinctive *noren* (half-length curtains over the doorway). *Sentō noren* usually bear the hiragana (ゆ, *yu*) for hot water (occasionally, it may be written in kanji: 湯). At the bottom of the *noren,* look for the kanji for men (男) and for women (女).

Once you've located a *sentō,* determine the men's or women's side, take off your shoes, place them in a locker in the entryway and slide open the door to the changing room. As you enter, you'll see the attendant, who sits midway between the men's and women's changing rooms, collecting the entry fee. *Sentō* usually cost between ¥300 and ¥400. Most are open from around 3pm to midnight.

In the changing room, you'll see a bank of lockers and stacks of wicker or plastic baskets. Grab a basket and drop your clothes into it. Find one of the common *senmenki* (washbowls) and place your toiletries in it, then place your basket in a locker (these have keys on elastic bands). Now you're ready for your bath.

Do not step into the bath until you have thoroughly washed your body. This is done at the banks of low showers and taps that line the walls of the place. Grab a low stool and plant yourself at an open spot.

Once you've washed thoroughly and removed all the soap, you are ready for a soak in the tubs. At a good *sentō,* you'll have a choice of hot tub, scalding tub, cold tub, whirlpool bath, sauna and, believe it or not, electric bath (which is meant to simulate swimming with electric eels!).

After soaking away the strains of the day, if you've done everything correctly, you will have achieved a state called *yude-dako* (boiled octopus). Now stagger home and collapse onto your futon.

KOMPARU-YU ONSEN Map pp290-1

☎ 3571-5469; 8-7-5 Ginza, Chūō-ku; admission ¥400; 2pm-midnight Mon-Sat; Ginza or JR Yamanote Line to Shimbashi (exit 1)

The fact that this straightforward, Meiji-era bath manages to keep its wits about it even as real estate prices continue to climb in the ritzy Ginza that surrounds it, must be one of Tokyo's best jokes. The bath mistress is a daunting battle-axe – no kidding, this gal chews tacks. With this in mind, make sure you scrub extra hard behind your ears, and don't even think about wearing the plastic slippers intended for the toilet out into the general locker room. This place has only old-school sit-down showers, so grab a plastic stool on your way in. As at other *onsen*, towels, soap and shampoo and fresh underwear are for sale at the door.

KOSHI-NO-YU SENTŌ Map p286

☎ 3404-2610; 1-5-22 Azabu-Jūban, Minato-ku; admission ¥400; 11am-11pm Wed-Mon; Namboku or Toei Ōedo Line to Azabu-Jūban (exits 4 & 7)

This simple place is overseen by a tough-as-nails bath mistress who watches the men's and women's sides closely for any serious bathing infractions or attempted voyeurism. If you've forgotten soap, shampoo or a clean pair of underwear, she'll be glad to help you out for a small fee. Upstairs is the fancier **Azabu-Jūban Onsen** (¥1260), which uses the same tea-coloured, mineral-rich water piped from 500m underground but also features a sauna, a cold bath and tatami rooms. If you're looking to hang out with the locals, though, the downstairs bathing area is really the thing.

Ō-EDO ONSEN MONOGATARI Map p289

☎ 5500-1126; 2-57 Aomi, Kōtō-ku; adult/child from ¥2800/1500, from 6pm-2am ¥1900/1500; 11am-9am; Yurikamome Line to Telecom Center (main exit) or Rinkai Line to Tokyo Teleport (free shuttle bus)

Ō-edo Onsen Monogatari does bill itself as an old Edo 'theme park', so come here for kitsch rather than authenticity. It's a good place to socialise in mixed groups, as there's an outdoor footbath area for relaxing in your *yukata* (light cotton robe). You wouldn't come here for a simple scrub, but if you'd like to make a day of it in Odaiba with some chums, this is a good place for an evening soak. See p108 for more information.

ROKURYU ŌNSEN Map pp296-7

☎ 3821-3826; 3-4-20 Ikenohata, Taitō-ku; admission ¥300; 3.30-11pm Tue-Sun; Chiyoda Line to Nezu (exit 2)

It may feel like a good neighbourhood *sentō*, but it's actually an *onsen* where the water is pleasantly hot, as opposed to scalding hot as it is at some other city hot springs. The bubbling amber water contains minerals that the many old timers who come here in the afternoon claim can cure a number of ailments. These same folk tell stories about the occasional ancient leaf that's worked its way up the pipes and into the tub. These leaves are in high demand and are reputed to be excellent for your skin. The bath is located down a small lane on the right; look for the traditional Japanese façade and the blue *noren*.

RUNNING

While Tokyo's city streets are generally too crowded for jogging – though they do make an excellent obstacle course in that respect – there are parks aplenty for runners. Some of the best places to run, with lots of greenery and long paths, include **Yoyogi-kōen** (p100), **Meiji-jingū Gyōen** (Map p284) and **Higashi-gyōen** (Imperial Palace East Garden; p62). If you prefer not to jog solo, and instead like your running to be a social event, try 'hashing' with the Tokyo members of that long-running (ouch) organisation.

HASH HOUSE HARRIERS

http://tokyohash.org

Formed in 1938, this worldwide club's activities are a mix of mad dashing and serious drinking done by cheeky joggers with sobriquets such as 'Sakura Sucker'. Several planned runs meander through a variety of routes each week. Bring your best drinking shoes.

SKATING

What could be better on a sweltering summer afternoon than gliding around an icy, indoor skating rink? If you would rather mentally score the double axels than execute them, the rinks sell 'observer' tickets (¥300 to ¥400) for those not taking to the ice.

TAKADANOBABA CITIZEN ICE SKATE RINK Map pp278-9

☎ 3371-0910; 4-29-27 Takadanobaba, Shinjuku-ku; adult/child ¥1300/800; noon-7.45pm Mon-Sat, 10am-7.45pm Sun; JR Yamanote Line to Takadanobaba (Waseda exit)

The people's skating rink, this 30m by 60m slab of ice is used for lessons, ice hockey, speed skating and general-purpose fun. Skate rental costs ¥500; discounts are taken off admission if you show up after 5pm. Head west out of Takadanobaba Station and walk about five minutes along Waseda-dōri; look for the big yellow sign to your left.

MEIJI-JINGŪ ICE SKATING RINK

Map p286

☎ 3403-3458; Gobanchi, Kasumigaoka, Shinjuku-ku; adult/child ¥1300/900; noon-6pm Mon-Fri, 10am-6pm Sat & Sun; Toei Ōedo Line to Kokoritsu-Kyōgijō (exit A2) or JR Chūō or JR Sōbu Line to Sendagaya (main exit)

Open year-round, Meiji-jingū Ice Skating Rink is there for a good twirl and glide around the rink. When you arrive you'll be given a choice between three types of skates – ice hockey, speed skating and figure skating (rentals cost ¥500). Choose whichever will help you move most gracefully across the NHL-sized rink. Discounts on admission are offered after 3pm.

SWIMMING & GYMS

In general, joining a Japanese gym is a cumbersome, expensive process best undertaken only by those who will be living in Tokyo (in which case we recommend it – most gyms have very good facilities and superb bathing areas that are especially tempting in winter). If you're just in the mood for a good swim or functional workout, the following spots should help you work up a good sweat. Most swimming pools require that swimmers wear bathing caps.

CHIYODA SOGO TAIKUKAN POOL

Map pp294-5

☎ 3256-8444; www.city.chiyoda.tokyo.jp/english/e-guide/sports.html; 2-1-8 Uchi-Kanda, Chiyoda-ku; pool/gym ¥600/350; 9am-9.30pm, closed 3rd Mon; Chiyoda, Hanzōmon or Marunouchi Line to Ōtemachi (exits A1, A2, C1 & C2)

A public pool and weight room are available for reasonable fees. The pool is open to the public from 5pm to 9pm on most days, but hours vary. Keep in mind that certain times during the day are reserved for those residing in Chiyoda. The website lists details in English.

CHŪŌ-KU SOGO SPORTS CENTRE

Map pp278-9

☎ 3666-1501; 2-59-1 Nihombashi-Hamachō, Chūō-ku; pool/gym ¥500/400; 9am-8.30pm; Toei Shinjuku Line to Hamachō

Another of Tokyo's public gyms, this one in Chūō-ku has gym facilities and a swimming pool. *Kyūdo* (Japanese archery) practice also takes place at the sports centre; though no lessons are given, spectators are welcome to watch this graceful discipline if anyone is practising here.

TOKYO METROPOLITAN GYMNASIUM INDOOR POOL Map p284

☎ 5474-2111; 1-17-1 Sendagaya, Shibuya-ku; admission ¥450; 9am-8pm, closed 3rd Mon; JR Sōbu Line to Sendagaya (main exit)

If all that movement on land has made you crave a few laps, head here. In addition to a pool there's a weights room, although its use requires an extra fee. The gymnasium and pool are located just to the northwest of the National Stadium in Harajuku, just a few minutes' walk from the Sendagaya JR Station.

YOGA

INTERNATIONAL YOGA CENTER

Map pp278-9

☎ 090-4596-7996; www.iyc.jp; 4th fl, 5-30-6 Ogikubo, Suginami-ku; sessions ¥3000; Marunouchi Line to Ogikubo (south exit)

Drop in to do the downward dog at the International Yoga Center, which has branches across Tokyo. Ninety-minute classes in Ashtanga and Iyengar yoga are given in Japanese, but you can check the website for a list of English-speaking instructors and where and when they'll be teaching.

WATCHING SPORT

SUMŌ

Sumō is a fascinating, highly ritualised activity steeped in Shintō tradition. Perhaps sumō's continuing claim on the national imagination lies in its ancient origins and elaborate rites; it's the only traditional Japanese sport that still has enough clout to draw big crowds and dominate primetime TV.

When a tournament isn't in session, you can enjoy the **Sumō Museum** (p106), next door to the stadium. Displays include humungous wrestler hand-prints and the referees' ceremonial clothing. Unfortunately, there are no English explanations, and during tournaments the museum is open only to attending ticket-holders.

RYŌGOKU KOKUGIKAN Map pp278-9

☎ 3623 5111; www.sumo.or.jp/eng/index.html; 1-3-28 Yokoami, Sumida-ku; admission ¥500-45,000; opening ceremonies 8.30am, ticket office 10am-6pm; JR Sōbu or Toei Ōedo Lines to Ryōgoku

Tokyo's *bashō* (sumō wrestling tournaments) take place at this stadium in January, May and September. Unless you're aiming for a big match on a weekend you should be able to secure a ticket: *bashō* take place over 15 days. The best seats are bought up by those in the know who also happen to have the right connections, but upstairs seats are usually available and cost from ¥2300 to ¥7000. Nonreserved seats at the back sell for ¥1500, and if you don't mind standing, you can get in for around ¥500. Tickets can be purchased up to a month prior to the tournament or you can simply turn up on the day of the match. It's advisable to get there early, as keen punters start queuing the night before. Note that only one ticket is sold per person, a clever device used to foil scalpers. The stadium is adjacent to JR Ryōgoku Station, on the north side of the railway tracks. If you can't go in person, NHK televises sumō from 3.30pm daily during tournaments.

BASEBALL

Baseball is Japan's most popular sport and six of Japan's 12 pro-baseball teams are based in Tokyo. A trip to one of the local ballparks is truly a cultural (or perhaps a religious?) experience – the crowd behaviour is completely unlike what you're probably used to at home. The home team's fans often turn up in matching *happi* (half-length coats) and perform intricate cheering rituals in perfect unison led by special cheerleaders, one for each section, who make a job out of whipping fans into a well-ordered frenzy. Sitting in the cheap seats will put you right in the middle of it.

Baseball season starts at the end of March or the first week of April and runs until October. Tokyo Dome is probably the most exciting place to take in a game, though Jingū Stadium can make for a fun afternoon out when the weather is fair.

See also the **Japanese Baseball Hall of Fame** (p88) and see p17 for some history of the sport in Japan.

JINGŪ BASEBALL STADIUM Map p286

Jingū Kyūjo; ☎ 3404-8999; 13 Kasumigaoka, Shinjuku-ku; tickets ¥1500-3900; games start 6pm; Ginza Line to Gaienmae (north exit)

Now home for the Yakult Swallows, Tokyo's number two team, Jingū Baseball Stadium was originally built to host the 1964 Olympics. When not hosting Yakult Swallows games, the baseball stadium is sometimes used for high-profile Little League and intercollegiate championships. You can buy tickets from the booth in front of the stadium; outfield tickets can cost as little as ¥1500.

TOKYO DOME Map pp278-9

Big Egg; ☎ 5800-9999; www.tokyo-dome.co.jp/e; 1-3-61 Kōraku, Bunkyō-ku; admission ¥1200-5900; JR Chūō or JR Sōbu Line to Suidōbashi (west exit)

The 'Big Egg', as it's affectionately known, is the best place to catch a baseball game in the city, as it's the home turf of Japan's most popular baseball team, the Yomiuri Giants. Night games tend to be well-attended and can be especially exciting. There are ticket booths on three sides of the Big Egg; after purchasing your ticket, navigate to the gate you want.

Baseball souvenirs, Tokyo Dome (above)

J-LEAGUE SOCCER

Japan was already soccer crazy when the World Cup came to Saitama and Yokohama in 2002. Now it's a chronic madness, and five minutes of conversation with any 10-year-old in Tokyo about why they like David Beckham should clear up any doubts you might have to the contrary. J-League games are generally played outside of the city. If you'd like to catch an international match, try the National Stadium.

NATIONAL STADIUM Map p286

Kokuritsu Kyōgijō; ☎ 3403-1151; Kasumigaokamachi, Shinjuku-ku; admission ¥2000-5000; JR Chūō Line to Sendagaya (east exit)

Completed in 1958 and used as one of the primary venues for the 1964 Olympics, National Stadium now hosts the annual Toyota Cup (November or December) and other international soccer events.

HORSE RACING

There are two big racing tracks in the Tokyo area, offering weekend gamblers a good chance to wager (and lose) some money. Gambling is illegal in Japan except in sanctioned contexts – horse racing being one of them. If you're itching to take your chances, look up the Japan Racing Association's English guide online at www.jair.jrao.ne.jp/howtobet/main.html on how to bet. Races are generally held on weekends from 11am to 4pm and are a hot destination for young couples on dates.

ŌI KEIBAJŌ

☎ 3763-2151; 2-1-2 Katsushima, Shinagawa-ku; general admission ¥100, reserved seats ¥500-2000; Tokyo Monorail to Ōi-Keibajōmae

Each year from April to October, Ōi Keibajō offers night-time 'Twinkle Races'. The races are lit by mercury lamps, whose diffused light draws young couples out on hot dates. Though the popularity of horse racing has declined over the past decade, some lucky record-breaker won over ¥13 million from a mere ¥100 bet here in May 2005.

TOKYO KEIBAJŌ Map pp278-9

Fuchū Racecourse; ☎ 0423-633 141; 1-1 Hiyoshichō, Fuchū-shi; admission varies; Keiō Line to Fuchūkeiba-Seimonmae (pedestrian overpass)

More popularly known as Fuchū Racecourse, Tokyo Keibajō's 500m-long home straight is the longest in the country and can make for exciting, win-by-a-nose finishes. This track is where most major and international races take place.

Shopping

Shopping

There's something about consumer culture in Tokyo that is definitive of the city itself. People here shop as they work – long and hard – and while much of the booty is taken home and eventually worn or indulged in by the buyer, an equal amount is used as gifts to grease the wheels of complex social and business relationships.

The central dispensers of most goods are multistorey *depāto* (department stores), many of which are owned by the companies that also operate the train lines (p53) – hence the sprawling retail clusters around the busiest train stations. Over the decades, many have become local institutions. Of course, department store culture isn't for everyone and Tokyo has an abundance of smaller, more eccentric shops. Many are found on the backstreets of Harajuku and Ebisu and display items that are as lovingly designed and crafted as they are unique. Even trendy Shibuya, a haven for teenagers on the lookout for the day's latest trend at knock-off prices, has its share of original storefronts tucked between chain stores.

If you are in Tokyo for only a few days, head for Omote-sandō or Harajuku, which has some of the city's most interesting high- and low-fashion boutiques. For status shopping, go straight to Ginza glam. If you've got more time, roam through Ebisu, Shibuya and the odd little craft shops on the side streets and in the alleys of Asakusa. Foreign *otaku* (geeks) should definitely hit Akihabara (also see p77) and Shinjuku for manga and electronics. And a stroll down one of Tokyo's shopping streets can reveal unexpected finds (p181).

Lastly, though bargaining is the norm in most of Asia, in Japan it's simply not done – except at flea markets and the occasional electronics store.

ANTIQUE FAIRS & FLEA MARKETS

After days of white-gloved attendants in Tokyo's perfectly ordered department stores, one longs for the colourful anarchy and dust of a good flea market. Tokyo has loads of flea markets and antique fairs, many held on temple or shrine grounds, where you can spend hours among the bric-a-brac. Don't get your hopes up about finding treasures, though, for gone are the days when astute buyers could cart off antique *tansu* (wooden chests) or virtuosic lacquerware worth thousands of dollars. More likely, you'll find some quirky gifts at considerable savings over department store prices. Things to look for include old kimono, *obi* (belts used to fasten kimono), scrolls, pottery, old Japanese postcards, Chinese snuff bottles, antique toys and costume jewellery. Though bargaining is permitted, remember that it's considered bad form to drive too hard a bargain. If your Japanese is lacking, bring a pencil and paper.

The following are some of Tokyo's better flea markets and antique fairs. Check with the Tourist Information Center (TIC; p248) before going, as shrine and temple events sometimes interfere with the scheduling of markets.

Aoyama Oval Plaza Antique Market (Map p284; 6am-dusk 3rd Sat of the month; Chiyoda, Ginza or Hanzōmon Line to Omote-sandō, exit B2) This market houses an assortment of dealers in antique ceramics, prints and furniture; a good place to start an antique hunt.

Azabu-jūban Antique Market (Map p286; from 8am 1st Sat of the month; Namboku or Toei Ōedo Line to Azabu-jūban) This flea market is held on the patio above Azabu-jūban Station.

Hanazono-jinja Flea Market (Map p282; dawn-dusk Sun; Marunouchi or Shinjuku Line to Shinjuku-sanchōme, exit B3 or B5) A good mix of old and new feature at this market, ranging from antique ceramics to new junk jewellery and used *yukata* (light cotton summer kimono).

Nogi-jinja Flea Market (Map p286; dawn-dusk 2nd Sun of the month; Chiyoda Line to Nogizaka, main exit) The place to go for *ukiyo-e* (wood-block prints) and antiques from Asia and Europe.

Roppongi Antique Fair (Map p286; 8am-7pm 4th Thu & Fri of the month; Hibiya or Toei Ōedo Line to Roppongi, exit 3) Another antique market that happens rain or shine; find good ceramics and quality dealers here.

Tōgō-jinja Fine Arts Market (Map p284; 4am-3pm 1st, 4th & 5th Sun of the month; JR Yamanote Line to Harajuku, Takeshita exit) Rummage through this trove of authentic antique wares and kimono, and odds and ends of various vintages.

Duty-Free Tokyo

Most major department stores and many of the well-known tourist shops offer tax-exempt shopping for foreign tourists making purchases of more than ¥10,000. In order to qualify, you must present your passport and a customs document will then be attached to it (this will be checked and removed as you exit the country). Most of the big stores have special tax-exemption counters where staff will be able to speak some English or at the very least have information that you can read.

IMPERIAL PALACE & MARUNOUCHI

MITSUKOSHI Map pp294-5 Department Store

☎ 3241-3311; 1-4-1 Nihombashi-Muromachi, Chūō-ku; 10am-7pm; Ginza or Hanzōmon Line to Mitsukoshimae (exits A2, A3, A5, A7 & A8)

Though there are branches of this department store in Ikebukuro (Map p280), Ginza (Map pp290–1) and Ebisu (Map p288), the flagship store in Nihombashi is still the most elegant. Check out the floor dedicated to the art of the kimono or peruse the morsels in the *depachika* (department store food floor; p124). For the full effect, arrive at 10am for the bells and bows that accompany each day's opening.

TOP FIVE TRADITIONAL CRAFTS SHOPS

- Bingoya (p180) Looking for quality folk arts? Bingo – you've found the place.
- Japan Traditional Craft Center (p188) Museum, craft demos and folk-arts shop rolled into one lovely venue.
- Yoshitoku (p179) Dollmaker to the emperor – not a bad endorsement.
- Takumi (p178) Take or leave the Ginza glitz, but take a few minutes to browse Takumi's handicrafts.
- Oriental Bazaar (p185) Sure-fire, last-minute souvenir shopping in one stop.

GINZA

It's true that Ginza is the poshest shopping district in Tokyo – one look around Wakō or Mitsukoshi will testify to this. But tucked in between some of the more imposing façades are simpler pleasures like fine papers and shelves full of ingenious toys. This is probably the one neighbourhood where shopping options truly reflect the breadth and depth of the city's consumer culture, which is equal parts high fashion glitz and down-to-earth dedication to craft.

HAKUHINKAN TOY PARK

Map pp290-1 Toy Shop

☎ 3571-8008; www.hakuhinkan.co.jp; 8-8-11 Ginza, Chūō-ku; 11am-8pm; JR Yamanote Line to Shimbashi (Ginza exit) or Toei Asakusa Line to Shimbashi (exits 1 & 3)

One of Tokyo's most famous toy stores, this layer cake of a 'toy park' is crammed to every corner with this year's models of character toys, the hottest squawking video games, seas of colourful plastic and the softest plush toys ever invented. Hakuhinkan also harbours child-friendly restaurants and even a theatre in this huge children's attention-deficit paradise.

ITŌYA Map pp290-1 Art Supplies

☎ 3561-8311; 2-7-15 Ginza, Chūō-ku; 9.30am-7pm Mon-Sat, 9.30am-6pm Sun; Ginza or Hibiya Line to Ginza (exits A12 & A13)

Nine floors of stationery-shop love await visual-art professionals, as well as paper and paperclip fanatics, at Itōya. In addition to a comprehensive collection of *washi* (fine Japanese handmade paper), there are Italian leather agendas, erasable pens in your signature colour and even *tenugui* – beautifully hand-dyed, all-purpose handkerchiefs.

MATSUYA Map pp290-1 Department Store

☎ 3567-1211; 3-6-1 Ginza, Chūō-ku; 10.30am-7.30pm; Ginza, Hibiya or Marunouchi Line to Ginza (exits A12 & A13)

Matsuya offers fine men's and women's clothing on the 1st floor and a good breadth of traditional Japanese crafts, pottery and knick-knacks on the 7th. Boons for foreign visitors are the international shipping service, tax-exemption assistance and useful, in-store English-speaking guides. There's another branch in Asakusa (Map pp296–7).

GIFT BOX

As with many customs in Japan, gift-giving is akin to a complex art form, fraught with symbolism and intricate design. While most Japanese will graciously forgive the faux pas of a foreigner, some basic etiquette is its own gift.

If invited to someone's home, go bearing a small gift as a gesture of appreciation to your host. Flowers are a good choice, as is a pretty package of sweets (you'll score points for presentation) from a *depachika* – avoid giving green tea, as this is typically reserved for funerals. Bringing along some quality trinkets and speciality items from your home country to give as gifts will delight Japanese friends or hosts, but err on the side of modesty, as anything extravagant might embarrass the recipients or make them feel obligated to reciprocate in kind. Avoid anything in sets of unlucky four or nine, and don't wrap gifts in funeral-connoting white.

When you are offered a gift, the polite response is to initially refuse it so as not to appear greedy. Conversely, when you offer a gift, expect to do a bit of gentle urging before it's accepted. In group situations, give something to everyone (a shared box of biscuits, for example) but give individual gifts in private. It's good form to give and receive with both hands (see p15 for other tips). And unless the giver insists you open it, politely resist the temptation to tear into it – until your gleeful arrival home.

MATSUZAKAYA Map pp290-1 Department Store

☎ 3572-1111; 6-10-1 Ginza, Chūō-ku; 10am-8pm Mon-Sat, 10am-7.30am; Ginza, Hibiya or Marunouchi Line to Ginza (exit A3)

For 300 years Matsuzakaya has been selling traditional garments and crafts. Today the range is broader, though the store still has a first-rate kimono shop. Matsuzakaya is one of those grand department stores with a fabulous *depachika* in the basement. Find other branches in Ueno (Map pp296–7) and Ebisu (Map p288).

MIKIMOTO PEARL Map pp290-1 Jewellery

☎ 3535-4611; www.mikimoto.com/html/en; 4-5-5 Ginza, Chūō-ku; 11am-6.30pm Ginza, Hibiya or Marunouchi Line to Ginza (exit B5)

The most famous of Tokyo's pearl shops, Mikimoto Pearl was founded by Mikimoto Kokichi, who invented the cultured pearl in 1893 after a painstaking process of trial and error. Aiming to drape the necks of all the women in the world with pearls, which he saw as the antidote to cases of hysterics, he opened his first store in Ginza in 1899.

TAKUMI Map pp290-1 Craft

☎ 3571-2017; www.ginza-takumi.co.jp in Japanese; 8-2-4 Ginza, Chūō-ku; 11am-7pm Mon-Sat; JR Yamanote Line to Shimbashi (Ginza exit) or Toei Asakusa Line to Shimbashi (exits 1 & 3)

Takumi has been around for more than 60 years, and has acquired an elegant selection of toys, textiles, ceramics and other traditional folk crafts from around Japan. Ever thoughtful, the shop also encloses information detailing the origin and background of its pieces if you make a purchase.

WAKŌ Map pp290-1 Department Store

☎ 3562-2111; 4-5-11 Ginza, Chūō-ku; 10.30am-6pm; Ginza, Hibiya or Marunouchi Line to Ginza (exits A9, A10 & B1)

Built in 1932 on Ginza's main strip, Wakō is housed in one of the only buildings in the neighbourhood to have survived the fiery air raids during WWII. Today, it still occupies its original neo-Renaissance digs and sells some of the city's finest jewellery and apparel. Stop by for a look at the famous clock tower and the elegant, prewar interior.

ASAKUSA

Asakusa was once the heart of Edo's low city, home to artisans, merchants and prostitutes. Its small lanes and winding alleyways are still full of surprises, from venerable doll shops to virtuosic drum makers such as Taiko-kan (p87). For straight gift shopping, Nakamise-dōri is probably the best choice, although the long stretch of Kappabashi-dōri also yields promising discoveries in its little culinary-supply shops.

KAPPABASHI-DŌRI Map pp296-7 Market

Ginza Line to Tawaramachi (exit 3)

It's most famous for its shops selling plastic food models, but Kappabashi-dōri supplies many a Tokyo restaurant in bulk, selling matching sets of chopsticks, woven bamboo tempura trays and tiny ceramic *shōyu* (soy sauce) dishes glazed in iron oxide and blue. This makes it the perfect street for stocking up if you're setting up an apartment or seeking small, useful souvenirs. See p87 for other details on this famous shopping street.

Geta *(traditional wooden sandals)*

NAKAMISE-DŌRI Map pp296-7 Market

Nakamise-dōri, the long, crowded pedestrian lane running from Kaminarimon gate to Hōzōmon gate, has more than 80 stalls that for centuries have been helping the Japanese people fulfil their gift-giving obligations. The wide alley is chock-a-block with small shops selling temple paraphernalia as well as traditional items of varying beauty and quality. The little arcade of Nakamise-dōri is also the place to pick up locally made, salty *sembei* (crispy rice crackers).

YOSHITOKU Map pp296-7 Traditional Dolls

☎ 3863-4419; 1-9-14 Asakusabashi, Taitō-ku; 10am-5pm; JR Sōbu or Toei Asakusa Line to Asakusabashi (exit A2 or main exit)

Once known as doll-maker to the emperor, Yoshitoku has been crafting and distributing dolls since 1711. The 1st floor is filled with miniatures that depict kabuki actors, geisha and sumō wrestlers in minute detail and exquisite dress. Figures are historically accurate rather than cartoonish and are designed with the serious collector, rather than children, in mind.

ASAKUSA TRADITIONAL PRODUCTS

The following shops specialise in only-in-Asakusa traditional products. If there are other crafts you're interested in, and there are dozens more, visit the Edo Shitamachi Dentō Kōgeikan (Shitamachi Traditional Crafts Museum; p84) or visit www.asakusa-e.com/dentokoge/dentokoge_e.htm.

Bengara (Map pp296–7; ☎ 3841-6613, 1-35-6 Asakusa, Taitō-ku; 10am-6pm Thu; Ginza Line to Asakusa (exit 1) or Toei Asakusa Line to Asakusa (exit A5)) Sells *noren*, the curtains that hang in front of shop doors. Some *noren* are very artful, with the spirit of the *mingei* movement (p23). It's one block east of Nakamise-dōri.

Kanesō (Map pp296–7; ☎ 3844-1379; 1-18-12 Asakusa, Taitō-ku; 10.30am-7pm Thu; Ginza Line to Asakusa (exit 1) or Toei Asakusa Line to Asakusa (exit A5) This place has been selling knives since the early Meiji period. In a country where knives are a serious business, this shop is known as being a favourite of the pros.

Miyamoto Unosuke Shoten (Map pp296–7; ☎ 3844-2141, 2-1-1 Nishi Asakusa, Taitō-ku; Ginza Line to Tawaramachi, exit 3) If it's festival products you're after, Miyamoto is one-stop shopping, from *mikoshi* (portable shrines) to drums, clappers and festival masks. It's on the ground floor of the building and downstairs from the drum museum (p87).

WEST OF THE IMPERIAL PALACE

A few stops east of Shinjuku, the altitudes of the surrounding buildings descend to a more human scale. A stroll up the Kagura-zaka slope from Iidabashi Station will turn up several shops selling *geta* (traditional wooden sandals) and drawstring purses made from lavish kimono fabric. Elsewhere in the area, wedged in unexpected places between pharmacies, groceries and *pachinko* (vertical pinball-game) parlours, are shops carrying goods like Czech puppets and handpainted kites.

BINGOYA Map pp278-9 — Craft

☎ 3202-8778; www.quasar.nu/bingoya; 10-6 Wakamatsuchō, Shinjuku-ku; 10am-7pm Tue-Sun; Toei Ōedo Line to Wakamatsu-kawada

Richly dyed *washi* (handmade paper), vibrant batik textiles, regional ceramics and a quality assortment of folk crafts fill out the five floors of this wonderful shop. Find handmade glassware, cushions and Japanese tea cups for feathering your nest, or painted fans, *happi* (half-length coats) and *washi*-covered tea canisters for gifting to loved ones. This shop is especially dangerous as it accepts credit cards.

PUPPET HOUSE Map pp294-5 — Speciality Store

☎ 5229-6477; www.puppet-house.co.jp in Japanese; 1-8 Shimomiyabi-chō, Shinjuku-ku; 11am-7pm Tue-Sat; JR Chūō or JR Sōbu Line to Iidabashi (east exit)

Possibly slightly scary for small children or puppet-fearing adults, this is otherwise a wondrous workshop of functional, not just decorative, marionettes. Peopled by an international collection of puppets, this place is run by a super-friendly couple who are happy to talk shop. Look for the sign of Punch in an alley near Mizuho Bank.

ROPPONGI

Though Roppongi is best known as a few square blocks of bars, clubs and pick-up joints, it's also home to a few of the city's most interesting and idiosyncratic shops and showrooms, and its most frequented new shopping mega-mall, Roppongi Hills. Of special interest in Roppongi are the Axis showroom, showcasing contemporary design, and Japan Sword, which displays and sells the exquisite weaponry of the samurai.

AXIS Map pp290-1 — Craft

☎ 3587-2781; 5-17-1 Roppongi, Minato-ku; 11am-7pm Mon-Sat; Hibiya or Toei Ōedo Line to Roppongi (exit 3)

Salivate over some of Japan's most innovative interior design at this Roppongi design complex. Of the 20-odd galleries and retail shops selling art books, cutting-edge furniture and other objets d'interior design, highlights are **Yoshikin** (☎ 3568-2356; 2nd fl) for beautifully crafted, inexpensive kitchenware and **Kisso** on the 3rd floor, specialising in ceramics.

BLUE & WHITE Map p286 — Craft

☎ 3451-0537; 2-9-2 Azabu-jūban; 11am-8pm Wed-Mon; Namboku or Toei Ōedo Line to Azabu-jūban (exit 4)

Taking inspiration from classic Japanese colours, the expat American behind this small crafts store sells traditional and contemporary items like indigo-dyed *yukata* (light cotton kimono or robe) and painted chopsticks, all in blue-and-white. Pick through tiny dishes of ceramic beads or collect bundled-up swatches of fabric for your own crafty creations. Ready-made and custom-tailored clothing also make unique gifts.

DON QUIXOTE Map p286 — Department Store

☎ 5786-0811; www.donki.com/index.php; 3-14-10 Roppongi, Minato-ku; 11am-10pm; Hibiya or Toei Ōedo Line to Roppongi (exit 3)

The Roppongi branch of this jam-packed, bargain castle is the best of the bunch with its outdoor seating underneath a giant fish tank – a welcome respite from the sensory overload inside. Don Quixote sells everything from household goods to Halloween costumes, usually at cut-rate prices. Though you'll need to sort through some junk, it's possible to find funky gifts here.

JAPAN SWORD Map pp290-1 — Antiques

☎ 3434-4321; www.japansword.co.jp; 3-8-1 Toranomon, Minato-ku; 9.30am-6pm Mon-Fri, 9.30am-5pm Sat; Ginza Line to Toranomon (exit 2)

Tokyo's most famous seller of samurai swords and weaponry attracts both Japanophiles and Quentin Tarantino fanatics. It sells the genuine article – such as antique sword guards and samurai helmets dating from the Edo period – as well as convincing replicas crafted by hand. The shop usually has exhibits of impressive armour or swords on display.

MUJI Map p286 Clothes & Homewares

☎ 3478-5800; www.muji.net; 2-12-18 Kita-Aoyama, Minato-ku; 10am-8pm; Hibiya or Toei Ōedo Line to Roppongi (exits 1c & 3)

It's ironic that Tokyo's famously understated no-name brand has become one of the hippest names in Paris. Despite the fanfare, Muji still sells simple, unadorned clothing and accessories for men and women. It also carries a decent selection of hard-to-find M and L sizes (though these, too, are small). It's also a good place to buy well-designed, reasonably priced kitchen- and home-wares.

ROPPONGI HILLS Map p286 Shopping Mall

☎ 6406-6000; Roppongi 6-chōme; Hibiya or Toei Ōedo Line to Roppongi (exits 1c & 3)

In the first three months after its opening in April 2003, Roppongi Hills (p93) saw a staggering 26 million visitors pass through its doors. After a year, the count was up to a cool 46 million. The 200 retail stores, Mori Art Museum (p92) and nine-screen cinema (p148) still draw the crowds.

EBISU & AROUND

Wonderful Ebisu is often overlooked, though its shops, like its restaurants, are some of the most forward-thinking and interesting in the city. Yebisu Garden Place, an open-air mall connected to the Ebisu JR Station by a series of enclosed, moving walkways, is a good place to start prowling around. If you're more interested in one-of-a-kind wares and would like a glimpse into the ingenuity of the neighbourhood's small shopkeepers, hot-foot it up the hill toward Daikanyama and Hachiman-dōri (right).

ALOHALOHA Map p288 Children's Clothes

☎ 5457-1360; 1-17-12 Ebisu-Nishi, Shibuya-ku; 11am-7pm Mon-Sat; Hibiya or JR Yamanote Line to Ebisu (exit 4 & west exit)

Many a hip mama and papa live in Ebisu, where this little shop comfortably fills a niche for colourful, cute kids' clothes. A classy look is the rule for the children's clothes here, though there are some outright funky numbers to start the little ones with a taste for quirky fashion – as appropriate for Ebisu.

SHOPPING STREETS

Ameyoko Arcade (p79) One of Tokyo's only old-fashioned, open-air pedestrian markets, and a good place for bargains – from spices to shoes.

Hachiman-dōri (Map p288) Lined with shops purveying high and low fashion trends, this street is a delightful treasure hunt for local designs.

Kappabashi-dōri (p178) Food, food everywhere, and nary a rice grain to eat – because it's plastic.

Nakamise-dōri (p179) Leading up to the grand gate that opens onto Sensō-ji, this is home to countless trinket, snack and knick-knack shops.

Omote-sandō (Map p184) Known as the centre of Tokyo's *haute couture* culture, Omote-sandō is the place to take in Tokyo fashion on parade.

Takeshita-dōri (p186) Takeshita-dōri is to teenagers what Omote-sandō is to dilettantes.

DAIKANYAMA ADDRESS

Map p288 Shopping Mall

☎ 3461-6492; 17 Daikanyamachō, Shibuya-ku; 11am-8pm; Hibiya or JR Yamanote Line to Ebisu (exit 4 & west exit)

Just northwest of Daikanyama Station, this small retail complex is notable for its clever suspension bridges and four dozen or so designer boutiques selling clothing, eyewear and other sartorially stylish accessories. The open-air plaza is a treat on quiet afternoons, and weekends tend to be relatively free of mad throngs of shoppers.

HACKNET Map p288 Bookshop

☎ 5728-6611; www.hacknet.tv in Japanese; 1-30-10 Ebisu-Nishi, Shibuya-ku; 11am-8pm; Hibiya or JR Yamanote Line to Ebisu (exit 4 & west exit)

This is a bookshop for serious designers, or those who can get high off the fumes of elegant design. Hacknet specialises in cutting-edge design books from across disciplines and around the world. The small, well-lit space is excellent for browsing and the staff is incredibly studiously unobtrusive.

TOKYO'S BOOKSHOPS

The English-language sections of several of the larger Tokyo bookshops would put entire bookshops in many English-speaking cities to shame. A few of the most notable shops, which are happy to let you thumb through their selection, are listed here.

Aoyama Book Centre (Map p286; ☎ 3479-0479; 6-1-20 Roppongi, Minato-ku; 10am-5am Mon-Sat, 10am-10pm Sun; Hibiya or Toei Ōedo Line to Roppongi, exit 3) Open till the small hours of the morning, this spot near Roppongi crossing carries books and mags to keep you engaged until the trains start running again.

Blue Parrot (Map p280; ☎ 3202-3671; www.blueparrottokyo.com; 3rd fl, 2-14-10 Takadanobaba, Shinjuku-ku; 11am-9.30pm; JR Yamanote Line to Takadanobaba, main exit) A fabulous resource of English books, magazines, DVDs, children's books and Internet access.

Book 246 (Map p286; ☎ 5771-6899; B1 fl, 1-2-6 Minami-Aoyama, Minato-ku; 11am-11pm; Ginza, Hanzōmon or Toei Ōedo Line to Aoyama-itchōme, exit 4) Right behind Aoyama-itchōme Station, this classy little bookshop specialises in art and architecture, mostly in Japanese and a shuffle of European languages. Connected to 246 Café, with an outdoor dining area.

Crayon House (Map p284; ☎ 3406-6409; www.crayonhouse.co.jp in Japanese; 3-8-15 Kita-Aoyama, Minato-ku; 11am-10pm Chiyoda, Ginza or Hanzōmon Line to Omote-sandō, exits B2 & B4) Carries one of the sweetest, multilingual selections of children's books in the city. Browsing aisles and reading areas are perfectly kid-sized.

Good Day Books (Map p288; ☎ 5421-0957; www.gooddaybooks.com; 3rd fl, 1-11-2 Ebisu, Shibuya-ku; 11am-8pm Mon & Wed-Sat, 11am-6pm Sun; JR Yamanote Line to Ebisu, east exit) The best selection of used English-language books in Tokyo: a wide range of paperbacks and some hardcover tomes and magazines.

Issei-do (Map pp294–5; ☎ 3292-0071; 1-7 Kanda-Jimbōchō, Chiyoda-ku; 10am-6.30pm Mon-Sat; Toei Mita or Toei Shinjuku Line to Jimbōchō, exits A6 & A7) An antiquarian bookseller, this one with a wonderful selection of old texts. The 2nd floor has many well-weathered volumes in English.

Kinokuniya (Map p282; ☎ 5361-3301; Takashimaya Times Square, 5-24-2 Sendagaya, Shinjuku-ku; 10am-8pm; JR Yamanote Line to Shinjuku, south exit) One of the best selections of English-language titles on the 6th floor, with another nearby branch in Shinjuku.

Kitazawa Books (Map pp294–5; ☎ 3263-0011; 2-5 Kanda-Jimbōchō, Chiyoda-ku; 11am-6.30pm Mon-Sat; Toei Mita or Toei Shinjuku Line to Jimbōchō, exits A6 & A7) Kitazawa has a good selection of political, philosophical and literary works, some dressed in ancient dust covers.

Mandarake (Map pp278–9; ☎ 3228-0007; www.mandarake.co.jp/english/shop/nkn.html; 5-52-15 Nakano, Nakano-ku; noon-8pm; JR Chūō Line to Nakano, west exit) A must-stop for manga maniacs, Mandarake has more than a dozen shops spread throughout the Nakano Broadway mall. There's also another branch in **Shibuya** (Map p284; ☎ 3477-0777; B2 fl, Shibuya Beam Bldg, 31-2 Udagawachō, Shibuya-ku; www.mandarake.co.jp/english/shop/sby.html; noon-8pm; JR Yamanote Line to Shibuya, Hachikō exit).

Maruzen (Map pp294–5; ☎ 5288-8881; Oazo Bldg, 1-6-4 Marunouchi, Chiyoda-ku; 9am-9pm; JR Yamanote Line to Tokyo (Marunouchi north exit) Established in 1869, this is Japan's oldest Western bookshop and has one of the best selections of English-language books in Tokyo. Should move back to its original Nihombashi location (Map pp294–5; 2-3-10 Nihombashi, Chūō-ku) in 2007.

NADiff (Map p284; ☎ 3403-8814; 4-9-8 Jingūmae, Shibuya; 11am-8pm; Chiyoda, Ginza or Hanzōmon Line to Omote-sandō, exit A2) The city's best collection of design and art books, many in English.

Tokyo Random Walk (Map pp294–5; ☎ 3291-7071; 1-3 Kanda-Jimbōchō, Chiyoda-ku; 10.30am-8pm Mon-Sat, 11am-7pm Sun; Toei Mita or Toei Shinjuku Line to Jimbōchō, exits A6 & A7) This antiquarian bookstore carries a respectable selection of English books, many of them titles on Japan and Asia. Other branches in Akasaka (Map pp290–1) and Roppongi (Map p286).

Tower Records (Map p284; ☎ 3496-3661; 1-22-14 Jinnan, Shibuya-ku; 10am-10pm; JR Yamanote Line to Shibuya, east exit) Has a good range of English books and magazines, and probably the city's best selection of imported music publications.

Yaesu Book Center (Map pp290–1; ☎ 3281-1811; 2-5-1 Yaesu, Chūō-ku; 10am-9pm Mon-Sat, 10am-7pm Sun) Stocks a good selection of English-language books as well as some French and German titles.

Q FLAGSHIP EBISU-NISHI

Map p288 Clothes

☎ 5456-9117; www.qshop.jp in Japanese; B1 fl, 1-30-10 Ebisu-Nishi, Shibuya-ku; ⏰ noon-8pm; Ⓜ Hibiya or JR Yamanote Line to Ebisu (exit 4 & west exit)

Sharing a building with Hacknet, Q Flagship Ebisu-Nishi presents its clothing and accessories like candy, or jewellery. Many pieces are originals by local and international designers from as far abroad as Australia and Italy, but the shop also designs a house collection. Sizes are limited generally to those fitting svelte Daikanyama figures.

YEBISU GARDEN PLACE

Map p288 Shopping Mall

☎ 5423 7111; www.gardenplace.co.jp/english; 4-20-3 Ebisu, Shibuya-ku; Ⓜ JR Yamanote Line to Ebisu (east exit to Skywalk)

This large mall, which has its own exit from the train station, has loads of upper-end shops and a basement full of good restaurants. Most of the wares here are the usual department store fare – high-quality, glitzy and somewhat characterless. But the lovely alfresco courtyard and the openness of the space are a welcome departure from more crowded shopping districts.

SHIBUYA

Shibuya is as much the centre of the cities live-music phenomenon as it is one of the epicentres of teen trendiness and, not surprisingly, many of the shops around Shibuya cater to one of the two scenes. Music shops and cheap, outrageous apparel are everywhere, as are the hip kids who come to primp, pose and listen. A day of window shopping here, especially near the station, will give most people a feel for the pulse of the city's constantly changing youth culture. On the weekends, the street in front of the 109 Building closes to all but foot traffic.

One of the few spots for grownups is Tōkyū Hands, the local institution that bills itself as a lifestyle store. Happily, the weirder this multilevel funhouse becomes, the more successful it seems to be, this while also supplying practical hardware and housewares. It provides a marvellous diversion on an idle afternoon.

CISCO Map p284 Music

☎ 3462-0366; 2nd fl, 11-1 Udagawachō, Shibuya-ku; ⏰ noon-10pm Mon-Sat, 11am-9pm Sun; Ⓜ JR Yamanote Line to Shibuya (Hachikō exit)

Nearly every DJ in town drops by for an occasional chat with the incredibly well-informed staff. The stock at this shop generally covers hip-hop and R&B, but clustered around the main store are separate buildings specialising in techno, reggae and house from Japan and abroad. Most new selections are sold on CD, though some vinyl records are also available. Be sure to thumb through the bargain boxes.

LOFT Map p284 Department Store & Homewares

☎ 3462-3807; www.loft.co.jp in Japanese; 21-1 Udagawachō, Shibuya-ku; ⏰ 10am-9pm Mon-Sat, 10am-8pm Sun; Ⓜ JR Yamanote Line to Shibuya (Hachikō exit)

Loft's multiple levels of housewares, accessories, travel supplies and stationery are more compact than at Tōkyū Hands, and, aimed toward younger shoppers, the bias leans toward fun rather than function. Stylish bedding and blob-shaped vases distract the shopper from titanium jewellery and trendy makeup before the *kawaii* (cute) plastic toys and mobile-phone charms do 'em in. Another branch is in Ikebukuro (Map p280).

PARCO I, II & III Map p284 Department Store

☎ 3464-5111; 15-1 Udagawachō, Shibuya-ku; ⏰ 10am-9pm; Ⓜ JR Yamanote Line to Shibuya (Hachikō exit)

Parco, divided into several stores located smack in the middle of Shibuya, carries contemporary designs for a very young crowd. In Parco I, you'll find a good magazine and bookstore on the 7th floor and edgy shops on floors three through six. Parco III, mainly known for its art gallery and cinema complex, also houses some small shops. There's another branch in Ikebukuro (Map p280).

SHIBUYA 109 Map p284 Clothes

Ichimarukyū; ☎ 3477-5111; www.shibuya109.jp in Japanese; 2-29-1 Dōgenzaka, Shibuya-ku; ⏰ 10am-9pm Mon-Fri, 11am-10.30pm Sat & Sun; Ⓜ JR Yamanote Line to Shibuya (Hachikō exit)

Tokyo's fad-obsessed fashionistas come to 109's circular tower for the season's freshest looks. Most of the clientele is under 20;

the punk fabrics and wild designs reflect this – it's a sample of what kids are wearing on the street at any given moment and what kids in other parts of the world may be donning next month.

TŌKYŪ HANDS Map p284 Department Store

☎ 5489-5111; 12-18 Udagawachō, Shibuya-ku; 10am-8.30pm; JR Yamanote Line to Shibuya (Hachikō exit)

This is Tokyo's favourite DIY store, with hardware and materials for home projects. What defines it is the sheer diversity of eccentric goodies: clocks that tick backwards, hand-blown glass pens and vibrating reflexology slippers, all under one roof. This is eight floors of oddball, functional stuff you never realised you needed. If you hit one store during your stay, let this be it. There's another huge store in Shinjuku's Takashimaya Times Square (Map p282).

TSUTSUMU FACTORY Map p284 Craft

☎ 5478-1330; 37-15 Udagawachō, Shibuya-ku; 11am-7pm Mon-Sat; JR Yamanote Line to Shibuya (Hachikō exit)

It's the wrapping-paper centre of the packaging-excess capital: Tsutsumu, which translates into 'wrapping', carries hundreds of kinds of gorgeous *washi* as well as other kinds of paper, lovely ribbons, bows and perfectly shaped boxes. It's just up the street from Shibuya's teen shopping district.

OMOTE-SANDŌ

Home to the famed Harajuku girls, Takeshita-dōri and the alleys packed with small, independent designers' shops and secondhand stores, Omote-sandō is the most eclectic, experimental neighbourhood in Tokyo. In addition to its bountiful backstreet boutiques showcasing indie designs, the area also has a number of excellent antique stores and novelty shops.

High fashion rules the Aoyama end of Omote-sandō, where 'fashionable' has an entirely different meaning than for the hipsters of Harajuku layering *haute couture* with secondhand finds. Creatively active but solidly established, the air permeating well-to-do Aoyama is grown-up and refined while retaining a sense of innovation. It's no wonder some of the more artistic designers and high fashion flagship stores have chosen to make the area their creative home.

CHICAGO THRIFT STORE Map p284 Clothes

☎ 3409-5017; 11am-8pm; 6-31-6 Jingūmae, Shibuya-ku; 11am-7pm; JR Yamanote Line to Harajuku (Omote-sandō exit) or Chiyoda Line to Meiji-jingūmae (exit 4)

Stuffed to the rafters with funky hats, ties and coats, Chicago is a treasure trove of vintage clothing and used duds stacked high and priced low. Of special note is the extensive collection of used kimono and *yukata* in the basement. Sort through the standing racks for just the right fabric, but keep an eye out for stains.

COMMES DES GARÇONS

Map p284 Designer Wear

☎ 3406-3951; 5-2-1 Minami-Aoyama, Minato-ku; 11am-8pm; Chiyoda, Ginza or Hanzōmon Line to Omote-sandō (exit A5)

The architectural eccentricity of Kawakubo Rei's flagship store (see p115) should come as no surprise – her radical designs have been refiguring the fashion landscape for more than 20 years. Both men's and women's fashions are on display. Most available sizes are quite small, but a quick circuit of the shop is interesting in itself.

CONDOMANIA Map p284 Speciality Store

☎ 3797-6131; 6-30-1 Jingūmae, Shibuya-ku; 10.30am-10.30pm; Chiyoda, Ginza or Hanzōmon Line to Omote-sandō (exit A5)

Occupying a prime corner of the Omote-sandō and Meiji-dōri intersection, the Condomania storefront may be Tokyo's cheekiest rendezvous point. Inside are condoms of all colours, sizes and flavours. Just look for the smiling, bright-yellow condom character adorning the windows.

FUJI-TORII Map p284 Antiques

☎ 3400-2777; www.fuji-torii.com; 6-1-10 Jingūmae, Shibuya-ku; 11am-6pm Wed-Mon, closed 3rd Mon of the month; JR Yamanote Line to Harajuku (Omote-sandō exit) or Chiyoda Line to Meiji-jingūmae (exit 4)

For more than half a century, this discriminating antique dealer has specialised in providing authentic lacquerware, ceramics, scrolls and *ukiyo-e* (wood-block prints) to interested buyers. The authenticity of everything in the store is guaranteed and the English-speaking staff is happy to answer your questions.

CLOTHING SIZES

Measurements approximate only, try before you buy

Women's Clothing						
Aus/UK	8	10	12	14	16	18
Europe	36	38	40	42	44	46
Japan	5	7	9	11	13	15
USA	6	8	10	12	14	16
Women's Shoes						
Aus/USA	5	6	7	8	9	10
Europe	35	36	37	38	39	40
France only	35	36	38	39	40	42
Japan	22	23	24	25	26	27
UK	3½	4½	5½	6½	7½	8½
Men's Clothing						
Aus	92	96	100	104	108	112
Europe	46	48	50	52	54	56
Japan	S		M	M		L
UK/USA	35	36	37	38	39	40
Men's Shirts (Collar Sizes)						
Aus/Japan	38	39	40	41	42	43
Europe	38	39	40	41	42	43
UK/USA	15	15½	16	16½	17	17½
Men's Shoes						
Aus/UK	7	8	9	10	11	12
Europe	41	42	43	44½	46	47
Japan	26	27	27½	28	29	30
USA	7½	8½	9½	10½	11½	12½

HANAE MORI BUILDING ANTIQUE MARKET Map p284 — Antiques

B1 fl, 3-6-1 Kita-Aoyama, Minato-ku; 11am-8pm; Chiyoda, Ginza or Hanzōmon Line to Omote-sandō (exit A1)

More than 30 antique stalls have made their home in the cool, dark basement of the Hanae Mori building (p115). Vendors carry both Japanese and Western antiques, with some specialising in woodwork, swords or Tiffany glass.

HYSTERIC GLAMOUR Map p284 — Clothes

3409-7227; 6-23-2 Jingūmae, Shibuya-ku; 11am-8pm; JR Yamanote Line to Harajuku (Omote-sandō exit) or Chiyoda Line to Meiji-jingūmae (exits 1 & 4)

It's actually attitudinous tongue-in-cheek rather than hysteric glamour, but whatever you want to call it, it's sexy and fun. These designer confections are a good place to start for hip fashion with a Tokyo twist. There's even a toddler line, the ultimate in designer punk for your little rocker.

ISSEY MIYAKE Map p284 — Designer Wear

3423-1407; www.isseymiyake.com; 3-18-11 Minami-Aoyama, Minato-ku; 10am-8pm; Chiyoda, Ginza or Hanzōmon Line to Omote-sandō (exit A4)

Before Issey Miyake put Tokyo on the fashion map, Japanese designers were known to copy Western trends after they'd already hit the runway. Miyake's work has changed such conceptions. Check out the A-POC garments – each made from a single piece of fabric.

KIDDYLAND Map p284 — Toy Shop

3409-3431; 6-1-9 Jingūmae, Shibuya-ku; 10am-8pm, closed 3rd Tue of the month; Chiyoda Line to Meiji-jingūmae (exit 4)

Eep, Kiddyland: six floors of appealing products for your children to fall in lust with and which you may still be paying for next year. In fact, you yourself may be regressively seduced by plastic-bobbled barrettes, Pokémon paraphernalia or nostalgia-inducers like her feline highness Hello Kitty or Ultraman. Claustrophobes should avoid the store on weekends when it teems with teens.

LAFORET BUILDING Map p284 — Shopping Mall

5411-3330; 1-11-6 Jingūmae, Shibuya-ku; 11am-8pm; JR Yamanote Line to Harajuku (Omote-sandō exit) or Chiyoda Line to Meiji-jingūmae (exit 5)

This rounded '70s edifice must be the teen shopping capital of the world. The mall's hundreds of shops sell the trendiest garb, meant to be worn for a fleeting season and then tossed into the trash. Sizes here fit tiny Tokyo teens, so unless you're very petite, this will be a window-shopping, people-watching venture.

ORIENTAL BAZAAR Map p284 — Craft

3400-3933; 5-9-13 Jingūmae, Shibuya-ku; 10am-7pm Fri-Wed; Chiyoda Line to Meiji-jingūmae (exit 4)

Carrying a wide selection of antiques and tourist items at very reasonable prices, Oriental Bazaar is an excellent spot for easy one-stop souvenir shopping. Good gifts to be found here include fans, folding screens, pottery, porcelain and kimono. The branch at Narita airport opens at 7.30am for last-chance suit-of-armour purchases. The entire staff at both branches speaks fluent English.

EVERYWHERE VENDORS

No prizes for guessing that Tokyo has the largest number of vending machines in the world – six million and counting. Amazingly, whether they carry liquor, soft drinks or cigarettes, they go mostly unmolested. The most ubiquitous machines sell tea and coffee (magically hot in winter, cold in summer) while less common ones sell goods ranging from rice and bouquets to neckties and software. There are also the occasional machines outside pharmacies that sell condoms and those that purvey pornography (mostly magazines and videos). In love hotels, they even dole out sex toys.

SHISEIDO COSMETICS GARDEN

Map p284 — Cosmetics

☎ 5474-1534; www.shiseido.co.jp/garden in Japanese; 4-26-18 Jingūmae, Shibuya-ku; 🕑 11am-7.30pm Tue-Sun, closed 2nd Tue of the month; Ⓜ Chiyoda, Ginza or Hanzōmon Line to Omote-sandō (exit A2)

Based on the idea that not selling you lipstick is the best way to sell you lipstick, Shiseido's glamorous showroom displays the entire range of the cosmetic giant's line without selling any of it to anyone. Feel free to spread, sniff and sample to your heart's content – if you speak Japanese, sign up for a makeover consultation.

SPIRAL RECORDS Map p284 — Music

☎ 3498-1224; www.spiral.co.jp in Japanese; 🕑 11am-8pm; 5-6-23 Minami-Aoyama, Minato-ku; Ⓜ Chiyoda, Ginza or Hanzōmon Line to Omote-sandō (exit B1)

Located just inside the entrance of the Spiral building, Spiral Records is both a vendor and an experimental label. The listening stations feature avant-garde tunes both new and old. The staff spins records while you browse.

TAKESHITA-DŌRI Map p284 — Market

Ⓜ JR Yamanote Line to Harajuku (Takeshita-dōri exit)

If you're struck with a sudden urge to fit into one of Tokyo's youth subcultures, passing through the flowered arches of Takeshita-dōri will reveal all you need. You'll find salons to pouf your hair into a gigantic fro, white platform Mary Janes to go with your bloody nurse's outfit and creative inspiration in the members of these teen tribes passing noisily by.

UNDERCOVER Map p286 — Streetwear

☎ 3407-1232; 5-3-18 Minami-Aoyama, Minato-ku; 🕑 11am-8pm; Ⓜ Chiyoda, Ginza or Hanzōmon Line to Omote-sandō (exit A5)

Former punk band frontman Jun Takahashi's take on youth-minded streetwear is still crazy after all this time. His Undercover Lab, designed by architect Astrid Klein, is just up from Yohji Yamamoto (below).

UNIQLO Map p284 — Clothes

☎ 5468-7313; 6-10-8 Jingūmae, Shibuya-ku; 🕑 11am-9pm; Ⓜ Chiyoda Line to Meiji-jingūmae (exits 1 &4)

Like Muji (p181), Uniqlo has made a name for itself by sticking to the basics. Offering inexpensive, quality clothing with clean, simple style, this chain has taken Tokyo by typhoon. You'll find the original outpost in Omote-sandō, and you'll stumble over dozens more all over town. Sizes run small.

YOHJI YAMAMOTO Map p286 — Designer Wear

☎ 3409-6006; www.yohjiyamamoto.co.jp; 5-3-6 Minami-Aoyama, Minato-ku; 🕑 11am-8pm; Ⓜ Chiyoda, Ginza or Hanzōmon Line to Omote-sandō (exit A5)

Wander down Omote-sandō to check out Yohji Yamamoto's bold, timeless designs. Though there's no sign on it, his flagship store is recognisable by its distinctive bronze façade, which you'll want to get past for a look at the experimental interior.

Corner of Omote-sandō & Aoyama-dōri

SHINJUKU

Let's face it: shopping in Shinjuku can be overwhelming. From the moment you step out of the train station (which is itself encased by a giant mall, My City), the lights and noise make the whole place seem like the interior of a bustling casino. But beyond this first impression, there is another. Two branches of the Kinokuniya bookstore (p182) are here, as is stately Isetan, one of Tokyo's most revered department stores that caters to the young set. Shinjuku is also one of a few pilgrimage points for audiophiles – Shibuya being the other – and the haunt of bargain-hunting shutterbugs.

DISK UNION Map pp294-5 Music

☎ 3352-2691; www.diskunion.co.jp in Japanese; 3-18-1 Shinjuku, Shinjuku-ku; 11am-8pm; Marunouchi or Toei Ōedo Line to Shinjuku-sanchōme (exit A1)

The stairwell at Disk Union is papered with posters of old glam and punk bands. The place is known by local audiophiles as Tokyo's best used CD and vinyl store. Six storeys carry a variety of musical styles. More genre-specific branches can be found elsewhere, especially around Meiji University in Kanda.

ISETAN Map p282 Department Store

☎ 3352-1111; 3-14-1 Shinjuku, Shinjuku-ku; 10am-8pm; Marunouchi or Toei Shinjuku Line to Shinjuku-sanchōme (exits B3, B4 & B5)

In addition to its stunning food hall in the basement, Isetan boasts an excellent *yukata* department as well as several floors of designer goods. Check out the store's I-club, a free service that provides English-speaking staff for visiting shoppers. The membership desk for this service is located on the 7th floor of the Isetan annexe building.

SAKURAYA CAMERA Map p282 Photography

☎ 5368-1717; 3-17-20 Shinjuku, Shinjuku-ku; 10am-8.30pm; Marunouchi Line to Shinjuku (exits B7, B8 & B9)

With a few branches around Shinjuku, this is main rival to **Yodobashi Camera** (see right). Like Yodobashi, it offers an incredible selection of lenses and digital cameras, and prices are similar at both shops.

SEKAIDŌ Map p282 Art Supplies

☎ 5379-1111; 3-1-1 Shinjuku, Shinjuku-ku; 9.30am-9pm; Marunouchi or Toei Shinjuku Line to Shinjuku-sanchōme (exit C1)

Sekaidō, whose entrance is marked by a banner depicting the *Mona Lisa*, sells a broad array of art supplies such as pens, brushes and easels, as well as fine paper and a vast selection of manga.

YODOBASHI CAMERA

Map p282 Photography

☎ 3346-1010; 1-11-1 Nishi-Shinjuku, Shinjuku-ku; 9.30am-9.30pm; JR Yamanote Line to Shinjuku (west exit)

Yodobashi is well-stocked and is Tokyo's largest and most highly regarded camera emporium. Its prices are very competitive and tourists are waived Japanese consumption tax if a valid passport is shown. It's also one of the rare shops in the city where some bargaining is considered acceptable. Make sure you know competitors' prices beforehand; the clerk helping you will know the score.

IKEBUKURO

Though two of the largest department stores in the world are here, humble Ikebukuro has never quite taken off as a shopping destination. Perhaps it's proof that little speciality shops, such as those found in Omote-sandō and Ebisu, really do have something that people crave, or that bigger doesn't necessarily imply better. Whatever the case, Ikebukuro can still be a good hunting ground for bargains on wares you'll find in other parts of the city.

BIC CAMERA Map p280 Photography

☎ 3988-0002; 1-11-7 Higashi-Ikebukuro, Toshima-ku; 10am-8pm; Marunouchi Line to Ikebukuro (exits 23, 29 & 30)

Bic Camera carries lots of delicious food for shutterbugs. Bins of bargain film can be found in front and a variety of Japanese cameras are on display. The top floors stock a fairly extensive array of audio and video equipment, most of it at prices comparable to those in Akihabara (see p77). There are three other Bic stores in the neighbourhood.

HMV Map p280 Music

☎ 5953-6711; 3rd fl, 1-22-10 Higashi-Ikebukuro, Toshima-ku; ⏲ 10.30am-10.30pm; Ⓙ JR Yamanote Line to Ikebukuro (east exit)

HMV has branches all over Tokyo, but this one is probably the best for its focus on J-pop and other contemporary Japanese music. You could spend a few hours at the listening stations getting a good earful of Tokyo's musical landscape that month.

JAPAN TRADITIONAL CRAFT CENTER

Map p280 Craft

☎ 5954-6066; www.kougei.or.jp/english/center.html; 1st & 2nd fl, Metropolitan Plaza Bldg, 1-11-1 Nishi-Ikebukuro, Toshima-ku; ⏲ 11am-7pm; Ⓙ JR Yamanote Line to Ikebukuro (Metropolitan exit)

Though this spot bills itself as a museum (p103), it's primarily a shop that carries traditional crafts in a variety of media. Fine lacquerwork, ceramics, natural-bristle paintbrushes and knives are on display and for sale. Nearly everything has been made by hand, and in-store demonstrations are often given by expert craftspeople.

SEIBU Department Store

☎ 5956-3281; 1-28-1 Minami-Ikebukuro, Toshima-ku; ⏲ 10am-9pm Mon-Sat, 10am-8pm Sun; Ⓙ JR Yamanote Line to Ikebukuro station (east exit)

One of the original big two of Ikebukuro's department stores, Seibu occupies a huge block on the east side of Ikebukuro station and purveys all the usuals, with an impressive *depachika* for the foodies.

TŌBU Map p280 Department Store

☎ 3981-2211; 1-1-25 Nishi-Ikebukuro, Toshima-ku; ⏲ 10am-8pm; Ⓙ JR Yamanote Line to Ikebukuro (west exit)

This is one of Ikebukuro's two big department stores, with a whopping 29 floors. Of particular note are the larger-than-average-sized togs (by Tokyo standards) to be found in the central building. This doesn't mean an availability of plus sizes, but that some items will be larger than a typical small.

ODAIBA

Odaiba was designed as an entertainment and shopping mecca, so it should come as no surprise that two of its main attractions are malls with views over the water. You'll find both big-name designers and small shops (some carrying local designers). Venus Fort is worth a peek to take in its timed sunrise and sunset.

DECKS TOKYO BEACH

Map p289 Shopping Mall

☎ 3599-6500; www.odaiba-decks.com; 1-6-1 Daiba, Minato-ku; ⏲ 11am-9pm; Ⓙ Yurikamome Line to Odaiba Kaihin-kōen (main exit)

Decks is divided into two malls, Island and Seaside. Both house a rainy day's worth of browsing, and if you're hungering for Chinese food, the Island Mall boasts **Daiba Little Hong Kong** (p141). There's also Tokyo Joypolis, a high-tech amusement park run by Sega, with virtual reality games and indoor rollercoasters: bring on the overstimulation.

VENUS FORT Map p289 Shopping Mall

☎ 3599-1735; www.venusfort.co.jp/multi/index_e.html; 1 Aomi, Minato-ku; ⏲ 11am-9pm Sun-Fri, 11am-10pm Sat; Ⓙ Yurikamome to Aomi (main exit) or Rinkai Line to Tokyo Teleport (main exit)

Shopping officially became recreation when Venus Fort declared itself a retail theme park just for women. The faux Italian Villa and the staged sunrise and sunset every few hours add to the idea, though in the end, the effect is more Vegas than Venice. Among the hundreds of shops, Gaultier has a presence here, as does Donna Karan.

Sleeping

Sleeping

From capsules to skyscrapers, Tokyo has thousands of places to sleep. As a general rule you get what you pay for, so if you've come here on a budget, expect a bit of noise and perhaps a longer walk from the train station. If expense is not so much an issue, choose from a myriad of decadent rooms – many of which boast incredible city views.

Central neighbourhoods like Ginza, Shinjuku and Akasaka are ideal, with loads of high-end options as well as a few in the midrange. Reasonably priced business hotels exist all along the Yamanote loop, while some excellent inns await in slightly more out-of-the-way locales. Cheap Sleeps are listed by neighbourhood, but you'll find more on the outer fringes of central Tokyo. Check out Worth the Trip (p193) for some sweet budget deals.

Though most of the accommodation in Tokyo is Western-style, a few traditional inns and hotels are probably unlike anything you've seen. For full definitions of each type of lodging, check out p235. Note that most Tokyo ryokan (traditional Japanese inns) don't fit the traditional mould as elsewhere in Japan. Typical amenities at midrange to top-end Western- and Japanese-style accommodation usually includes a *yukata* (light cotton robe) and slippers, basic toiletries and often little extras like hair ties, cotton swabs and disposable razors (though sometimes not shaving foam).

Rack rates are quoted in this chapter, but prices can vary drastically. Most business and high-end hotels offer discounts, often quite significant, for reservations made in advance via phone or Internet; check their websites for seasonal deals. Rates at budget places usually remain as quoted, though small discounts may sometimes apply if business is slow. Keep in mind that during Golden Week (29 April to 5 May), as at other national holidays (see p242 for details), rooms may be booked out or, if available, may be very expensive.

PRICE GUIDE

¥¥¥	over ¥16,000 a night
¥¥	¥6500 to ¥16,000 a night
¥	under ¥6500 a night

Tax

A 5% consumption tax applies to room rates across all accommodation categories, with the exception of *gaijin* houses (see p235) and some of the other budget options. On high-end accommodation (generally rooms costing over ¥16,000), a 3% local tax is also added to the 10% to 15% service charge. Prices quoted in this chapter are not inclusive of these taxes. Finally, the Tokyo Metropolitan Government now tacks on a small per-person accommodation tax on rooms costing more than ¥10,000: ¥100 for rooms costing up to ¥14,999 and ¥200 for rooms costing from ¥15,000.

Reservations

Working closely with the Japan National Tourist Organization (JNTO; p248), **Welcome Inn Reservation Center** (www.itcj.jp) staff at TICs (Tourist Information Centers) offer a free reservations service for accommodation at member hotels, ryokan and *minshuku* (Japanese B&B), or you can reserve via the centre's website.

You can also secure *minshuku* lodging through the **Japan Minshuku Center** (Map pp278–9; ☎ 5858-0103; www.minshuku.jp; 3-11-8 Hirai, Edogawa-ku; Mon-Sat, closed national holidays; JR Sōbu Line to Hirai) in the lobby of Hotel Tōka. Staff will handle all reservations and payments, and will give you a map to your *minshuku*.

BOOK ACCOMMODATION ONLINE

For more accommodation reviews and recommendations by Lonely Planet authors, check out the online booking service at www.lonelyplanet.com. You'll find the true, insider lowdown on the best places to stay. Reviews are thorough and independent. Best of all, you can book online.

Longer-Term Rentals

Renting an apartment in Tokyo from a Japanese agency will require putting down a substantial deposit. The agency's fee will most likely be a month's rent. After that, you will be expected to produce the landlord's *reikin* (key money – two to three months' rent), usually required again after two years. This money is never returned. After this, plan for the deposit (one or two months' rent) and an up-front payment of one or two months' rent.

If you do decide to rent, there are English-speaking real-estate agents in Tokyo who specialise in helping foreigners find rentals in *gaijin* houses; the following places are worth seeking out. Rents may be a bit higher at these agencies because you're receiving the apartment without the burden of the hefty deposit.

Kimi Information Center (Map p280; ☎ 3986-1604; www.kimiwillbe.com) Connected in name and spirit to Kimi Ryokan (p206), Kimi Information Center can help place you in a reasonably priced apartment. Kimi charges an agency fee equal to one month's deposit. Locations tend to be around working-class Ikebukuro.

Sakura House (Map p282; ☎ 5330-5250; www.sakura-house.com; 2nd fl, 7-2-6 Nishi-Shinjuku, Shinjuku-ku; JR Yamanote Line to Shinjuku, east exit) Sakura House has extensive listings of well-maintained apartments. Staff members are fluent in English, Korean and Chinese, and they'll escort you to apartments or shared housing for viewing. Rooms and apartments are available to rent for a minimum occupancy of one month.

Serviced Apartments

If you're based in Tokyo for more than a month or two, serviced apartments can be more comfortable and affordable than living in a hotel. Look in the *Japan Times* or *Tokyo Journal*. Prices vary dramatically depending on size, location and services provided. No key money is required, but you generally pay a one-month deposit. For good apartments in good locations, be prepared to spend between ¥100,000 and ¥180,000 per month.

TOKYO STATION AREA

Because of its proximity to the Marunouchi district and the Imperial Palace, the area around Tokyo Station has a few fine hotels and some good midrange places designed for short-term business travellers. This business district is quieter in the evenings and provides quick access to the rest of the city via the JR Yamanote Line.

TOP FIVE PLACES TO SLEEP

- Cerulean Tower Tōkyū Hotel (p201) This upscale addition to the Shibuya skyline manages to be stunning and stunningly unpretentious.
- Park Hyatt Tokyo (p204) It's the epitome of understated elegance, imbued with *Lost in Translation* glamour.
- Ryokan Shigetsu (p197) Shigetsu honours the beautiful basics, for travellers on a budget.
- Sukeroku No Yado Sadachiyo (p198) Tokyo's most traditional ryokan (traditional Japanese inn) glows with gorgeous ambience and lovely proprietors.
- Yama-no-Ue (Hilltop) Hotel (p195) Long the haunt of eccentrics and jolly outcasts, the wood-trimmed Hilltop is also notable for its vintage furnishings and piped-in negative ions.

MARUNOUCHI HOTEL

Map pp294-5 Luxury Hotel ¥¥¥

☎ 3215-2151; www.marunouchi-hotel.co.jp/english/index.html; Oazo Bldg, 1-6-3 Marunouchi, Chiyoda-ku; s/d from ¥23,300/31,385; JR Yamanote Line to Tokyo (Marunouchi north exit)

Housed in the brand-new Oazo Building opposite Tokyo Station, the newest version of the Marunouchi Hotel deftly synthesises modern conveniences with definite Japanese style. Paper *shōji* (sliding rice-paper screens) over windows and gorgeous inlaid wood furnishings accent simple, unfussy rooms, while undulating curves echo from atriums to marble countertops to retro alarm clocks. Oh-so-civilised restaurants and bars round out its chic appeal.

PALACE HOTEL

Map pp294-5 Luxury Hotel ¥¥¥

☎ 3211-5211; www.palacehotel.co.jp/english; 1-1-1 Marunouchi, Chiyoda-ku; s/d from ¥25,200/33,600; Chiyoda, Marunouchi, Toei Mita or Tōzai Line to Ōtemachi (exit C13b)

Directly alongside the Imperial Palace, the Palace Hotel has an old-fashioned atmosphere and arguably the best location in Tokyo. Many rooms command impressive views over the palace and gardens. The service is predictably wonderful, the hotel's restaurants are among Tokyo's best, and the hotel's quaint time warp is an immediate balm against whatever cut-throat action your day has hurled at you.

TOKYO INTERNATIONAL YOUTH HOSTEL Map pp294-5 Youth Hostel ¥

☎ 3235-1107; www.tokyo-yh.jp/eng/e_top.html; 1-1 Kagurakashi, Shinjuku-ku; dm adult/child ¥3500/2400; JR Yamanote Line to Iidabashi (west exit);

It may be a dorm, but these dorm rooms have spectacular five-star views over Shinjuku-ku. Though the interior of the hostel's two floors feels like an anonymous office (there's even a conference room), it's a model hostel outfitted with laundry, Internet access and the best budget views in Tokyo.

TOKYO STATION HOTEL

Map pp294-5 Business Hotel ¥¥

☎ 3231-2511; www.tshl.co.jp/top_e.html; 1-9-1 Marunouchi, Chiyoda-ku; s/d from ¥11,600/19,600; JR Yamanote Line to Tokyo (Marunouchi central exit)

Built in 1914 of red brick, this hotel's looks are distinctive – elegant interiors feature high ceilings, wood trim and red carpets. Bypass the cheaper modern rooms for the classically designed rooms on the second floor. Light sleepers should request rooms on the west side, furthest from the trains.

YAESU RYŪMEIKAN Map pp294-5 Ryokan ¥¥

☎ 3271-0971; www.ryumeikan.co.jp.yaesu_e.htm; 1-3-22 Yaesu, Chūō-ku; s ¥10,500-13,500, d ¥17,600-19,000; JR Yamanote Line to Tokyo (Yaesu north exit) or Tōzai Line to Nihombashi (exit A3);

Yaesu Ryūmeikan's comfortable Japanese-style rooms are a steal in this locale, especially since a full Japanese breakfast is included in the price. Though slightly worn around the edges, it's a cosy spot with friendly staff, and it does have conveniences like broadband Internet hook-ups. Book in advance, as this place is often packed.

USEFUL JAPANESE

capsule hotel カプセルホテル
hotel ホテル
minshuku 民宿
ryokan 旅館
youth hostel ユースホステル

YAESU TERMINAL HOTEL

Map pp294-5 Business Hotel ¥¥

☎ 3281-3771; www.yth.jp; 1-5-14 Yaesu, Chūō-ku; s/d ¥11,340/16,590; JR Yamanote Line to Tokyo (Yaesu north exit)

This attractive business hotel has sleek lines and a contemporary, somewhat minimalist aesthetic. Though room sizes are most definitely on the microscopic end, they're decently priced for this neighbourhood and very clean. Rooms are simple and unadorned, calling to mind a never-at-home bachelor's digs. A cut above, it's also a short walk away from Tokyo Station and Ginza.

GINZA

Ginza, and the latest revitalisation of nearby Shiodome, offer some of Tokyo's poshest accommodation. Along with the ultraluxe, however, are some sleek, midrange hotels. Expect rates here to be higher than in the rest of the city – Ginza real estate is some of the priciest on the planet.

GINZA MERCURE Map pp290-1 Luxury Hotel ¥¥¥

☎ 4335-1111; www.mercureginza.com in Japanese; 2-9-4 Ginza, Chūō-ku; s/d from ¥18,375/24,150; Yūrakuchō Line to Ginza-itchōme (exit 11);

Popular with ladies from out of town who come in for Ginza shopping expeditions, the petite Mercure is ideally placed for dragging spoils back from Chanel, Mitsukoshi and Tiffany. Vanilla-hued marble floors and chunky red furnishings offset the tasteful use of floral décor. Broadband Internet access and double-paned windows for quiet also make it classy headquarters for businesspeople.

GINZA NIKKŌ HOTEL

Map pp290-1 Business Hotel ¥¥

☎ 3571-4911; www.ginza-nikko-hotel.com/english/index.html; 8-4-21 Ginza, Chūō-ku; s/d from ¥13,960/27,920; JR Yamanote Line to Shimbashi (Ginza exit) or Ginza Line to Shimbashi (exit 5);

Though this Ginza hotel has been around for 45 years, it's looking fine and bright after a thorough remodel several years ago. All of the spotless rooms come equipped with LAN Internet access and full-sized bathtubs. A smart and solid business hotel, it's perfectly placed for a dawn stroll to Tsukiji Central Fish Market, midday shopping in Ginza, and evening *izakaya* (bar)-hopping.

WORTH THE TRIP

Though the bulk of Tokyo's accommodation is located in the central neighbourhoods we've listed, those looking to get off the beaten track might seek out these options.

Andon Ryokan (Map pp278–9; ☎ 3873-8611; www.andon.co.jp; 2-34-10 Nihonzutsumi, Taitō-ku; r per person ¥8190; Ⓜ Hibiya Line to Minowa, exit 3; 💻) Fabulously designed in form and function, the minimalist and modern Andon Ryokan has tiny but immaculate tatami rooms. Pluses include free Internet access, DVD players, cheap breakfasts and laundry facilities. This gem is run by the same people who established the more downmarket New Koyo (below).

Four Seasons Hotel Chinzan-sō (Map pp278–9; ☎ 3943-2222; www.fourseasons.com; 2-10-8 Sekiguchi, Bunkyō-ku; s/d from ¥45,150/47,250; Ⓜ Yūrakuchō Line to Edogawabashi, exit 1a) Ridiculously opulent with Japanese antiques and a European feel, the Four Seasons Chinzan-sō is built on the grounds of a Meiji-era ornamental garden.

Hotel Bellclassic (Map pp278–9; ☎ 5950-1200; www.hotel-bellclassic.co.jp; 3-33-6 Minami-Ōtsuka, Toshima-ku; s/d ¥14,700/23,100; Ⓜ JR Yamanote Line to Ōtsuka, south exit) One stop from Ikebukuro, this churchy-looking business hotel has immaculate, plain-vanilla rooms that are a smidge wider than those at standard business hotels. Room rates go down off season.

Hotel New Koyo (Map pp296–7; ☎ 3873-0343; www.newkoyo.com; 2-26-13 Nihonzutsumi, Taitō-ku; r ¥2500-4800; Ⓜ Hibiya Line to Minowa, exit 3) Tokyo's cheapest rooms, worth the stay if you're seriously short on yen.

Juyoh Hotel (Map pp278–9; ☎ 3875-5362; www.juyoh.co.jp; 2-15-3 Kiyokawa, Taitō-ku; s/d ¥3200/6400; Ⓜ Hibiya Line to Minami-Senju, south exit) The three tiny doubles and numerous singles fill up fast at this little spot in the old city. Reservations and directions are available on the excellent website.

Ryokan Sansuiso (Map pp278–9; ☎ 3441-7475; www.sansuiso.net; 2-9-5 Higashi-Gotanda, Shinagawa-ku; s/d from ¥4900/8600; Ⓜ JR Yamanote Line to Gotanda, east exit) This sweet, seven-room ryokan gets a bit of rail noise from the JR tracks nearby, but with that comes the experience of staying in a real Japanese home.

HOTEL SEIYŌ GINZA

Map pp290-1 Luxury Hotel ¥¥¥

☎ 3535-1111; www.seiyo-ginza.com; 1-11-2 Ginza, Chūō-ku; r ¥45,000-200,000; Ⓜ Yūrakuchō Line to Ginza-itchōme (exit 7) or Ginza Line to Kyōbashi (exit 2)

The Seiyō Ginza resembles a rambling mansion (in the non-Japanese sense of the word) hosting several parties of guests. Each room comes with a personal butler attending to guests' needs around the clock – the only hotel in Tokyo to provide such a service. For those requiring rarefied isolation, the Seiyō can be your secret hideaway in the middle of Ginza.

IMPERIAL HOTEL

Map pp290-1 Luxury Hotel ¥¥¥

☎ 3504-1111; www.imperialhotel.co.jp; 1-1-1 Uchisaiwaichō, Chiyoda-ku; s/d from ¥35,750/40,950; Ⓜ Chiyoda, Hibiya or Toei Mita Line to Hibiya (exit A13); 💻

The Imperial Hotel's present building replaces Frank Lloyd Wright's 1923 masterpiece, and small tributes to Wright – in the form of a chair or a modernist motif – adorn the lobby. Large rooms in the newest Imperial floor have been updated with features like large-screen plasma TVs and high-speed Internet while maintaining the refined design of this venerable hotel.

MITSUI URBAN HOTEL GINZA

Map pp290-1 Business Hotel ¥¥

☎ 3527-4131; www.mitsuikanko.co.jp; 8-6-15 Ginza, Chūō-ku; s/d from ¥14,500/25,000; Ⓜ JR Yamanote Line to Shimbashi (Ginza exit) or Ginza Line to Shimbashi (exit 3); 💻

Starting with the eccentric mirrored elevator, the Mitsui Urban's sparkly personality blinds you with polish. But the relatively spacious rooms, toned in sepia and bone, are a reprieve from the shiny-surfaced public areas. Flat-screen TVs accent the urban décor and some rooms come with broadband Internet access. Two floors of restaurants cover you from breakfast to nightcap.

SHIODOME

Revitalised Shiodome, a sliver of slick development shoulder-to-shoulder with Shimbashi and Hama Rikyū Onshi-teien (Detached Palace Garden), provides an upscale, high-rise accommodation alternative to the smaller hotels of Ginza.

CONRAD HOTEL Map pp290-1 Luxury Hotel ¥¥¥

☎ 6388 8000; www.conradtokyo.co.jp; 1-9-1 Higashi-Shimbashi, Minato-ku; s/d from ¥52,000/57,000; Ⓜ JR Yamanote, Ginza or Toei Asakusa Line to Shimbashi (Shiodome exit)

Impressive, in a word. One of the gigantic, glittery gems comprising the new Shiodome development adjacent to Hama Rikyū Onshi-teien, the Conrad Hotel is definitely a new contender for the attentions of upscale travellers looking for that central, supersophisticated base in Tokyo. The garden or city views are equally spectacular, as are the varnished hardwood interiors and floor-to-ceiling glassed-in bathrooms of the hotel. Understated *and* over-the-top.

HOTEL VILLA FONTAINE SHIODOME

Map pp290-1 Business Hotel ¥¥

☎ 5339-1200; www.villa-fontaine.co.jp/eng/shiodome/index.html; 1-9-2 Higashi-Shimbashi, Minato-ku; s & d ¥10,000-18,000; Ⓜ JR Yamanote, Ginza or Toei Asakusa Line to Shimbashi (Shiodome exit); 💻

Cone-shaped floor lanterns light the high-ceilinged, black marble lobby. Sculptural red blobs and flame-themed art on the walls lead to decidedly less spooky, upscale rooms with Internet TV and partial views of Hama Rikyū Onshi-teien. A slightly eccentric and excellent deal in one of Tokyo's newest revamped neighbourhoods, rates include the rarity of a buffet breakfast.

KANDA & AROUND

Kanda is not the most appealing of the city's neighbourhoods, but it does have some good midrange bargains. Nearby are Tokyo's finest traditional restaurants (see p127 for listings) and Jimbōchō's millions of antique manuscripts (see p182 for more information).

HOTEL NEW KANDA

Map pp294-5 Business Hotel ¥¥

☎ 3258-3911; www.hotelnewkanda.com in Japanese; 2-10 Kanda Awajichō, Chiyoda-ku; s/d from ¥9975/12,600; Ⓜ JR Chūō or JR Sōbu Line to Ochanomizu (Hijiribashi exit); 💻

Posher than your average business hotel, the New Kanda offers all the basics in a comfortable, upscale setting. An easy, five-minute walk from either of two JR stations, and with a Family Mart and in-house restaurant downstairs, it's convenient from any angle. Taller guests will appreciate the larger semidouble beds. Internet access can be arranged at check-in.

NEW CENTRAL HOTEL

Map pp294-5 Business Hotel ¥¥

☎ 3256-2171; www.pelican.co.jp; 2-7-2 Kanda-Tachō, Chiyoda-ku; s/d/tw from ¥7350/7875/10,080; Ⓜ JR Yamanote Line to Kanda (west exit)

A cheap choice near several railway lines, the accommodation at the New Central won't wow anyone. But what sets this otherwise just-OK place apart are its homely communal bath facilities. Catering to the salaryman, the

ALTERNATIVES TO SLEEPING

If you've missed the last train back to your hotel, that ¥3000 in your pocket might be better spent staying out all night than on a taxi ride home. Happily, nocturnal Tokyo has options for insomniacs. You could pay the cover at a club, nurse your one free drink for an hour, and then tear up the dance floor until dawn.

Those feeling less groovin' might look for a nearby manga (comic book) café. Full-night rates at manga cafés are a bargain, comparable to those at capsule hotels. You can while away the wee hours watching DVDs, reading manga, surfing the Internet and having a bite to eat – or napping in your lounge chair. Staff make regular rounds to ensure a safe environment.

Café J Net New New (Map p284; ☎ 5458-5935; 7th fl, Saito Bldg, 34-5 Udagawachō, Shibuya-ku; 🕑 24hr; Ⓜ JR Yamanote Line to Shibuya, Hachikō exit)

Manga Hiroba (Map p286; ☎ 3497-1751; 2nd fl, Shuwa Roppongi Bldg, 3-14-12 Roppongi, Minato-ku; 🕑 24hr; Ⓜ Hibiya or Toei Ōedo Line to Roppongi, exit 3)

Manga@Cafe-Gera Gera (Map p282; ☎ 5285-0585; 1-23-1 Kabukichō, Shinjuku-ku; 🕑 24hr; Ⓜ JR Yamanote Line to Shinjuku, east exit).

men's bath is roomier than the bamboo-floored women's. Westerners should opt for the larger doubles, as singles are not only closet-sized but also lack showers.

TOKYO GREEN HOTEL OCHANOMIZU

Map pp294-5 Business Hotel ¥¥

☎ 3255-4161; www.greenhotel.co.jp/ochanomizu_e.html; 2-6 Kanda-Awajichō, Chiyoda-ku; s/d from ¥8400/13,000; JR Chūō or JR Sōbu Line to Ochanomizu (Hijiribashi exit)

A few blocks south of Kanda-gawa, this immaculate spot is the nicest in Kanda. Rooms are comfortable and spotless, staff are friendly and polite, and the quiet surroundings are conducive to a good night's sleep. Its visual appeal, with details like sliding window screens and varnished woods, makes it a lovely break from the monotonous concrete jungle.

YAMA-NO-UE (HILLTOP) HOTEL

Map pp294-5 Luxury Hotel ¥¥¥

☎ 3293-2311; www.yamanoue-hotel.co.jp; 1-1 Kanda-Surugadai, Chiyoda-ku; s/d from ¥15,750/23,100; JR Chūō or JR Sōbu Line to Ochanomizu (Ochanomizu exit)

One of Japan's most esteemed authors, Mishima Yukio, wrote his last few novels here. For your own literary endeavours (or daily itinerary-planning), the older, unpretentious rooms in the main building come with antique writing desks and inviting, overstuffed chairs. Negative ions circulated throughout the rooms supposedly promote relaxation but may not be worth the expense for some.

Cheap Sleeps

SAKURA HOTEL Map pp294-5 Hostel ¥

☎ 3261-3939; www.sakura-hotel.co.jp; 2-21-4 Kanda-Jimbōchō, Chiyoda-ku; dm/s/d from ¥3780/6090/8400; Marunouchi, Toei Mita or Toei Shinjuku Line to Jimbōchō (exit A6);

A sunny spot literally and figuratively, the Sakura Hotel is a reliable cheapie with a sociable atmosphere. Staff are bilingual and helpful, and the rooms, though pretty basic, are comfortable and clean. There's a 24-hour café, and laundry and Internet access, but bookworms will appreciate it most for its location in the bookshop district of Jimbōchō.

UENO

Families travelling with kids will find Ueno easy to access and full of attractions. Keisei trains from Narita airport run directly to Ueno, and the park is stuffed with museums, Ueno Zoo, buskers and paddleboats on the pond. Travellers looking for nightlife and a more central location should consider Shibuya or Shinjuku instead.

HOTEL PARKSIDE Map pp296-7 Business Hotel ¥¥

☎ 3836-5711; www.parkside.co.jp; 2-11-18 Ueno, Taitō-ku; Western-style s/d from ¥9200/14,000, Japanese-style r from ¥18,000; JR Yamanote Line to Ueno (Shinobazu exit)

The Parkside has some of the best midrange accommodation in this neighbourhood, as well as green views of the gigantic lily pads on Shinobazu Pond. Choose from either Western- or Japanese-style rooms, but make sure to get a spot above the 4th floor for the best views. The doubles were remodelled in 2005 with larger bathrooms and attractive, contemporary wood detailing.

SOFITEL TOKYO Map pp296-7 Luxury Hotel ¥¥¥

☎ 5685-7111; www.sofiteltokyo.com; 2-1-48 Ikenohata, Taitō-ku; s/d from ¥30,000/35,000; Chiyoda Line to Nezu (exit 2) or Yushima (exit 1)

You can't miss this kooky Lego-land Christmas tree looming over the paddleboats on Shinobazu-ike. Big beds, beautiful décor and a low-profile Shitamachi location make it a smart, if not exactly hidden, hideaway. Its location is less than central, but it's close enough to Ueno Station and a cluster of subway stations to get you anywhere in the city fairly quickly.

SUIGETSU HOTEL ŌGAI-SŌ

Map pp296-7 Business Hotel ¥¥

☎ 3822-4611; www.ohgai.co.jp/index-e.html; 3-3-21 Ikenohata, Taitō-ku; Western-style s/d ¥7980/11,550, Japanese-style r from ¥18,000; Chiyoda Line to Nezu (exit 2)

Well-placed for museum visits from the western edge of Ueno-kōen, this is a reasonably priced blend of East and West. With mostly Japanese-style tatami rooms, the hotel is set around a serene Japanese garden. Western-style rooms incorporate well-selected traditional touches, like sliding screens over the windows. Don't miss a soak in one of the hotel's lovely, large *sentō* (public bath).

UENO FIRST CITY HOTEL

Map pp296-7 Business Hotel ¥¥

☎ 3831-8215; www.uenocity-hotel.com; 1-14-8 Ueno, Taitō-ku; s/d from ¥8000/13,000; Ⓜ Chiyoda Line to Yushima (exit 4)

Unlike most hotels, the tatami rooms here are the same price as the Western rooms and unlike most ryokan, they also have ensuite bathrooms. Simple rooms of both types are functional, clean and cosy, and new tatami was recently installed in the Japanese-style quarters. Though it's a 15-minute hike from Ueno Station, this unassuming spot is a great deal in Ueno.

Cheap Sleeps

RYOKAN KATSUTARŌ

Map pp296-7 Ryokan ¥

☎ 3821-9808; www.katsutaro.com; 4-16-8 Ikenohata, Taitō-ku; s/d ¥5200/8400; Ⓜ Chiyoda Line to Nezu (exit 2); 💻

Ryokan Katsutarō's family-style atmosphere is a low-key introduction to Tokyo. With only seven tatami rooms, it feels that much homier than larger ryokan but still comes with perks like laundry machines and free Internet. Family-run and family-friendly, it's located in a quaint, quiet neighbourhood near Ueno-kōen and the zoo. Basic breakfasts are ¥500 and it even accepts credit cards.

RYOKAN KATSUTARŌ ANNEX

Map pp296-7 Ryokan ¥

☎ 3828-2500; www.katsutaro.com; 3-8-4 Yanaka, Taitō-ku; s/d ¥6300/10,500; Ⓜ Chiyoda Line to Sendagi (exit 2); 💻

More a modern incarnation than the strict country-inn version of a ryokan, this spotless place has all tatami rooms with Western-style baths attached. There's LAN access in each room, but the lobby has both free Internet access *and* free coffee. Call ahead for directions in English, or print out a map from the website. Happily, major credit cards are accepted.

SAWANOYA RYOKAN

Map pp296-7 Ryokan ¥

☎ 3822-2251; www.sawanoya.com; 2-3-11 Yanaka, Taitō-ku; s/d from ¥4935/9240; Ⓜ Chiyoda Line to Nezu (exit 1); 💻

The efficient staff at this family-run ryokan work their matter-of-fact magic to make you feel at home. Set on a narrow street in quiet Yanaka, it's a pleasant walk to Ueno-kōen.

STAYING AT A RYOKAN

With a few exceptions, most Tokyo ryokan (traditional Japanese inns) don't offer the full-on traditional experience with meals and futon-folding; however, knowing the drill will come in handy for travels outside of Tokyo.

On arrival at the ryokan, you leave your shoes at the entrance steps, you don a pair of slippers, and you are shown to your tatami-floored room by a maid. Slippers are taken off before entering tatami rooms. Instead of using numbers, rooms are often named after auspicious flowers, plants or trees.

The room usually contains a *tokonoma* (alcove), decorated with a flower display or a calligraphy scroll. One side of the room will contain a cupboard with sliding doors for the bedding; the other will have *shōji* (sliding rice-paper screens) and may open onto a veranda with a garden view.

A tray is provided with a towel, *yukata* (light cotton robe) and *obi* (belt), which you put on before taking your *o-furo* (traditional Japanese bath). Remember to close the left side of the *yukata* over the right – the reverse order is used for dressing the dead. In colder weather, there will also be a *tanzen* (outer jacket). You can wear the *yukata* in both private and public areas of the ryokan.

Some ryokan offer rooms with private baths, but the communal ones are often designed with 'natural' pools or a window looking onto a garden. Bathing is communal, but sexes are segregated. Make sure you can differentiate between the bathroom signs for men and women, (although ryokan will often have signs in English).

At traditional ryokan, dinner is usually laid out in the guest rooms – in some ryokan, dinner is provided in a separate room. Along with rice, dinner usually includes standard dishes such as miso soup, *tsukemono* (pickles), *sunomono* (vegetables in vinegar), *zensai* (hors d'oeuvres), *sashimi* (fish either grilled or raw), and perhaps tempura and a stew. Meals at a ryokan can become flamboyant displays of local cuisine or refined arrangements of *kaiseki* (see p42 for more information). After dinner, the maid will clear the dishes and prepare your bedding. A futon is placed on the tatami floor and a quilt put on top.

In the morning, the maid will knock to make sure you are awake, then come in to put away the bedding before serving breakfast. Breakfast usually consists of pickles, *nori* (dried seaweed), raw egg, dried fish, miso soup and rice, though many places are now offering a more Western menu. After breakfast, the day is yours.

Japanese-style room, Ryokan Shigetsu (below)

Most rooms share the house's Japanese-style baths. Along with free tea and coffee in the bright lounge area, you'll find free Internet access and friendly itinerary advice.

SUZUKI RYOKAN Map pp296-7 Ryokan ¥

☎ 3821-4944; www.itcj.jp; 7-15-23 Yanaka, Taitō-ku; s without bath ¥4000, d with bath ¥8000; JR Yamanote Line to Nippori (south exit)

The *obasaan* (grandmotherly ladies) running this show don't speak English, but that won't stop them from efficiently getting you settled. This traditional but quirky house, with its astroturf stairs and a bumpy stone-and-wood-cobbled floor, is weirdly charming. Make reservations through the Welcome Inn Reservation Center, unless you speak enough Japanese to call the ryokan yourself. Unfortunately, visitors from Iran and Iraq have reported being turned away at the door.

ASAKUSA

If you're only in Tokyo for a short time, Asakusa is a great, laid-back area to stay. Though not the centre of Tokyo, it's the heart of Shitamachi, which was depicted in the millions of *ukiyo-e* (wood-block prints) that were pressed within its quarters. You'll also find two wonderful, classic ryokan here, near Sensō-ji.

ASAKUSA VIEW HOTEL

Map pp296-7 Luxury Hotel ¥¥¥

☎ 3847-1111; www.viewhotels.co.jp/asakusa/english; 3-17-1 Nishi-Asakusa, Taitō-ku; Western-style s/d from ¥13,650/29,400, Japanese-style r ¥42,000-63,000; Ginza Line to Tawaramachi (exit 3)

If you're keen on staying in the area but are not into the ryokan, the Asakusa View is by far the ritziest place in the neighbourhood. From the lacquer-patterned elevator walls to the Japanese cypress and granite baths, the hotel is lavishly designed. While the spacious rooms aren't particularly striking, their large windows overlook nearby Sensō-ji in the east or west to Shinjuku in the distance.

RYOKAN SHIGETSU Map pp296-7 Ryokan ¥¥

☎ 3843-2345; www.shigetsu.com; 1-31-11 Asakusa, Taitō-ku; Japanese-style r ¥8400/26,250, Western-style r ¥7665-14,700; Toei Asakusa or Toei Ōedo Line to Asakusa (exit 1)

South of Asakusa-kōen, this spotless and atmospheric ryokan has mostly Japanese-style rooms. The entire inn is immaculate, with carpeted entryways and *shōji*-screened doors and windows. Absolutely required is taking at least one bath here; however, two are recommended to fully savour the views from each *o-furo* (traditional Japanese bath): one over the city, the other toward the five-storey pagoda at Sensō-ji.

SUKEROKU NO YADO SADACHIYO

Map pp296-7 Ryokan ¥¥

☎ 3842-6431; www.sadachiyo.co.jp; 2-20-1 Asakusa, Taitō-ku; s/d ¥12,000/17,600; Ⓜ Ginza or Toei Asakusa Line to Asakusa (exit 1)

This stunning ryokan virtually transports its guests to old Edo. Gorgeously maintained tatami rooms are spacious for two people, and all come with modern, Western-style bathrooms. Splurge on an exquisite meal here, and make time for the *o-furo*, one made of fragrant Japanese cypress and the other of black marble. Lighter sleepers should book on higher floors, away from the alley's strains of karaoke.

Cheap Sleeps

CAPSULE HOTEL RIVERSIDE

Map pp296-7Capsule Hotel ¥

☎ 3844-1155; 2-20-4 Kaminarimon, Taitō-ku; capsules ¥3300; Ⓜ Ginza or Toei Asakusa Line to Asakusa (exit 6)

For a pittance, the very clean Riverside sells an encapsulated night's sleep. Unlike most capsule hotels, it accepts both women and men, with the 8th floor reserved for female guests only. Separate sauna and bath facilities are provided for both sexes, and credit cards are accepted with a small surcharge. Enter round the back of the building.

SAKURA RYOKAN Map pp296-7 Ryokan ¥

☎ 3876-8118; www.sakura-ryokan.com/index-en.html; 2-6-2 Iriya, Taitō-ku; s&d ¥5500-11,000; Ⓜ Hibiya Line to Iriya (exits 1 & 2)

Rooms are clean and comfortable at this unpretentious inn. Since Western- and Japanese-style rooms are comparably priced, do yourself the favour of choosing a tatami one. While half the rooms have attached bathrooms, all have access to the communal baths – which, like the dining area, offer little superfluous charm but feel like part of a typical suburban home.

TAITŌ RYOKAN Map pp296-7 Ryokan ¥

☎ 3843-2822; www.libertyhouse.gr.jp; 2-1-4 Nishi-Asakusa, Taitō-ku; r per person ¥3000; Ⓜ Ginza Line to Tawaramachi (exit 3)

Taitō Ryokan is just the place for wandering souls more concerned with meeting kindred spirits than, say, quiet and luxury. This 1950s-era wooden house is one of the cheapest places around, with tatami rooms and decorative, carved wood trim. All rooms share one shower, and there isn't much noise privacy, but you're free to come and go at all hours.

AKASAKA

Who knows how many political deals have been made in the hushed rooms of Akasaka's luxury hotels. The location is mostly exclusive, though you'll see listed here a few functional, though not outstanding, options in the midrange bracket.

AKASAKA PRINCE HOTEL

Map pp294-5 Luxury Hotel ¥¥¥

☎ 3234-1111; www.princehotelsjapan.com/akasakaprincehotel/; 1-2 Kioi-chō, Chiyoda-ku; s/d from ¥29,000/38,500; Ⓜ Ginza or Marunouchi Line to Akasaka-mitsuke (exit 7), or Hanzōmon, Namboku or Yūrakuchō Line to Nagatachō (exits 5, 7 & 9)

This towering landmark, designed by architect Tange Kenzō to echo the shape of a Japanese fan, has over 700 spacious rooms providing excellent views. As well as its naturally-aged, retro '80s appeal, the princely address still carries a certain cachet. The lobby is done up in marble and mirrors, while rooms are simple in design and large.

AKASAKA YŌKŌ HOTEL

Map p286 Business Hotel ¥¥

☎ 3586-4050; www.yokohotel.co.jp in Japanese; 6-14-12 Akasaka, Minato-ku; s/d ¥9345/13,650; Ⓜ Chiyoda Line to Akasaka (exit 7)

This is a reasonably priced business hotel about midway between Akasaka and Roppongi. Although it's quite simple, the modest rooms are clean and comfortable and the staff are friendly. From the Yōkō, you're close enough to walk to Roppongi for a wild night out, but far enough to retire peacefully to quieter pastures afterwards.

ANA HOTEL TOKYO

Map pp290-1 Luxury Hotel ¥¥¥

☎ 3505-1111; www.anahoteltokyo.jp/e/; 1-12-33 Akasaka, Minato-ku; s/d from ¥28,350/36,750; Ⓜ Ginza Line to Tameike-sannō (exit 13) or Namboku Line to Roppongi-itchōme (exit 3)

With an enormous, chandelier-hung lobby in the Ark Hills area, the plush 37-storey

Ana Hotel Tokyo is in the process of refined refurbishment by degrees. With an outdoor pool, a small gym and an excellent business centre, this remains a sleek and sophisticated choice. Elegant rooms are large and well appointed, some with views of Mt Fuji.

ASIA CENTER OF JAPAN

Map p286 Business Hotel ¥¥

☎ 3402-6111; www.asiacenter.or.jp; 8-10-32 Akasaka, Minato-ku; s/d from ¥8200/10,800; Ⓜ Ginza, Hanzōmon or Toei Ōedo Line to Aoyama-itchōme (exit 4); 💻

Down a narrow road in a quiet Akasaka neighbourhood, the Asia Center covers the basics of a business hotel – omitting the oppressively cramped quarters. Old-annexe rooms come with wood-planked walls and an airy, simple charm. Served by four subway lines within a five-minute walk, the Asia Center is also a quick walk to Roppongi. It also offers coin-operated Internet access and laundry facilities, as well as cheap ¥795 breakfasts. It's also a quick walk to Roppongi.

CAPITOL TŌKYŪ HOTEL

Map pp290-1 Luxury Hotel ¥¥

☎ 3581-4511; www.capitoltokyu.com/english; 2-10-3 Nagatachō, Minato-ku; s/d ¥26,000/55,000; Ⓜ Ginza or Namboku Line to Tameike-sannō (exit 5)

Sitting on the same hill as Hie-jinja, this refined hotel is constructed around a fine Japanese garden. Several good restaurants and bars, warmly decorated with gleaming wood interiors, take in the lovely garden views. In warmer months, you can lounge around the outdoor swimming pool. The hotel's glossy, eminently comfortable accommodation is a relaxing haven from business and government deal-making in Akasaka.

HOTEL NEW ŌTANI Map p286 Luxury Hotel ¥¥¥

☎ 3265-1111; www1.newotani.co.jp/en/tokyo/index.html; 4-1 Kioi-chō, Chiyoda-ku; s/d from ¥31,000/36,000; Ⓜ Ginza or Marunouchi Line to Akasaka-mitsuke (Belle Vie exit)

There's definitely a whiff of pretension about the New Ōtani, but it's somewhat justified, loaded as it is with large, luxurious rooms, upscale restaurants, boutiques and gift shops. This august establishment even has its own art museum and an immaculately manicured, 10-acre, 400-year-old Japanese garden surrounding it, for which it is renowned (see p91 for more information).

HOTEL ŌKURA Map pp290-1 Luxury Hotel ¥¥¥

☎ 3582-0111; tokyo.okura.com; 2-10-4 Toranomon, Minato-ku; s/d from ¥34,125/42,000; Ⓜ Ginza Line to Toranomon (exit 3)

A preferred landing place for visiting dignitaries and businesspeople, the unpretentious but graceful Hotel Ōkura exudes old-school elegance. Lovely and lived-in, the inviting feel of the hotel's décor and low-lying architecture are matched by personable staff who take a warm but discreet approach. There are excellent business facilities, and the beautiful Japanese garden and top-notch restaurants complete the picture.

HOTEL SUNROUTE AKASAKA

Map pp290-1 Business Hotel ¥¥

☎ 3589-3610; www.sunroute.jp; 3-21-7 Akasaka, Minato-ku; s/d from ¥13,125/15,225; Ⓜ Ginza or Marunouchi Line to Akasaka-mitsuke (Belle Vie exit); 💻

A bright, friendly spot with well-designed rooms all equipped with high-speed Internet access, this is conveniently located near the Akasaka-mitsuke subway station and is a fifteen-minute walk from Roppongi nightlife. There's no restaurant, but there's an Excelsior Café (akin to Starbucks) downstairs.

Cheap Sleeps

CAPSULE HOTEL FONTAINE AKASAKA Map pp290-1 Capsule Hotel ¥

☎ 3583-6554; 4-3-5 Akasaka, Minato-ku; capsules men/women Mon-Fri ¥4800/4500, Sat & Sun ¥4500; Ⓜ Ginza or Marunouchi Line to Akasaka-mitsuke (Belle Vie exit)

This upmarket capsule hotel is one of the few in Tokyo that accept women. It also happens to be one of the more luxurious, featuring lovely bath and sauna facilities and comfortable, bright sitting areas. On weekends, women sometimes take over several capsules for sleepovers – the baths here are perfect for soaking, steaming and socialising till all hours.

ROPPONGI

While Roppongi is an attractive place to base yourself if you plan on carousing in local bars and clubs until the wee hours, the pricey accommodation reflects the area's popularity. That said, there are a few excellent midrange hotels handily placed close to Roppongi Crossing, in addition to the more upscale choices nearby.

ARCA TORRE Map p286 — Business Hotel ¥¥

☎ 3404-5111; www.arktower.co.jp; 6-1-23 Roppongi, Minato-ku; s ¥11,000-13,000, d ¥14,000-21,000; Ⓜ Hibiya or Toei Ōedo Line to Roppongi (exit 3)

Excellently placed yet reasonably priced, the cosy Arca Torre is made for hard-partiers and heavy sleepers. Beds are on the hard side, but even standard singles are furnished with semi-double beds. As it's steps away from Roppongi Crossing, the soundtrack of heavy traffic seeps in from all sides, but it's an easy, central stumble home.

GRAND HYATT TOKYO

Map p286 — Luxury Hotel ¥¥¥

☎ 4333-8800; www.grandhyatttokyo.com; 6-10-3 Roppongi, Minato-ku; s/d from ¥47,250/52,500; Ⓜ Hibiya or Toei Ōedo Line to Roppongi (exits 1c & 3)

Architecturally open and bright despite its somewhat labyrinthine layout, the Grand Hyatt is warmly, gorgeously chic. Smooth mahogany and natural fabrics give an organic flavour to the rooms, while its Roppongi Hills location imparts it with vibrant energy. Even the bathrooms feature rainshower fixtures and rough-cut stone, carrying on a nature-in-architecture motif. It has easy sophistication well-suited for business and pleasure.

HOTEL IBIS Map p286 — Business Hotel ¥¥

☎ 3403-4411; www.ibis-hotel.com; 7-14-4 Roppongi, Minato-ku; s/d from ¥13,382/16,023; Ⓜ Hibiya or Toei Ōedo Line to Roppongi (exit 4a)

Ideally placed for those who want to be close to Roppongi nightlife, the Ibis is comfortable spot to settle in after a debauched night. There's also a fancy karaoke lounge based here, with private themed rooms. Just this side of noir, the interior suggests some dark drama lurking underneath. Lighter sleepers should request a quiet room not facing the back.

ROPPONGI PRINCE HOTEL

Map pp290-1 — Luxury Hotel ¥¥¥

☎ 3587-1111; www.princehotelsjapan.com/roppongiprincehotel; s/d ¥19,500/24,500; Ⓜ Namboku Line to Roppongi-itchōme (exit 1)

One of those rare hotels in Tokyo that hasn't reinvented itself fifty times since 1970, the Roppongi Prince retains its cred like an aging rock star who shuns a facelift. Its curvy, groovy courtyard boasts a heated outdoor swimming pool. This Prince is only a 10-minute walk from the excesses of Roppongi.

EBISU

Just up the JR Yamanote Line from Shibuya, Ebisu is an excellent location from which to explore Tokyo. The neighbourhood is funky and playful and also features an array of crazy, locally designed architecture. Staying in Ebisu will give you a good idea of how the smart and stylish folk in Tokyo live. Accommodation options vary in price, though all are within striking distance of the central train station.

HOTEL EXCELLENT Map p288 — Business Hotel ¥¥

☎ 5458-0087; 1-9-5 Ebisu-nishi, Shibuya-ku; s/d ¥9100/11,550; Ⓜ JR Yamanote Line to Ebisu (west exit) or Hibiya Line to Ebisu (exit 3); 💻

Thirty seconds away from the JR Ebisu Station, this hotel may not be excellent but it is a perfectly adequate place to stay. This is a bare-bones joint in one of Tokyo's most idiosyncratic central neighbourhoods. While it offers no laundry, no breakfast, and no personality, the hotel does have free LAN Internet access and clean, smoke-free rooms at your request.

KYOWA KAIKAN Map p288 — Ryokan ¥¥

☎ 3464-2262; 1-10-5 Ebisu-nishi, Shibuya-ku; Western-style s/d ¥7300/11,000, Japanese-style r ¥19,000; Ⓜ JR Yamanote Line to Ebisu (west exit) or Hibiya Line to Ebisu (exit 3)

Just up the street from Ebisu-jinja, this functional little inn is not on the normal tourist routes, but it has a few Japanese-style rooms. The family that runs the place is stern but warm, but not everyone speaks English. Doors shut at midnight unless you ask the staff ahead of time to leave a door unlocked for you.

WESTIN HOTEL TOKYO

Map p288 Luxury Hotel ¥¥¥

☎ 5423-7000; www.westin-tokyo.co.jp/en/; 1-4-1 Mita, Meguro-ku; s/d ¥35,000/40,000; Ⓙ JR Yamanote Line to Ebisu (Atré exit)

This Westin could be a beautiful hotel in New York, Paris or Munich except for the ikebana (flower arrangement) the size of a baby elephant in the lobby. The rooms have a lovely, laid-back European panache, and the clientele is grown-up but hip. From the station, take the Skywalk to Ebisu Garden Place and head towards the road round back.

SHIBUYA

Clustered around Shibuya Station and the streets spoking away from it are a variety of great midrange and high-end hotels. Naturally enough, it's still the neighbourhood where visiting rock stars put up camp after a big show at NHK Hall or a smaller gig at one of Shibuya's myriad live-music houses.

ARIMAX HOTEL Map p284 Luxury Hotel ¥¥¥

☎ 5454-1122; www.arimaxhotelshibuya.co.jp in Japanese; 11-15 Kamiyamachō, Shibuya-ku; s/d from ¥22,145/27,920; Ⓙ JR Yamanote Line to Shibuya (Hachikō exit)

This plush little corner of European pomp and polish is just minutes away from Shibuya Crossing's super-trendy promenade. Small and cushy, the Arimax is inviting in a way its vaguely incongruous name might not suggest. Neoclassical furnishings arranged in the lobby and its 23-room scale create its intimate atmosphere on the outskirts of wild Shibuya.

CERULEAN TOWER TŌKYŪ HOTEL

Map p284 Luxury Hotel ¥¥¥

☎ 3476-3000; www.ceruleantower-hotel.com/en/; 26-1 Sakuragaokachō, Shibuya-ku; s/d ¥27,720/36,960; Ⓙ JR Yamanote Line to Shibuya (south exit)

Sprawl out on huge beds and drink deeply of the big views, because there's room to breathe in these enormous rooms. The sleek lobby opens onto a garden view, an organic complement to the sleek modern aesthetic of this place. Arts fiends take note: quality *nō* (stylised dance-drama) and jazz performances take place at the impressive in-house theatre and jazz club (p166).

CHILDREN'S CASTLE HOTEL

Map p284 Business Hotel ¥¥

☎ 3797-5677; www.kodomono-shiro.or.jp/english/hotel; 5-53-1 Jingūmae, Shibuya-ku; Western-style s/d ¥6720/9975, Japanese-style r ¥21,420; Ⓙ JR Yamanote Line to Shibuya (east exit)

Though you may be disappointed to learn that it's not actually a castle, this small, *über* child-friendly hotel (known as Kodomo-no-Shiro in Japanese), is perfect for families – though childless guests are also welcome. The 'castle' itself is a paradise of play, with art projects, swimming pool, puppet shows and endless amusements for kids, *and* it's comfortable and childproof (see p96).

CRESTON HOTEL Map p284 Business Hotel ¥¥¥

☎ 3481-5800; www.crestonhotel.co.jp in Japanese; 10-8 Kamiyamachō, Shibuya-ku; s/d from ¥15,115/22,145; Ⓙ JR Yamanote Line to Shibuya (Hachikō exit)

Rumour has it that many a rock star has crashed here after the show at nearby NHK. Unassumingly chic and central enough to Shibuya without being in the middle of the party scene, the Creston has a laid-back, classy ambience. It's tucked down an alley that won't get much pedestrian traffic but gives easy access to Shibuya nightlife, restaurants and neighbourhood action.

HOTEL METS SHIBUYA

Map p284 Business Hotel ¥¥

☎ 3409-0011; www.hotelmets.jp/shibuya; 3-29-17Shibuya, Shibuya-ku; s/d from ¥11,000/18,000, wheelchair-accessible ¥19,000; Ⓙ JR Yamanote Line to Shibuya (new south exit); 💻 ♿

Super-convenient, Shibuya-central, and squarely comfortable, the Hotel Mets is strategically located adjacent to the hub that is Shibuya Station. It's worth laying out the extra ¥500 for a roomier deluxe single. Rates include free broadband Internet and the rarity of a free buffet breakfast.

Remember to book one of the pleasant, vanilla-toned rooms not facing the heavily-trafficked tracks.

SHIBUYA CITY HOTEL

Map p284 Business Hotel ¥¥

☎ 5489-1010; www.shibuya-city-hotel.com in Japanese; 1-1 Maruyamachō, Shibuya-ku; s/d from ¥9450/18,900; JR Yamanote Line to Shibuya (Hachikō exit);

Night owls will love this hotel, strategically located on the lower slope of Love Hotel Hill and a short downhill roll from loads of good live-music venues and clubs. For such a prime location, the prices are a fabulous deal. It has comfortable, spacious rooms, a superb Shibuya base, and even a tricked-out wheelchair-friendly room (¥14,800).

SHIBUYA TŌBU HOTEL

Map p284 Business Hotel ¥¥

☎ 3476-0111; www.tobuhotel.co.jp/shibuya in Japanese; 3-1 Udagawachō, Shibuya-ku; s/d from ¥13,960/19,635; JR Yamanote Line to Shibuya (Hachikō exit);

Roll into the smooth marble and wood-trimmed lobby to be greeted by a more airy, stylish atmosphere than at average business hotels. As with many hotels of this standard, it's worth spending up for the nicer singles, which have bigger, more comfortable semidouble beds. Rooms facing Kōen-dōri get some slight street noise, but it's otherwise a cool, reliable midrange choice.

SHIBUYA TŌKYŪ INN

Map p284 Business Hotel ¥¥

☎ 3498 0109; www.tokyuhotels.co.jp/en/; 1-24-10 Shibuya, Shibuya-ku; s/d from ¥13,440/21,420; JR Yamanote Line to Shibuya (east exit)

This quality chain hotel has some style, with clean lines and sliding window screens in pleasing primary colours. Shibuya Tōkyū Inn is close to Shibuya Station without being on top of the chaos, with double-paned windows blocking out station and street noise. Spacious singles are a superb deal, credit cards are accepted, and there's free dialup or paid broadband Internet access.

SHINJUKU

East and west Shinjuku are different worlds when it comes to accommodation. The west has the lion's share of luxury hotels, while the east generally offers the better deal and the more central location. Capsule hotels and manga cafés (p194) provide alternative accommodation.

CENTURY HYATT TOKYO

Map p282 Luxury Hotel ¥¥¥

☎ 3349-0111; www.tokyo.century.hyatt.com; 2-7-2 Nishi-Shinjuku, Shinjuku-ku; s/d from ¥23,000/32,000; Toei Ōedo Line to Tochōmae (exits A7 & C4)

Don't judge this place by its institutional exterior – though not in the same stratosphere as the Park Hyatt, this nonstop-marble behemoth holds its own as one of Shinjuku's best high-end accommodation options. Always housing a healthy population of international businesspeople, the Century Hyatt now has the added attraction of its swank new 'Regency Club' rooms and lounges.

CITY HOTEL LORNSTAR

Map p282 Business Hotel ¥¥

☎ 3356-6511; www.thehotel.co.jp/en/lornstar/index.php; 2-12-12 Shinjuku, Shinjuku-ku; s ¥7350-8400, d ¥10,500-15,750; Marunouchi or Toei Shinjuku Line to Shinjuku-sanchōme (exit C8)

No-frills but friendly, the dimensions here are small and the rooms fairly simple at the Lornstar. Located in the heart of Tokyo's gay district, Shinjuku-nichōme, it's also known as the queerest lodging in the city. Unusually for this standard of business hotel, credit cards are accepted and a basic continental breakfast is laid out in the mornings.

HILTON TOKYO Map p282 Luxury Hotel ¥¥¥

☎ 3344-5111; www.hilton.com; 6-6-2 Nishi-Shinjuku, Shinjuku-ku; r from ¥19,000; Marunouchi Line to Nishi-Shinjuku (exit C8) or Toei Ōedo Line to Tochōmae (exit C8)

Another of Shinjuku's large, upscale digs for business folk, the Hilton covers all the bases. Comforts like firm mattresses and full-sized bathtubs are complemented by aesthetically pleasing elements like *shōji* over the windows. A warren of shops, restaurants and bars lies downstairs, and stressed-out

Park Hyatt Tokyo (p204)

professionals can work it off in the indoor heated pool, tennis courts or gym.

HOTEL CENTURY SOUTHERN TOWER

Map p282 Business Hotel ¥¥¥

☎ 5354-0111; www.southerntower.co.jp/english; 2-2-1 Yoyogi, Shibuya-ku; s/d from ¥16,000/22,000; JR Yamanote Line to Shinjuku (south & new south exits);

With winter views of Mt Fuji possible from one side and the green space of Shinjuku-gyōen on the other, this monolith is very reasonably priced for its central location and the intangible sense of space its wide windows bestow. Free broadband Internet access, low-slung bathtubs and a variety of restaurants inside; fast access to Shinjuku Station outside.

HOTEL SUNLITE SHINJUKU

Map p282 Business Hotel ¥¥

☎ 3356-0391; www.sunlite.co.jp/top-e.htm; 5-15-8 Shinjuku, Shinjuku-ku; s ¥8715-9345, d ¥12,075-18,900; Marunouchi or Toei Shinjuku Line to Shinjuku-sanchōme (exit C7)

Though the small rooms at the Sunlite are typical of lesser business hotels in its class, they're well-maintained and comfortable. Small details like triangular bay windows and trapezoidally shaped rooms lend a funky air to an otherwise ordinary place. Prices won't break the budget, and its east Shinjuku location is central to transport, shopping and the nocturnal life of Kabukichō.

HOTEL SUNROUTE TOKYO

Map p282 Business Hotel ¥¥

☎ 3375-3211; www.sunroute.jp/index.html in Japanese; 2-3-1 Yoyogi, Shibuya-ku; s/d ¥12,500/17,000; Toei Ōedo or Toei Shinjuku Line to Shinjuku (exit A1)

Southwest of Shinjuku Station and adjacent to the Toei Shinjuku subway station, the Sunroute was under renovation when we visited. Though prices should rise somewhat, they should reflect improvements to what were formerly blandly clean but quality rooms.

KEIŌ PLAZA HOTEL

Map p282 Luxury Hotel ¥¥¥

☎ 3344-0111; www.keioplaza.com; 2-2-1 Nishi-Shinjuku, Shinjuku-ku; Western-style s/d from ¥22,000/26,000, Japanese ste from ¥84,000; Toei Ōedo Line to Tochōmae (exit B1);

Conveniently central in west Shinjuku, the 47-storey Keiō Plaza has old-fashioned style, all red carpets and gilded surfaces. Updated rooms feature the cleaner lines of more modern luxury hotels, and all have excellent city views. With a wonderful business centre and free high-speed Internet in every room, it also caters to busy travellers with its wealth of quality restaurants.

PARK HYATT TOKYO

Map p282 Luxury Hotel ¥¥¥

☎ 5322-1234; http://tokyo.park.hyatt.com; 3-7-1-2 Nishi-Shinjuku, Shinjuku-ku; r/ste from ¥55,650/68,250; Toei Ōedo Line to Tochōmae (exit A4)

The setting will look familiar, as it was the backdrop for the film *Lost in Translation*. Views are stunning, day and night, and appear to be part of another world from these serene heights. Dignified but relaxed, the stylishly understated rooms are done in naturally-finished wood, fabric and marble. Staff are gracefully, discreetly attentive and the restaurants are some of Tokyo's best.

SHINJUKU PARK HOTEL

Map p282 Business Hotel ¥¥

☎ 3356-0241; www.shinjukuparkhotel.com in Japanese; 5-27-9 Sendagaya, Shibuya-ku; Western-style s&d ¥7900-10,400, Japanese-style r ¥24,800; JR Yamanote Line to Shinjuku (new south exit)

Park views (be sure to request one), easy access to two stations on the Yamanote loop, and several shopping megaliths are within minutes of this low-key but warm business hotel. Japanese-style rooms here are a steal, and regular rooms are a terrific deal for the price. Solo foreign travellers will find the beds more comfortably proportioned in the larger singles.

SHINJUKU WASHINGTON HOTEL

Map p282 Business Hotel ¥¥

☎ 3343-3111; www.shinjyuku-wh.com in Japanese; 3-2-9 Nishi-Shinjuku, Shinjuku-ku; s/d from ¥10,000/15,000; JR Yamanote Line to Shinjuku (south exit)

This is a large, bustling business hotel whose curvaceous exterior conceals considerably less exciting, basic rooms. However, the views from the upper floors are excellent, and there's automatic check-in and check-out available downstairs for regulars; everyone else will need to approach the desk.

STAR HOTEL

Map p282 Business Hotel ¥¥

☎ 3361-1111; www.starhotel.co.jp in Japanese; 7-10-5 Nishi-Shinjuku, Shinjuku-ku; s/d ¥9450/17,850; JR Yamanote Line to Shinjuku (west exit)

In west Shinjuku, this hotel is very conveniently located near the station and the bright lights of the neighbourhood, but the rooms are capital-G generic – not a bad thing, necessarily, and certainly it's a fair deal for clean, basic accommodation. The staff are helpful, and there are even several decent restaurants in-house.

Cheap Sleeps

GREEN PLAZA SHINJUKU

Map p282 Capsule Hotel ¥

☎ 3207-5411; www.hgpshinjuku.jp in Japanese; 1-29-3 Kabukichō, Shinjuku-ku; s ¥4500; JR Yamanote Line to Shinjuku (east exit)

Smack in the middle of sleazy Kabukichō, Green Plaza Shinjuku offers standard-issue capsules as a last resort – note, these are for men only. However, the ladies' sauna on the 9th floor allows women to check in for the night (¥2800-3400) to soak, steam and snooze in a safe place. Tattooed individuals are strictly prohibited from entering the baths, but if you're discreet you should be OK.

TAKADANOBABA

Though Baba is just a few stops away from bustling Shinjuku, it is mostly a student haunt and is lacking in accommodation for those not here to study. Both options are easily accessed from the JR station.

HOTEL SUNROUTE TAKADANOBABA

Map p280 Business Hotel ¥¥

☎ 3232-0101; www.sunroutehotel.jp/takadanobaba; 1-27-7 Takadanobaba, Shinjuku-ku; s/d from ¥9500/16,800; JR Yamanote Line to Takadanobaba (Waseda-dōri exit);

Perfectly acceptable digs for those who've graduated from student budgets, this business hotel is one of the clean, reliable Sunroute chain found throughout Tokyo. High-speed Internet access is zapped into every blandly comfortable room, and the place is surprisingly quiet for being in a neighbourhood abuzz with university activity.

Cheap Sleeps

TAMA RYOKAN Map p280 Ryokan ¥

☎ 3209-8062; www.tamaryokan.com; 1-25-33 Takadanobaba, Shinjuku-ku; s/d ¥4500/8000; Ⓢ JR Yamanote Line to Takadanobaba (Waseda-dōri exit)

Four traditional tatami rooms fill out the second floor of this lovely private home, kept by a sweet, no-nonsense couple. The ryokan is up a small alley about five minutes' walk from Takadanobaba Station. While it lacks a traditional bath, there's a local *sentō* nearby. Email in advance for reservations, as this smashing deal is often booked.

IKEBUKURO

Ikebukuro is home to many a cheap hotel, but the trick is to avoid the flea pits in favour of spots near enough to the station for quick getaways to the more happening 'hoods. We've listed many good midrange options, along with posher digs and perhaps the city's best budget accommodation.

CROWNE PLAZA METROPOLITAN HOTEL Map p280 Luxury Hotel ¥¥¥

☎ 3980-1111; www.metropolitan.jp; 1-6-1 Nishi-Ikebukuro, Toshima-ku; s/d from ¥16,500/22,000; Ⓢ JR Yamanote Line to Ikebukuro (west exit)

The Metropolitan's commodious rooms make it the only worthwhile high-end hotel in Ikebukuro, which generally isn't much of a destination neighbourhood. It's a two-minute walk to the JR station but has both gym and outdoor pool (summer only) for more strenuous workouts. Upgraded rooms have a clean, modern look, but hipper rooms can be found in more compelling neighbourhoods.

HOTEL CLARION TOKYO

Map p280 Business Hotel ¥¥

☎ 5396-0111; 2-3-1 Ikebukuro, Toshima-ku; s/d from ¥14,000/20,000; Ⓢ JR Yamanote Line to Ikebukuro (west exit) or Yūrakuchō Line to Ikebukuro (exit C5); 💻

Rooms at the Hotel Clarion are quite spacious and fresh-looking, in contrast to the more common tired feel of most comparable business hotels. The staff are helpful, high-speed Internet access is available in all rooms and major credit cards are accepted. Navigate towards its teal-coloured roof; it's just steps from the C5 subway station exit.

HOTEL GRAND CITY

Map p280 Business Hotel ¥¥

☎ 3984-5121; www.grand-city.gr.jp in Japanese; 1-30-7 Higashi-Ikebukuro, Toshima-ku; s ¥7980-8800, d ¥13,860-17,000; Ⓢ JR Yamanote Line to Ikebukuro (east exit)

On the east side of Ikebukuro, this is a standard but friendly business hotel with relatively inexpensive rates and even a ladies-only floor. Rooms are definitely on the small side, and the hotel doesn't have too much flavour apart from its location next door to an entertainment complex featuring billiards, bowling and batting cages going strong well into the night.

HOTEL SUNROUTE IKEBUKURO

Map p280 Business Hotel ¥¥

☎ 3980-1911; www.sunroute-ikebukuro.com in Japanese; 1-39-4 Ikebukuro, Toshima-ku; s/d from ¥10,395/15,120; Ⓢ JR Yamanote Line to Ikebukuro (east exit); 💻

Just up the street from the main Bic Camera store, this Sunroute branch in Ikebukuro has pleasant, clean rooms and friendly staff, some of whom speak English. All rooms have free LAN Internet access, and though the beds are a bit on the hard side, the rooms feel less spartan than the standard.

Cheap Sleeps

HOUSE IKEBUKURO Map p280 Ryokan ¥

☎ 3984-3399; www.housejp.com.tw/english index.htm; 2-20-1 Ikebukuro, Toshima-ku; r ¥6000-12,000; Ⓢ JR Yamanote Line to Ikebukuro (west exit), or Marunouchi or Yūrakuchō Line to Ikebukuro (exit C1)

Spotless tatami rooms are the rule at House Ikebukuro, which does a brisk business at housing backpackers in a quiet Ikebukuro alley. Though common areas are more functional than inviting, the place is cheery in its busyness. Reserve well ahead, as this popular inn is often fully booked. All singles share bath facilities, but some doubles have private bathrooms.

KIMI RYOKAN Map p280 Ryokan ¥

☎ 3971-3766; www.kimi-ryokan.jp; 2-36-8 Ikebukuro, Toshima-ku; s ¥4500, d ¥6500-7500; JR Yamanote Line to Ikebukuro (west exit)

One of the best budget ryokan in Tokyo, this convivial inn provides an affordable and welcoming base for travellers discovering Tokyo. Fragrant tatami rooms are small but not cramped, and the large, wood-floored lounge area provides a comfortable place to hang out and meet fellow travellers over green tea. Clean showers and toilets are shared, and there's a lovely traditional Japanese bath. Book well in advance.

TOYOKO INN Map p280 Business Hotel ¥

☎ 5960-1045; www.toyoko-inn.com/eng; 2-50-5 Ikebukuro, Toshima-ku; s/d ¥6800/8800; JR Yamanote Line to Ikebukuro (north exit);

The Toyoko Inn is one of the most appealing choices of the standard business hotels in this area. Rooms are tidy, if tiny, and Japanese rooms with tatami mats are available. Free high-speed wireless Internet service is provided in the lobby, and it even throws in a simple breakfast with the room rates.

Excursions

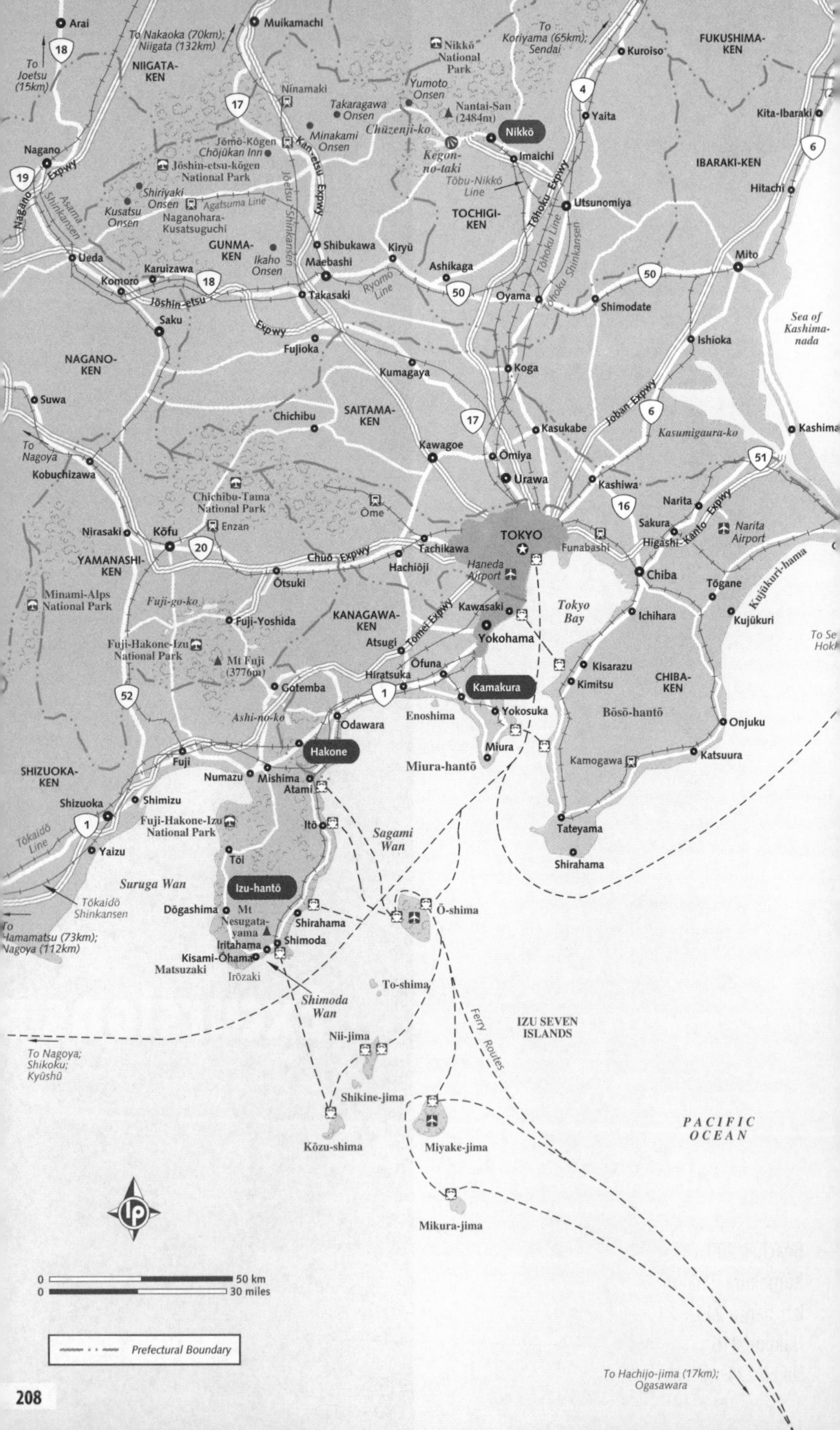

Arai
To Nakaoka (70km); Niigata (132km)
Muikamachi
To Joetsu (15km)
NIIGATA-KEN
Nikkō National Park
To Koriyama (65km); Sendai
Kuroiso
FUKUSHIMA-KEN
Ninamaki
Yumoto Onsen
Takaragawa Onsen
Nantai-San (2484m)
Yaita
Kita-Ibaraki
Minakami Onsen
Chūzenji-ko
Nikkō
Jōmō-Kōgen
Chōjūkan Inn
Kegon-no-taki
Imaichi
Nagano
Jōshin-etsu-kōgen National Park
Tōbu-Nikkō Line
IBARAKI-KEN
Shiriyaki Onsen
Agatsuma Line
Utsunomiya
Hitachi
Kusatsu Onsen
Naganohara-Kusatsuguchi
TOCHIGI-KEN
Asama Shinkansen
Joetsu Shinkansen
Kan-etsu Expwy
Tōhoku Expwy
Tōhoku Line
Tōhoku Shinkansen
GUNMA-KEN
Shibukawa
Kiryū
Ueda
Ikaho Onsen
Maebashi
Mito
Karuizawa
Ashikaga
Komoro
Ryomo Line
Jōshin-etsu Expwy
Takasaki
Oyama
Shimodate
Saku
Sea of Kashima-nada
Ishioka
Fujioka
NAGANO-KEN
Kumagaya
Koga
Suwa
Chichibu
SAITAMA-KEN
Joban Expwy
To Nagoya
Kasukabe
Kasumigaura-ko
Kashima
Kawagoe
Ōmiya
Kobuchizawa
Urawa
Kashiwa
Chichibu-Tama National Park
Ōme
Narita
Narita Airport
Sakura
Higashi-Kanto Expwy
Nirasaki
Kōfu
Enzan
TOKYO
Funabashi
YAMANASHI-KEN
Chūō Expwy
Tachikawa
Hachiōji
Haneda Airport
Chiba
Kujūkuri-hama
Ōtsuki
Tōgane
Minami-Alps National Park
Fuji-go-ko
Kawasaki
Tokyo Bay
Ichihara
Kujūkuri
Fuji-Yoshida
KANAGAWA-KEN
Tomei Expwy
Yokohama
Atsugi
Fuji-Hakone-Izu National Park
Mt Fuji (3776m)
Ōfuna
Kisarazu
Kimitsu
CHIBA-KEN
Hiratsuka
Kamakura
Gotemba
Yokosuka
Bōsō-hantō
Ashi-no-ko
Enoshima
Odawara
Onjuku
Miura
Hakone
Katsuura
Fuji
Kamogawa
Miura-hantō
SHIZUOKA-KEN
Numazu
Mishima
Atami
Shimizu
Shizuoka
Fuji-Hakone-Izu National Park
Itō
Sagami Wan
Tateyama
Tōkaidō Line
Yaizu
Tōi
Shirahama
Suruga Wan
Izu-hantō
Tōkaidō Shinkansen
Ō-shima
Dōgashima
Mt Nesugata-yama
Shirahama
To Hamamatsu (73km); Nagoya (112km)
Shimoda
Iritahama
Kisami-Ōhama
Matsuzaki
Irōzaki
To-shima
Shimoda Wan
IZU SEVEN ISLANDS
Ferry Routes
To Nagoya; Shikoku; Kyūshū
Nii-jima
Shikine-jima
PACIFIC OCEAN
Kōzu-shima
Miyake-jima
Mikura-jima
0
50 km
0
30 miles
Prefectural Boundary
To Hachijo-jima (17km); Ogasawara

Excursions

The Tokyo machine is a marvel of efficiency – on-time trains on the move, whisking people this way or that as they email away on their *keitai* (mobile phones). As you step up to this manic pace with your own agenda of places to go and people to see, Tokyo can be fantastically fulfilling, but also hugely overwhelming. Between the soaring heights of towering buildings and the tangled maze of the city subways, it's easy to feel a bit lost amid the ever-teeming crowds in the megalopolis. No matter how much you love the nonstop action, the city can eventually leave you longing to breathe deeply of some fresh air. Thankfully, just an hour or two away by train are some of Japan's best travel destinations, offering some sweet relief from the big city.

Foremost among the destinations beyond Tokyo's boundaries are Kamakura and Nikkō, each of which boast numerous temples and shrines – some rivalling those found in the cultural meccas of Kyoto and Nara. Also nearby is the Hakone region, a cluster of mountain towns best known for harbouring countless hot springs and dramatic views of Mt Fuji (when it's not obscured by clouds). The area can be congested at weekends and national holidays, but time it right, and a day or two here can feel like a rebirth. A bit further away, and equally frequented by tourists from Tokyo, is the Izu-hantō area. Like Hakone, this is primarily a hot-springs resort, a place where urbanites come for the weekend to soak, steam and unwind. Izu is one of the prime destinations for young Japanese couples heading for a romantic weekend. And, if some beach time is all you need, you're well covered.

Places listed in this chapter can be visited as day trips, although if you're planning on being in Tokyo for a week or more, an overnight stay can make these excursions infinitely more relaxing.

BEACHES

If you're seeking sun but shunning crowds, don't head for the beach on weekends and holidays when there's a predictable inflow of city-dwellers (and their sometimes appalling penchant for littering). When school's out for summer (mid-July through August), students will also be flocking to the shoreline. Surfers can find respectable waves along the Pacific coast of the Bōsō peninsula, in Chiba prefecture, and sunbathers will find decent beaches on both Bōsō-hantō and Izu-hantō. Be warned that many beaches have very strong rip currents.

Kamakura has its own beach at **Zaimokuza** and **Enoshima Island** (p214) can be visited on a weekday when it's less crowded.

There are some lovely beaches near **Shimoda** (p215) on the Izu peninsula. Ten minutes north of town by bus, **Shirahama** (白浜) can see good surf, but if the tides are uncooperative the expansive, beautiful beach awaits your towel. Buses from Shimoda leave hourly (¥320). Ten minutes south of Shimoda are a string of lovely beaches, of which **Iritahama** (入田浜) and **Kisami-Ōhama** (吉佐美大浜) are favourites with surfers and sunbathers. Further around to the western side of the peninsula, **Dōgashima** (堂ヶ島; p215) is another charming town.

Underrated and untainted by overdevelopment, the Bōsō peninsula boasts some of the best, mellow beaches near Tokyo. **Onjuku** (御宿) is the nicest of those most easily accessed from Tokyo, with beachfront cafés, a laid-back coastal vibe and lots of white sand and decent waves. South of Onjuku, **Katsuura** (勝浦) and **Kamogawa** (鴨川) also get good swells. Wakashio trains (*tokkyū*, ¥3700, 80 minutes) to Onjuku Station depart from the southeast end of Tokyo Station on the JR Keiyō Line. About half the cost, but much slower, are the regular trains on the JR Sotobō Line.

North of Onjuku, **Kujūkuri-hama** (九十九里浜) has over 60km of smooth, sandy, sparsely-peopled beaches. To access them, take the JR Sotobō Line to Oami Station, transfer to the Tōgane Line, and disembark at Kujūkuri town. Frequent buses ply Kujūkuri-hama's coastal towns, and you can hop off when you see a spot that appeals to you.

KAMAKURA

Kamakura had a spell of glory as the nation's capital from 1192 to 1333 when Japan's seat of power temporarily relocated here from Kyoto. The Minamoto and later the Hōjo clans ruled Japan from Kamakura for more than a century, until finally in 1333, weakened by the heavy cost of maintaining defences against the threats of attack from Kublai Khan in China, the Hōjo clan fell from power at the hands of the forces of Emperor Go-Daigo. Although the restoration of imperial authority was somewhat illusory, the capital nevertheless shifted back to Kyoto, and Kamakura disappeared temporarily from the history books.

TRANSPORT

Train The JR Yokosuka Line runs to Kamakura (¥890, 55 minutes) and Kita-Kamakura (¥780) Stations. On clear days, you may be able to catch intermittent glimpses of elusive Fuji. Once here, you can continue on to Enoshima via the scenic Enoden (Enoshima Dentetsu) Line from Kamakura Station or by bus from stop No 9 in front of the station. The train (¥250, 25 minutes) is the simpler and cheaper option.

Bus The transportation hub here is the Kamakura train station, from which most of the local buses depart. A lack of English-language signposting makes the bus network hard to use, but the station's Travel Information Centre (TIC) has the latest details on which boarding spots serve which destinations.

Today Kamakura's wealth of notable temples and elegant shrines makes it one of Tokyo's most rewarding day trips, and one that is most often undertaken by locals. In order to take in the area's sights, perhaps the best route to take is the one that starts at Kita-Kamakura Station and continues on to Kamakura proper. This trek will allow you to visit at leisure the temples and shrines that dot the surrounding landscape. Particularly pleasant in spring and autumn when the weather is temperate, this moderately easy walk also takes in some of the area's indigenous flora. To begin, exit the station at Kita-Kamakura, where vendors sell bilingual maps that can be useful for veering off the beaten track.

A footpath to your right just outside the station leads you back along the tracks and finally across them where you'll see the entrance to **Engaku-ji**, one of the five main Rinzai Zen temples in Kamakura. Once inside, you can stroll along the cypress-lined walks and through the majestic main gate, which was built in the 1780s. This structure bears a framed calligraphic inscription penned by Emperor Fushimi, who ruled Japan during the second half of the 13th century. The temple's main treasure, one of Buddha's teeth, is enshrined up the hill but is off-limits to the public (although you can peer into the courtyard). Engaku-ji dates from 1282.

Across the tracks from Engaku-ji is **Tōkei-ji**, an old nunnery that was established by Kakusan-ni, the young widow of a regent who herself came from a distinguished family. For 600 years, Tōkei-ji was known as the Divorce Temple, the only place in Japan where abused or disgruntled wives could seek refuge from unhappy marriages (local lore has it that nearby residents helped by pointing the way to the temple to any woman who seemed to be in a hurry). The main object of worship here is a statue of Shaka Nyorai (the Enlightened Buddha). The statue is believed to date back to the 14th century and, according to temple records, it escaped a great fire in 1515.

A couple of minutes further on from Tokei-ji is **Jōchi-ji**, another temple with tranquil surroundings. Founded in 1283 by Hojo Morotoki, it is considered the fourth of Kamakura's five great Zen temples. As you climb the worn stone stairs and approach the entrance, notice the main gate's unique belltower. The bell on the 2nd floor was cast in 1340. Also near the entrance is Kanro-no-ni, one of Kamakura's 10 revered wells. The interest in this muddy little pond, whose name translates to 'sweet water', is mostly historical, but photographers still swarm its edges looking for the perfect shot. Before leaving, peek into the main hall for a look at the trio of statues that depict Amida, Shaka and Miroku figures, which respectively represent past, present and future.

About a 10-minute walk beyond Jōchi-ji you'll come upon **Kenchō-ji**, the first and grandest of Kamakura's Zen temples, which today serves as the head of the more than 500 smaller temples that belong to the Kenchō-ji school of the Rinzai sect. As you enter, stop for a moment to observe the gnarled, braided cypress trees whose seeds were brought from China by the temple's founding priest, Lah-hsi Tao-lung, 700 years ago. A bit further on, you'll see

KAMAKURA

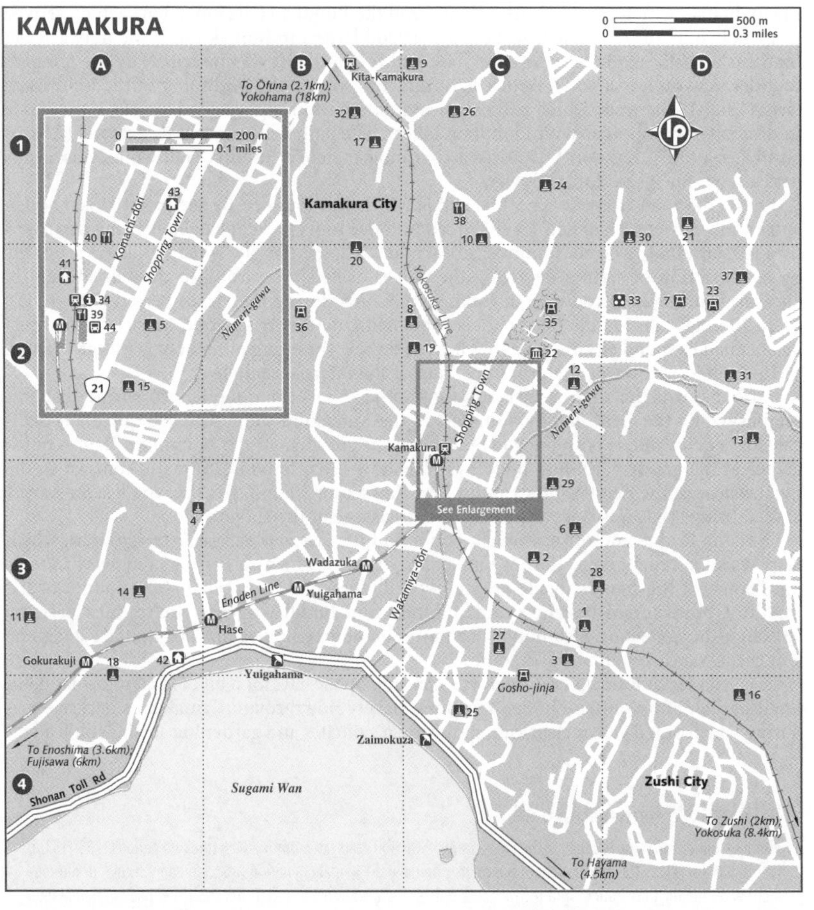

SIGHTS & INFORMATION
Ankokuron-ji 安┌論寺 1 C3
Anyô-in 安養院 2 C3
Chôshô-ji 長勝寺 3 C3
Daibutsu (Great Buddha) 鎌倉大┌ 4 A3
Daigyô-ji 大巧寺 5 A2
Daihô-ji 大┌寺 6 C3
Egara Tenjinja 荏柄天神社 7 D2
Eishô-ji 英勝寺 8 C2
Engaku-ji 円┌寺 9 C1
Ennô-ji 円┌寺 10 C1
Gokuraku-ji 極┌寺 11 A3
Hôkai-ji ┌戒寺 12 C2
Hôkoku-ji 報┌寺 13 D2
Hase-dera 長谷寺 14 A3
Hongaku-ji 本┌寺 15 A2
Hosshô-ji 法性寺 16 D4
Jôchi-ji ┌智寺 17 B1
Jôju-in 成就院 18 A3
Jufuku-ji ┌福寺 19 C2
Kaizô-ji 海┌寺 20 B2
Kakuon-ji ┌園寺 21 D1
Kamakura National Treasure Museum 鎌倉┌┌館 22 C2
Kamakura-gû 鎌倉宮 23 D2
Kenchô-ji 建長寺 24 C1
Kyûhin-ji 九品寺 25 C4
Meigetsu-in 明月院 26 C1
Myôchô-ji 妙長寺 27 C3
Myôhô-ji 妙法寺 28 C3
Myôhon-ji 妙本寺 29 C3
Raigô-ji ┌迎寺 30 D1
Sugimoto-dera 杉本寺 31 D2
Tôkei-ji 東慶寺 32 B1
Tomb of Minamoto Yoritomo 源┌朝の墓 33 D2
Tourist Information Center ┌光案┌センタ┌ 34 A2
Tsurugaoka Hachiman-gû 鶴岡八幡宮 35 C2
Zeniarai-benten ┌洗弁天 36 B2
Zuisen-ji 瑞泉寺 37 D2

EATING
Chaya-kado 茶屋かど 38 C1
Komachi-Ichiba 小町市場 39 A2
T-Side ティ┌サイド 40 A1

SLEEPING
Hotel New Kamakura ホテルニュ┌カマクラ 41 A2
Kamakura Kagetsuen Youth Hostel 鎌倉花月園ユ┌スホステル 42 A3
Kamakura Marriage Avenue ホテル鶴が丘┌館 43 A1

TRANSPORT
Bus Station バス停 44 A2

the main hall, which travelled from Kyoto, and the Buddha Hall (Butsuden), which arrived from Tokyo in 1647. The temple bell, the second largest in Kamakura, is the only artefact that was actually made here. A close look will reveal that it was inscribed by the temple's founder. As you leave, you'll notice signs directing you to the beginning of the **Ten-en hiking course** (13km). The walk, which makes a pleasant detour through shaded forests, is moderate in difficulty and popular with mountain bikers. The path will take you by **Kakuon-ji** (2.5km) and **Zuisen-ji** (5m). Kakuon-ji features a charming thatched Buddha Hall while Zuisen-ji is best known for its perennial flowers.

Across the road from Kenchō-ji is **Ennō-ji**, which was founded by the priest Dokai Soden some time between 1250 and 1309. Forced to move to its present site after being destroyed by a tsunami that ravaged Zaimokuza beach in 1703, the temple is distinguished primarily by its collection of statues depicting the judges of hell. According to the Juo concept of Taoism, which was introduced to Japan from China during the Heian period (794–1185), these 10 judges decide the fate of souls, who, being neither truly good nor truly evil, must be assigned to spend eternity in either heaven or hell. Presiding over them is Emma (Yama), a Hindu deity known as the gruesome king of the infernal regions.

Further down the road is **Tsurugaoka Hachiman-gū**, a carnivalesque Shintō shrine that was established by the Genji family, founders of the Kamakura shōgunate. The shrine is dedicated to a deity who is both the god of war and the guardian of the Minamoto clan. A quick glance at the gaudy vermilion buildings will show them to be in dramatic contrast to the quiet repose of the Zen temples around Kita-Kamakura Station. Nearby, you'll see a steeply arched bridge that was once reserved for the passage of the shōgun alone.

Over the bridge and off to the left, you'll find the **Kamakura National Treasure Museum,** which displays an excellent collection of Kamakura art, most of which is cloistered away in temples. Some of the figures inside are the typically peaceful *jizō* (small stone statues of the Buddhist protector of travellers and children) and Buddha figures you're most used to, although the collection also houses a number of compelling sculptures that are energetic and carnal, and sometimes gruesome.

Once you reach Kamakura proper, you can stop by the TIC for a bit of local information in English, then jump on the Enoden Line for a rickety ride through Kamakura's backstreets – during which you'll gain a clear view of the town's ditches and gardening sheds. You'll alight

BUDDHISM IN KAMAKURA

Although Buddhism came to Japan in the 6th century, it was 500 years later, during the Kamakura period (1185–1333), that Buddhism finally spread throughout the country. Initially the Kamakura period was marked by secular disillusionment with Buddhist institutions and the monastic orders, and a widespread belief that the world had entered Mappō (the Later Age), a period of Buddhist decline when individuals would no longer be able to achieve enlightenment through their own efforts alone. This led to the flourishing of alternatives to established Buddhist doctrine – notably Zen and the Pure Land school of Buddhism.

The Pure Land Jōdō school preached that in the Later Age, salvation could be achieved only through devotion to the transcendent Amida Buddha – all who called on him sincerely would achieve salvation in the Pure Land after death. This populist stroke opened Buddhism in Japan to the masses, who had previously been largely excluded from the more esoteric branches of Buddhism. This also contrasted with Zen, which sought Buddhahood through meditative practice aimed at the empty centre of the self.

With its rigorous training and self-discipline, Zen found support among an ascendant warrior class and made a considerable contribution to the samurai ethic. Differences on the question of whether *satori* (enlightenment) could be attained suddenly or whether it was a gradual process accounted for Zen breaking into the Rinzai and Sōtō sects.

The contending schools of Pure Land and Zen, along with the views of charismatic leaders such as the influential 13th-century priest Nichiren, led to the revitalisation of Buddhism within Japan during the Kamakura period. The major Japanese Buddhist sects can trace their antecedents to that era.

You will find numerous temples around Kamakura, including: Ankokuron-ji, Chōshō-ji, Daigyō-ji, Daihō-ji, Eishō-ji, Gokuraku-ji, Hongaku-ji, Hosshō-ji, Jufuku-ji, Kaizō-ji, Kyūhin-ji, Myōchō-ji, Myōhon-ji, Myōhō-ji and Raigō-ji. Anyō-in is a temple known for its azalea blooms in spring; Joju-in is another temple known for its blooms in May; Meigetsu-in is a 13th-century temple; and Zeniarai-benten is a Shintō shrine famed for its ability to double money washed in its spring.

at Hase Station, which is near the *Daibutsu* (Great Buddha) and Hase-dera. The **Daibutsu** (Great Buddha) was completed in 1252 and is Kamakura's most famous sight. Once housed in a huge hall, the statue today sits in the open, its home having been washed away by a tsunami in 1495. Cast in bronze and weighing close to 850 tonnes, the statue is 11.4m tall. Its construction was inspired by the even bigger *Daibutsu* in Nara, although it's generally agreed that the Kamakura bronze is artistically superior. If you're not claustrophobic, you can enter the Buddha's belly through a small door that opens from his side. The privilege costs a measly ¥20.

Daibutsu (left), Kamakura

Back towards Hase Station is the small lane leading to **Hase-dera.** The temple grounds begin with a garden and then open onto a grand view of the bay. Inside the temple is a 9m-tall, gold-leafed **Kannon statue**, which is said to have washed up from the sea in the early 8th century. The statue represents the Buddhist goddess of mercy whose compassion is often invoked as a source of succour to the bereaved and aggrieved. Unfortunately, although the hall containing this statue is open to the public, the statue itself is normally off-limits. If you've come during the afternoon, you may want to stop in for tea.

Also worth a look are the poignant thousands of small *jizō* statues. Mothers who have miscarried or aborted fetuses, or lost their children, often dress *jizō* in warm clothing or offer toys or food as offerings in supplication for helping those lost children negotiate the underworld.

Once you've returned to Kamakura Station, you may want to explore some of Kamakura's more remote temples. **Egara Tenjinja**, which was founded at the beginning of the 12th century, is popular with students who come to pray for academic success. Like other Tenjin shrines, Egara is dedicated to the memory of Michizane Sugawara, a Kyoto scholar of noble birth who was born in the middle of the 9th century. Many students who make the pilgrimage write their academic aspirations on *ema* (small wooden plaques), which are then hung to the right of the shrine. At the end of January each year, the shrine holds a memorial service for honoured writing instruments, such as bamboo calligraphy brushes and school children's pencils. These implements are ritually burned in the temple's oven. Buses from stop No 6 in front of Kamakura Station run out to Egara Tenjinja; get off at the Tenjin-mae bus stop.

While you're here, check out **Zuisen-ji**, which affords relaxing strolls through gardens laid out by the temple's founder, Musō Kokushi, during the Kamakura era (1185–1333). It's a 15-minute walk from Egara Tenjinja; turn right where the bus turns left in front of the shrine, take the next left and keep following this road.

Also of interest is **Sugimoto-dera**, Kamakura's oldest temple, said to have been established by Empress Komei sometime in the mid-8th century. The famous ancient steps lead to ferocious guardian figures *(niō)* poised at the entrance. The main hall, with its quaint thatched roof, houses three Kannon statues that are said to have miraculously escaped a 12th-century fire by hiding themselves behind a tree. To get to Sugimoto-dera, take a bus from the No 5 bus stop in front of Kamakura Station and get off at Sugimoto Kannon.

Finally, down the road from Sugimoto-dera, is **Hōkoku-ji**, a Rinzai Zen temple with quiet landscaped gardens where you can relax under a parasol with a cup of green tea in hand. The temple is particularly known for its forest of vibrant, perennial bamboo. It regularly holds *zazen* (meditation) classes for beginners.

Information

Post Office (1-10-3 Komachi; 🕑 9am-7pm Mon-Fri, 9am-3pm Sat) Has ATMs inside.

Tourist Information Centre (☎ 0467-22-3350; 1-1-1 Komachi; 🕑 9am-5.30pm Apr-Sep, 5pm Oct-Mar) Located just outside the east exit of Kamakura Station.

Sights

Daibutsu (Great Buddha; admission ¥200; 🕑 7am-6pm Mar-Nov, 7am-5pm Dec-Feb)

Egara Tenjinja (☎ 0467-25-1772; admission free; 🕑 7.30am-6.30pm)

Engaku-ji (☎ 0467-22-0487; admission ¥200; 🕑 8am-5pm Apr-Sep, 8am-4pm Oct-Mar)

ENOSHIMA DETOUR

Unless you're a surfer and plan on being in the water for most of the day, it's best to avoid this popular beach at weekends, when its sand is completely packed with day-tripping escapees from Tokyo. At the end of the beach is a bridge to **Enoshima Island**, where **Enoshima-jinja** (☎ 0466-22-4020; 🕑 9am-4pm) is reached by an outdoor escalator, although it is possible, and pleasant, to walk the whole way. The shrine houses a *hadaka-benzaiten* – a nude statue of the Indian goddess of beauty. Other sights around the island include the Enoshima **Shokubutsu-en** (Tropical Garden; ☎ 0466-22-0209; adult/child ¥200/100; 🕑 9am-5pm) and some sea caves on the far side of the island.

Enoshima's beaches are good for some meditative wandering, particularly around the rocky headlands on the southern side of the island. On fair days, Mt Fuji is clearly visible from the south and west sides of the island. In the late afternoon, you can stop for a drink at one of the cliff-side restaurants where couples often come to watch the sun set over the mountain.

Transport

Train The rustic Enoden railway runs between Kamakura and Enoshima (¥250, 25 minutes). Alternatively, Enoshima can be reached from Shinjuku Station in Tokyo with the use of Odakyū Line's Enoshima Kamakura Free Pass (¥1430, 90 minutes). JR also offers a Kamakura Enoshima Free Pass (¥1970, 55 minutes), which is valid for two days.

Ennō-ji (admission ¥200; 🕑 9am-3.30pm Nov-Mar, 9am-4pm Apr-Oct)

Hase-dera (☎ 0467-22-6300; admission ¥300; 🕑 8am-5.30pm Mar-Sep, 8am-4.30pm Oct-Feb)

Hōkoku-ji (☎ 0467-22-0762; admission to garden ¥200; 🕑 9am-4pm)

Jōchi-ji (☎ 0467-22-3943; admission ¥150; 🕑 9am-4.30pm)

Kakuon-ji (☎ 0467-22-1195; admission with guided tour ¥300; 🕑 10am-4pm, closed in Aug) Tours begin on the hour; the last one starts at 3pm.

Kamakura National Treasure Museum (Kamakura Kokuhōkan; ☎ 0467-22-0753; 2-1-1 Yukinoshita; admission ¥310; 🕑 9am-4.30pm Tue-Sun)

Kenchō-ji (☎ 0467-22-0981; admission ¥300; 🕑 8.30am-4.30pm)

Sugimoto-dera (☎ 0467-22-3463; admission ¥200; 🕑 8am-4.30pm)

Tōkei-ji (☎ 0467-22-1663; admission ¥100; 🕑 8.30am-5pm Apr-Oct, 8.30am-4pm Nov-Mar)

Tsurugaoka Hachiman-gū (☎ 0467-22-0315; general admission free, exhibition hall ¥100; 🕑 9am-4pm, closed last Mon each month)

Zuisen-ji (☎ 0467-22-1191; admission ¥100; 🕑 9am-5pm)

Eating

Chaya-kado (☎ 0467-23-1673; mains from ¥800; 🕑 10am-5pm, may close without notice) Serving up hot, hearty soup, this humble *soba* (buckwheat noodles) spot is conveniently located on the route from Kita-Kamakura to Kamakura, just before you reach Kenchō-ji. During low-season, the restaurant may open only for lunch.

Komachi-Ichiba (☎ 0467-24-7921; lunch/dinner from ¥980/1700; 🕑 11.30am-2pm & 4-10.30pm) This restaurant, located on the 2nd floor of the station building above the tourist information centre, dishes up tasty meal sets at terrific prices. The sister tempura shop next door has the same hours of operation.

T-Side (☎ 0467-24-9572; sets from ¥2100; 🕑 11am-9.30pm) T-Side's varied and delicious Indian menu is a find in Kamakura. Unlike most local eateries in town, which close just after 8pm or so, this little spot stays open later.

Sleeping

Hotel New Kamakura (☎ 0467-22-2230; 13-2 Onarimachi; s/d from ¥7000/10,000) Reservations are recommended at this friendly, wood-floored hotel near the station. Both Western- and Japanese-style rooms are available.

Kamakura Kagetsuen Youth Hostel (☎ 0467-25-1238; 27-9 Sakanoshita; dm/s/d ¥3308/7300/10,400) This hostel has good ocean views from its Western- and Japanese-style rooms. You can walk to the hostel from Hase-dera or take an Enoden train to Hase Station and walk five minutes southwest of the station along the seafront (the hostel is inside Kagetsuen Hotel).

Kamakura Marriage Avenue (Tsurugaoka Kaikan; ☎ 0467-24-1111; 2-12-27 Komachi; s/d ¥8500/17,000) The lobby and rooms of this fancy, fancifully-renamed hotel look as if they were decorated by a glamorous grandmother, although some Japanese-style accommodation is available.

IZU-HANTŌ

Eighty kilometres southwest of Tokyo, Izu-hantō, with its abundant *onsen* (mineral hot springs) and rugged coastline, is one of Japan's most popular resort destinations. This means that things can get pretty crowded at weekends and holidays, particularly in summer. Luckily, once you get past the touristy resort of Atami, the crowds usually thin out. And over on the west coast, where transport is by bus only, things are always a lot quieter.

Atami is known as a hot-spring naughty-weekend destination for Japanese couples, although one well-known *gaijin* (foreigner), John Wayne, got off his horse and drank his sake here for the filming of *The Barbarian & the Geisha*. Other than its numerous hot springs, its prime attraction is the **MOA Art Museum**, which houses a collection of Japanese and Chinese art. Take a bus from the No 4 bus stop outside the station to the MOA Bijutsukan. **Itō** is another hot-springs resort and is famous as the place where Anjin-san (William Adams), the hero of James Clavell's book *Shōgun*, built a ship for the Tokugawa shōgunate. Atami is especially popular with amorous twosomes, and is best avoided if you're wanting peace and quiet.

If you have time for only one town on the peninsula, skip Atami, pass by Itō and head for **Shimoda**, the most pleasant of the surrounding *onsen* towns. Shimoda is famous as the residence of the American Townsend Harris, the first Western diplomat to set up house in Japan. The Treaty of Kanagawa, which resulted from Commodore Matthew Perry's visit (p52), ended Japan's centuries of self-imposed isolation by forcing the nation to open the ports of Shimoda and Hakodate to US ships. An American consulate was established in Shimoda in 1856.

About 700m south of Shimoda Station is **Ryōsen-ji**, which is now famous as the site where Commodore Perry and representatives of the Tokugawa shōgunate signed a treaty whose conditions (favourable to the USA, of course) supplemented those outlined in the Treaty of Kanagawa, which was signed earlier, in 1854. Located next to the temple is a **small museum** which displays exhibits relating to the arrival of Westerners in Japan. These include a series of pictures depicting Okichi-san, a courtesan who was forced to give up the man she loved in order to attend to the needs of the brutal barbarian, Harris. When Harris left Japan five years later, Okichi-san was stigmatised for having had a relationship with a foreigner and she was eventually driven to drink and suicide. Next door to Ryōsen-ji is **Chōraku-ji**, a pleasant little temple that is worth a quick look. Nearby **Hōfuku-ji** has a museum that commemorates the tragic life of Okichi-san. Other ways to take in Shimoda include taking a **cable car** up 200-metre tall Nesugata-yama, walking along one of the many beaches, or taking one of the tongue-in-cheek **Black Ship cruises** around the bay. These cruises take about 20 minutes and depart from Shimoda Harbour every 30 minutes. There are three boats per day (9.40am, 11am and 2pm) that leave on a course for Iro-zaki. You can leave the boat at Iro-zaki (one way ¥1530, 40 minutes) and travel by bus northwards up the peninsula, or stay on the boat to return to Shimoda. Note, three boats per day leave on Monday, Friday, Saturday and Sunday; during holiday seasons the schedule is daily.

EAST TO WEST IZU-HANTŌ DETOUR

From Shimoda's No 5 bus stop in front of the station, it's a very scenic bus journey to **Dōgashima**, a small, charming fishing town on the western side of the peninsula. Along the way is **Matsuzaki**, a cape recommended for its traditional-style houses and quiet sandy beach. The bus to Dōgashima takes about 30 minutes (¥1360).

The main attractions at Dōgashima are the dramatic **rock formations** that line the seashore. The park just across the street from the bus stop has some of the best views. It's also possible to take a boat trip (¥900) from the nearby jetty to visit the town's famous **shoreline cave**, which has a natural window in its roof that allows light to pour in. You can look down into the cave from paths in the aforementioned park.

South of the bus stop in Dōgashima, you will find the stunning **Sawada-kōen onsen** (admission ¥500; 7am-7pm Wed-Mon) which is perched high on a cliff overlooking the Pacific Ocean. You should go early in the day if possible; around sunset, it's standing room only.

TRANSPORT

Atami

Train JR trains run from Tokyo Station to Atami on the Tōkaidō Line: *futsū* (¥1890, two hours), Kodama *shinkansen* (¥3570, 50 minutes), Odoriko *tokkyū* (¥4070, 80 minutes). It's also possible to approach Atami via Shinjuku Station via the Odakyū Line to Odawara (¥850, 70 minutes) and then connecting with the JR Tōkaidō Line to Atami (¥400, 30 minutes).

Itō

Train Itō is connected to Atami by the JR Itō Line (¥320, 25 minutes). The JR Odoriko *tokkyū* service also runs from Tokyo Station to Itō (¥4090) and takes about two hours.

Shimoda

Train Shimoda is as far as you can go by train on the Izu-hantō peninsula. You can take the Izu Kyūkō Line from Itō (¥1670, 90 minutes) or the Odoriko *tokkyū* from Tokyo Station (¥6160, three hours).

Information

Main Post Office (10am-5pm; Shimoda) Has an international ATM.

Shimoda Tourist Association (0558-22-1531; 1-4-28 Shimoda; 10am-5pm; Shimoda)

Volunteer English Guide Association (0558-23-5151; maimai-h@i-younet.ne.jp; Shimoda; 8.30am-5.15pm Tue-Sun) Offers free guided tours of the area.

Sights

Black Ship Tours (0558-22-1151; Shimoda; 20-min cruise ¥920) Departing from Shimoda Harbour approximately every 30 minutes from 9.10am to 3.30pm.

Chōraku-ji (admission free; 8.30am-5pm)

Hōfuku-ji (museum; 0558-22-0960; Shimoda; admission ¥300; 8am-5pm)

MOA Museum of Art (0557-84-2511; www.moaart.or.jp; Atami; admission ¥1600; 9.30am-4.30pm Fri-Wed, closed 6-10 Jan & 25-31 Dec)

Nesugata-yama cable car (Shimoda; admission ¥1200)

Ryōsen-ji (museum; 0558-22-0657; Shimoda; admission ¥500; 8.30am-5pm)

Eating

Gorosaya (0558-23-5638; 1-5-25 Shimoda-shi, Shimoda; lunch/dinner ¥1575/3150; 11.30am-2pm & 5-9pm Wed-Mon) This slightly upscale restaurant serves very good seafood; look for the wooden fish at the entrance.

Matsu Sushi (0558-22-1309; Shimoda; sets from ¥1500; 11am-8pm Thu-Tue) Stop by this place for well-priced, fresh sushi and sashimi.

Musashi (0558-22-0934; Shimoda; mains from ¥800; 11am-2pm & 5.30-7.30pm Wed-Mon) Musashi serves most Japanese favourites, including tempura *soba.*

Sleeping

Kokumin-shukusha New Shimoda (0558-23-0222; 1-4-13 Nishi-Hongo, Shimoda; r per person with/without meals ¥7480/4855) This nondescript economy inn does have its pros: tatami floors and a spacious *onsen*. Take a right out of the station, another right at the first light, continue for 2½ blocks and find it on your right.

Ōizu Ryokan (0558-22-0123; 3-3-25 Shimoda-shi, Shimoda; r per person ¥3500) With a tiny hot-spring bath and small, simple Japanese-style rooms, this popular ryokan is on the south side of Shimoda. It's two blocks north of Perry Rd and four from the waterfront.

Shimoda Tōkyū Hotel (0558-22-2411; www.tokyuhotels.co.jp; 5-12-1 Shimoda-shi, Shimoda; s/d from ¥14,000/16,000) Two kilometres south of Shimoda, this posh hotel has *onsen* and a swimming pool and boasts a cliffside location with ocean views. Rates include a free shuttle to and from the station, as well as two free meals.

Station Hotel Shimoda (0558-22-8885; 1-1-3 Nishi-Hongo, Shimoda; s/d ¥5800/9800) Right next to the station, this is a reasonably priced, no-frills business hotel that will do for a short stay.

HAKONE

If the weather cooperates and Mt Fuji is clearly visible, the Hakone region can make a memorable day trip from Tokyo. You can enjoy cable-car rides, visit an open-air museum, poke around smelly volcanic hot-water springs and cruise Ashi-no-ko (Lake Ashi).

Once you've arrived at Hakone-Yumoto Station, it's possible to board the delightful two-car mountain train that slowly winds through the forest to Gōra. Between Odawara and Gōra on the toy-train Hakone-Tōzan Line is the **Hakone Open-Air Museum.** You might want to stop in at the Hakone-Yumoto **TIC** before you start exploring; it's a five-minute walk west of the station. This art museum is a short walk from Chōkoku-no-mori Station, just before Gōra. As well as paintings, the museum has a 70,000 sq metre outdoor sculpture park that features works by artists such as Auguste Rodin and Henry Moore. The outdoor bronzes are particularly lovely in the winter under a light blanket of snow.

Gōra is at the end of the Hakone-Tōzan Line and the start of the funicular and cable-car trip to Togendai on the shore of Ashi-no-ko. There's nothing to see at Gōra, and you'll probably want to wander on. Further up the hill, 10 minutes from Gōra Station, is the **Hakone Museum of Art**, which has an interesting moss garden and a collection of ceramics from Japan and across Asia.

Once finished with the museum, take the funicular from Gōra up **Sōun-zan** (10 minutes). If you don't have a Hakone Free Pass, you'll need to buy a ticket (¥400) at the booth to the right of the platform exit. Sōun-zan is the starting point of a dramatic 4km cable-car ride to **Togendai.** On the way, the car passes through **Ōwakudani**, which you'll know you're approaching when you catch the first eggy whiff of sulphur. You can get out at this point and take a look at the volcanic hot springs where the steam continually rises. The water from these hot springs is responsible for the black shells of many a boiled egg. If the weather is clear, there are grand views of Mt Fuji, both from the gondolas and from Ōwakudani. The journey from Gōra to Togendai costs ¥1300/2300 one way/return; make sure to hold on to your ticket if you pause at Ōwakudani. If you're curious about the geology of the region, the **Ōwakudani Natural Science Museum** will fill you in about the formation of this volcanic valley more than 3000 years ago. From Ōwakudani, the car continues to **Ashi-no-ko**, a pretty lake that on clear days serves as a reflecting pool for majestic Mt Fuji, which rises imperiously above the surrounding hills. The best way to take in the views and cross the lake is to board one of the incongruous black **Ashi-no-ko Pirate Ships** at Tōgendai. These kitschy ships cruise the length of Ashi-nō-ko in 30 minutes.

Near where the boats dock in Hakone-machi is the old **Hakone Checkpoint**, run by the Tokugawa regime from 1619 to 1869 as a means of controlling the movement of people and ideas in and out of Edo. The present-day checkpoint is a recent reproduction of the original, and can be interesting for history buffs.

From here, nearby buses run from Moto-Hakone back to **Odawara** (¥1070, 50 minutes). Odawara is billed as an old castle town, which it is – although it's generally agreed that the castle is an uninspiring reconstruction of the original. If you're still interested, **Odawara castle** is a 10-minute walk from Odawara Station.

There are many bathing options in Hakone's numerous *onsen* areas. Along with a multitude of *onsen* there are also many *onsen ryokan* (traditional hot-spring inns), some of which welcome day visitors. See the Honourable Bath (p219) for more information.

TRANSPORT

There are three ways to get to the Hakone region: the Odakyū express bus service, departing from the bus terminal on the west side of Shinjuku Station; JR service, which runs regularly from Tokyo Station; and the private Odakyū train line, which departs from Shinjuku Station.

Train JR trains run on the Tōkaidō Line between Tokyo Station and Odawara Station. *Futsū* trains (¥1450, 90 minutes) run every 15 minutes or so, while *tokkyū* trains (¥2900, 70 minutes) leave less frequently. *Shinkansen* (¥3640, 40 minutes) leave Tokyo Station every 20 minutes, but you'll need to make sure you're on the train that stops at Odawara (the Kodama does, others do not).

Trains also run to Odawara from Shinjuku Station on the Odakyū Line. The quickest and comfiest option is the Romance Car (¥1690, 75 minutes), which leaves every half-hour. There's also a *tokkyū* service (¥850). At Odawara, you can change to the Hakone-Tōzan Line, a two-car toy train that will eventually deposit you at Gōra (¥650). Alternatively, if you are already on the Odakyū Line, you can continue on to Hakone-Yumoto and change to the Hakone-Tōzan Line (¥390 to Gōra) by crossing the platform.

Bus The Odakyū express bus service has the advantage of running directly into the Hakone region, to Ashi-no-ko (Lake Ashi) and to Hakone-machi (¥1950, two hours). The disadvantage is that the bus trip is much less interesting than the combination of Romance Car, toy train (Hakone-Tōzan Line), funicular, cable car (ropeway) and ferry. Buses leave from bus stop No 35 in front of Odakyū department store on the west side of Shinjuku Station.

Hakone Free Pass The Odakyū Line offers a Hakone Free Pass (Monday to Thursday ¥4700; Friday to Sunday ¥5500); this excellent ticket allows you to use any mode of transport (except for Seibu buses) within the Hakone region for three days and provides discounts on some of the major sights. The fare between Shinjuku and Hakone-Yumoto Station is also included in the pass, although if you're seeking the comforts of the Romance Car, you'll have to pay a surcharge (¥870). If you have a Japan Rail Pass, you'd be advised to buy a Free Pass in Odawara (¥3410/4130). Altogether it's a good deal for the Hakone circuit.

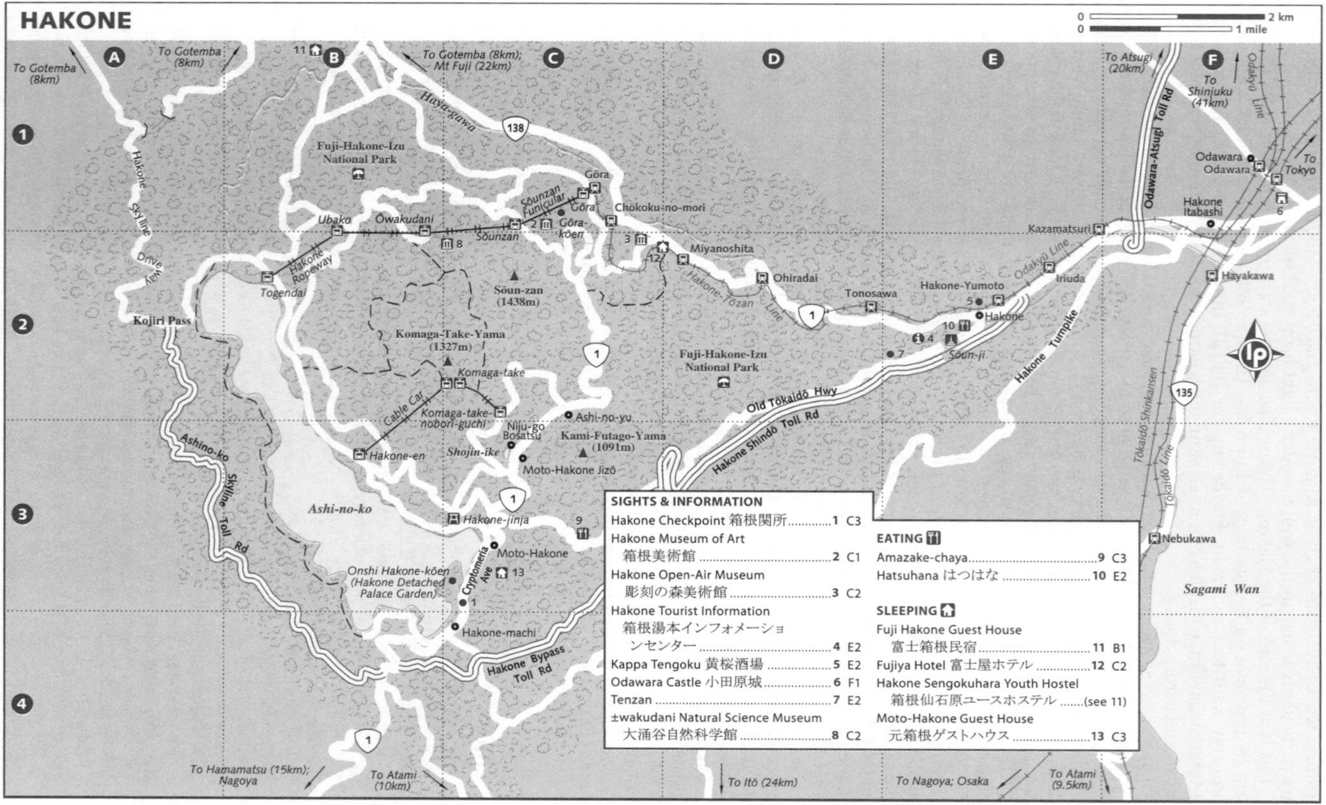

HAKONE

0 — 2 km
0 — 1 mile

SIGHTS & INFORMATION

- Hakone Checkpoint 箱根関所 1 C3
- Hakone Museum of Art 箱根美術館 2 C1
- Hakone Open-Air Museum 彫刻の森美術館 3 C2
- Hakone Tourist Information 箱根湯本インフォメーションセンター 4 E2
- Kappa Tengoku 黄桜酒場 5 E2
- Odawara Castle 小田原城 6 F1
- Tenzan 7 E2
- ±wakudani Natural Science Museum 大涌谷自然科学館 8 C2

EATING

- Amazake-chaya 9 C3
- Hatsuhana はつはな 10 E2

SLEEPING

- Fuji Hakone Guest House 富士箱根民宿 11 B1
- Fujiya Hotel 富士屋ホテル 12 C2
- Hakone Sengokuhara Youth Hostel 箱根仙石原ユースホステル ......(see 11)
- Moto-Hakone Guest House 元箱根ゲストハウス 13 C3

THE HONOURABLE BATH

Getting naked with total strangers is not, for most of us, the cultural norm, and those not from Japan often feel self-conscious at first. But shy *gaijin* (foreigners) should know that the Japanese perceive bathing as a great social leveller; company presidents rub naked shoulders with truck drivers, priests with publicans – and all revel in the anonymity that nudity allows. Only the *yakuza* (Japanese mafia) stand out with their magnificent *irezumi* (tattoos) or, in *yakuza* parlance, *iremono*.

The baths themselves come in as many different shapes and sizes as the customers, varying from the deluxe to the primitive. Essentially, you will either visit solely for an *o-furo* (literally the 'honourable bath'); or stay at an *onsen ryokan* (traditional hot-spring inn) to enjoy good food, copious amounts of alcohol, karaoke and a soak in the establishment's private baths, which may be located either indoors or outside. Ryokan will often allow you to have a soak even if you aren't staying there (ask for *ofuro-nomi*), although late-night privileges are often reserved for guests. This is an excellent and affordable way to experience some beautiful, traditional baths. Unfortunately, bathing is also big business and rampant commercialism has marred many once-lovely *onsen*.

There are two excellent books devoted to hot springs: *A Guide to Japanese Hot Springs* by Anne Hotta and Yoko Ishiguro and *Japan's Hidden Hot Springs* by Robert Neff. Both are worth seeking out for anyone looking to *onsen*-hop their way through Tokyo's outlying hot-spring resorts. Holders of the JR Pass can use JR lines to hop to hot springs far afield from Tokyo, utilising the *shinkansen* (bullet train) to get out of the city as swiftly as possible.

But the star in the Kantō area hot-spring firmament is Gunma-ken, where water bubbles out of the ground wherever you poke a stick into it. Get to Gunma from Ueno Station in Tokyo via Takasaki (*shinkansen* ¥4600, 45 minutes; *tokkyū* ¥3190, 75 minutes; *futsū* ¥1890, 110 minutes) and Jōmō-Kōgen Stations (*shinkansen* ¥5550, 70 minutes) on the Jōetsu *shinkansen* line, or via Maebashi (*tokkyū* ¥3190, 100 minutes; *futsū* ¥1890, two hours) and Shibukawa (*tokkyū* ¥3570, 100 minutes; *futsū* ¥2210, 2¼ hours) on the Takasaki and Ryomo or Agatsuma Lines, respectively.

The following Gunma springs are highly recommended and within a day's journey via *shinkansen*.

Chōjūkan Inn (☎ 0273-85-6634; 650 Nagai, Niiharu-mura) To get to this gorgeous, wood-walled inn at Hoshi Onsen, take the Jōetsu *shinkansen* from Tokyo Station to the Jomo-Kogen train station (¥5750, 75 minutes). From there, take the bus for Sarugakyo Onsen (30 minutes). At the last stop, take another bus for Hoshi Onsen (25 minutes). Try to arrive around noon to sample the inn's mountain-vegetable steamed rice. Women can sneak into the (far superior) men's bath here. In fact, it's almost expected.

Ikaho Onsen Great public bath with views of Mt Haruna. To get there, take the Jōetsu Line from Takasaki to Shibukawa Station (*tokkyū/futsu* ¥1410/400, 20/30 minutes), and then a local bus to the *onsen* (¥550, 20 minutes).

Kusatsu Onsen This is a quintessential old-time *onsen* town. Take the Agatsuma Line from Takasaki to Naganohara-Kusatsuguchi Station (*tokkyū/futsū* ¥2520/1110, 60/100 minutes), then local bus to the *onsen* (¥670, 30 minutes).

Minakami Onsen This is a thriving *onsen* town that is often frequented by couples. If you're not interested in a romantic rendezvous, you can white-water raft in the summer. To get there, take the Jōetsu Line from Takasaki to Minakami Station (*tokkyū/futsū* ¥2360/950, 60/90 minutes). From the station, the *onsen* is a pleasant 15-minute walk.

Shiriyaki Onsen Very odd and primitive, literally, the 'arse-burning' hot spring, favourite of haemorrhoid sufferers of the Heike clan. At this hot spring, you simply strip and climb into the river – not during spring, when the river is high and the water quite cold. Bring a *bentō* (boxed lunch) as there's nothing in the area, and start out early. To get there, take the Agatsuma Line from Takasaki to Naganohara-Kusatsuguchi Station (*tokkyū/futsū* ¥2520/1110, 60/100 minutes) where you can catch a local bus to Hanashiki Onsen (¥800, 30 minutes), from the bus stop, it's a 10-minute walk.

Takaragawa Onsen Complete with river bathing, Takaragawa has oft been voted the nation's best. To get there, take the Jōetsu Line from Takasaki to Minakami Station (*tokkyū/futsū* ¥2360/950, 60/90 minutes), where you will be able to catch a local bus to the *onsen* (¥1100, 40 minutes).

Information

Hakone-Yumoto Tourist Information Center (☎ 0460-5-8911; 698 Yumoto; ⏲ 9am-5pm) A five-minute walk from the Hakone-Yumoto train station.

Hakone-Yumoto Post Office (☎ 0460-5-5681; 383 Yumoto; ⏲ 9am-6pm Mon-Fri)

Sights

Ashi-no-ko Pirate Ships (30min cruise ¥840)

Hakone Museum of Art (☎ 0460-2-2623; 1300 Gora; admission ¥900; ⏲ 9am-4.30pm Fri-Wed)

Hakone Open-Air Museum (☎ 0460-2-1161; www.hakone-oam.or.jp; 1121 Ni-no-Taira; admission with/without Hakone

Free Pass ¥1400/1600; 9am-5pm Mar-Nov, 9am-4pm Dec-Feb)

Odawara Castle (0465-23-1373; admission adult/child ¥400/150; 9am-5pm)

Ōwakudani Natural Science Museum (0460-4-9149; admission ¥400; 9am-4.30pm)

Onsen

Kappa Tengoku (0460-5-6121; admission ¥750; 10am-10pm) Just up the hill from Hakone-Yumoto Station, this *rotemburo* (outdoor bath) is a nice one if it's not too crowded.

Tenzan (0460-6-4126; 208 Yumoto-Chaya; admission ¥900; 9am-11pm) This large, popular bath is 2km southwest of town; weekends and holidays can be busy. A free shuttle bus runs from the bridge near Hakone-Yumoto Station. After soaking in *rotemburo* of varying temperatures and designs (one is constructed to resemble a natural cave), the 20-minute walk back down the hill along the river is invigorating.

Eating

Amazake-chaya (0460-3-6418; amazake & snacks from ¥500) Since the Edo era, this tea house has been serving up *amazake* (warm, sweet sake) and light snacks. It's about 550m up the Old Tōkaidō Hwy from Moto-Hakone.

Hatsuhana (0460-5-8287; mains ¥750-1100; 10am-7pm) Slurp some *soba* at this pleasant eatery along the Haya-gawa. Hang a left on the next main street after passing the tourist information centre in Hakone-Yumoto; it's over the bridge on the left.

Sleeping

Hakone's popularity with Japanese weekenders in search of the ultimate spa experience is reflected in the high price of most accommodation in the area. With the exception of two youth hostels and a couple of ryokan, there are few budget and midrange options, although those that exist are comfortable and convenient for hiking and hot-spring hopping.

Fuji-Hakone Guest House (0460-4-6577; www.fujihakone.com; 912 Sengokuhara; r per person from ¥5250) Take a bus from stand No 4 of Odawara Station to the Senkyōrō-mae bus stop (¥1020, 50 minutes). There's an English sign nearby. A natural hot spa is available for private bathing, and night-time soaks are a treat, especially when the weather cools.

Fujiya Hotel (0460-2-2211; www.fujiyahotel.co.jp/english; 359 Miyanoshita; r from ¥20,000) The posh, wood-trimmed Fujiya Hotel, which has the rustic feel of a 19th-century hunting lodge, is famous as one of Japan's earliest Western-style hotels, and is highly rated on all fronts. The hotel is a five-minute walk from Miyanoshita Station on the Hakone-Tōzan Line; if you ring from the station, someone will give you directions in English.

Hakone Sengokuhara Youth Hostel (0460-4-8966; www.jyh.or.jp; 912 Sengokuhara; dm ¥3045) This friendly youth hostel is located just behind Fuji-Hakone Guest House. Check-in is from 4pm to 6pm. For directions, see Fuji-Hakone Guest House (above).

Moto-Hakone Guest House (0460-3-7880; www.fujihakone.com; 103 Moto-Hakone; r per person ¥5250) This homey, pleasant guest house is located near Ashi-nō-ko. From the bus terminal at Odawara Station, catch a bus from lane 3 to Ashinokoen-mae bus stop. The guest house is signposted from there.

Ashi-no-ko Pirate Ships (p217), Hakone

A WISE MAN'S CLIMB *Tony Wheeler*

I started out on a hot August night. At 10pm the temperature had been around 27°C (80°F), but by 4am it was below freezing and the wind was whistling past at what felt like hurricane speed. With a surprising number of other *gaijin* (foreigners) and a huge number of Japanese, I reached the top of Mt Fuji.

Climbing Mt Fuji is definitely not heroic: in the two-month 'season', as many as 180,000 people get up to the top – 3000-odd every night. Nor is it that much fun – it's a bit of a dusty slog, and when you get to the top it's so cold and windy that your main thought is about heading down again. But the climb and the views aren't really what you do it for. To Japanese Fuji-climbers, it's something of a pilgrimage; to *gaijin,* it's another opportunity to grapple with something uniquely Japanese.

Like many other climbers, I made my Fuji climb overnight. At 9.30pm I got off the bus at the Kawaguchi-ko 5th Station, which is where the road ends and you have to start walking. Surprisingly, about half the passengers on my bus were *gaijin,* most of them a group of Americans planning to convert the Japanese to Mormonism! I'd bought a litre of the isotonic drink Pocari Sweat and a packet of biscuits at a 7-Eleven in the town of Kawaguchi-ko, and wearing a shirt and a coat, I was all set. The night was clear but dark, and I was glad I'd bought some new batteries for my torch before I left Tokyo.

My experience of climbing holy mountains is that you always get to the top too early – you work up a real sweat on the climb and then you freeze waiting for dawn. So I hung around for a while before starting out.

Despite the hordes climbing the mountain, I managed to lose the path occasionally. By the time I reached 2390m I'd already stopped to unzip the lining from my coat. By 11pm I was past 2700m and thinking it was time to slow down if I wanted to avoid arriving too early. By midnight it was getting much cooler, and I zipped the jacket-lining back in place and added more clothes to my ensemble. I was approaching 3000m – virtually halfway – and at this rate I was going to be at the top by 2.30am, in line with the four hours and 35 minutes the tourist office leaflet said it was supposed to take! In Japan, even mountain climbing is scheduled to the minute.

Although I'd started on my own, some of the faces I met at rest stops were becoming familiar by this point, and I'd fallen in with two Canadians and a Frenchman.

Huts are scattered up the mountainside; some stations have a number of huts, and others have none. The proprietors are very jealous of their facilities, and prominent signs, in English and Japanese, announce that even if it is pouring with rain, you can stay outside if you aren't willing to fork over the overnight fee. Fortunately, at 1.30am we were virtually swept into one hut, probably in anticipation of the numerous bowls of *rāmen* (noodles in soup) we would order. We hung out in this comfortable 3400m-high hideaway until after 3am, when we calculated that a final hour and a bit of a push would get us to the top just before the 4.30am sunrise.

We made it and, looking back from the top, we saw hordes of climbers heading up towards us. It was no great surprise to find a souvenir shop (there is absolutely no place in Japan where tourists won't find a souvenir shop waiting for them). The sun took an interminable time to rise, but eventually it poked its head through the clouds, after which most climbers headed straight back down. I spent an hour walking around the crater rim, but I wasn't sorry to wave Fuji-san goodbye. The Japanese say you're wise to climb Fuji, but a fool to climb it twice. I've no intention of being a fool.

If you decide to go

Fuji-san can be reached via **Keiō Kōsoku bus** (☎ 5376-2222; ticket ¥1700), which takes 1¾ hours and departs from the long-distance bus station on the west side of Shinjuku Station, or via a more expensive and circuitous train route that takes at least two hours and involves hopping the JR Chūō Line for Ōtsuki (*tokkyū/futsū* ¥2230/1280) where you will then need to cross the platform to catch the local train to Kawaguchi-ko (¥1110, 50 minutes). Whether arriving by bus or train, Kawaguchi-ko is the place to catch the bus for the Kawaguchi-ko 5th Station (one of several departure points that are part-way up the mountain), where most climbers from Tokyo begin their evening hike. If you're a glutton for punishment you can start at the base of Fuji-san and climb all the way up Fuji via the Yoshida route. Keep in mind that the official climbing season starts on 1 July and ends on 31 August (although it is possible – but not advised – to go at other times). And, of course, remember common-sense hiking precautions: take water unless you intend to buy it during your climb, and make sure you pack gear that is appropriate for cold and wet weather – conditions can vary wildly between the bottom and top of the mountain.

NIKKŌ

Nikkō is not only one of the most popular day trips from Tokyo, it's also one of Japan's major tourist attractions due to the splendour of its shrines and temples, and the surrounding natural beauty. Nikkō can become extremely crowded, especially during spring and autumn foliage seasons. If it's at all possible, it's best to visit early on a weekday to avoid the crowds. Before you head to the shrine area either via bus or by foot, you may want to stop by the **Tōbu Nikkō station information centre** or the **Kyōdo Center Tourist Information office** to give yourself the lay of the land.

TRANSPORT

Train The best way to visit Nikkō is via the Tōbu-Nikkō Line from Asakusa Station. The station is in the basement of the Tōbu department store (it's well signposted from the subway). All seats are reserved on *tokkyū* trains (¥2740, 110 minutes), but you can usually get tickets and reservations just before setting out. Trains run every 30 minutes or so from 7.30am to 10am; hourly after 10am. *Kaisoku* trains (¥1320, two hours, hourly from 6.20am to 4.30pm) require no reservation. (Note, passengers should ensure they ride in the first two carriages of the train as only these two reach all the way to Nikkō.) For trains other than the *tokkyū*, you may have to change at Imaichi.

Travelling by JR is costly and time-consuming, and is really of interest only to those who have purchased a JR Pass at home. The quickest way to Nikkō via JR is to take the *shinkansen* from Tokyo to Utsunomiya (¥4800, 50 minutes), where you will then change for a *futsū* train to Nikkō (¥740, 45 minutes).

Nikkō-Kinugawa Free Pass This economical pass (¥5000) is valid for four days and is available from Tōbu railways in Asakusa. The pass includes transport from Asakusa to Nikkō, unlimited Tōbu bus usage on certain Nikkō-area routes and some discounts at local shops.

Bus Once you arrive in Nikkō, you can either do the 30-minute uphill (and fairly featureless) walk to the temple and shrine area, or you can hop on bus 1 or 2 (¥190).

Nikkō's history as a sacred site stretches back to the middle of the 8th century when the Buddhist priest Shōdō Shōnin established a hermitage here in 782. For many years it was known as a famous training centre for Buddhist monks, although after a time it declined into obscurity. Nikkō remained forgotten until it was chosen as the site for the mausoleum of Tokugawa Ieyasu (p224), the warlord who took control of all Japan and established the shōgunate that ruled for 250 years until Commodore Perry (p52) and his American ships arrived in Tokyo Bay, just in time to usher in the Meiji Restoration and the end of the feudal era.

Tokugawa Ieyasu was laid to rest among Nikkō's towering cedars in 1617, but it was his grandson Tokugawa Iemitsu who, in 1634, commenced work on the imposing shrine that can be seen today. The original shrine, Tōshō-gū, was completely rebuilt using an army of 15,000 artisans from all over Japan. The work on the shrine and mausoleum took two years to complete, and the results continue to receive mixed reviews.

Tōshō-gū was constructed as a memorial to a warlord who devoted his life to conquering Japan. Tokugawa Ieyasu was a man of considerable determination and was not above sacrificing a few scruples, or a few people, in order to achieve his aims. He is attributed with having had his wife and eldest son executed because it was politically expedient for him to do so. Interestingly, Tokugawa's final resting place manages to reflect the imperiousness and the austerity of the powerful despot.

Today in Nikkō, close to the Tōshō-gū area is **Shin-kyō-bashi**. Shōdō Shōnin was reputedly carried across the river at this point on the backs of two huge serpents. Tourists not toted by reptiles can cross the bridge on foot.

The next stop is 1200-year-old **Rinnō-ji**, also founded by Shōdō Shōnin of the Buddhist Tendai sect. On its grounds is **Sambutsu-dō** (Three Buddha Hall), which houses a trio of huge, remarkable gold-lacquered images: a *senjū* (1000-armed Kannon); the central image of Amida Nyorai; and Batō, a horse-headed goddess of mercy. **Hōmotsu-den** (Treasure Hall), also in the temple grounds, has a splendid collection of temple artefacts, sculptures and scrolls. Admission to Hōmotsu-den includes entry to the lovely Edo-period garden **Shōyō-en**.

A huge stone torii (entrance gate to a Shintō shrine) marks the entrance to **Tōshō-gū**, while to the left is a **five-storey pagoda**. The pagoda dates from 1650 but, like so many structures destroyed by natural disasters, was reconstructed in 1818. The pagoda is remarkable for its lack of foundations – the interior contains a long suspended pole that apparently swings like a pendulum in order to maintain equilibrium during an earthquake.

The true entrance to Tōshō-gū is through the torii at **Omote-mon**, which is protected on either side by the Deva kings. Through the entrance to the temple to the right is **Sanjinko** (Three Sacred Storehouses). The upper storey of this building is renowned for the imaginative relief

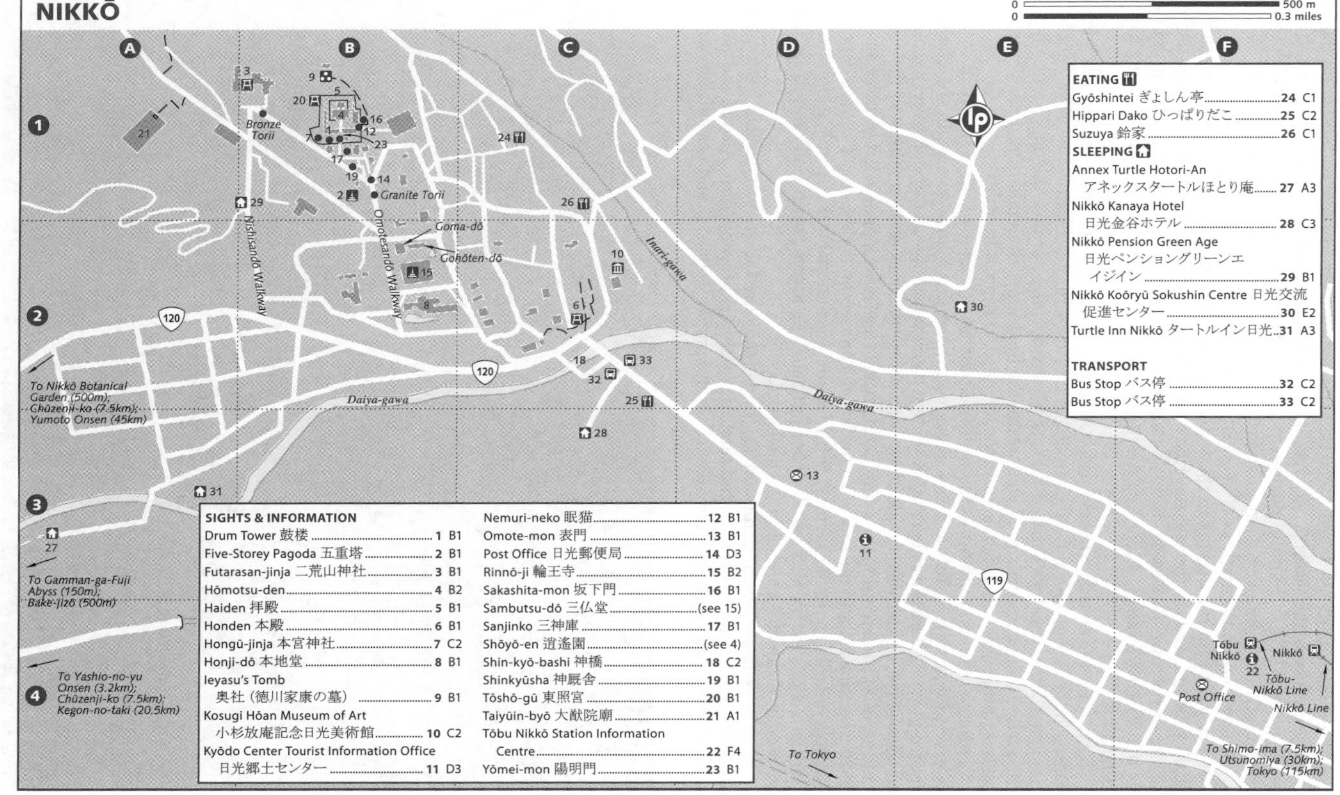
NIKKŌ
0 500 m
0 0.3 miles
A
B
C
D
E
F
1
2
3
4
EATING
Gyōshintei ぎょしん亭 24 C1
Hippari Dako ひっぱりだこ 25 C2
Suzuya 鈴家 26 C1
SLEEPING
Annex Turtle Hotori-An アネックスタートルほとり庵 27 A3
Nikkō Kanaya Hotel 日光金谷ホテル 28 C3
Nikkō Pension Green Age 日光ペンショングリーンエイジイン 29 B1
Nikkō Koōryū Sokushin Centre 日光交流促進センター 30 E2
Turtle Inn Nikkō タートルイン日光 31 A3
TRANSPORT
Bus Stop バス停 32 C2
Bus Stop バス停 33 C2
SIGHTS & INFORMATION
Drum Tower 鼓楼 1 B1
Five-Storey Pagoda 五重塔 2 B1
Futarasan-jinja 二荒山神社 3 B1
Hōmotsu-den 4 B2
Haiden 拝殿 5 B1
Honden 本殿 6 B1
Hongū-jinja 本宮神社 7 C2
Honji-dō 本地堂 8 B1
Ieyasu's Tomb 奥社（徳川家康の墓） 9 B1
Kosugi Hōan Museum of Art 小杉放庵記念日光美術館 10 C2
Kyōdo Center Tourist Information Office 日光郷土センター 11 D3
Nemuri-neko 眠猫 12 B1
Omote-mon 表門 13 B1
Post Office 日光郵便局 14 D3
Rinnō-ji 輪王寺 15 B2
Sakashita-mon 坂下門 16 B1
Sambutsu-dō 三仏堂 (see 15)
Sanjinko 三神庫 17 B1
Shōyō-en 逍遙園 (see 4)
Shin-kyō-bashi 神橋 18 C2
Shinkyūsha 神厩舎 19 B1
Tōshō-gū 東照宮 20 B1
Taiyūin-byō 大猷院廟 21 A1
Tōbu Nikkō Station Information Centre 22 F4
Yōmei-mon 陽明門 23 B1
Bronze Torii
Granite Torii
Goma-dō
Gohōten-dō
Nishisandō Walkway
Omotesandō Walkway
Inari-gawa
Daiya-gawa
Daiya-gawa
120
120
119
To Nikkō Botanical Garden (500m); Chūzenji-ko (7.5km); Yumoto Onsen (45km)
To Gamman-ga-Fuji Abyss (150m); Bake-jizō (500m)
To Yashio-no-yu Onsen (3.2km); Chūzenji-ko (7.5km); Kegon-no-taki (20.5km)
To Tokyo
Tōbu Nikkō
Nikkō
Tōbu-Nikkō Line
Nikkō Line
Post Office
To Shimo-ima (7.5km); Utsunomiya (30km); Tokyo (115km)

carvings of elephants by an artist who had apparently never seen the real thing. To the left of the entrance is the **Shinkyūsha** (Sacred Stable), a suitably plain building housing a carved white horse. The stable's only adornment is an allegorical series of relief carvings depicting the lifecycle of the monkey. They include the famous 'hear no evil, see no evil, speak no evil' trio that is now emblematic of Nikkō and a favourite subject for shutterbugs.

Once you're finished taking in the stable, pass through another torii and climb another flight of stairs, and on the left and right you will see a **drum tower** and a belfry. To the left of the drum tower is **Honji-dō**, with its huge ceiling painting of a dragon in flight known as the Roaring Dragon. According to legend, the dragon will roar if you clap your hands beneath it.

Next comes **Yōmei-mon**, whose interior is adorned with a multitude of reliefs of Chinese sages, children, dragons and other mythical creatures. So much effort and skill went into the gate that its creators worried that its perfection might arouse the anger and envy of the gods. To appease their predicted wrath, the final supporting pillar on the left side was placed upside down as a deliberate error intended to express humility.

Through Yōmei-mon and to the right is **Nemuri-neko** (Sleeping Cat). This small carving is easy to miss – look to the beam above your head just before you begin the climb to Ieyasu's tomb. **Sakashita-mon** here opens onto a path that climbs up through towering cedars to **Ieyasu's Tomb**, a relatively simple affair considering the boundless ambition of the person entombed. If you are using the combination ticket (see Sights, opposite), it will cost an extra ¥520 to see the cat and the tomb. To the left of Yōmei-mon is Jinyōsha, a storage depot for Nikkō's *mikoshi* (portable shrines), which come out and bring the temple ground to life during Nikkō's merry May and October festivals. The **Honden** (Main Hall) and **Haiden** (Hall of Worship) can also be seen in the enclosure.

Nearby is **Futarasan-jinja**, dedicated to Nantai-san, the tall mountain that rises above Chūzenji-ko, its consort Nyotai and their mountainous progeny Tarō. Also in the vicinity is **Taiyūin-byō**, which enshrines Ieyasu's grandson Iemitsu (1604–51) and is a smaller version

A forest near Chūzenji-ko (opposite), Nikkō

of the grander Tōshō-gū. The smaller size gives it a less extravagant air, and some consider it more aesthetically worthy than its larger neighbour.

The **Kosugi Hōan Museum of Art** has a collection of landscape paintings by local artist Kosugi (1920–64) and is a good rainy-day option.

To take a break from the colour and the crowds, take a 20-minute walk over to **Gamman-ga-Fuji Abyss,** which houses an interesting collection of statues of *Jizō*. One of the statues, Bake-jizō, mocks travellers foolish enough to count the number of statues (it's said to be constantly changing to frustrate such attempts).

A bit further afield, and ideal on a quiet day if you've thoroughly explored Nikkō, is the 50-minute bus trip up to **Chūzenji-ko** (¥1100) along a winding road; buses depart from either Nikkō or Tōbu Nikkō train stations. There's some beautiful scenery, including the 97m-high waterfall Kegon-no-taki; an elevator (¥530 return) drops down to a platform where you can observe the full force of the waterfall. Also worth a visit is the third of the trio of Futarasan-jinja, complementing those near Tōshō-gū and on Nantai-san.

Information

Kyōdo Center tourist information office (☎ 0288-53-3795; 591 Gokomachi; 🕑 8.30am-5pm) Providing lots of useful pamphlets and maps, the office also has helpful English-speaking staff. Internet access costs ¥100 per 30 minutes.

Nikkō Post office (🕑 9am-6pm Mon-Fri) Three blocks northwest of the Kyōdo Center tourist information office, this post office has an international ATM.

Tōbu Nikkō station information centre (☎ 0288-53-4511; 🕑 8.30am-5pm) At the Nikkō train station, there's a small information desk where you can pick up a town map and get help in English to find buses, restaurants, and hotels.

Sights

Although you can buy separate tickets to each of Nikkō's attractions, it makes sense to buy a combination ticket (¥1000), which is valid for two days. The ticket covers entry to Rinnō-ji and to Tōshōgū and Futarasan-jinja; however, the following special exhibits or sights require an additional entrance fee.

Kosugi Hōan Museum of Art (☎ 0288-50-1200; 2388-3 Sannai; admission ¥700; 🕑 9.30am-5pm Tue-Sun)

Nemuri-Neko & Ieyasu Tomb (admission ¥520; 🕑 8am-4.30pm)

Hōmotsu-den (Rinnō-ji; admission ¥300; 🕑 8am-4pm)

Onsen

Yashio-no-yu Onsen (やしおの湯温泉; ☎ 0288-53-6611; adult/child ¥500/free; 🕑 10am-9pm Fri-Wed) This modern hot-spring complex has open-air baths, saunas and a large indoor bath. Take a Chūzenji-bound bus from either train station in Nikkō; it's a 12-minute ride to the Kiyomizu-itchōme stop. Walk back toward Nikkō, under the bypass and across the bridge.

Yumoto Onsen (湯元温泉; admission ¥500) Although Nikkō is not generally thought of as a place to hit the hot springs, it does have its own little pocket of thermal activity. This quiet hot spring is about 30 minutes from Chūzenji-kō by bus (¥840) and can be a good way to wrap up a day spent trudging between temples and shrines.

Eating

Gyōshintei (☎ 0288-53-3751; dishes ¥2000; 🕑 noon-8pm) Set on the garden grounds of Meiji-no-Yukata, Gyōshintei serves elegant Buddhist vegetarian cuisine.

Hippari Dako (☎ 0288-53-2933; dishes ¥800; 🕑 11am-7pm) Good, cheap *yakitori* (skewers of grilled chicken) and *yaki-udon* (fried noodles) and friendly staff has made Hippari Dako a favourite travellers' spot for years. The walls are papered with business cards and testimonies to the virtues of hot sake.

Suzuya (☎ 0288-54-0293; set lunch ¥1400) Stop by for a bowl of *soba*, or try the local speciality *yuba* (bean curd, skimmed off the top of soy milk), which is used in much of Nikkō's local cuisine.

Sleeping

Annex Turtle Hotori-An (☎ 0288-53-3663; www.turtle-nikko.com; 8-28 Takumi-chō; r per person from ¥6800) This place, with mostly tatami rooms, is to the west of Turtle Inn Nikkō (p226), over the river but on the same road. The bath house looks out onto the forest surrounding the inn.

Nikkō Kanaya Hotel (☎ 0288-54-0001; www.kanayahotel.co.jp/nkh/index-e.html; 1300 Kami-Hastuishi-machi; r from ¥10,000) Overlooking Shin-kyō-bashi, Nikkō's classiest hotel is decent value if you feel like a little civilised splendour. During peak holiday periods the rates nearly double.

Nikkō Kōryu Sokushin Centre (☎ 0288-54-1013; www city.nikko.tochigi.jp/nyh/; 2845 Tokorono; r with/without bathroom ¥5000/4100) Japanese- and Western-style rooms have views at this popular hostel. It's a 10-minute walk from the Shiyakusho-mae bus stop, on the southern side of the Daiya-gawa.

Nikkō Pension Green Age Inn (☎ 0288-54-3636; 10-9 Nishi-Sandō; r per person with/without breakfast & dinner ¥9800/5800) A Tudor-style mansion near the temples.

Turtle Inn Nikkō (☎ 0288-53-3168; www.turtle-nikko.com/turtle/index_en.html; 2-16 Takumi-chō; s with/without bathroom from ¥5900/5100) Far and away the most popular of Nikkō's pensions is the Turtle Inn **Nikkō**, which is located beside the river and beyond the shrine area. From the station, you are able take a bus to the Sōgō-kaikan-mae bus stop, then you can backtrack around 50m to the fork in the road and then follow the river for around five minutes.

Directory

Directory

TRANSPORT

Tokyo's world-class, public-transport system will get you anywhere you need to go. Most places worth visiting are conveniently close to a subway or Japan Railways (JR) station. Where the rail network lets you down (though it really shouldn't), there are usually bus services – although using these can be challenging if you can't read kanji.

Most residents and visitors use the railway system far more than any other means of transport. It is reasonably priced and frequent (generally five minutes at most between trains on major lines in central Tokyo), and stations have conveniences such as left-luggage lockers for baggage storage. The only drawback is that the system shuts down at midnight or 1am and doesn't start up again until 5am or 6am.

Subway trains have a tendency to stop halfway along their route when closing time arrives. People who are stranded face an expensive taxi ride home or have to wait for the first morning train. Check schedules posted on platforms for the last train on the line if you plan to be out late.

Avoiding Tokyo's rush hour is a good idea, but might be impossible if you're on a tight schedule. Commuter congestion tends to ease between 10am and 4pm, when travelling around Tokyo – especially on the JR Yamanote Line – can actually be quite pleasant. Before 9.30am and from about 4.30pm onward there'll be cheek-to-jowl crowds on all major train and bus lines.

Flights, tours and rail tickets can be booked online at www.lonelyplanet.com/travel_services.

AIR

International flights from all over the world land in Japan, most of them arriving in Tokyo. Tokyo is also the hub of air travel within Japan, which is extensive, reliable and safe. In many cases, flying can be faster – and not significantly more expensive – than riding the *shinkansen* (bullet train). Flying can also help you get from Japan's main hubs, like Tokyo, to some of the small islands near the coast.

Customs and immigration procedures are usually straightforward, although they're more time-consuming for *gaijin* (foreigners) than for Japanese. A neat appearance will speed your passage through passport control and customs, whereas those with even a slightly 'hippy' look is asking for a visit to 'the room'. Everything at Narita is clearly signposted in English and you can change money in the customs halls of either terminal or in the arrival halls. The rates will be the same as those offered in town.

Airports

Tokyo has two airports: Narita, which handles most international traffic, and Haneda, which is used primarily for domestic flights.

Narita airport (flight information ☎ 0476-34-5000, general information ☎ 0476-32-2802) is 66km east of Tokyo, but aside from its inconvenient location, it's an excellent, modern airport with a plethora of services. It is divided into two terminals, which are connected by a free shuttle-bus service. From Terminal 1 board this bus at the No 0 bus stop, and from Terminal 2 board at the Nos 8 and 18 stops. Note that some of the airport's services are available only in the newer Terminal 2.

At both terminals there are post offices, currency-exchange counters (generally open 7am to 10pm, although the one in Terminal 2 on the 1st floor is open until 11pm), health clinics and lots of restaurants and duty-free shops. Both terminals also offer left-luggage services and efficient baggage-courier services (see p237).

In both Terminals 1 and 2, the travel-weary (and -dirty) will find showers and day-rooms for napping, and free children's playrooms available to departing passengers who have completed emigration formalities. Both playrooms include computer games and well-designed play areas.

There are several information counters in both terminals, and the staff speak English; the main counter for foreign visitors is in Terminal 2 on the 1st floor (☎ 0476-34-6251; ⌚ 9am-8pm).

GETTING INTO TOWN

Narita Airport

Getting into town from Narita can take anything from 50 minutes to two hours, depending on your mode of transport. Because the two terminals at Narita are fairly distant from one another, be sure to get off at the correct terminal – all airport transport prominently displays lists of airlines and the terminal they use.

Both the private Keisei Line and Japan Railways (JR East) offer a choice of services to get from Narita to Tokyo. Conveniently, all trains depart from stations directly under both airport terminals.

On the private **Keisei Line** (☎ 0476-32-8501; www.keisei.co.jp/keisei/tetudou/keisei_us/top.html), two services run between Narita airport and Tokyo: the comfortable, fast **Skyliner service** (¥1920, 56 minutes), which runs nonstop to Nippori and Ueno Stations (Map p281); and the **tokkyū service** (limited express; ¥1000, 75 minutes). The Keisei Stations in Terminals 1 and 2 are clearly signposted in English. From Nippori or Ueno (the final stop), you can change to the JR Yamanote Line. Ueno Station is on both the JR Yamanote Line and the Hibiya and Ginza subway lines. If you're travelling to Ikebukuro or Shinjuku, it's more convenient to get off one stop before Ueno at Nippori Station, also on the JR Yamanote Line.

Going to the airport from Ueno, the Keisei Ueno Station is right next to the JR Ueno Station. You can buy advance tickets here for the Skyliner service, or purchase tickets for the Keisei *tokkyū* service from the ticket machines. JR Nippori Station has a clearly signposted walkway to the Keisei Nippori Station.

Japan Railways (JR East; ☎ 3423-0111; www.jreast.co.jp/e/nex/index.html) runs **Narita Express** (N'EX; ¥2940, 53 minutes) and **JR kaisoku** (rapid express; ¥1280, 85 minutes) services into Tokyo Station (Map pp294–5), from where you can change for almost anywhere. N'EX is swift, smooth and comfortable, but it doesn't run as frequently as the private Keisei Line. N'EX trains leave Narita approximately every half hour between 7am and 10pm for Tokyo Station, and they also run less frequently into Shinjuku (Map p282) and Ikebukuro (Map p280; ¥3110), or to Japan's second-largest city, Yokohama (¥4180). All seats are reserved, but tickets can usually be bought just before departure; if the train is already full, you can buy a standing ticket for the same price.

The JR *kaisoku* service is part of the local transit network and so stops at many local stations. This service is the slowest and cheapest into Tokyo Station, leaving about once an hour.

Friendly Airport Limousine buses (☎ 3665-7220; www.limousinebus.co.jp/e) can be found in both wings of the arrival building of Narita airport. Don't get too excited about the name – they're ordinary buses. They take 1½ to two hours (depending on traffic) to travel between Narita airport and a number of major hotels around Tokyo. Check departure times before buying your ticket; buses depart every 15 to 30 minutes.

The fare to hotels in Ikebukuro, Akasaka, Ginza, Shibuya or Shinjuku is ¥3000. You can also go straight to Tokyo Station (one hour 20 minutes) or to Shinjuku Station (one hour 25 minutes) for ¥3000. You can also take the bus into **Tokyo City Air Terminal** (TCAT; Map pp278–9; ☎ 3665-7111; 42-1 Hakozakichō, Chūō-ku) in Nihombashi, although departing from TCAT is probably more convenient than arriving here. Those transferring to domestic flights departing from Haneda airport can take a limousine bus direct (¥3000, 75 minutes) from Narita. Allow plenty of extra time as traffic conditions in Tokyo are seldom ideal. Limousine buses also offer services between Narita and **Yokohama City Air Terminal** (YCAT; ☎ 045-459-4800) at Yokohama Station. Buses from YCAT, departing every 20 minutes or so, take around 90 minutes and cost ¥3500.

A taxi to Narita airport from Tokyo will cost about ¥30,000 and, battling traffic all the way, will usually take longer than the train.

Haneda Airport

The simplest, cheapest way to get from Haneda into Tokyo is to hop on the JR monorail to Hamamatsuchō Station on the JR Yamanote Line. Trains (¥470, 20 minutes) leave every 10 minutes. Limousine buses also connect Haneda with TCAT (direct ¥900, 30 minutes) and hotels around central Tokyo; buses to Ikebukuro and Shinjuku, for example, cost ¥1200 and take about one hour). Of course you could shell out around ¥7000 for a taxi if you prefer.

The airport **Tourist Information Center** (TIC; ☎ 0476-34-6251; 🕑 9am-8pm) is a key stop if you haven't yet booked any accommodation. While you're there, pick up a subway map and the *Tourist Map of Tokyo*. There's a TIC on the 1st floor in each terminal. Narita airport also has a JR office where you can make bookings and exchange your Japan Rail Pass voucher for a pass, if you're planning to start travelling straight away.

Check-in procedures are usually very efficient at Narita, but you should arrive at the airport at least two hours before your departure time. Passport control and security procedures are similarly efficient (bring your embarkation card, which you should have received upon arrival; if you don't have one, you can get a blank form before going through passport control).

Haneda airport (information ☎ 5757-8111) is the airport Tokyo expats wish was still Tokyo's main air hub. Unfortunately, all international traffic now goes via Narita airport, and only domestic flyers and charter flights can make use of this conveniently located airport.

Haneda doesn't have Narita's services infrastructure, but there are post offices, banks, left-luggage services and baggage-shipping companies. Nor does Haneda have a dedicated English-language information counter, although there is usually someone who can answer your questions in English.

FLIGHT BOOKING

You'll find a number of travel agencies in Tokyo where English is spoken. For an idea of current prices, check the *Japan Times* or *Metropolis*.

Across Traveller's Bureau (www.across-travel.com) Ikebukuro (Map p280; ☎ 5391-3227; 3rd fl, 1-11-1 Higashi-Ikebukuro, Toshima-ku); Shibuya (Map p284; ☎ 5467-0077; 3rd fl, 1-14-14 Shibuya, Shibuya-ku); Shinjuku (Map p282; ☎ 3340-6745; 2nd fl, 1-19-6 Nishi-Shinjuku, Shinjuku-ku)

No 1 Travel (www.no1-travel.com) Ikebukuro (Map p280; ☎ 3986-4690; 4th fl, 1-16-10 Nishi-Ikebukuro, Toshima-ku); Shibuya (Map p284; ☎ 3770-1381; 7th fl, 1-11-1 Jinnan, Shibuya-ku); Shinjuku (Map p282; ☎ 3200-8871; 7th fl, 1-16-5 Kabukichō, Shinjuku-ku)

STA Travel (Map p280; ☎ 5391-2922; www.statravel.co.jp/english/index.html; 7th fl, 1-16-20 Minami-Ikebukuro, Toshima-ku)

BICYCLE

Despite the tangled traffic and often narrow roads, bicycles are still one of the most common forms of transit in Tokyo. Theft does happen, especially of cheap bicycles, so go ahead and lock up your bike. Ride with your bag or pack on your person, as opportunists on motorbikes do swipe stuff from those front-mounted baskets.

Some ryokan and inns rent bicycles to their guests, but if your lodgings don't, you can rent a bicycle in Asakusa for ¥200 per day. There's a bicycle-rental lot on the Sumida river bank near Azumabashi (the bridge just outside Asakusa Station).

See p168 for location-specific leisure-ride bike rentals.

BOAT

Water taxis are one of the most dramatic ways to take in the city. For more information on cruises down the Sumida River see p87.

BUS

Many Tokyo residents and visitors have never set foot on a bus, as the rail system is so convenient. Bus services tend to finish around 10pm, especially in more remote areas, but bus stops are clearly marked and buses generally have English-language signs indicating the destinations.

Bus fares are ¥200 for Tokyo Metropolitan (Toei) buses; you can pick up a copy of the *Toei Bus Route Guide,* including a route map and timetable, at any Toei subway station. Buses run by private companies and hotels might require you to pay a different fare, and others might ask that you prepurchase a ticket. Children's rates are half those of adult fares. Deposit your fare into the box next to the driver as you enter the bus; you can get change for ¥1000 notes and coins. A tape recording announces the name of each stop as it is reached, so listen carefully and press the button next to your seat when yours is announced.

The one-day Tokyo Combination Ticket (p233) can be used on Toei buses as well as the subway and JR railway lines.

CAR & MOTORCYCLE

Driving yourself around Tokyo is by no means impossible but akin to stabbing yourself in the eye with a chopstick. Parking space is limited and expensive, traffic moves in slow-mo, traffic lights are posted virtually every 50m, and unless you can navigate the city in your sleep, expect to get lost. You're better off taking advantage of Tokyo's excellent public transport – but if you do intend to drive in Japan, note first of all that driving is on the left side. If you do decide to drive, pick up a copy of the eminently useful *Rules of the Road,* available from the **Japan Automobile Federation** (www.jaf.or.jp/e/index.htm).

Many foreigners living in Tokyo end up getting themselves a motorbike. It's a good way to get around town, especially after the trains have stopped running. The best place to take a look at what's available and get some information in English is the area of motorbike shops on Korinchō-dōri, near

Ueno Station (Map pp296–7). Some of the shops there have foreign staff.

If you buy a motorbike, you will need a motorbike licence (for motorbikes up to 400cc, your foreign licence is transferable) and your bike will need to be registered. Bikes up to 125cc are registered at your ward office; bikes of more than 125cc are registered with the Transport Branch Office. Further information can be obtained through the Tokyo Metropolitan Government's service for foreign residents living in Tokyo (☎ 5320-7744).

Hire

Car-rental agencies in Tokyo will hire you one of their vehicles upon presentation of an international driving licence. Small cars average ¥8000 per day. The following rental agencies will usually have English-speaking staff on hand.

Dollar Rent-a-Car (☎ 3567-2818)

Nippon Rent-a-Car (☎ 3485-7196)

Toyota Rent-a-Car (☎ 5954-8008)

TAXI

Taxis are so expensive that you should use them only when you have no alternative. Rates start at ¥660, which buys you 2km (after 11pm it's 1.5km), then the meter rises by ¥80 every 274m (every 220m or so after 11pm). You also click up about ¥80 every two minutes while you relax in a typical Tokyo traffic jam. Taxi vacancy is indicated by a red light in the corner of the front window; a green light means there's a night-time surcharge; and a yellow light means that the cab is on call.

If you have to get a taxi late on a Friday or Saturday night, be prepared for delays and higher prices. The same applies any day of the week for the first hour or so after the last trains run. At these times, most stranded commuters stand in long queues (sometimes up to an hour) in order to get a taxi home.

Tokyo taxi drivers rarely speak any English, so, if you don't speak Japanese, it's a good idea to have your destination written down in Japanese. Even if your destination has an English name, it is unlikely the driver will understand your pronunciation. Don't slam the door shut when you get in or leave – the door will magically shut itself.

TRAIN

The Tokyo train system can be a bit daunting at first, but you soon get the hang of it. Much initial confusion arises from the fact that Tokyo is serviced by a combination of JR lines, private and municipal inner-city subway lines and private suburban lines. This sometimes means switching between both trains and train systems. It's not as bad as it sounds, however, as the lines are well integrated and can often be traversed with just one purchase of a special combination ticket (see p233). To get around Tokyo, you'll probably only need to use the JR lines and subway lines.

Train destinations are usually written in both Japanese and English on the side of the train and on the platform departure board, and announcements or electronic displays inside the train are made in both Japanese and English.

Most of Tokyo's train lines now reserve women-only carriages at weekday rush hours and on weekend nights. The carriages are marked with signs (usually pink in colour) in both Japanese and English, or in some cases by illustrations showing the silhouette of a man standing outside of a women-only carriage. Boys older than 12 are not allowed on women-only carriages.

Once you get off the JR Yamanote Line and the subway lines, watch for express services. Generally, the longer the route, the more likely you are to find faster train services. The fastest 'regular' trains (ie slower than a *shinkansen*, or bullet train) are *tokkyū* (limited express services), then followed by *kyūkō* (ordinary express), which usually stop at only a limited number of stations. A variation on *kyūkō* trains are the *kaisoku* (rapid service trains). The slowest trains, which stop at all stations, are called *futsū*.

Since the faster trains do not stop at all stations, you must determine whether your destination is serviced by an express train before boarding it. There is usually a board on the platform indicating exactly which trains stop where. Trains are colour-coded, and you can usually tell what's what even if you don't read Japanese (although smaller destinations are frequently not written in English, so it's a good idea to have your destination written down in kanji before setting out). See the Tokyo Subway Route Map for details (Map pp276–7).

Japan Railways (JR) Lines

CHŪŌ & SŌBU LINES

The JR Chūō Line (Map pp276–7) cuts its way through the centre of the JR Yamanote Line between Shinjuku and Tokyo Stations. Trains on this line are coloured orange. This line is continuous with the JR Sōbu Line until Ochanomizu Station where the lines split – the Chūō heading down to Tokyo Station and the Sōbu heading out to the eastern suburbs. Trains on the JR Sōbu Line are yellow, so telling them apart is easy. The JR Chūō Line is about the fastest route between Shinjuku and Tokyo Stations (only rivalled by the Marunouchi subway line).

YAMANOTE LINE

Making a 35km loop around central Tokyo, the JR Yamanote Line is a mostly aboveground circuit that makes a great introduction to the city. Buy the cheapest fare (¥130), disembarking at the same station where you start, and you'll get a solid, one-hour overview of Tokyo's main areas of interest. Most fares within the Yamanote loop are either ¥160 or ¥190. JR Yamanote Line trains are silver with a green stripe.

In Tokyo's larger train stations, look for the green JR signage to find the correct ticket machines. Machines have an English option; if you can't parse the station maps above the ticket machines, simply select the cheapest fare and pay the balance at your destination at the fare adjustment machines (see p234).

JR stations in Tokyo have clear English signage directing you to the platform you want. If plan to travel on JR lines for more than a few days, consider buying a prepaid JR IO card. IO cards come in denominations or ¥1000, ¥3000 and ¥5000 and can be purchased from some JR ticket machines. Instead of calculating fares and counting change each time you travel, you can simply insert the IO card into the wicket, which automatically debits your fare.

Those planning to spend an extended period of time in Tokyo should strongly consider getting a Suica smart card (see opposite).

When determining where to get off the train, look for station names clearly marked in both Japanese and English on platform signs and/or posts. These may sometimes be difficult to see, but inside the trains there are electronic signs indicating the next station in Japanese and English. Additionally, automated announcements are made both inside the trains, as well as at the station when the doors open.

OTHER LINES

The JR Yokosuka Line runs south to Kamakura from Tokyo Station via Shimbashi and Shinagawa Stations. The JR Tōkaidō Line also travels in the same direction from Tokyo Station, providing access to Izuhantō (p215).

Some of the other main lines are the northbound lines (Takasaki, Keihin-Tōhoku, Saikyō) to the Saitama-ken and beyond, the JR Jōban and JR Narita Lines to the northeastern satellite towns in the Saitama and Chiba prefectures, and the JR Sōbu and JR Keiyō Lines that head out east towards Chiba city (and Tokyo Disneyland) and the convention city at Makuhari Messe.

Subway Lines

There are 13 subway lines, of which eight are Tokyo Metro Company lines and four are Toei lines. It is not particularly important to remember this distinction as the services are essentially the same and have good connections from one to the other, although they do operate under separate ticketing systems. The colour-coding and regular English signposting make the system easy to use – you soon learn that the Ginza Line is orange and that the Marunouchi Line is red. Perhaps the most confusing part is figuring out where to surface when you have reached your destination – there is almost always a large number of subway exits. Fortunately, the exits are numbered and maps are posted, usually close to the ticket turnstiles.

Generally, the subway system is indispensable for getting to areas that lie inside the loop traced by the JR Yamanote Line. The central Tokyo area is served by a large number of lines that intersect at Nihombashi, Ōtemachi and Ginza, making it possible to get to this part of town from almost anywhere. All Tokyo Metro Company information counters (found near the automated turnstiles) have a very useful English map and brochure, *Tokyo Metro Guide*, explaining the system in detail.

See opposite for ticketing requirements.

Private Lines

YURIKAMOME LINE

The Yurikamome Line services the Tokyo Bay area's Odaiba Ariake developments (Map p289). This driverless, elevated train departs from Shimbashi, just south of Ginza, crosses the Rainbow Bridge and terminates in Ariake, on an artificial island in Tokyo Bay. The Shimbashi terminal is above ground and on the eastern side of JR Shimbashi Station (Map pp290–1). Ticket machines provide ample English explanation; the fare from Shimbashi to Aomi and Ariake is ¥370 and is money well spent, as you get spectacular views of the bay during the ride. If you're planning on hopping on and off the Yurikamome, a day pass (¥800) is a good deal.

OTHER LINES

Most of the private lines service suburban areas outside Tokyo, but some of them also connect with popular sightseeing areas. The private lines almost always represent better value for money than the JR lines. The ones you are most likely to use are Shibuya's Tōkyū Tōyoko Line, which runs south to Yokohama; Shinjuku's Odakyū Line, which runs southwest out to Hakone (p216); and Asakusa's Tōbu Nikkō Line, which goes north to Nikkō (p221).

Tickets & Passes

You'll need different tickets for the two subway systems, but the automated ticket machines sell transfer tickets (¥70), which allow you to transfer from one system to another for without buying another full-price ticket. The button for this ticket is usually marked only in Japanese (のり換え; *norikae*). To save yourself time and hassle, don't bother with transfer tickets – buy a Passnet card or Tokyo Combination Ticket instead.

The **Japan Travel Bureau** (JTB; Map pp278–9; ☎ 5796-5454; 2-3-11 Higashi-Shinagawa, Shinagawa-ku) can help with transport bookings.

JR

The Suica card (¥2000, including a ¥500 deposit) is the one that most commuters use for daily rides. Fares are automatically deducted at the end of a journey and you can replenish the value of the card as needed. Purchase Suica cards at vending machines or at ticket counters in JR stations. Conveniently, the Suica card can be swiped over the wicket without being removed from a wallet or bag. You can even use it to pay for items in stores, vending machines and baggage lockers in JR stations. When you return your Suica card at a JR station office, you'll be refunded the ¥500 deposit that was included with the initial ¥2000 purchase.

Another pass offered by JR is the Japan Rail Pass, allowing for unrestricted travel on JR trains throughout Japan. This pass costs ¥23,300 and must be purchased *before* arriving in Japan. If you're planning on spending most of your time in Tokyo, this pass will not be of benefit to you. If you are planning on visiting other cities or on making some short day trips (see p209), it could save you a little money.

PASSNET CARD

Good on all subway lines but *not* on JR, the Passnet card is a boon for anyone travelling the Tokyo subways. Passnet cards are sold by Tokyo Metro (SF Metro Card) or the Toei subway system (T-Card). These prepaid cards are valid for all the different subway lines and eliminate the need to buy several tickets for one journey. Purchase Passnet cards from ordinary automated ticket machines with a 'Passnet' logo (look for an orange-and-white running figure – presumably zipping through turnstiles). Cards are sold in denominations of ¥1000, ¥3000 and ¥5000. Insert the amount, push the Passnet button, then the cash amount button.

Insert the card into the automated turnstiles as you would a normal ticket, but don't forget to grab it as you exit the turnstile! The turnstiles will automatically deduct the minimum fare (¥160 to ¥170, depending on the subway system) as you enter the subway system and then any amount above that figure, if necessary, as you transfer and/or exit. If you have less than ¥160 left on the card, you will not be able to enter the subway system. Take the card to a ticket machine, then insert the card and whatever amount is necessary to bring the total on the card to ¥160. The machine will then spit out a new ticket and the now worthless Passnet card.

TOKYO COMBINATION TICKET

A Tokyo Combination Ticket (¥1580) is a day pass that can be used on all JR, subway and bus lines within the Tokyo metropolitan area. It is available at Pass offices, which can be found in most JR and subway stations.

Train Stations

Modern Japanese spend a good part of their lives in train stations, and this fact is reflected in the wide range of services at most stations. Most importantly, there is the ticket office. In the case of JR stations, there will be signs (sometimes but not always in both English and Japanese) indicating the Midori-no-Madoguchi (Green Window) ticket counter, which is usually posted with a green sign. Here you can buy your tickets and make reservations; in smaller stations this is where you ask for information as well. Stations also have one or more banks of automated ticket machines.

Most stations also have left-luggage lockers, which can hold medium-sized bags (backpacks won't usually fit). These lockers often come in several sizes and cost from ¥200 to ¥600. Storage is good for 24 hours, after which your bags will be removed and taken to the station office.

All train stations have toilets, almost all of which are free of charge (Shinjuku has a few that cost ¥100). Bring toilet paper, as it is not usually provided (this is why advertising in the form of tissue packets handed out on street corners is big business); it's also a good idea to pick up a handkerchief at the ¥100 shop, as paper towels or hand driers are not usually provided. At many stations you can also find several options for food. The smallest of these are kiosks, which sell snacks, drinks, magazines, newspapers (many have copies of Japan's English dailies), film etc. Next up are stores selling *ekiben* (train-station boxed lunches; p42); larger stations also have *tachi-kui* (stand-and-eat) restaurants. Most of these places require that you purchase a food ticket from a vending machine, which you hand to an attendant upon entry (most machines have pictures on the buttons to help you order). Large stations might also have a choice of several sit-down places, most of which will have plastic food models displayed in the front window.

BUYING A TICKET

For all local journeys, tickets are sold by vending machines called *kippu jidō hanbaiki*. Above the vending machines is a rail map with fares indicated next to the station names. Unfortunately for visitors, the names on the map are often in kanji only. The best way around this problem is to put your money in the machine and push the lowest fare button (¥130 on JR, ¥160 to ¥170 on subway lines). When you get to your destination, you can correct the fare at an attended ticket gate or at a fare-adjustment machine (see below).

All vending machines for all lines accept ¥1000 notes and most accept ¥10,000 (there are pictures of the bills accepted on the machines). Don't forget to pick up the bills you get in change.

Two buttons on the machine could come in handy if you completely bungle the operation. First is the *tori-keshi* (取り消し; cancel) button, which is usually marked in English. The second is the *yobidashi* (呼び出し; call) button, which will alert a staff member that you need assistance (staff sometimes pop out from a hidden door between the machines – it can be surprising).

FARE ADJUSTMENT

Many travellers and even long-term residents never bother to figure out the appropriate fare when buying tickets, particularly for short inner-city hops. They just grab the cheapest ticket and are on their way. If you choose to do this, you have two choices upon arrival at your destination: an attended ticket gate or the fare-adjustment machine.

At an attended gate, simply hand over your ticket and the attendant will inform you of the additional fare. A fare-adjustment machine is just as simple and saves time if the gate is congested. Look for fare-adjustment machines, usually lit up with yellow signs, near the exit turnstiles. Insert your ticket into the slot near the top of the machine. The screen will tell you how much to pay, then spit out your change (if any) and a new ticket. Insert this ticket into the exit turnstiles, and off you go. Fare-adjustment machines usually have English instructions, and they are sited slightly apart from the ticket machines to avoid congestion.

STATION EXITS

Navigating your way around train stations in Tokyo can be confusing, particularly at some of the more gigantic and complex stations like Shinjuku Station. The key is to know where you're going before you get to the station. Most stations have adequate English signposting, with large yellow signs on the platforms posting exit numbers and often including local destinations, such as large hotels, department stores and embassies. When possible, find out which exit to use when you get directions to a destination. Street maps of the area are usually posted near each exit.

Many stations simply have four main exits: north, south, east and west. Since one station will usually have several different exits, you should get your bearings and decide where to exit while still on the platform. If you have your destination written down, you can go to an attended gate and ask the station attendant to direct you to the correct exit. To help you along we've included in this guidebook exit details for each listing where possible.

PRACTICALITIES

ACCOMMODATION

In this guide, accommodation listings have been organised alphabetically and by neighbourhood. Midrange to high-end options are listed within the main part of each neighbourhood's sleeping options. Budget options follow under the category 'Cheap Sleeps'. Cheap sleeps are rooms costing ¥6500 or less; midrange rooms cost between ¥6500 and ¥16,000; and top-end rooms will cost more than ¥16,000. For general listings see p190, and for details on making reservations see p190. A child for the purposes of hotels and other accommodation options is under 15 years of age.

Business Hotels

A common form of midrange accommodation is the so-called 'business hotel' – usually as functional and economical as the name would suggest. Geared to the lone traveller on business, the typical Tokyo business-hotel room will have pay TV (sometimes pay-per-view, and occasionally a fee for simply turning on the set) and a tiny bathroom, and cost between ¥7000 and ¥12,000. Some business hotels accept credit cards, but you should always ask when you check in. There is no room service, and you will usually be required to check in after 3pm or 4pm and check out at 10am or 11am. Some of the nicer business hotels have large shared baths and saunas in addition to the private ones in the guest rooms.

Although you can't necessarily expect much English from the staff at more low-rent business hotels, if you smile and speak slowly you should be OK.

Capsule Hotels

Of course they're small – they're capsules, after all – but they're roomy enough to recline in, and each capsule is fitted with bed, reading light, TV and alarm clock. Despite their size, prices still range from ¥3500 to ¥5000, depending on the area and the facilities; capsules are also cash only. Most of their business comes from drunken office workers who have missed the last train home, but their novelty value attracts the odd foreigner. Many capsule hotels have a well-appointed bath area similar to a good local *sentō* (public bath).

Gaijin Houses

If you're a budget traveller planning on settling in Tokyo, you might consider landing first at a *gaijin* (foreigner) house while getting your bearings. These are private dwellings that have been partitioned into rooms or apartments and rented out to *gaijin*. See p191 for reputable agencies.

Love Hotels

You've heard of love hotels – with bondage trapezes hung from the ceiling, sex-toy vending machines and themed rooms ranging from Hello Kitty to African safari. Married couples, teenage lovers and less-licit trysting pairs check into love hotels for a little privacy away from prying eyes and ears.

Love hotels are distinguished by their discreet entrances – high bushes, opaque or nonexistent windows, underground parking and so on – all so that patrons can duck in and out in complete anonymity. Once inside, the anonymity continues: you choose a room from a bank of illuminated pictures on the wall. If the picture is not illuminated, the room's already taken. Once you've decided, either push a button or say the number to a hidden clerk and make your payment through a slot in the wall. Once you've paid, you'll be given a key and must make your own way to the room.

Posted outside love hotels are signs indicating the rates for a one- or two-hour stay, referred to as a *kyūkei* (rest), or *tomari* (for an overnight stay). Overnight rates are fairly reasonable (around ¥8000; no credit cards accepted), but most places will not allow you to check in for an overnight stay until 10pm or 11pm. Though some love hotels are not used to dealing with foreigners, mustering a little Japanese (saying 'kyūkei' or 'tomari' will suffice), you should have no problems. Same-sex guests might be refused at some love hotels. If this happens, insist that you are travelling as *tomodachi* (friends) and you might get in.

Luxury Hotels

In the top-end bracket, you can expect to find the amenities of deluxe hotels anywhere in the world, and you're spoilt for choice. From the most exclusive boutique hotels to the biggest, baddest behemoths, the styles run the gamut while providing for every comfort. Expect satellite TV beaming in CNN and the BBC, high-speed Internet access and, luxury of luxuries in space-starved Tokyo, enough square metres in which to properly unwind. The staff speak English, the rooms are spotless and the service is impeccable. In addition, most of Tokyo's luxury hotels have several good restaurants and bars on their premises, many of which offer outstanding views over the city.

Minshuku

Similar to ryokan, but generally simpler in décor and cheaper, are *minshuku* (similar to Western-style B&Bs) These are private homes that accept visitors and offer food, usually both breakfast and dinner. They are friendly places, and you can often get to know other travellers, both Japanese and foreign, especially in places where meals are taken communally in a dining room.

Minshuku in Tokyo generally cost about ¥6000 to ¥8000 per person (cash only), including two meals, making these one of your better travel bargains. Few *minshuku* owners speak English, but they'll welcome you warmly.

Ryokan

For those who crave a really traditional Japanese experience with tatami (woven-mat floor) rooms and futon instead of beds, the ryokan (traditional Japanese inns) have it. Although the more exclusive establishments can charge upwards of ¥25,000, there are a number of relatively inexpensive ryokan in Tokyo. These places are generally more accustomed to foreigners than their counterparts in more remote parts of Japan and the rules tend to be a bit more relaxed as a result. The trade-off is that you don't usually get the strictly traditional experience, with Japanese meals and the diurnal stowing away of your futon.

Although some ryokan will allow you to pay by credit card, you should always ask at check-in if you hope to do so. The ryokan listed in this book are generally budget and midrange; those wishing to stay in top-end ryokan should inquire at the Japan National Tourist Organization (JNTO; p248), which has listings and will handle reservations (also see p190).

Youth Hostels

Tokyo's youth hostels are much like youth hostels elsewhere: a bit noisy, not much atmosphere and a mixture of dorms and private rooms. On the plus side, they are used to foreigners and are cleaner than many of their overseas counterparts. A room in a typical youth hostel is about ¥3200, cash only. Membership is often not required.

Other Options

The TIC (p248) can give you information about several other lodging options in and around Tokyo, including *shukubō* (staying on the grounds of a temple), *onsen* (hot-spring resorts) and converted farmhouses or *kokumin-shukusha* (people's lodges). It also has information for travellers with special needs, eg seniors or disabled visitors, and those with children.

BUSINESS CARDS

Business cards *(meishi)* carry much more weight in Japan than they do in the West. Information about a person's status and, perhaps even more importantly, their connections can be obtained from business cards, which are ritually exchanged on first meeting. It's good form to accept cards with both hands and examine them before tucking them away into your purse or wallet. If attending a meeting, the card should be left on the table until the end of the meeting, and only afterwards be respectfully put away.

BUSINESS HOURS

Banks are normally open 9am to between 3pm and 5pm Monday to Friday. Most businesses open 9am to 5pm Monday to Friday, although some are also open on Sat-

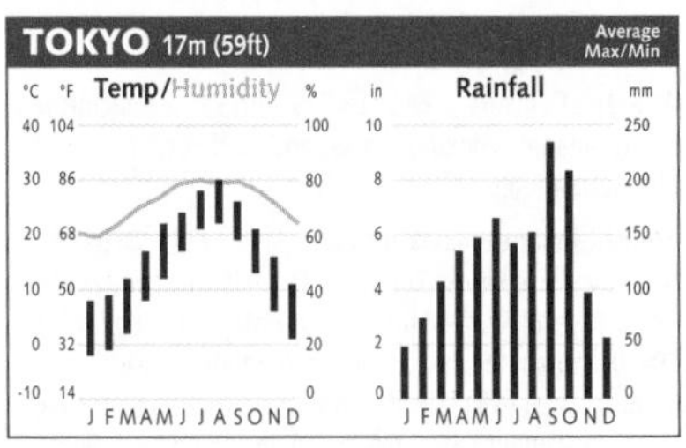

urday. Restaurants are generally open for lunch 11.30am or noon to 2.30pm or 3pm and for dinner 6pm or 6.30pm to 9pm or 10pm, with last orders taken about half an hour before closing. Shops and supermarkets are usually open 10am to 8pm daily.

Variations on the above opening hours are listed in reviews.

CHILDREN

Tokyo, like the rest of Japan, is unreservedly child-friendly. In addition to loads of kid-centred activities (see the boxed text, p96), the city also offers numerous playgrounds and parks where children, and parents, can unwind. If you're travelling with small children, common items like nappies (diapers) can be found at any pharmacy. Formula and special dietary needs, of course, will be labelled in Japanese, so bringing such items from home could save a bit of time and frustration.

Baby-sitting

If you're staying at a hotel, staff there might be able to refer you to a reliable babysitter. Listed are a few recommended services providing English-speaking sitters. Though some require an annual membership fee, they may waive it if you ask for introductory or trial rates.

Japan Baby-Sitter Service (☎ 3423-1251; www.jbs-mom.co.jp in Japanese; per 3hr ¥4200) One of Japan's oldest – and considered one of its most reliable – services.

Poppins Service (☎ 3447-2100; www.poppins.co.jp/english/index.html; per hr ¥2500) Nannies versed in early child development and first aid can also speak English, French, German or Italian.

Tokyo Domestic Service Center (☎ 3584-4769; per 8hr ¥12,000) All sitters required to have at least 10 years experience with children. Call a day ahead to arrange an English-speaking sitter.

Tom Sawyer Agency (☎ 3770-9530; per 3hr ¥3000) Sitters available (24 hours) for newborns to 12-year-olds; arrange services by 8pm the day before.

CLIMATE

Tokyo kicks off its year with cold winter days and rare snowfalls. Although temperatures occasionally drop below freezing, winter (December to February) is usually reasonable if you have the right kind of clothes. Spring (March to May) brings pleasant, warm days, and of course the cherry blossoms (see Tokyo in Bloom, p12) – early April is probably the best time to view the blooms. Summer (June to August) is hot and muggy, a time when overcrowded trains and long walks can feel irritating. Late June can see torrential rains that pound the city during monsoon seasons, and the temperature and humidity are at their worst in August. After spring, autumn (September to November) is the most pleasant season as temperatures cool down to a cosy level and days are often clear and fine. Autumn also means the return of the dramatic foliage season, when the parks and green areas of the city mellow into varying hues of orange and red.

COURIER SERVICES

Baggage couriers provide next-day delivery of your large luggage from Narita airport to any address in Tokyo (costs around ¥2000 per large bag). They can also deliver luggage to points beyond Tokyo so you don't have to haul it through trains and stations all over the countryside. Couriers can also pick up luggage for delivery to the airport, but be sure to call two days before your flight to arrange a pick-up. The companies listed here have counters in both terminals of Narita airport; some operators speak English.

ABC (☎ 0120-9191-20)

NPS Skyporter (☎ 3590-1919)

Yamato (☎ 0476-32-4755)

COURSES

If you've got a bit of time to spend in Tokyo, you might want to look into studying the language or a traditional art or martial art form. Listed are some suggestions to get you started.

Cooking

A Taste of Culture (☎ 5716-5751; http://tasteofculture.com) Japanese cooking courses and market tours with Ms Elizabeth Andoh.

Konishi Japanese Cooking Class (Map p288; ☎ 3714-8859; www.seiko-osp.com/private/sekigu/kjcc/index.htm; 1405 Nissei Meguro-Mansion; 3-1-7 Meguro, Meguro-ku; JR Yamanote Line, or subway Namboku or Mita Line to Meguro, west exit) Friendly English instruction with small class sizes; about ¥4500 per lesson, including ingredients.

Ikebana

Ohara School of Ikebana (International Division; Map p284; ☎ 5774-5097; www.ohararyu.or.jp/english/class/index2.htm; 5-7-17 Minami-Aoyama, Minato-ku; Chiyoda, Ginza or Hanzōmon Line to Omote-sandō, exits B1 & B3) Ohara specialises in flower-arranging classes for students of all levels. One-timers and short-term visitors are welcome, as are those who'd just like to watch.

Sōgetsu Kaikan (Map p286; ☎ 3408-1151; www.sogetsu.or.jp/english/index.html; Sōgetsu Kaikan Bldg, 7-2-21 Akasaka, Minato-ku; 10am-5pm Mon-Thu & Sat, 10am-8pm Fri; Ginza, Hanzōmon or Toei Ōedo Line to Aoyama-itchōme, exit 4) An avant-garde ikebana school, with ikebana displays, a bookshop and coffee shop. Call ahead for class information. Also see p91 for more details.

Language

Academy of Language Arts (Map pp294–5; ☎ 3235-0071; www.ala-japan.com; 5th fl, 2-16-2 Agebachō, Shinjuku-ku; Namboku, Tōzai, Yūrakuchō or Toei Ōedo Line to Iidabashi, exit B1)

East West Japanese Language Institute (Map pp278–9; ☎ 3366-4717; www.eastwest.ac.jp; 2-36-9 Chūō, Nakano-ku; Marunouchi Line to Nakano-sakaue)

Sendagaya Japanese Institute (Map p280; ☎ 3232-6181; www.jp-sji.org; 7th fl, 1-31-18 Takadanobaba, Shinjuku-ku; JR Yamanote Line to Takadanobaba, main exit)

Martial Arts

All-Japan Judō Federation (Map pp278–9; Zen Nihon Judo Renmei; ☎ 3818-4199; www.judo.or.jp; c/o Kodokan, 1-16-30 Kasuga, Bunkyō-ku) See Kōdōkan Judō Institute, right for details.

International Aikidō Federation (Map pp278–9; ☎ 3203-9236; www.aikido-international.org; c/o Aikikai Foundation, 17-18 Wakamatsuchō, Shinjuku-ku; 6am-7.30pm Mon-Sat, 8.30-11.30am Sun; Toei Ōedo Line to Wakamatsu-Kawada)

Japan Kendō Federation (Map pp294–5; ☎ 3211-5804; www.kendo.or.jp; c/o Nippon Budokan, 2-3 Kitanomaru-kōen, Chiyoda-ku)

Kōdōkan Judō Institute (Map pp278–9; ☎ 3818-4172; www.kodokan.org; 1-16-30 Kasuga, Bunkyō-ku; open practice 3.30-8pm Mon-Fri, 4-7.30pm Sat; Toei Mita or Toei Ōedo Line to Kasuga, exits A1 & A2)

Kyūmeikan (Map pp278-9; ☎ 3930-4636; 2-1-7 Akatsuka-Shinmachi, Itabashi-ku; Yūrakuchō Line to Chikatetsu-Narimasu, main exit)

World Union of Karate-dō Organisation (Map pp290–1; ☎ 3503-6640; www.wuko-karate.org; 4th fl, Sempaku Shinkokaikan Bldg, 1-15-16 Toranomon, Minato-ku; Ginza Line to Toranomon, exit 2)

CUSTOMS

Customs allowances include the usual tobacco products plus three 760mL bottles of alcoholic beverages, 57g of perfume, and gifts and souvenirs up to a value of ¥200,000 or its equivalent. You must be older than 20 years to qualify for these allowances. The penalties for importing drugs are very severe.

Although the Japanese are no longer censoring pubic hair in domestically produced pornography, customs officers will still confiscate any pornographic materials in which pubic hair is visible.

There are no limits on the importation of foreign or Japanese currency. The export of foreign currency is also unlimited, but there is a ¥5 million export limit for Japanese currency. Visit **Japan Customs** (www.customs.go.jp/index_e.htm) for more information on Japan's customs regulations.

DISABLED TRAVELLERS

Many new buildings in Tokyo have access ramps, traffic lights have speakers playing melodies when it is safe to cross, train platforms have raised dots and lines to provide guidance and some ticket machines have Braille. Some attractions also offer free entry to disabled people and a companion. A fair number of hotels, from the higher end of midrange and above, offer a 'universal' (meaning 'universally accessible') room or two. Still, Tokyo can be rather difficult for disabled people to negotiate, especially visitors in wheelchairs who are often asked to negotiate stairs or to re-route.

For more information check out the following websites.

Accessible Japan (www.wakakoma.org/aj) Details the accessibility of hundreds of sites in Tokyo, including hotels, sights and department stores, as well as general information about getting around Japan.

BRINGING GUIDE DOGS TO JAPAN

Japanese regulations on the importation of live animals are very strict, and are not waived for guide dogs. Dogs brought from countries in which rabies has been eradicated need not be quarantined, provided their owners can show a *yūshutsu shomeisho* (exportation certificate). Dogs arriving from countries in which rabies occurs will be placed into quarantine for up to six months, unless their owners can supply an exportation certificate, veterinary examination certification and written proof of rabies vaccination.

Japanese Red Cross Language Service Volunteers (Map pp290–1; ☎ 3438-1311; http://accessible.jp.org; 1-1-3 Shiba Daimon, Minato-ku, Tokyo 105-8521) Has loads of useful information, and it also produces an excellent guide called *Accessible Tokyo*, which can be requested by email, mail or telephone – or found on its website.

ELECTRICITY

Plugs & Sockets

Japanese plugs are the flat two-pin type, which are identical to two-pin North American plugs (appliances with a flat two-pin plug will work without an adaptor, but may be a bit sluggish).

Voltage & Cycles

The Japanese electric current is 100V AC, an odd voltage found almost nowhere else in the world. Tokyo and eastern Japan are on 50Hz. Transformers are easy to find at one of Japan's plentiful electronics shops. Check www.kropla.com for detailed information on matters of voltage and plugs.

EMBASSIES & CONSULATES

Australia (Map pp278–9; ☎ 5232-4111; www.dfat.gov.au/missions/countries/jp.html; 2-1-14 Mita, Minato-ku)

Belgium (Map pp278–9; ☎ 3262-0191; www.diplomatie.be/tokyo; 5 Nibanchō, Chiyoda-ku)

Canada (Map p286; ☎ 5412-6200; www.dfait-maeci.gc.ca/ni-ka/menu-en.asp; 7-3-38 Akasaka, Minato-ku)

France (Map pp278–9; ☎ 5420-8800; www.ambafrance-jp.org; 4-11-44 Minami-Azabu, Minato-ku)

Germany (Map pp278–9; ☎ 5791-7700; www.tokyo.diplo.de/ja/Startseite.html; 4-5-10 Minami-Azabu, Minato-ku)

Ireland (Map pp294–5; ☎ 3263-0695; www.embassy-avenue.jp/ireland; 2-10-7 Kōjimachi, Chiyoda-ku)

Italy (Map pp278–9; ☎ 3453-5291; www.embitaly.jp; 2-5-4 Mita, Minato-ku)

Malaysia (Map pp278–9; ☎ 3476-3840; www.kln.gov.my; 20-16 Nanpeidaichō, Shibuya-ku)

Netherlands (Map pp290–1; ☎ 5401-0411; www.oranda.or.jp; 3-6-3 Shiba-kōen, Minato-ku)

New Zealand (Map pp278–9; ☎ 3467-2271; www.nzembassy.com; 20-40 Kamiyamachō, Shibuya-ku)

South Korea (Map pp278–9; ☎ 3452-7611; www.mofat.go.kr; 1-2-5 Minami-Azabu, Minato-ku)

UK (Map pp294–5; ☎ 5211-1100; www.uknow.or.jp/be_e; 1 Ichibanchō, Chiyoda-ku)

USA (Map pp290–1; ☎ 3224-5000; http://tokyo.usembassy.gov; 1-10-5 Akasaka, Minato-ku)

EMERGENCY

Although most emergency operators you'll reach in Tokyo don't speak English, the operators will immediately refer you to someone who does. Japan Helpline is a service that provides assistance to foreigners living in Japan.

Ambulance (☎ 119)

Fire (☎ 119)

Japan Helpline (☎ 0120-461-997)

Police (☎ 110)

GAY & LESBIAN TRAVELLERS

With the possible exception of Thailand, Japan is Asia's most enlightened nation with regard to the sexual orientation of foreigners. While a few particularly gay-friendly venues are scattered within the listings in this book, Tokyo is a tolerant city where the bars, clubs and restaurants host folks of all predilections. Tokyo does have an active gay scene and a small but very lively gay quarter (Shinjuku-nichōme). Check *Tokyo Classified* or *Tokyo Journal* for listings of gay and lesbian clubs. Outside Tokyo, you will find it difficult to break into the local scene unless you spend considerable time in a place or have local contacts who can show you around.

Same-sex couples probably won't encounter too many problems travelling in Japan. Some travellers have reported being turned away or grossly overcharged when checking into love hotels with a partner of the same sex. Apart from this, it's unlikely that you'll run into difficulties. There are no legal restraints to same-sex sexual activities of either gender in Japan, although it does pay to be discreet with public displays of affection.

Cineastes visiting in the summer should check the local listings for screenings of the **Tokyo International Lesbian & Gay Film and Video Festival** (☎ 6475-0388; lgff@tokyo.office.ne.jp).

Websites well worth perusing when planning your travels:

Fridae (www.fridae.com/cityguides/tokyo/tk-intro.php)

Gay Scene Japan (www.members.tripod.co.jp/GSJ)

Utopia Asia (www.utopia-asia.com)

HEALTH

by Dr Trish Batchelor

Health conditions in Tokyo are good with an excellent standard of medical care. Air pollution is one health issue, but apart from travellers with chronic lung conditions, this is unlikely to affect most people. Travellers have a low risk of contracting infectious diseases but should ensure that their basic vaccinations are up to date and that they carry a basic medical kit to deal with simple problems such as respiratory infections, minor injuries and stomach upsets.

At the time this book went to press, human cases of Avian influenza (bird flu) in Japan were extremely limited, and the risk to travellers was low. The strain in question is known as 'Influenza A H5N1' or simply 'the H5N1 virus', a highly contagious form of Avian influenza. Travellers to the region should avoid contact with any birds and should ensure that any poultry is thoroughly cooked before consumption. See the World Health Organization website (www.who.int/en/) for the latest information.

It's also a good idea to consult your government's travel-health website before departure.

Australia (www.dfat.gov.au)

Canada (www.travelhealth.gc.ca)

New Zealand (www.moh.govt.nz)

UK (www.dh.gov.uk)

USA (www.cdc.gov/travel/)

Insurance

If your health insurance doesn't cover you for medical expenses incurred overseas, ensure you purchase supplemental travel insurance before leaving home. Evacuations in an emergency can cost well over US$100,000.

Recommended Vaccinations

No vaccinations are required for Japan. Your routine vaccinations should be up to date.

Adult diphtheria/tetanus (ADT) A booster is recommended if it is more than 10 years since your last shot. Side effects include a sore arm and fever in about 10% of people.

Measles/Mumps/Rubella (MMR) Two doses of MMR are recommended unless you have had the diseases. Many young adults under the age of 35 require a booster. Occasionally a rash and flu-like illness can occur about a week after vaccination.

Varicella (Chickenpox) If you have not had chickenpox you should discuss this vaccine with your doctor. Chickenpox can be a serious disease in adults with complications such as pneumonia and encephalitis. Vaccination involves two injections six weeks apart.

Under certain circumstances or for those that are at special risk, the following vaccinations are recommended. These should be discussed with a doctor specialising in travel medicine:

Hepatitis B For those staying long term or who might be exposed to body fluids via sexual contact, acupuncture, dental work etc, or for health-care workers.

Influenza If you are older than 50 or have a chronic medical condition such as diabetes, lung disease or heart disease you should have a flu shot annually.

Japanese B encephalitis There is no risk in Tokyo, but there is risk in rural areas of all islands. The risk is highest in the western part of the country from July to October.

Pneumonia (Pneumococcal) This vaccine is recommended to travellers over the age of 65 or those over 55 with chronic lung or heart disease.

Tick-borne encephalitis This is present only in the wooded areas of Hokkaidō and is transmitted between April and October. This vaccine is readily available in Europe but can be difficult to find elsewhere.

Diseases

AIDS & STDS

AIDS and STDs can be contracted anywhere in the world. People carrying STDs often show no signs of infection. Always wear a condom with a new partner; however, some diseases such as herpes and warts cannot be prevented even by using condoms. If after a sexual encounter you develop any rash, lumps, discharge or pain when passing urine seek medical attention immediately. If you have been sexually active during your travels have a check-up on your return home.

Rates of HIV infection in Japan have increased significantly in the last couple of years. It is predicted that this trend will continue, due in part to poor government awareness programmes. The majority of cases in Japan are contracted via sexual contact, and more than 60% of newly infected people are under 25 years of age.

Condoms are widely available in Tokyo, but generally only locally produced varieties, which tend to be on the small side. If you think you're going to need them, it's a good idea to bring your own, since foreign-made condoms can be difficult to find.

DIARRHOEA

Tokyo is a low-risk destination, and the tap water is safe to drink. You could still be unlucky, however, so carrying some anti-diarrhoea medication in your medical kit is a good idea.

HEPATITIS B

Hepatitis B is a virus spread via body fluids, eg through sexual contact, shared needles or unclean medical facilities. Hepatitis B is also the only sexually transmitted disease that can be prevented by vaccination. In the short-term hepatitis B can cause the typical symptoms of hepatitis – jaundice, tiredness, nausea – but long-term consequences can include liver cancer and cirrhosis. Long-term travellers or those who might be exposed to body fluids should be vaccinated.

INFLUENZA

Influenza is transmitted from November to April. The flu is caused by a virus and gives you a high fever, general body aches and generalised respiratory symptoms such as cough, sore throat and runny nose. If you get the flu you should rest up and take symptomatic treatment such as pain killers – antibiotics won't help. All high-risk individuals should ensure that they have been vaccinated before travelling, and all travellers should consider the vaccine if visiting in the winter months. Under some circumstances your doctor might recommend taking antiviral drugs to treat the flu.

JAPANESE B ENCEPHALITIS

Japanese B encephalitis (JBE) is not present in Tokyo, but is found in the rural areas of all of the islands, particularly in the west. It is a viral disease transmitted by mosquitoes and is present during the summer months of July to October. If you are intending to spend more than a month in an affected rural area you should consider getting vaccinated. JBE is a serious disease without any specific treatment – 30% of those infected will die and a third will suffer permanent brain damage.

Environmental Hazards

AIR POLLUTION

Air pollution is a problem in Tokyo, although the government is taking steps to improve the situation. If you have a lung condition such as asthma or chronic airways disease speak to your doctor before you travel, and ensure that you have enough of your regular medication with you.

FUGU (PUFFER FISH)

This famous delicacy (also known as blowfish or globefish) is strictly controlled, and there have been no deaths related to its ingestion for more than 30 years.

Medications

Some medications cannot be taken into Japan. If you take any regular medication you should check with your Japanese embassy whether there is any restriction on taking it into the country.

Traditional Medicine

If you decide to have any traditional medical treatments, make sure you tell your practitioner if you are taking any Western medicines. The two best-known forms of traditional Japanese medicine are shiatsu and *reiki*.

REIKI

Reiki claims to heal by charging the life force *(ki)* with positive energy, thus allowing it to flow in a natural, healthy manner. In a standard treatment *reiki* energy flows from the practitioner's hands into the client. The practitioner places their hands on or near the client's body in a series of positions that are held for between three and 10 minutes. People become practitioners after receiving an 'attunement' from a *reiki* master.

SHIATSU

Shiatsu is a form of manual therapy incorporating gentle manipulations and stretches derived from physiotherapy and chiropractic, combined with pressure techniques exerted through the fingers or thumbs. The philosophy underlying shiatsu is similar to many traditional Asian medical systems and involves the body's vital energy *(ki)* flowing through the body in a series of channels known as meridians. If the *ki* is blocked from flowing freely, illness can occur; hence shiatsu is used to improve the flow of *ki*. Shiatsu was officially recognised by the Japanese government as a therapy in its own right in 1955.

HOLIDAYS

Japan has 15 national holidays. When a public holiday falls on a Sunday, the following Monday is taken as a holiday. You can expect travel and lodgings to be fully booked during Shōgatsu (New Year; 29 December to 6 January), Golden Week (29 April to 5 May) and the O-Bon festival in mid-August; see p8 for more information on festivals. Also, during this time, about the only places open are convenience stores and fast-food joints; if you don't want to survive on potato chips and fries, make appropriate preparations.

Japan's national holidays:

Ganjitsu (New Year's Day) 1 January

Seijin-no-hi (Coming-of-Age Day) Second Monday in January

Kenkoku Kinem-bi (National Foundation Day) 11 February

Shumbun-no-hi (Spring Equinox) 20 or 21 March

Midori-no-hi (Green Day) 29 April

Kempō Kinem-bi (Constitution Day) 3 May

Kokumin-no-Saijitsu (Adjoining Holiday Between Two Holidays) 4 May

Kodomo-no-hi (Children's Day) 5 May

Umi-no-hi (Marine Day) Third Monday in July

Keirō-no-hi (Respect-for-the-Aged Day) Third Monday in September

Shūbun-no-hi (Autumn Equinox) 23 or 24 September

Taiiku-no-hi (Health & Sports Day) Second Monday in October

Bunka-no-hi (Culture Day) 3 November

Kinrō Kansha-no-hi (Labour Thanksgiving Day) 23 November

Tennō-no-Tanjōbi (Emperor's Birthday) 23 December

INTERNET ACCESS

Modems and phone jacks are similar to those used in the USA (RJ11 phone jacks). Conveniently, many of the grey IDD pay phones in Tokyo have a standard phone jack and an infrared port so that you can log on to the Internet just about anywhere in the city. If you use dial-up, it's best to download a list of dial-up numbers for major Internet service providers before leaving home. Most hotels have in-room LAN ports and can rent or sell you a LAN cable; electronics shops also carry them for about ¥500.

If you haven't brought your own laptop, you'll find an abundance of Internet cafés in every major neighbourhood in Tokyo. Rates vary, usually ranging from ¥200 to ¥700 per hour, and most connections are fast DSL or ADSL.

When using Internet cafés around Tokyo, travellers should avoid conducting such sensitive business as online banking or credit-card transactions. In 2003, a pair of hackers using keystroke-capture devices at public Internet terminals around Tokyo successfully stole over US$100,000 by transferring it to their own account.

WI-FI ACCESS

For a city as efficiency-obsessed as tech-loving Tokyo, wi-fi access is less than widespread. But for the millions emailing away via the *keitai* (mobile phones) attached to their thumbs, wi-fi is probably irrelevant.

Still, you needn't search too hard for wi-fi hotspots. NTT Communications sells 24-hour passes (¥500) to its wireless network, with hotspots throughout Tokyo. Prepaid cards can be purchased at some branches of Bic Camera and Prince Hotels; check NTT Communication's website for hotspot locations and purchasing information. Some hotels offer wi-fi, but frequently for a fee: from ¥1000 to ¥2000.

Free wi-fi is scattered around Tokyo in cafés, public buildings and JR stations – check the Freespot access map (www.freespot.com/users/map_e.html) for locations offering fee-free wi-fi.

LEGAL MATTERS

Japanese police have extraordinary powers compared with their Western counterparts. For starters, Japanese police have the right to detain a suspect without charging them for up to three days, after which a prosecutor can decide to extend this period for another 20 days. Police can also choose whether to allow a suspect to phone their embassy or lawyer, although if you find yourself in police custody you should insist that you will not cooperate in any way until allowed to make such a call. Your embassy is the first place you should call if given the chance.

Police will speak almost no English; insist that a *tsuyakusha* (interpreter) be summoned; police are legally bound to provide one before proceeding with any questioning. Even if you do speak Japanese, it's best to deny it and stay with your native language.

For legal counselling in English and some other languages, seek out these resources:

Human Rights Counseling Center for Foreigners (☎ 5689-0518; ⏲ 1-4.30pm Tue & Thu) Free consultation and English–Japanese translation on problems regarding human rights.

Tokyo English Life Line (TELL; ☎ 5774-0992; ⏲ 9am-11pm)

Tokyo Foreign Residents Advisory Center (☎ 5320-7744; ⏲ 9.30am-noon & 1-4pm Mon-Fri)

MAPS

Stop by the tourist information centre of the Japan National Tourist Organization (JNTO; p248) to pick up a free copy of its superb *Tourist Map of Tokyo*. To successfully interpret and navigate Tokyo's challenging address system, longer-term visitors might consider looking up Kodansha's *Tokyo City Atlas*, a bilingual guide stocked by larger bookshops. Both Kodansha and Shobunsha (Japanese publishers) publish bilingual atlases and fold-out maps (prices start at ¥700) that are available at most of Tokyo's bookshops (see p182 for listings).

The Tokyo Metro Company puts out the free *Tokyo Metro Guide*, with English-language explanations on buying tickets and special deals. Find these near the ticket machines and turnstiles in most subway stations.

MEDICAL SERVICES

A national health-insurance plan covers Japanese who wish to visit a doctor as well as foreign residents who are legally employed. When seeking medical care, be sure to bring proof of your travel or health insurance that clearly indicates that you're covered for any treatment you receive. If you arrive without insurance, it's possible to see a doctor at either a hospital or a clinic, but you will be expected to pay in full at the time of service.

Foreign travellers to Japan should be warned that medical services in Japan might not be on par with those of other developed nations. For simple complaints, you should be fine; for emergencies, you might have no choice. For elective procedures and anything else that can wait until you get home, we suggest you do just that.

Most hospitals and clinics do not have doctors and nurses on staff who speak English, but we've listed a few good ones that do. See also Pharmacies (p245).

Clinics

International Medical Center of Japan (Map p280; ☎ 3202-7181; www.imcj.go.jp in Japanese; 1-21-1 Toyama, Shinjuku-ku; Ⓜ Toei Ōedo Line to Wakamatsu-kawada, main exit) Though the website's in Japanese, operators on the phone speak English.

National Medical Clinic (Map pp278–9; ☎ 3473-2057; www.nmclinic.net; 2nd fl, 5-16-11 Minami-Azabu, Minato-ku; Ⓜ Hibiya Line to Hiro-o, exits 1 & 2) English-speaking physicians practise general medicine here, along with a few specialised services.

Tokyo British Clinic (Map p288; ☎ 5458-6099; www.tokyobritishclinic.com; 2nd fl, Daikanyama Y Bldg, 2-13-7 Ebisu-Nishi, Shibuya-ku; emergency service ⏲ 24hr; Ⓜ Hibiya or JR Yamanote Line to Ebisu, west exit) Founded and run by a British physician, this clinic also offers paediatric, ob/gyn and referral services.

Tokyo Medical & Surgical Clinic (Map pp290–1; ☎ 3436-3028, emergency ☎ 3432-6134; www.tmsc.jp; 2nd fl, Mori Bldg 32, 3-4-30 Shiba-kōen, Minato-ku; emergency service ⏲ 24hr; Ⓜ Hibiya Line to Kamiyachō, main exit) This well-equipped clinic is staffed with English-speaking Japanese and foreign physicians.

Emergency Rooms

Japanese Red Cross Medical Centre (Map pp278–9; ☎ 3400-1311; www.med.jrc.or.jp in Japanese; 4-1-22 Hiro-o, Shibuya-ku; ⏲ 24hr; Ⓜ Hibiya Line to Hiro-o, exits 1 & 2)

Seibo International Catholic Hospital (Map pp278–9; ☎ 3951-1111; www.seibokai.or.jp in Japanese; 2-5-1 Nakaochiai, Shinjuku-ku; Ⓜ JR Yamanote Line to Mejiro, main exit)

St Luke's International Hospital (Map pp290–1; ☎ 3541-5151; www.luke.or.jp in Japanese; 9-1 Akashichō, Chūō-ku; ⏲ 24hr; Ⓜ Hibiya Line to Tsukiji, exits 3 & 4)

MONEY

Be warned that cold hard cash is the way to pay in Tokyo. Although credit cards are becoming more common, cash is still the payment of choice, and travellers cheques are rarely accepted outside of large hotels. Do not assume that you can pay with a credit card, and always carry sufficient cash. The only places where you can count on paying by credit card are department stores and large hotels.

For those without credit cards, it's a good idea to bring some travellers cheques as a back-up. As in most other countries, the US dollar is still the preferred currency for exchanging cash and cashing travellers cheques. For more information on costs see p18.

The currency in Japan is the yen, and banknotes and coins are easily identifiable. There are ¥1, ¥5, ¥10, ¥50, ¥100 and ¥500 coins; and ¥1000, ¥2000, ¥5000 and ¥10,000 banknotes (the ¥2000 note is very rarely seen). The ¥1 coin is an aluminium lightweight coin; the ¥5 and ¥50 coins have a punched hole in the middle (the former is coloured bronze and the latter silver). Note that some vending machines do not accept older ¥500 coins. Prices may be listed using the kanji for yen: 円.

ATMs

ATMs are almost as common as vending machines in Tokyo. Unfortunately, most of these do not accept foreign-issued cards. Even if they display Visa and MasterCard logos, most accept only Japan-issued versions of these cards and 24-hour ATMs are exceedingly rare.

Fortunately, Citibank operates 24-hour international ATMs in major areas including Roppongi, Harajuku, Omote-sandō and Shinjuku. Better still, the Japanese postal system has recently linked all of its ATMs to the international Cirrus and Plus cash networks (and some credit-card networks), making life a breeze for travellers to Tokyo. Most larger post offices have **postal ATMs** (9am-5pm Mon-Fri, 9am-noon Sat, closed Sun & holidays). Press the handy button marked 'English Guidance' for English instructions.

Exchanging Money

In theory, banks and post offices will change all major currencies. In practice, some banks refuse to exchange anything but US-dollar cash and travellers cheques. Note also that the currencies of neighbouring Taiwan (New Taiwan dollar) and Korea (*won*) are not easy to change, so you should change these into yen or US dollars before arriving in Japan.

With a passport you can change cash or travellers cheques at an Authorised Foreign Exchange Bank (signs are displayed in English), major post offices, some large hotels and most big department stores. Note that you receive a better exchange rate when withdrawing cash from ATMs than when exchanging cash or travellers cheques in Tokyo; be aware that many banks place a limit on the amount of cash you can withdraw in one day (often around US$400).

Exchange rates are listed on the inside front cover of this guide.

Credit Cards

As Japan is very much a cash-based economy, never assume you can pay using a credit card. If you bring one with you, Visa is most widely accepted, followed by MasterCard, American Express and Diners Club. Getting a cash advance using your foreign-issued credit card is nearly impossible, but Sumitomo Mitsui banks (SMBC) give cash advances if you bring your passport with you. The main credit-card offices are in Tokyo.

American Express (24hr ☎ 0120-020-120)

MasterCard (☎ 5728-5200)

Visa (24hr ☎ 00531-44-0022)

International Transfers

In order to make an international transfer you'll have to find a Japanese bank associated with the bank transferring the money. Start by asking at the central branch of any major Tokyo bank. If it doesn't have a relationship with your bank, it can usually refer you to a bank that does. Once you find a related bank in Tokyo, you'll have to give your home bank the exact details of where to send the money: the bank, branch and location. A credit-card cash advance is a worthwhile alternative.

Post Office & Bank Accounts

Opening a regular bank account is difficult for foreign visitors on a temporary visitor visa. Most banks ask to see an Alien

Registration Card, and some might also require a name stamp (*hanko* or *inkan*, easily available at speciality stores). A much better option for long-term visitors or those who don't want to bother with changing money all the time is a *yūbin chokin* (postal savings account). You can open these accounts at any major post office in Tokyo. With a postal savings account you'll be issued a cash card that enables you to withdraw funds from any post office in Japan (and these are everywhere). You should be able to get things started by using the phrase: *'yūbin chokin no kōza o hirakitai desu'* (I would like to open a post office savings account).

NEWSPAPERS

The three English dailies listed serve the city's international community and are sold at most of the big train-station kiosks. Two English magazines, the weekly *Metropolis* and the quarterly *Tokyo Journal*, round out coverage of local news, dining and entertainment.

Asahi Shimbun/International Herald Tribune (www.asahi.com/english/english.html)

Daily Yomiuri (www.yomiuri.co.jp/dy)

Japan Times (www.japantimes.co.jp)

PHARMACIES

Pharmacies are located throughout Tokyo, although a bit of Japanese helps in getting the medication or item you need. Japanese law prohibits them from selling medications from other countries, but pharmacists will generally be able to help you find a Japanese medication that is either identical with or similar to the one you take at home. The pharmacies listed cater to English-speaking customers.

American Pharmacy (Map pp294–5; ☎ 5220-7716; www.tomods.jp in Japanese; B1F, Marunouchi Bldg, 2-4-1 Marunouchi, Chiyoda-ku; 🕒 9am-9pm Mon-Fri, 10am-9pm Sat, 10am-8pm Sun & holidays; Ⓜ JR Yamanote or Marunouchi Line to Tokyo, Marunouchi exits) The American Pharmacy is staffed by English-speaking pharmacists, and credit cards are accepted. There's another branch inside Ueno Station (Map pp296–7) on the JR Yamanote Line.

National Azabu Supermarket Pharmacy (Map pp278–9; ☎ 3442-3495; 4-5-2 Minami Azabu, Minato-ku; 🕒 9.30am-7pm; Ⓜ Hibiya Line to Hiro-o, exit 2) Inside the National Azabu supermarket (p123).

PHOTOGRAPHY & VIDEO

Tokyo is one of the best places in the world to buy film and camera equipment. You'll have no problem finding print film in Tokyo, and high-quality slide film is widely available at camera shops (see p187). A 36-exposure roll of print film costs anywhere from ¥400 to ¥800. A 36-exposure roll of Kodachrome slide film costs about ¥950 without processing; Fuji slide film, such as Velvia and Provia, is similarly priced.

Film processing is fast and economical and standards are usually high. A 36-exposure roll of print film typically costs around ¥600 to have developed. A 36-exposure roll of slide film usually costs around ¥900 to have developed and mounted, or ¥600 to have developed only.

Digital photographers will find all manner of memory media, batteries and digital cameras widely available. Japan's photo shops also offer a wide range of services for digital photographers, like high-quality prints from digital files.

Most photo-processing shops, as well as department stores and even 7-11 convenience stores, can also transfer digital shots onto CD for you; there's usually a two-day turnaround period.

Serious photographers might want to pick up a copy of Lonely Planet's *Travel Photography*.

POST

The Japanese postal system is reliable and efficient and, for regular postcards and airmail letters, has rates similar to those of other developed countries.

The symbol for post offices is a red T with a bar across the top on a white background (〒). District post offices (the main post office in a ward) are normally open 9am to 7pm weekdays and 9am to 3pm Saturday and are closed Sunday and public holidays. Local post offices are open 9am to 5pm weekdays and are closed Saturday, Sunday and public holidays. Main post offices in the larger cities might have an after-hours window open 24 hours.

Postal Rates

The airmail rate for postcards is ¥70 to any overseas destination; aerograms cost ¥90. Letters less than 25g are ¥90 to other countries within Asia, ¥110 to North America,

Europe or Oceania (including Australia and New Zealand) and ¥130 to Africa and South America. One peculiarity of the Japanese postal system is that you will be charged extra if your writing runs over onto the address side (the right side) of a postcard.

Receiving & Sending Mail

Although any post office will hold mail for collection, the poste restante concept is not well known and can cause confusion in smaller neighbourhoods. The **Tokyo Central Post Office** (Map pp294–5; ☎ 3560-1139) can give you more information about large post offices that can receive and handle your mail. Letters are usually held for only 30 days before being returned to sender. When inquiring about mail for collection ask for *kyoku dome yūbin.*

Mail can be sent to, from or within Japan when addressed in Roman script *(rōmaji)*, but it should, of course, be written as clearly as possible.

TELEPHONE

The country code for Japan is ☎ 81. Japanese telephone codes consist of an area code (Tokyo's is ☎ 03) plus a local number; Tokyo numbers usually consist of eight digits. The area code is not used if dialling a Tokyo number from within Tokyo. You do not dial an area code's first 0 if dialling from abroad. For example, when dialling Tokyo from abroad, dial the international access code of the country from which you are calling, then 81-3. If you're calling within Japan, dial 03 and then the number. Toll-free numbers begin with ☎ 0120. Also see the Quick Reference (inside front cover) for a list of area codes for some main cities and tourist areas covered in this guide.

The Japanese public telephone system is very well developed; there are a great many public phones and they work almost 100% of the time. Local calls cost ¥10 for three minutes. Long-distance or overseas calls require a handful of coins or a telephone card, which are used up as the call progresses; unused ¥10 coins are returned after the call is completed, but no change is given on ¥100 coins. It's more economical to make domestic calls by dialling outside the standard hours.

For local calls it's still much easier to buy a *terefon kādo* (prepaid phone card) than to worry about having enough coins, as most pay phones will accept phone cards. Prepaid cards are available from vending machines and convenience stores in ¥500 and ¥1000 denominations (the latter throws in an extra ¥50 in calls). They can be used in most grey or green pay phones, and the phones will display the remaining value of your card when it is inserted.

International Calls

Paid overseas calls are best made using a prepaid international phone card (see opposite). You can also call overseas on grey international ISDN phones, usually found in phone booths marked 'International & Domestic Card/Coin Phone'. Unfortunately, these are rare; look for them in the lobbies of top-end hotels and at airports. Reverse-charge (collect) overseas calls can be made from any pay phone.

You can save money by dialling late at night. Economy rates, with a discount of 20%, apply 7pm to 11pm weekdays, and 8am to 11pm on weekends and holidays. Discount rates of 40% off the regular rate apply 11pm to 8am.

In some youth hostels and guesthouses, you will also find pink coin-only phones from which you cannot make international calls (although you can receive them).

If you find a public phone that allows international calls, it's more convenient to use a phone card rather than coins. Calls are charged by six-second units, so if you don't have much to say, you can make a quick call home for the minimum charge of ¥100.

HOME COUNTRY DIRECT

One option for making international calls is to dial ☎ 0039 for home country direct, which takes you straight through to a local operator in the country dialled (your home country direct code can be found in phone books or by calling ☎ 0051). You can then make a reverse-charge call or a credit-card call with a phone card valid in that country.

Dialling codes:

Country	Home Country Direct Dial
Australia	0039-61
Canada	0039-1
China	0039-86
France	0039-33
New Zealand	0039-64
UK	0039-44
USA	0039-1

OPERATOR-ASSISTED CALLS

To place an international call through the operator, dial ☎ 0051 (international operators almost always speak English). To make the call yourself, dial ☎ 001 (KDDI), ☎ 0041 (ITJ), ☎ 0061 (IDC) or ☎ 0033 (NTT) – there's very little difference in their rates – then the country code, the local code and the number.

PREPAID PHONE CARDS

The easiest way to place international calls is by using a prepaid international phone card. You can purchase prepaid cards at convenience stores and some hotels.

With the exception of the IC Card, the following cards can be used with any regular pay phone in Japan.

Global Card These cards are only available at discount ticket shops and some guesthouses.

IC Cards Sold from machines that accompany IC card phones, these cards can only be used with the orange IC phones.

KDDI Superworld Card Find these cards at almost any convenience store in Japan.

Directory Assistance

For local directory assistance dial ☎ 104; to place a domestic collect call dial ☎ 106. For international directory assistance in English, dial ☎ 0057.

Mobile Phones

Before you stash your mobile (cell) into your carry-on, consider that your fancy tri-band GSM phone won't work in Japan, unless it's *so* fancy that it also supports the non-ubiquitous CDMA standard. The good news is that several companies now offer short-term mobile-phone rentals for travellers and businesspeople. Rates are quite reasonable, from around ¥3000 per week. Many offer free delivery or have rental counters at Narita airport; check out the following outfits.

DoCoMo (☎ 0120-680-100; www.docomosentu.co.jp/Web/english/rental/)

GoMobile (www.gomobile.co.jp/index_e.html)

PuPuRu (☎ 0120-919-226; www.pupuru.com/en/index_en.html)

Rentafone Japan (☎ 080-3240-9183; www.rentafonejapan.com)

Vodafone (☎ 03-3560-7330; www.vodafone-rental.jp)

TIME

Tokyo local time is nine hours ahead of Greenwich Mean Time (GMT). When it's noon in Tokyo, it's 7pm (the day before) in Los Angeles, 10pm in Montreal and New York, 3am (the same day) in London, 4am in Frankfurt, Paris and Rome, 11am in Hong Kong, 3pm in Melbourne and 5pm in Wellington. Japan does not observe daylight savings time, so remember to subtract one hour when working out the time difference with a country using daylight savings time.

TIPPING & BARGAINING

There is little of either in Japan. If you want to show your gratitude to someone, give them a gift rather than a tip. If you do choose to give someone a cash gift (a maid in a ryokan, for instance), place the money in an envelope first. Bargaining is largely restricted to flea markets and discount electronics shops (where a polite request will often bring the price down by around 10%).

TOILETS

In Japan you will come across everything from bidet-and-blow-dry Western-style toilets to the humbler Asian squat toilets. When you need to squat, the correct position is facing the hood, away from the door. Make sure the contents of your pockets don't spill out! Toilet paper isn't always provided, so always graciously accept those small packets of tissue handed out on the street, a common form of advertising.

In many bathrooms in Japan, separate toilet slippers are often provided just inside the toilet door. These are for use in the toilet only, so remember to shuffle out of them when you leave.

It's quite common to see men urinating in public – the unspoken rule is that it's acceptable at night time if you happen to be drunk. Public toilets are free and can usually be found in or around most train stations. If you're not near a station, department stores are always a good bet, and convenience stores have clean public toilets that are often available 24 hours a day.

TOURIST INFORMATION

Japan's tourist information services (┌光案┌所; *kankō annai-sho*) are first rate, and the Tokyo branch of the Japan National Tourist

Organization (JNTO; below) is the best of the bunch.

Other helpful places about town:

Asakusa Tourist Information Center (Map pp296–7; ☎ 5246-1151; 4-5-6 Higashi-Ueno, Taitō-ku; 🕑 10am-5pm; Ⓜ Ginza or Toei Asakusa Line to Asakusa, exit A4) Awaiting you in Asakusa, this excellent place is staffed with friendly local experts who can arrange free neighbourhood tours with English-speaking guides.

TIC Tochō (Map p282; Tokyo Metropolitan Government Offices, North Tower, 1st fl, 2-8-1 Nishi-Shinjuku, Shinjuku-ku; Ⓜ Toei Ōedo Line to Tochōmae, exit A4)

Tokyo Convention & Visitors Bureau (TCVB; Map pp294–5; ☎ 3287-7024; 1st fl, 3-2-2 Marunouchi, Chiyoda-ku; 🕑 10am-5pm Mon-Fri, 10am-4pm Sat, Sun & holidays; Ⓜ Chiyoda, Hibiya or Toei Mita lines to Hibiya, exit B7) Another great local resource is the tourist information centre here, where you can pick up a **Grutt Pass** (p60).

If you're looking to use a licensed, professional tourist guide you could contact the **Japan Guide Association** (☎ 3213-2706; www.jga21c.or.jp/f_introduction.html).

Japan National Tourist Organization (JNTO)

The **Japan National Tourist Organization** (JNTO; www.jnto.go.jp) is the main English-language information service for foreign travellers to Japan. JNTO produces a great deal of useful literature, which is available from its overseas offices and its Tourist Information Centers (TICs) inside Japan. Most publications are available in English and, in some cases, other European and Asian languages. JNTO's website is very useful for planning your journey.

JNTO operates two main TICs in Tokyo:

Narita (☎ 0476-34-6251; 1st fl, Terminals 1 & 2, Narita airport, Chiba; 🕑 9am-8pm).

Tokyo (Map pp290–1; ☎ 3216-1901; 10th fl, Kōtsū Kaikan Bldg, 2-10-1, Yūrakuchō, Chiyoda-ku; 🕑 9am-5pm Mon-Fri, 9am-noon Sat, closed Sun & national holidays; Ⓜ JR Yamanote Line to Yūrakuchō, exit A8).

TIC staff cannot make transport bookings; they can, however, direct you to agencies that can, such as the Japan Travel Bureau (JTB).

In addition to its main offices listed, JNTO operates 111 English-language Tourist Information Centers throughout Japan. The centres are usually found in the main train stations of major Japanese cities. Look for the red question mark with the word 'information' printed beneath it.

TOURIST OFFICES ABROAD

JNTO has a number of overseas offices:

Australia (☎ 02-9251 3024; www.jnto.go.jp/syd/index.html; Level 18, Australia Square Tower, 264 George St, Sydney, NSW 2000)

Canada (☎ 416-366 7140; info@jntoyyz.com; 165 University Ave, Toronto, ON M5H 3B8)

France (☎ 01 42 96 20 29; 4 rue de Ventadour, 75001 Paris)

Germany (☎ 069-20353; fra@jnto.de; Kaiserstrasse 11, 60311 Frankfurt am Main)

UK (☎ 020-7734 9638; www.seejapan.co.uk; Heathcoat House, 20 Savile Row, London W1S 3PR)

USA (www.japantravelinfo.com) Los Angeles (☎ 213-623 1952; 515 South Figueroa St, Suite 1470, Los Angeles, CA 90071); New York (☎ 212-757 5640; One Rockefeller Plaza, Suite 1250, New York, NY 10020); San Francisco (☎ 415-292 5686; 1 Daniel Burnham Court, Suite 250C, San Francisco, CA 94109)

VISAS

Generally, visitors who are not planning to engage in income-producing activities while in Japan are exempt from obtaining visas and will be issued a *tanki-taizai visa* (temporary visitor visa) on arrival.

Stays of up to six months are permitted for citizens of Austria, Germany, Ireland, Mexico, Switzerland and the UK. Citizens of these countries will almost always be given a 90-day temporary visitor visa upon arrival, which can usually be extended for another 90 days at immigration bureaux inside Japan (see Visa Extensions, opposite).

Citizens of the USA, Australia and New Zealand are granted 90-day temporary visitor visas, while stays of up to three months are permitted for citizens of Argentina, Belgium, Canada, Denmark, Finland, France, Iceland, Israel, Italy, Netherlands, Norway, Singapore, Spain, Sweden and a number of other countries.

For additional information on visas and regulations, contact the nearest Japanese embassy or consulate (p239), or visit the website of the **Japan Ministry of Foreign Affairs** (www.mofa.go.jp) where you can check out the Guide to Japanese Visas, read about working-holiday visas and find details on the Japan Exchange and Teaching (JET) programme, which sponsors native English-speakers to teach in the Japanese public-school system. You can also contact the **Immigration Information Center** (Tokyo Regional

Immigration Bureau Office; Map pp278–9; ☎ 5796-7112; www.moj.go.jp/ENGLISH/index.html; 5-5-30 Kōnan, Minato-ku; 9am-noon & 1-4pm Mon-Fri; Tokyo Monorail or Rinkai Line to Tennozu Isle).

You can get up-to-date visa information through the links on Lonely Planet's website www.lonelyplanet.com. Navigate to Travel Links and click on Embassies & Visas under Practical Planning.

Alien Registration Card

Anyone – and this includes tourists – who stays for more than 90 days is required to obtain a *gaikokujin torokushō* (Alien Registration Card). This card can be obtained at the municipal office of the city, town or ward in which you're living, but moving to another area requires that you reregister within 14 days.

You must carry your Alien Registration Card at all times as the police can stop you and ask to see the card. If you don't have it, you could be hauled off to the station to wait until someone fetches it for you – providing you have one.

Visa Extensions

With the exception of those nationals whose countries have reciprocal visa exemptions and can stay for six months, the limit for most nationalities is 90 days. To extend a temporary visitor visa beyond the standard limit, apply at the Immigration Information Centre (Tokyo Regional Immigration Bureau Office; opposite). You must provide two copies of an Application for Extension of Stay (available at the immigration office), a letter stating the reasons for the extension and supporting documentation as well as your passport. There is a processing fee of ¥4000.

Many long-term visitors to Japan get around the extension problem by briefly leaving the country, usually by going to South Korea. Be warned, however, that immigration officials are wise to this practice, and many 'tourist visa returnees' are turned back at the entry point.

Working-Holiday Visas

Citizens of Australia, Canada, France, Germany, Korea, New Zealand and the UK can apply for a working-holiday visa if they're between 18 and 30 (the upper age limit for UK citizens is officially 25, but this is negotiable). This visa allows a six-month stay and two six-month extensions. The visa is designed to enable young people to travel extensively during their stay; thus, employment is supposed to be part-time or temporary. In practice, many people work full time.

A working-holiday visa is much easier to obtain than a work visa and is popular with Japanese employers. Single applicants must have the equivalent of US$2000 of funds, a married couple must have US$3000, and all applicants must have an onward ticket from Japan. For details, inquire at the nearest Japanese embassy or consulate (p239).

Work Visas

Ever-increasing demand has prompted much stricter work-visa requirements than previously. Arriving in Japan and looking for a job is quite a tough proposition these days, although people still do it. There are legal employment categories for foreigners that specify standards of experience and qualifications.

Once you find an employer in Japan who is willing to sponsor you, it is necessary to obtain a Certificate of Eligibility from your nearest Japanese immigration office. The same office can then issue your work visa, which is valid for either one or three years. This procedure can take two to three months.

WOMEN TRAVELLERS

Japan is one of the safest countries in which to travel – if you're a man. Japan is not as safe for women travellers, who primarily face dangers and annoyances of a sexual nature: sexual harassment, molestation, attempted rape and rape. Although some expats will assure you that it's safe to walk the streets of any Tokyo street alone at night, follow your common sense: keep to streets with heavier foot traffic, stay in groups etc.

Women who have spent some time in Japan have probably experienced some type of sexual harassment. Jam-packed trains can provide opportunities for the roving hands of *chikan* (gropers on crowded trains). A loud complaint usually shames the perpetrator into retreating. To avoid the possibility altogether, ride in the women-only train carriages during rush hour (see p231).

Although statistics show low rates of violent crimes against women, many Japanese women's organisations and media attribute this to under-reporting. If you or someone you know is raped, be forewarned that Japanese police and medical personnel, like those in other countries, can be insensitive to the needs of a woman who has been assaulted. Insist on receiving necessary medical care, and know that you are entitled to help from a translator if you need to file a police report.

If you find the local police unhelpful, call the **Human Rights Counseling Center for Foreigners** (p243).

Finally, an excellent resource for any woman setting up in Japan is Caroline Pover's book *Being A Broad in Japan*; find it in bookstores or order from her website (www.being-a-broad.com).

WORK

Finding work in Tokyo is possible, but it's not as easy nor lucrative as it used to be. Teaching English is still the most common job for Westerners, but bartending, hostessing, modelling and various writing/editorial jobs are also possible.

Whatever line of work you choose, it's essential to look neat and tidy for interviews – appearances can make or break you in Japan. You'll also need to be determined, and you should have a sizable sum of money to float on while you're looking for work, and possibly to get you out of the country if you don't find any (it happens). Foreigners who have set up in Japan over the last few years maintain that a figure of around US$5000 or more is necessary to make a go of it. People do it with less, but they run the risk of ending up penniless and homeless before they find a job.

English Teaching

Teaching English has always been the most popular job for native English speakers in Japan. While it's a fairly common option, competition for the good jobs is very tight since many English schools have failed as a result of Japan's weakened economy. A university degree is an absolute essential as schools cannot sponsor you for a work visa without one (be sure to bring the actual degree with you to Japan). Teaching qualifications and some teaching experience will be of huge advantage when job hunting.

Consider organising a job before arriving in Japan. Big schools like **Geos** (www.geoscareer.com) or **Nova** (www.teachinjapan.com) have recruitment programmes in the USA and the UK. A downside to the big 'factory schools' that recruit overseas is that working conditions are often pretty dire compared with smaller schools that recruit within Japan.

Travellers who can take advantage of the Japanese working-holiday visa (p249) are in a slightly better position. Schools are happier about taking on unqualified teachers if it means they don't have to bother with sponsoring a teacher for a work visa.

For job listings, start here:

Dave's ESL Café (www.eslcafe.com)

ELT News (www.eltnews.com)

Japan Times (http://classified.japantimes.com/career/)

Language

Language

It's true – anyone can speak another language. Don't worry if you haven't studied languages before or that you studied a language at school for years and can't remember any of it. It doesn't even matter if you failed English grammar. After all, that's never affected your ability to speak English! And this is the key to picking up a language in another country. You just need to start speaking.

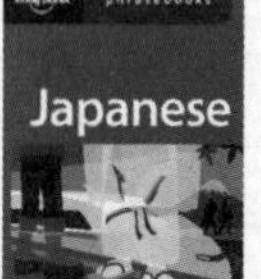

Learn a few key phrases before you go. Write them on pieces of paper and stick them on the fridge, by the bed or even on the computer – anywhere that you'll see them often.

You'll find that locals appreciate travellers trying their language, no matter how muddled you may think you sound. So don't just stand there, say something! If you want to learn more Japanese than we've included here, pick up a copy of Lonely Planet's comprehensive but user-friendly *Japanese Phrasebook.*

PRONUNCIATION

Pronounce double consonants with a slight pause between them, so that each is clearly audible. Vowel length affects meaning, so make sure you distinguish your short and long vowels clearly. Certain vowel sounds (like **u** and **i**) aren't pronounced in some words, but are included as part of the official Romanisation system (which employs a literal system to represent Japanese characters). In the following words and phrases these 'silent' letters are shown in square brackets to indicate that they aren't pronounced.

a	short, as the 'u' in 'run'
ā	long, as the 'a' in 'father'
e	short, as in 'red'
ē	long, as the 'ei' in 'rein'
i	short, as in 'bit'
ī	long, as in 'marine'
o	short, as in 'pot'
ō	long, as the 'aw' in 'paw'
u	short, as in 'put'
ū	long, as in 'rude'

SOCIAL

Meeting People

Hello/Hi.
konnichi wa　　こんにちは。
Goodbye.
sayōnara　　さようなら。
Yes.
hai　　はい。
No.
iie　　いえ。
Please.
(when offering something)
dōzo　　どうぞ。
(when asking a favour or making a request)
onegai shimasu　　お願いします。
Thank you (very much).
(dōmo) arigatō (gozaimas[u])　　(どうも)ありがとう(ございます)。
You're welcome.
dō itashimash[i]te　　どういたしまして。
Excuse me. (to get attention or to get past)
sumimasen　　すみません。
Sorry.
gomen nasai　　ごめんなさい。

Could you please …?
… kuremasen ka?
…くれませんか?
repeat that
kurikaeshite
繰り返して
speak more slowly
motto yukkuri hanash[i]te
もっとゆっくり話して
write it down
kaite
書いて

What's your name?
o-namae wa nan des[u] ka?
お名前は何ですか?
My name is …
watashi no namae wa … des[u]
私の名前は…です。
Do you speak English?
eigo ga hanasemas[u] ka?
英語が話せますか?

Do you understand?
wakarimash[i]ta ka?
わかりましたか?
Yes, I do understand.
hai, wakarimash[i]ta
はい、わかりました。
No, I don't understand.
iie, wakarimasen
いいえ、わかりません。

Going Out

What's on ...?
... wa nani ga arimas[u] ka?
…は何がありますか?

locally
kinjo ni 近所に
this weekend
konshū no shūmatsu 今週の週末
today
kyō 今日
tonight
konya 今夜

Where can I find ...?
doko ni ikeba ... ga arimas[u] ka?
どこに行けば…がありますか?

clubs
kurabu クラブ
gay venues
gei no basho ゲイの場所
Japanese-style pubs
izakaya 居酒屋
places to eat
shokuji ga dekiru tokoro 食事ができる所
pubs
pabu パブ

Is there a local entertainment guide?
jimoto no entāteimento gaido wa arimas[u] ka?
地元のエンターテイメントガイドはありますか?

PRACTICAL

Question Words

Who?
dare?/donata? だれ?/どなた? (polite)
What?/What is this?
nan?/nani? 何?/なに?
Which?
dochira? どちら?
When?
itsu? いつ?
Where?
doko? どこ?
How?
dono yō ni? どのように?
How much does it cost?
ikura des[u] ka? いくらですか?

Numbers

0	zero/rei	ゼロ/零
1	ichi	一
2	ni	二
3	san	三
4	shi/yon	四
5	go	五
6	roku	六
7	shichi/nana	七
8	hachi	八
9	ku/kyū	九
10	jū	十
11	jūichi	十一
12	jūni	十二
13	jūsan	十三
14	jūshi/jūyon	十四
15	jūgo	十五
16	jūroku	十六
17	jūshichi/jūnana	十七
18	jūhachi	十八
19	jūku/jūkyū	十九
20	nijū	二十
21	nijūichi	二十一
22	nijūni	二十二
30	sanjū	三十
40	yonjū	四十
50	gojū	五十
60	rokujū	六十
70	nanajū	七十
80	hachijū	八十
90	kyūjū	九十
100	hyaku	百
200	nihyaku	二百
1000	sen	千

Days

Monday	getsuyōbi	月曜日
Tuesday	kayōbi	火曜日
Wednesday	suiyōbi	水曜日
Thursday	mokuyōbi	木曜日
Friday	kinyōbi	金曜日
Saturday	doyōbi	土曜日
Sunday	nichiyōbi	日曜日

Banking

I'd like to ...
... o onegai shimas[u]
…をお願いします。

cash a cheque
kogitte no genkinka
小切手の現金化
change a travellers cheque
toraberāz[u] chekku no genkinka
トラベラーズチェックの現金化
change money
ryōgae
両替

Where's …?
… wa doko des[u] ka?
…はどこですか?
an ATM
ētīemu
ATM
a foreign exchange office
gaikoku kawase sekushon
外国為替セクション

Post

Where is the post office?
yūbin kyoku wa doko des[u] ka?
郵便局はどこですか?

I want to send a/an …
… o okuritai no des[u] ga
…を送りたいのですが。

letter	
tegami	手紙
parcel	
kozutsumi	小包
postcard	
hagaki	はがき

I want to buy a/an …
… o kudasai
…をください。

aerogram	
earoguramu	エアログラム
envelope	
fūtō	封筒
stamp	
kitte	切手

Phones & Mobiles

I want to …
…tai no des[u] ga
…たいのですが。
buy a phonecard
terefon kādo o kai
テレフォンカードを買い
call (Singapore)
(shingapōru) ni denwa shi
(シンガポール)に電話し
make a (local) call
(shinai) ni denwa shi
(市内)に電話し
reverse the charges
korekuto-kōru de denwa shi
コレクトコールで電話し

I'd like a …
… o onegai shimas[u]
…をお願いします。
charger for my phone
keitaidenwa no jūdenki
携帯電話の充電器
mobile/cell phone for hire
keitaidenwa no rentaru
携帯電話のレンタル
prepaid mobile/cell phone
puripeido no keitaidenwa
プリペイドの携帯電話
SIM card for your network
shimukādo
SIMカード

Internet

Where's the local Internet café?
intānetto-kafe wa doko des[u] ka?
インターネットカフェはどこですか?

I'd like to …
… shitai no des[u] ga
…したいのですが。
check my email
īmēru o chekku
Eメールをチェック
get Internet access
intānetto ni akuses[u]
インターネットにアクセス

Transport

When's the … (bus)?
… (bas[u]) wa nan-ji des[u] ka?
…(バス)は何時ですか?

first	
shihatsu no	始発の
last	
saishū no	最終の
next	
tsugi no	次の

What time does it leave?
kore wa nan-ji ni demas[u] ka?
これは何時に出ますか?
What time does it get to ...?
kore wa ... ni nan-ji ni tsukimas[u] ka?
これは...に何時に着きますか?

Is this taxi available?
kono tak[u]shī wa kūsha des[u] ka?
このタクシーは空車ですか?
Please put the meter on.
mētā o irete kudasai
メーターを入れてください。
How much is it to …?
… made ikura des[u] ka?
…までいくらですか?
Please take me to (this address).
(kono jūsho) made onegai shimas[u]
(この住所)までお願いします。

FOOD

breakfast	
chōshoku	朝食
lunch	
chūshoku	昼食
dinner	
yūshoku	夕食
snack	
kanshoku	間食
to eat	
tabemas[u]	食べます
to drink	
nomimas[u]	飲みます

Can you recommend a …?
doko ka ii … o shitte imas[u] ka?
どこかいい…を知っていますか?

bar	
bā	バー
café	
kafe	カフェ
restaurant	
restoran	レストラン

Is service included in the bill?
sābis[u] ryō komi des[u] ka?
サービス料込みですか?

For more detailed information on food and dining out, see Food & Drink on p33 and Eating on p121.

EMERGENCIES

Help!
tas[u]kete!
たすけて!
It's an emergency!
kinkyū des[u]!
緊急です。
Call the police!
keisatsu o yonde!
警察を呼んで。
Call a doctor!
isha o yonde!
医者を呼んで。
Call an ambulance!
kyūkyūsha o yonde!
救急車を呼んで。
Could you please help?
tas[u]kete kudasai?
たすけてください。
Where's the police station?
keisatsusho wa doko des[u] ka?
警察署はどこですか?

HEALTH

Where's the nearest …?
kono chikaku no … wa doko des[u] ka?
この近くの…はどこですか?

(night) chemist	
(nijūyojikan eigyō no) yakkyoku	(24時間営業の)薬局
doctor	
isha	医者
hospital	
byōin	病院

I need a doctor (who speaks English).
(eigo ga dekiru) o-isha-san ga hitsuyō des[u]
(英語ができる)お医者さんが必要です。

I'm allergic to …
watashi wa … arerugī des[u]
私は…アレルギーです。

antibiotics	
kōsei busshitsu	抗生物質
aspirin	
as[u]pirin	アスピリン
bees	
hachi	蜂
nuts	
nattsurui	ナッツ類
penicillin	
penishirin	ペニシリン

Symptoms

I have …
watashi wa … ga arimas[u]
私は…があります。

diarrhoea	
geri	下痢
a headache	
zutsū	頭痛
nausea	
hakike	吐き気
a pain	
itami	痛み

GLOSSARY

For a glossary of more food and drink terms see p34.

aka-chōchin – red lanterns, typically used outside pubs
anime – animated films

-bashi – suffix for 'bridge'; see also *hashi*
basho – sumō wrestling tournament
bentō – boxed lunch or dinner, usually of rice, fish or meat and vegetables
bijutsukan – art museum; see also *hakubutsukan*
bosozoku – motorcycle gangs who dye their hair and wear bright, flashy clothes.
bunraku – classical puppet theatre using life-sized puppets to enact dramas similar to those of *kabuki*
butō – a relatively modern form of Japanese dance
butsu – Buddha statue (as in Kamakura's Daibutsu, or Great Buddha)

chimpira – a punk, often a *yankii* who has taken rebellion a step further and hopes to become a junior *yakuza*
chō – an area of a city, subdivision of a *ku*; made up of many *chōme*
chōme – city area of a few blocks
cos-play – costume play (also called *kosu-purē*); typically high school girls who dress up to attract attention

-dera – suffix meaning Buddhist temple; see also *-ji*
Daibutsu – Great Buddha
daimyō – feudal lords under the *shōgun*
depachika – department store food floor
depāto – department store
dōri – avenue or street (also *dōro*)

Edo – pre–Meiji Restoration name for Tokyo
Edokko – literally 'children of Edo' but also an informal name for modern-day Tokyoites
eki – train station
ekiben – *bentō* lunch boxes sold at train stations
ema – small votive plaques hung in shrine sanctuaries as petitions to resident deities
enka – often referred to as Japanese country and western; ballads about love and loss that are popular with the older generation

freeter – people in their 20s with little ambition
fugu – poisonous blowfish (also called globefish or puffer fish), elevated to *haute cuisine* with a bite
furigana – Japanese syllabic script used as an aid to pronouncing *kanji*; see also *hiragana* and *katakana*
futsū – literally, 'ordinary'; also refers to basic stopping-at-all-stations train service

gaijin – literally, 'outside person'; the usual term for a foreigner; contracted form of *gaikokujin* (outside country person)
-gawa – suffix for river (also see *kawa*)
geisha – a woman versed in the arts and other cultivated pursuits who entertains guests
geta – traditional wooden sandals
gochisō-sama desh[i]ta – after-meal expression of thanks (literally 'it was a feast')
-gu – suffix indicating a Shintō shrine

haiden – hall of worship in a shrine
haiku – 17-syllable poem (five syllables in the first line, seven in the second and five in the third)
hakubutsukan – museum, except for art museum (see *bijutsukan*)
hanami – cherry-blossom viewing
hanko – personal stamp or seal used to authenticate documents; carries the same weight as a signature in the West
hantō – peninsula
hashi – chopsticks; bridge (which sometimes also includes the suffix *-bashi*)
heya – room; also a sumō stable
higashi – east
hiragana – *furigana* commonly for verb endings, prepositions, conjunctions etc; see also *kanji* and *katakana*
honden – main building or hall of a shrine
hondō – main building or hall of a temple

ichiba – market; see also *shijō*
IDC – International Digital Communication
ike – pond
ikebana – art of flower arranging
inkan– personal name stamp, similar to *hanko*
irezumi – a tattoo or the art of tattooing
itadakimas[u] – literally, 'I will receive'; before-meals expression
ITJ – International Telecom Japan
izakaya – Japanese version of a pub; beer, sake and lots of snacks available in a rustic, boisterous setting

-ji – suffix indicating a Buddhist temple (see also *-dera*)
jikokuhyō – book of timetables; usually for trains
jinja – shrine (also *jingū* or *gū*)
Jizō – Buddhist deity, protector of travellers and children, often seen as stone statues wearing bibs
JNTO – Japan National Tourist Organization
JR – Japan Railways; regional JR companies operate above-ground trains in Tokyo and throughout Japan
JTB – Japan Travel Bureau

kabuki – form of Japanese theatre drawing on popular tales and characterised by elaborate costumes, stylised acting and the use of male actors for all roles
Kabukichō – Tokyo's infamous red-light district in Shinjuku
kaikan – hall; a more majestic building than an average house or office building
kaiseki – Japanese banquet cuisine in which every small detail of the repast is carefully controlled
kaisoku – rapid express train
kami – Shintō gods or spirits associated with natural phenomena

kamikaze – literally, 'wind of the gods'; the typhoon that sank Kublai Khan's 13th-century invasion fleet and the name adopted by Japanese suicide bombers in the waning days of WWII
kampai – 'cheers', as in a drinking toast
-kan – suffix meaning building or hall
kanji – literally, 'Chinese writing'; Chinese ideographic script used for writing Japanese; see also *furigana*, *hiragana* and *katakana*
Kannon – Buddhist goddess of mercy (Guanyin in Chinese, Avalokiteshvara in Sanskrit)
katakana – Japanese script used for foreign and loan words (see also *furigana*, *hiragana* and *kanji*)
katana – Japanese sword
kawa – river (also called *gawa*)
KDDI – Kokusai Denshin Denwa; telephone company offering international service
keiretsu – a business cartel
keitai – mobile phone
-ken – suffix meaning prefecture
kendō – 'the way of the sword'; fencing technique based on the two-handed *samurai* sword
kita – north
-ko – suffix meaning lake
kōban – local police box; a common sight in Tokyo
kōen – park
koi – carp; considered a brave, tenacious fish; see also *koinobori*
koinobori – windsocks flown around Boy's Day (5 May) in honour of sons whom it is hoped will inherit the virtues of the *koi*
konbini – convenience store
kosu-purē – costume play; see *cos-play*
kōyō – autumn foliage season
ku – city ward; an administrative area
kyūkō – ordinary express train (faster than *futsū*, stopping only at certain stations)

machi – literally 'town', subdivision of a city that often serves the same function as a *chō*
manga – Japanese comics
matsuri – festival
meishi – business card; very important in Japan
mikoshi – portable shrines (or ceremonial palanquins) carried around by phalanxes of sweaty men during festivals
minami – south
mingei – often referred to as folk crafts; also a philosophy that everyday household objects should bring pleasure through their aesthetics, touch and use
minshuku – Japanese equivalent of a B&B
mizu shōbai – see *water trade*
mukekkon sedai – nonmarriage generation; see also *parasite single*

N'EX – Narita Express
NHK – Japan Broadcasting Corporation
Nihon – the most commonly used name for Japan, meaning literally 'Source of the Sun'; see also *Nippon*
niō – temple guardians
Nippon – a slightly more formal version of the name for Japan (similar to *Nihon*); this version sometimes carries a whiff of nationalism
nishi – west
nō – classical Japanese mask drama performed on a bare stage
noren – door curtains or cloth awning, usually for restaurants, usually printed with the name of the establishment
NTT – Nippon Telegraph & Telephone Corporation

obasan – aunt or older woman
obaasan – grandmotherly type
obatarian – this word combines the Japanese word *obasan* and the English suffix '-genarian', as in someone who has reached a certain age; known for shouldering their way onto trains and buses, terrorising shop assistants and generally getting their way
o-furo – traditional Japanese bath (literally 'the honourable bath'); see also *sentō*
ojisan – uncle or older man; similarly *'ojiisan'* is a grandfatherly type
ojitarian –male equivalent to *obatarian*; are generally uncommunicative and sour, wear unfashionable clothes and pick their teeth in public
ojōsan – a young woman, usually a college student or graduate, who is middle class and headed for marriage to a young *salaryman*
OL – common term which stands for office lady; female employee of a large firm, usually a clerical worker
onsen – mineral hot spring with bathing areas and accommodation
otaku – someone unusually obsessed, usually with something technological or having to do with manga or *anime*

parasite single – single women who continue to live with their parents well into their 20s and 30s; sometimes referred to as part of the *mukekkon sedai*

rakugo – performances of stand-up comedy or long tales; a traditional art that is dying out
ryokan – traditional Japanese inn

sadō – tea ceremony (literally 'way of tea')
salaryman – male employee of a large firm; white-collar businessman
samurai – Japan's traditional warrior class
sembei – soy-flavoured crispy rice crackers often sold in tourist areas
sentō – public bath
setto – set menu or set meal; see also *teishoku*
shamisen – traditional three-stringed instrument, similar to a banjo
shi – city
shijō – market; see also *ichiba*
shimbun – newspaper

shinkansen – bullet train
Shitamachi – low-lying plebeian quarters of old Edo, centred around Ueno and Asakusa
shodō – Japanese calligraphy; literally, 'the way of writing'
shōgun – military ruler of pre-Meiji Japan
shokudō – Japanese-style cafeteria; cheap restaurant
sumō – Shintō-derived sport where two wrestlers wearing ceremonial clothing collide in a ring

taikō – drums
tatami – tightly woven floor matting on which shoes or slippers should not be worn
TCAT – Tokyo City Air Terminal
tera – Buddhist temple
teishoku – a set meal in a restaurant (usually lunch)
terefon kādo – prepaid phone card
TIC – Tourist Information Center
tokkyū – limited express train; faster than *kyūkō*
torii – entrance gate to a Shintō shrine

ukiyo-e – wood-block prints; literally, 'pictures of the floating world'
uyoku – right-wing groups that yearn for the good old imperial days

waka – 31-syllable poem
washi – fine Japanese handmade paper
water trade – the world of bars, entertainment and sex for sale; also called *mizu shōbai*

yakuza – Japanese mafia
yakyū – baseball
Yamanote – historically refers to the high-city region of old Edo; now also the train line that loops around the city centre
yamato-e – a term of much debated origins that refers to the Japanese world, particularly in contrast to things Chinese
yan-mama – a woman who has had children at a very young age and continues to dress in miniskirts and platform shoes
yankii – pronounced 'yahn-kee'; a member of this tribe prefers blond or brown hair, sports flashy clothes and has a mobile phone permanently glued to one ear
YCAT – Yokohama City Air Terminal
yokozuna – sumō grand champion
yukata – like a dressing gown, a light cotton robe or kimono, worn for lounging after a bath; standard issue at ryokan and some hotels; can also be used as pyjamas

Behind the Scenes

THE LONELY PLANET STORY

The story begins with a classic travel adventure: Tony and Maureen Wheeler's 1972 journey across Europe and Asia to Australia. There was no useful information about the overland trail then, so Tony and Maureen published the first Lonely Planet guidebook to meet a growing need.

From a kitchen table, Lonely Planet has grown to become the largest independent travel publisher in the world, with offices in Melbourne (Australia), Oakland (USA) and London (UK). Today Lonely Planet guidebooks cover the globe. There is an ever-growing list of books and information in a variety of media. Some things haven't changed. The main aim is still to make it possible for adventurous travellers to get out there – to explore and better understand the world.

At Lonely Planet we believe travellers can make a positive contribution to the countries they visit – if they respect their host communities and spend their money wisely. Every year 5% of company profit is donated to charities around the world.

THIS BOOK

This 6th edition was written by Andrew Bender and Wendy Yanagihara. Philip Brophy wrote the boxed text Manga & Anime (p29). The 5th edition was written by Kara Knafelc, the 4th by John Ashburne. Dr Trish Batchelor wrote the Health section (p240). This guide was commissioned in Lonely Planet's Melbourne office, and produced by the following people:

Commissioning Editor Rebecca Chau

Coordinating Editor Gina Tsarouhas

Coordinating Cartographer Kusnandar

Coordinating Layout Designer Laura Jane

Managing Cartographer Corinne Waddell

Assisting Editors Yvonne Byron, Monique Choy, Gennifer Ciavarra, Margedd Heliosz, Lauren Rollheiser

Assisting Cartographers Diana Duggan

Cover Designer Nic Lehman

Project Manager Glenn van der Knijff

Language Content Coordinator Quentin Frayne

Thanks to Sally Darmody, Mark Germanchis, Raphael Richards, Suzannah Shwer, Kayoko Todd, Celia Wood

Cover photographs: Sunlight on skyscrapers, Photolibrary (top); Woman on scooter on pedestrian crossing, Warwick Kent/Photolibrary (bottom); Geisha in kimono signing autograph for fan, Greg Elms/Lonely Planet Images (back).

Internal photographs by Lonely Planet Images and Greg Elms except for the following: p2 (#3), p9, p70 (#2) Adina Tovy Amsel; p157 (#3) Antony Giblin; p213, p224 Bob Charlton; p155 (#2), p169 Brent Winebrenner; p157 (#2) Chris Mellor; p71 (#4) Christian Aslund; p69 (#2), p72 (#2 & 3), p76, p155 (#3), p156 (#1), p158 (#2 & 3), p159 (#2) John Ashburne; p69 (#1), 89, 107 Martin Moos; p71 (#3) Michael Taylor; p37 Oliver Strewe; p220 Staeven Vallak. All images are the copyright of the photographers unless otherwise indicated. Many of the images in this guide are available for licensing from Lonely Planet Images: www.lonelyplanetimages.com.

THANKS

ANDREW BENDER

Thanks go to Yohko Scott, Carol Wong and the staff at the JNTO Los Angeles, Keiko Garrison, Marian Goldberg, Suzuki Tomoya, Nakamichi Yumi, Miyazawa Kōji, Kasahara Michiko, the volunteer guide service, Steve Beimel and Nancy Craft. In-house thanks go to Rebecca Chau, Gina Tsarouhas and Kusnandar, and to Wendy Yanagihara for being such a trouper and so easy to work with.

WENDY YANAGIHARA

Many thanks to the hundreds of Tokyoites who lent me a helping hand, imparted insights into their vibrant city and shared slices of their lives with me. Special thanks go to the

LONELY PLANET AUTHORS

Why is our travel information the best in the world? It's simple: our authors are independent, dedicated travellers. They don't research using just the Internet or phone, and they don't take freebies in exchange for positive coverage. They travel widely, to all the popular spots and off the beaten track. They personally visit thousands of hotels, restaurants, cafés, bars, galleries, palaces, museums and more – and they take pride in getting all the details right, and telling it how it is. For more, see the authors section on **www.lonelyplanet.com**.

Kagurazaka crew, and to my ever-wonderful aunt Shigeko and cousins Kiku-chan and Miho-chan. I am also sincerely grateful to Bec and Gina, whose sensitivity and flexibility were invaluable to me on this project.

I would like to dedicate my work on this book to my mother, Michiko Yanagihara (1941–2005), who started me on the road and inspired my love for travel before I could walk – and who left us all behind a little too soon.

OUR READERS

Many thanks to the hundreds of travellers who used the last edition and wrote to us with helpful hints, useful advice and interesting anecdotes:

Talia Abrams, Bruce Anderton, Mary Beth Bursey, Daniel Corrales, Philip Crosby, Patricia Decker, Carl Dobias, Benjama Feisthauer, Debra Flippin, Aleksandr Gekht, Tomas Gradin, John Hunter, Tsuyodino Inohara, Dympna Kelly, Robert Kerkhofs, Matthew Keyes, Greta Kobayashi, Joanne Louis, Suvi Makela, Marilyn Marler, Eric Medina, Jordan Menzies, Brian Micek, Rachel Pennay, Jody Lee Potvin-Jones, Rebecca Butler Power, Collin Redmond, Ron Robinson, Ru Sam, Karen Sandness, Wendy Schaffer, Pietro Slavich, Chris Sorensen, Andrew Thompson, Stéphanie Tiffon, Shinichiro Uehara, Vincent Ursem, Andy Wuenn, Kuramasu Yutaka,David Zentgraf, Gianni Zoccatelli, Lukas Zweifel

SEND US YOUR FEEDBACK

We love to hear from travellers – your comments keep us on our toes and help make our books better. Our well-travelled team reads every word on what you loved or loathed about this book. Although we cannot reply individually to postal submissions, we always guarantee that your feedback goes straight to the appropriate authors, in time for the next edition. Each person who sends us information is thanked in the next edition – and the most useful submissions are rewarded with a free book.

To send us your updates – and find out about Lonely Planet events, newsletters and travel news – visit our award-winning website: www.lonelyplanet.com /feedback.

Note: We may edit, reproduce and incorporate your comments in Lonely Planet products such as guidebooks, websites and digital products, so let us know if you don't want your comments reproduced or your name acknowledged. For a copy of our privacy policy visit www.lonelyplanet.com/privacy.

ACKNOWLEDGMENTS

Many thanks to the following for the use of their content:
Tokyo Metro Map © Tokyo Metro 2002

Notes

Notes

Notes

Index

See also separate indexes for Eating (p271), Entertainment (p271), Shopping (p272) and Sleeping (p272).

000 map pages
000 photographs

H

I

000 map pages
000 photographs

000 map pages
000 photographs

U

V

000 map pages
000 photographs

Index

000 map pages
000 photographs

SHOPPING

SLEEPING

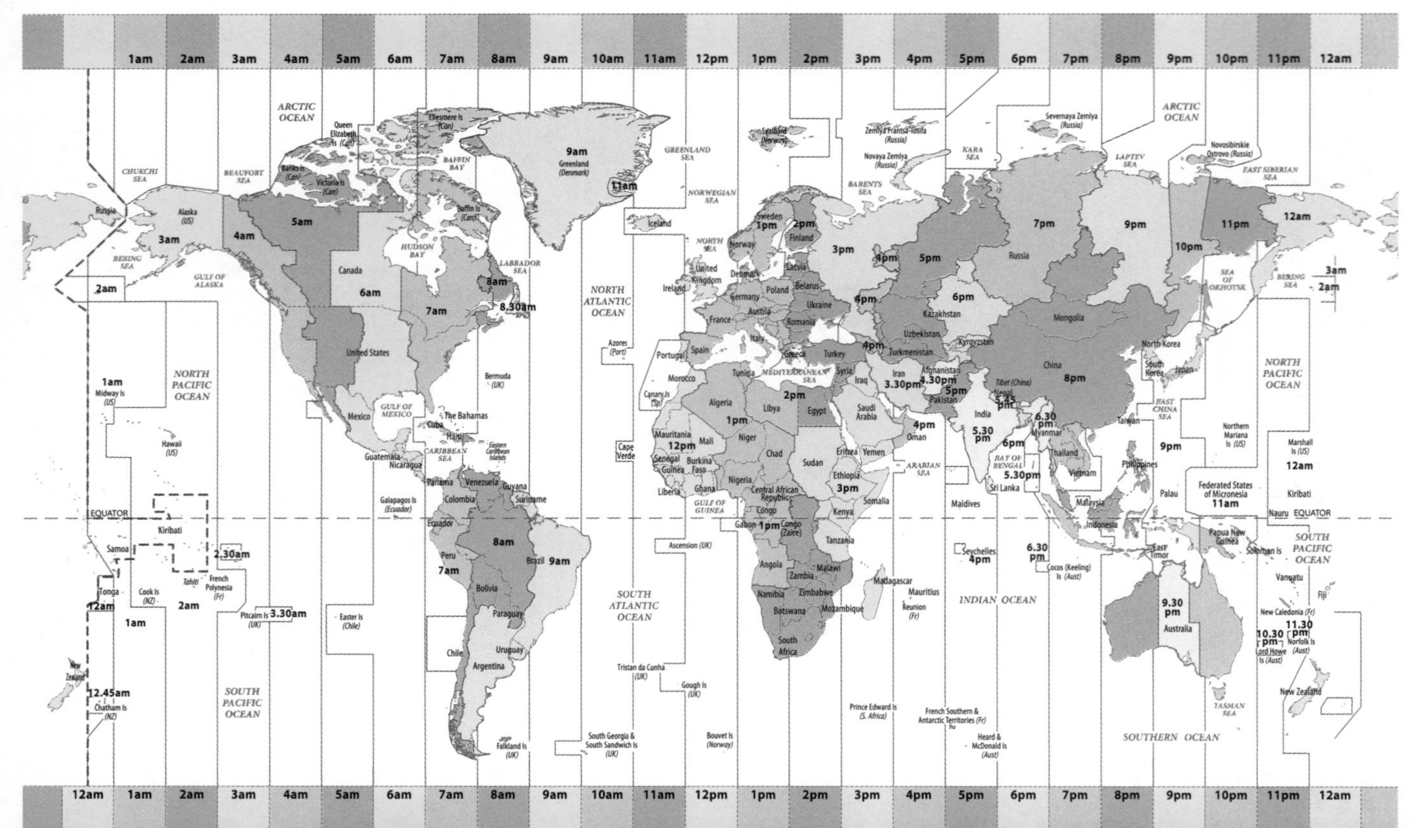

1am
2am
3am
4am
5am
6am
7am
8am
9am
10am
11am
12pm
1pm
2pm
3pm
4pm
5pm
6pm
7pm
8pm
9pm
10pm
11pm
12am
ARCTIC OCEAN
CHUKCHI SEA
BEAUFORT SEA
BERING SEA
GULF OF ALASKA
Russia
Alaska (US)
3am
4am
5am
2am
Queen Elizabeth Is (Can)
Banks Is (Can)
Victoria Is (Can)
Ellesmere Is (Can)
BAFFIN BAY
Baffin Is (Can)
HUDSON BAY
Canada
6am
7am
LABRADOR SEA
8am
8.30am
9am
Greenland (Denmark)
11am
United States
Mexico
GULF OF MEXICO
The Bahamas
Cuba
Haiti
Eastern Caribbean Islands
CARIBBEAN SEA
Guatemala
Nicaragua
Panama
Venezuela
Guyana
Suriname
Colombia
Ecuador
Peru
7am
Bolivia
8am
Brazil
9am
Paraguay
Chile
Uruguay
Argentina
Falkland Is (UK)
Galapagos Is (Ecuador)
Easter Is (Chile)
Bermuda (UK)
1am
Midway Is (US)
NORTH PACIFIC OCEAN
Hawaii (US)
EQUATOR
Kiribati
Samoa
2.30am
Tahiti
French Polynesia (Fr)
Tonga
12am
Cook Is (NZ)
2am
1am
Pitcairn Is (UK)
3.30am
New Zealand
12.45am
Chatham Is (NZ)
SOUTH PACIFIC OCEAN
NORTH ATLANTIC OCEAN
Azores (Port)
Cape Verde
SOUTH ATLANTIC OCEAN
Ascension (UK)
Tristan da Cunha (UK)
Gough Is (UK)
South Georgia & South Sandwich Is (UK)
Bouvet Is (Norway)
GREENLAND SEA
NORWEGIAN SEA
NORTH SEA
Iceland
Ireland
United Kingdom
Portugal
Spain
Canary Is (Sp)
Morocco
France
Svalbard (Norway)
Norway
Sweden
1pm
Finland
2pm
Denmark
Germany
Poland
Latvia
Belarus
Ukraine
Austria
Romania
Italy
Greece
Turkey
Tunisia
MEDITERRANEAN SEA
Algeria
Libya
2pm
Egypt
1pm
Mauritania
12pm
Mali
Niger
Senegal
Guinea
Burkina Faso
Ghana
Liberia
Nigeria
Chad
Sudan
Central African Republic
GULF OF GUINEA
Gabon
1pm
Congo
Congo (Zaire)
Angola
Namibia
Botswana
South Africa
Zambia
Zimbabwe
Malawi
Mozambique
Tanzania
Kenya
Ethiopia
3pm
Eritrea
Yemen
Somalia
Madagascar
Mauritius
Reunion (Fr)
Prince Edward Is (S. Africa)
French Southern & Antarctic Territories (Fr)
Heard & McDonald Is (Aust)
Zemlya Frantsa-Iosifa (Russia)
Novaya Zemlya (Russia)
BARENTS SEA
KARA SEA
3pm
4pm
5pm
Russia
Kazakhstan
6pm
Uzbekistan
Turkmenistan
Kyrgyzstan
4pm
Syria
Iraq
Iran
3.30pm
Saudi Arabia
Oman
4pm
ARABIAN SEA
Afghanistan
4.30pm
Pakistan
5pm
India
5.30 pm
Nepal
5.45 pm
Tibet (China)
BAY OF BENGAL
Sri Lanka
5.30pm
6pm
Maldives
Seychelles
4pm
INDIAN OCEAN
6.30 pm
Cocos (Keeling) Is (Aust)
Myanmar
6.30 pm
Thailand
Vietnam
Malaysia
Indonesia
Severnaya Zemlya (Russia)
7pm
Mongolia
China
8pm
LAPTEV SEA
9pm
ARCTIC OCEAN
Novosibirskie Ostrovo (Russia)
EAST SIBERIAN SEA
10pm
11pm
12am
SEA OF OKHOTSK
BERING SEA
3am
2am
North Korea
South Korea
Japan
EAST CHINA SEA
Taiwan
Philippines
9pm
Palau
East Timor
Papua New Guinea
Australia
9.30 pm
SOUTHERN OCEAN
TASMAN SEA
NORTH PACIFIC OCEAN
Northern Mariana Is (US)
Marshall Is (US)
12am
Federated States of Micronesia
11am
Kiribati
Nauru
EQUATOR
SOUTH PACIFIC OCEAN
Solomon Is
Vanuatu
Fiji
New Caledonia (Fr)
11.30 pm
Norfolk Is (Aust)
10.30 pm
Lord Howe Is (Aust)
New Zealand

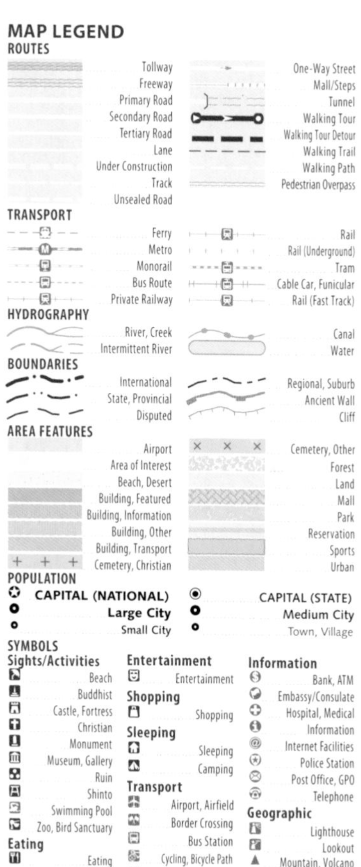
MAP LEGEND
ROUTES
Tollway
Freeway
Primary Road
Secondary Road
Tertiary Road
Lane
Under Construction
Track
Unsealed Road
One-Way Street
Mall/Steps
Tunnel
Walking Tour
Walking Tour Detour
Walking Trail
Walking Path
Pedestrian Overpass
TRANSPORT
Ferry
Metro
Monorail
Bus Route
Private Railway
Rail
Rail (Underground)
Tram
Cable Car, Funicular
Rail (Fast Track)
HYDROGRAPHY
River, Creek
Intermittent River
Canal
Water
BOUNDARIES
International
State, Provincial
Disputed
Regional, Suburb
Ancient Wall
Cliff
AREA FEATURES
Airport
Area of Interest
Beach, Desert
Building, Featured
Building, Information
Building, Other
Building, Transport
Cemetery, Christian
Cemetery, Other
Forest
Land
Mall
Park
Reservation
Sports
Urban
POPULATION
CAPITAL (NATIONAL)
Large City
Small City
CAPITAL (STATE)
Medium City
Town, Village
SYMBOLS
Sights/Activities
Beach
Buddhist
Castle, Fortress
Christian
Monument
Museum, Gallery
Ruin
Shinto
Swimming Pool
Zoo, Bird Sanctuary
Eating
Eating
Drinking
Drinking
Café
Entertainment
Entertainment
Shopping
Shopping
Sleeping
Sleeping
Camping
Transport
Airport, Airfield
Border Crossing
Bus Station
Cycling, Bicycle Path
General Transport
Petrol Station
Taxi Rank
Information
Bank, ATM
Embassy/Consulate
Hospital, Medical
Information
Internet Facilities
Police Station
Post Office, GPO
Telephone
Geographic
Lighthouse
Lookout
Mountain, Volcano
National Park
River Flow
Waterfall

Maps

TOKYO SUBWAY MAP

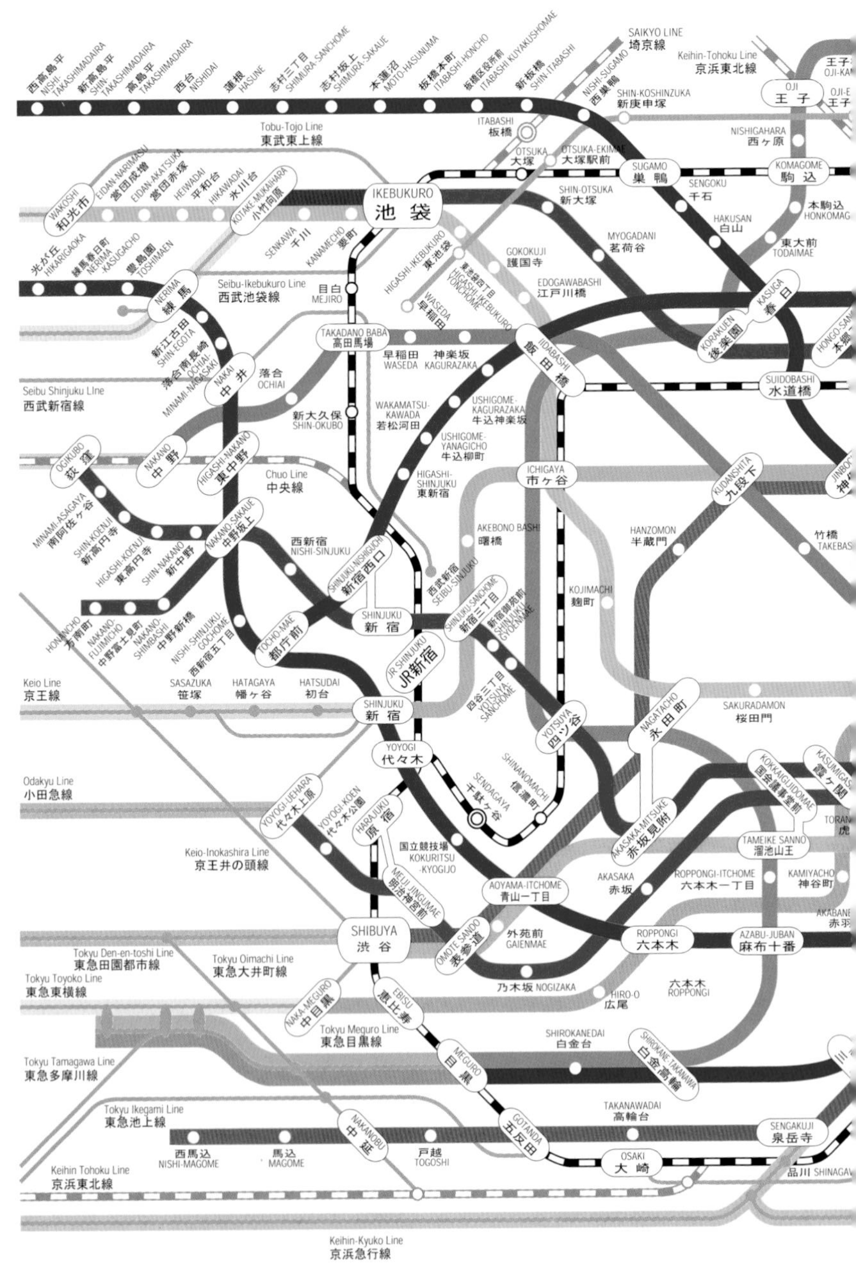

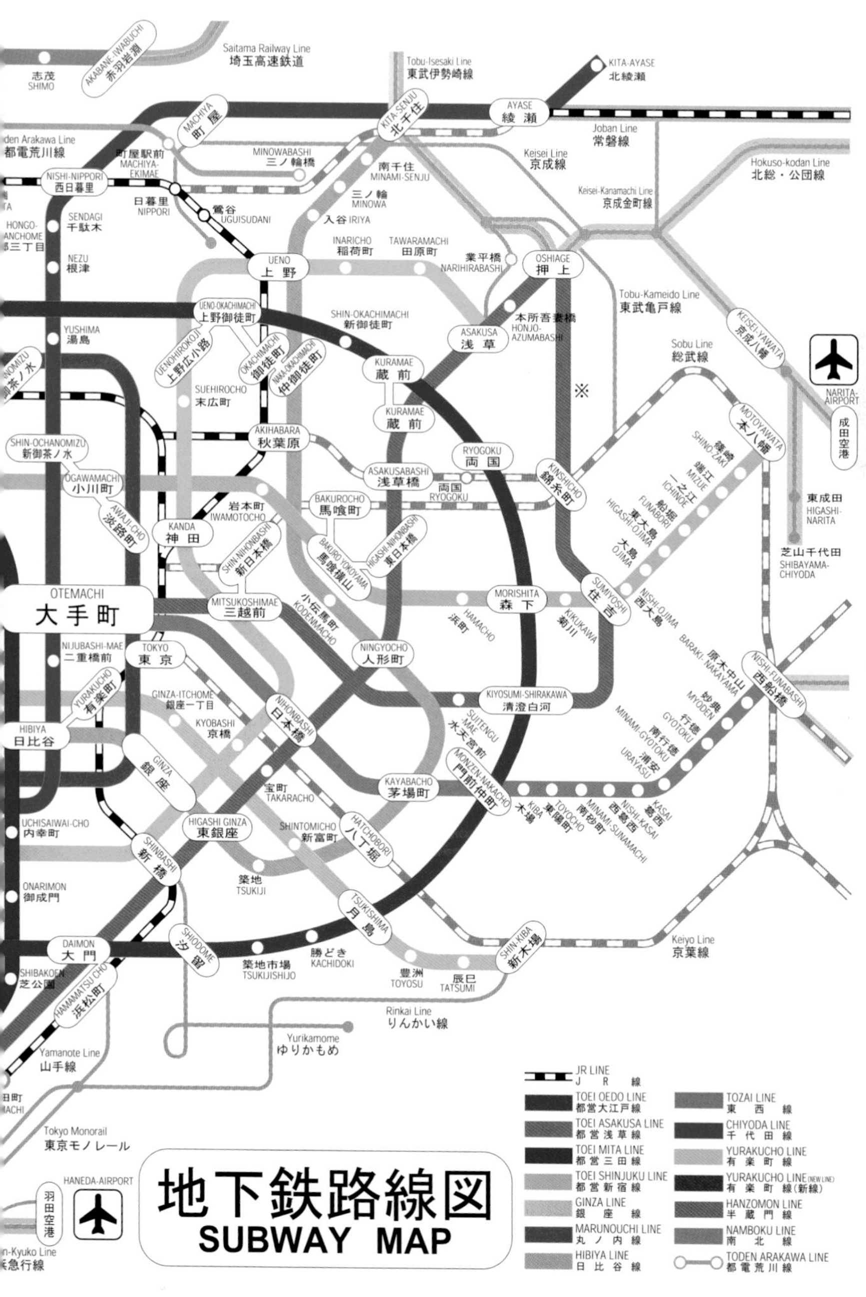
地下鉄路線図
SUBWAY MAP
Saitama Railway Line
埼玉高速鉄道
Tobu-Isesaki Line
東武伊勢崎線
KITA-AYASE
北綾瀬
AYASE
綾 瀬
Joban Line
常磐線
Keisei Line
京成線
Hokuso-kodan Line
北総・公団線
Keisei-Kanamachi Line
京成金町線
Tobu-Kameido Line
東武亀戸線
Sobu Line
総武線
Keiyo Line
京葉線
Rinkai Line
りんかい線
Yurikamome
ゆりかもめ
Yamanote Line
山手線
Tokyo Monorail
東京モノレール
志茂
SHIMO
AKABANE-IWABUCHI
赤羽岩淵
MACHIYA
町 屋
KITA-SENJU
北千住
町屋駅前
MACHIYA-EKIMAE
MINOWABASHI
三ノ輪橋
南千住
MINAMI-SENJU
三ノ輪
MINOWA
入谷 IRIYA
NISHI-NIPPORI
西日暮里
日暮里
NIPPORI
鶯谷
UGUISUDANI
SENDAGI
千駄木
NEZU
根津
UENO
上 野
INARICHO
稲荷町
TAWARAMACHI
田原町
業平橋
NARIHIRABASHI
OSHIAGE
押 上
UENO-OKACHIMACHI
上野御徒町
UENOHIROKOJI
上野広小路
OKACHIMACHI
御徒町
NAKA-OKACHIMACHI
仲御徒町
SHIN-OKACHIMACHI
新御徒町
本所吾妻橋
HONJO-AZUMABASHI
ASAKUSA
浅 草
YUSHIMA
湯島
KURAMAE
蔵 前
SUEHIROCHO
末広町
AKIHABARA
秋葉原
RYOGOKU
両 国
両国
ASAKUSABASHI
浅草橋
KINSHICHO
錦糸町
SHIN-OCHANOMIZU
新御茶ノ水
OGAWAMACHI
小川町
AWAJI-CHO
淡路町
岩本町
IWAMOTOCHO
BAKUROCHO
馬喰町
KANDA
神 田
SHIN-NIHONBASHI
新日本橋
BAKURO-YOKOYAMA
馬喰横山
HIGASHI-NIHONBASHI
東日本橋
OTEMACHI
大手町
MITSUKOSHIMAE
三越前
小伝馬町
KODENMACHO
MORISHITA
森 下
SUMIYOSHI
住吉
KIKUKAWA
菊川
HAMACHO
浜町
NINGYOCHO
人形町
NIJUBASHI-MAE
二重橋前
TOKYO
東 京
YURAKUCHO
有楽町
GINZA-ITCHOME
銀座一丁目
KYOBASHI
京橋
NIHONBASHI
日本橋
KIYOSUMI-SHIRAKAWA
清澄白河
SUITENGU-MAE
水天宮前
HIBIYA
日比谷
GINZA
銀 座
宝町
TAKARACHO
KAYABACHO
茅場町
MONZEN-NAKACHO
門前仲町
KIBA
木場
TOYOCHO
東陽町
MINAMI-SUNAMACHI
南砂町
NISHI-KASAI
西葛西
KASAI
葛西
UCHISAIWAI-CHO
内幸町
HIGASHI GINZA
東銀座
SHINTOMICHO
新富町
HATCHOBORI
八丁堀
SHINBASHI
新 橋
ONARIMON
御成門
築地
TSUKIJI
TSUKISHIMA
月 島
SHIN-KIBA
新木場
DAIMON
大 門
SHIODOME
汐 留
築地市場
TSUKIJISHIJO
勝どき
KACHIDOKI
豊洲
TOYOSU
辰巳
TATSUMI
SHIBAKOEN
芝公園
HAMAMATSU-CHO
浜松町
HANEDA-AIRPORT
羽田空港
KEISEI-YAWATA
京成八幡
MOTOYAWATA
本八幡
NARITA-AIRPORT
成田空港
SHINOZAKI
篠崎
MIZUE
瑞江
ICHINOE
一之江
FUNABORI
船堀
HIGASHI-OJIMA
東大島
OJIMA
大島
NISHI-OJIMA
西大島
東成田
HIGASHI-NARITA
芝山千代田
SHIBAYAMA-CHIYODA
BARAKI-NAKAYAMA
原木中山
NISHI-FUNABASHI
西船橋
MYODEN
妙典
GYOTOKU
行徳
MINAMI-GYOTOKU
南行徳
URAYASU
浦安
JR LINE
J R 線
TOEI OEDO LINE
都営大江戸線
TOEI ASAKUSA LINE
都営浅草線
TOEI MITA LINE
都営三田線
TOEI SHINJUKU LINE
都営新宿線
GINZA LINE
銀座線
MARUNOUCHI LINE
丸ノ内線
HIBIYA LINE
日比谷線
TOZAI LINE
東西線
CHIYODA LINE
千代田線
YURAKUCHO LINE
有楽町線
YURAKUCHO LINE (NEW LINE)
有楽町線(新線)
HANZOMON LINE
半蔵門線
NAMBOKU LINE
南北線
TODEN ARAKAWA LINE
都電荒川線

See Ikebukuro & Takadanobaba Map (p280)
See Shinjuku Map (p282)
See Kanda, Tokyo Station Area & Imperial Palace Map (pp294-5)
See Shibuya & Omote-sandō Map (p284)
See Roppongi Map (p286)
See Akasaka, Ginza, Tsukiji & Shiodome Map (pp290-1)
See Ebisu & Meguro Map (p288)
To East West Japaness Institute (1.5km); Kyūmeikan (8.5km)
To International Yoga Centre (3km)
To Mandarake (1.5km); Kōenji (3.5km); Ghibli Museum(10km); Mt Takao (45km)
To Tokyo Keibajō (16km)
To Suzunari Theatre (500m)
To Mingei Museum (1.5km)
To Setagaya Public Theatre (2km)
To Hara Museum (500m)
To Tama River (8.5km)
Ikebukuro
Takadanobaba
Waseda
Shinjuku
Shibuya
Ebisu
Meguro
Gotanda
Shinagawa
Tamachi
Hamamatsuchō
Shimbashi
Tokyo
Kanda
Suidōbashi
Ochanomizu
Sugamo
Komagome
Tabata
Koishikawa Botanical Garden
Fukiage Imperial Gardens
Shinjuku-gyōen
Meiji-jingū Gyōen
Shinjuku-ku 新宿区
Bunkyō-ku 文京区
Chiyoda-ku 千代田区
Shibuya-ku 渋谷区
Minato-ku 港区
Meguro-ku 中目黒
Shinagawa-ku 品川区
Toshima-ku 豊島区
Kita-ku 北区
Tokyo Bay 東京湾
Rainbow Bridge
Daiba-kōen
See Odaiba/Tokyo Bay Area Map

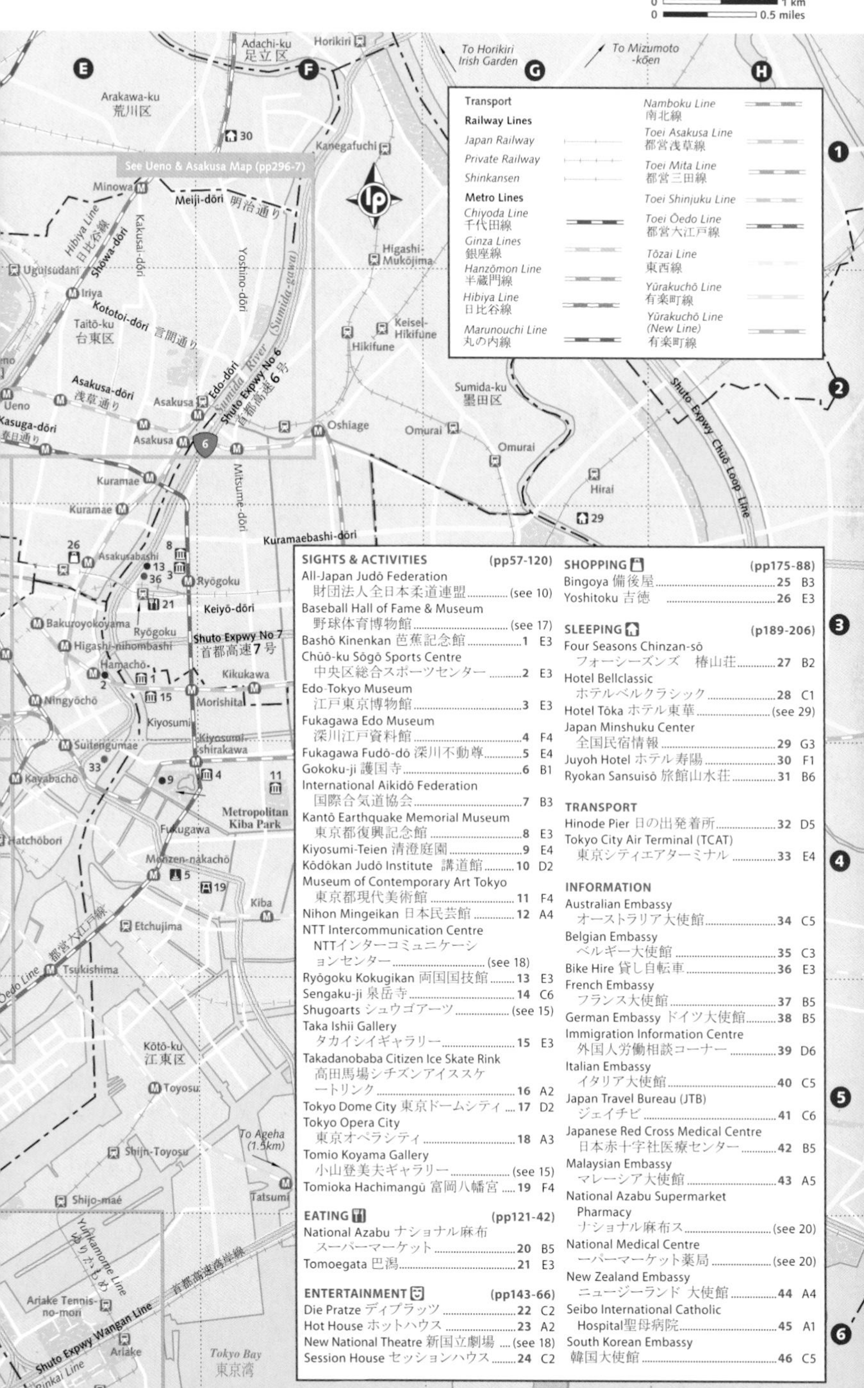

0 1 km
0 0.5 miles
Transport
Railway Lines
Japan Railway
Private Railway
Shinkansen
Metro Lines
Chiyoda Line 千代田線
Ginza Lines 銀座線
Hanzōmon Line 半蔵門線
Hibiya Line 日比谷線
Marunouchi Line 丸の内線
Namboku Line 南北線
Toei Asakusa Line 都営浅草線
Toei Mita Line 都営三田線
Toei Shinjuku Line
Toei Ōedo Line 都営大江戸線
Tōzai Line 東西線
Yūrakuchō Line 有楽町線
Yūrakuchō Line (New Line) 有楽町線
See Ueno & Asakusa Map (pp296-7)
Adachi-ku 足立区
Arakawa-ku 荒川区
Taitō-ku 台東区
Sumida-ku 墨田区
Kōtō-ku 江東区
To Horikiri Irish Garden
To Mizumoto -kōen
To Ageha (1.5km)
Sumida River (Sumida-gawa)
Tokyo Bay 東京湾
Metropolitan Kiba Park
SIGHTS & ACTIVITIES (pp57-120)
All-Japan Judō Federation 財団法人全日本柔道連盟 (see 10)
Baseball Hall of Fame & Museum 野球体育博物館 (see 17)
Bashō Kinenkan 芭蕉記念館 1 E3
Chūō-ku Sōgō Sports Centre 中央区総合スポーツセンター 2 E3
Edo-Tokyo Museum 江戸東京博物館 3 E3
Fukagawa Edo Museum 深川江戸資料館 4 F4
Fukagawa Fudō-dō 深川不動尊 5 E4
Gokoku-ji 護国寺 6 B1
International Aikidō Federation 国際合気道協会 7 B3
Kantō Earthquake Memorial Museum 東京都復興記念館 8 E3
Kiyosumi-Teien 清澄庭園 9 E4
Kōdōkan Judō Institute 講道館 10 D2
Museum of Contemporary Art Tokyo 東京都現代美術館 11 F4
Nihon Mingeikan 日本民芸館 12 A4
NTT Intercommunication Centre NTTインターコミュニケーションセンター (see 18)
Ryōgoku Kokugikan 両国国技館 13 E3
Sengaku-ji 泉岳寺 14 C6
Shugoarts シュウゴアーツ (see 15)
Taka Ishii Gallery タカイシイギャラリー 15 E3
Takadanobaba Citizen Ice Skate Rink 高田馬場シチズンアイススケートリンク 16 A2
Tokyo Dome City 東京ドームシティ 17 D2
Tokyo Opera City 東京オペラシティ 18 A3
Tomio Koyama Gallery 小山登美夫ギャラリー (see 15)
Tomioka Hachimangū 富岡八幡宮 19 F4
EATING (pp121-42)
National Azabu ナショナル麻布スーパーマーケット 20 B5
Tomoegata 巴潟 21 E3
ENTERTAINMENT (pp143-66)
Die Pratze ディプラッツ 22 C2
Hot House ホットハウス 23 A2
New National Theatre 新国立劇場 (see 18)
Session House セッションハウス 24 C2
SHOPPING (pp175-88)
Bingoya 備後屋 25 B3
Yoshitoku 吉徳 26 E3
SLEEPING (p189-206)
Four Seasons Chinzan-sō フォーシーズンズ 椿山荘 27 B2
Hotel Bellclassic ホテルベルクラシック 28 C1
Hotel Tōka ホテル東華 (see 29)
Japan Minshuku Center 全国民宿情報 29 G3
Juyoh Hotel ホテル寿陽 30 F1
Ryokan Sansuisō 旅館山水荘 31 B6
TRANSPORT
Hinode Pier 日の出発着所 32 D5
Tokyo City Air Terminal (TCAT) 東京シティエアターミナル 33 E4
INFORMATION
Australian Embassy オーストラリア大使館 34 C5
Belgian Embassy ベルギー大使館 35 C3
Bike Hire 貸し自転車 36 E3
French Embassy フランス大使館 37 B5
German Embassy ドイツ大使館 38 B5
Immigration Information Centre 外国人労働相談コーナー 39 D6
Italian Embassy イタリア大使館 40 C5
Japan Travel Bureau (JTB) ジェイチビ 41 C6
Japanese Red Cross Medical Centre 日本赤十字社医療センター 42 B5
Malaysian Embassy マレーシア大使館 43 A5
National Azabu Supermarket Pharmacy ナショナル麻布スーパーマーケット薬局 (see 20)
National Medical Centre (see 20)
New Zealand Embassy ニュージーランド 大使館 44 A4
Seibo International Catholic Hospital聖母病院 45 A1
South Korean Embassy 韓国大使館 46 C5

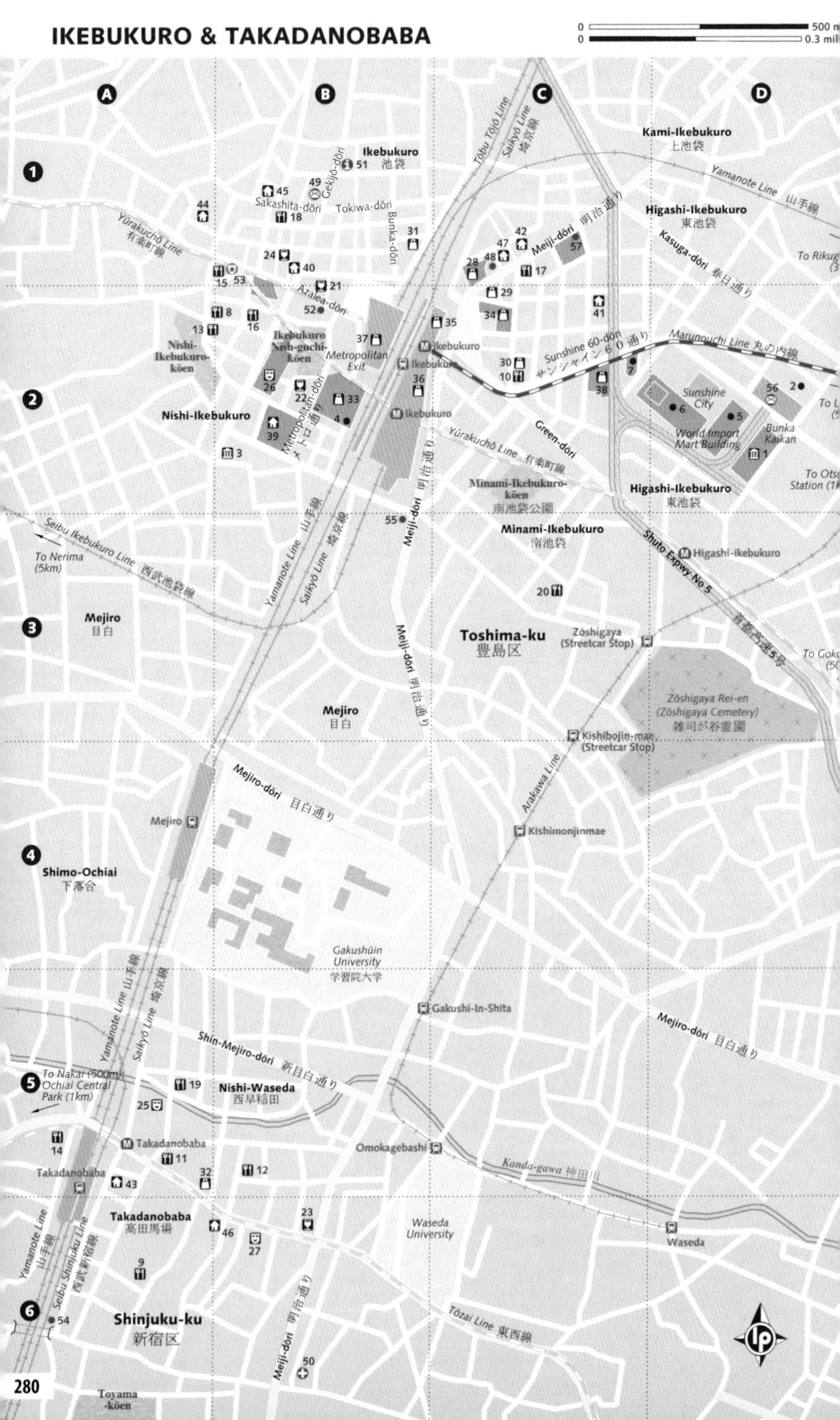
IKEBUKURO & TAKADANOBABA
0 500 m
0 0.3 miles
Ikebukuro
池袋
Kami-Ikebukuro
上池袋
Higashi-Ikebukuro
東池袋
Nishi-Ikebukuro
Nishi-Ikebukuro-kōen
Ikebukuro Nishi-guchi-kōen
Metropolitan Exit
Minami-Ikebukuro-kōen
南池袋公園
Minami-Ikebukuro
南池袋
Sunshine City
World Import Mart Building
Bunka Kaikan
Toshima-ku
豊島区
Mejiro
目白
Shimo-Ochiai
下落合
Zōshigaya (Streetcar Stop)
Zōshigaya Rei-en (Zōshigaya Cemetery)
雑司が谷霊園
Kishibojin-mae (Streetcar Stop)
Kishimonjinmae
Gakushūin University
学習院大学
Gakushi-In-Shita
Nishi-Waseda
西早稲田
Takadanobaba
高田馬場
Omokagebashi
Waseda University
Waseda
Shinjuku-ku
新宿区
Toyama-kōen
Tōbu Tōjō Line
Saikyō Line 埼京線
Yamanote Line 山手線
Yūrakuchō Line 有楽町線
Marunouchi Line 丸の内線
Seibu Ikebukuro Line 西武池袋線
Seibu Shinjuku Line 西武新宿線
Arakawa Line
Tōzai Line 東西線
Shuto Expwy No 5 首都高速5号
Meiji-dōri 明治通り
Sunshine 60-dōri サンシャイン60通り
Kasuga-dōri 春日通り
Green-dōri
Gekijō-dōri
Sakashita-dōri
Tokiwa-dōri
Bunka-dōri
Azalea-dōri
Metropolitan-dōri メトロ通り
Mejiro-dōri 目白通り
Shin-Mejiro-dōri 新目白通り
Kanda-gawa 神田川
To Nerima (5km)
To Nakai (500m); Ochiai Central Park (1km)
To Rikug
To Otsu Station
To Gokoku
To Toden

IKEBUKURO & TAKADANOBABA

SIGHTS & ACTIVITIES (pp57-120)
Ancient Orient Museum 古代オリエント博物館 1 D2
Cup Ice Museum カップアイス博物館 .... (see 5)
Ice Cream City アイスクリームシティー .... (see 5)
Ikebukuro Bōsai-kan 池袋防災館 2 D2
Ikebukuro Bōsai-kan 池袋防災館 3 B2
Japan Traditional Craft Center 全国伝統的工芸品センター 4 B2
Namco Namjatown ナムコなんじゃタウン 5 D2
Sunshine 60 サンシャイン６０ .... (see 6)
Sunshine City サンシャインシティ展望台 6 D2
Sunshine International Aquarium サンシャイン国際水族館 .... (see 6)
Sunshine Starlight Dome サンシャインスターライトドーム .... (see 5)
Tokyo Chou Crème Hatake 東京シュークリーム畑 .... (see 5)
Toyota Amlux トヨタアムラックス 7 C2

EATING (pp121-42)
Akiyoshi 秋吉 8 B2
Ben's Café ベンズカフェ 9 A6
Hikarichō Rāmen Meisakuza ひかりちょうラーメンめさくざ 10 C2
Ikebukuro Gyōza Stadium 餃子スタディアム .... (see 5)
Kao Thai カオ·タイ 11 A5
La Dinette ラディネット 12 B5
Malaychan マレーチャン 13 A2
Marmara ママラ 14 A5
Myun ミュン 15 B1
Ootoya 大戸屋 16 B2
Saigon サイゴン 17 C1
Sushi Kazu 寿司和 18 B1
Taverna タベルナ 19 A5
Tonchin 屯ちん 20 C3

DRINKING (pp143-66)
Bobby's Bar ボビーズバー 21 B2
Dubliners ザダブリナーズ 22 B2
Fiddler ザフィドラー 23 B6
Sasashū 笹周 24 B1

ENTERTAINMENT (pp143-66)
Jazz Spot Intro ジャズズポットイントロ 25 A5
Tokyo Metropolitan Art Space 東京芸術劇場 26 B2
Waseda Shochiku 早稲田松竹 27 B6

SHOPPING (pp175-88)
Bic Camera (Main Store) ビックカメラ本店 28 C1
Bic Camera PC Store ビックカメラＰＣストア 29 C2
Bic Camera ビックカメラ 30 C2
Bic Camera ビックカメラ 31 B1
Blue Parrot ブルーパロット 32 A5
HMV エイチエムヴィー 33 B2
Loft ロフト .... (see 36)
Mitsukoshi 三越 34 C2
Parco パルコ 35 C2
Seibu 西武 36 B2
Tōbu 東武 37 B2
Tōkyū Hands 東急ハンズ 38 C2

SLEEPING (pp189-206)
Crowne Plaza Metropolitan Hotel ホテルメトロポリタン 39 B2
Hotel Clarion Tokyo ホテルクラリオン東京 40 B1
Hotel Grand City ホテルグランドシティ 41 C2
Hotel Sunroute Ikebukuro ホテルサンルート池袋 42 C1
Hotel Sunroute Takadanobaba ホテルサンルート高田馬場 43 A5
House Ikebukuro ハウス池袋 44 A1
Kimi Ryokan 貴美旅館 45 B1
Tama Ryokan 多摩旅館 46 B6
Toyoko Inn 東横イン 47 C1

INFORMATION
Across Traveller's Bureau アクロストラベル 48 C1
Ikebukuro Post Office 池袋郵便局 49 B1
International Medical Center of Japan 国立国際医療センター 50 B6
Kimi Information Center 貴美インフォメーションセンター 51 B1
No 1 Travel ナンバーワントラベル 52 B2
Police 警察署 53 B1
Sendagaya Japanese Institute 千駄ヶ谷日本語教育研究所 54 A6
STA Travel エスティーエートラベル 55 B3
Toshima Post Office 豊島郵便局 56 D2
Toshima-ku Ward Office 豊島区役所 57 C1

TOKYO WARDS (KU)

0 — 12 km
0 — 7 miles

SAITAMA-KEN
CHIBA-KEN
KANAGAWA-KEN
Arakawa
Edogawa
Tamagawa
Sumida River (Sumida-gawa)
Ikebukuro
Ueno
Shinjuku
Tokyo
Tokyo Bay 東京湾

NFORMATION
ta-ku大田区 1 C3
dachi-ku足立区 2 C1
rakawa-ku荒川区 3 C1
unkyō-ku文京区 4 C2
hūō-ku中央区 5 C2
hiyoda-ku千代田区 6 C2
dogawa-ku江戸川区 7 D2
abashi-ku板橋区 8 C1
ōtō-ku 江東区 9 D2
atsushika-ku葛飾区 10 D1
ita-ku北区 11 C1
eguro-ku目黒区 12 B2
inato-ku港区 13 C2
akano-ku中野区 14 C2
erima-ku練馬区 15 B1
etagaya-ku世田谷区 16 C2
hibuya-ku渋谷区 17 C2
hinagawa-ku品川区 18 C2
hinjuku-ku新宿区 19 C2
uginami-ku杉並区 20 B2
umida-ku墨田区 21 D2
aitō-ku台東区 22 C2
oshima-ku豊島533A 23 C1

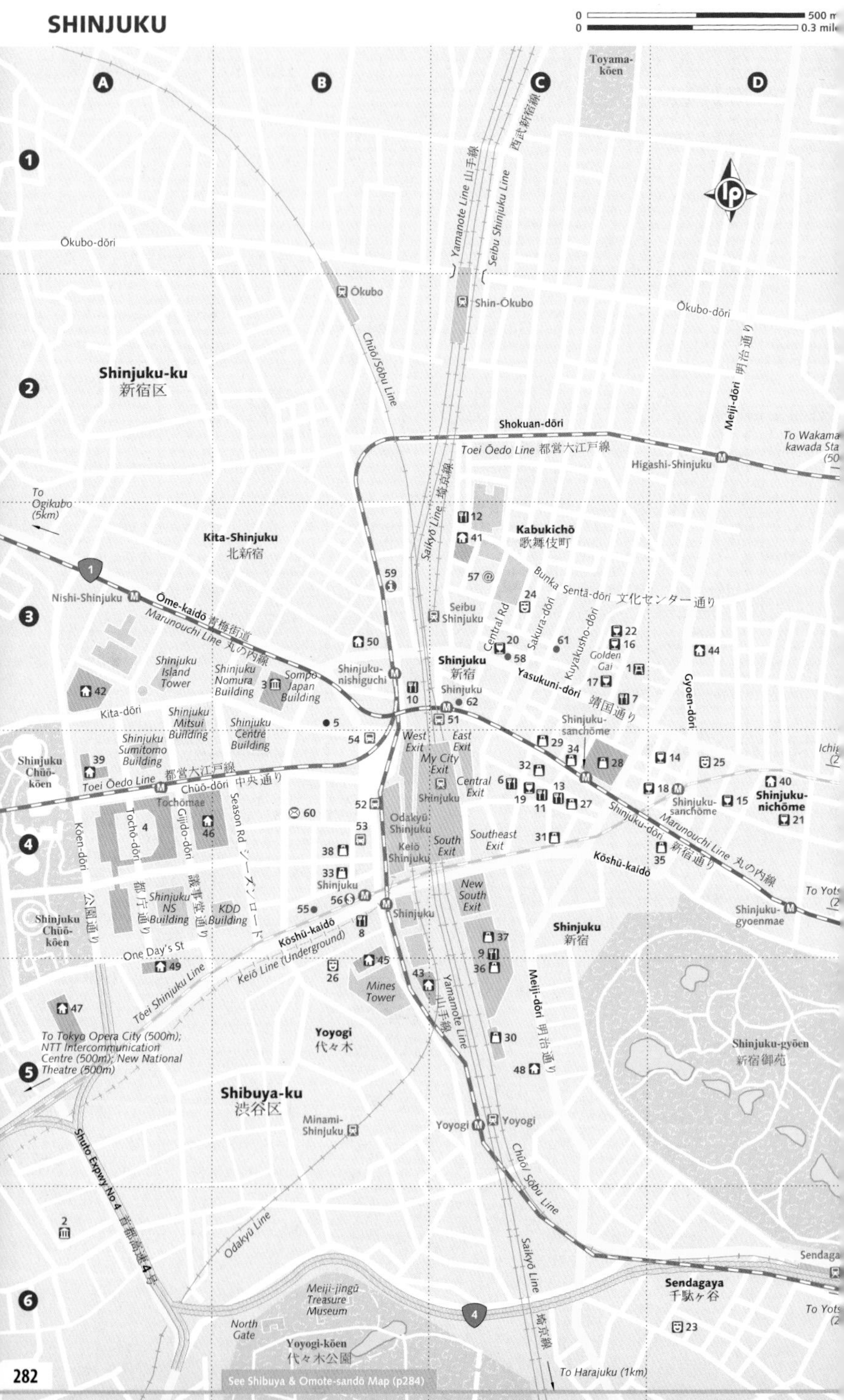

See Shibuya & Omote-sandō Map (p284)

SHINJUKU

SIGHTS & ACTIVITIES **(pp57-120)**
Hanazono-jinja 花園神社 **1** C3
Japanese Sword Museum
刀剣博物館 **2** A6
Sompo Japan Museum of Art
損保ジャパン東郷青児
美術館 **3** B3
Tokyo Metropolitan Government
Offices 東京都庁 **4** A4
Toto Superspace 新宿Lタワー
(TOTOスーパースペース) **5** B3

EATING **(pp121-42)**
Capricciosa カプリチョーザ **6** C4
Christon Café クリストンカフェ **7** C3
Court Lodge コートロッジ **8** B4
Imahan 今半 **9** C4
New York Grill
ニューヨークグリル ....(see 47)
Omoide-yokochō 思い出横丁 **10** B3
Raj Mahal ラジマハル **11** C4
Shinjuku Negishi 新宿根岸 **12** C3
Tsunahachi つな八 **13** C4

DRINKING **(pp143-66)**
Advocates Bar
アドヴォケッツバー **14** D4
Arty Farty
アーティファーティ **15** D4
Aurora Lounge
オーロララウンジ .... (see 46)
Bar Plastic Model バープラスチックモ
デル **16** C3
Bon's ボンズ **17** C3
Clubhouse クラブハウス **18** D4
Dubliners ダブリナーズ **19** C4
Garam ガラム **20** C3
Kinswomyn キンズウミン **21** D4
La Jetée ラジェッテイ **22** C3
New York Bar
ニューヨークバー ....(see 47)
Sky Bar Polestar
スカイバーポールスター ....(see 46)

ENTERTAINMENT **(pp143-66)**
Kokuritsu Nō-Gakudō
(National Nō Theatre)
国立能学堂 **23** D6
Loft ロフト **24** C3
Shinjuku Pit Inn 新宿PIT INN **25** D4
Space Zero スペースゼロ **26** B5

SHOPPING **(pp175-88)**
Disk Union ディスクユニオン **27** C4
Hanazono-jinja Flea Market
花園神社フリーマーケット ....(see 1)
Isetan 伊勢丹 **28** C4
Kinokuniya 紀伊国屋書店 **29** C4
Kinokuniya 紀伊国屋書店 **30** C5
Mitsukoshi (New Branch)
三越（新店） **31** C4
Mitsukoshi (South Building)
三越南館 **32** C4
Sakuraya Camera
カメラのサクラヤ **33** B4
Sakuraya Camera
カメラのサクラヤ **34** C4
Sekaidō 世界堂 **35** D4
Tōkyū Hands 東急ハンズ **36** C5
Takashimaya Times Square
高島屋タイムズスクエア **37** C4
Yodobashi Camera
ヨドバシカメラ **38** B4

SLEEPING **(pp189-206)**
Century Hyatt Tokyo センチ
ュリー ハイアット東京 **39** A4
City Hotel Lornstar
シティーホテルロンスター **40** D4
Green Plaza Shinjuku
グリーンプラザ新宿 **41** C3
Hilton Tokyo ヒルトン東京 **42** A3
Hotel Century Southern Tower
ホテルセンチュリー サザン
タワー **43** B5
Hotel Sunllight Shinjuku
ホテルサンライト新宿 **44** D3
Hotel Sunroute Tokyo
ホテルサンルート東京 **45** B5
Keiō Plaza Hotel
京王プラザホテル **46** A4
Park Hyatt Tokyo
パークハイアット東京 **47** A5
Shinjuku Park Hotel
新宿パークホテル **48** C5
Shinjuku Washington Hotel
新宿ワシントンホテル **49** A5
Star Hotel スターホテル **50** B3

TRANSPORT
Haneda Limousine Bus Stop
羽田リムジンバス乗り場 ....(see 53)
Haneda Limousine Bus Stop
羽田リムジンバス停 ....(see 53)
Hato Bus Stop
はとバス乗り場 **51** C3
Keiō Kōsoku Bus
京王高速バス ....(see 54)
Narita Limousine Bus Stop
成田リムジンバス停 **52** B4
Shinjuku Highway Bus Terminal
新宿高速バスターミナル **53** B4
Shinjuku Main City Bus Stop
新宿西口バスターミナル **54** B4

INFORMATION
Across Traveller's Bureau
アクロストラベル **55** B4
Citibank シティバンク **56** B4
Manga@Cafe-Gera Gera
マンガカフェゲラゲラ **57** C3
No 1 Travel
ナンバーワントラベル **58** C3
Sakura House サクラハウス **59** B3
Shinjuku Main Post Office
新宿中央郵便局 **60** B4
Shinjuku Ward Office
新宿区役所 **61** C3
Studio Alta Building
スタジオアルタ **62** C3

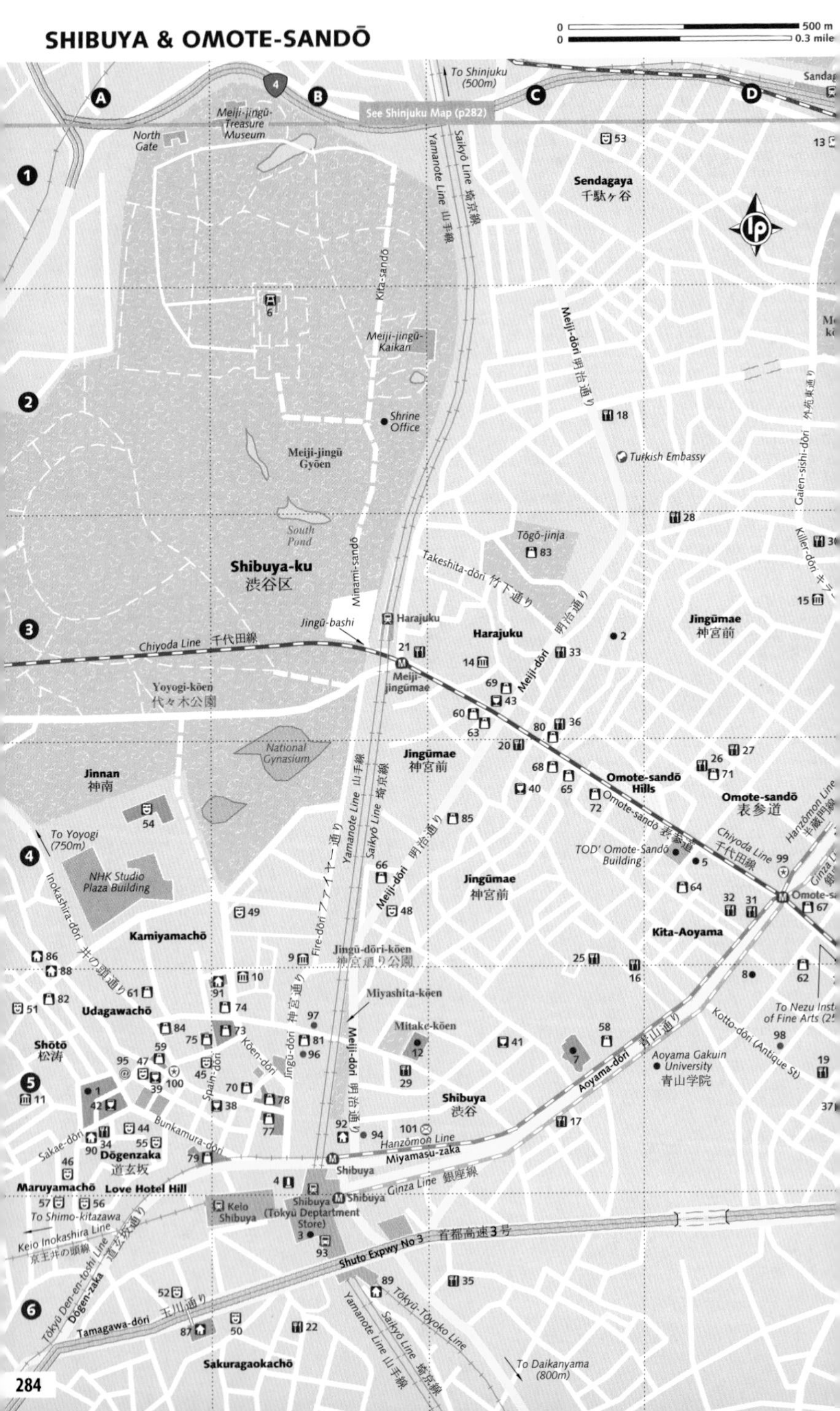
0 500 m
0 0.3 miles
To Shinjuku (500m)
See Shinjuku Map (p282)
Meiji-jingū Treasure Museum
North Gate
Sendagaya
千駄ヶ谷
Saikyō Line 埼京線
Yamanote Line 山手線
Kita-sandō
Meiji-jingū Kaikan
Shrine Office
Meiji-jingū Gyōen
South Pond
Shibuya-ku
渋谷区
Minami-sandō
Meiji-dōri 明治通り
Turkish Embassy
Tōgō-jinja
Takeshita-dōri 竹下通り
Gaien-nishi-dōri 外苑西通り
Killer-dōri
Harajuku
Jingū-bashi
Chiyoda Line 千代田線
Meiji-jingūmae
Jingūmae
神宮前
Yoyogi-kōen
代々木公園
National Gymnasium
Jinnan
神南
Omote-sandō Hills
Omote-sandō
表参道
Omote-sandō 表参道
TOD' Omote-Sandō Building
Hanzōmon Line 半蔵門線
Ginza Line 銀座線
To Yoyogi (750m)
NHK Studio Plaza Building
Inokashira-dōri 井の頭通り
Fire-dōri ファイヤー通り
Kamiyamachō
Kita-Aoyama
Jingū-dōri-kōen
神宮通り公園
Miyashita-kōen
Mitake-kōen
To Nezu Institute of Fine Arts
Udagawachō
Shōtō
松涛
Kōen-dōri
Spain-dōri
Jingū-dōri 神宮通り
Aoyama-dōri 青山通り
Kotto-dōri (Antique St)
Aoyama Gakuin University
青山学院
Shibuya
渋谷
Sakae-dōri
Bunkamura-dōri
Dōgenzaka
道玄坂
Hanzōmon Line
Miyamasu-zaka
Maruyamachō
Love Hotel Hill
Keio Shibuya
Shibuya (Tokyū Deptartment Store)
To Shimo-kitazawa
Keio Inokashira Line
京王井の頭線
Shuto Expwy No 3 首都高速3号
Tōkyū Den-en-toshi Line
Dōgen-zaka 道玄坂通り
Tamagawa-dōri 玉川通り
Tōkyū-Tōyoko Line
Yamanote Line 山手線
Saikyō Line 埼京線
To Daikanyama (800m)
Sakuragaokachō

SHIBUYA & OMOTE-SANDO

SIGHTS & ACTIVITIES (pp57-120)

- Bunkamura 文化村 ... 1 A5
- Design Festa デザイン·フェスタ ... 2 C3
- Eight Rent エイトレント ... 3 B6
- Hachikō the Dog Statue 八千公像 ... 4 B5
- Hanae Mori Building ハナエモリビル ... 5 D4
- Meiji-jingū 明治神宮 ... 6 B2
- National Children's Castle こどもの城 ... 7 C5
- On Sundaysオンサンデーズ ... (see 15)
- Spiral Building スパイラルビル ... 8 D5
- Tepco Electric Energy Museum 電力館 ... 9 B4
- Tobacco & Salt Museum たばこと塩の博物館 ... 10 B5
- Toguri Museum of Art 戸栗美術館 ... 11 A5
- Tokyo Metropolitan Children's Hall 東京都児童会館 ... 12 B5
- Tokyo Metropolitan Gymnasium Indoor Pool 東京体育館 プール ... 13 D1
- Ukiyo-e Ota Memorial Art Museum 浮世絵大田記念美術館 ... 14 C3
- Watari-um (Watari Museum of Contemporary Art) ワタリウム美術館 ... 15 D3

EATING (pp121-42)

- Cam Chien Grippe カム·シャン·グリッペ ... 16 C5
- El Castellano エルカステリャーノ ... 17 C5
- Fonda de la Madrugada フォンダ·デ·ラ·マドルガダ ... 18 C2
- Fu-min フミン ... 19 D5
- Fujimamas フジママス ... 20 C4
- Hiroba 広場 ... (see 64)
- Home ホーム ... (see 64)
- Jangara Rāmen じゃんがらラーメン ... 21 B3
- Kantipur カンティプール ... 22 B6
- Kinokuniya Interim Store 紀ノ国屋 ... 23 D4
- Kinokuniya International Supermarket 紀ノ国屋 ... 24 D4
- Las Chicas ラスチカス ... 25 C4
- Le Bretagne ル·ブルターニュ ... 26 D4
- Maisen まい泉 ... 27 D4
- Mominoki House モミノキハウス ... 28 D3
- Myōkō 妙高 ... 29 B5
- Natural Harmony Angolo ナチュラルハーモニーアンゴロ ... 30 D3
- Natural House 紀ノ国屋 ... 31 D4
- News Deli ニューズデリ ... 32 D4
- Pampkin Cook Katsura パンプキンクックカツラ ... 33 C3
- Sakana-tei 酒菜亭 ... 34 A5
- Shizenkan II 自然館 ... 35 C6
- Sonoma ソノマ ... (see 55)
- Spyro's スピロス ... 36 C3

DRINKING (pp143-66)

- Bello Visto ベロビスト ... (see 87)
- Bunkamura Theatre Cocoon 文化村シアターコクーン ... (see 1)
- Den Aquaroom デンアクアルーム ... 37 D5
- Hub Pub ハブパブ ... 38 B5
- Insomnia 2インソムニア ... 39 A5
- Oh God オーガッド ... 40 C4
- Pink Cow ... 41 C5
- Shibuya Tōkyū Honten 渋谷東急本店 ... 42 A5
- Tokyo Apartment Café 東京アパートメントカフェ ... 43 C3

ENTERTAINMENT (pp143-66)

- Aoyama Enkei Gekijō 青山円形劇場 ... (see 7)
- Cerulean Tower Nō Theatre セルリアンタワー能楽堂 ... (see 87)
- Cine Amuse East/West シネアミューズ ... 44 A5
- Cinema Riseシネマライズ ... 45 A5
- Club Asia クラブアジア ... 46 A5
- Club Quattro クラブクアトロ ... 47 A5
- Crocodile クロコダイル ... 48 B4
- Eggman エッグマン ... 49 B4
- Eurospace ユーロスペース ... 50 B6
- JZ Brat ジェイゼットブラット ... (see 87)
- Kanze Nō-gakudō (Kanze Nō Theatre) 観世能楽堂 ... 51 A5
- La mama ラママ ... 52 A6
- National Nō Theatre (Kokuritsu Nōgakudō) 国立能学堂 ... 53 C1
- NHK Hall NHKホール ... 54 A4
- Ruby Room ルビルーム ... 55 A5
- Shibuya O-East オンエアーイースト ... 56 A6
- Womb ウーム ... 57 A6

SHOPPING (pp175-88)

- Aoyama Oval Plaza Antique Market ┌山アンティ┌クマ┌ケット ... 58 C5
- Beam Building ビームビル ... 59 A5
- Chicago Thrift Store シカゴ ... 60 C3
- Cisco シスコ ... 61 A5
- Commes des Garçons コムデギャルソン ... 62 D5
- Condomania コンドマニア ... 63 C3
- Crayon House クレヨンハウス ... 64 D4
- Fuji-Torii ふじとりい ... 65 C4
- Hanae Mori Building Antique Market ハナエモリビル アンティーク通り ... (see 5)
- Hysteric Glamour ヒステリックグラモー ... 66 B4
- Issey Miyake 三宅一生 ... 67 D4
- Kiddyland キディーランド ... 68 C4
- Laforet Building ラフォーレビル ... 69 C3
- Loft ロフト ... 70 B5
- Mandarakeまんだらけ ... (see 59)
- NADiff ナディフ ... 71 D4
- Oriental Bazaar オリエンタルバザール ... 72 C4
- Parco I パルコパート1 ... 73 B5
- Parco II パルコパート2 ... 74 B5
- Parco III パルコパート3 ... 75 A5
- Prada Aoyamaプラダ青山 ... 76 D5
- Seibu (A Building) 西武（A館） ... 77 B5
- Seibu (Main Building) 西武（本店） ... 78 B5
- Shibuya 109 渋谷１０９ ... 79 A5
- Shiseido Cosmetics Garden 資生堂コスメティックガーデン ... 80 C3
- Spiral Records スパイラルレコード ... (see 8)
- Tower Records タワーレコード ... 81 B5
- Tsutsumu Factory 包む工房 ... 82 A5
- Tōgō-jinja Fine Arts Market 東郷神社骨董市 ... 83 C3
- Tōkyū Hands 東急ハンズ ... 84 A5
- Uniqlo ユニクロ ... 85 C4

SLEEPING (pp189-206)

- Arimax Hotel アリマックスホテル ... 86 A4
- Cerulean Tower Tōkyū Hotel セルリアンタワー東急ホテル ... 87 A6
- Children's Castle Hotel 子供の城ホテル ... (see 7)
- Creston Hotel クレストンホテル ... 88 A5
- Hotel Mets Shibuya ... 89 B6
- Shibuya City Hotel 渋谷シティホテル ... 90 A5
- Shibuya Tōbu Hotel 渋谷東武ホテル ... 91 B5
- Shibuya Tōkyū Inn 渋谷東急イン ... 92 B5

TRANSPORT

- Shibuya Bus Terminal 渋谷バスターミナル ... 93 B6

INFORMATION

- Across Traveller's Bureau アクロストラベル ... 94 B5
- Café J Net New New カフェジェイネットニューニュー ... 95 A5
- HIS Travel HIS旅行代理店 ... 96 B5
- No 1 Travel ナンバーワントラベル ... 97 B5
- Ohara School of Ikebana 小原流いけばな ... 98 D5
- Police Box 交番 ... 99 D4
- Police Box 交番 ... 100 A5
- Shibuya Post Office 渋谷郵便局 ... 101 B5

ROPPONGI

0 500 m
0 0.3 miles
A
B
C
D
1
2
3
4
5
6
Shinjuku-ku
新宿区
Shinanomachi
Shuto Expwy No 4
首都高速4号
Kokuritsu-Kyōgijō
Gaien-higashi-dōri
外苑東通り
Jingū Gaien
神宮外苑
Jingū Kyūjo (Jingū Stadium)
Prince Chichibu Memorial Rugby Stadium
Ichō-Namiki
Nambоku Line
南北線
Marunouchi Line
丸ノ内線
Benkei Moat
Hanzōmon Line 半蔵門線
Aoyama-dōri 青山通り
Ginza Line 銀座線
Aoyama-itchōme
Gaienmae
Minato-ku
港区
Tokyo Broadcasting Station (TBS)
To Akasaka Metro Station
Akasaka-dōri
Toei Ōedo Line
都営大江戸線
Nogi-jinja
Aoyama Rei-en (Aoyama Cemetery)
青山霊園
Nogizaka
Hikawa-jinja
Roppongi
六本木
Minami-Aoyama
Chiyoda Line
千代田線
Aoyama-kōen
Sejiōki-dōri
Roppongi Crossing
To Roppongi Hills
Gaien-nishi-dōri
Roppongi Hills
Maman
TV Asahi
Keyaki-zaka
TV Asahi-dōri
Imoarai-zaka
Torii-zaka
To Tokyo Tower
Shuto Expwy No 3 首都高速3号
Roppongi-dōri 六本木通り
Hibiya Line 日比谷線
Nishi-Azabu
Moto-Azabu
Chinese Embassy
Singaporean Embassy
Azabu-Jūban
麻布十番
Austrian Embassy
Azabu-jūban
To Hiro-o Metro Station (500m)
See Shibuya & Omote-sandō Map (p284)

ROPPONGI

SIGHTS & ACTIVITIES (pp57-120)
Akasaka Detached Palace 迎賓館 1 C1
Azabu-jūban Onsen 麻布十番温泉 2 D6
Complex コンプレックス 3 D5
Jingū Baseball Stadium 明治神宮野球場 4 A2
Koshi-no-Yu Sentō 腰の湯銭湯 (see 2)
Meiji-jingū Ice Skating Rink 明治神宮アイススケート場 5 A1
Mori Art Museum 森美術館 6 C5
National Stadium 国立競技場 7 A1
Nezu Institute of Fine Arts 根津美術館 8 A5
Roppongi Hills 六本木ヒルズ 9 C5
Sōgetsu Kaikan 草月会館 10 C2
Sōgetsu School of Ikebana (see 10)
Tokyo City View 東京シティビュー (see 6)

EATING (pp121-42)
Asterix アステリクス 11 D3
Bikkuri Sushi びっくり寿司 12 D5
Bindi ビンディー 13 A6
Bistrot de la Cité ビストロ·ド·ラ·シテ 14 B6
Fukuzushi 福寿司 15 D5
Gino's ギノス 16 D5
Inakaya 田舎屋 (see 29)
Lilla Dalarna リルラダラマ 17 D5
Meidi-ya 明治屋 18 C5
Monsoon Café モンスーンカフェ 19 B5
Moti モティ 20 C5
Nobu 信 21 A6
Roppongi Hills 六本木ヒルズ (see 9)
Sicilia シシリヤ (see 52)

DRINKING (pp143-66)
Agave アガベ 22 C5
BuL-Lets ブレッツ 23 C5
Gas Panic Bar ガスパニックバー 24 D5
Motown House 1 & 2 モータウンハウス 25 D5
Paddy Foley's パディーフォーリーズ 26 D5
Propaganda プロパガンダ (see 12)
Tokyo Sports Café 東京スポーツカフェ 27 C5

ENTERTAINMENT (pp143-66)
Blue & White ブルアンドワイト (see 2)
Blue Note ブルーノート 28 A5
Cavern Club カバーンクラブ 29 D5
Club 328 さんにぱ３２８ 30 B5
Lexington Queen レキシントンクイーン 31 D5
Salsa Caribe サルサカリベ 32 D5
Salsa Sudada サルサスダダ 33 C5
Space Lab Yellow スペースラボイエロー 34 B5
Sweet Basil 139 (Stb139) スイートバジル１３９ 35 D5
Vanilla ヴァニラ 36 C5
Virgin Toho Cinemas Roppongi Hills ヴァージンTOHO シネマズ六本木ヒルズ (see 9)

SHOPPING (pp175-88)
Aoyama Book Centre 「山ブックセンタ「 37 C5
Book 246 ブック２４６ 38 C3
Don Quixote ドンキホーテ 39 D5
Muji 無地 40 C6
Nogi-jinja Flea Market 乃木神社フリーマーケット 41 C4
Roppongi Antique Fair 六本木アンティークフェア 42 D5
Roppongi Hills 六本木ヒルズ (see 9)
Tokyo Random Walk (Striped House) 東京ランダムウォーク ストライプハウス店) 43 D5
Undercover アンダーカバー 44 A5
Yohji Yamamoto 山本耀司 45 A5

SLEEPING (pp189-206)
Akasaka Yōkō Hotel 赤坂陽光ホテル 46 D3
Arca Torre アルカトーレ 47 D5
Asia Center of Japan アジア会館 48 C3
Grand Hyatt Tokyo グランドハイアット東京 49 C5
Hotel Ibis ホテルアイビス 50 D5
Hotel New Ōtani ホテルニューオータニ 51 D1

INFORMATION
Almond アーモンド 52 D5
Canadian Embassy カナダ大使館 53 C3
Citibank シティバンク 54 D5
Dai-ichi Kangin Bank 第一勧業銀行 55 C5
Manga Hiroba まんが広場 56 D5
Nishi-Azabu Post Office 西麻布郵便局 57 B5
Police Box 交番 58 D5

EBISU & MEGURO (p288)

SIGHTS & ACTIVITIES (pp57-120)
Beer Museum Yebisu 恵比寿麦酒記念館 1 D3
Daien-ji 大円寺 2 C6
Ebisu-jinja 恵比寿神社 3 B2
Meguro Gajoen 目黒雅叙園 4 C6
Meguro Museum of Art Tokyo 目黒区美術館 5 B5
Meguro Parasitological Museum 目黒寄生虫館 6 B6
Sapporo Breweries HQ サッポロビール本社 (see 1)
Shizen Kyōiku-en 自然教育園 7 D4
Tokyo Metropolitan Museum of Photography 東京都写真美術館 8 C4
Tokyo Metropolitan Teien Art Museum 東京庭園美術館 9 D5

EATING (pp121-42)
Bikkuri Sushi びっくり寿司 10 C2
Café Artifagose カフェアルトファゴス 11 A2
Caffé Michelangelo カフェミケランジェロ 12 A2
Good Honest Grub グッドオネストグラブ 13 C3
Ippūdō 一風堂らーめん 14 D2
Katsuyoshi かつ好 15 D4
Kazuki Rāmen 香月 16 B2
KM Fils カーエムフィス 17 B2
Monsoon モンスーンカフェ 18 C3
Mushroom マッシュルーム 19 B2
Nanaki Soba なな樹そば 20 B2
Tonki とんき 21 D6

DRINKING (pp143-66)
Footnik フットツニック (see 28)
Space Punch スペーイスパンチ 22 B2
What the Dickens ワットザディケンズ 23 B2

ENTERTAINMENT (pp143-66)
Liquid Room リキッドルーム 24 C2
Milk ミルク (see 23)
Yebisu Garden Cinema 恵比寿ガーデンシネマ 25 D3

SHOPPING (pp175-88)
Alohaloha アロハロハ 26 B2
Daikanyama Address 代官山 ADDRESS 27 A2
Good Day Books グッドデイブックス 28 C2
Hacknet ハックネット 29 B2
Matsuzakaya 松坂屋 30 B3
Mitsukoshi 三越百貨店 31 D3
Q Flagship Ebisu-nishi ハックネット (see 29)
Yebisu Garden Place 恵比寿ガーデンプレース 32 D3

SLEEPING (pp189-206)
Hotel Excellent ホテル エクセレント 33 B2
Kyowa Kaikan 協和会館 34 B2
Westin Hotel Tokyo ウェスティンホテル東京 35 D4

TRANSPORT
Taxi Stop タクシー乗り場 36 C3

INFORMATION
Ebisu Eki-mae Post Office 恵比寿駅前郵便局 37 B2
Konishi Japanese Cooking Class 小西ジャパニーズクッキングクラス 38 B5
Kōseichūō Hospital 厚生中央病院 39 C4
Post Office 郵便局 40 C2
Tokyo British Clinic 東京ブリティッシュクリニック 41 B1

0 500 m
0 0.3 miles
A
B
C
D
1
2
3
4
5
6
See Shibuya & Omote-sandō Map (p284)
To Shibuya (1.5km)
Shibuya-ku
渋谷区
Daikanyama
代官山
Hiro-o
広尾
Hachiman-dōri
Tōkyū Tōyoko Line
Saikyō Line 埼京線
Yamanote Line 山手線
Meiji-dōri 明治通り
Ebisu Prime Square Plaza
To Hiro-o Station
Daikanyama
Hibiya Line 日比谷線
Ebisu-Nishi
恵比寿西
Ebisu
West Exit
Ebisu-hagashi kōen
Ebisu
恵比寿
ATRE Building
Komazawa-dōri
Hibiya Line 日比谷線
To Minami-Aoyama (1.5km)
Naka-meguro
Neonat Building
Ebisu-Minami
恵比寿南
Ebisu-minami kōen
恵比寿南公園
America-bashi
Kusunoki-dōri 楠木通り
Yamanote Line 山手線
Naka-Meguro
中目黒
Yamate-dōri 山手通り
Defense Agency Technical Research & Development Institute
プラタナス通り
Platanus-dōri
Mita-bashi
Mita
三田
Meguro-gawa 目黒川
Chaya-zaka (slope)
Shuto Expway No 2
首都高速2号
Meguro-ku
目黒区
Shinagawa-ku
品川区
Yamate-dōri 山手通り
Meguro
目黒
Toei Mita Line 都営三田線
Nomboku Line 南北線
To Shirokanedai Station (300m)
Gonnosuke Zaka (slope)
Meguro
Meguro
Meguro-dōri 目黒通り
Kami-Ōsaki
上大崎
Shimo-Meguro
下目黒

ODAIBA/TOKYO BAY AREA

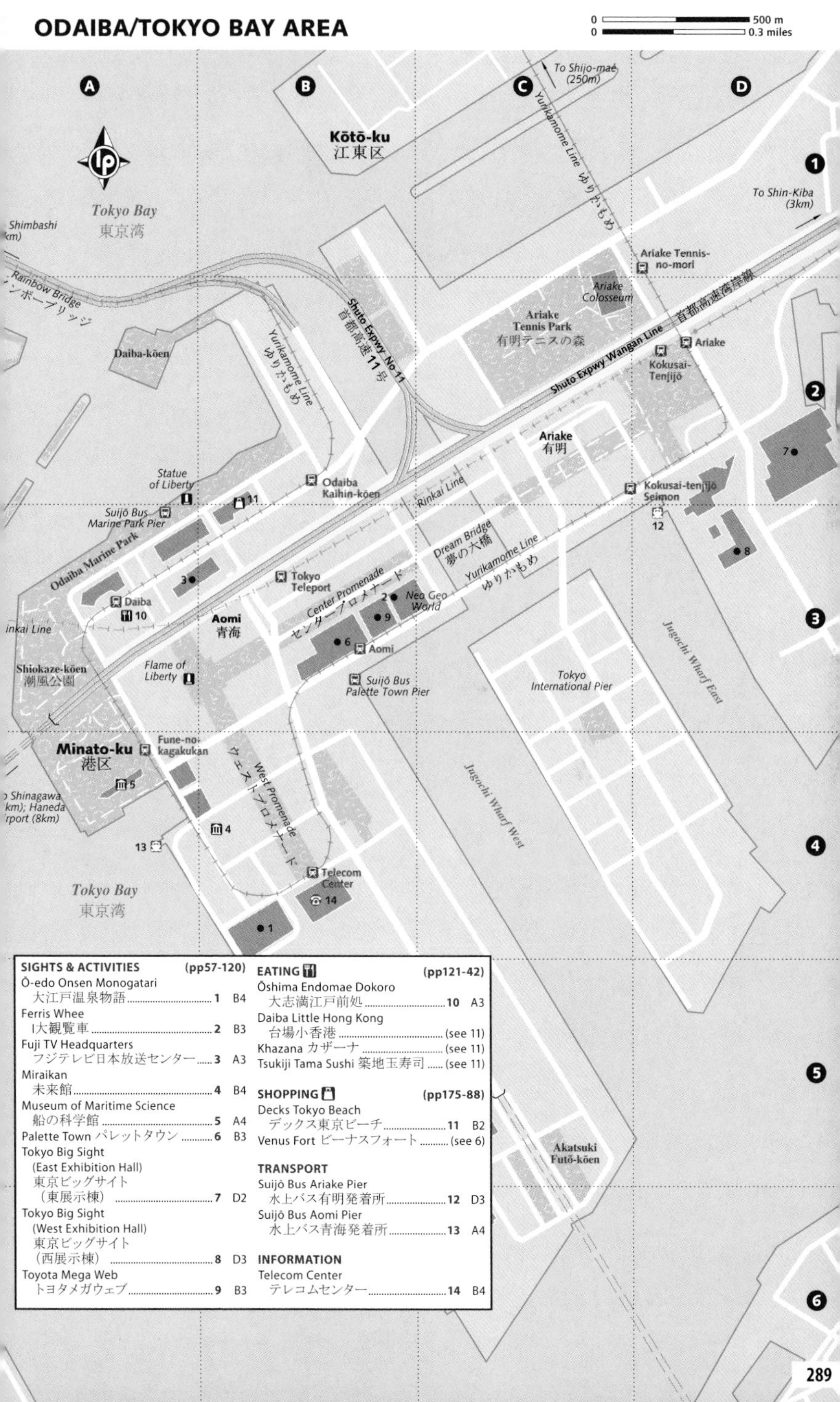

SIGHTS & ACTIVITIES (pp57-120)

Ō-edo Onsen Monogatari 大江戸温泉物語 ... 1 B4
Ferris Whee 大観覧車 ... 2 B3
Fuji TV Headquarters フジテレビ日本放送センター ... 3 A3
Miraikan 未来館 ... 4 B4
Museum of Maritime Science 船の科学館 ... 5 A4
Palette Town パレットタウン ... 6 B3
Tokyo Big Sight (East Exhibition Hall) 東京ビッグサイト（東展示棟） ... 7 D2
Tokyo Big Sight (West Exhibition Hall) 東京ビッグサイト（西展示棟） ... 8 D3
Toyota Mega Web トヨタメガウェブ ... 9 B3

EATING (pp121-42)

Ōshima Endomae Dokoro 大志満江戸前処 ... 10 A3
Daiba Little Hong Kong 台場小香港 ... (see 11)
Khazana カザーナ ... (see 11)
Tsukiji Tama Sushi 築地玉寿司 ... (see 11)

SHOPPING (pp175-88)

Decks Tokyo Beach デックス東京ビーチ ... 11 B2
Venus Fort ビーナスフォート ... (see 6)

TRANSPORT

Suijō Bus Ariake Pier 水上バス有明発着所 ... 12 D3
Suijō Bus Aomi Pier 水上バス青海発着所 ... 13 A4

INFORMATION

Telecom Center テレコムセンター ... 14 B4

A
B
C
D
1
2
3
4
5
6
Akasaka-mitsuke
Nagatachō
永田町
Akasaka
赤坂
Tokyo Broadcasting Station
Akasaka-dōri
Akasaka
Namboku Line 南北線
Kokkaimae Garden (Western Style)
国会前庭洋式庭園
National Diet Building
Kokkaimae Garden (Japanese Style)
国会前庭和式庭園
Sakuradamon
Tokyo Metropolitan Police Department
Chiyoda-ku
千代田区
Tokyo High Court & Distric Court
Kasumigaseki
Uchibori-dōri 内堀通り
Ministry of Foreign Affairs
Marunouchi Line 丸の内線
Chiyoda Line 千代田線
Kokkai-gijidōmae
Diet Press Centre
Kokkai-dōri
Roppongi-dōri 六本木通り
Kasumigaseki
Sotobori-dōri 外堀通り
Tameike-sannō
Chiyoda Line
千代田線
Akasaka
赤坂
Ginza Line 銀座線
Toranomon
Sotobori-dōri 外堀通り
Uchisaiwaichō
Ginza Line
銀座線
Shuto Expwy Loop Line
Ark Mori Building
Ark Hills
Toranomon
虎ノ門
Hotel Ōkura Annex
Sakurada-dōri 桜田通り
Hibiya Line 日比谷線
Toei Mita Line 都営三田線
Shimbashi
新橋
Roppongi-dōri 六本木通り
Roppongi-itchōme
Roppongi
六本木
See Roppongi Map (p286)
Post Office
Namboku Line 南北線
Kamiyachō
Gaien-Higashi-dōri 外苑東通り
Onarimon
Toei Asakusa Line 都営浅草線
Azabudai
麻布台
Noa Building
Russian Embassy
Sakurada-dōri 桜田通り
Tokyo Tower
Minato-ku
港区
Higashi-Azabu
To Roppongi (1.5km)
Shiba Kōen
芝公園
Shiba-kōen
芝公園
Toei Ōedo Line 都営大江戸線
Daimon
Shiba Daimon
芝大門
Azabu-jūban
Shuto Expwy Loop Line
Akabanebashi
Hamamatsuchō
Shibakōen
67
77
57
28
34
62
5
10
61
37
74
22
29
41
38
43
31
75
88
60
83
69
68
8
72
50
45
47
79
81
86
20

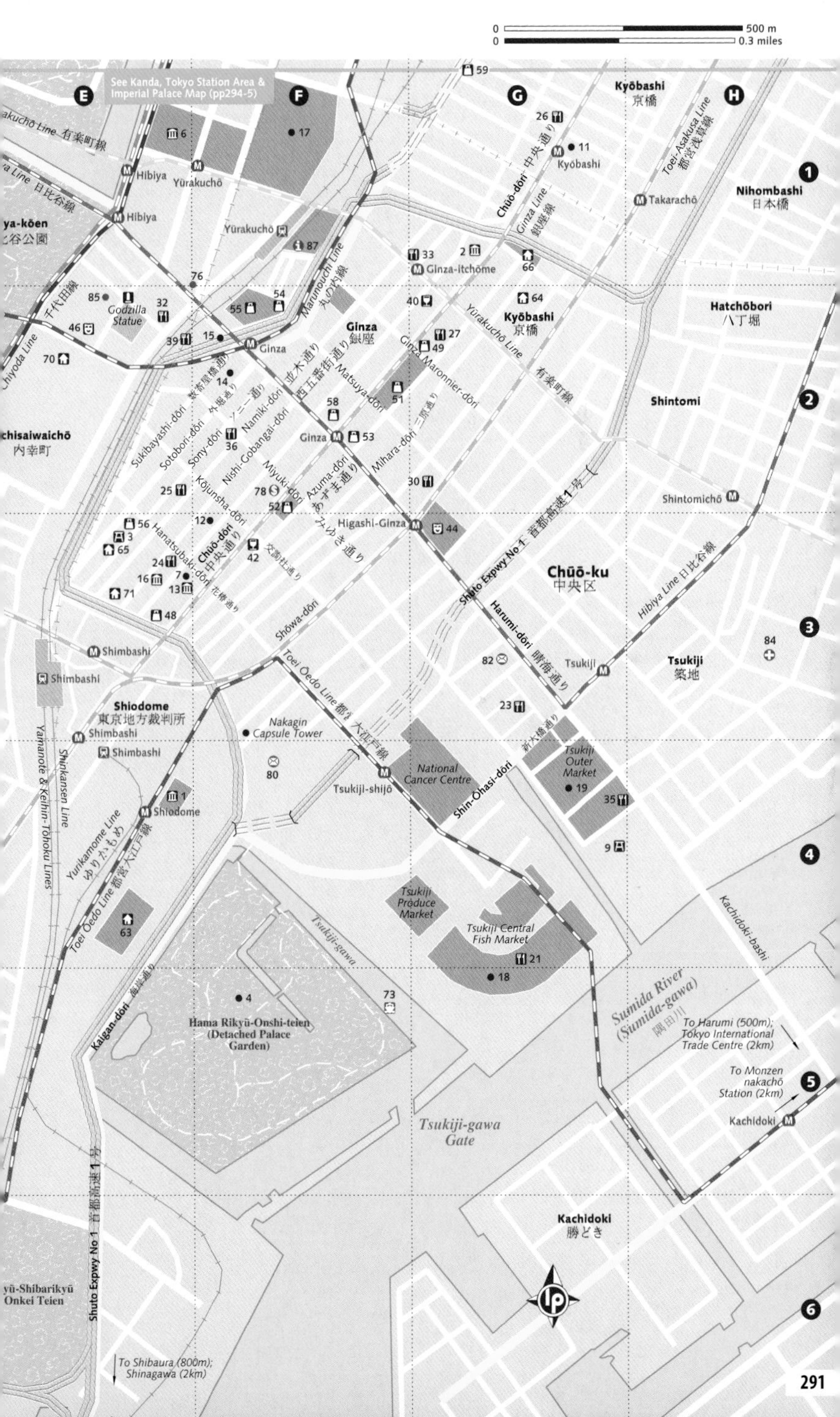

0 500 m
0 0.3 miles
See Kanda, Tokyo Station Area & Imperial Palace Map (pp294-5)
E
F
G
H
1
2
3
4
5
6
Kyōbashi 京橋
Nihombashi 日本橋
Hatchōbori 八丁堀
Shintomi
Ginza 銀座
Kyōbashi 京橋
Chūō-ku 中央区
Tsukiji 築地
Shiodome
東京地方裁判所
Kachidoki 勝どき
Uchisaiwaichō 内幸町
Hibiya
Yūrakuchō
Ginza-itchōme
Takarachō
Shintomichō
Higashi-Ginza
Shimbashi
Shiodome
Tsukiji-shijō
Kachidoki
Yūrakuchō Line 有楽町線
Hibiya Line 日比谷線
Chiyoda Line 千代田線
Marunouchi Line 丸の内線
Ginza Line 銀座線
Toei-Asakusa Line 都営浅草線
Toei Ōedo Line 都営大江戸線
Yurikamome Line ゆりかもめ
Shinkansen Line
Yamanote & Keihin-Tōhoku Lines
Chūō-dōri 中央通り
Harumi-dōri 晴海通り
Shōwa-dōri
Shuto Expwy No 1 首都高速1号
Sukibayashi-dōri
Sotobori-dōri 外堀通り
Sony-dōri ソニー通り
Namiki-dōri 並木通り
Nishi-Gobangai-dōri 西五番街通り
Matsuya-dōri
Ginza Maronnier-dōri
Mihara-dōri 三原通り
Azuma-dōri あずま通り
Miyuki-dōri みゆき通り
Kōjunsha-dōri 交詢社通り
Hanatsubaki-dōri 花椿通り
Shin-Ōhasi-dōri 新大橋通り
Kaigan-dōri 海岸通り
Kachidoki-bashi
Godzilla Statue
Nakagin Capsule Tower
National Cancer Centre
Tsukiji Outer Market
Tsukiji Produce Market
Tsukiji Central Fish Market
Tsukiji-gawa
Tsukiji-gawa Gate
Hama Rikyū-Onshi-teien (Detached Palace Garden)
Sumida River (Sumida-gawa) 隅田川
To Harumi (500m); Tokyo International Trade Centre (2km)
To Monzen nakachō Station (2km)
To Shibaura (800m); Shinagawa (2km)
Kyū-Shibarikyū Onkei Teien
Hibiya-kōen
比谷公園

AKASAKA, GINZA, TSUKIJI & SHIODOME (pp290-1)

SIGHTS & ACTIVITIES (pp57-120)

Advertising Museum Tokyo 電通 1 E4
AXIS Gallery アクシスギャラリー .... (see 47)
Gallery Koyanagi ギャラリー小柳 2 G1
Hachiman-jinja 八幡神社 3 E3
Hamarikyū-teien 浜離宮庭園 4 F5
Hie-jinja 日枝神社 5 A1
Idemitsu Museum of Arts 出光美術館 6 E1
Imperial Theatre 帝国劇場 .... (see 6)
Konparu-yu Onsen こんぱる湯 7 E3
Musée Tomo 智美術館 8 B3
Namiyoke-jinja 波除神社 9 G4
National Diet Building 国会議事堂 10 B1
Pen Station ペンステーション 11 G1
Shiseido Art House 資生堂アートハウス 12 F3
Shiseido Gallery 資生堂ギャラリー 13 E3
Sony Building ソニービル 14 F2
Sukiyabashi Crossing 数寄屋橋交差点 15 F2
Tokyo Gallery 東京画廊 16 E3
Tokyo International Forum 東京国際フォーラム 17 F1
Tsukiji Central Fish Market 築地市場 18 G5
Tsukiji Outer Market 場外市場 19 G4
Zōjō-ji 増上寺 20 C6

EATING (pp121-42)

Daiwa Sushi 大和寿司 21 G4
Delhi デリー 22 A2
Edogin 江戸銀 23 G3
Kisso 吉左右 .... (see 47)
Kyūbei 久兵衛 24 E3
L'Osier レストランロオジェ 25 E2
Meidi-ya 明治屋 26 G1
Meidi-ya 明治屋 27 G2
Moti モティ 28 A1
Moti モティ 29 A2
Nair's ナイル 30 G2
Nataraj ナタラジ .... (see 78)
Rakutei 楽亭 31 A2
Robata 炉端 32 E2
Sakata 坂田 33 G1
Sushi-sei 寿司清 34 A1
Takeno たけの食堂 35 G4
Ten-Ichi 天一 36 F2
Tōfu-ya 豆腐屋 37 A1
Yamaya やまや赤坂店 38 A2
Yūrakuchō Yakitori Alley 有楽町焼き鳥横丁 39 E2

DRINKING (pp143-66)

ANA Hotel Beer Garden 全日空ホテルビアガーデン .... (see 60)
Aux Amis des Vins オザミ·デ·ヴァン 40 G2
Hobgoblin ホブゴブリン 41 A2
Lion Beer Hall ライオンビアホール 42 F3

ENTERTAINMENT (pp143-66)

B-Flat ビーフラット 43 A2
Kabuki-za 歌舞伎座 44 G3
Roppongi Pit Inn 六本木ピットイン 45 A4
Takarazuka Gekijō 東京宝塚劇場 46 E2

SHOPPING (pp175-88)

AXIS アクシスビル 47 A4
Hakuhinkan Toy Park 博品館 48 E3
Itōya 伊東屋 49 G2
Japan Sword 日本刀剣 50 C3
Matsuya 松屋 51 F2
Matsuzakaya 松坂屋 52 F2
Mikimoto Pearl ミキモト真珠 .... (see 58)
Mitsukoshi 三越 53 F2
Seibu Annex 西武アネックス 54 F2
Seibu 西武 55 F2
Takumi たくみ 56 E3
Tokyo Random Walk 東京ランドムォーク 57 A1
Wakō 和光 58 F2
Yaesu Book Center 八重洲ブックセンター 59 G1

SLEEPING (pp189-206)

ANA Hotel Tokyo 全日空ホテル東京 60 A3
Capitol Tōkyū Hotel キャピトル東急ホテル 61 B1
Capsule Hotel Fontaine Akasaka カプセルホテル フォンテーヌ赤阪 62 A1
Conrad Hotel コンラッドホテル 63 E4
Ginza Mercure メルキュールホテル銀座 64 G2
Ginza Nikkō Hotel 銀座日航ホテル 65 E3
Hotel Seiyō Ginza ホテル西洋銀座 66 G1
Hotel Sunroute Akasaka ホテルサンルート赤坂 67 A1
Hotel Villa Fontaine Shiodome ホテルヴィラフォンテーヌ汐留 .... (see 63)
Hotel Ōkura Annex ホテルオークラ別館 68 B3
Hotel Ōkura ホテルオークラ 69 B3
Imperial Hotel 帝国ホテル 70 E2
Mitsui Urban Hotel Ginza 三井アーバンホテル銀座 71 E3
Roppongi Prince Hotel 六本木プリンスホテル 72 A3

TRANSPORT

Water Bus Pier 水上バス乗り場 73 F5

INFORMATION

Akasaka Post Office 赤坂郵便局 74 A2
American Embassy アメリカ大使館 75 B3
American Express アメリカンエキスプレス 76 F1
Citibank シティバンク 77 A1
Citibank シティバンク 78 F2
Dutch Embassy オランダ大使館 79 B4
Ginza Post Office 銀座郵便局 80 F4
Japanese Red Cross Language Service Volunteers 日本赤十字社 81 D5
Koyasu Drug Store Hotel Ōkura U子安ドラッグストアー ホテルオークラ .... (see 69)
Kyōbashi Post Office 京橋郵便局 82 G3
Roppongi Post Office 六本木郵便局 83 A3
St Luke's International Hospital 聖路加病院 84 H3
Tokyo Disney Resort Ticket Center 東京ディズニーリゾートチケットセンター 85 E2
Tokyo Medical & Surgical Clinic 東京クリニック 86 C5
Tourist Information Center (JNTO) 東京交通会館 87 F1
World Union of Karate-dō Organisation 88 C3

KANDA, TOKYO STATION AREA & IMPERIAL PALACE (pp294-5)

SIGHTS & ACTIVITIES (pp57-120)

Akihabara Electric Town 秋葉原電気街 **1** G2
All Japan Kendō Federation 全日本剣道連盟 (see 45)
Bijutsukan Kōgeikan (Crafts Gallery) 美術館工芸館 **2** C4
Bridgestone Museum of Art ブリヂストン美術館 **3** G6
Chiyoda Sogo Taikukan Pool 千代田区総合体育館プール **4** F4
Hide & Seek Alleys かくれんぼ横丁 **5** B1
Higashi-Gyōen 東御苑 **6** D5
Hirakawa-mon 平川門 **7** E4
Imperial Household Agency 宮内庁 **8** D5
Imperial Palace 皇居 **9** D6
Ishimaru Denki 石丸電気 **10** G2
JCII Camera Museum 日本カメラ博物館 **11** B5
Kagaku Gijitsukan (Science Museum) 科学技術館 **12** D4
Kanda Myōjin 神田明神 **13** F1
Kitahanebashi-mon 北桔橋門 **14** D4
Kokuritsu Kindai Bijutsukan (National Museum of Modern Art) 国立近代美術館 **15** D4
Laox ラオックス **16** G2
Museum of Imperial Collections 三の丸尚蔵館 **17** E5
Nicholai Cathedral ニコライ堂 **18** F2
Nijū-bashi 二重橋 **19** D6
Onoden オノデン **20** G2
Sato Musen サトウムセン **21** G2
Tayasu-mon 田安門 **22** C3
Tokyo Anime Center 東京アニメセンター **23** G2
Tokyo Stock Exchange 東京証券取引所 **24** H6
Tokyo Wonder Site トーキョーワンダーサイト **25** E1
Transportation Museum 交通博物館 **26** G3
Yamagiwa ヤマギワ **27** G2
Yamagiwa ヤマギワ **28** G2
Yamatane Bijutsukan (Yamatane Museum of Art) 山種美術館 **29** B4
Yasukuni-jinja 靖国神社 **30** B3
Yushima Seidō 湯島聖堂 **31** F2
Ōte-mon 大手門 **32** E5

EATING (pp121-42)

Botan ぼたん **33** F3
Canal Café カナルカフェ **34** B1
Hana Noren 花暖簾 **35** B1
Isegen いせ源 **36** G3
Jangara Rāmen じゃんがらラーメン **37** G2
Kanda Yabu Soba 神田やぶそば **38** F3
Kua 'Aina クアアイナ **39** E6
Le Bretagne ルブルターニュ **40** B1
Marugo Tonkatsu とんかつ丸五 **41** G2
Matsuya まつや **42** F3
Mikuni's Café Marunouchi ミクニズカフェ丸の内 **43** E6
Muang Thai Nabe ムアンタイなべ **44** E3
Muito Bom ムイトボン (see 44)

DRINKING (pp143-66)

Top of Akasaka トップ·オブ·アカサカ (see 55)

ENTERTAINMENT (pp143-66)

Nihon Budōkan 日本武道館 **45** C3

SHOPPING (pp175-88)

Disk Union ディスクユニオン **46** E3
Issei-dō 一誠堂 **47** E3
Kitazawa Books 北沢書店 **48** D3
Maruzen (Old Location) 丸善 **49** G6
Maruzen 丸善 **50** F5
Mitsukoshi 三越 **51** G5
Puppet House パペットハウス **52** B1
Takashimaya 高島屋百貨店 **53** G6
Tokyo Random Walk 東京ランダムウォーク **54** E3

SLEEPING (pp189-206)

Akasaka Prince Hotel 赤坂プリンスホテル **55** A6
Hotel New Kanda ホテルニュー神田 **56** F2
Marunouchi Hotel 丸ノ内ホテル (see 50)
New Central Hotel ニューセントラルホテル **57** F3
Palace Hotel パレスホテル **58** E5
Sakura Hotel サクラホテル **59** D3
Tokyo Green Hotel Ochanomizu 東京グリーンホテル御茶ノ水 **60** F3
Tokyo International Youth Hostel 東京国際ユースホステル **61** B1
Tokyo Station Hotel 東京ステーションホテル **62** F6
Yaesu Ryūmeikan 八重洲龍名館 **63** G5
Yaesu Terminal Hotel 八重洲ターミナルホテル **64** G6
Yama-no-Ue (Hilltop) Hotel 山の上ホテル **65** E2

TRANSPORT

JR Highway Bus Station ＪＲ高速バスターミナル **66** F6
TCAT Airport Limousine Bus Stop ＴＣＡＴ空港リムジンバス停 **67** F6

INFORMATION

Academy of Language Arts アカデミーオブランゲージアーツ **68** B1
American Pharmacy アメリカンファーマシー (see 39)
Babasakimon Police Box 馬場先門交番 **69** E6
Bank of Japan 日本銀行 **70** G5
Bank of Tokyo-Mitsubishi 東京三菱銀行 **71** G5
British Council ブリティッシュカウンシル **72** B1
British Embassy イギリス大使館 **73** B5
Indian Embassy インド大使館 **74** C3
Irish Embassy アイルランド大使館 **75** B5
Jimbōchō Post Office 神保町郵便局 **76** E3
Kanda Post Office 神田郵便局 **77** G2
Police 交番 (see 7)
Post Office 郵便局 **78** G6
Tokyo Central Post Office 東京中央郵便局 **79** F6
Tokyo Convention & Visitors Bureau (TCVB) 東京観光財団 **80** E6
Tokyo International Post Office 東京国際郵便局 **81** F5
Tokyo-Mitsubishi Bank 東京三菱銀行 **82** G2

KANDA, TOKYO STATION AREA & IMPERIAL PALACE

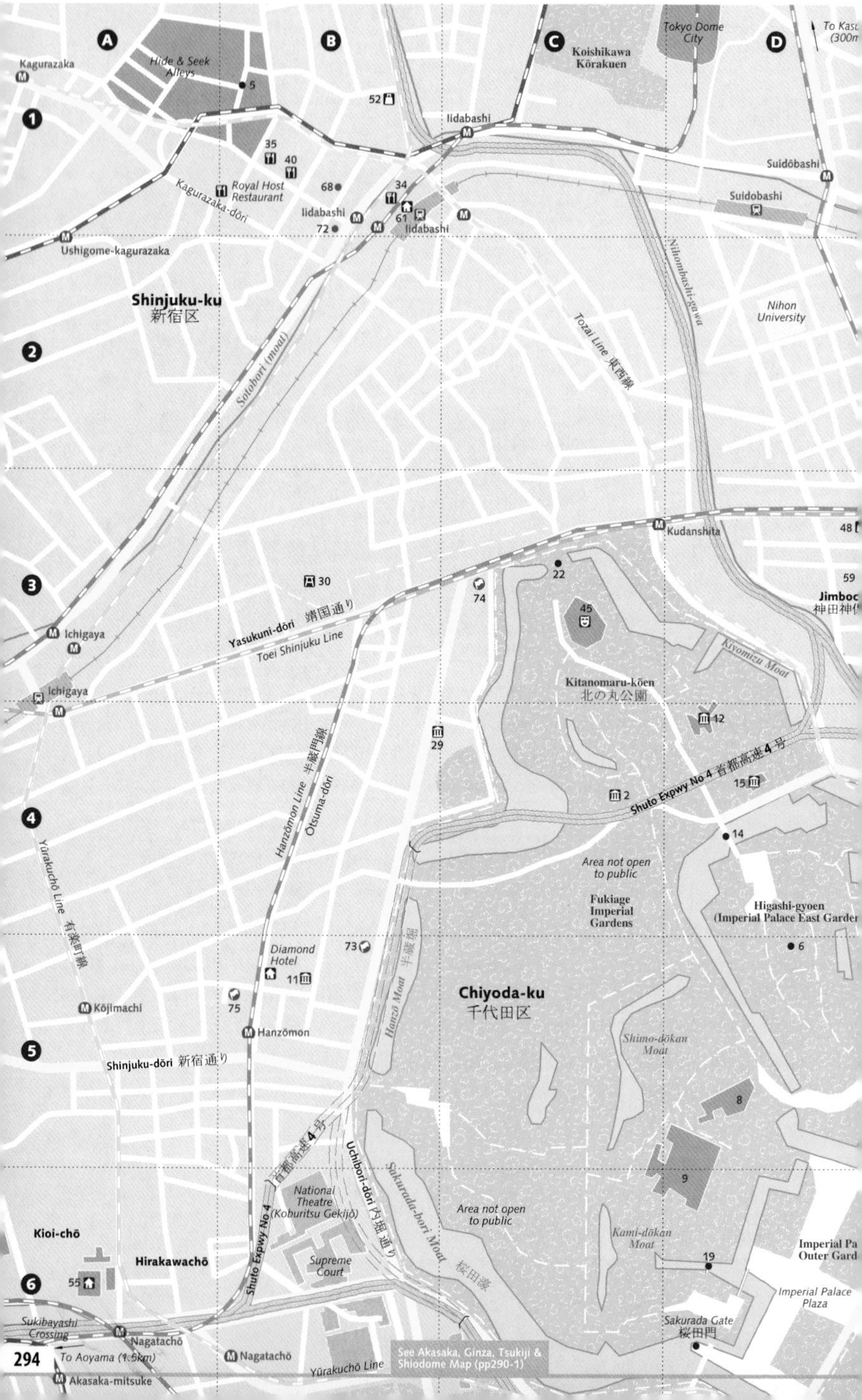

A
B
C
D
1
2
3
4
5
6

Kagurazaka
Hide & Seek Alleys
5
52
Iidabashi
Koishikawa Kōrakuen
Tokyo Dome City
To Kasu (300m
35
40
Royal Host Restaurant
68
Kagurazaka-dōri
34
Iidabashi
61
Iidabashi
72
Suidōbashi
Suidobashi
Ushigome-kagurazaka
Shinjuku-ku
新宿区
Nihombashi-gawa
Tozai Line 東西線
Nihon University
Sotobori (moat)
Kudanshita
48
22
30
74
59
Jimboc
神田神
45
Yasukuni-dōri 靖国通り
Toei Shinjuku Line
Ichigaya
Ichigaya
Kiyomizu Moat
Kitanomaru-kōen
北の丸公園
12
29
Hanzōmon Line 半蔵門線
Ōtsuma-dōri
Shuto Expwy No 4 首都高速4号
15
2
Yūrakuchō Line 有楽町線
14
Area not open to public
Fukiage Imperial Gardens
Higashi-gyoen (Imperial Palace East Garde
Diamond Hotel
73
6
11
Hanzō Moat 半蔵濠
75
Chiyoda-ku
千代田区
Kōjimachi
Hanzōmon
Shimo-dōkan Moat
Shinjuku-dōri 新宿通り
8
首都高速4号
Uchibori-dōri 内堀通り
9
National Theatre (Koburitsu Gekijō)
Sakurada-bori Moat
Area not open to public
Kioi-chō
Kami-dōkan Moat
Imperial Pa Outer Gard
Supreme Court
桜田濠
19
Shuto Expwy No 4
Hirakawachō
55
Imperial Palace Plaza
Sukibayashi Crossing
Nagatachō
Sakurada Gate 桜田門
To Aoyama (1.5km)
Nagatachō

See Akasaka, Ginza, Tsukiji & Shiodome Map (pp290-1)

Yūrakuchō Line
Akasaka-mitsuke

0 500 m
0 0.3 miles
To Hongo San-chōme (300m)
See Ueno & Asakusa Map (pp296-7)
Suehirochō
Kuramaebashi-dōri
Hongō-dōri
Sotobori-dōri 外堀通り
Chūō & Sōbu Lines
Tokyo Medical & Dental University
Chiyoda Line 千代田線
Shōheibashi-dōri
Shuto Expwy No 1 首都高速1号
Hibiya Line 日比谷線
Showa-dōri
rugakuchō 猿楽町
Ochanomizu
Kanda-gawa 神田川
UDX Building
Akihabara
Asakusabashi 浅草橋
Ochanomizu
Nichidai Hospital
Meiji University
Electronics Neighbourhood
To Yoshitoku (250m)
Bookshop Neighbourhood 神田書店街
Shin-ochanomizu
Jimbōchō
Sporting Goods Neighbourhood スポーツ用具店街
Meidai-dōri
Yasukuni-dōri 靖国通り
Suzuran-dōri
Awajichō
Ogawamachi
Iwamotochō
Iwamotochō 岩本町
Kanda
Kanda-Nishikichō
Kanda-Keisatsu-dōri
Kodenmachō 小伝馬町
Shuto Expwy No 5 首都高速5号
Uchi-Kanda
Ōtemachi
akebashi
Chūō Lines
Yamanote & Keihin-Tōhoku Lines
North-bound Shinkansen Line
Chūō-dōri 中央通り
Sōbu Line
Kodemmachō
ōkyo-Gaien
Marunouchi Line 丸ノ内線
Ginza Line 銀座線
Nihombashi-Muromachi 日本橋室町
Ōtemachi
Toei Mita Line 都営三田線
Eitai-dōri 永代通り
Mitsukoshimae
To Asakusa-bashi JR Station
Hanzōmon Line 半蔵門線
Wadakura Square
Tōzai Line 東西線
Marunouchi OAZO Building
Nihombashi (Bridge)
Nihombashi 日本橋
Shin-Marunouchi Building
Shuto Expwy No 6 首都高速6号
Tokyo
Sotobori-dōri 外堀通り
Sakura-dōri 桜通り
Marunouchi Central Exit
Marunouchi Building
Babasaki Moat
Nijūbashimae
Yaesu Central Exit
Yaesu Underground Arcade
Toei-Asakusa Line 都営浅草線
Marunouchi 丸の内
Yaesu 八重洲
Yaesu-dōri
Kyōbashi 京橋
Kayabachō
Hibiya-dōri
To Tokyo International Forum (250m)
See Akasaka, Ginza, Tsukiji & Shiodome Map (pp290-1)

UENO & ASAKUSA

Nishi-Nippori
Chiyoda Line 千代田線
To Kita-Senju (2.5km)
To Keisei Machiya (1.8km)
Suwa-jinja
Senkō-ji
40
Yōfuku-ji
Keiō-ji
Keisei Nippori
Nippori
1
64
25
Kaizō-in
72
Tennō-ji
20
Chōan-ji
79
Jōzai-ji
Yanaka Cemetery 谷中霊園
To Sendagi (500m)
Negishi 根岸
Yanaka 谷中
Kototoi-dōri 言問通り
19
Uguisudani
50
Bunkyō-ku 文京区
Tokugawa Shōgun Rei-en (Tokugawa Shōgun Cemetery) 徳川将軍家霊所
Tokyo National University of Fine Arts & Music
14
Iriya
68
Keisei Line
Ueno-Sakurgai
15
31
24
Hakubutsukan Dōbutsuen
13
65
29
43
Nezu
32
Ueno-kōen 上野公園
Ikenohata
Rinnō-ji
35
Chiyoda Line 千代田線
Great Fountain
7
70
12
22
Yamanote & Keihin-Tōhoku Lines
Takasaki & Jōetsu Lines
Tōhoku Main Line & Jōban Line
Tōhoku & Jōetsu Shinkansen
Shuto Expwy No 1 首都高速1号
Monorail
34
Ueno 上野
23
Aesop Bridge
Daibutsu Pagoda
82
17
Tokyo Metropolitan Festival Hall 東京文化会館
Gojō-jinja
Korinchō Rd
Kita-Ueno 北上野
Suijōdobutsu-ike
Dōbutsuen-dōri
Ueno
Kōen Exit
69
Benten-bashi
Ueno-no Mori Art Museum
Hibiya Line 日比谷線
33
Tokyo University
21
Hirokō-ji Exit
81
Bōto-ike
5
Tokyo University Branch Hospital
Keisei Ueno
26
Asakusa Exit
Ginza Line 銀座線
Ueno
Shinobazu-dōri
Shinobazu-ike
Inarichō
Asakusa-dōri 浅草通
Chūō-dōri 中央通り
Eki-mae-dōri
Ueno Okachimachi chūō-dōri
Hongō 本郷
28
Tokyo Regional Court
Shinobazu-dōri 不忍通り
46
Arcade
63
53
Nakamachi-dōri
Ueno Naka-dōri
Shōwa-dōri 昭和通り
Higashi-Ueno 東上野
45
42
Ueno 上野
Ameyoko アメ横
Yushima
Kasuga-dōri 春日通り
36
Ueno-okachimachi
Toei Ōedo Line 都営大江戸線
58
Okachimachi
74
Naka-okachimachi
Shin-okachimachi
Ueno 上野
Ueno-hirokōji
Kasuga-dōri 春日通り
Yushima 湯島
Taitō 台東
To Akihabara (1km)

See Kanda, Tokyo Station Area & Imperial Palace Map (pp294-5)

Suehirochō

0 500 m
0 0.3 miles

UENO & ASAKUSA (pp296-7)

SIGHTS & ACTIVITIES (pp57-120)

Asakura Chōso Museum 朝倉彫塑館 ... **1** A2
Asakusa Eikō-dō 浅草寺影向堂 ... **2** F4
Asakusa Kannon Onsen 浅草観音温泉 ... **3** F4
Asakusa-jinja 浅草神社 ... **4** F4
Benten-dō 弁天堂 ... **5** B5
Benten-dō 弁天堂 ... **6** F5
Children's Playground こどもの広場 ... **7** B4
Chingodō-ji 鎮護寺 ... **8** F5
Dembō-in 伝法院 ... **9** F5
Edo Shitamachi Dentō Kōgeikan 江戸下町伝統工芸館 ... **10** F4
Five-Storey Pagoda 五重塔 ... **11** F5
Five-Storey Pagoda 五重塔 ... **12** B4
Gallery of Hōryū-ji Treasures 法隆寺宝物館 ... **13** B3
Heiseikan 平成館 ... **14** C3
Hyōkeikan 表慶館 ... **15** B3
Hōzōmon 宝蔵門 ... **16** F5
Ikenohata-mon 池之端門 ... **17** A4
Jakotsu-yu 蛇骨湯 ... **18** E5
Kanei-ji 寛永寺 ... **19** B3
Kannon-ji 観音寺 ... **20** A2
Kiyōmizu Kannon-dō 清水観音堂 ... **21** B5
Kokuritsu Kagaku Hakubutsukan (National Science Museum) 国立科学博物館 ... **22** C4
Kokuritsu Seiyō Bijutsukan (National Museum of Western Art) 国立西洋美術館 ... **23** C4
Rokuryu Ōnsen 六竜温泉 ... **24** A3
Ryūsen-ji 龍泉寺 ... **25** A2
Saigō Takamori Statue 西郷隆盛像 ... **26** B5
Sensō-ji 浅草寺 ... **27** F4
Shitamachi Museum 下町風俗資料館 ... **28** B5
Tōyōkan (Gallery of Eastern Antiquities) 東洋館 ... **29** C4
Taiko-kan 太鼓館 ... **30** E5
Tokyo Kokuritsu Hakubutsukan (Tokyo National Museum) 東京国立博物館 ... **31** C3
Tokyo Metropolitan Museum of Art 東京都美術館 ... **32** B4
Tokyo University ... **33** A5
Tōshō-gū 上野東照宮 ... **34** B4
Ueno Zoo 上野動物園 ... **35** B4
Yushima Tenjin 湯島神社 ... **36** A6

EATING (pp121-42)

Asakusa Imahan 浅草今半 ... **37** E5
Asakusa Manos 浅草マノス ... **38** F5
Capricciosa カプリチョーザ ... **39** F5
Chalet Swiss Mini シャレスイスミニ ... **40** A1
Daikokuya 大黒屋 ... **41** F5
Daikokuya 大黒屋 ... (see 66)
Futaba ふたば ... **42** B5
Hantei はん亭 ... **43** A4
Ichimon 一文 ... **44** F4
Ikenohata Yabu Soba 池之端やぶそば ... **45** B5
Izu-ei 伊豆栄 ... **46** B5
Komagata Dojō 駒形どぜう ... **47** F6
Namiki Yabu Soba 並木やぶそば ... **48** F5
Omiya おみや ... **49** F5
Sasa-no-Yuki 笹乃雪 ... **50** D3
Sometaro 染太郎 ... **51** E5

ENTERTAINMENT (pp143-66)

Asakusa Engei Hall 浅草演芸ホール ... **52** E5

SHOPPING (pp175-88)

Ameyoko Centre Building アメ横センタービル ... **53** B5
Bengara べんがら ... **54** F5
Kanesō かね惣 ... **55** F5
Maiduru まいづる ... **56** E5
Matsuya 松屋 ... **57** F5
Matsuzakaya 松坂屋 ... **58** B6
Miyamoto Unosuke Shoten 宮本卯之助商店 ... (see 30)
Satō Sample サトウサンプル ... **59** E4

SLEEPING (pp189-206)

Asakusa View Hotel 浅草ビューホテル ... **60** E4
Capsule Hotel Riverside カプセルホテルリバーサイド ... **61** F5
Hotel New Kōyō ホテルニュー紅陽 ... **62** G1
Hotel Parkside ホテルパークサイド ... **63** B5
Ryokan Katsutarō Annex アネックス 旅館勝太郎 ... **64** A2
Ryokan Katsutarō 旅館勝太郎 ... **65** A4
Ryokan Shigetsu 旅館指月 ... **66** F5
Sakura Ryokan 桜旅館 ... **67** D3
Sawanoya Ryokan 澤の屋旅館 ... **68** A3
Sofitel Tokyo ホテルソフィテル東京 ... **69** A5
Suigetsu Hotel Ōgai-sō 水月ホテル鴎外荘 ... **70** A4
Sukeroku no Yado Sadachiyo 助六の宿貞千代 ... **71** F4
Suzuki Ryokan 鈴木旅館 ... **72** B2
Taitō Ryokan 台東旅館 ... **73** E5
Ueno First City Hotel 上野ファーストシティホテル ... **74** A6

TRANSPORT

Suijo Bus Pier 水上バス発着所 ... **75** G5
Sumida-gawa Cruise (Suijō Bus) Pier 隅田川水上バス発着所 ... **76** F5

INFORMATION

Asakusa Post Office 浅草郵便局 ... **77** E5
Asakusa Tourist Information Center (JNTO) 浅草観光案内センター ... **78** F5
Police Box 交番 ... **79** B2
Sensō-ji Hospital 浅草寺病院 ... **80** F4
Taitō-ku Ward Office 台東区役所 ... **81** C5
Ueno-kōen Information Centre 上野公園 インフォメーション センター ... **82** C4